An Introduction to the Philosophy and Religion of Taoism

Pathways to Immortality

道可道。非常道。

The *Tao* that can be spoken of
is not the eternal *Tao*

An Introduction to the Philosophy and Religion of Taoism
Pathways to Immortality

JEANEANE FOWLER

sussex
ACADEMIC
PRESS
Brighton • Chicago • Toronto

Copyright © Jeaneane Fowler, 2005, 2015

The right of Jeaneane Fowler to be identified as Author of this work has been asserted in accordance with the Copyright, Designs and Patents Act 1988.

2 4 6 8 10 9 7 5 3

First published in 2005, reprinted 2105, in Great Britain by
SUSSEX ACADEMIC PRESS
PO Box 139
Eastbourne BN24 9BP

and in the United States of America by
SUSSEX ACADEMIC PRESS
Independent Publishers Group
814 N. Franklin Street, Chicago, IL 60610

and in Canada by
SUSSEX ACADEMIC PRESS (CANADA)
24 Ranee Avenue, Toronto, Ontario M6A 1M6

All rights reserved. Except for the quotation of short passages for the purposes of criticism and review, no part of this publication may be reproduced, stored in a retrieval system or transmitted in any form or by any means, electronic, mechanical, photocopying, recording or otherwise, without the prior permission of the publisher.

British Library Cataloguing in Publication Data
A CIP catalogue record for this book is available from the British Library.

Library of Congress Cataloging-in-Publication Data
Fowler, Jeaneane D.
  An introduction to the philosophy and religion of Taoism :
  pathways to immortality / Jeaneane Fowler.
    p. cm.
  Includes bibliographical references and index.
  ISBN 978-1-84519-086-6 (pbk. : alk. paper)
  1. Taoism. I. Title.
  BL1920.F685 2005
  299.5'14—dc22
                                                              2005002181

Cover illustration: Courtesy of Jeffrey Grupp, who explains that the artwork comes from research into the theory of abstract atomism which views ultimate (partless) non-physical particles as the metaphysical atoms that make up reality, but which are only directly apprehended in nirvanic consciousness. While research to date has focused on Indian Buddhist atomism, the "activity" of the momentary Indian Buddhist atoms clearly have conceptual similarities to the philosophy of the Tao, especially when represented artistically.

MIX
Paper from
responsible sources
FSC® C013056

Typeset and designed by G&G Editorial, Brighton.
Printed by TJ International, Padstow, Cornwall.

Contents

Preface and Acknowledgements   viii

Introduction   1

1 The Origins of Taoism: Ancient China   4
Taoism: the nature of the word   4
The Chinese psyche   7
The roots of Taoism in ancient practices   9
The Chinese dynasties   12
The Hsia/Xia "dynasty"   13
The Shang dynasty   15
The Chou/Zhou dynasty   22
The age of philosophers   29
Confucius   30
Early Taoists   32

2 The Interconnected Cosmos: The *I Ching/Yijing*   34
The *Book of Changes*: the *I Ching/Yijing*   34
Historical development   36
Reality as perpetual flux and change   44
The *Pa-kua/Bagua* or Eight Trigrams   47
The hexagrams   54
Consulting the *I Ching/Yijing*: finding the hexagram of the moment   59

3 Creative Forces: *Yin* and *Yang* and the Five Agents   65
Yin and *yang*   65
The origins of *yin* and *yang*   66
Yin   69
Yang   69
The interplay of *yin* and *yang*   70
Diversity in unity   75
Creation   77
The wider applications of the *yin* and *yang* theory   80

CONTENTS

Evaluating *yin* and *yang*	83
The Five Agents	84
Historical development of the Five Agents	85
The Five Agents as cosmological functions	88
The characteristics of the Agents	90
The theory of correspondences	91
Wider influences	93

4 *Tao* and its Early Philosophers — **95**

Lao-tzu/Laozi and the *Tao Te Ching/Daodejing*	96
Chuang-tzu/Zhuangzi	102
Lieh-tzu/Liezi	105
Tao	106
Creation	110
Te/De	116
Wu-wei: non-action	119
Tzu-jan/ziran: naturalness and spontaneity	121
The functioning of *Tao* in life	124

5 Taoism in Imperial China — **129**

Imperial China: Early period	129
The Ch'in/Qin dynasty	131
The Han dynasty	132
The period of the Three Kingdoms	141
The Chin/Jin dynasty	144
The period of disunity: the Six Dynasties	148
The Sui dynasty	153
Imperial China: Middle period	153
The T'ang/Tang dynasty	153
Imperial China: Late period	155
The period of the Five Dynasties	156
The Sung/Song dynasty	156
The Yüan/Yuan, Ming and Ch'ing/Qing dynasties	158

6 Alchemy — **160**

What is alchemy?	160
The origins of alchemical ideas	163
The Golden Elixir	166
Outer alchemy	167
The Taoist anatomy of the body	170
The Three Treasures	175
The Spirit Embryo	178
Sexual alchemy	179
Inner alchemical praxis	181

Returning to *Tao*	183
Meditation	184
The firing process	187
Becoming the Void	193

7 Life beyond Earth: Ancestors, Deities, Immortals and Sages — **194**

Ancestors	195
Deities	197
Immortals	214
The Eight Immortals (*Pa-hsien/Baxian*)	216
Sages	223

8 Religious Taoism — **226**

The eclectic nature of religious Taoism	226
Schools of Taoism	229
Priests	223
Spirit mediums	236
Exorcists	237
Divination	238
Temples	239
Ritual	240
The *chiao/jiao* ceremonies	243
Worship	245
The calendar	247
Festivals	248
Symbols	256
Life-cycle rites	259

9 Taoism Today — **263**

Communist China	263
Taoism in the West	267
T'ai Chi Ch'üan/Taijiquan	267
Feng-shui	270

Notes	276
Glossary of Chinese Names and Terms	309
Bibliography	316
Index	335

Preface and Acknowledgements

At the dawn of the third millennium, many human beings find themselves caught in the rapid pace of daily life. We travel greater distances to work. We work longer hours and often bring work home with us. We have to take on someone else's work who has left, been sacked or made redundant, and not been replaced. We have to worry about whether we will still have a job the following year, or whether we will be lucky enough to get one. And we have to put up with the pressures of management without means of redress. At home, there are different pressures, but no less a fast pace of life. These seem to be common issues in today's busy world. For some people, such a way of life provides interesting challenges, for others a feeling of being ill at ease with life. And the more we pack into the day, the faster time seems to hurtle ahead. It is perhaps for these reasons that so many individuals are searching for answers to the deeper questions of life, and are searching for the kinds of things that will juxtapose serenity and quietude with the bustle of life in the third millennium. It is in this context that ancient books such as the Taoist *Tao Te Ching/Daodejing* find a meaningful place on the bookshelves of ordinary people. For all the materialism that many have found in the West, there has been a deficit of spirituality – not religious spirituality, but a sense of being out of touch with the deeper meanings of life. Part of the purpose in writing this book is to share with others a search for some of these deeper meanings through an exploration of Taoism – a philosophy and religion that embraces just about every possible facet of spiritual experience.

In the academic realm of the third millennium the trend is very much in favour of specialisms. Perhaps I am fortunate not to be bound by academic institutional aims, and can independently enjoy the pleasures of exploring human spiritual, cultural and religious expressions from a broader canvas than can some of my colleagues. Those who have read some of my other books will identify the same aim in them as here: to explore how others answer fundamental questions about our existence. Why are we here as human beings? What is our purpose and function in life? How do we create the best balances in our lives? What are the ultimate goals of our existence? What are the proximate goals that will help us evolve towards our ultimate aim? Why do we suffer? Why do we feel dis-ease? Each religious culture will have a different approach to some of these questions, but there are also cross-cultural similarities, even identical concepts. It is the purpose of this book to examine the philosophy and religious practices of Taoism with a view to providing an insight into how the Chinese approached the religious and spiritual dimensions of human existence.

PREFACE AND ACKNOWLEDGEMENTS

I am indebted to the *Library and Learning Resources Centre* at the University of Wales, Newport for their help in the preparatory research of this text, especially to Nigel Twomey, who has always been so thoroughly helpful and efficient in procuring texts from interlibrary loans. I am also indebted to Sarah Norman and Jamie Creswell at *The Institute of Oriental Philosophy European Centre* at Taplow Court, near Maidenhead, Berkshire, for their invaluable help. The library there boasts an excellent range of texts on eastern religion and philosophy, and exquisite surroundings in which to work. I am grateful indeed to Jeffrey Grupp, Associate Editor of *Philo*, for permission to use his superb design for the jacket and cover of this book. My sincere thanks are due also to Tony and Anita Grahame and the team at Sussex Academic Press for their production of this text and for the excellent rapport that is always maintained between the publishing team and its authors. For any mistakes in the text, I take full responsibility.

Finally, my interest in Taoism came about many years ago through conversations with an Israeli homeopath, Jeremy Sherr. I know not where he is now, but he is an outstanding homeopathic practitioner, and an equally outstanding philosopher, from whom I have acquired a good slice of wisdom. It is to Jeremy that I dedicate this book with grateful thanks for the legacy of his thought in my own life.

Wentwood View
Autumn 2004

If you do not seek the great way to leave the path of delusion, even if
you are intelligent and talented you are not great. A hundred years
is like a spark, a lifetime is like a bubble. If you only crave
material gain and prominence, without considering
the deterioration of your body, I ask you, even if
you accumulate a mountain of gold can you
buy off impermanence?

Chang Po-tuan
Understanding Reality

Every human being, whether big or small, humble or great, young
woman or old man, musician, herbalist, clown, or scholar, may –
on the sole condition of finding his or her own mountain –
quit the treadmill of progress towards death and discover
the return towards life. It is not even necessary to act
intentionally: luck and a certain predisposition may
sometimes be the only needed conditions,
but nothing is guaranteed.
It is necessary, however, to at all times be open and prepared to
recognize, at a given moment of one's life, the mountain or
the initiating Immortal, which some day is to be found
on everyone's life path. It is in this readiness and
openness that we find all possible latitude
for individual free will and faith.

Kristofer Schipper
The Taoist Body

If all things do not have emptiness in the centre, if they do not have
form as substance, if *yin* does not have *yang*, how can they come
into being? Know the light and hold on to the dark. This is
the secret of existence. Those who know this intuitively
know the wondrous way of *Tao*.

Kuo-p'u
Ch'ing-lung-ching

Introduction

I have long believed that cultures beyond one's own have so much to offer in encouraging the expansion of the ways in which we view ourselves, our aims, our perspectives of life and the ways we might want to live life. Too often, the human being is bound by the restrictions of a conditioned life – by family, friends, society, and institutions. But once we step out of the boundaries of our own culture, providing we can do so without too much baggage and an open mind, we can learn so much that can assist us in the often turbulent passage of life. This is not to say that we should abandon all baggage and float freely with nothing! Some wise words from Lama Anagarika Govinda here are very pertinent: "It is beautiful to believe in something that gives us strength and confidence, to trust in the wisdom of life, but it is a sign of immaturity, of intolerance, nay outright stupidity, narrowness and mental overbearing to regard one's beliefs as infallible or as superior to other beliefs."[1] In the light of these words, this book is informed by two aims. First, it represents part of my own exploration of different cultures, another piece of the jigsaw in the understanding of others who share with me the definition of being human beings. Secondly, it has the educational aim, too, of helping others to open their minds to different cultures.

As a former tutor of Religious Studies I found Taoism a delight to teach, and it was well received by students. While I am not a sinologist, I firmly believe that a student beginning Religious Studies needs a broad understanding of what religion is before specializing in greater depth. This book, therefore, is directed to such enquiry with the hope that it will broaden the horizons of students of Religious Studies, and provide comprehensive coverage of Taoism that will encourage tutors to include Taoism in their courses. But the book is written as an introduction to Taoism; it assumes no previous knowledge and explains terms throughout, with a *Glossary of Chinese Names and Terms* at the end for reference. It is, therefore, a book that can act as an introduction for any individual who might wish to explore or expand their vision of Taoism. If I may steal some words from Ware's *Preface* to his *Alchemy, Medicine and Religion*, they are very apt for he or she embarking on new exploration: "Since I have no extraordinary talent but do happen to like the pursuit of action that constitutes perfect freedom, by deploying my wings I might well traverse the dark heavens, and by speeding my feet move over the landscape with the speed of wind."[2] Such is just what the mind can do when it explores new things.

In addition to expanding our own minds in the study of other cultures, there is hope, too, that we can achieve wider tolerance of others. Consider the following words of Charles Moore: "One of the hopeful signs in these otherwise hectic times in which we are living is

INTRODUCTION

the long-overdue realization of the need for mutual understanding of the people of the East and those of the West. Genuine understanding of the people who are separated from us by great distance or who differ from us in language, in way of life, in social custom, is difficult to achieve, even for those who are sincerely dedicated to this task."[3] These words were written a decade short of half a century ago and referred to the understanding of Chinese academic history and philosophy. Nevertheless, they are words that are (perhaps rather sadly) no less applicable to the world in which we live today. And they are words even more applicable today in the need for flexible interchange between different cultures, and the failure of different races and factions to engage in constructive mutual understanding.

Taoism is a multifaceted religion in the same way that most religions are varied by distinct yet sometimes blurred sectarian characteristics. Taoism is, however, perhaps more multifaceted than most religious cultures for it was involved with so many divergent strands of Chinese enquiry – geography, astronomy, pharmacology, herbology, medicine, as well as more religious quests such as self-cultivation, divination and the search for immortality. Taoism touched all aspects of Chinese life – often remarkably deeply. Whoever we are there will be some aspect of Taoism that will attract us. Most of all, there is an even more attractive call to a stillness of the inner self that is increasingly hard to glimpse in a world of domestic and societal pressures; yet we instinctively recognize its possibility. But since Taoism is so multifaceted its stillness and harmony are also balanced with colour, vibrancy, sound, magic and visionary journeys in the macrocosm of space and the microcosm of the self.

Because Taoism infiltrated so much of Chinese life, some space is given in the pages that follow to the historical background of Taoism in China. Chapter 1 encompasses the China of antiquity wherein lie the roots of Taoism in attitudes to nature and the concomitant practices that complemented such belief. Many people will be familiar with the *Book of Changes*, the *I Ching/Yijing*, the theories of which have informed so much of Taoist practice, though the original text predated Taoism by a long period of time. This text is the subject of chapter 2. Few have not heard of the concept of *yin* and *yang*, which forms the content of chapter 3, though the complementary theory of the Five Agents may be less well-known. The content of chapter 4 will be familiar to those who have heard of the *Tao Te Ching/Daodejing*; many of the important philosophical terms of Taoism are explained and examined. Chapter 5 returns to the historical background of Taoism in Imperial China and the rise of religious Taoism. The next step is to tour the inner microcosm of the body in chapter 6, which deals with the alchemy traditions of China. Life beyond Earth is the subject of chapter 7. Here, there are charming stories about deities, immortals (including the famous Eight Immortals of Taoism), and ancestors. The vast topic of religious Taoism – colour, vibrancy, sound and magic – is the subject of chapter 8. Finally, Taoism today in the East and the West provides material for the concluding chapter, including the practices of T'ai Chi Ch'üan/Taijiquan, so well known now in the West, and *feng-shui*, which is also becoming more widely known.

A few words on the romanization of Chinese characters are essential here. The Chinese language consists of a large number of pictorial symbols. The characters that compose these can be rendered into western sounds by two methods. One is called the Wade–Giles method, and the other Pinyin. The former is the older of the two systems and has been popular in the West for many years. Hence, we are used to spellings like Taoism and, for those who have some knowledge of Taoism, Lao-tzu and Chuang-tzu, the great sages of classical Taoism. But Pinyin is becoming very popular, and is much closer to the real sounds of words. It is the method of romanization that is used officially in China, and so many writers today use this system. So Taoism becomes Daoism, *Tao* becomes *Dao*, and the sages Lao-tzu and Chuang-tzu, Laozi and Zhuangzi respectively. Sometimes, the difference is minimal or even non-existent, but on other occasions the difference is so radical that the names bear little similarity. I have decided to use both forms throughout, the Wade–Giles form first, followed by Pinyin, thus Lao-tzu/Laozi. The reader who is used to one form rather than the other is then able to ignore the less familiar form. However, since texts often use one or the other and rarely both, the student will not be bewildered by an unfamiliar form when reading a quotation, or another book. Despite the decision to use both Wade-Giles and Pinyin romanization throughout, the text would become very cumbersome should *every* Chinese word be written in both methods. I have therefore decided to leave the word Taoism in Wade-Giles alone, as also *Tao*. The reader should note, however, that *D*aoism and *D*ao are the correct pronunciations. Romanization throughout follows the table in the *Peoples Republic of China: Administrative Atlas*.[4]

Sometimes we meet things and events, beliefs and practices that are strange to us. To understand these we often have to get behind the surface to the deeper meanings and rationales that make such beliefs and practices important to those close to them. To be educated is not to arrive at an educated state but to travel with different and transforming points of view, points of view that are ever widening, exploring, evolving. The more flexible we can become, the more we are open-minded, tolerant and willing to communicate with sympathy and sincere interest in cultures other than our own.

1
The Origins of Taoism: Ancient China

Taoism: the nature of the word

Taoism originated in China – a land so vast that it is almost the same size as Europe. China has had a long period of prehistory and history and multiple expressions of what it is to be Chinese. Taoism has grown out of that prehistory and history. It is difficult to trace the beginnings of the Taoist religion, partly because its roots are varied and complex, but also because of the unique interaction of the different religious strands of Chinese culture. China has embraced four religious genres from antiquity – Confucianism, which has been the dominant culture; Taoism; Buddhism, which infiltrated China at the beginning of the first millennium; and popular religion, the religion of the ordinary folk. While each of these has had its own particular characteristics the cross-fertilization of beliefs and practices between all four has been prolific resulting, almost, in a fifth genre – Chinese religion. Thus, it is often difficult to extract Taoism from Confucian, Buddhist and popular beliefs and practices. And since, too, Taoism has encompassed so many beliefs and practices it is difficult to define it. Julia Ching aptly remarks that it "may designate anything and everything"[1] – a point that will be seen throughout the pages of this book as we examine the heights of mystical philosophy on the one hand, and such things as the search for alchemical potions to ensure immortality on the other.

There are also problems with the word "Taoism" itself. The term Taoism was first used to refer to a religious school of thought in the second century BCE. The historian Ssu-ma T'an/Sima Tan, who wrote about the six main schools of thought at that time, referred to the school of *Tao-te/Daode*. Thereafter, this school was called the Taoist school. The first part of the word *Tao*, lies at the heart of what we call Taoism, and we shall spend some time examining it in a later chapter, but it is the *-ism* that is problematic. The Chinese used the term *tao* in all sorts of contexts so it was a term that pervaded all Chinese thought and that predated Taoism. Tao-*ism*, however, really refers to two kinds of religious belief, *Tao-chia/Daojia*, which is early philosophical Taoism, and *Tao-chiao/Daojiao*, which is the later religious and ritualistic Taoism. Using the word *Taoism* unites the two, but somewhat anachronistically and ambiguously. The Chinese character that represents the word *Tao* is made up of two parts, one representing a human, and the other representing forward movement. Thus, *Tao* suggests a "Way" in a very fundamental sense. In Taoist philosophy and metaphysics, *Tao* represents Reality at its ultimate, and all existence both as the "Way" that emanates from that Reality, and as the return to it. In its ordinary senses, however, the word has very wide meanings, and it is important to remember, also, that the word *Tao* is not exclusive to the religion we call Taoism. Confucius used it, for example, as meaning the ultimate in social order and moral behaviour.

Despite the multiple facets of Taoism, it can conveniently be divided into the two aspects noted above – one early, partly philosophical and metaphysical, the other later, overtly religious and ritualistic. While it is quite acceptable to see the later religious Taoism as a multifaceted religion there is much to be said for regarding the earlier, philosophical Taoism of those such as Lao-tzu/Laozi and Chuang-tzu/Zhuangzi as a non-religion. For these sages, *Tao* is not a deity to be worshipped, nor is it an indescribable Absolute in the same sense as the mystical Absolute of Hinduism. As Joseph Wu remarks of this early thought, "Tao is neither religiously available; nor is it even religiously relevant".[2] Indeed, it is difficult to create a religion around an inexplicable principle underpinning all other principles. Such philosophical Taoism, *Tao-chia/Daojia* or "school of the Way" will absorb considerable space in chapter 8. *Tao-chiao/Daojiao* or "religion of the Way" will be dealt with in a later chapter. Some see the later, religious Taoism as a degeneration of the earlier philosophical thought; others accept their complementary natures. These are issues that will need to be examined in due course.

Tao-chia/Daojia, associated especially with Lao-tzu/Laozi and Chuang-tzu/Zhuangzi – both of whom we shall meet in chapter 4 – belongs to the period of classical Taoism. Little is known historically of Lao-tzu/Laozi and Chuang-tzu/Zhuangzi, or how much of the texts bearing their names are authentic, but their works are seminal to philosophical Taoism. Inevitably, in writing of *Tao* there is an element of mysticism in these works – Lao-tzu/Laozi's *Tao Te Ching/Daodejing* and Chuang-tzu/Zhuangzi's *Chuang-tzu/Zhuangzi* – but there is also much that is grounded in naturalism and humanism. Thus, Lao-tzu/Laozi has advice for the ruler and for warfare, and Chuang-tzu/Zhuangzi's writings are full of the humour associated with life itself. Wu calls this blend of mysticism and humanism "esthetic mysticism"[3] to distinguish it from the religious mysticism that we associate with other meditative and introspective religions. On the other hand, Bishop describes philosophical Taoism as transcendentalist "if by transcendental we mean, first, going beyond the usual or ordinary and, second, excelling or being excellent in oneself".[4] This is not a denial of the ordinary, non-transcendental self in the sense that many religions interpret the phrase; it is more recognition of a different self that is a natural part of the universe – a self rooted in *Tao*.

While philosophical *Tao-chia/Daojia* has certain basic characteristics, subsequent Taoism in the form of *Tao-chiao/Daojiao*, religious Taoism, is anything but a unified phenomenon. Taken together, they illustrate the many varied facets of Taoism – philosophical, magical, alchemical, priestly, ritualistic, for example. Isabelle Robinet points out that we cannot think of Taoism as a whole, nor can we trace a neat linear growth of it:

It took shape only gradually, during a slow gestation that was actually a progressive integration of various ancient lines of thought. No precise date can be set for its birth, and the integration of outside elements into the religion has never ceased. If we add to this the enrichment of Taoism throughout its history with new revelations or new inspirations, we can see how open a religion it is, constantly progressing and evolving, and how difficult it is not only to date its first appearance but also to define its boundaries.[5]

Despite such obscure development and varied beginnings, there are characteristics in the archetypal Chinese psyche that are to be found in Taoist thought and practice throughout its history right through to present times – albeit characteristics overlaid by accumulated ideas and practices. These characteristics seem to emerge despite the great regional variations in belief and language in the vast lands of China. Underpinning the varied threads that make up the multifaceted religion of Taoism are some strands that reach back to antiquity. Perhaps this is because the Chinese culture adds and borrows new elements without necessarily replacing old ones, and because it has great reverence for its ancient past. Robinet puts this point sensitively when she says that Taoism "has never stopped moving, transforming, absorbing. Its history shows us how ceaselessly it has proceeded by 'recursive loops', taking up its past like a bundle under its arm in order to travel farther toward new horizons and, as it goes, gleaning all sorts of treasures along the way".[6] It is precisely the "recursive loops" that enable the characteristics embedded in the Chinese psyche to re-emerge again and again. Ssu-ma T'an/Sima Tan, cited above, demonstrates well the eclectic nature of what he termed Taoism in his own day: "As to its techniques, it conforms with the great yin and yang; it selects the good points of the Literati and Mohists; it chooses the essentials from the School of Terms and the School of Totalitarians." Taoists, he says, "change with the times and respond to the transformations of things-and-beings".[7]

From what has been said so far, then, while we might want to see the term Taoism as indicative of a religion that has a formulated, characterized set of beliefs, it is not so. Just as religions like Christianity, Judaism, Hinduism and Buddhism – to name but a few – are characterized by great diversity, so, too, is Taoism. While its origins stretch back into antiquity, Taoism is a term encompassing a whole spectrum of beliefs and practices. So when Taoism is referred to as a religion of China, the term may be likened to water that encompasses seas, oceans, streams, rivers, rain and clouds. It is the water that is Taoism while its facets are many and varied. In Taoism, then, there are many pathways, sometimes to the same goal and sometimes to different ultimate goals. In fact, such a perspective reflects well the heart of Taoism for, just as water never flows the same way twice, so Taoism would find one route or path a totally one-sided religious perspective. We should view Taoism, then, as one facet of Chinese religion, and the latter as unique in being a special blend of Confucianism, Taoism, Buddhism, and popular practices. In examining Taoism as a specific aspect of Chinese religion the particular influences and characteristics that inform such a unique blend always have to be borne in mind. For many individuals the preference for Confucian, Taoist or Buddhist praxis has always been a pragmatic one. Allinson makes the valid point, "we are reminded of the generalized folk saying that every Chinese person is a Confucian, a Taoist, and a Buddhist. He is a Confucian when everything is going well; he is a Taoist when things are falling apart; and he is a Buddhist as he approaches death".[8]

The influence of Confucianism is certainly evident from the earliest times, and of

Buddhism, even though it arrived on the scene much later. And in the area of popular religious beliefs and practices the dividing line between them and Taoism is often extremely difficult to define. Many writers extract Taoism from the popular culture, seeing the latter as something separate. Saso, for example, describes Chinese popular religion as "a cultural system that governs the rites of passage and the annual festivals celebrated by the people of China".[9] He thus sees Chinese popular religion as something different from the three religions – Taoism, Confucianism and Buddhism – and as associated with Chinese culture. Such a distinction is aided by the fact that popular religion is not so much a belief system as a way of life, a way of life that incorporates different aspects of the three strands, but cannot really be slotted into any one of them. But the three strands have borrowed so much from each other, and from popular belief and praxis, that such a neat demarcation between popular religion and Taoism (or Buddhism, or Confucianism) is hardly possible.

Robinet was categorical that Taoism was quite open in its borrowings from Confucianism and Buddhism. She wrote: "It has enriched itself at their expense, enlarging and extending itself, without ever abandoning its own cosmological vision and without ever forgetting its goal: to sublimate humanity and not to leave it behind."[10] She believed that Taoism evolved marginally and somewhat separately and elitist as a way of life.[11] However, I do not think the aims of Taoism have ever been so clear cut. Nor do I think that Taoism can be extrapolated from the everyday existence of the Chinese people so easily. Taoism is by nature generally syncretistic and the Chinese psyche is equally so. Chinese popular religion is informed by much that is Taoist, and Taoism is equally informed by the religious needs of the populace. This is surely true of religious Taoism. The religion of the people was a mongrel religion, but it was as much Taoist as Confucian and Buddhist. It is just that the boundaries became so lost in cultural tradition and syncretism that no one religion could ever really be properly stranded out. And apart from the early philosophical *Tao-chia/Daojia*, Taoism has been very much people orientated. Barrett describes it as "a natural outgrowth of native ways of thought and action":[12] essentially, it was very much a *Chinese* phenomenon, close to the psyche of the Chinese people.[13] We should, then, be wary of distinctly demarcating Taoism from popular religion itself.

The Chinese psyche

So what are the strands in the Chinese nature that reach back into antiquity and inform Taoism? Perhaps the most important is an inherent affinity with nature and the natural world. Bodde rightly commented: "For the Chinese, this world of nature, with its mountains, its forests, its storms, its mists, has been no mere picturesque backdrop against which to stage human events. On the contrary, the world of man and the world of nature constitute one great indivisible unity."[14] Bodde considered that this perspective of nature stemmed from the agrarian nature of the Chinese existence in antiquity. Thus, just as the Judeo-Christian and Muslim religions sprang from patriarchal male-dominated tribal religions, and have retained the masculinity of their concept of deity to this day, so the ancient agrarian background of the Chinese instilled into their psyche a closeness to, and need for harmony with, all nature. It was a harmony that saw the same animation and spirit in nature as in human beings. Mountains, springs, rivers, trees – all had their animated forces that might or might not co-operate with humans. It was such beliefs that led to worship and propitiation of all kinds of gods and spirits through dance, chant, sorcery, sacrifice and shamanism. The corners of the home and the niches of the environment had their spirits good and evil – house deities, earth deities, territorial deities, demons, were abundant. But the dominant idea in these practices was a need to harmonize oneself, one's home, family and clan with natural and supernatural forces in order for life to run smoothly.

Combined with such a perspective of nature was a profound belief in the spirits of ancestors – a belief that surfaced as much in political intrigue and status as in popular religious worship in later times. Belief in a spirit world, in the ongoing existence of deceased ancestors in spirit form, and a quest for harmony with nature and its forces, are part of the legacy of the ancient past to the Chinese people throughout their history. Ancestor veneration, especially, united the living and the dead in the *present*, not in a mere remembrance of the departed by the living, but in a mutual reciprocity emerging from the belief that each could affect the other in the here and now. Ancestor veneration has been a dynamic and continuous aspect of the Chinese psyche, one that held together families, clans, territories and dynasties in the long years of Chinese history, and one that was coupled with Confucian respect for familial ties. What emerged was a reverence for the ancient past and a retention of ancient beliefs in the present psyche.

The ancient conception of an orderly universe in which all is harmonized in interconnected, though hierarchized, relationships is continuously reflected in Chinese thought. Nature is characterized by incessant, regular change that conforms to self-perpetuating rhythms, patterns and cycles: individual, familial and societal life needed to reflect the same kind of harmony. In social terms, the Chinese have accepted that such harmonious living does not necessarily mean equality of living. A hierarchized existence is as essential in the physical, earthly realm as in the divine or spirit world, and to experience harmony is to accept one's social position and function in society and family. This does not suggest that social mobility is impossible, for belief in the inherent goodness and possible perfection of human beings is inherited from the time of Confucius. Psychologically, harmonious living is found in the search for harmony of the mind and body, and physiologically in the harmony of the energies that maintain and preserve the body. The *yin* and *yang* theories, associated with Chinese and Taoist religion, reflect these inner searches for balance and harmony.

The human being is not estranged from nature or from a reality that is so ultimate that he or she is worthlessly lost. Reality is experienced in the patterns and harmonies of nature and life. Derk Bodde believed that it is ethics and not religion that informs the spiritual life of the Chinese,[15] and such a view is certainly evident in the meticulous expression of order, right behaviour, ritual practice, honour to ancestors, and so on, which have characterized Chinese life. Fulfilling the best in one's own nature and accepting the unique difference of oneself from another is what it means to be a relevant part of an interconnected and harmonized whole. Bodde considered it was for this reason that Taoists were not too interested in salvation, for they knew that very few were equipped with the nature of a sage.[16] The concept of a retributive deity, of rewarding heavens and punishing hells, was an innovation brought to the Chinese by Buddhism; it was a thought originally somewhat alien to the Chinese mind.

Yet a belief in fate seems to be characteristic, a belief perhaps informed by the capriciousness and overwhelming force that nature often displays. It was this that engendered the need to remain in harmony with nature, and to use the medium of shamans and sorcerers, as well as priests and ritual to maintain the harmonious rhythms of familial, agricultural, political and societal life. The sociologist Granet put this succinctly long ago when he said: "The sense that the natural world and human society are closely bonded has been the basic element of all Chinese beliefs."[17] The intimate connection between spirit and human worlds is reflected in the divinatory practices that have been popular from ancient to present times. Keightley's comment that: "The oracular impulse lies deep in Chinese culture",[18] is indeed so. We find it in all kinds of expression from interpreting cracks on tortoise shells and animal bones in the ancient past, to the visits of people to the many fortune-tellers in temples in present times. Again, the underlying concept is one of creating and maintaining harmony between oneself and nature. This seems to have been the underpinning philosophy that informs Chinese beliefs. Indeed, Allinson makes the point that such philosophy has been far more important than set doctrines. He writes, "the reason why the Chinese mind has not developed strongly in the direction of the construction of theoretical proof structures is that Chinese philosophy has, from the beginning, seen man as being at home in nature".[19] The Chinese goal is harmony of the self with nature, and of Heaven with oneself. This would be true whether from a Taoist, Confucian or Buddhist perspective.

The foregoing is not to say that we can stereotype the Chinese psyche. Indeed, contradictions to these generalized characteristics will surely abound. Yet, they are indicators of what we might want to look for in the nature of Taoism in so far as it relates to Chinese culture in general. They are also indicators of the ancient ideas that have contributed to Taoist beliefs and practices that survived to the last century in China. The respect that the Chinese had for their ancient past has meant that the connnective tissue of centuries of tradition has grounded some beliefs firmly in the Chinese psyche – ancestor reverence is a case in point, and there are aspects of festivals that reflect the most ancient of ideas. We shall need to look for these links in the pages that follow, and that is why we need to turn first to the ancient past, to ancient China that predates any form of Taoism, though it contains its seeds.

The roots of Taoism in ancient practices

If we look more specifically for the roots of Taoism we shall find them not only in the variety of beliefs that have coloured the Chinese character down through the centuries, but also in a variety of practices from the very earliest strata of Chinese prehistory and history. But this is not to say that those roots can be specifically identified: indeed, the roots of Taoism are multifarious, and it is possible here to highlight only some of the major practices that were endemic in the ancient past. These practices serve more to highlight the kind of ethos that pervaded early thought, the kinds of practices to which the early Chinese were attracted and, more importantly, why. Examining these roots will help to create an understanding of the later phenomenon that came to be known as Taoism. However, because Taoism is something of an eclectic phenomenon, its roots are not only ancient, for it gleaned as it progressed and changed, and newer roots will need to be pointed out along the way in later chapters.

Three practices stand out as precursors of later trends: divination, shamanism and sorcery, and ancestor reverence – and they are linked by the same kind of human psychological needs. The practice of divination, as noted earlier, is closely associated with the bond between humans and nature, and the need to know the outcome of a certain action. It is an attempt to understand fate, what will happen in the future, and was widely practised in ancient China. As will be seen later, it was often limited to a negative or a positive response – no or yes. But this was important for the undertaking of serious matters – waging war, for example.

Shamanism was also a major precursor of Taoism; indeed, it was probably the foundation of many religions. Palmer, for example, considers it to have been the world's first major religion,[20] beginning about eight thousand years ago in Siberia, where the term *shamanism* originated, and spreading from there into many parts of Asia and to North and Central America. Such is its influence that it is not too difficult to see the traces of shamanism in many religions, for it really epitomizes humankind's deep-rooted subconscious beliefs and fears about the world in which we live.[21] Shamanism views the universe as an interconnectedness of spirit and matter. Humans live in the world of matter, along with the phenomena of that world – mountains, trees, the sun, moon, plants, rocks, animals, and so forth. It is the interconnected nature of, and interaction between, the two worlds of spirit and matter that are at the root of shamanist belief and practice. Every entity in existence is affected by the spiritual forces on the "other side". Thus, sickness, health, natural disasters, good harvests and the whole welfare of human and agricultural life are dependent on the benevolent or malevolent forces of the spirit world.

So far, this would make life a very arbitrary existence: it would be difficult to know how, when, and which spirits had been offended in order to produce bad luck, or for what reasons life was going well. It was in situations such as these that the role of shamans became crucial as mediums of contact between the physical and spiritual worlds. Through entering into a trance, they were able to come into contact with the spirits, talk to them, and mediate with them for other mortals. Or, a spirit could enter a shaman's body in order to communicate more directly to people. Shamans could ascertain why spirits were offended and, more importantly, what could be done to put things right. Indeed, it was believed that shamans could contact the spirits *before* something was undertaken so that people could proceed with their plans with confidence. Shamanism, therefore, revealed more than divination. Awareness of the fact that life and nature can so easily be hostile, and the need to tread respectfully so as not to offend the spirits of the other world made shamans a necessary force in society.

Shamanism has influenced Taoism in a number of ways. First, it bequeathed to *Tao-chia*, the philosophical Way of Taoism, a deep reverence for nature that sees humankind as needing to interact with the whole of the natural world in a very harmonious way. Shamans professed to be very close to nature, to understand it, and to interact with it. Shamanism also involved the everyday life of the people, their ups and downs, their need to make sense of their environment, and their need to be assured that there was something they could *do* in order to make sense of life. We shall also see much later the influence of shamanism in many of the practices of institutional forms of Taoism – the retained beliefs in a hierarchized pantheon of gods and spirits; in the use of magical practices, talismans and the like; in modern festivals such as the Chinese New Year; and in deities such as the "Kitchen God", for example. At heart, shamanism is an attempt to gain some harmony with, and some control over, the natural forces of the world around, but "control" in the sense of being able to work *with* nature by assisting the physical and spirit worlds to return to harmony. Palmer puts this point well when he says that shamanism at a philosophical or spiritual level had

> the sense of a relationship between the laws of nature and the ultimate power of the universe. The idea that harmony and balance within nature reflects the harmony and balance of the universe is as central to shamanism as it is to Taoism. Associated with this is the concept that change cannot be forced but only revealed or experienced. The shamanist is not in control of the spirits. They are in charge of him or her. Through the shaman they help humanity to repair any damage it has done and thus to return to the Way. The idea of flowing with the Way, of bending and thus surviving, reflects the shamanistic attitude to life around us.[22]

However, despite Palmer's words, there is an element of control over spirits by the shaman, because he or she is able to communicate with a spirit *at will*. And that interaction with a spirit is a very *ecstatic* one, not one in which the shaman is passive. For this reason shamans were often referred to as sorcerers and sorceresses, perhaps because their collective skills were multiple.[23] They were often believed to fly through the sky, visit the gods or the underworld, bring rain, exorcise demons, cure diseases and expel evil. Female shamans, especially, became associated with rain-making. Early ritual, then, "pointed symbolically, and sometimes also actually to a primeval union between the human being and the gods, a union that was shamanic and ecstatic".[24]

Reverence for ancestors has characterized Chinese religions from the earliest times. The continued interaction between the living and the dead meant that the living were protected by their ancestors, who remained interested in the affairs of the family. Conversely, the dead continued to be cared for by the living, with sacrificial offerings bestowed with respectful and meticulous ritual. Ancestor veneration gave particular emphasis to the role, unity and stability of the family. It also engendered filial respect and reverence. Bishop's comments concerning this fundamental belief are particularly apt: "Religion was predicated on a view of reality as monistic and moral and a belief in the continuity of life and organic natural processes. There was no sharp division between a person and his ancestors. Life flowed on from one generation to another. Similarly, there was no absolute break between past, present and future."[25] Such concepts reinforce the monistic unity in the universe that was to underpin later philosophical Taoism. But, for the moment, it is important to note that ancestor reverence was essential to the ordinary person. Bodde called it "the most vital and sincere form of religious feeling" in early Chinese civilization.[26]

The Chinese dynasties

Precise dates for the earliest period of Chinese prehistory and history are impossible to ascertain with any certainty, and they vary from source to source – often considerably. In particular, events important in Taoist history have not really been chronicled by official Chinese historians. Such difficulties need not concern us too much, in that it will be the philosophical and contextual ideas related to Taoism that will be the main concern of this book. Nevertheless, some backdrop of time is needed against which to set the events in Taoist development and character. The present chapter serves to provide such detail with regard to ancient China, normally agreed to have ended with the Chou/Zhou dynasty when feudalism gave way to imperialism. The earliest period is mainly legendary, though evidence of a Stone Age and following Neolithic culture has been brought to light by archaeological expertise. It is China that can boast the discovery of "Peking Man", a being likely to date back to the Pleistocene era, 400,000 or 500,000 BCE. Even earlier, approximately a million years ago, some kind of humanoid may have lived in south-west China, judging by fossil teeth discovered in 1965.[27]

Some early Neolithic sites have been discovered in China, possibly dated to 7000–8000 BCE. Here, coarse, plain pottery has been found, along with implements suggesting the use of cereals, and the domestication of animals.[28] The Yang-shao culture, from the late sixth to the third millennium BCE, has revealed evidence of a farming culture, with the village being the social unit.[29] From the Lung-shan/Longshan culture, dating roughly to the whole of the fourth millennium BCE, archaeological discoveries have unearthed evidence of divination by the use of animal bones, inscribed pottery, early altars and clay phallic objects. These last have suggested to some the worship of male ancestors.[30] What is interesting is that many different Neolithic sites have been found in China, suggesting that the streams that fed Chinese civilization were varied and regional. The Neolithic people lived in villages in the river basins where the soil was fertile, or on the higher slopes where water was available but where they were safe from frequent floods. However, a common factor would have been dependency on agriculture, a fact that might presuppose an emphasis on fertility and nature. In a world where people were so dependent on the negative and positive powers of nature, it might be expected that earthly and heavenly phenomena were ascribed animated powers. And in the processes of birth, decay and death, it is perhaps here that we see the need for a cult of ancestors who would protect and aid the family and clan. It seems, too, that domesticated animals – dogs, pigs, sheep and cattle – were part of the earliest known cultures. As time advanced, towns were built, pottery became more advanced with the invention of the potter's wheel, and the time became right for a more centralized ruling power, the Shang dynasty. The Lung-shan/Longshan culture preceded the better-known Shang, the former having considerable influence on the latter.[31] Of course, the Shang civilization that followed, being a Bronze Age culture, was more advanced, as we shall see. What seems to have occurred was the natural progression from segregated to integrated village cultures, which eventually developed into wider, more complex state cultures. Some brief dates of this development might be helpful here.

Hsia/Xia dynasty	*Somewhere between 22nd–20th down to the 18th–16th centuries* BCE
Shang (Yin) dynasty	*17th–11th centuries* BCE *(traditionally 1766–1123* BCE*) probably 1600–1027* BCE
	Confirmed by archaeological findings
	Religion characterized by divination and sacrifice, including human sacrifice
	Ancestor veneration evident
	Worship of nature via spirits
Chou/Zhou dynasty	*11th–3rd centuries* BCE *(c. 1027–256* BCE*)*
	Beginnings of feudalism in China
Western Chou/Zhou	*11th–8th centuries* BCE *(traditionally 1122–771* BCE*) probably c. 1027–771* BCE
	Founder King Wu
	Duke of Chou/Zhou's regency
Eastern Chou/Zhou	*8th–3rd centuries* BCE *(c. 771–256* BCE*)*
	Chou/Zhou King becomes central power (722–481 BCE) – the "Spring and Autumn" period
	6th–5th centuries BCE: Confucius (*c.* 551–479 BCE)
	5th–3rd centuries BCE: Warring States period (*c.* 403–221 BCE)
	Age of classical philosophy
	4th–3rd centuries BCE: Lao-tzu/Laozi and the *Tao Te Ching/Daodejing* (traditional dates 604–531 BCE)
	4th–3rd centuries BCE: the *Chuang-tzu/Zhuangzi* (369–286 BCE)

The Hsia/Xia "dynasty"

China has always accepted its ancient beginnings as Three Dynasties – the Hsia/Xia, Shang and Chou/Zhou. Many have considered the Hsia/Xia dynasty to be completely mythical, but Chang Kwang-chih is one author who accepts the political existence of a Hsia/Xia "dynasty". He considers that the political forces of the Hsia/Xia and Shang were "chronologically parallel – or at least overlapping – political groups".[32] The same could be said of the Shang and the Chou/Zhou. Chang identifies the Hsia/Xia with the Erh-li-t'ou/Erlitou culture in the north-west of Honan.[33] So while not exactly a "dynasty" as we would think of the term, a Hsia/Xia existence is not completely out of the question.

While there is sound evidence of Stone Age and Neolithic cultures, however, traditional Chinese prehistory is mostly legendary, full of mythical heroes and legendary emperors and sages. Of the legendary rulers of ancient China, most arising from Shang myths, the most celebrated in the history of Taoism as much as Chinese religion in general is the figure known as the Yellow Emperor, Huang-ti/Huangdi, whom legend dates at around 2500 BCE. He is said to have had secret and divine knowledge. Although the famous

THE ORIGINS OF TAOISM: ANCIENT CHINA

Taoist sage Chuang-tzu/Zhaungzi frequently mentions the Yellow Emperor, real evidence to suggest his existence outside myth is impossible to find. But what is important about the Yellow Emperor is that traditionally he is said to have been the founder of Taoism. Although it was Lao-tzu/Laozi who gave Taoism its metaphysical and mystical emphasis, Chinese themselves see the Yellow Emperor as beginning it all. Blofeld wrote: "The majestic figure of the Yellow Emperor looms through the swirling mists of time, for he was one of the Five Emperor-Sages belonging to China's Golden Age . . . who presided over the birth of the Empire, endowing it with such precious skills as the use of fire, of ploughs, of silk-looms. He personally is credited with having discovered and transmitted the secret of immortality."[34] He was also said to be an expert at *feng-shui*, "earth magic".

While the Yellow Emperor was the most important of the legendary emperors, he was preceded by Three August Ones. One of these, Fu Hsi/Fu Xi, was the founder of animal husbandry and hunting, as well as the calendar, marriage, civil administration and, some claimed, the eight trigrams. Another was the ox-headed Shen-nung/Shennong, who founded agriculture and medicine. Yü/Yu is said to have founded the Hsia/Xia dynasty and was the founder of engineering and of the essential irrigation systems for agriculture. These were characteristics cast retrospectively on mythical Hsia/Xia times from much later periods. The time of these legendary characters was known traditionally as a Golden Age when people lived in harmony with nature and with each other in a life of tranquillity and peace. Since each person's consciousness was harmonized with all other aspects of life, society needed no rules for living; these were introduced only when the Golden Age declined and the consciousness of human beings deteriorated.

Such legendary sage-rulers, then, belong to the Hsia/Xia dynasty of China, the first and partially mythical dynasty. As has been seen, ancestor reverence has been of crucial importance to the way in which the Chinese have ordered their lives, and this was no less the case for the great emperors as the poorest peasants. Aristocratic positions in society were hereditary, and to have an ancient lineage was essential, especially for an emperor. Thus, it was to this mythical Hsia/Xia dynasty that the great families projected legendary founders – founders that varied from a great emperor to a hero or deity. And just as immediate ancestors were felt to grant prosperity in wealth, peace and war to their descendants, so the powerful mythical founders were believed to grant even greater favours. Dynastic families or leading aristocratic families adopted or created founders and legends to support their ancestral line. The Chou/Zhou dynasty, for example, took as its ancestor Hou-chi/Huji the founder and King of Millet. Sometimes, such originating ancestors were non-human – a bird with a human voice, a fish, a bear, a mastiff. As far as we know then, the Hsia/Xia dynasty was partially legendary or semi-mythical. The third dynasty, the Chou/Zhou dynasty, justified its overthrow of the previous Shang dynasty by the point that the Shang itself had overthrown the Hsia/Xia dynasty. It was such propaganda that entrenched in the Chinese mind the existence of a first Hsia/Xia dynasty that archaeology has never thoroughly verified. However, from the point of view of religious belief, the early, prehistoric period was probably characterized by a belief in spirits that presided over natural phenomena, as well as divination practices. Ancestor worship probably also had its origins in the early village life of prehistoric times.

Chinese history is characterized by dynastic cycles that waxed and waned. They were inaugurated with power struggles that brought periods of intense warfare, and were divided sometimes by more diffused power. They reflect the *yin* and *yang* of historical progression. The history of ancient China that follows is important in the search for the roots and real beginnings of Taoism. The Shang dynasty that began Chinese civilization reveals the basic ingredients that inform Chinese and Taoist religion and, therefore, deserves specific analysis in the pages that follow. The Chou/Zhou dynasty is even more important, for it included the age of classical China and produced some of its greatest thinkers – Confucius, Lao-tzu/Laozi and Chuang-tzu/Zhuangzi. Ancient, classical China, then, refers to these two dynasties of the Shang and the Chou/Zhou.

The Shang dynasty

The Shang dynasty was an advanced Bronze Age culture. Despite being a literate culture, few documents survived, so that the second to first century BCE court historian, Ssu-ma Ch'ien/Sima Qian, had little to utilize in his survey of Shang history.[35] Thus, it is mainly through inscriptions, rather than texts, that knowledge about the Shang dynasty is gleaned. It was informed by the interaction of different locational cultural characteristics – what Needham called "culture-complexes".[36] These "culture-complexes" served to make the overall Shang culture multifarious. China is a vast country and the differences between North and South alone are considerable. The North, with its notable Yellow River, is temperate with warm summers, cold winters and little rainfall. The South, on the other hand, is subtropical and the rainfall heavy. It is easy to see how the different geographical circumstances might produce variants in religious beliefs and practices that were felt to be essential for the healthy agriculture of each locality. But the Shang and Chou/Zhou times were mainly concentrated around the Yellow River valley, with not too extensive expanding geographical power.

It is with the Shang dynasty that we have the dawn of Chinese history. According to tradition, the last of the princes of the Hsia/Xia dynasty was a tyrant who was overthrown by one of his vassals, the Prince of Shang. This began the Shang dynasty, later to be known as the Yin dynasty, from the name of its last capital. It is likely that the people of the early Shang period also gained their living through agriculture. Needham noted that milk has been absent from the Chinese diet from ancient times, and a pastoral life is therefore unlikely even at this early period.[37] Apart from rice and millet, wheat also seems to have been cultivated. Cowrie shells were used as a means of exchange. While no books survive from the period, short inscriptions on stone or bone bear testimony to the ability to record important events, particularly religious ones. There seems to have been continuity of religious practices with pre-Shang times – a belief in ancestors, divination, and a developed sacrificial ritual – but an advancement that makes the Shang dynasty the first real Chinese civilization. Traditionally, the dynasty is supposed to have begun in 1766 BCE, though it is more likely that it spanned the centuries from about the beginning of the sixteenth or early fifteenth century to the eleventh century BCE. Archaeology has gleaned much about the period from oracle inscriptions, particularly from later Shang times. It is the later period of the Shang dynasty that has revealed an advanced Bronze Age culture, particularly through excavations at the earlier Shang capital at Anyang in the Honan valley. This mature culture had large buildings in its cities, and produced some beautifully and expertly crafted bronze utensils for religious ritual, for war, and as luxury items. It is from the decorative representations on some of these bronzes that we are able to glean something of the life at the time. Indeed, the bronze work and woven silks are indicative of sensitivity to art and culture, and increased specialization.

Divination, which was focused around the king and the court diviners, was an important part of the religious cult, and the practice of it in different ways both preceded the Shang dynasty and stretched down the centuries after it. In Shang times, the undershells of tortoises and turtles or shoulder-blades of animals were heated so that the cracks could be "read" by trained priests, who would then relay the decision of the gods. While only "yes" or "no" or "favourable" or "unfavourable" answers could be given, diviners seem to have been fairly meticulous about keeping records of their transactions, inscribing the divinatory request or statement alongside the cracks and, on occasion, how a king had interpreted it.[38] Also included, where divination concerned sacrifices for ancestors, were genealogical lists. We know that in early Shang times questions would be asked about the weather, the beginning of a campaign of war, setting out on a journey, the sex of a child, an illness, interpretation of the king's dreams,[39] for example. However, in Sarah Allan's view, Shang divination was not so much a desire to know the outcome of a future event as an attempt to control it.[40] It is a sensible deduction, given that if the former were the case, there would be little that could be done to avoid the outcome.

In fact, there was more to Shang divinatory praxis than a first glance reveals. Keightley makes the point that Shang divination is set against a view of reality that was orderly. The hollows bored in the shell or bone were done in such a way that the diviner knew exactly where the cracks would occur: "No crack could appear where the Shang diviner did not want it to. The powers could not reveal themselves in unexpected ways. The supernatural responses were rigorously channeled."[41] The ancestors/deities to whom divination was made were part of the same rational order as humanity and, therefore, *could* be divined.[42] Smith considers that divination specialists were an occupational group in Neolithic northern China in the third millennium BCE. So by Shang times, divination had developed to a fine art.[43]

The divinatory question or statement could be made both positively and negatively on the same shell or bone. In late Shang times, statements were paired in very positive and mildly negative terms, for example, "Help will be received" (positive), and "Perhaps help will not be received" (mildly negative). The nature of the words as statements not requests is important. According to Keightley, it seems an increasing number of scholars are maintaining that divinations were *not* questions but statements of intent. The divination removed doubts by "posing two complementary, alternative charges in the indicative mood".[44] Thus, the statements may have been made in order to authenticate decisions already made.

By late Shang times, the king himself interpreted the cracks as a demonstration of his power and, thus, by these times inscriptions certainly show statements of the king's intent – not a wish to know what would happen in the future, but an action to ensure something would take place. "Divination was not just a matter of determining what the spirits wanted; it was a way of telling the spirits what man wanted, and of seeking reassurance from the fact that the spirits had been informed."[45] Thus, the mildly negative of paired statements was abandoned, and the divining act became more of a "magical charm" against disaster.[46] Needless to say, the results of the divination always proved the king to be right. So whereas early Shang divination was concerned with disease, the harvest, dreams, hostile attack and the like, by late Shang times it was concerned mainly with statements of ritual sacrifices to be performed, or announcements of royal hunts. Keightley makes the interesting point here that: "We must assume, not that the Shang were no longer troubled by such questions as successful childbirth, victorious alliances, or the significance of dreams, but that other systems, like that represented by the *Yi-ching*, grew up to handle them."[47] Considering the prevalence and importance of divination in Taoism down through the centuries, it is a very valid supposition.

So as the Shang dynasty unfolded, divination inscriptions became less elaborate, more formalized, and with auspicious rather than inauspicious content. The emphasis on correct ritual sacrifice suggests that control of the future – the rains, the harvest and malign influences – must have been paramount. Ancestors and gods satisfied by sacrificial offerings would be supportive to the best kind of outcome. The inscriptions on the thousands of oracle bones that have been discovered have yielded about five thousand characters, but only about one and a half thousand have been deciphered.[48] It was the beginnings of writing for China and East Asia, and represents the seeds of divination praxis in Taoism.

The kings of the Shang dynasty were numerous. Ssu-ma Ch'ien/Sima Qian listed thirty of them, who centred their rule in as many as seven towns at various times. Yin, near today's Anyang, was its last capital. It is with the developing Shang dynasty that we begin to see the patriarchal role of the ruler in relation to his subjects. A primitive feudalism begins here and was developed in Chou/Zhou times. Like the father of a small family the king had complete control over his subjects as the wider family of his state. A hierarchized bevy of officials assisted the king, and formed the nobility, the aristocracy. Important diviners also assisted him. The role of the king was paramount in religious ritual, which took the form of leading the people in appeasing, and requesting the assistance of, the many spirits, deities and ancestors. It was critical that the sanction of these spirits and deities was obtained before any venture, and that they were appropriately thanked on its successful completion or placated if it were to go wrong. The divinatory inquiries by the king, along with his ritual sacrifices, ceremonies and respect to ancestors, were conceived of as the most powerful form of contact with Heaven and the spirits of the other world.

Important to note is the meticulous sense of order and correctness in conducting ritual before the arrival on the historical scene of Confucius and the emphasis on moral and social order and etiquette that marked his beliefs. Such meticulous praxis in Shang times is described by Allan. She writes. "Not only did the ancestor have to be worshipped on the proper day, but the ceremony, animal or combination of animals (including humans), their preparation, number, sex, color were all suitable subjects of divination."[49] Gradually, as Allan goes on to say, ritual became increasingly ordered and codified. It is clear, too, that such prescribed order needed a large number of officials. These aristocrats lived in cities and contrasted considerably with the rural peasants. They were frequently engaged in warfare, hunted, and supported the king not only in life but also in death, for they were immolated with the king when he died. Clearly life was thought to continue much the same after death as it had before for the Shang ruler and his nobility.

From what has been briefly mentioned concerning religious belief and practice, it is clear that Shang religion was pluralistic and polytheistic. It was, after all, the many nature deities and ancestral spirits that were felt to be closest to the needs of the people, and it was the forces of nature, both benign and malevolent, that were so critical to daily existence. While archaeological discoveries cannot project a philosophy of life onto physical artefacts, Donald Bishop has the following to say about the early Chinese direct experience with nature:

> Each day, as the farmer plants his fields and tills the land, he is directly aware of and apprehends the working of nature. But, and very important, intuitive insight is present also. Closely identifying himself with her, the farmer unconsciously knows or is aware of the nuances of nature. He is sensitive to her inner forces. Knowing what the day would bring weatherwise, when the right time to plant the seed is, whether the coming winter will be harsh or mild was a skill so highly developed, among some, that it seemed as if they had an almost miraculous insight into the ways of nature or mother earth.[50]

Bishop's words provide a very simple but interesting reiteration of how the Chinese were early attuned to nature and, as we shall see, it was these simpler affinities with nature that engendered the later, deeper, metaphysical philosophies. Bishop notes this, too, and specifies "order, regularity, correlates, interrelatedness, cause and effect, parts and whole, harmony, vitalism, change and beneficence",[51] as the outcomes of an underpinning affinity with nature. And it is these outcomes that will be so evident in later Taoist philosophy, particularly in the classical philosophy of the Chou/Zhou dynasty. However, the interrelation between Heaven and Earth – between the spirit world and the physical, human one – was always paramount. The harmony between the human and spirit world was as essential for effective agriculture, for health, longevity and success, as the harmony between the farmer and the soil. Indeed both were part of the interrelated cosmic pattern. It was in the person of the king that harmony between Heaven and Earth was centred, and his earthly abode was the fulcrum for the important rites that linked the two: the king was the Son of Heaven and prime mediator.

To turn now to an analysis of more specific religious beliefs and practices, we need to look first at the supreme divine being that emerged during this time. He was Ti/Di, "Lord" or Shang-ti/Shangdi, "Lord-on-High". All ancestors were known as *ti/di*, but Shang-ti/Shangdi became the supreme *Ti/Di*. He was believed by the Shang to be their founder ancestor, the first and primeval ancestor spirit of the Shang aristocracy. While Shang-ti/Shangdi was the supreme god, he was not directly consulted through divination or ritual. Instead, intermediary spirits and lesser deities were summoned by the king to act as intercedents. As the supreme deity, Shang-ti/Shangdi presided over these ancestor spirits, as well as over a host of other deities of the natural world. He had the power to grant favours, but he could also bring disease. He controlled nature – the wind, rain, thunder and drought, and the king was sufficiently linked to him to be dethroned should he not rule well – so the following Chou/Zhou conquerors claimed. Since he could both reward and punish it was essential that sacrificial ritual associated with him, and with the ancestral spirits who interceded with him, was carried out meticulously. But, despite the central role of *ti* in religion, and of Shang-ti/Shangdi in particular, the ancestral gods were only vaguely depicted and not greatly anthropomorphized. Indeed, as ancestors became more remote in time, they blended in with the mass of others and lost individual identity. As the king presided over a hierarchized officialdom, just so Shang-ti/Shangdi presided over an equally hierarchized spiritual world: the microcosm on Earth reflected the macrocosm of Heaven.

Below Shang-ti/Shangdi, then, were the many ancestral spirits, in addition to nature deities, ghosts and even mythical monsters. Anything that went wrong in the natural order, anything that seemed strange, was seen as an omen that all was not well in the spirit world. It was here that the diviners could help to ascertain the wishes of the spirits and restore balance and harmony in daily events. But it was only the ancestral spirits of the aristocracy that became divine or semi-divine beings worthy of worship. For the poorer rural peasant of the time we know little, but their ancestors, or *kuei/gui*, were probably thought of as more mundane ghosts who, nevertheless, could affect the family fortunes adversely without appropriate respect and ritual.

Then, too, there were many nature deities, gods of the sun and moon, of the rain, the wind, lakes and of clouds. But earthly gods were also very important, not only of rivers, mountains and such natural phenomena, but also of the earth itself, for gods of the soil and of the grain were more immediately effective in daily existence. Earth gods came to be distinctly parochial, a deity for the ground inhabited by each different group of people. Again, these would have been hierarchized in terms of their degree of territorial space and the prestige of the people who inhabited it. So each *home* would have its earth deity, its god of the soil. Each family *group* would have a higher-status earth god. Each community *area* would have a god; each geographical *country*; and so on until we have, at the top of the pyramid, the Earth God of the ruler himself, the ultimate Earth God. It is interesting that the ancient Chinese did not feminize their earth deities; they were clearly male, despite the emphasis on agriculture and fertility. Such a concept is perhaps indicative that the patriarchal, hierarchized life of the early Chinese people dominated societal interchange and thought at very radical levels. This is not to say that female deities were entirely absent, but they do not seem to have featured widely at this early period.

Ancient Chinese religion lacks the development of a rich mythical pantheon of deities for their role was more pragmatic.[52] At the level of the ordinary peasant it would have been the household gods and local earth gods that would have been all important, as well as the immediate ancestors. Although we have no real written evidence of the popular religion during the Shang we know that the later customs found in Chou/Zhou times obtained also in the Shang. Each household would have had a number of gods of its own, a major earth god, gods of the entrances and of the well. There would also be gods of the village and local fields. Such gods were probably more "forces" than anthropomorphized characters – another interesting feature of Chinese religion. Perhaps the *territorial* nature of such gods rendered such amorphous characters a necessity, for once a home was destroyed, so too were its gods. Similarly, should a territory be conquered, its gods usually disappeared. Such temporality was enhanced by the fact that earth gods had their homes on the land, or in a forest, marked only by a rather temporary mound. Thus, it was difficult to anthropomorphize them in legend and myth. Then, too, while it is true to say that deities were thought of as anthropomorphized beings, there were too many of them for the characters to be really clear. Some were animals or part human, part animal. However, one nature deity that was to develop a more personalized nature was the Count of the River, Ho-po/Hebo. He presided over the Yellow River, a dangerous river that claims many lives, not least through its floods. But for the ordinary peasant earth gods and immediate ancestral spirits would have been seen as essential to the ongoing work in the fields. The rain was needed at the right time, and the forces of winter and summer were treated respectfully, "the fecundity of the earth and that of families were interlinked".[53] But it would have to be claimed that we know little of the ordinary peasant in ancient China, for the information we have of the Shang and Chou/Zhou dynasties refers only to the higher class. What we do know is that the family was and always remained extremely important, what Maspero termed "the fundamental cell of ancient Chinese society".[54]

The necessary harmony between Heaven, Earth and humankind was effectuated through royal ritual. Such ritual ensured the success of the harvest, the rhythm of the seasons and of reproductive life. Ritual surrounding death was especially important. The spirit was believed to hang around the deceased until the body disintegrated. Given the importance of ancestors, the spirit was essential for the welfare of the remaining descendants, so it was prudent to keep the body as well preserved as possible, so that the spirit would remain with it. Smith wrote: "Though there is no evidence of the art of embalming, as practised by the Egyptians, the elaborate preparation of the corpse, the use of what were believed to be life-preserving agencies such as jade, the stopping up of all the orifices of the body, all witness to the attempt to provide the soul of the deceased with as permanent a home as possible."[55] The spirit, ghost or *kuei/gui*, of the deceased was offered food and drink to keep it happy in case it disturbed and harmed its living descendants. But the eventual fate of the souls of lower mortals was the earth. For aristocratic souls, Heaven and the company of Shang-ti/Shangdi were the ultimate fate. Either way, we see ideas of preservation of life energies as an important belief emerging from this era.

Since the souls of noble ancestors became *ti/di*, their tombs were filled with necessities for their lives with Shang-ti/Shangdi after death – lives very much like their earthly ones. These necessities even amounted to weapons of war and chariots, though ritual objects were also included. Human sacrifice was also practised, for wives, servants, slaves were certainly immolated with kings, as well as horses. Jade – the Chinese symbol of immortality – was also to be found in the tombs, again, to promote preservation and eternal life in Heaven. Some captives taken in war were certainly sacrificed to ancestors, and some were beheaded so that they could not rise to fight again in the world beyond death. But sacrifice was also a part of the general religious cult. Maspero called such sacrifices "marking-posts at particularly critical moments of the periodic cycle".[56] That is to say, they supported the rhythms of agricultural life as much as ancestor observance. Animal sacrifice was abundant. For the aristocracy at least all such ritual was meticulous, carried out with elaborate correctness – *li* as it came to be known.

The medium for dialogue with gods, spirits and ancestors were the shaman-diviners, called *chen/zhen*, *jen/ren* or *wu-jen/wuren*. The Chinese used the term *wu* for a shaman, a term that had much to do with dancing, bird-like men or women evidenced on divination bones. Needham noted the similarity with the character of Chinese *hsien/xian*, the immortals who often were to be seen clothed in feathers and who flew up into the clouds.[57] We shall meet them in chapter 7. Strictly speaking, *wu* referred to women, while the term for men was *hsi/xi*. *Wu* tended to have more to do with the common people. The shaman-diviners had various other functions – rainmaking, exorcism, dream interpretation, fortune-telling, healing and prophesying. Then there were masters of ceremonies, or ceremonial officiants, *chu/zhu*, who made certain that proceedings and sacrifices were carried out correctly. Sorceresses were particularly employed for rain-making. The great centre of the state was the temple, and it was there that ceremonial feasts were held to which gods and ancestors were invited and entertained with meticulous ritual and correctness of ceremony. All important state events centred around the temple. Many ceremonies were connected with the agricultural year, others with the seasons, equinoxes and solstices, others, again, with ancestors. Campaigns of war, the illness of the king, strange events, all had their appropriate ceremonies.

Festivals were centred around the agricultural year, the year being divided up into unequal periods. Maspero depicted this well:

> There was the time of nature's great labour, which it was the aim of religion to help and sustain, and there was the time of her great repose, when – work in the fields ended and agricultural life suspended – nothing remained but to give thanks for harvests past and to pray for harvests to come. The festivals were linked once and for all to the proper season. Displacing them would have meant disordering the whole universe, thus bringing about unprecedented cataclysms.[58]

As Maspero pointed out ritual was not for the benefit of individuals but to create order and harmony in the world.[59] Such ritual was undertaken by the aristocracy and local lords on behalf of all the people. Of importance to the whole population were the festivals that marked the end of winter and the beginning of spring, that came to mark the New Year – a highly auspicious occasion. It was marked with exact ritual, sacrifices, music and dancing and involved a whole series of ceremonies. Importantly, the gods of the earth had to be notified of all events. Winter forces that were antagonistic to spring and summer activity were ritualistically driven out, and the home fires ritually extinguished and taken outside, before the people left their homes to dwell in huts in their working fields. The springtime was the time for marriages. At the autumn, similar festivals and rituals marked the close of the hard work in the fields; a new fire was kindled in the homes to which the people returned and *everyone* was sealed in his or her home for the winter weeks, the doors of the houses being sealed with clay. The rationale for such an action was beautifully, if a little imaginatively, described by Marcel Granet:

> When men take their rest they give rest also to things, and they conceive this rest of nature in the likeness of their own. Because they live during the winter snug in their homes, shut up in their clan village, they look upon the dead season as a period of universal confinement, during which all things return to their original dwellings, ... The earth, dedicated, no longer yields to human toil; exclusive rights of ownership no longer hold good at a distance; there are no longer any ties save between beings in close proximity and of the same nature. While men are reviving their powers in the intimacy of their family circle, and, in contact with their

own people, are restoring in themselves the genius of their race, they believe that in the same way the various classes of beings, also dwelling among their intimates, regain their particular attributes, and that their revived nature is being prepared for the spring.[60]

Interspersed with the many festivals and ceremonies related to agriculture were the ongoing rituals for ancestor worship, which served to reunite the deceased with their descendants. Marriages had to have the sanction of ancestors, baby sons presented to them, and initiation into manhood had to take place before them.

Archaeological discovery is continuing to build on our present information about the Shang. To date, excavations have revealed new Shang cities like that called Huanbei near modern Anyang, where the wall has been traced around a city of two square miles. Huanbei dates to about the fourteenth century BCE.[61] What is interesting is that excavations in the last two decades suggest that the Shang "dynasty" consisted of many cultural centres. It may, in fact, have been small in geographical terms, though much larger culturally, the outreaches importing and exchanging both materials and ideas. Lady Hao, who features in late Shang divination inscriptions, was the wife of King Wu-ting/Wuding. Her tomb was excavated in the 1970s and was the first major tomb not to have been previously looted. The tomb revealed "195 bronze vessels, of which over a hundred were marked with Lady Hao's name. There were also 271 weapons, tools, and small bronzes, as well as 755 jade objects – the most jades ever found in a Shang tomb. The pit contained 16 human skeletons, along with six dogs. Lady Hao's bronze collection weighed over 3,500 pounds."[62] We know a good deal about Lady Hao, too, from the divinatory inscriptions that mention her.[63]

Thus we have the Shang dynasty. Many of its customs were continued in the ensuing Chou/Zhou dynasty, which itself allows us to project back some ceremony into Shang times. Of the Shang customs and beliefs that emerge as important for future Chinese centuries, we need to single out the emphases on balance and harmony with nature, ancestor worship, harmony of heavenly spirits and earthly beings, a sense of order, divination, and magic. The belief seems to have emerged, too, that rulership was divinely permitted, provided it were morally effected. It is Keightley's view that Shang traditions and culture were still influential a millennium after the end of the dynasty. "Every idea, every pattern of thought, has its genealogy, and many of the mental habits central to Chou and Han culture can be traced back ... to the ideas and thought of the Shang."[64] The Shang dynasty was overthrown by King Wu and broken up in parts to be given to loyal vassals. According to Chou/Zhou tradition, Heaven had withdrawn its Mandate from the tyrannical Shang kings and transferred it to the Chou/Zhou, a tributary state of the Shang.

The Chou/Zhou dynasty

The new ruler of the Chou/Zhou dynasty died shortly after the conquest of the Shang, and the state was ruled by the Duke of Chou/Zhou. He is an important figure because his rule was seen in subsequent centuries as a model one. Chinese regarded him highly and in many ways he came to be thought of as an ideal sage-ruler. He predates

Confucius by several centuries, though some Confucian ideas seem to have been preempted by him. The king (*wang*) was the "Son of Heaven", ruling by the Mandate of Heaven and, therefore, was mediator between Heaven and his subjects. He must rule well, lest the Mandate would be withdrawn. The conquest of the Shang had been justified by a prudent statement that the supreme Lord of Heaven had commanded the Chou/Zhou to overthrow the last, allegedly corrupt, ruler of the Shang and end his dynastic line. Bearing in mind the prevalent necessity to rule with the sanction of the supreme God and high ancestral spirits, this was a necessary tactical step to gain authenticity for the change in dynastic rule. We know little about the origins of the Chou/Zhou, but they seem to have come from the north-western part of China, to which they retired after their conquest of the Shang and other areas, ruling the country from there. In fact, things went on much as before their conquest, and areas were allowed to continue their normal existence without too much interference. The important corollary of such a policy was a good deal of continuity in religious ideas and practices. By about the eighth century BCE, a good many small states existed, each with its major walled city outside of which the peasants lived on the surrounding land.

Our knowledge of the Chou/Zhou is much more detailed than that of the Shang because they left us literary sources. Indeed in the later years of the Chou/Zhou dynasty we have the great age of classical literature. One source that tells us a good deal about everyday life is the *Book of Poetry* or *Songs*, the *Shih Ching/Shijing*, which is a record of popular songs sung in the court, as well as by ordinary folk, and also contains more ceremonial hymns for special occasions. We also have a *Book of Documents*, the *Shu Ching/Shujing* (or *Shang shu*), which is concerned with history, government and royal power, and is the earliest extant Chinese text. Then there is the famous *Book of Changes* the *I Ching/Yijing*; the *Book of Rites* or *Rituals*, the *Li Chi/Liji*, which gives details of ceremonies; and the *Annals of Spring and Autumn*, the *Lü-shih Ch'un-ch'iu/ Lüshih Chunqiu*, which contains a chronicle of events of the principality of Lü. Collectively, these are known as the *Five Classics*, and all pre-date Confucius. Several other historical texts, as well as the works of the philosophers of the age, contribute to our knowledge of this dynasty.

Non-textual sources are also important for our knowledge of the Chou/Zhou. Towards the end of the Shang dynasty it became fashionable to make inscriptions on bronze vessels, a fashion that reached its peak in the Western Chou/Zhou. Such inscriptions were cast in order to celebrate the appointment of, or royal favour granted to, noblemen. When the Chou/Zhou court disintegrated, the noblemen fled, leaving their inscribed vessels in underground vaults for the future; but they never returned.[65] It is interesting that Eastern Chou/Zhou bronze inscriptions celebrate personal triumphs, not royal favour, and secular rather than religious occasions.[66] Noblemen came to cast their own bronze vessels and inscribed them with their own merits for the benefit of both their ancestors and their descendants.[67]

With the consolidation of the Chou/Zhou dynasty we find a semi-feudal state being set up. While not a fully feudal state, the Chou/Zhou developed the proto-feudalism of the Shang considerably. The Chou/Zhou rulers had to divide the state into manageable principalities under the rulership of favoured aristocratic vassals. What prevents the Chou/Zhou dynasty from being fully feudal is the fact that these vassals did not then enfeoff their own vassals, and so on. The old Shang emphasis on ancestral lineage was never broken, and each clan felt the ties of familial and societal obligations through its own clan, and its religious obligations were to the ancestors of that clan. Inevitably, as time went on, some of the vassals became strong and others weak, and there was much annexing of the weaker territories by the stronger ones. In the eighth century BCE this went as far as creating a strong enough alliance to oust the king from his capital for a short period. After this hiatus, the Chou/Zhou regained its power and we have the beginnings of the Eastern Chou/Zhou (as opposed to the earlier Western Chou/Zhou), since a new capital was set up in the more easterly lower Yellow River valley.

The history of the Chou/Zhou dynasty need not concern us too much here, but a few points might set the context for a more detailed look at the religious beliefs and practices. It was seen above that the whole Chou/Zhou dynasty was divided into Western and Eastern. The Eastern Chou/Zhou (771–256 BCE) is itself divided into two periods, the Spring and Autumn period as it is called,[68] from the eighth to the fifth centuries BCE (722–481 BCE), and then the Warring States period, from the fifth to the third centuries BCE (403–221 BCE). From a different point of view, the Chou/Zhou dynasty is divided into pre-classical times, down to about the mid-sixth century, and the classical period that followed. It is in the classical period that we meet the great philosophers. In the eighth century BCE, the Chou/Zhou capital was transformed to Lo-i/Luoyi, today's Loyang/Luoyang in Honan.

The Warring States period was probably enhanced by the use of iron, the Iron Age being dated roughly to the middle of the Chou/Zhou dynasty. By the time Confucius was born in the sixth century BCE four powerful states had emerged that were constantly at war in an endless struggle for further power. Increasingly, warfare became more ruthless and brutal, involving vast armies. It created a wretched existence for those caught in the middle, and a breakdown of normal social order and good government. The philosophy of Confucius was set against this backdrop. And yet, the period was not without its successes. Needham noted the advances in craft skills, the animal-drawn plough, the growth in markets, improved economy, military expertise, and irrigation, for example. He saw the period as one of political and economic consolidation.[69] Cultural changes were evident in the increased elaboration of decorated bronzes, in music, and by sophisticated artefacts that were buried with the dead. Clearly, civilized progress was accompanying the terrors of warfare.

In spite of the changes that were taking place at the political level, the religious traditions still maintained some of their earlier characteristics. The practice of hierarchizing deities and ancestors in Shang times was entrenched with the feudal system that itself had a clear, hierarchized bureaucracy. Sacrificial ceremony was as important as ever, for without it, the ruler of a state, or the king himself, might be defeated in war if he disrespected the gods. Religion and politics were, therefore, inseparable. As in Shang times, religious ceremony was a public and not personal occasion, undertaken by the nobility on behalf of the respective clans. As Maspero commented: "It was an expression of religious life in defined social grouping where each person's place was determined by his role in society – the lords to carry on the worship, the subjects to take part in it following their lord. It allowed no room whatever for personal feeling."[70] However, it is likely that the more personal problems of the peasants were presented to such as the local shaman-diviners, the sorcerers and magicians, who were believed to have power over disease, fearful phenomena, and so on, through their intercessionary powers with departed spirits and the spirits of nature. Smith wrote: "Everywhere shaman-diviners engaged themselves in ritual dances and incantations designed to bring back the spirits of the sick and the dead, or to induce trances in which they wandered freely in the spirit world, or drew down the gods of stars, rivers and mountains to their assistance."[71] This, indeed, would have been the religion of the ordinary folk.

For the early Chou/Zhou, Shang-ti/Shangdi remained the overarching, all-powerful supreme deity. Some myths about Shang-ti/Shangdi emerge from the Chou/Zhou period, and we know more about him through the poems of the *Shu Ching/Shujing*. He was a huge giant, evidenced by his occasional footprints left on earth. He had his palace in the constellation of the Great Bear, though he sometimes entertained guests on Earth. He had a family, and the ancestors of the powerful clans as his vassals. Life in his palace was thought to be the same as that in the earthly king's palace, and like the king ruled his subjects, so Shang-ti/Shangdi supervised the whole world, assisted by the *ti/di*, the deceased ancestors who were once great ministers and rulers themselves. Of these, five Lords stand out, the Blue Lord in the East, the White Lord in the West, the Red Lord in the South, the Dark Lord in the North, and the Yellow Lord, Huang-ti/Huangdi in the centre. A host of other nature gods was added.

As time went on Shang-ti/Shangdi was replaced by T'ien/Tian, "Heaven", though both deities seem to have existed as "conscious but relatively impersonal forces".[72] Later still, the name Shang-ti/Shangdi came to mean "high god" or "high gods", and a synonym of T'ien/Tian.[73] Above all, T'ien/Tian demanded moral righteousness in a ruler, and good government, for the ruler would have been chosen and, therefore, supported by him. The ruler was, thus, a vassal of God, to whom he owed constant allegiance. The idea that the earthly ruler held his place by the Mandate of Heaven was developed by the Chou/Zhou; after all, it was with such a theory that they had justified the overthrow of the Shang. Consequently, the king was sometimes called T'ien-tzu/Tianzi "Son of Heaven". As T'ien/Tian regulated all life, so the king regulated the sacrifices and ceremonies that perpetuated that order as the Mandate of T'ien/Tian. The king thus existed for the sake of good government of his people and linked Heaven and Earth. It was a concept that promoted further the idea of the unity of Heaven and Earth and the interconnectedness of all things. By late Chou/Zhou times Tsao Chun/Zaozhun, the god of the stove, the "Kitchen God", seems to have been well established, and was to remain an important deity in Taoism throughout the centuries that followed. He was a "Master of Destinies" who kept an eye on the good and evil done by the inhabitants of the home. He kept a register of these actions and then reported them to T'ien/Tian. The length of an individual's life was then extended or reduced, depending on the report. In the words of the time: "*T'ien* inspects the people below, keeping account of their righteousness, and regulating accordingly their span of life. It is not *T'ien* who destroys men. They, by their evil doing, cut short their own lives."[74]

As in Shang times, there were an abundant number of other gods, spirits of nature and ancestors who were the object of attention in order to gain their benevolence and avert their hostility. Also to be found were the gods involved with human life – the god of marriage, of occupations, of the doors of the home, the hearth and the well, as we have seen probably existed in Shang times. It seems also that three grand deities were worshipped in Chou/Zhou times: T'ai-i/Taiyi "Grand Unity", T'ien-i/Tianyi "Heavenly Unity" and Ti-i/Diyi "Earthly Unity". These three presided over an increasingly larger hierarchized pantheon of gods. The overall God of the Earth, and the hierarchized other earth gods continued to flourish. There were also gods of the guilds of craftspeople. Belief in demons and evil forces continued and rocks, mountains, trees, stones and swamps, and so on, were believed to be infested with demons ready to lead humans astray or devour them.[75] The actual *nature* of all these supernatural beings never really troubled the Chinese; they were all simply superhuman beings with inherent powers, but none too clearly demarcated. The fact that ancestors – once human beings themselves – became deified reveals how deities were rather like humans, not terribly reliable and prone to mood swings if all did not go well! It would have been impossible to pay respect to *all* these deities and spirits, hence the responsibility of the clan leader to conduct ceremonies for the main gods of his own clan, and the need for individuals to conduct their specific rites in their homes for their gods and ancestors. There must also have been considerable coming and disappearing of local territorial gods in a period that was infested with warfare. Importantly, the nobles, or patricians (*shih/shi*) of any clan (*hsing/xing*) claimed virtuosity as nobles from the power and virtue, or *te/de*, of their founding deified ancestor. This word *te/de* is an important concept and will be examined later, but it is worthwhile noting here the way in which it was used generally in Chou/Zhou times.

The shaman-diviners remained at the official level as much as at the popular level of religion, but since there were official priests that oversaw ceremonies, the shamans were closer to the ordinary folk than the priests. They also came to be associated with ideas of immortality and the concoction of elixirs and drugs to procure it.[76] Priests assisted with ritual. Each head of state, each prince and the king himself, had his own official clergy. They were responsible for divining, for reciting prayers and carrying out sacrifices. They called the gods to the sacrifice and ceremony and had a certain amount of social esteem. Their offices were probably hereditary, the ritual prayers and ceremonial ritual being learned meticulously and passed on from generation to generation. There were different priests for different functions – prayer, sacrifice, the hunt, war, treaties and contracts, funerals, rites to the Earth God and many others. They are indicative of the importance placed on precise ritual and the proper means of conducting ceremonies involving gods, ancestors and the spirit world. Such official priests contrasted very much with the shaman-diviners, the sorcerers and sorceresses.

Because they were characterized by ecstatic dancing, trances, emotional outbursts and less precise ritual, shaman practices came to be looked on with fear and suspicion. The profession was normally a hereditary one, judging by the term for the diviners, *wu-chia/wujia*, "shaman-family" and, as noted earlier, included women as much as men. The shaman was important enough to be sacrificed if an urgent situation arose, the thought being that he could more speedily intercede for restoration of harmony! Unlike the shamans, the priests could not summon the gods or spirits; neither could they go to the abodes of the spirits and gods in the same way that shaman-sorcerers could, or accompany the soul of a deceased person, guiding it to Heaven. The priests were not chosen by spirits and gods as mediums, and so were never possessed. The shamans, however, were summoned to their profession by their own gods and spirits, and had *power*. However much the nobility came to distrust and despise shamans, they were often quick to call on their services when sickness invaded a household. Specialized sorcerers were also essential for expelling evil forces such as at the great exorcism that took place at the end of winter and the beginning of spring to rid the old year of all malign evils. Then, too, princes would not venture out of their territories without a sorcerer to protect them. In later times, the state continued to have the same ambivalence in its attitude to shamans. At the popular level, however, they remained in demand. Shamans and sorcery diminished in popularity amongst the nobility by the end of the Chou/Zhou dynasty, but remained embedded in folk practices. It was particularly in the South that religious cultures clung to shamanism for a good deal longer than in the more sophisticated North. Astronomy and astrology were also a feature of religious practice. It was believed that the planets exerted their influence on human affairs.

The Chou/Zhou dynasty continued the practice of divination along late Shang lines, and diviners continued to be important in the functioning of the state. The diviners took to the use of yarrow stalks for divining, rather than the bones of animals and shells of tortoises as in Shang times, though the richer persons might resort to the latter. It is likely that, as time went on, the practice of divination with yarrow sticks was adopted more widely by non-professional patricians, since it became a philosophical practice as much as a ritual one. This will be seen when the *I Ching/Yijing* is examined in detail in chapter 2. It was partly through the medium of divination that King Wu of the Chou/Zhou justified his overthrow of the Shang. As we have seen, Wu claimed that the Mandate of Heaven gave him the right to rule, instead of the unjust Shang ruler. But this meant that it was exigent to maintain harmony between state, Heaven and people. Richard Smith thus makes the point: "For this reason, the Zhou state, and all subsequent Chinese regimes made every effort to divine Heaven's will with the milfoil and turtle shell, to predict the movements of the sun, moon, stars and planets, and to interpret portents correctly. Chinese astrology, astronomy, divination and calendrical science coalesced into a single administratively-grounded science."[77] The trend in the Shang to focus divination at the court was reversed during Chou/Zhou times, and by the Spring and Autumn period, divination was widespread outside court circles.[78]

There was, thus, a good deal of continuity in religious tradition from Shang to Chou/Zhou times. The differences were of emphasis rather than radical alteration. But the religious cult became more elaborate under the Western Chou/Zhou. Ceremonies were characterized by sacrificial offerings of animals, prayer, incantation, dance and music. Ritual purity and perfection of detail were essential not to offend the gods and not to bring about disorder as a result. The specialism demanded for the ceremonies further entrenched the notion that the nobles were acting on behalf of a large number of people. But the ordinary people took no part in the proceedings. The aim was to ensure order in the world and support for the clan, not to assist individuals. Ceremonial burials, however, did change. Fewer humans and animals were immolated with their masters, though the tombs were still filled with everything needed for an ancestral life with T'ien/Tian. It was the Earth God, in particular, who expected animal and sometimes human sacrifices – the latter usually supplied in the form of prisoners of war, though the custom of human sacrifice was certainly in decline by the later years of the Chou/Zhou. Girls were also sacrificed to the deity the Count of the Yellow River.

No temples have been bequeathed to us by the Chou/Zhou. Where they existed, they were built in wood and clay and so have long disappeared. But in any case, apart from the palace temple and the mounds to the Earth God in the temple confines, other deities had altar mounds – usually square, since the earth was believed to be so – in open spaces. However, the temples for ancestors were always housed within a dwelling. After all, ancestors were part of the family and the clan. The royal temple, of course, was much grander than those of the nobility, though all were similar in structure. The royal temple would also have more shrines for ancestors, unlike leading nobility who would have had just three shrines, for father, grandfather and great-grandfather.

Religious ritual was rhythmic; it complemented the seasons and agricultural cycles on the one hand, and the needs of ancestor worship on the other. It segmented the year[79] into patterns and balances that were predictable, and that were believed to bring about the necessary harmony for existence. By conforming to the rhythms of nature and the patterns for care and veneration of ancestors, life was ensured in a self-creative way. The religious festivals, especially, were intimately linked with agriculture. However, as feudalism gave way to imperial state control during Chou/Zhou times, and state organization reduced the number of feudal localities to ten principalities, religion shifted from the many small localities to major state centres, so removing ceremony, festival, and ritual, away from local practice. As we shall see in chapter 5, this was a major factor in the beginnings of a religious Taoism that, once again, returned religious praxis to the ordinary individual.

The ritual surrounding death was extensive and meticulous. Whereas in Shang times the wives, servants, slaves, horses and a host of objects might be placed in the great tombs, only representations of these came to be used towards the end of the Chou/Zhou dynasty, except for the burial of kings and later emperors, when many real and costly items were placed in their tombs. It was particularly the lack of an appropriate afterlife for the masses of peasants that attracted many to Taoism in years to come, for Taoists were to formulate a satisfactory possibility for the fate of the soul after death. It would be a short leap from preventing the soul's departure from the body in death, to the same prevention in life and, hence, to a belief in immortality. But, being deprived of the right to sacrifice and carry out appropriate ritual to the higher gods and spirits, the fate of the souls of the peasants after death was a depressing one. In all, as Maspero commented, ideas of afterlife "were clumped together into such a confused mass in the Chinese mind that any description must falsify if it tries to define them precisely"[80] and Matthias Eder writes: "We see that the Chinese dealt with the enigma of death in a confused way, baffled by this great dissonance in human existence."[81]

Veneration of ancestors was as orderly and hierarchized as the rest of the Chou/Zhou culture. The homage paid to a person in life was mirrored in equal veneration in death, reflecting that person's position and status. The importance of sons cannot be overemphasized in this patriarchal tradition where male ancestors were important for the further protection of the family. As Eder stated: "Ancestor worship is not only care for the dead; it is care for the living as well. The ancestor soul is the family's most favorably disposed guardian-god, the worship of whom at the same time enhances the social standing of the family."[82] Filial piety, or *hsiao/xiao*, was essential in this process, and respectful obedience to parents and ancestors was a particularly ethical expression of Chou/Zhou life. It was a sign of virtue, *te/de*. On the wider scale, ancestor worship linked the clan, and bound it as a religious unit as much as a social one. Thus, bringing a new bride into a home was only legitimized after a sacrifice had been made to the ancestors: a trial period had to be undergone before such an important event could take place, and before a woman could be brought into the clan. So important was ancestor reverence that it did not differ fundamentally in principle with the rich and the poor. It was just that the poor had not so many ancestors to whom they gave offerings, and the offerings were according to their means. And just as the earth gods were notified of agricultural activities, so the ancestors were notified of all events, agricultural and otherwise. Ancestor reverence was essential to all Chinese religion.

The age of the philosophers

The sixth century BCE onwards under the Chou/Zhou witnessed a superb intellectual flowering, producing some of the greatest thinkers and philosophers in the world. There were said to be a hundred schools of philosophers, and their counsel was sought by great nobles at a time of political unrest and social conflict. The age was a crucial period for Taoism proper and, therefore, I shall only deal with these important Chou/Zhou times briefly, for there are major developments that need separate chapters. Throughout the Chou/Zhou dynasty there had been a growing literati, and by the sixth century BCE such intellectuals had become increasingly concerned with more abstract thought, a sense of universal order, and an ideal social order. Confucius was to retain the idea of *tao* as a universal social morality, while the Taoists projected it to an indescribable principle. The projection of religion to an abstract level was probably influenced by the instability of the time, the corrupt Chou/Zhou rulers, and the feeling that T'ien/Tian was impotent in the face of the suffering of so many people. The literati, then, were beginning to be concerned with naturalistic, humanistic and ethical philosophy in contrast to ritualistic religion. Coupled with this was the desire of some to withdraw from the political arena, commune with nature, and follow a more cosmic path.

Many of the concepts that were accepted by the Taoists have their roots here in the Chou/Zhou dynasty long before the advent of philosophers like Lao-tzu/Laozi. *Te/de* was one; it was the special power by which the Chou/Zhou rulers were able to receive the Mandate of T'ien/Tian to rule. *Te/de* was a charismatic power of personality, a godlike quality, but it also came to mean the virtue by which the king ruled and was permitted to rule by T'ien/Tian. Then, too, the aristocratic ancestral heritage of the nobility granted it a certain amount of *te/de*, which ordinary people without the same powerful and virtuous ancestors lacked. Theories of *yin* and *yang*, the complementary forces that govern life and whose interaction produces all the phenomena of life, are very old, as is the theory of Five Agents that inform all life, though both were developed considerably in the late Chou/Zhou period. *Yin* and *yang* were related to the agricultural year in particular, to its festivals, and to humans themselves; indeed, the theory was expanded to explain everything in life. The Confucians and the Taoists accepted these theories of *yin* and *yang* and the Five Agents to explain the universe and the way in which they dynamically supported life. They are theories important enough to need separate and more detailed examination in a later chapter, as is the related *I Ching/Yijing*.

But there were other streams of thought and practice that were also feeding into what was eventually to become the expansive sea of Taoism. A passion for longevity was taken up by some and cultivated by control and exercise of the body, along with breathing exercises. Ideas of immortality had also gained ground, concomitant with harmony of the inner forces of the body. Death, it was believed, occurred because of the disharmony of *yin* and *yang* material forces in the body. But if these forces could be kept in perfect harmony and retained, death would be averted. Morality, virtue, fasting, control of breath – were all thought to promote such harmony.

Confucius

Confucianism was to become the orthodox doctrine of China for most of the latter's long history. In retrospect, later ages were to look back at the figure of Confucius, who looms so large in the history of Chinese thought and practice, and give to him all sorts of greatness, wisdom, sagacity and even divine status. But he was not a founder of a religion in his time. Indeed, his life ended in disappointment and ineffectiveness. It was only posthumously that fame was accorded him. The debate as to whether his beliefs were based on a religious or totally humanist framework still engages scholars. Primarily, it seems, he was interested in ideal ethical social living and, therefore, we find in his ideas no doctrines of afterlife, no religious ritual, priests, scriptures, and little to say about the concept of God. However, there are passages of the *Analects* where he mentions Heaven, T'ien/Tian, and these illustrate that he seems to regard T'ien/Tian as the source of virtue, *te/de*. Perhaps there was a "deep sense of man's dependence upon a supreme deity"[83] that underpinned his social, ethical and political perspectives, but it is difficult to know how far he took this, given his emphasis on social concerns. The earliest biography of the great thinker was not undertaken until centuries after his death, and even his famous *Analects* was compiled long after his demise. Perhaps we need to take for granted his acceptance of the ritualistic respect given to the gods and ancestors, it is difficult to say. The chaos of the time needs to be borne in mind along with the scepticism that accompanied it concerning the nature of the divine beings and supreme God who seemed to be absent. Such factors may have influenced Confucius in his promulgation of a humanistic and social ethic, rather than an overtly religious one.

Details of the life of Confucius need only detain us briefly here. Hagiography has played an enormous part in embellishing and distorting the life of one of China's greatest figures, and we have to rely on the collections of sayings in the *Analects* to provide a picture of the man. So important was this text to the Chinese that many memorized its sayings – even peasants preserved some of them as proverbs. His words are no less applicable today, despite the passage of time. A few examples might suffice:

> Those who are possessed of understanding from birth are the highest type of people. Those who understand things only after studying them are of the next lower type, and those who

learn things from painful experience are the next. Those who have painful experiences but do not learn from them are the lowest type of people.[84]

Honourable people are modest in what they say but surpassing in what they do.[85]

Honourable persons seek things within themselves. Small-minded people, on the other hand, seek things from others.[86]

As a whole, his teachings influenced Chinese society on dramatic levels. He was born in 551 BCE and came from the state of Lü, and he died in 479 BCE. He was probably one of a rising class of scribes who were learned men not necessarily of the nobility class. His name was not really Confucius; this is simply the easiest westernized pronunciation of it. His real name was K'ung Fu-tzu/Kong Fuzi. He must have been an outstanding teacher, if unorthodox. He taught that any person could become a *chün-tzu/junzi*, a "son of the ruler", "superior man" or "gentleman" – noble, unselfish, kind, just – irrespective of birth. Such an idea was perhaps to be expected, given the instability of social order in the times in which he lived, but he trained his students to become gentlemen and chose them from all walks of life, rich and poor. This tended, however, to impose class structure by education rather than birth, and Confucians never courted any notion of equality. He came to accept that correctness in aspects of life, and proper behaviour in every person, would bring about the kind of stability necessary for a wholesome and peaceful existence. Although he failed in his lifetime to bring any degree of order to society and was unable to convince any ruler of his teachings, his ideas were accepted by many and were later to affect Chinese society immensely and fundamentally. He held only a minor government post, which he abandoned in order to travel from state to state to find a ruler that might accept his ideas. Unsuccessful, he retired to his home state of Lü and spent his time teaching.

Essentially Confucius believed in the right kind of actions and behaviour between king and minister, father and son, husband and wife, elder brother and younger brother and between friend and friend – the Five Relationships of Confucianism. Thus, Confucianism is associated with social stability and moral uprightness. His message was one advocating the intrinsic *humanity* in each person, and the need for a sense of propriety in all dealings in life. The need for an altruistic concern for others in each person was an important element of his teaching. Such a concern was to be generated by an inner moral strength of character that set an example and aided others in becoming the same. External standards for living life were not felt to be sufficient. An internalizing rationale for one's behaviour and beliefs was essential: this was following the path or way, the *tao*, the harmonizing of one's inner self with the way nature meant people to be, and the way society ought to be. *Tao* was the right way, the moral way, the way that led to health and well-being for all. However, Confucius did not seem to be interested in the metaphysical problems of a search for ultimate reality, or the ultimate fate of the self as these came to be seen in the Taoist interpretation of *Tao*. We have a choice of seeing the *way* of Confucius as a purely humanistic path through life or, of seeing it as the *Way* of Heaven, of T'ien/Tian. But however we see it, the same concepts of propriety, love, loyalty, sincerity, moral rectitude, wisdom and correct social interaction characterize the *tao* as the products produced by it in successful interactive living.

Two other major terms accentuated by Confucius need some explanation here. These are *li* and *jen/ren*. *Li* is propriety or the ritual associated with it. In the establishing of a gentleman, it can also mean etiquette or courtesy. Creel noted that the original meaning of *li* was "to sacrifice"[87] suggesting its original use in connection with correct ritual practice in the service of the gods and ancestors. What Confucius did was to internalize the concept and make it an inner attitude that was naturally expressed by the true gentleman, rather than an outward conformity to ritual practice. But he also gave the word a moral dimension by externalizing it as conformity to high moral and social norms. Those who could do this were the individuals that could make society effectively moral. And there were certainly moral outcomes of his teaching. It was the Confucians who managed to oust the last vestiges of human sacrifice, and who stressed the need for universal education. After all, to govern effectively rulers and officials needed to be men of character and educated, and these criteria should not preclude the poorest man from rising to high-ranking places in the government, to assist the hereditary rulers.

The other major term is *jen/ren*, "love". It is an inner quality, one that proceeds from the heart of an individual and that externalizes as serenity and grace in living. It was what Smith termed the "inner dynamic" of *li*.[88] *Jen/ren* is goodness in the sense of its outgoingness to others; it is benevolence and humanity in its fullest expression in an individual. It was a central concept of Confucius' teachings, and might be said to be the fundamental characteristic from which all other qualities develop.

Confucius must have died feeling something of a failure in life. He left a legacy to his disciples and a whole way of thinking and living for all the Chinese generations after him, but he was never to know that. He was certainly a deeply humanistic man, and as Creel commented: "He took as his basis, therefore, neither theological dogma nor religious hope but the nature of man and society as he observed them."[89] What emerged in Confucianism was the idea that each person should know his or her role in life and effectuate it without friction to others and in a way that would be of benefit to other individuals and to society at large. Family cohesiveness and mutual support became paramount and the fabric and essence of Chinese societal life. Famous interpreters of Confucius were to consolidate and expand Confucian ideas. The main proponents here were Mencius (379–289 BCE) and Hsün Tzu/Xun Zi (298–238 BCE). In the centuries to follow, Confucius became a role model, like the Duke of Chou/Zhou. In time, Confucius became deified. Palmer writes of this event: "K'ung, who had virtually denied the relevance of the spiritual and of the gods, was busy being worshipped by the end of the first century BC and in AD 59 the Emperor formalized this by decreeing that sacrifices could and indeed should be offered to K'ung".[90]

Early Taoists

The late Chou/Zhou period saw the rise of more metaphysical thoughts about life. What was behind all the flux and change of life? Was there something behind the constant transformations of *yin* and *yang* in the cosmos? For some thinkers, the wealth and power, the ritual and pomp of ceremony were rejected for a naturalistic perspective of the cosmos. Coupled with this was a belief that life was precious and should be preserved. Death was not the inevitable fate of all. Then, too, the interconnectedness of life gave it a unity, and all things in that unity had their natural "way". As in the case of Confucius it is never really clear whether those who thought this way were religious thinkers or philosophical humanists. For they certainly turned their backs on religious propriety in the sense of conforming to norms of ritual practice. Chuang-tzu/Zhuangzi, for example, was found singing to himself while beating time on a wooden bowl after his wife died, instead of conforming to the usual funeral rites. It is the early sages like Lao-tzu/Laozi and Chuang-tzu/Zhuangzi, set in the late Chou/Zhou dynasty, who will absorb a later chapter. With Confucius, Lao-tzu/Laozi and Chuang-tzu/Zhuangzi and others in the three centuries after Confucius, we have the age of classical China, the age of the great philosophers and thinkers in Chou/Zhou times.

The end of the Chou/Zhou dynasty came in 256 BCE after years of weakening power by the central government. Its semi-feudalism was to give way to a political unity in the form of the first Chinese empire begun by the Ch'in/Qin dynasty. But, before examining these later historical events, it is necessary to turn back to some of the important ideas that remained Chinese and Taoist, which had their origins in the Chou/Zhou. The following chapters, then, will deal with the book of divination that has been handed down to us from Chou/Zhou times, the *I Ching/Yijing*, with the well-known theories of *yin* and *yang*, and the important Five Agents that inform all life.

2

The Interconnected Cosmos
The I Ching/Yijing

The Book of Changes: the *I Ching/Yijing*

The *I Ching/Yijing* is probably one of the oldest known books, some parts of it being perhaps about three thousand years old. Yet, despite its antiquity, it has been in constant use over the millennia right up to the present day. Its prestige in China has been unsurpassed by any other text, and its easy availability in bookshops in the West is a measure of its continued popularity. Adopted widely in Korea, Vietnam and Japan, it was essential reading for Japanese militarists down to the last century. The psychologist Carl Jung was sufficiently impressed by the book to endorse its contents in the *Foreword* to Richard Wilhelm's translation of it.[1] It is certainly the oldest of the Chinese *Classics*, being incorporated into the Confucian *Classics* during the Han dynasty. Not only does the *I Ching/Yijing* predate Confucius, but it is also antecedent to formative Taoism by a long period. In its beginnings, it was more of a Chinese phenomenon than the prerogative of any particular school of religious or socio-political thought. And yet, there was much in it that was eventually to appeal to Confucianism and Taoism in such a way as to make the *I Ching/Yijing* an essential text to both. Taoism, especially, was to become closely involved with the philosophy underpinning the *I Ching/Yijing*, appropriating its ideas to render a Taoist view of the cosmos. Taoists were also particularly attracted by the divinatory and mystical characteristics of the text. In his seminal work on the *I Ching/Yijing*, Richard Wilhelm referred to the "seasoned wisdom of thousands of years" that comprise the *I Ching/Yijing* we have today. He wrote, too: "Nearly all that is greatest and most significant in the three thousand years of Chinese cultural history has either taken its inspiration from this book, or has exerted an influence on the interpretation of its text."[2]

So what exactly is the *I Ching/Yijing*? *I/Yi* (pronounced *ee/yee* not "eye") means "transformations", "changes", and *ching/jing* means "warp". *Ching/jing* is a Chinese character portraying a loom and is, thus, associated with weaving, specifically the *warp* of the material that is fundamental to the whole. This is *classic* literature that is different from "woof" literature, or *wei*, which is supportive and apocryphal. Fung Yu-lan explains the usage of both well: "Used in apposition to each other as names of literary genres, the two terms metaphorically denote the latitudinal and longitudinal threads of knowledge which, when woven together, were regarded by the Chinese as a unified fabric covering all human wisdom."[3] It is the ideas of change and transformation that are the key to the Taoist and modern understanding of the *I Ching/Yijing*. Many scholars argue extensively that it is not a fortune-telling oracle – even if it began, as we shall see, as a divinatory text. The main reason for such an objection is that, while one has to *consult* the text in the same way as one might a fortune teller, the response the text gives describes the state of things as they are and as they are becoming. But there is no suggestion that something *must* happen in the future, or that things cannot change. Thus, it permits active changing of the course of one's life, not sitting back to await unavoidable results. It is more a response to "How can I handle the situation in which I find myself?" rather than "What is going to happen in the future?" It permits freedom to choose the appropriate path. Then, too, the other objection to depicting the *I Ching/Yijing* as a fortune-telling oracle is the fact that its responses are believed to be *morally* geared to the evolution of the self and of society. If the need to develop virtue is presupposed by the *I Ching/Yijing*, then it is concerned with the best directions for shaping life, and the pathways that conform best to the changing patterns of the universe. The messages it gives are cryptic, leaving the reader to relate the words to his or her particular life-condition in time. But the advice given will essentially be concerned with establishing the right balance and harmony in life.

Such views reflect the philosophical and ethical dimensions of the *I Ching/Yijing*. They represent some of the developed, traditional theories about the text. However, recent scholarship is beginning to demonstrate a much more layered development of the *I Ching/Yijing* in which, when the cosmological, ethical and philosophical meanings are peeled away, a more basic, pragmatic, divinatory text is to be found underneath as evidence of its ancient past. Both – the divinatory and the philosophical – inform the book today. In its origins the *I Ching/Yijing*, as we shall see, was clearly a divination text. But between these extremes of time, the *I Ching/Yijing* developed into a text that was believed to encapsulate the patterns and transformations of life itself. It became on the one hand a philosophical text and, on the other, a pseudo-scientific one that professed to explain the law of existence in the interrelation and interaction of all things in the universe. It served to relate the individual, familial or societal situation to what was happening in the cosmos, and to suggest how co-operation with the prevailing cosmic forces might best be achieved. In Blofeld's words:

> From this it is clear that, could we but analyse the pattern of changes governed by this Law and could we but relate our affairs to the right point in the everlasting process of ebb and flow, increase and decrease, rising and falling, we should be able to determine the best action to be taken in each case. Then, by peacefully according with the necessity to advance, remain stationary awhile or retreat, by cheerfully accepting the promise of gain or loss when each is due, we could come close to being masters of our lives![4]

But while the divinatory nature of the text may have been rejected by many in favour of a more philosophical conception,[5] it is likely that the text has maintained its complementary, divinatory character alongside its deeper associations. Those who preferred the latter saw the *I Ching/Yijing* as a book of wisdom and, as such, it acted as an inspiration to a number of eminent philosophers and thinkers.

Perhaps one of the reasons for the *I Ching/Yijing*'s timeless survival is its uniqueness in not being associated with a particular religion or, indeed, any religion at all. Indeed, it is a very humanistic text, centring on the interrelation of the human being with a changing universe. Deborah Sommer aptly writes: "Human action is not circumscribed by dualities of good and evil but is guided by the principles of appropriateness and timeliness, qualities that mirror the seasonal periodicity of the natural world."[6] If there are hints of divine dispensation in the *I Ching/Yijing*, they are minimal. It is preoccupation with the reality of nature that is the essence of the developed concepts of the *I Ching/Yijing*. The work represents Heaven and Earth constantly in states of transformation through their interaction with each other, and represents each, and all the possible results of their interaction – the "cosmic archetypes", as one writer calls them[7] – in dynamic images. The *I Ching/Yijing* is believed to guide the individual who consults it according to the cosmic principles of the universe. Every individual or entity in the universe has its own vital essence and its own path that brings it into line with the cosmic laws. The *I Ching/Yijing* states the way things are at the moment, in what ways one has deviated from this norm, and points out the changes necessary to return to that norm. Such changes might demand passivity or activity, withdrawal or advance, and so on – all dependent on the nature of the moment. Jung, in his *Foreword* to Wilhelm's work on the *I Ching/Yijing*, suggested that at any moment in time we are caught up in the particular conditions that obtain in the universe; we are like a series of connected atoms in a cosmic whole. How we are in one moment is not isolated from the rest of the universe but reflects our degree of harmony or disharmony with the cosmic norms. The *I Ching/Yijing* points to this condition and, if necessary, how it can be improved, because it connects the moment of time of the individual with the moment of time of the cosmic process. It is, to use Fung Yu-lan's words, "a reflection in miniature of the entire universe".[8] Such an idea presupposes that the individual *subconscious* affects the moment as much as the *conscious* inquirer. Perhaps this is what fascinated Jung about the *I Ching/Yijing*. In closing his *Foreword* to Wilhelm's book, Jung wrote: "To one person its spirit appears as clear as day; to another, shadowy as twilight; to a third, dark as night. He who is not pleased by it does not have to use it, and he who is against it is not obliged to find it true. Let it go forth into the world for the benefit of those who can discern its meaning."[9]

Historical development

What we now know as the *I Ching/Yijing* is the result of a development in content and philosophy that evolved over thousands of years. Its beginnings are veiled in mystery and legend. There are two ways in which the history of the *I Ching/Yijing* can be approached. The first is academic, stripping away the text to as much of its bare bones as can possibly be revealed given its ancient origins. In what follows there must be, in the interests of a search for truth, some measure of this approach. The second is traditional and, since it is traditional beliefs that inform Taoist reverence for, and belief in, the *I Ching/Yijing*, in my view it is an approach that has valid meaning for an understanding of Taoism. I shall, therefore, adopt both approaches. Let us look at the traditional view first. According to this, the ancient sages responsible for its earliest stratum attempted an explanation of life in terms of their own experience of the patterns and cycles of earthly and heavenly phenomena that existed in time. As Jou comments: "They looked at the world around them and sought to understand why and how change occurs. They did not look beyond reality or ascribe all events to the 'hand of God.' Instead, they found enlightenment through the very practical process of examining the concepts of space and time."[10] In the words of the *Ta-chuan/Dazhuan*, *The Great Treatise* appended to the *I Ching/Yijing*: "The holy sages were able to survey all the confused diversities under heaven. They observed forms and phenomena, and made representations of things and their attributes. These were called the Images."[11] But it was particularly the changing patterns of the phenomena of the universe that interested the sages, and such change was replicated in the archetypal images of the hexagrams. These representations will be examined later.

The Chou I/Zhouyi

From a more academic view, however, we must go back to the ancient practices of divination that were prolific in Shang and early Chou/Zhou times discussed in chapter 1. Early divinatory practices were an attempt to validate future events in the context of a particular need of the moment or regular ritualistic praxis. While the *I Ching/Yijing* is known for its multiples of *yang* ——— and *yin* —— —— lines – three to form trigrams and six to form hexagrams – the early divinators recorded results with numerical symbols. Richard Smith indicates that the practice was very early. He states, "there is growing evidence to support the view that the Shang Chinese developed a numerical system capable of producing linear hexagrams even prior to the invention of trigrams. This numerical system seems also to have been related to the practice of divination by milfoil stalks, also known as yarrow sticks."[12] It is bone and bronze inscriptions from Chou/Zhou times that supply the evidence here, with oracles recorded in sets of six numerals with a resemblance to the hexagrams. Exactly when this system developed into the *yin* and *yang* lines that we know is uncertain, but the latter system was in place well before the time of Confucius, and was encapsulated in a text with sixty-four hexagrams, a brief statement of the image of each hexagram, and statements concerning the six lines in the hexagrams. This early *I Ching/Yijing* was known as the *Chou I/Zhouyi*, "*The Changes of the Chou/Zhou*". It dates perhaps to the late second or early first millennium BCE, though there is no certainty of its age. There may, indeed, have been an oral transmission of some of its contents in the prognostications and sayings of the divinators before these were committed to written form. Linguistically, the *Chou I/Zhouyi* matches the language of Western Chou/Zhou bronze inscriptions,[13] so a finer date of about 825–800 BCE is possible. Customs presupposed by the *Chou I/Zhouyi* fit well into that period. Whatever its origins, a primary text, the *Chou I/Zhouyi*, came into being, predating Confucius by many centuries, but lacking the accompanying commentaries that we find in the received text today.

What we seem to have is originally a divination system that served the purely pragmatic need for prognostication at the Shang and Chou/Zhou royal courts – the *Chou I/Zhouyi*. Then, the original system was developed to provide greater philosphical and moral content in what we know as the *I Ching/Yijing*. As to the original *Chou I/Zhouyi*, according to Shaughnessy: "In general it can be said that while moralistic implications are not necessarily absent in the *Chou i*, no coherent or developed philosophy is presented in the text."[14] Similarly, the word *tao* occurs in the *Chou I/Zhouyi* with its basic meaning of "road, way" not, as in the developed material, with the metaphysical sense of *Tao* as it came to be understood in Taoism. Richard Rutt has also attempted to peel away the later philosophical meanings in an effort to find the original contexts of the Chinese characters in the *Chou I/Zhouyi*. Stripped of its commentaries appended to the book in later times, and the attempts to apply abstract symbolism to the hexagrams, the *Chou I/Zhouyi* seems to be a guide for official royal diviners with content very similar to the context of Bronze Age divination that we explored in chapter 1 – and there was nothing "philosophical" about that.[15] Rutt claims, too, that the documents surviving from the Chou/Zhou – the *Book of Documents (Shu Ching/Shujing), Book of Poetry or Songs (Shih Ching/Shijing)*, a chapter of the *I-Choushu/Yi Zhoushu*) and the *Chou I/Zhouyi*) – are *all* government documents.[16] This presupposes that the *Chou I/Zhouyi* was a document for official divination, and nothing else.

The *Shuo-kua/Shuogua*, the *Discussion of Trigrams*, one of the appendices to the *I Ching/Yijing*, gives the traditional view of its authorship:

> In ancient times the holy sages made the Book of Changes thus:
> They invented the yarrow-stalk oracle in order to lend aid in a mysterious way to the light of the gods. To heaven they assigned the number three and to earth the number two; from these they computed the other numbers.
> They contemplated the changes in the dark and the light and established the hexagrams in accordance with them. They brought about movements in the firm and the yielding, and thus produced individual lines.
> They put themselves in accord with tao and its power, and in conformity with this laid down the order of what is right. By thinking through the order of the outer world to the end, and by exploring the law of nature to the deepest core, they arrived at an understanding of fate.[17]

From these words it can be seen that it is to the additions to the *Chou I/Zhouyi* that we have to look in order to find its moral and philosophical content. Traditionally, the Chinese have long regarded the *I Ching/Yijing* to have been compiled by Fu Hsi/Fu Xi, King Wen, the Duke of Chou/Zhou, and Confucius. The first of these, Fu Hsi/Fu Xi, as we saw in chapter 1 is probably completely legendary. He was a deity sometimes described as half man and half snake, though he may have been an early chieftain. He is credited with introducing crafts to humankind, as well as the eight trigrams that form the basis of the *I Ching/Yijing* images. The *Ta-chuan/Dazhuan, The Great Treatise* (in which Fu Hsi/Fu Xi is called Pao Hsi/Baoxi) states:

> When in early antiquity Pao Hsi ruled the world, he looked upward and contemplated the images in the heavens; he looked downward and contemplated the patterns on earth. He contemplated the markings of birds and beasts and the adaptations to the regions. He

proceeded directly from himself and indirectly from objects.[18] Thus he invented the eight trigrams in order to enter into connection with the virtues of the light of the gods and to regulate the conditions of all beings.[19]

Then, traditionally, came the contributions of King Wen and the Duke of Chou/Zhou in the early Chou/Zhou dynasty. King Wen was responsible for the addition of explanations to the hexagrams – the so-called *Judgements*. Tan/Dan, the Duke of Chou/Zhou, and son of King Wen, is believed to have added comments on the individual lines of the hexagrams. Regardless of disputes about their respective roles in creating the *I Ching/Yijing*, these contributions by the early Chou/Zhou rulers were thought to have shifted the emphasis from a primarily divinatory purpose to one that was far more philosophical. The change in emphasis empowered freedom of choice, and offered the possibility of evading the negativities of the future by recourse to correct actions. Wilhelm wrote of this change:

> They endowed the hitherto mute hexagrams and lines, from which the future had to be divined as an individual matter in each case, with definite counsels for correct conduct. Thus the individual came to share in shaping fate. For his actions intervened as determining factors in world events, the more decisively so, the earlier he was able with the aid of the Book of Changes to recognize situations in their germinal phases. The germinal phase is the crux. As long as things are in their beginnings they can be controlled, but once they have grown to their full consequences they acquire a power so overwhelming that man stands impotent before them.[20]

Wilhelm, like many, accepted the traditional view. However, while a date of the early Western Chou/Zhou is likely for the *Chou I/Zhouyi* (late ninth century BCE), the authorship of King Wen and the Duke of Chou/Zhou is currently dismissed. As Shaughnessy comments, "it is generally assumed that the *Chou i* represents the accumulated experiences of divination of Western Chou court scribes".[21] It was Ssu-ma Ch'ien/Sima Qian, the second to first century BCE historian, who stated that King Wen was responsible for creating the hexagrams from the trigrams to form the *Chou I/Zhouyi*, as well as the hexagrams and line statements. Later, Ma Jung/Ma Rong (79–166 CE) presented what became the accepted view that King Wen was responsible for the hexagram statements and the Duke of Chou/Zhou the line statements. The theory was suggested and rigidified that the hexagrams came first, then their statements, then the line statements. But Rutt warns, "the idea that the hexagram drawings, hexagram statements and line statements were created in that order was no more than an inference from the order in which they appear on the page. It is just as likely that the oldest things in *Zhouyi* are some of the line statements, which were probably common sayings and proverbs that became attached to the divinatory hexagrams."[22] Whether the *Chou I/Zhouyi* evolved through the collective skills of many diviners – the current academic view – or the efforts of Wen and Tan/Dan – the traditional view – the extension of its use from pure divination to a philosophy of change was well under way. While the term *i/yi* "change" is common to both the earlier and later titles of the text, the addition of *Appendices* to the *Chou I/Zhouyi* completed the process of applying a highly philosophical dimension that was not present in the early text.

The Ten Wings

It is to Confucius and his later followers that the *Appendices* of the *I Ching/Yijing* are traditionally credited. He is believed to have edited and annotated the *Chou I/Zhouyi*, producing what are called the *Ten Wings (Shih-i/Shiyi)*, the ten sections and *Appendices* to the work. These consist of seven texts, three of which are divided into two, resulting in ten texts. It was probably a number of his followers that accredited Confucius with the authorship of the important extraneous material. However, the contradictory and variant nature of the material contained in the *Ten Wings* is not at all suggestive of a single author or of having been written at a particular time: the Warring States period is perhaps the most favoured. Rutt thinks it highly unlikely that Confucius knew of the *Chou I/Zhouyi* and that the only line of his *Analects* given as evidence is suspect. His point is: "Since in his lifetime the book was almost certainly extant in only one copy or very few copies, kept by the Zhou diviners, there is little likelihood that he would have seen it or known what was in it."[23] The book probably remained a divination manual at court until Han times, and survived the Ch'in/Qin book burning as such.

The value of these commentaries of the *Ten Wings* lies in the philosophical analyses they provide, analyses essential to an original text that contains only brief and ambiguous statement. While their content, also, is often extremely ambiguous, and they survive in only a fragmentary way with repetitions, gaps and contradictions, they incorporate many cosmological ideas that complement the earlier material. Maspero commented that these *Appendices* gave the Chinese of later centuries a philosophical vocabulary, and were the only parts of the *Classics* to deal with metaphysics.[24] Inevitably, however, the *Ten Wings* provided fertile material for all kinds of further outgrowth of ideas and commentaries on the *I Ching/Yijing*. The *Chou I/Zhouyi* is written in Early Old Chinese; the *Wings* in Middle Chinese. By the time the *Wings* were written no one really understood the archaic statements of the *Chou I/Zhouyi*. Rutt thus comments: "The whole understanding of the book was changed: the hexagrams became a source of supposedly Confucian metaphysics; both hexagrams and oracles were reinterpreted as the source of a philosophy concerned more with change than with being, more with ethics than with prognostication. *Yijing*, the expansion of *Zhouyi*, was becoming the most revered book in China and began spawning an immense literature of comment and criticism."[25] The emphasis on philosophy and ethics replaced the wholly pragmatic divinatory nature of the original work and, as Rutt states, "the spell was cast more by the Ten Wings than by *Zhouyi*".[26]

Briefly, the *Ten Wings* or *Appendices* are as follows:

- The *T'uan-chuan/Tuanzhuan* or "Commentary on the Judgements" is, as its name suggests, a commentary on the *Judgements* or statements in each hexagram. It gives some explanation for the words in the *Judgements* and the characteristics of the hexagrams in relation to their constituent trigrams and lines.
- The *Hsiang-chuan/Xiangzhuan* "Commentary on the Images or Symbols" is in two parts. The "Greater" examines the images presented by the constituent trigrams and the hexagrams they inform, and the "Lesser" comments on the hexagram lines.

- The *Ta-chuan/Dazhuan*, "The Great Treatise", is also known as the *Hsi-tz'u-chuan/Xicizhuan*, "Appended Judgements", and is in two parts. It comments on the *I Ching/Yijing* as a whole, and was "the catchall for all sorts of pronouncements", as one writer put it,[27] emerging from the Confucian school. It deals with wider philosophical issues and enters into discussions on the importance of the *I Ching/Yijing*, social and moral development, and discussion concerning the images.
- The *Shuo-kua-chuan/Shuoguazhuan* "Discussion of Trigrams", is also in two parts. It also discusses *Tao*.
- The *Hsü-kua-chuan/Xuguazhuan* "Sequence of Hexagrams".
- The *Tsa-kua-chuan/Zaguazhuan* contains miscellaneous comments on the hexagrams.
- The *Wen-yen-chuan/Wenyanzhuan*, the "Commentary on the Words" was a collection of commentaries, now mainly lost, though parts relating to the first two hexagrams are extant.

The oldest extant copy of the received text is on stone tablets dated to second century Han times. By this time, the *Ten Wings* had become an accepted appendage to the *Chou I/Zhouyi*. Reading the *Wings* the impression gained is one of philosophical depth and insight into nature and humanity, and very Taoist concepts. Concerning the analysis of nature in *The Great Treatise*, Rutt writes:

> Westerners may find this schema strangest at the point where patterns are discerned in the skies, the earth and man. Britons especially, because they live in a land of few cloudless nights, their sight further dimmed by ubiquitous artificial lighting that pollutes the darkness, find it hard to imagine the clear night skies of north-east Asia, where the brilliant patterns of the asterisms gave primitive man some of the first linear designs he discerned. The stratification of rocks and soil showed him parallel lines, his own body taught him symmetry. Such details in the Great Treatise are perceptive and accurate."[28]

The subsequent history of the *I Ching/Yijing* need not detain us long. In the time of Ch'in Shih Huang-ti/Qinshi Huangdi, the *Chou I/Zhouyi* became very popular, and it is at this time that the Yin–Yang school attached its extensive theories to interpreting it. The *Chou I/Zhouyi* was to survive the book burning of Ch'in Shih Huang-ti/Qinshi Huangdi, and after the fall of the first Ch'in/Qin dynasty at the beginning of the Han, its title was changed to *I Ching/Yijing*. It was at this time, too, that the *I Ching/Yijing* became the fifth Chinese *Classic*, and in form was very much the same as the book we have today. Being raised to the status of *Classic* meant that many eminent scholars of Han times were keen to write their own thoughts on the ancient text, some of which have survived to the present day. It is Wang Pi/Wang Bi's third century commentary and text, the *Chou-i-chu/Zhouyizhu*, which provided the basis for all future work on the *I Ching/Yijing*. Since Wang Pi/Wang Bi accepted the philosophical and ethical dimensions of the *I Ching/Yijing*, and it is his text, and versions of it, that is transmitted to us, it is inevitable that philosophical interpretations are endemic and entrenched. As Rutt points out, "his influence set the general course of *Yijing* study for two thousand years".[29]

Thus, we have both the traditional and academic views of the origins of the *I Ching/Yijing*. Xinzhong Yao and Helene McMurtrie believe that it is unwise to strip the *I Ching/Yijing* entirely of its historical philosophical development. In their view:

> It stands as a monument to the power of human thought, which for over two thousand years has attached itself to an ancient oracle and is associated with Confucian–Daoist worldviews. The resulting philosophy has inspired and changed people's awareness of themselves, their environment; it has provided a document of unsurpassed wisdom in a more or less mystic language. The fact that it may have originated from a terrifying society preoccupied with war and human sacrifice, demonstrates how far society has changed and how many changes have been made to the understanding of the Zhouyi itself.[30]

The *I Ching/Yijing* became important in the study of alchemy, chemistry, biology, physiology, and even art, for example, and was consulted in times of war. It was particularly taken up by the alchemists of the Sung/Song dynasty, and it was this dynasty edition by Chu Hsi/Zhu Xi that became the orthodox edition for over half a century.[31] What is important for our purposes, however, is its long acceptance by Taoists. Many Taoists had written their own texts related to the *I Ching/Yijing*, and some of these, along with the *I Ching/Yijing* itself, found their way into the Taoist canon, the collection of accepted, orthodox Taoist texts, by Ming times. In 1715, during the Ch'ing/Qing dynasty, a final, standard, orthodox *I Ching/Yijing* was produced by imperial edict, to replace the earlier one of Chu Hsi/Zhu Xi. It is from the 1715 edition that present-day translations in the West stem. Palmer, O'Brien and Kwok Man Ho give words of warning about this final edition. They point out that, while the ancient text is kept intact:

> The *I Ching* of 1715 is first and foremost a sociopolitical book published to support a particular line. Thus while it does indeed draw upon many of the great commentaries, the reasons for choosing some and not others lie in the political game which was being fought – a game the prize for which was the right to rule. Therefore we should be very careful in seeing in the Imperial edition of 1715 an objective, totally unbiased document, apparently distilling for us, without prejudice, all the greatest wisdom of the ages about the *I Ching*.[32]

But while the vast body of commentaries on the *I Ching/Yijing* serve to distort its original sayings in the light of prevailing socio-political agendas of different times, and the different interpretations of it are legion, the ancient core now has philosophical meaning, and its purpose remains fairly clear. Hellmut Wilhelm suggested that this purpose is threefold: "Devotion to the system of changes imparts the repose and joyous freedom characteristic of the superior man. Meditation on its images and judgments imparts the knowledge that arms him for all situations, and the augury given him by the oracle imparts the decision on his action."[33]

The ancient nature of the core corpus of the *I Ching/Yijing* need not preclude its relevance to modern times. Cleary demonstrates this well in his translation of, and comments on, Cheng I/Zhengyi's *The Tao of Organization*. Cheng I/Zhengyi was an eleventh century commentator on the *I Ching/Yijing* who was interested in its "inner design". In Cleary's own comments on the text he states: "Because it is a structure of structures, the design of the *I Ching* can generate analytic systems of potentially infinite complexity and variety, and can be applied to any conceivable realm or situation."[34] In correlating the life-conditions of the moment with the more macrocosmic pattern of things, "it becomes possible to bring about mutual understanding and cooperation among people, thus making possible the effective accomplishment of the tasks facing the group".[35] In its original time context, the content of the *I Ching/Yijing* often dealt with rulership, with military issues and administration of the empire. Right conduct and virtue in a ruler were as essential for societal well-being as much as for individual living. But these kinds of contexts need to be translated into the present-day for those who wish to consult the *I Ching/Yijing* today.

Accompanying interpretations of each of the hexagrams of the *I Ching/Yijing* are often indirect rather than direct, subtle rather than obvious. This makes the *I Ching/Yijing* difficult to understand. And since the original Chinese characters cannot convey singular or plural, nouns or verbs, verbal tenses or pronouns, and the language of the whole is, in any case, archaic, the scope for differences in translation is considerable. There is breadth of choice, too, between the polarities of translating the text literally and rigidly on the one hand, and translating it liberally by attempting to apply some kind of interpretation and meaningful sense to the text, on the other. Very different translations can, then, occur. The greatest of Chinese philosophers have found the text complex and impossible to fathom in many places. There were even different schools founded on the strength of different interpretations of the *I Ching/Yijing*. Such factors sometimes make the *I Ching/Yijing* difficult to use; though it might be said that we would at least gain some impression of the favourability or non-favourability of advancing forward quickly, gently, standing still or retreating, in consulting it. Thus, at least minimally, we gain some idea of good or ill fortune in present actions. Despite difficulties in reading and finding appropriate meaning in the text, Cleary believes that the *I Ching/Yijing* can be applied to any system of organization – the family, a societal group, a political group, a culture, for example. He writes: "The *I Ching* analyzes the interplay of relations as functions of qualities, roles, and relative standing. It is therefore extremely versatile in handling both individual and collective perspectives; and since all standing is relative, it can be applied internally to any system of human organization, regardless of scale or configuration."[36] Such a view suggests a basic, pragmatic purpose for the *I Ching/Yijing*. In the long history of the last empire of China, the Ch'ing/Qing dynasty, the *I Ching/Yijing* was not only used for very serious concerns of state but also for such simple things as appropriate assistance for toothache![37] But from a more philosophical point of view, Blofeld had the following to say about the purpose of the *I Ching/Yijing*:

> It is the function of the *Book of Change* so to interpret the various interlocking cycles of change that the progress of individual transformations can be deduced from them and the enquirer thereby receive a firm support which will help him to avoid being swept through the vortex like a leaf carried by angry waters. Though we cannot, by holding up our hand and using Words of Power, bid the winds and waves to cease, we can learn to navigate the treacherous currents by conducting ourselves in harmony with the prevailing processes of transformation; thus we can safely weather successive storms in this life and in all lives to come until that probably remote time when, having penetrated to the heart of change, we enter the immutable, undifferentiated stillness which is at once the womb and the crown of being.[38]

Blofeld's words suggest an inner role for the *I Ching/Yijing* in the context of today's world, a role that might promote inner harmony, and it is this kind of thought that is so much in line with Taoism. Taoists accepted the philosophy that fed into the *I Ching/Yijing*, particularly the need for harmony with the incessant interplay of complementary and opposing forces on the canvas of change and flux that characterizes the universe. Cleary writes: "For Taoists, to harmonize with the celestial in human life means to deal with each 'time', each combination of relations and potentials, in such a way as to achieve an appropriate balance of relevant forces and their modes of manifestation."[39] This is living life with one's finger on the pulse of the universe.

For Taoists, too, there is a cosmogonic message informing the *I Ching/Yijing*. Time is not linear but cyclical in the sense that the universe is constantly regenerating itself. It is a universe that is dynamically changing in its process of generation and regeneration, and it is with that backdrop in mind that the inquirer of the *I Ching/Yijing* seeks to harmonize the condition of the moment with the macrocosm of the universe. The *I Ching/Yijing* presents options, opens the mind to different perspectives and possibilities, and expects the inquirer to use reason to apply its contents to the moment in life. What we have today in the *I Ching/Yijing* is a composite, though heterogeneous collection of Chinese wisdom throughout the ages. The resultant *I Ching/Yijing* is thus built up of many strata. In Hellmut Wilhelm's words: "Archaic wisdom from the dawn of time, detached and systematic reflections of the Confucian school in the Chou era, pithy sayings from the heart of the people, subtle thoughts of the leading minds: all these disparate elements have harmonized to create the structure of the book as we know it."[40]

Reality as perpetual flux and change[41]

The view of reality presented in the *I Ching/Yijing* is that everything in the universe is subject to change. Nothing can ever be static, but is *dynamically* and *perpetually* changing. Hellmut Wilhelm put this point forcefully when he wrote: "The world of this book is a changing world; every static expression, every binding form appears here as a frozen image that is opposed to life."[42] Such change, however is not haphazard but rhythmic, and the rhythms of the universe are subject to certain fundamental laws that ensure its change conforms to certain patterns. As we have seen, it is the word *I/Yi* of the *I Ching/Yijing* that means "change" or "transformation". In the Chinese character for the word the upper part means "sun" and the lower "moon", thus reflecting the passage of time in the perpetual contrasts and opposing interplay of day and night.[43] But just as day and night have their own particular pattern, so the patterns of the whole universe resonate and interact according to their respective laws of change in an organic whole. So acorns become oak trees according to their specific patterns of change, just as season follows season, old age follows youth, and so on. Each one of us is involved in multiple processes of transformations in the forces of living and gradually dying. In order to find meaning in such processes, in the words of Stephen Karcher: "The world we live in is changing and we are involved in a deep shift in the ground of our being. We search for hidden significance in events, seeking the meaning of the crossroads we confront."[44] That all reality is flux and change is the fundamental law of the *I Ching/Yijing*. And if there *is* anything that is changeless in the cosmos, it is the very fact that all is subject to change. The *I Ching/Yijing* is believed to reflect the resonating cosmos. If individuals are able to align themselves with that resonance, then they will have the potential to bring harmony to their lives and actions and find the "ground of our being". Blofeld wrote:

> Every single thing is either coming into existence, developing, decaying or going out of existence. . . . Change, which is never-ending, proceeds according to certain universal and observable rules. In relying upon the *I Ching* to reveal the future, we are not dealing with magic but calculating the general trend of events and seeking the best way to accord with that trend by relating whatever matter we have in mind to the predictable cycle (or cycles) of events to which it belongs.[45]

However, since change characterizes everything in the cosmos, then the situation at one particular time in life is different from that which is coming to be; each situation is one in process, only to be changed in the succeeding moment, hour, day, or spell of life. But the change that takes place is rhythmic, patterned, predictable, though not necessarily predetermined. In the words of Hellmut Wilhelm: "Change is not something absolute, chaotic, and kaleidoscopic; its manifestation is a relative one, something connected with fixed points and given order."[46]

Since change is the reality that underpins the universe, there is no divine being that begins it all. There is no creation in time that brings about the universe, that oversees it and, perhaps, brings it to an end. Any personal gods like T'ien/Tian or *ti/di* operated within the structure of change no less than humans. They did not create the changing universe. The universe is a changing, dynamic, self-perpetuating phenomenon, sustained by its own patterns and rythyms. And if it dies? Then it can regenerate all over again. The *I Ching/Yijing* is concerned with cyclical movement and not with the equilibrium of the point at which all is still, as *Tao* was frequently portrayed. It is concerned with balance and with aligning the self to that balance. In a sensitive passage, Lama Anagarika Govinda writes that change

> is necessitated by a slight divergence from the state of perfect balance, an incommensurable irregularity which causes a movement toward adjustment, an oscillation of forces, comparable to the up-and-down-swinging scales of a balance. But unlike a balance, which after all has only to adjust itself and soon comes to a standstill after having found its equilibrium, the world is composed of innumerable forces; and the displacement of one means the immediate reaction of all. This reaction is not of equal strength in all factors, but it affects them according to the value, the importance or nearness of their relationship. In this way, continuous movement is ensured which is interminable, since the factors involved are infinite in numbers and unlimited in space.[47]

So while change is the changeless basis to all existence its interplay and interconnectedness permits our continued existence, with freedom to conform to the patterns of the universe or to diverge from them.

Change, and the interplay of the forces of life are described in the *I Ching/Yijing* as *the firm* (*kang/gang*) and *the yielding* (*jou/rou*). More by transference of idea than any synonymy between the meanings of the words, *the firm* later came to be called *yang*, and *the yielding, yin*. But in the early *Chou I/Zhouyi* and the earliest commentaries, *yin* and *yang* do not occur. The firm and the yielding represent the opposites of activity and receptivity, or movement and stillness, and the tension between both informs all the processes of life. Throughout our daily lives, thoughts advance and subside, arise and disappear. We advance to do this or that and retreat after our efforts. We are active during the day and passive during the night. And we know that the basis of our ability to advance, to act, to think well, to achieve, is dependent on the strength we acquire in the rest and stillness we have in sleep. Receptivity and passivity, stillness and calm are therefore the dynamic processes of change that prepare us for the more active times of our daily lives. And the tension between the two will always operate to create new experiences or different nuances of old ones. It is this that is the unchanging law of the whole cosmos. In the words of Wu Yao-yü: "The movings and flowings of the yin and yang atoms do not halt for even the blink of an eye, nor does the transformation of the myriad things-and-beings halt for the blink of an eye. However, this fundamental principle of transformation is itself eternally unchanging."[48] Changes, then, are the tensions infused with dynamism between the firm and the yielding; they are "the imperceptible tendencies to divergence that, when they have reached a certain point, become visible and bring about transformations".[49] What this suggests is that events in time are perceptible in the future because they are in the process of coming to be. And by assessing the way in which that process is taking place, it is possible to align the balance of the activity and receptivity in the self to harmonize with events in a positive way. This is what proponents of the *I Ching/Yijing* claim the book can do. Further, the events that we see unfolding in our individual lives are connected to the deeper levels of reality in a relational way that is more to do with the cosmic nature of things than with the time-scale of ordinary perceived reality. Each moment in time is a blend of interrelated and interacting fragments. The *I Ching/Yijing*, therefore, is believed to set a moment in time on the wider canvas of a constantly changing cosmic reality.

Later in its historical setting, that which informed all the transformations in the cosmos was posited as *Tao*. The *Appendices*, the *Ten Wings* of the *I Ching/Yijing*, write of *Tao* as the root from which all the transformations spring, "the immutable, eternal law at work in all change . . . the course of things, the principle of the one in the many".[50] It was sometimes called *T'ai Chi/Taiji*, "Supreme Ultimate", *chi/ji* meaning "ridgepole", the essential part of a building that tied it all together. *Tao* as *T'ai Chi/Taiji* is that which generates the tension between opposites, that which makes changes and transformations, possible, and the power that renews that tension from moment to moment. It is the quiet, spontaneous power that eternally gives energy to the cosmos, to the rhythmic composition of the stars and planets as much as to the energy that a tiny seed needs for germination.

When the *I Ching/Yijing* was fused with notions of *Tao*, the language used to describe it was similar to that used to depict *Tao*. Thus, the *Ta-chuan/Dazhuan* combines the two in the following words: "The Book of Changes is vast and great. When one speaks of what is far, it knows no limits. When one speaks of what is near, it is still and right. When one speaks of the space between heaven and earth, it embraces everything."[51] Since the *I Ching/Yijing* is believed to be in complete harmony with *Tao* it is able to provide representational images of the patterns of the cosmos to which individuals can relate their immediate life-conditions and change their lives to bring them into harmony and accord with *Tao*. And harmonizing oneself with *Tao* lies at the heart of what Taoism is. It is no wonder, then, that the *I Ching/Yijing* was adopted as an essential text of Taoism.

Fundamental to the *I Ching/Yijing* is the complementary dynamic relationship between Heaven and Earth – the former the firm, the active, creative and energizing principle, eventually the *yang*, and the latter the yielding, the receptive and passive, eventually the *yin*. Heaven is light, incorporeal, and the macrocosm, and is the determinant of what happens on Earth. Earth is its opposite, dark and corporeal. It is the microcosm, and is receptive to what is determined by its upper opposite. The complementary interplay between these opposites is the basis of all the other possibilities of change. Each individual is a microcosmic image correspondent to the macrocosm, a replica of the universe. The *I Ching/Yijing* acts as the medium that illuminates the interchange between them. However, the *I Ching/Yijing* only clarifies the events, the choice of going with the current or against it always lies with the individual. And since change is the nature of reality, nothing is fixed; fate is never decreed. The *I Ching/Yijing* does not seem to suggest that the future is unchangeable. Within the vast patterns of change there is plenty of room for manoevring.

The *Pa-kua/Bagua* or Eight Trigrams

We must turn now to examine the trigrams and hexagrams of the *I Ching/Yijing* in a little more detail. A text of the *I Ching/Yijing* itself would be valuable to the reader in conjunction with this chapter and translations of the text are to be found in the *Bibliography* at the end of this book. Here, I might point out that an inexpensive and easy copy to use, though without the full *Appendices* included in other volumes, can be found in the Richard Wilhelm, Cary Baynes translation *The Pocket I Ching* noted in the *Bibliography*.

It is by no means certain that, historically and chronologically, trigrams preceded hexagrams, but for simplicity's sake, I think it preferable to begin with the simpler three-line trigrams. The *Pa-kua/Bagua*, "Eight Trigrams", are images of processes of change. Each consists of three lines placed one on top of the other in combinations of firm ———— and yielding —— —— . And there are only eight different possibilities of combination; hence the *Pa-kua/Bagua*. *Kua/gua* is the word the Chinese use for "trigram", the latter being a more modern, foreign description. Similarly, hexagrams are *liu-shih-ssu-kua/liushisigua*. *Kua/gua* means "yarrow-stick divination".[52] Neither firm nor yielding lines are unchangeable. The firm line is active, moving outwards so that it breaks apart and becomes a yielding line. The yielding line does the opposite by moving inwards so that it eventually becomes a firm line.[53] Of the three lines, in whatever combination of firm and yielding, the top one always represents Heaven, the bottom one Earth, and the middle one, humanity. Being in the middle, humanity has the option of looking upward to Heaven and to spirituality, or of being focused downwards to Earth. The eight trigrams, then, are as follows:

THE INTERCONNECTED COSMOS THE *I CHING/YIJING*

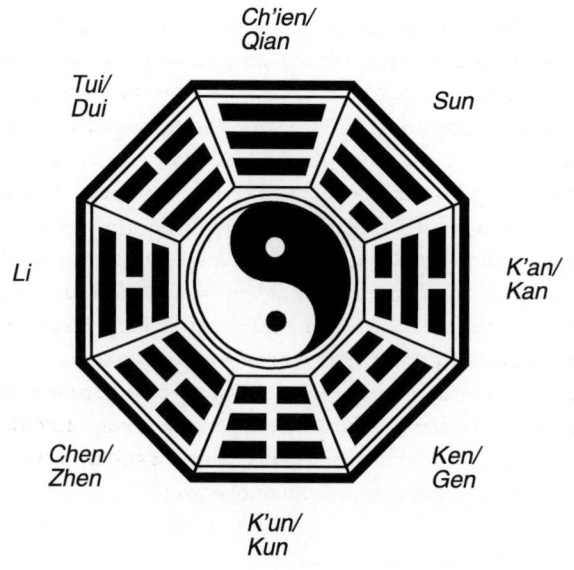

    The arrangement of the trigrams above is the earlier, former, primal, or prior to Heaven arrangement, attributed to Fu Hsi/Fu Xi. It is also called the "Yellow River Map" or *ho-t'u/hetu*, and remains an important symbol in Taoist ritual. As can be seen from the arrangement, the trigrams at both ends of each axis are complementary opposites. So *Ch'ien/Qian* is South and summer, while *K'un/Kun* is North and winter (the Chinese inverted North and South). *K'an/Kan* is West and autumn, while *Li* is East and spring. *Ken/Gen* is mountain, and its opposite *Tui/Dui* is lake. *Chen/Zhen* is thunder, an awakening force, while its opposite, *Sun*, is wind, which drives things away.

    According to tradition, King Wen rearranged the trigrams to represent the motion of change through the cycle of the year. His order is known as the later, or later than Heaven arrangement, beginning in the springtime with *Chen/Zhen*:

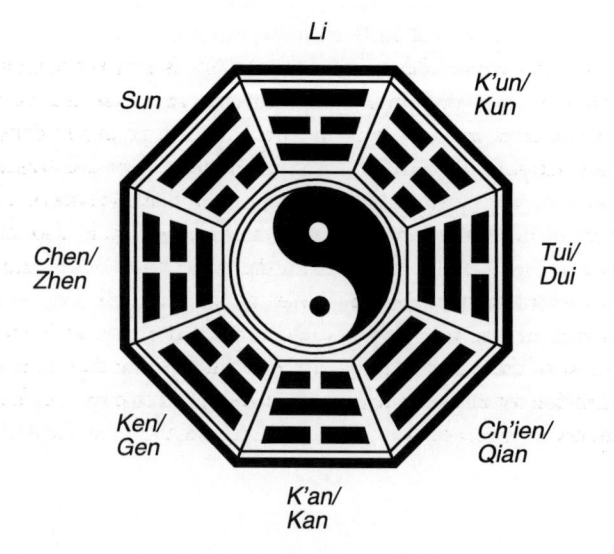

Spring begins the year like the morning begins the day, so *Chen/Zhen*, thunder, wakens the energies of the earth. Then comes *Sun* with its gentle winds, which melt the ice of winter and bring about a time of growth. Then we have summer, *Li*, a time of maturity in the yearly cycle, and of noon in the daily cycle. It is followed by the fruitful time of *K'un/Kun*, the time of harvest, and then the passing into autumn with *Tui/Dui*. *Tui/Dui* also represents the evening, the time for rest after the day's work, just as the work of the year ends following the harvest. Then, according to the *Shuo-kua/Shuogua* a battle takes place between the creative force of *Ch'ien/Qian* and the darker forces of cold and winter. It is a time for spiritual reflection within in the face of the darkness without. It is a time followed by the depth of winter itself, *K'an/Kan*. Finally, the trigram *Ken/Gen* is the point of stillness before the whole cycle begins again.

The characteristics of each trigram, each state of change in the universe, are represented in the arrangement of the three lines of the trigram. Each trigram has its name, its image (given below in italics) a corresponding family relationship, and a number of general characteristics, the main ones being given in the following:[54]

Ch'ien/Qian The Creative

Heaven. The three strong lines of this trigram represent the attribute of strength. Additionally, sublimity, success, beauty, goodness, furthering perseverance and consistency are in its nature. It is a male representation of strength, the father in the family; the king of a nation; action; causality; and in *yin* and *yang* terms is wholly *yang*. It is associated with the dragon and all kinds of horses, the fruits of trees, and Metal in the Five Agents or Elements. It represents South in the early Fu Hsi/Fu Xi arrangement of the trigrams and north-west in the later one, in which it matches late autumn and late evening. It came to be associated with deep red, with the head in the human body; with jade; clarity; the coldness of ice; and with characteristics of roundness and expansiveness, like the fullness of autumn time. It represents productive energy in life. It is the place where opposites meet.

Tui/Dui The Joyous

Lake. The two firm lines underlying the broken line is a sign of stability within, and is associated with joy, happiness and wisdom. In the primal arrangement, the trigram represents a son, but in the later arrangement, it represents the youngest daughter. This is because the yielding, feminine, *yin* line is last, and at the top of the trigram (and so is youngest). The whole is a *yin* trigram. The associative animal is the sheep, the broken line above two firm lines representing its horns to some. The image is also suggestive of a yielding outer nature. Thus, it can also represent the concubine. Water and Metal are its Agents. It is south-east in the primal arrangement of trigrams and West in the later one, making it mid-autumn in the year and the evening of the day. It is associated with enchantresses, in view of the strange things it can hold, and that can be enticed from its depths. It is related to the mouth and tongue of the body, and to pleasure. Since it is a deep and still lake, it reflects images, and so symbolizes deep reflection in life itself.

Li   The Clinging   ☲

Fire. Here darkness is enveloped in light, the sun, and heat, shown by the two firm or *yang* lines enclosing the yielding or *yin* line. It is thus a light-giving trigram and is associated with external phenomena like the sun, lightning and fire, and internal aspects like the evolution of consciousness, devotion, beauty and purity. It is a *yang* trigram associated in the primal arrangement of trigrams with a son, but in the later one with the middle daughter, since its yielding line is in the middle of the trigram. The pheasant, the toad, crab, snail, turtle and tortoise are associated with this trigram, and Fire is its Agent. In the primal arrangement of trigrams it is the East, in the later one the South, and so, here, is summer, midday, and intense heat. It is associated with the eye of the body, with weapons, drought, the withered tree, and brightness. It is also associated with self-consciousness, and the corollaries of that in clinging and possessiveness, though it is also indicative of intelligence and understanding. Fire can only rise towards the sky, unlike its opposite of water, which can only go downwards.

Chen/Zhen   The Arousing   ☳

Thunder. The strong lowest line with two yielding lines above represents energy and light rising up, reaching through the dark, and so the attributes of this trigram are movement, speed, energy, power and impulse. It is associated with the springtime. Despite its predominantly *yin* lines, it represents the eldest son in the family, indicated by the single firm line being at the bottom and, thus, first in the trigram. It is associated with the dragon in flight, rising up to the sky, or the galloping horse, both represented by the firm line rising upwards. Wood is its Agent. It is the north-east in Fu Hsi/Fu Xi's primal arrangement, the North in the later one, and hence associated with mid-winter, midnight, and with thieves who steal at the dark time of the night. It is connected with the ear of the human body and with the colour dark yellow. Generally, it signifies danger. However, it is essentially a creative and dynamic trigram, representing youth that is rapidly developing.

Sun   The Gentle   ☴

Wind and *Wood.* The firm upper two lines based on a yielding line characterize the trigram as gentle and penetrating like the wind. It is related to what is spiritual, to the intellect and the mind. It is a *yang* trigram and in the family is associated with the eldest daughter, its yielding line being first and at the base of the trigram. It is associated with the cockerel amongst animals, and with the Agent of Wood. It is south-west in the primal arrangement of trigrams and south-east in the later one, corresponding to late spring and early summer during the year and morning time in the day. It is connected with merchants, with the colour white and with the thigh and eyes of the body. It relates to steady progress in tasks, or the growth of trees and vegetation. It represents growth and productivity and times of vitality, but also purity and wholeness.

K'an/Kan   The Abysmal   ☵

Water. The firm line representing strength and light is surrounded by darkness with the yielding lines above and below. The picture is representative of winter; darkness; instability; and danger of being enveloped. It is a predominantly *yin* representation, and is a daughter in the primal arrangement of trigrams but is the middle son of the family in the later arrangement, because the firm line is in the middle position. Water always seeks the lowest point, but it can symbolize spiritual depth as much as the darkness of an abyss. *K'an/Kan* is the darkness of a deep gorge into which water penetrates, or water flowing rapidly through a gorge, thus showing penetrating and piercing characteristics. Water is cold and dark, but it can be heated and can absorb light. The pig is associated with this trigram because it lives in mud and water, and the thief, who hides himself in the watery ditch. The human being who is low in spirits is *K'an/Kan*, as are sickly horses, but also courageous horses. It has curvature, and ability to bend – like water that fits any shape – in its nature, so it is the bow and the moon. It is West in the early arrangement and North, mid-winter, midnight, and the time of struggle before the light dawns again in the later.

Ken/Gen   Keeping Still

Mountain. Resting and standing fast is the nature of this trigram. The two yielding lines supporting the uppermost firm one suggest passive immovability at the roots. The firm upper line is rooted in the earth of the two lowest yielding lines. In the family it represents the youngest son in the later arrangement of trigrams, being third and top in the trigram, though it is a daughter in the earlier, primal arrangement. Despite the two *yin* lines, it is a *yang* trigram. It is associated with the dog as the faithful guard, the rat, and some birds. Its Agent is Wood. While representing north-west in the early arrangement of trigrams, the later one places it in the north-east, early spring and early morning when night is ending. It was associated with the gatekeepers of the cities, the entrances, with the hand and finger of the human body and with fruits, seeds and knotty trees. While it can represent the stillness of stagnation, it can also represent the stillness of meditative reflection. It is a calm, quiet and restful trigram, but also a firm one.

K'un/Kun   The Receptive

Earth. The three yielding or *yin* lines represent pure femininity and, thus, the mother and the queen of a nation. The trigram personifies receptivity, passivity, devotion and a yielding nature, and is a pure *yin* trigram. The animals associated with the trigram are the mare and the ox. Earth is its Agent. It is North in the primal arrangement of trigrams and south-west in the later one, here representing late summer when fruits ripen, the warm sun of early autumn, and the afternoon in late summer. Its associative colour is black, and the part of the body connected with it is the abdomen. Characteristics are squareness, flatness, docility, harmony, accord, and receptivity. In the *Shuo-kua/Shuogua* of the *Appendices* to the *I Ching/Yijing* it is cloth, a kettle, frugality, level, a cow with calf, a large wagon, form, multitude, a shaft, and black soil.[55]

Similar symbols of firm (*yang*) or yielding (*yin*) lines represented a divination result in the archaic past, the firm line being a positive, lucky outcome, and the yielding line an unlucky outcome. Visually, the trigrams became meaningful to the Chinese. Smith cites an old folk rhyme describing them: "Qian is three [lines] connected; Kun is six broken. Zhen is a bowl turned upward; Gen is a bowl overturned. Li is empty in the middle; Kan is full in the middle. Dui has a space on top; Sun is broken on the bottom."[56] Once established in the *I Ching/Yijing*, trigrams became subject to wide interpretation and analysis.

Importantly, the trigrams represented a fluid and not static picture. They were believed to be changing constantly into each other, and thus depicted the flow of cosmic change. According to the *Shuo-kua/Shuogua*: "Heaven and earth determine the direction. The forces of mountain and lake are united. Thunder and wind arouse each other. Water and fire do not combat each other. Thus are the eight trigrams intermingled."[57] Such transformations enabled the life-condition of the moment to be related to the process of change. However, each trigram has its positive and negative characteristics. These have to be taken into account when the trigrams are combined together into hexagrams:

	Positive	**Negative**
Heaven	strength; firmness; creativity	aggression; force; dominance
Lake	enjoyment	selfishness; complacency
Fire	understanding; wisdom; illumination; beauty; brightness	superficiality; fixation
Thunder	active understanding	erroneous knowedge; perilousness
Wind	moving on the right path	conditioning; desires; aversions
Water	problem solving	inability to cope with problems
Mountain	balanced reflection	passivity
Earth	receptivity; flexibility; submission	lack of personal autonomy; weakness; dependence[58]

Both the positive and negative qualities, as well as the breadth of characteristics embodied in the nature of each trigram permit all sorts of combinations of meanings dependent on the situation at the time. In the earlier arrangement of trigrams attributed to Fu Hsi/Fu Xi, Heaven and Earth are the two major trigrams, and the South/North axis from which all the others spring. In the later arrangement, Fire and Water provide the South/North axis. But Heaven and Earth represent just that – the whole cosmos, the Father and Mother of all things. Heaven and Earth came to be the *yang* and *yin* interactive forces that composed all things in an ever-shifting manner. The interrelation of Heaven and Earth is beautifully expressed by Liu I-ming/Liu Yiming in *The Book of Balance and Harmony*:

> Openness is the form of Heaven, tranquility is the form of Earth. Unceasing self-strengthening is the openness of Heaven, rich virtue supporting beings is the tranquility of Earth. Boundless spaciousness is the openness of Heaven, boundless breadth is the tranquility of earth. The Tao of Heaven and Earth is openness and tranquility; when openness and tranquility are within oneself, this means Heaven and Earth are within oneself.[59]

As Cleary points out in relation to Liu I-ming/Liu Yiming's words: "Thus concentration in stillness and active contemplation are regarded as complementary procedures. Certain exercises have traditionally been employed in Taoist practice to clarify, unify, and stabilize the mind so as to achieve the attunement represented as embodiment of Heaven and Earth."[60]

Ch'ien/Qian as Heaven is more than we would generally understand by the term "Heaven". For on the one hand it is the formlessness that expresses non-being, complementing Earth, which epitomizes the phenomenal forms of existence. On the other hand it represents the phenomena of the sun, the moon, wind and thunder – those aspects of the universe observable to the ancient Chinese. But Heaven in the sense that the word is normally understood is a created phenomenon, a produce of *Ch'ien/Qian* and *K'un/Kun*.[61] There is a "maleness" and "femaleness" about *Ch'ien/Qian* "Heaven" and *K'un/Kun* "Earth" respectively. Together they create; Earth is the source of all that is born, though it is restrained by the power of Heaven, bringing things into being on behalf of the power of Heaven. This process of bringing into being is incessant. As things come to an end, they begin again in endless change, like the seasons, good and bad fortune and day and night. Nothing goes away that does not return. According to the *Ta-chuan/Dazhuan*, *The Great Treatise* on the *I Ching/Yijing*:

> The Creative and the Receptive are the real secret of the Changes. Inasmuch as the Creative and the Receptive present themselves as complete, the changes between them are also posited. If the Creative and the Receptive were destroyed, there would be nothing by which the changes could be perceived. If there were no more changes to be seen, the effects of the Creative and the Receptive would also gradually cease.[62]

While The Creative and The Receptive are Father and Mother of all things, the other six trigrams represent the "family" that springs from them. In the primal arrangement of trigrams attributed to Fu Hsi/Fu Xi, this is always determined by the bottom line of the three in the trigram. Thus, *Chen/Zhen*, The Arousing, *Li* The Clinging and *Tui/Dui* The Joyous are all sons, while *Sun* The Gentle, *K'an/Kan* The Abysmal and *Ken/Gen* Keeping Still are the daughters. In the later arrangement, however, Li The Clinging and *Tui/Dui* The Joyous become female and *K'an/Kan* The Abysmal and *Ken/Gen* Keeping Still become male. The others remain the same. The logic behind the later sequence is based on the position of the firm (*yang*) line for sons. When at the bottom with two yielding (*yin*) lines above it represents the eldest son. In the middle with two yielding lines either side, it represents the middle son, and when at the top, with two yielding lines beneath, it represents the youngest son. Trigrams and hexagrams, remember, are always read from the bottom. The same sequence occurs for the eldest, middle and youngest daughter with the movement of the yielding (*yin*) line from base to top, with otherwise firm lines. The sons and daughters of The Creative and The Receptive are differentiated profiles of the changes that occur in nature. The trigrams of the sons are considered to be light, despite the two dark yielding lines with which they form trigrams. Conversely, the trigrams of the daughters are dark, despite the predominance of firm lines. The reasoning behind this is to do with numbers allocated to the lines composing the trigrams. A yielding or *yin* line considered to be a "moving" line was given the even number six, and a firm, but "moving" *yang* line the odd number nine. These two lines are lines in the greatest state of change; they are moving to their opposites. Other yielding and firm lines are at rest, and not, at present, moving. The yielding line at rest is given the even number eight, the firm line at rest, the number seven. When the numbers of each of the three lines in a trigram add up to an even number the trigram is "dark". When they add up to an odd number, it is "light".

The juxtaposition of dark and light or yielding and firm lines predates the use of *yin* and *yang*. These terms, as will be seen in the following chapter, were introduced into the interpretation of the *I Ching/Yijing* at a later date. However, they are so well known now in relation to the *I Ching/Yijing* and other Chinese aspects, and even some western philosophy, that it seems pragmatic to use them here occasionally from now on. Indeed, the *Ten Wings*, the *Appendices* to the *I Ching/Yijing*, make extensive use of the terms. Richard Wilhelm pointed out that *yang* originally meant "banners waving in the sun" and came to be applied to the light side of a mountain. The original meaning of *yin* was "the cloudy", "the overcast", and came to be applied to the dark side of a mountain.[63] Ultimately, however, *yin* and *yang* came to represent the varying configurations present in cosmic phenomena, their interplay creating the moment, and their changing course what was becoming. *Yin* and *yang* became the two forces from which all else emerged.

The hexagrams

Traditionally and scholastically it has always been believed that the hexagrams were derived from the combination of trigrams and were a later development of them. The eight trigrams combined with each other form sixty-four possible combinations, each a hexagram, a set of six lines placed one on top of the other. The fact that two trigrams make up a hexagram seems to support a trigram > hexagram development. However, hexagrams were probably used before trigrams, the latter becoming important in the late Warring States period for the understanding of the hexagrams themselves.[64] The inscriptions on late Shang oracle bones and Western Chou/Zhou bronzes, with sets of six numerical components very similar to the hexagrams, suggest that they may be prior to the trigrams, and certainly prior to the *yin* and *yang* lines that we now know.[65] It seems, then, that hexagrams were not a natural development of placing two trigrams together. Indeed, it is even possible that hexagrams and trigrams may have been co-existent from very early times. Xinzhong Yao and Helene McMurtrie certainly think so: "Ancient diviners may have consulted their deities by directly forming a hexagram or a trigram. Both trigrams and hexagrams might well have been tools for divination and other religious rituals, either independently or jointly together."[66]

Each of the sixty-four hexagrams (*kua-hua/guahua*) is given a name or "tag", and much conjecture has taken place over the centuries of the history of the *I Ching/Yijing* to find symbolic meaning between each hexagram tag, the hexagram, and even its line statements. Many of the names of the hexagrams reflect life situations such as Youthful Folly, Possession, Waiting, Opposition. Some reflect social situations such as The Marrying Maiden, The Well, Fellowship with Men. Others embody personal characteristics like Modesty, Enthusiasm and Grace. Rutt thinks that the names of hexagrams have been overlaid with philosophical meaning in such a way that they have been stripped of their basic ritualistic intentions. To him, the hexagram names were probably simply just that, "a convenient shorthand mnemonic reference".[67] It is his view that the names have nothing to do with the body of the text. Others, like Stephen Karcher, see the names of the hexagrams "not only important, but as implicitly repeated in each line statement".[68] Then, too, Rutt claims that: "No discernible pictorial connection exists between any of the hexagrams and the texts that accompany them."[69] And as far as hexagram 50, which many consider resembles a cooking pot, a *ting/ding*, is concerned, he considers, "one must very much want to believe in the similarity in order to be convinced about it; and even if the similarity were accepted, a single example would be no more than coincidental. Pictorially, the hexagrams are meaningless".[70] Each hexagram has a statement attached to it. Hexagram statements are *t'uan/tuan*[71] and were probably originally connected with sacrifice, ritual and divination. Rutt considers that they were not summative of the line statements and may not have been connected with them at all. Nor do we know when they were first placed in the text.[72] He believes that the line statements may well have originally referred to warfare, though they have been overlayed with philosophical meaning in the light of the content of the *Ten Wings*.

When we look at the texts of the *I Ching/Yijing* today, each hexagram has a number. The Chinese, however, do not number the hexagrams; they are known to them by their names, their tags. Numbering merely assists referencing. In 1973, a silk manuscript of the *I Ching/Yijing*, dated to second century BCE Han times, came to light at Ma-wang-tui/Mawangdui in Honan/Henan. In this text the hexagrams are placed in a different order from the traditional and received text.[73] However, it seems likely that, while the Ma-wang-tui/Mawangdui is the earliest extant copy that we have, extraneous evidence suggests that its order of hexagrams, while logical, was a rearrangement of an earlier, traditional order, the one we know today.[74] The earliest extant established or received order of hexagrams is on the second-century Han stone tablets. This order – not reflected in the text at Ma-wang-tui/Mawangdui – arranges the hexagrams where possible in pairs, by a process of inversion, the second of a pair being the inversion of the first. Karcher sees inversion, rotation, transformation and conversion into its opposite as informing the order and specific matrix of the hexagrams.[75]

The traditional view makes exactly these kinds of philosophical connections that Rutt, above, is so critical of. The arrangement of the hexagrams alternates in pattern, nature and meaning, representing the *yin* and *yang* of life and nature. They are believed to be sequential, mirroring the ebb and flow of existence. Their specific order has a tendency to reflect opposing forces, each juxtaposed with the one before and the one following in contrasting ways. This is because the pendulum of life experiences is never static. At each high point it has to swing back in the other direction, though perhaps with momentary rest before the change in the opposite direction occurs. So success can only be followed by failure, strife by peace, beginning by completion, abundance by scarcity, creativity by passivity and so on: the pendulum always swings back the other way. Understanding such a principle of life encourages optimism in moments of despair and caution in excessive success. The hexagram that emerges following consultation of the *I Ching/Yijing* places the individual psyche in the appropriate context of such ebb and flow, such process of change and transformation, indicating in which direction life is flowing, and how best to deal with it.

Hexagrams express even more finely, and with mathematical precision, the permutations of transformations extant in the world of phenomena. Importantly, just as the trigrams are believed to interact with each other through processes of transformation, so too the hexagrams are images of states of change. They are considered to represent the fundamental laws and possible states of existence. The firm transforms to the yielding, the yielding to the firm, alternating in rhythmic pattern to form the cycles of life and death, day and night, heat and cold, summer and winter, pleasure and sorrow. So one hexagram changes to another in constant flux, each hexagram representing the moment in time in the process of change – and discovered at the time of consultation. Jung called this the "synchronicity" and interdependence of one object with another, including the psyche of the observer, the individual consulting the *I Ching/Yijing*.[76] The acceptance of such "synchronicity" is one essential factor in the validity of the *I Ching/Yijing*, the other essential factor being the acceptance of the hexagrams as reflecting states of change in a particular moment in time. The concept of the interrelation of all things lies at the heart of the philosophy of the *I Ching/Yijing*. Such interrelation is "between all things in the universe from solar systems lying beyond our ken to objects so small that even the microscope has not discovered all of them". In this case, "the same fundamental laws govern worlds, nations, groups of entities, single entities and microscopic parts of entities".[77] Four of the hexagrams are special and timeless, and we shall look at them below. It is the remaining sixty that represent time, their six lines amounting to the number of days in a lunar year (360), and it is these, especially, that symbolize the rhythmic phases of phenomenal life.

Just as in the trigrams the lines were divided into Heaven, Earth and humanity so the top two lines of the hexagrams represent Heaven, the bottom two Earth, and the middle two humankind. And just as trigrams *Ch'ien/Qian* Heaven, and *K'un/Kun* Earth, were the most important, so too are the hexagrams of the same name. Heaven as pure *yang* and Earth as pure *yin* are the two hexagrams from which all the others are derived. These two hexagrams and those of *T'ai/Tai*, Peace (Contentment), which has three *yang* lines supporting three *yin* lines, and *P'i/Pi* Standstill (Stagnation), which has three *yin* lines supporting three *yang* lines, are considered to be the four timeless hexagrams. The particular balance between them is obvious:

Ch'ien/Qian   **K'un/Kun**   **T'ai/Tai**   **P'i/Pi**

The ideal hexagram is number 63 *Chi Chi/Jijii*, After Completion (Order). This hexagram has, reading from its base a *yang* and *yin* line alternately. It represents temporary perfection and a state of harmonious balance and order in the three areas of Heaven, Earth and humanity. Conversely, the next hexagram, number 64, *Wei Chi/Weiji*, Before Completion is the least harmonious, since all its lines are in the wrong places.

Of the two trigrams that combine to form a six-lined hexagram, the lower tends to refer to what is in the process of happening, to what is being created, to the inner self and behind. The upper refers to what is receding or dissolving, what is above, the external environment, and in front, or in the future. The lines of the upper trigram are "going" while the lower ones are "coming". Within a hexagram there are also what are called "nuclear" trigrams. If we read a hexagram from the bottom, the second, third and fourth lines themselves form a trigram, as do lines three four and five. So there are two nuclear trigrams in every hexagram, and these, too, have some bearing on the way in which a hexagram is "read". They provide an "inner" situation to the whole hexagram, and are taken into consideration when interpreting a hexagram. Nuclear trigrams were identified probably in about the beginning of the first millennium.[78]

The lines of hexagrams

It is not only a hexagram as a whole, and its nuclear trigrams, which present a particular cosmic pattern but the individual lines of the hexagram. Firm, unbroken lines are "odd" (because they are single) and *yang*. Yielding and broken lines are "even" (because they are dual) and *yin*. Such lines are important with reference to their specific places in the hexagram, their relation to other lines, and their order from bottom to top. The numbering of the lines, it should be remembered, begins at the bottom of the hexagram. Odd-numbered lines are superior to even-numbered ones. Combining the placement of the line with its odd or even nature gives a further opportunity for interpretation. But if the overall interpretation demands firmness, then yielding lines, even in the right place, are not particularly favourable, as would firm lines be in a situation that required one to yield.[79] In the ideal hexagram of *Chi Chi/Jiji*, all the lines are in their most fortuitous places.

Then, too, certain lines are relationally linked to others – the first and fourth, the second and fifth, and the third and sixth. It is particularly favourable if these lines are opposites, *yin* and *yang*, symbolizing balance. The first, third and fifth lines are considered to be light, and are therefore favourable if they are *yang* lines in the hexagram. The second, fourth and sixth are dark and, similarly, are favourable if they are *yin* in the hexagram. But if *yang* places are occupied by *yin* lines, and *vice versa*, then the result is generally unfavourable. The second and fourth lines refer to officials, sons or women, the fourth line being superior. The fifth line represents a person in high authority, like a ruler, though the third line is also one indicating authority because it is at the top of the lower trigram. The middle lines of both trigrams in the hexagram are also important features in the analysis of the hexagram, being positive if they are *yin* or *yang* lines in the right places, and negative if in the wrong places. Their importance may have something to do with the fact that both lines represent humankind in their respective trigrams. Where *yin* and *yang* are in the wrong places, the line is said to be "unsuitable", or "improper", though such unsuitability may not be the case in the light of the character of the hexagram as a whole.[80]

The top line is superior to all the others; the bottom line is inferior. In ancient times the top line tended to represent the sage and the higher lines stood for members of the ruling class or officials. Today the higher lines have been applied to all sorts of socio-political positions, with the ruler at the top and the mass of people represented by the bottom line.[81] However, a position of authority, normally a *yang* line, may be designated by a *yin* line if the other lines of the hexagram point to such a necessity. Similarly, a *yang* line badly placed, may indicate an inferior, not superior, person. The bottom and top lines are peripheral to the hexagram, the bottom one not quite entering into the scene, and the top one being almost out of it. They can also represent the beginnings and ends of things, respectively.

The second line represents the person balanced between the work-face and "middle management", or those in the work-face who excel. The third line represents those in charge of the work-face, the "middle managers" or "manageresses" themselves. Cleary comments on this line: "Many tensions and conflicts arise at the border between the lower and upper ranks, for this is where there exist the greatest differences between the status of the line in the context of its own trigram and its status in the context of the hexagram as a whole."[82] Although the fourth line is in the upper trigram and represents a strong position of leadership in relation to the lower trigram, in its own context it is at the base of the upper one and represents the difficult situation of importance on the one hand and subordination to high-powered leadership, represented by the fifth line, on the other.[83] Cheng I/Zheng Yi summed up the relation of lines to the context of social groups more applicable to the modern world in the following way:

> First: workers, peasants, artisans, small businesses
> Second: educated and skilled people from among unenfranchised people, artists and intellectuals, grass-roots organizers, trade unions
> Third: middle classes, lower and middle management, large local landlords and developers
> Fourth: upper managerial levels, academic establishments, functionaries of social, cultural, business, and political organizations with responsibilities on organization-wide, national, or global scales
> Fifth: central directorates
> Top: the aged, the retired, the emeriti, extremists and diehards[84]

Thus, the way in which the firm and yielding lines are placed in a hexagram suggest strengths and weaknesses in relation to the social or working situation. The lines will suggest positive or negative conditions, depending on the overall character of the hexagram. However, a firm line in the right place may suggest over-aggression and an overbearing nature that is clearly wrong in the life-situation. Similarly, a yielding line may be in its right place, but the overall hexagram may indicate too much yielding, withdrawal, and a distinct lack of firmness when it is most needed. It is the overall hexagram that will reveal such anomalies. Unbroken, firm or *yang* lines are indicative of movement, their opposite of broken, yielding or *yin* lines are indicative of rest. It is the changing places of these lines, their ascent and descent, the changing of weak lines to strong ones, and strong ones to weak ones, that mark the ebb and flow of life's situations.[85]

A whole hexagram has to be seen as a fluid, dynamic picture that pulsates through its lines. The first line is the beginning of a process of change, the second, the internal nature of a situation. The third line is that point at which what is internal in the outer trigram is becoming external in the upper one. Thus it is a line representing tension and crisis. The fourth line represents the start of the externalization of the situation, and the fifth, which corresponds to the third line of the "internal", lower, trigram, fully externalizes the situation. The sixth line is the completion or the point at which things turn into their opposite.

When the *I Ching/Yijing* is used, the resulting hexagram may contain what are called "moving" lines, mentioned briefly above. These are lines that are in the process of change from yielding to firm or *vice versa*. The process of change is strong enough to result in a new hexagram obtained by changing the moving lines to their opposites. How this occurs will be seen below. Such moving lines are indicators of a radically dynamic changing situation, an almost immediate state of change for an individual. A moving firm or *yang* line is represented by ———o———, and is an "old *yang*" and a moving *yin* line, an "old *yin*", by ———x———. Non-moving lines are "young" lines. In analysis, *two* hexagrams are interpreted, the first with its moving lines giving the situation at the moment, and the second, when the old lines have been changed into their opposites, the state into which things are rapidly moving. Moving lines are sufficiently important to override the whole hexagram if there is any contradiction in the interpretation. As noted earlier, lines that are not moving lines are given the numbers seven (*yang*) and eight (*yin*). These are "resting" lines. A *yang* line that is moving to a *yin* one is given the number nine. A *yin* line moving to a *yang* is given the number six.

In summation, *yang* lines are representative of Heaven, of activity and motion, of the male, firmness, strength and light. They are positive indicators. *Yin* lines are indicative of Earth, of passivity, receptivity, and are yielding, weak and dark. They are negative indicators. In the *Ten Wings* of the *I Ching/Yijing*, *yin* and *yang* were accepted as the two interacting forces that inform all phenomenal existence, produced from *Tao* the Ultimate Source of all.

Consulting the *I Ching/Yijing*: finding the hexagram of the moment

How, then, is the *I Ching/Yijing* consulted? How do we find where we are at the moment in time and the best way forward from the present into the future? The oldest method, and still one used today, was by the use of yarrow sticks. The use of yarrow sticks or milfoil[86] in divination was used alongside, but gradually replaced, the divination methods of cracks on animal bones and tortoise or turtle shells. The traditional method of finding a hexagram by the use of yarrow sticks is the most complicated of methods. Fifty sticks are used (though one is put to one side), and through divisions, subdivisions and countings the hexagram is built up from the bottom.[87] Since this system is mainly used for ritual temple use, and is lengthy to explain, it will be left to the interested reader to glean its details elsewhere. Suffice it to say here that the traditional method is still extant today, and is also adapted for more popular use.[88]

The ways in which the use of yarrow stalks has been adapted to modern use have been described by Palmer, O'Brien and Kwok Man Ho.[89] In some cases, the inquirer visits a temple where he or she is given a special container in which are placed a hundred numbered sticks. After prayers and offerings, the container is shaken until one stick falls out, the inquirer asking his or her chosen god for an answer to a specific question during the process. A professional fortune-teller then interprets the answer from the number on the stick. However, two other methods are very common, these being the use of just twelve sticks, or the use of coins. With the former, six of the sticks are marked with a *yang* line and the remaining six with *yin*. From the twelve, one stick at a time is drawn out forming the hexagon, building it up from the bottom. With this system, however, there can be no moving lines.

The coin-tossing method traditionally goes back to the fourth century BCE and was invented by a Taoist named Wang Hsü/Wang Xu.[90] The use of three coins is perhaps the best known in the West. These need to be three like coins. In pre-revolution China, Chinese coins were round, representing Heaven with a square hole in the centre, representing Earth. One side was inscribed and was considered to be *yin*, the uninscribed side being *yang*. With coins outside China it is often difficult to ascertain which should be the inscribed side. Perhaps the side giving its value should be regarded as inscribed. Most, indeed, regard the head side as *yang* and the reverse side as *yin*.[91] The three coins are thrown down six times, one for each line of the hexagram, beginning at the bottom. The *yang* side of the coin is given three points and the *yin* side two points. Each throw will give one of four possible results:

$2 + 2 + 2 = 6$ = moving *yin* ———x———
$2 + 2 + 3 = 7$ = young *yang* ——————
$2 + 3 + 3 = 8$ = young *yin* ——— ———
$3 + 3 + 3 = 9$ = moving *yang* ———o———

Where moving *yin* and *yang* lines occur, then *two* hexagrams have to be taken into account. The first will be the current situation, and the second, the dominant situation into which events are moving. Young *yin* and *yang* have no moving characteristics at all, and so reflect the situation more firmly as it is.

There is also an eight-coin method of using the *I Ching/Yijing*. With this method, called the *Pa Ch'ien/Baqian* method, the *Pa-kua/Bagua* of Fu Hsi/Fu Xi is used. Using eight like coins, one of which is marked in some way, and beginning with *Ch'ien/Qian* at the top (which is South to the Chinese), a coin is placed in an anti-clockwise direction until the bottom, North position is reached. Then the inquirer returns to the top and proceeds clockwise after *Ch'ien/Qian*. Wherever the marked coin turns up, that is the lower trigram. The process is then repeated to find the upper trigram. No moving lines can be indicated by the process so far. However, the line indicating the moving *yin* or *yang* is found by a similar method. Two unmarked coins are removed. The remaining six are shuffled and then placed one by one on top of each other. When the marked coin occurs, the corresponding line of the hexagram is the line indicating the specific degree of change and the answer to the inquirer's question.[92]

Those who use the *I Ching/Yijing* as part of their religious belief system treat it with great respect and conduct their inquiries of it with a degree of reverence. Washing the hands before using it is usual, as is the use of incense. But very important is the state of mind of the inquirer, which should be calm and receptive. Some people use the *I Ching/Yijing* for quiet reflection and to gain wisdom. Others may use it for meditation purposes. Some may even open it at random to help solve a particular problem. Palmer, O'Brien and Kwok Man Ho, who have studied the contexts in which the *I Ching/Yijing* is used, point out that it is *not* frequently consulted, unlike the Chinese almanac, but that it would be used in times of crisis.[93] However, the traditional rituals surrounding its use are very exact as to the way to face, the utensils to use, and the precise way in which the yarrow stalks are handled and subdivided.[94] Traditionally, the *I Ching/Yijing* is kept wrapped in a cloth on which it rests when being used, and it should not be kept anywhere lower than a person's shoulders. The yarrow sticks, too, are kept in a special container and are not otherwise used. Special ritual also accompanies the end of the consultation.

The *I Ching/Yijing* is generally understood to be underpinned by a profound morality that promotes a better state, improvement from the moment to the best possible outcome, or in negative circumstances, the most moral way forward. The lines of the hexagram, especially, indicate the *yin* or *yang* deviations and aberrations from the ideal trigrams of Heaven and Earth. But a good deal of developed intuition is necessary in interpreting each hexagram in relation to the question posed. Shchutskii illustrated this point well:

> The elements of the *Book of Changes* are elements of imagery. Instead of speaking of the appropriateness of collective action, the *Book of Changes* says, "When the reed is plucked, the other stalks follow after it, since it grows in a bunch. Firmness brings happiness. Development." Instead of speaking of the vanity of an undertaken action, the *Book of Changes* says, "The nobody has to be powerful; the nobleman has to perish. Firmness is terrifying. When the goat butts the fence, its horns stick in it."[95]

These are vivid images indeed! They serve to illustrate admirably the ways in which the *I Ching/Yijing* symbolizes the moment in time, and the necessity to apply a hexagram to the personal life-situation in a reflective manner.

How, then, do we evaluate the *I Ching/Yijing* in a final analysis. The *I Ching/Yijing* presupposes that the microcosmic realm of Earth has its mirror image in the macrocosmic world of heavenly ideas beyond the senses. Such a concept is the metaphysical reality underpinning the *I Ching/Yijing*. Wilhelm wrote: "The holy men and sages, who are in contact with those higher spheres, have access to these ideas through direct intuition and are therefore able to intervene decisively in events in the world. Thus man is linked with heaven, the suprasensible world of ideas, and with earth, the material world of visible things, to form with these a trinity of the primal powers."[96] It is not unusual for cultures to project such "higher spheres" in mythological and religious attempts to explain creation and the universe in terms of the outcome of divine power. Concomitant with such a view is the search, too, for an *unchanging* divine power and reality that underpins an observable world of change. But the *I Ching/Yijing* does neither of these things. On the contrary, change and transformation *are* the reality of the universe according to the *I Ching/Yijing*, and it is in the context of that change and transformation that the human being is placed.

The theories informing the *I Ching/Yijing* thus replaced the usual mythological basis for interpreting life in ancient China. Indeed, China has few myths in comparison to most cultures. Hellmut Wilhelm put this succinctly when he wrote that the *I Ching/Yijing* "is an attempt to come nearer to the same universal problems whose reflection in other cultures has led to the insights expressed in their various mythologies; in particular, it is an attempt to come near to a solution for the ever-present problem of duration and change, of being and becoming".[97] And since change and transformation constitute reality, the *I Ching/Yijing* cannot impose fixed laws, it can only present guidelines in relation to the particular flow of events or movement of the universe at a moment in time. It can only encourage self-reflection and responsibility in terms of the present condition in life. Raymond Van Over's words here are especially apt: "If the oracle wishes to direct our action in a specific direction or through a particular channel it will tell us how a Superior Man would conduct himself. In this subtle way our actions are directed toward a positive goal while still allowing us the free will to choose our own ultimate destiny."[98] There is, thus, a self-evolutionary value to working with the *I Ching/Yijing*.

The interrelation and interconnectedness of all things in the universe, both material and subtle, are presupposed by the *I Ching/Yijing*. The changing universe is not a chaotic backdrop on which the human being is placed, but a vast canvas on which the interplay of all things forms patterns and rhythms of growth and decay, coming and going, resisting and yielding, expansion and contraction, and so on. Going with the flow of things, rather than in the face of things, is the easier path. The *I Ching/Yijing* is presented as a means by which this is possible, a tool that assists in shaping life.

So the ultimate aim underpinning the *I Ching/Yijing* is to achieve the kind of harmony and balance in life that results in the wisdom of the sage, or the well-being of the *chün-tzu/junzi*, Confucius' gentleman, or superior person,

> one who is perfectly self-controlled and self-sufficient, wholly free from self-seeking and able to stand freely and serenely among forces which toss lesser men to and fro like shuttlecocks, despite their tears and screams. Cheerfully impervious to loss or gain, he acts vigorously when action is needed and willingly performs the much harder task of refraining from action when things are much better left alone.[99]

Becoming such a sage, and the embodiment of wisdom, harmony, naturalness, and particularly virtue, was the ultimate aim of Taoists. Like water that finds its way around obstacles, the sage flows with the negative and positive changes that occur in life, in harmony with the ever-transforming universe. For Taoists, this was being in accord with *Tao*; it was identifying oneself with the transformations initiated by *Tao* as the phenomena of all life, at the same time experiencing the oneness of *Tao* in all things. Such a life-condition points to inner stillness while engaged in outward activity, inner harmony while engaged in the ordinary events of the day.

The perfection embodied in the sage or the enlightened immortal was the ultimate goal of the Taoist. However, while the *I Ching/Yijing* was essentially a Chinese text, it was, in its early phases, more readily connected with Confucianism. Yet, in time, the Taoists themselves came to accept the *Book of Changes* as essential to their religion. Taoists were particularly attracted to the symbolic thought contained in the *I Ching/Yijing*. They were also attracted to the whole concept of transformation. Indeed, Shchutskii believed such a concept – embodied in the *Book of Changes* – enhanced the Taoists' interests in alchemy considerably, and also contributed to Taoist theories of the universe.[100] It was particularly the *Ta-chuan/Dazhuan* text, however, *The Great Treatise* with its wide philosophical explorations, which had an affect on Taoism. The fundamental philosophy of the *I Ching/Yijing* as a whole is certainly evident in Taoist thought. Using Shchutskii's words here, such correlation of thought might be summed up in three important points:

(a) the world is both changeability and immutability and, what is more, the natural unity of them; (b) at the basis of this lies the polarity which runs throughout the world, the antipodes of which are as opposed to each other as they are attracted to each other: in their relationship the world movement appears as a rhythm; (c) thanks to the rhythm, that which has been established and that which has not yet been established unite into one system, according to which the future already exists in the present as a "sprout" of coming events.[101]

If *Tao* is seen as underpinning each of these views, then we have in capsule form Taoist cosmogony, but I shall leave it to chapter 4 to explore the immensity of *Tao*. It was not just on Taoists that the *I Ching/Yijing* exerted a massive influence. It is Smith's view that it "exerted more influence in China than any other Confucian classic",[102] and was "an important intellectual and cultural common denominator" of Taoism, Buddhism and Confucianism.[103]

The hexagrams of the *I Ching/Yijing* continually point to the goal of perfection with all kinds of advice, such as developing integrity in one's conduct and helping others to do the same (hexagram 29), or cultivating virtue for the benefit of the world (hexagram 30). Thus, at least the *I Ching/Yijing* contains advice on moral behaviour, on the ways in which the self can evolve. Even if its more active role of response to inquiry is set aside, the more passive role of being an inherently moral guide is of immense value. For there is positive encouragement to do what is good without being harsh on the self, without being unnaturally good. Liu I-ming/Liu Yiming's commentary on the *I Ching/Yijing* brought this factor out well:

> Of old it has been said, always extinguish the stirring mind, do not extinguish the shining mind. When the mind is unstirring it is shining, when the mind does not stop it is astray. The shining mind is the mind of Tao, the straying mind is the human mind. The mind of Tao is subtle and hard to see; the human mind is unstable and uneasy.
> Although there is the mind of Tao in the human mind, and there is the human mind in the mind of Tao, it is just a matter of persistence in the midst of action and stillness: If the shining mind is always maintained, the straying mind does not stir; the unstable is stabilized, and the subtle becomes apparent.[104]

Joseph Needham called the *I Ching/Yijing* a "cosmic filing-system"[105] and a "mischievous handicap"[106] that rather prevented scientific development. *Scientifically* this may well be true. But those who put their faith in the *I Ching/Yijing* are not looking for scientific answers to life's problems. On the contrary, they are trying to explore ways in which they can solve the socio-psychological problems that life is presenting at a moment in time. They are trying, also, to gain greater perception of the particular way in which their present space–time situation harmonizes with the interconnected cosmos. Raymond Van Over put this sensitively when he wrote:

> The writers of the *I Ching* recognized this archetypal and ardent striving for universal identification. They looked not at transient values, or superficial answers such as commercial and social success, but rather at the rhythm of the flower as it thrusts from the ground, blossoms, spreads its seed, wilts, and returns from whence it came. Such, to the writers of the *I Ching*, held a profound meaning. Where there was only mystery for many and fear of the transience of life for others, there resided an eternal truth for a few. This movement of life,

its necessary ultimate destruction and eternal recurrence, its polarity of principles and energies, dictated a way of life that could, if based upon insight and wisdom, pattern itself after the cosmos.[107]

Such words epitomize rather well the inner meaning of the *I Ching/Yijing* for those who accept its validity. To regard it scientifically, or even too academically, is to miss the *spiritual* connectedness with the cosmos that its proponents wish to achieve. At the end of the day, there will be those who will view the *I Ching/Yijing* as no more than the fanciful ramblings of ancient soothsayers; others will find it a useful guide. And in Hellmut Wilhelm's words: "Even if we shrink from approaching the book with the willing faith of an oracle seeker, we can still meditate on this image of the cosmos for its own sake and seek to understand it."[108] One fact remains, the *I Ching/Yijing* seems to have stood the test of three millennia of time, and that in itself is remarkable. In the context of Taoism, it is an accepted text that Taoists took ownership of from their distant beginnings to present times.

3
Creative Forces:
Yin *and* Yang *and the Five Agents*

Yin and yang

Our understanding of the world around us is generated by relationships between opposites. We know what darkness is, because we know what light is; we know what heat is, because of its opposite of cold. And between such opposites we have the variables of shade, dusk, brightness, dullness, as well as coolness, iciness, burning heat or gentle warmth. The Chinese view of the cosmos, from the heavens to human beings, the seasons and the hours of the day, was one based on the interplay of such bipolarities. Generically, they were called *yin* and *yang*. So important was this fundamental principle in the Chinese understanding of the universe that one author describes it as "one of the most fruitful and useful ever devised by the mind of man for making sense out of the infinite multitude of diverse facts in the universe".[1] The theory of *yin* and *yang* is not only a philosophical perspective of reality but is also a theory of inherent power in all phenomena – a changing, dynamic power that alters from one polarity to another. It was adopted by the Chinese from ancient times onwards, and came to be accepted by both Confucians and Taoists. Indeed, we might view these two belief systems themselves as *yin* and *yang* polarities within Chinese culture: the former, Confucianism, being the social, ritualistic, and more rigid system, while Taoism was more religious, mystical at times, fluidly creative and colourful. And between the two extremes came about a wealth of beliefs and practices that reflected the interplay between them. Cooper writes:

> Taoism is based on rhythm and flux, on the natural, the unconventional, the freedom-loving detachment from worldly things and its product is the poet, the artist, the metaphysician, the mystic, together with all that is laughter-loving and light-hearted. Confucianism is concerned with the stable order, the formal, the conventional and the practical administration of worldly affairs; the one idealistic, the other realistic, but together the perfect combination offsetting and correcting each other and preventing too unconstrained an informalism on the one side or too arid and rigid a classicism on the other.[2]

To these words should be added the fact that between these two polarities are the many religious expressions emerging from the interplay between Confucianism and Taoism. But all these are the interplay between the more active *yang* of Confucianism and the *yin* passivity of Taoism. And in Taoism itself, we find the passive *yin* of its mystical periods juxtaposed with the *yang* of its later religious ritual.

The *yin* and *yang* theory arose naturally from a people that felt deeply about the rhythm of the seasons, the expression of nature in rhythmic patterns, and the need to harmonize societal, agricultural and religious life with those natural rhythms. Even Chinese history seemed to follow the natural swing of the pendulum from one polarity to its opposite. Allan notes this in the early history of China. The Hsia/Xia, she writes, "were originally the mythical inverse of the Shang, associated with water, dragons, the moons, darkness and death, as opposed to the fire, birds, suns, light and life, with which the Shang were associated".[3] The waning and waxing of dynastic rule, of war and peace, of upheaval and stability are the *yin* and *yang* of Chinese historical patterns.

The theory of *yin* and *yang* provided an abstract conceptual framework that could be applied to the world of matter in the form of essences that informed all things. It arose from the descriptors given to the sunny side of a mountain or river as *yang* and the shady side as *yin*. The sunny side is warm and dry. It is bright and encourages growth activity in plant life. The warmth of the sun also encourages the evaporation of water to provide moisturizing mists to nourish the ground. The *yin* side of a mountain, on the other hand, is cool, shady, dark, cloudy and overcast. There is nothing to lift the moisture so it moves downwards into the earth, making it damp. The roots of plants are fed by the moisture but their growth is passive without the warmth of the sun. These, then, are the origins of the terms *yin* and *yang*, but we must search further back in time for the roots of the theory that the two terms came to embody.

The origins of *yin* and *yang*

Traditionally, the origins of *yin* and *yang* have been cast back to the time of Fu Hsi/Fu Xi, the mythical founder of the Hsia/Xia dynasty and of the *Pa-kua/Bagua*, the eight trigrams. While this is certainly not true, the simplicity of the idea of two fundamental forces operating in nature suggests an ancient origin, even if the terms *yin* and *yang* were not applied until later. The ancient need to understand life in terms of the balance and harmony of nature, as opposed to imbalance and disharmony, is ingrained in the Chinese psyche, as we saw in chapter 1. Indeed, according to Allan: "Within the Shang myth system, there was also a dualism, the antecedent of later *yin-yang* theory, in which the suns, sky, birds, east, life, the Lord on High were opposed to the moons, watery underworld, dragons, west, death, the Lord below".[4] Allan thus believes that the origins of the *yin* and *yang* theory lie in Shang times.[5]

By the early Chou/Zhou dynasty divination using yarrow or milfoil stalks with long stalks representing firmness, and two short ones the opposite character of yielding, became the basis of the trigrams and hexagrams of the *I Ching/Yijing*. But the earliest strata of the *I Ching/Yijing* do not use the terms *yin* and *yang*, though the theory behind their use is clearly in place. It is in the *Great Treatise* appended to the *I Ching/Yijing* that the terms *yin* and *yang* are applied.[6] However, the whole concept of balance and rhythm that underlies *yin* and *yang* is common to the philosophy of the *I Ching/Yijing* and to the agricultural and religious practices of the ancient Chinese. Maspero put this point particularly well in describing ancient Chou/Zhou times:

> If life contracted in winter, if one was not to work in the fields, it was because that was the time dominated by the *yin*, repose; if life expanded in summer, if all was opened in that season, if one laboured in the fields, it was because that was the time when the *yang*, activity, was predominant. The *yang* was indeed in the ascendent and the *yin* on the decline until the summer solstice, after which they waxed and waned inversely until the winter solstice. The equinoxes were their times of equality. If the Son of Heaven [the king] had to dwell each season in a different pavilion of the Sacred Palace, he did this in order to follow the movements of the *yin* and the *yang* across the seasons: he punished in autumn (*yin*) and rewarded in spring (*yang*).[7]

But exactly how the terms *yin* and *yang* came to be associated with the *I Ching/Yijing* remains uncertain. They seem to be ancient terms, ones that predate the *Yin–Yang* school that will be examined below. Perhaps, as Pas suggests, their first usage as descriptors of the shady and dark sides of a mountain, valley or river bank might then have been extended to Heaven and Earth; to male and female; father and mother; ruler and subjects; summer and activity; winter and passivity; and so on.[8] But it was probably not until early Han times that the *yin–yang* concept was applied to the *I Ching/Yijing*. Indeed, Fung Yu-lan points out that the cosmological system of the *I Ching/Yijing* could stand as it was without the addition of *yin* and *yang* correlates.[9] Nevertheless, as noted above, the idea of balance and harmony between interchanging opposites underpinning the philosophy of both was sufficient to promote an easy amalgamation of concepts. Graham, too, thinks that while there is no evidence of *yin* and *yang* dualism *per se* prior to the school that developed the concept to its full, the *concept* itself is deeply rooted in earlier times.[10] Yet it has to be admitted that there is only scant reference to *yin* and *yang* prior to the school of Tsou Yen/Zou Yan that developed it. All later references also seem to be a product of the school itself.[11]

It was in the Warring States period of the fifth to third centuries BCE that the so-called One hundred Schools of Philosophy arose. It was as one of these schools that the *Yin–Yang chia/jia*, "Yin–Yang school" came about, at a time when circling ideas and theories were being gathered together as more organized philosophies. Another school had developed the cosmological theory of the Five Agents – of which, more below – and while the Five Agents school was originally separate from the *Yin–Yang* school, by the time of the Han dynasty, they were thoroughly coalesced. *Yin* and *yang*, then, are early ideas that pre-dated Taoism, but were to become widely adopted. They began as specialized terms outside the use of everyday life, in currency in the more elitist circles of one or more philosophical schools.[12]

The *Yin–Yang* school probably originated in the ranks of the practitioners of magical arts, those who later became the *fang-shih/fangshi*, who practised divination, medicine and magic in their early history, but who branched out into music, astronomy and other specialist areas in their later history. The founder of the school was Tsou Yen/Zou Yan, who seems to have organized some of the beliefs of the divergent groups of his time into a coherent and systematic cosmology. His efforts were sufficient to give Taoism and Confucianism their later allegiance to the theories of *yin* and *yang*. Tsou Yen/Zou Yan is dated somewhere in the third century BCE. He came from the state of Ch'i/Qi, but was also influential in the state of Yen/Yan. He seems to have been on the fringe of the established philosophers, perhaps because of his attachments to the popular practices of magicians and diviners, or because he was a newcomer in making his mark in court circles.[13] But he is mentioned by Ssu-ma Ch'ien/Sima Qian in his historical *Shih Chi/Shiji* about the end of the second and beginning of the first centuries BCE. Indeed, this is the only source to mention him by name; references to him are otherwise indirect, and none of his own writings is extant. He is likely to have been a Confucian, and this is perhaps one reason why his theory of *yin* and *yang* was wholeheartedly accepted by Confucians.[14] The *Shih Chi/Shiji* says of him:

> Thereupon he examined deeply into the phenomena of increase and decrease of the yin and the yang, and wrote essays totalling more than one hundred thousand words about strange permutations, and about the cycles of the great Sages from beginning to end. His words were grandiose and fanciful. He had first to examine small objects, and extended this to large ones until he reached what was without limit. . . . Moreover, he followed the great events in the rise and fall of ages, and by means of their omens and (an examination into their) institutions, extended his survey backward to the time when Heaven and Earth had not yet been born, to what was profound and abstruse and not to be examined.[15]

It is particularly the abstruse and non-examinable nature of that which existed prior to Heaven and Earth that would have been attractive to the Taoists, with their belief in the indescribable *Tao*.

The cosmology of the *Yin–Yang* school accepted the whole of the universe as the result of the intermingling of the two essences of *yin* and *yang* and, as we shall see below, of Five Agents, Elements or Phases. The basis of the cosmogony was one of nature. Since the Chinese lived in the northern hemisphere, the South was connected with heat and summer. Its opposite of North was associated with cold and winter. The sun rose in the East and was correlated with springtime, while sunset in the West correlated with autumn. The day, too, could be divided in the same way, morning as spring, noon as summer, evening as autumn and night as winter. While the terms *yin* and *yang* were hardly attested before the time of Tsou Yen/Zou Yan, the influence of the *Yin–Yang* school was to become considerable and was widespread in the Ch'in/Qin dynasty. After Tsou Yen/Zou Yan, other notable philosophers who developed the ideas of the school were Hsün-tzu/Xun Xi, who lived not long after Tsou Yen/Zou Yan, the Confucian Tung Chung-shu/Dong Zhongshu of the second century and, much later in the twelfth century, the Confucian Chu Hsi/Zhu Xi.[16]

Yin

Yin, often referred to as "White Tiger", is the yielding, receptive aspect in life. Thus it is the feminine essence, is gentle and beautiful, but also negative, cold and dark. It is autumn and winter time, from which its opposite emerges in the spring. Thus, cosmologically, it is the chaos of darkness from whence the light of creation was born: in some schools, it therefore precedes *yang* as the eternally creative element from which *yang* emerges. *Yin* is the mother aspect, passive, soft, wet, the flesh of the body, the shady, cool side of a valley, mountain, river bank or garden. Yet, such general passivity and receptivity are not weaknesses, for they can be more enduring than their opposite of *yang*. Taoism, indeed, teaches that strength is often to be found in apparent weakness. Ultimately, it is *yin* that allows *yang* to rise out of its quiescence.

Yin is the valley and the womb; it is depth and descent, receiving and accepting; yet from it, all emerges. Cooper writes: "It is because it is the lowest, humblest place that the valley receives the full force of the waters which fall into it from high *yang* places. Majestic waterfalls and turbulent mountain torrents, for all their power, come down to the lowly and are absorbed by it and converted into the deep-flowing, broad, quiet and irresistible forces of the rivers, lakes and oceans, the *yin* principle."[17] *Yin* is also square, its strict sides symbolizing immobility and passivity. The moon is *yin*, as is silver, the colour connected with the moon. Pearls, since they are obtained from water, are also *yin*. The physical spirits that survive after death are called *kuei/gui*, and since they return into the earth are also *yin*. In the human being, instinct, emotion and intuition are *yin*, as well as flexibility, openness and calmness. *Yin* is everything that is esoteric. Negatively, however, it can be weakness and stasis, pettiness and small-mindedness. The eighteenth century Taoist Liu I-ming/Liu Yiming had the following to say about the flexibility of character that is the nature of *yin* in a person:

> Flexibility is docility, yielding, self-mastery, self-restraint, self-effacement, humility, selflessness, consideration of others, absence of arbitrariness, pure simplicity, genuineness. Those who use flexibility well appear to lack what they are in fact endowed with, appear to be empty when they are in fact fulfilled. They do not take revenge when offended. They seek spiritual riches and are aloof of mundane riches; they do not contend with people of the world.[18]

Yang

Yang emerges from *yin* as the light that arises from darkness. It is the spirit, the intellect, the father, and thus male, and is the active principle in life. It is aggressive, hard, heat, dryness, the bone of the body, the hard, dry stone of the home, the south, sunny side of a valley or river bank, and the spring and summer time of the year. It is symbolized by the sun and is sometimes known as "Blue Dragon". It is round, indicative of its active ability to move. Roundness is also the symbol of Heaven, which is also *yang*. Gold, associated with the sun, is *yang* as is jade. The *shen* spirits that rise from the body at death into new life are

CREATIVE FORCES: *YIN* AND *YANG* AND THE FIVE AGENTS

yang unlike their *kuei/gui* and *yin* counterparts that are held in death. *Yang* is the right side of the body, the side that holds the sword, hence its aggression. *Yang* is experienced in the transcendence that sometimes floods the mind at odd times in life. The Taoist Huang-ch'i/Huangqi from Yüan/Yuan dynasty times explained this well:

> It may also happen that while you are reading books or reciting poetry, personal desires suddenly vanish and a unified awareness is alone present – this too is one aspect of the arising of yang.
>
> Also, sometimes when friends gather and talk, they reach a communion of the inner mind, and suddenly yang energy soars up and the true potential bursts forth – this is also one way in which yang arises.
>
> Furthermore, even when playing music, playing games, drawing, fishing, cutting wood, plowing fields, reading books, if you can harmonize spontaneously based on the natural essence, without seeking or desiring anything, there will be a serenity and contentment, clearing the mind so that you forget about feelings – this is in each case a form of arising of yang.[19]

However, despite the positivity of such transcendent experience, over-excitement, overdoing the experience, transforms into negativity. Similarly, firmness that becomes overbearing can become self-destructive. Cultivating the firmness of *yang* is the goal, but it has to be in the right ways. Liu I-ming/Liu Yiming explained what this means:

> What is firmness, first get rid of covetousness. Once covetousness is gone, firmness is established, and the pillars of the spiritual house are firmly stationed. Once the basis is firm and stable, there is hope for the great Tao.
>
> What is firmness? Cutting through sentiment and clearing the senses is firmness. Not fearing obstacles and difficulties is firmness. Putting the spirit in order and going boldly forward is firmness. Being harmonious but not imitative, gregarious yet nonpartisan, is firmness. Not doing anything bad, doing whatever is good, is firmness. Being inwardly and outwardly unified, working without ceasing, is firmness.[20]

Here, then, the characteristic of *yang* as the rising principle in life is applied to the spiritual evolution of the human being, and the goal of harmony of the inner and outer self. Liu I-ming/Liu Yiming's words show clearly how *yang* implies progress and growth in the best possible dimensions of living.

The interplay of *yin* and *yang*

Yin and *yang* are complementary essences or forces. Just as we cannot understand darkness without light or *vice versa*, and just as we need the variances of dark, light and shadow to see well, so *yin* and *yang* cannot exist without each other. So in being mutually dependent, *yin* and *yang*, like all opposites in Chinese thought, are complementary rather than oppositional. *Yin* and *yang* are *alternating* even "pulsating"[21] creative forces representing the interplay between physical and spiritual, emotion and intellect, passivity and activity, the yielding and the firm, resistance and generation. Rather than opposition between the two there is polarity in unity, like two sides of one coin – a harmonized unity of opposites.

There is tension between them and a mutual play and interaction that makes them too close to be outright opposites. And in that interaction there is never a state of perfect *yang* or *yin*. The goal may be balance between the two, but whatever exists is simply dominated by one or the other; it is the varying degree of *yin* or *yang* present in an entity, or in a period of time, that makes it what it is. Such mutual dependency is called *hsiang sheng/xiang sheng*. Lao-tzu/Laozi spoke of it thus:

> Everyone sees beauty as beauty only because there is ugliness.
> Everyone knows good as good only because there is evil.
>
> Therefore having and not having arise together.
> The difficult and the easy complement one another.
> Long and short contrast with each other;
> High and low depend on each other;
> Sound and silence harmonize with each other;
> Before and after follow one another.[22]

Not only, then, is our understanding of the world based on the interplay of polarities but, in the Chinese view of things, nothing can ever be wholly one polarity as opposed to its complementary opposite. All males have a certain amount of the female within their physical and psychic make-up, as do women have a degree of masculinity. Quite contrary to most western thought it is not the triumph of good over evil, of light over darkness, of the divine over the demonic that is the Chinese goal, but the perfect balance between *yin* and *yang* polarities that enables the self to transcend them in activity. Evil is but temporary disharmony, just as night is the temporary suspension of day.

The continuous transformation and rhythmic patterns of *yin* and *yang*, their waxing and waning, coming and going, rising and falling, are related to all phenomena in the universe. To use Chung-Ying Cheng's words: "*Yin* is always the phase of difference, and *yang* always the phase of identity in the process of change (*yin*). Therefore *yin* represents the potentiality changing into the actual and *yang* the actuality changing into potentiality."[23] The degrees of balance and tension created by *yin* and *yang* account for all things. Thus, *yin* and *yang* are the qualitative essences found in all entities in the universe, constantly reacting with each other. The energy they generate in doing so is the activity of *ch'i/qi*; it is the energy that is necessary for life, and for things to come into being. Their interaction controls the cycle of seasons, *yin* being the passive, cold seasons of autumn and winter, spring and summer being *yang*. So when winter is at its deepest – the time of maximum *yin* – *yang* begins to ascend once again, as far as the height of summer. *Yin* and *yang* affect all aspects of life, even the temperament of an individual, the nature of a society, war, and religion. They make life possible, their interaction creating the relativity necessary for existence. Rest and motion, contraction and expansion, advance and retreat are the dynamics of the universe.

The interrelation of the macrocosm of Heaven and the microcosm of human affairs was a critical one in Chinese thought. The ruler, especially, could influence natural events positively or negatively by proper or improper behaviour. Thus, it was exigent that he conducted his political and religious responsibilities at the correct times. The agricultural year was meticulously planned to coincide with the seasonal *yin* and *yang* changes. It was by such means that the *yang* of Heaven and the *yin* of Earth were balanced and harmonized. It was the *Yin–Yang* school, especially, that stressed the need for unity between the ruling power and the *yang* and *yin* of Heaven and Earth. There were even high government ministers who were responsible for advising the king on the ways in which *yin* and *yang* should be harmonized. A text known as the *Monthly Commands* set down exactly what the ruler should do in each month of the year. In the first month of spring, for example, the ruler was instructed thus:

> He [the sovereign] charges his assistants to disseminate [lessons of] virtue and harmonize governmental orders, so as to give effect to the expressions of his satisfaction and to bestow his favors to the millions of people. . . . Prohibitions are issued against cutting down trees. Nests should not be thrown down. . . . In this month no warlike operations should be undertaken; the undertaking of such is sure to be followed by calamities from Heaven. This avoidance of warlike operations means that they are not to be commenced on our side.[24]

The importance of harmonizing such affairs of state with the macrocosm of Heaven is underpinned by an acceptance of the interrelation and interdependence of all things. It is a belief that is fundamental to Taoism and points to the unity of all existence.

The idea of the relativity of opposites, reflected so much in nature and life, made sense to the Chinese psyche. As we saw earlier in this chapter, the world that we experience is one of multiplicity and plurality in which we differentiate between all things through a system of categorization by language and experience. In order to exist in the world we have to know what things are and what their properties are. We need to know that if something is hot that it can hurt, or that if music is beautiful, we may enjoy it. These perspectives that we have in life are *relative*: that is to say, we can only know what one thing is or means in relation to something else, usually its opposite. These are the dualities of life that help us to make sense of it. In much eastern religion, and certainly in classical Taoism, the ultimate goal in life is one that is involved with transcending these dualities. This is not to say that such dualities do not exist, that they are not there, but that we need to overcome the desires for, and aversions to, one thing rather than its opposite. To the Taoist, the perfect balance between *yin* and *yang* brings this about. Indeed, the enlightened being in much eastern thought is at the point of equilibrium between all opposites, and is able to flow in any direction in life without losing that equilibrium.

Since the relativity of opposites forms a considerable part of our space–time understanding of the world, if we focus on one thing too much we automatically highlight its opposite. If, for example, we concentrate on the good in life, we become even more aware of its opposite. If we imagine any pair of opposites pictorially as connected by a straight line, they become, as Capra described them, "extreme parts of a single whole".[25] The interdependence of polar opposites is what is behind the *yin* and *yang* principle. Their relativity means that nothing can exist in its own right. Lao-tzu/Laozi put this simply:

> That which contracts
> Must first expand.
> That which is weak
> Must first be strong.
> That which is cast down

Must first be raised up.
Before something is taken away
It must first be given.

This is called discernment of things.
The soft and weak overcome the hard and strong.
Fish should not leave deep waters,
A country's weapons should not be revealed.[26]

Human beings are constantly at some point other than the central equilibrium between all kinds of polarities. Only when dualities are transcended can the true perspective of reality be known. Jean Cooper pertinently points out: "No observation in the realm of duality can see the whole and therefore cannot be absolutely right. It is little wonder that so many of our judgements, both individual and social, produce such unfortunate results when they are based on the erroneous assumption that we can see the whole."[27]

While it is difficult to deny the complementary nature of opposites, the Chinese took the concept a stage further and, as noted earlier, accepted the *alternation* of opposites, *yin* becoming *yang* and *yang* becoming *yin* in endless cycles. As noted above, nothing is entirely *yin* or *yang* for each contains an element of its opposite. When one reaches its maximum, the other begins to increase until it, too, reaches its maximum point. Such a concept makes life like a pendulum swinging between multiple polarities. Metaphysically, the belief points to the perpetual flux of all life; it also highlights the point that anything taken to its extreme will automatically produce its opposite. The cyclical swing from *yin* to *yang* and *vice versa* is reflected in the hexagrams of the *I Ching/Yijing*, which are used also to depict the months of the year and the changing of the seasons.

Fu	*Lin*	*T'ai/ Tai*	*Ta-chuang/ Dazhuang*	*Kuai/ Guai*	*Ch'ien/ Qian*
11th	12th	1st	2nd	3rd	4th

Kou/ Gou	*Tun/ Dun*	*P'i/Pi*	*Kuan/ Guan*	*Po/ Bo*	*K'un/ Kun*
5th	6th	7th	8th	9th	10th

The diagram shows the beginning of the ascendancy of *yang* in the month of *Fu* after the predominance of *yin*, until it becomes predominant in the fourth month of *Ch'ien/Qian*. After this month, *yin* begins its ascent in the same way. Such alternation between *yin* and *yang* suggests that if you want to achieve something you should start from its opposite! Again, Lao-tzu/Laozi said:

Yield then overcome;
Bend and become straight;

Empty and become full;
Wear out and become new;
Have little and gain much;
Have much and be confused.[28]

Since all opposites are relative to, and interdependent on, each other, one can never be victor over the other. Indeed, recognizing the dynamic balance between opposites, between the *yin* and *yang* of things, and "flowing with them", is what Taoism is all about. The hexagrams of the above diagram show the essentially dynamic nature of life, for *yin* and *yang* are never static. They are not two irreconcilable, opposing forces, but are different, interdependent aspects of one whole, two parts of a unity, two sides of a coin. Their rhythm, to use Bodde's expression, is one of "eternal oscillation".[29]

Taking the gains and losses in our stride is the moral of a story told by Lieh-tzu/Liezi. An old man and his son lived together at the top of a hill. They were very poor. One day their horse strayed away. The neighbours came to express how sorry they were. But the old man said: "Why would you see this as misfortune?" Not long afterwards the horse returned bringing with it many other wild horses. This seemed good fortune indeed, so the neighbours all came to congratulate the old man. But the old man asked: "Why would you see this as good luck?" Having so many horses, the old man's son took to riding, but he fell off a horse and broke his leg. The accident left him lame. Once again, the neighbours gathered around to commiserate with the old man, but again he said: "Why would you see this as misfortune?" Some time later, war broke out and, of course, his young son was not able to go because he was lame.

The dominance of yang

Despite all that has been written above it would have to be admitted that *yang* generally appears to be superior to *yin*. The precedence of *yang* over *yin* is partially solved by Robinet, who wrote, "seen horizontally as two complementary poles in human life, they are clearly equals; if aligned vertically, Yang is always upper and dominates Yin, an indication that the desired fate of the human is transcendence of the self".[30] However, despite the predominance of *yang* Heaven over *yin* Earth, there are disparities in the "horizontal" perceptions of *yin* and *yang*. Graham, for example cites an early list of *yin* and *yang* characteristics from the ancient document *Ch'eng/Cheng*. Here, politically insignificant states are *yin* as opposed to important ones that are *yang*. And in terms of character, to be base as opposed to noble, being stuck where one is as opposed to getting on in the world, being controlled by others instead of controlling, are all *yin* in nature.[31] Metaphysically, too, *yin* is chaos from which *yang* as light and intellect emerges. In the Taoist rite of exorcism it is the *yang* energies that defeat and drive out the *yin kuei/gui*, and *yang* ritual items are used throughout.[32] *Yang* numbers are always odd, because they have undivided lines. The symbol is one of strength. Conversely, *yin* lines are weak, having no middle. They are always even numbers and thought of as "unlucky". The first odd number (other than one, unity) is three, and is assigned to *yang*. Nine, or three *yang* lines, are the optimum *yang*, the optimum light, and are indicative of Heaven, the *Ch'ien/Qian* trigram.

So while *yin* and *yang* can never replace each other there is what Bodde called "a cosmic hierarchy of balanced inequality" that informs the *yin* and *yang* relationship.[33] Given that the polarities of *yin* and *yang* probably arose from the observations of the seasons, Bodde comments, "it would be surprising indeed if the early Chinese, living in North China, with its rigorous winter climate, would have preferred the cold-bringing *yin* to the life-giving *yang*. Yet, confronted by the inexorable diurnal and annual alternation of the two, they were wise enough to see in them a pattern of movement necessary to the cosmic harmony rather than two irreconcilable warring forces".[34] The inconsistencies of hierarchizing *yin* and *yang* do not seem to have bothered Chinese and Taoist philosophers too much. Teiser comments: "Some interpreters of yin and yang choose to emphasize the nondualistic, harmonious nature of the relationship, while others emphasize the imbalance, hierarchy, and conflict built into the idea."[35] Pas suggests that the dominance of *yang* over *yin* and associative good over evil as respective correlates came about because *yang* is associated with life, health, Heaven and purity, as well as the *shen* spirit that is capable of rising to Heaven at death. *Yin* represents death, the realm of the dead, and the *yin p'o/po* soul is that which is confined to the earth and becomes a ghost.[36] But he also makes the pertinent point that, "if balance is created out of their union, both 'principles' must be necessarily good and positive".[37]

Diversity in unity

Those who accept the non-dual relationship of *yin* and *yang* stress the unity and oneness of the apparent polarities. One may be ascendant, but this only intensifies the dormant opposite. *Yin* and *yang* are a unity of complementary opposites whose interaction makes life simply expressions of their interplay. "Going with" that interplay is what it means to be a Taoist; it is bringing oneself in line with *Tao*. Trying to grasp at one aspect of a pair of opposites is futile, for life cannot be manipulated in such a way: desires and aversions, then, are a waste of time. The dualities we see only appear to be contradictory to each other, but it is to this separate appearance that we react, and on which we build our egos. What *is* real, is the present moment, a moment that is part of constant flux, constant movements between polarities. We can only go along with this movement, we cannot maintain a moment of it as our own, keep it, or recreate it.

The natural, non-differentiated state of the universe, then, is a dynamic one. It is a spontaneous flow of experiences bound within the natural order of the expression of *Tao* in the universe, the cyclical ebb and flow of all life and all in it. Things are always subject to change and extremes of one kind or another, but must always revert to their opposites. Ultimate Reality in Taoism, then, is at once the voidness of *Tao*, and the spontaneity of its essence, or *Te/De*, within existence – the continual flow and flux of all life. Separateness in manifest existence is an illusion brought about by the continued interplay between *yin* and *yang*. The unity of *yin* and *yang* provides what Chung-Ying Chen describes as "a core of rich meanings which is the source for all other meanings in the formation of Chinese metaphysics".[38] As the same author points out: "The unity of *yin* and *yang* hence implies unity of light and shade, unity of motion and rest, and unity of firmness and softness. From this fundamental unity the unity of difference and identity and the unity of being and becoming will arise."[39]

The unity of polarities and the interrelation of *yin* and *yang* are graphically displayed in the well-known *yin–yang* symbol of more modern times:

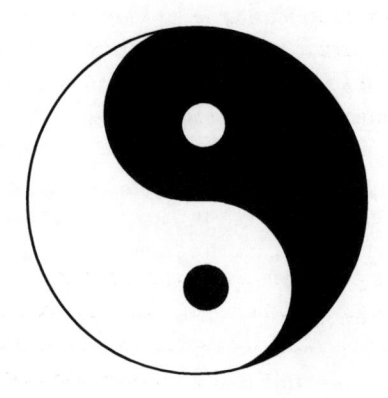

Here, *yin* and *yang* are enclosed in a circle representing their unity – the source of the two is One, though the One is not *Tao* as we shall see in a later chapter, for *Tao* is beyond even the One. The circle surrounding *yin* and *yang* symbolizes perfection, and in enclosing them, it encloses all the possibilities and potentialities of the cosmos, at the same time indicating their interrelation. Since neither *yin*, represented by the black (or sometimes blue) area, nor *yang*, represented by the light (or sometimes red), are able to exist without each other, a particle of each is present in its opposite. This rather neatly shows how good always contains the seed or potential for evil, the masculine for the feminine, and so on. In the symbol, too, *yin* and *yang* are intimately wrapped around each other, showing their mutual dependency and, again, that one can never entirely dominate the other. The symbol is indicative of the vital energy forces that provide the rhythm of life, for between them *yin* and *yang* are the products of *ch'i/qi*, the essential energy that makes material existence possible.

The *yin* characteristics of contraction, condensing, inertia and retreat are balanced with *yang* expansion, dispersion and advance. *Yin* and *yang* wane and wax, retreat and advance, go and come, close and open as the pendulum of creative rhythms swings between one and the other. The *yin–yang* symbol shows that, though dualities are evident in all existence, wholeness and completeness underpins the universe. The symbol of *yin* and *yang*, then, suggests the existence of both manifest dualities and of the unity of all opposites. Ultimately, reality is a unity not a plurality, and *Tao* and *ch'i/qi* are its unifying principles. It is because of the unity of the cosmos that disturbance in one aspect of it affects the whole. It was for this reason that rulers were felt to be critical to the harmony of societal life; they needed to be sages, who maintained the harmony of the microcosm with the macrocosm, Earth with Heaven.

The possibility of transcending the dualities of *yin* and *yang* in order to enter the sage-like state of immortal enlightenment was particularly attractive to Taoists. Stephen

Teiser notes that beings with unusual, numinous spirituality were thought to be impossible to characterize as *yin* or *yang*.⁴⁰ But it is the sage in whom the balance of *yin* and *yang* becomes such that *yin* and *yang* are transcended in the perfection that lies at the mid-point between all polarities. In being at this unperturbed point of equilibrium, experience of *Tao* as the ultimate source from which *yin* and *yang* originate is possible. Cooper writes, "it is the 'perfectly balanced union' which establishes an inner harmony in man and the universe, so that man becomes at peace with himself and the world about him, with the world within and the world without. It renders him harmless both to others and to himself. It produces the Perfect Man of Confucianism and the Sage of Taoism".⁴¹

Creation

Most religions and cultures have ancient creation myths to explain how the universe began and how humankind came into being. China, however, had no such creation myths in its ancient stratum. It was only towards the end of the classical age of China that a developed cosmology occurred. The only text to survive the book burning of China's first emperor towards the end of the third century BCE was the *I Ching/Yijing*. In the Han dynasty that followed, and with the acceptance of Confucian ideology, the *I Ching/Yijing* – especially its Confucian *Appendices*, the *Ten Wings* – became the basis of an official cosmology. The old belief in a three-tiered universe, however, with an upper Heaven, a middle world of humankind, and an underworld for the dead, was a legacy from Shang times. It was one that provided the basis for a number of three-tiered systems related to cosmic time, cosmic space, multiple heavens, and the three worlds of the immortals through which the soul on the spiritual path evolves.

The cosmogony of the second century *Huai-nan-tzu/Huainanzi* makes clear use of the *Yin–Yang* theory, dividing the *ch'i/qi* into heavenly clear and light *yang* energy, which soared up to make Heaven, and the heavier, grosser *ch'i/qi* that became the *yin* Earth:

> The hot *ch'i* of the accumulating Yang generated fire, the quintessence of the *ch'i* of fire became the sun; the cold *ch'i* of the accumulating Yin became water, the quintessence of the *ch'i* of water became the moon; the overflow of the quintessences of sun and moon became the stars. Heaven received the sun, moon and stars, Earth received the showers of water and the dust and dirt.⁴²

The *Huai-nan-tzu/Huainanzi* continues to describe Heaven as round, Earth as square. Heaven, *yang*, it says, sends *ch'i/qi* out and so transforms things; it also illuminates and lights up, like the fire and the sun. Earth, *yin*, holds *ch'i/qi* in and so is transformed rather than being the instrument of transformation, like *yang*. The forces of nature are presented as the interchanges of *yin* and *yang*:

> Of the *ch'i* inclining to Heaven, the raging became wind; of the combining *ch'i* of Heaven and Earth, the harmonious became rain. When Yin and Yang clashed, being roused they became thunder, crossing paths they became lightning, confusing they became mist. When the Yang *ch'i* prevailed, it scattered to become rain and dew; when the Yin *ch'i* prevailed, it congealed to become frost and snow.⁴³

Thus continues the text, describing how furry and feathered creatures are *yang*, while shelled and scaly ones, and hibernators are *yin*. Birds fly upwards and are *yang*; fish swim downwards and are *yin*. In short, the natural world is divided between the two essences of *yin* and *yang*, according to their respective natures. It was the *Huai-nan-tzu/Huainanzi* that set out the pattern of annual rhythms for *yin* and *yang* that became the generally accepted theory, though there were variations.

Absent from this scheme of things is a creator god or goddess. The rhythms of the cosmos are natural ones, self-perpetuating and regulating. The Taoist goal was not to emulate either a transcendent or an anthropomorphic deity, but to regulate personal life in conformity with cosmic patterns. Just as on the macrocosmic level the interplay and harmony between *yin*, the White Tiger, and *yang*, the Blue Dragon, are believed to create the rhythms of the cosmos, so, on the microcosmic level male and female are the living manifestations of the two forces. As miniatures of the cosmos, they need to be mediators of *Tao*. The natural society also blends the *yin* and *yang* – the intuitive, religious, gentle and mystical aspects of the female *yin* with the active, competitive, aggressive and rational aspects of the male. The interrelation of *yin* and *yang* as creative forces permeating from the macrocosm to the microcosm was superbly put by Robinet:

> The true nature of Heaven is to be pure and moving, and that of Earth is to be opaque and fixed. The pure and mobile Yang is the "yes," the Self, the principle of oneness (pure), of identity, of continuity, and thus of expansion and movement. The opaque and stable Yin is the opposing principle: it is the "no," the Other, the Two, which sets a limit on the expansion of the continuous. It is division, rupture, the different, the discontinuous, contraction, and immobility.... As a unit, the Yang "begins": all identity, every individual, begins in the One, in a principle of continuity, of identity with itself, opposing the Other, the different, which defines its limits. Thus the Yin "completes." One cannot exist alone; it needs the Other to show where it ends, to define its contours.[44]

These excellent descriptions of the interrelation of *yin* and *yang* show very well how the dynamism of change and transformation underpins all existence. Taoism accepts the cyclical regeneration of the macrocosm and microcosm in the same way that the seasons follow each other in rhythmic renewal. And just as all birth must contain the potential for death, so death contains the potential for regeneration; the beginning contains the end, and the end the beginning.

The aim of much philosophical Taoism was to understand the nature of the unity of opposites – a theory that was a legacy to much Taoist thought and practice down to present times. To view the world only from its manifest dualities is to miss the calm that is experienced from the point of balance between them, the point where things neither are nor are not. Poised between opposites, everything is as it is; there is total equanimity between life and death, sickness and health, good and evil, gain and loss. Such a state is experience of the tranquillity and stillness of *Tao*. Emptying the mind so that it is devoid of differentiation between opposites allows it to "go with" the flow of life that is *Tao*. It is not opting out of life but viewing the world from, as it were, the centre of a revolving circle where the world is active but the centre is still. Yet the centre is the only point from which all other parts of the circle can be understood, the only still point from which the active

CREATION

dynamism of the interchanges between *yin* and *yang* can be known. Movement in stillness is the result.

The pattern of movement from a primordial Source to the many phenomena of existence was carefully considered, and resulted in a number of posited Taoist cosmologies. One of the most popular is the following:

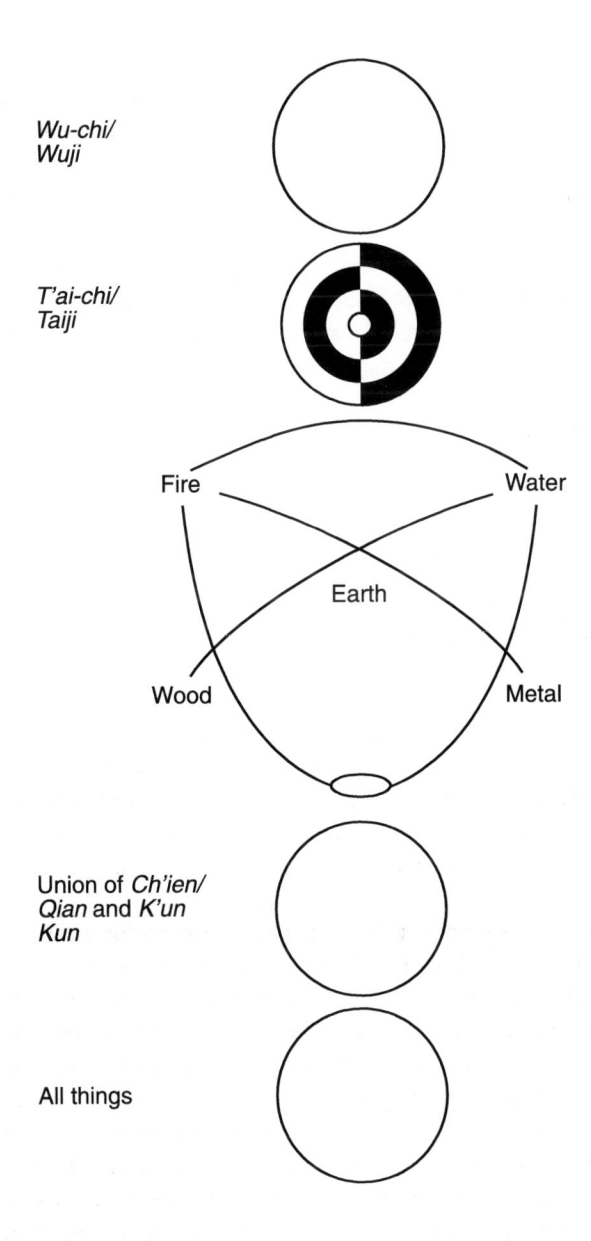

Wu-chi/
Wuji

T'ai-chi/
Taiji

Fire　　　　　　　Water

Earth

Wood　　　　　　Metal

Union of *Ch'ien/*
Qian and *K'un*
Kun

All things

Here, *Tao*, sometimes referred to as *Wu-chi/Wuji*, is the undifferentiated stillness that holds within it the potentialities of all existence. Below it is the older pictorialized symbol of *yin* and *yang*. The circle that encloses it still reflects the unity that underpins it, but *yin* and *yang* are more actively depicted here as the eye follows the circular pattern. *Yin* and *yang* are equally balanced in the three circles. The "Two" here have become *T'ai-chi/Taiji*, The "Supreme Ultimate" in some Taoist sects. The inner circle represents old *yin* and old *yang*. The middle circle represents greater *yin* and greater *yang*, and the outer circle lesser *yin* and lesser *yang*. These represent six of the trigrams of the *I Ching/Yijing*. Then follow the Five Agents – Fire, Water, Earth, Wood and Metal, which will be examined in more detail below. Finally, from the blend of *yang* Heaven (the trigram *Ch'ien/Qian*), and Earth (the trigram *K'un/Kun*) come all things. The human being, however, is important in the scheme of things, for humankind is the middle of the three worlds with Heaven above and Earth below. As such, human interaction with the two is critical to the interrelated harmony of all existence.

It is the emergence of all things in the universe – not only forms, but attitudes, concepts, emotions and so on – that gives rise to differentiation between this and that and the ensuing desires and aversions that involve the individual with one polarity rather than another. Thus we kick against the traces of what happens in life, wishing this or that were the case instead of dealing with the matter in hand and focusing on the moment in hand. The sophisticated interaction of *yin* and *yang* brings about the complexities of ideas – religious, philosophical, linguistic – and causes us to differentiate in abstract or ideological ways, as much as to differentiate between physical phenomena in existence. The more humankind identifies with these differentiated polarities, the more *Tao* is lost: the world of senses becomes important and Ultimate Reality and its oneness are blurred. Sense-based consciousness interferes with the natural order of things in the self and is inimical to harmony. Moreover, the continued interplay of *yin* and *yang* makes all life subject to change and impermanence. Everything emerges from *Tao* like waves arising in the ocean, only to be submerged in the ocean that gave rise to them. Things contract and expand, fill and empty, wax and wane, without ever gaining any permanence, and with a considerable measure of spontaneity. Even at the level of subatomic physics the behaviour of particles can only be predicted with probability but never with certainty. We cannot, then, take indefinite ownership of things, people and moments.

The wider applications of the *yin* and *yang* theory

As noted above, the origins of *yin* and *yang* lie partly in the natural observations of nature, particularly in the rhythmic patterns of the seasons. It was inevitable that the vision of the bright and sunny side of a hill or river bank should be applied to the summertime and, conversely, the dark side to the wintertime. Through the disciples of the *Yin–Yang* school the theory was used to depict all sorts of natural and supernatural phenomena. Fung Yu-lan saw the school as the genesis of Chinese scientific inquiry, albeit with many absurd ingredients. He wrote: "What I mean by this is that, underlying all the *yin–yang* thinking, was the fundamental aim of creating a truly inclusive system of thought – a system that would embrace and explain the phenomena of the entire universe. Granted that its methodology was faulty and its data inadequate, it was nevertheless scientific in spirit in its desire to organize and systematize universal phenomena, and to know their why and wherefore."[45] So important was the theory that it pervaded astronomy, medicine, mathematics, music, but if it provided the initial impetus for inquiry in many disciplines it also stifled inquiry beyond it, as Fung Yu-lan goes on to say.[46]

However, it was in its relation to human beings that the theory of *yin* and *yang* has played a particularly notable part. Taoists, especially, apply the theory to the human psyche. If the *yin–yang* balance in a person is good, then a greater degree of harmony will ensue. If perfectly balanced, then the individual will be at one with *Tao*. On the other hand, imbalance of *yin* and *yang* results in disharmony, discontent and failure physically, mentally, emotionally and spiritually: the art of life consists in keeping *yin* and *yang* in perfect balance. However, regardless of how difficult life may become, such difficulty cannot last, because its opposite must follow. The same applies on the wider scale to global events – war and peace, evil and good, the lull and the storm, famine and plenty – these are the *yin–yang* transformations of the earth itself.

In the life of any human the polarities of personality lie in the conscious and subconscious self. How close they sometimes are is revealed when we cry when we are happy, when we laugh hysterically when we are radically upset, and when we find laughter painful. In the complex web of interconnectedness and unity in manifest existence we build up from childhood a picture of dualities in existence and an egoistic desire for some things as opposed to others. Many people strive to be what they are not, and to have what they do not have, finding it difficult or impossible to be still for a moment and reflect on what is. Quiet reflection about life and times of stillness are all the more important when we think of the following words attributed to the Taoist philosopher Lieh-tzu/Liezi, though the allegory turns up in many cultures outside China. If we lived for a hundred years – and few of us do – then the bulk of the beginning of it is spent in immaturity, and the bulk of the end of it in senility. A third of life is spent in sleep, and another percentage in illness, anxiety, stress, and the struggle to achieve. Add to this the working world in whatever form that takes, and *life*, at least with any quality, seems rather short!

Yin and *yang* were also applied to the human body and have thoroughly influenced modern-day Chinese medicine, such as acupuncture. The body's liquid element is *ching/jing* and is *yin*. *Ching/jing* covers saliva, sweat, gastric juices, sweat and semen. The other element is the *yang ch'i/qi*, the vital essence essential to life. The third element comprising the human is the *yang* spirit, the *shen*, which at its best experiences *Tao* and at its worst is anxiety, worry and excessive mental activity. When *yin* or *yang* in the body become excessive or deficient, a physiological or pathological imbalance occurs that causes disease – dis-ease. Applied to the human body,

> yin corresponds to nutrient substances, and yang to functional activities. The nutrient substances remain in the interior, therefore "yin remains inside," while the functional activities manifest on the exterior, so "yang remains outside." The yang on the exterior is the manifestation of the substantial movement in the interior, so it is known as "the servant of yin." The yin in the interior is the material base for functional activities and is therefore called the "guard of yang."[47]

CREATIVE FORCES: *YIN* AND *YANG* AND THE FIVE AGENTS

The whole organic structure of the human body is explained in terms of *yin* and *yang*. The body is considered the unified whole that is animated by the interplay of *yin* and *yang*, and all the parts, organs and tissues are assigned to one or other of these forces. However, though the upper body is generally *yang* and the lower *yin*, organs have their *yin* and *yang* functions, so the principle of nothing being totally *yin* or *yang* is not forgotten. Good health results from maintaining the *yin–yang* balance throughout the body. This can be promoted by the right balance between sleep (*yin*) and wakefulness (*yang*), rest (*yin*) and activity (*yang*), salty foods (*yin*) and bitter foods (*yang*), in other words between all aspects of life. At death the *shen* souls that are *yang* move upwards towards Heaven, while the *p'o/po* or *yin* souls move down to Earth.

The physicians of ancient times explained the three major functions of the body – respiration, digestion and circulation – through *yin* and *yang* theories. Breathing is especially important in Taoist practice and in Chinese medical practice. Inhalation of breath is *yin* because it is thought to descend, and exhalation is *yang* because it ascends. The descent of the intaking *yin* breath takes *ch'i/qi* via the spleen to the liver and kidneys, while the *yang* exhales it via the kidneys, heart and lungs. Organs also have their "breaths", which facilitate their appropriate functions. But it was and is as part of Taoist meditation that breathing techniques – the control of the *yin* and *yang* within the body – are particularly relevant, and are essential to the practice of martial arts and their derivative practices to the present day. The classic Chinese medical text was the *Yellow Emperor's Classic of Internal Medicine*. It was not composed by the legendary Yellow Emperor Huang-ti/Huangdi, but was a product of Han dynasty times. Apart from relating all illnesses to the imbalances of *yin* and *yang* and giving explanations for cure, the text explains how good *yin–yang* balances can promote longevity. A sample of its pragmatic advice is the following:

> Experts in examining patients judge their general appearance; they feel their pulse and determine whether it is Yin or Yang that causes the disease. . . . To determine whether Yin or Yang predominates, one must first be able to distinguish a light pulse of low tension from a hard, pounding one. With a disease of Yang, Yin predominates. With a disease of Yin, Yang predominates. When one is filled with vigor and strength, Yin and Yang are in proper harmony.[48]

The physical body of the human being thus reflects the unity of the universe, and is a microcosm of the *yin* and *yang* balances that pervade it. No divine force directs this process, and the *yin–yang* theory stands as an impersonal system that explains the phenomena of the universe without the need of a divine creator. The natural state of humankind is one of harmony with the human being uniquely placed between the *yang* of Heaven and the *yin* of Earth. To be perfectly balanced between the two is the goal of the Taoist. The position of humankind in the cosmos is, therefore, unique in the Taoist scheme of things. The tortoise has always been the symbol for the three-tiered cosmos, its domed shell being Heaven, the bottom of the shell Earth, and the tortoise itself – which can expand outward or contract inward – humankind.

In ritual the emperor was the medium of harmonizing the *yin* and *yang* of Heaven and Earth. Indeed, this was the most important ritual of all. But the theory of *yin* and *yang* pervaded all kinds of religious and non-religious ritual in Taoist practices, and is to be found in its festivals, in Taoist alchemy, its deities and demons, even in its art and calligraphy. All these aspects will be taken up for discussion in greater detail in later chapters, where it will be seen how the theory of *yin* and *yang* pervaded other areas of Taoism.

Evaluating *yin* and *yang*

While many of the elaborate theories of Tsou Yen/Zou Yan were not to find their way into mainstream thought, and there were times when correlative thinking was not in vogue,[49] it would have to be claimed that even westerners understand the philosophy of *yin* and *yang*. This is so even if they have never heard of Taoism, and can only loosely connect the theory with China. Indeed, the two terms have now found their way into western dictionaries.

Tsou Yen/Zou Yan and his disciples combined theories of *yin* and *yang* with the Five Agents that will be looked at below, and the Three Powers of Heaven, Earth and humankind. As noted above, such cosmological theories were mainly atheistic, assigning the evolutionary cycles of the cosmos to impersonal and unconscious forces. These were ideas particularly attractive to Confucianism, though Taoism was to add its pantheon of deities alongside such cosmological theories. But it is the human being that is the lynchpin of the whole system. It is worth citing Maspero's words here concerning this central Power of humankind:

> And all will be perfect if Man, the only one of the Three Powers – and of all the forces which control the universe – to be personal and conscious does not sometimes throw disorder into it by the divagations of his conscious individuality. As long as he acts well, the well governed world progresses well, physically, socially, morally; but if he acts badly, his evil actions react upon the material world, bringing disorder to the round of the Five Elements, producing unseasonable excesses of *yin* and *yang* and disturbing the normal activity of Heaven and Earth, so that in the end everything goes very badly.[50]

Such a view suggests a teleological role for humankind, albeit that in China's imperial past it was left to the emperor to conduct himself in the proper way to produce the right results for the rest of humanity.

The importance of the *yin–yang* system in Chinese religion cannot be overestimated. Rites of passage, festivals, the layout of temples, and even the place where a home was built, were influenced by *yin* and *yang*. The influences are still evident today in many legacies of Chinese culture to the West, as in martial arts like T'ai Chi Ch'üan/Taijiquan, in Chinese medicine, and *feng-shui*, for example. The psychologist Jung was sufficiently interested in *yin* and *yang* to correlate them with the inner and outer personalities of the individual. In the West, we have only comparatively recently become aware of the way in which our daily lives have an impact on global issues – illustrating only too well the interconnectedness of the whole. Robinet described the Taoist world as "a closed whole, a sequence of nested enclosures in time and space".[51] As such it is an interconnected whole in which the interplay of dualities – the *yin* and *yang* of existence – "are lines of force, directions whose nature is to cross and mingle, to play against each other, both self-generating and self-propelling, disappearing and alternating; and their function is to define a double syntax of polarity and ambiguity".[52] Some may criticize the theory as non-personal and lacking ethical foundation. Wing-tsit Chan, however, points out that, "the yin yang theory has also put Chinese ethical and social teachings on a cosmological basis. It has helped the view that things are related and that reality is a process of constant transformation. The harmony of yin and yang accounts for much of the central emphasis on harmony in Chinese life and thought, and it has reinforced the doctrine of the Mean[53] common to Confucianism, Taoism, and Buddhism".[54] As ancient theories go, that of *yin* and *yang* was a rather developed perspective of reality that seems to have stood the test of time.

The Five Agents

As was seen with the analysis of the trigrams and hexagrams of the *I Ching/Yijing*, and the nature of *yin* and *yang* above, a cyclical motion of change underpins all life. And that cyclical motion of change is the only permanent reality: change and non-change are neatly juxtaposed. But in each repetition of a cycle the space for change is infinite; there is renewal without identical copying, alternation with difference. Just as no springtime can be the same as any other period of springtime in the past, so change characterizes the changeless cycles of the seasons, night and day, darkness and light, and the many dualities that make up existence. Such a view of the universe makes it self-creative and self-sustaining, with all phenomena caught up in the rhythm of cyclical motion. Thus, while plurality is self-evident in the universe, the totality of that plurality is interconnected and interrelated by the forces that inform it. These forces are the Five Agents – Wood, Fire, Earth, Metal and Water. Robinet commented on their importance in Chinese philosophy:

> All creatures are categorized, listed under one of these rubrics. All kinds of resonances and influences can be discovered in the system founded on this principle of classification, some of them opposing, some of them attracting. A basic guiding principle is that things which resemble each other go together. As a result, certain actions and interactions can be explained or predicted, both in space and in time, horizontally (from one end of the world to the other) as well as vertically (from earth to heaven).[55]

The Five Agents, then, underpin all nature and all life.

The Five Agents are known collectively as the *wu-hsing/wuxing*. *Wu* means "five", but the word *hsing/xing* is more problematic. Traditionally it has been translated as "Elements" much in line with the Greek and Indian conception of the elements of earth, air, fire and water as the constituents of manifest existence. But Chinese *hsing/xing* has a much more dynamic meaning. This can be seen instantly in its root meanings – to prosper; to begin; to increase; to rise; to raise; to walk; to do; to act; to travel.[56] Thus, *movement* is characteristic of each of the Agents. They are *activators*, each with its particular kind of movement. It is for this reason that the translation "Agents" more readily describes their cosmological function. Tsou Yen/Zou Yan called them *wu-te/wude* "Five Powers", because he related them to the rise and demise of dynasties. They were also called Five Processes, indicative of their properties – Fire rising and burning, Water saturating and sinking, for example.[57] In pre-Han times they were called Five Materials (*wu-ts'ai/wucai*),[58] and from Han times onwards, they were referred to as Five Phases, an appropriate term given the cyclical dominance of each of them in turn in all dimensions of life, as we shall see below. Such descriptors illustrate two points. The first is that the origins and growth of the concept of the Five Agents were not neatly linear and, second, that the Agents could be applied in a variety of ways. Indeed, it is this last point that we must take up in more detail below, for the theory of the Five Agents is very much alive in a number of fields in the present day and age. In all, the term *Agents* is perhaps the most all encompassing, and does the least to confine the overall use of all Five. The reader should note, however, that the terms Elements and Phases are widely used, the latter term by more modern, academic sources, though it is somewhat time orientated; the former being increasingly discarded because it is not suggestive of the dynamism of movement.[59] In martial arts, especially in T'ai chi Chüan/Taijiquan, however, the term "Elements" is the norm.

The Five Agents, then, are *active* motivators. They are functional, bringing into being and ending the phases and changes evident in the world. Through their mutual functioning all things come into being and pass away. Air is excluded for it is the all-pervasive oneness of *ch'i/qi*, the vital breath or energy from which *yin* and *yang* and the Five Agents themselves emerge. Instead, Wood is included because of its more obvious functional and indispensable role in existence, for it represents growth and the ability to flourish. So the Five Agents are both abstract principles and dynamic forces. The former prevents their being reduced to basic, static substances, and the latter ensures their active roles in informing the interconnection of all phenomena. All phenomena in life will correspond to one of these Agents.

Historical development of the Five Agents

Like so many aspects of Taoism and Chinese thought, the antecedents of the Five Agents must surely be found in the ancient observations of nature. The four seasons, especially, had their respective characters and rhythmic cycles, which four of the Agents, at least, could be seen to reflect. Earth came to be the central Agent that facilitated the activity of the other four. It is likely that the theory of Five Agents was imposed on older systems, gradually being applied to five deities and the four cardinal points around a centre.[60] Thus, it seems that the Five-Agent theory had some kind of origin prior to the time of Tsou Yen/Zou Yan who developed it. There is minimal evidence of the theory in the words of Lao-tzu/Laozi and Chuang-tzu/Zhuangzi and it was probably among the ranks of the *fang-shih/fangshi* that the cosmological theories relating to the Five Agents gathered ground. But Richard Smith notes that: "A number of Shang rituals, spiritual agencies, and terrestrial organizations were categorized according to groupings of five, indicating a possible affinity with later pentadic correlations in China."[61]

Our earliest sources of information regarding the Five Agents are two texts, the *Lü-shih Ch'un Ch'iu/Lüshi Chunqiu*, which contains what is called the *Monthly Commands* (extant also in the *Book of Rites*), and the *Hung Fan/Hongfan* or *Grand Norm* found in the *Book of Documents*, the *Shu Ching/Shujing*. The *Lü-shih Ch'un Ch'iu/Lushi Chunqiu* is the

CREATIVE FORCES: *YIN* AND *YANG* AND THE FIVE AGENTS

eclectic *Annals of Spring and Autumn,* composed in the late third century BCE by numerous scholars, and reflects the views of late Chou/Zhou philosophers. It is in this document that the phases of the Five Agents are correlated with dynasties and colours. Thus, the legendary Yellow Emperor ruled by the power of Earth with yellow as his colour. Earthworms and mole-crickets appeared before he rose to power to indicate the ruling Agent. Grass and trees appeared when Yü/Yu came to power. So Wood became his ruling Agent, and green his associative colour. Similarly, T'ang/Tang the founder of the Shang dynasty, was associated with Metal and the colour white since knife-blades appeared in the water. The appearance of a fiery flame and a red bird holding a red book in its mouth made King Wen rule by the Power of Fire, with red as his colour. The *Lü-shih Ch'un Ch'iu/Lüshi chunqiu* believed that Water would be the Power associated with the next ruler, along with the colour black, before the cycle revolved again to Earth. The early correspondents to the Five Powers were, therefore, to the respective dynasties and their correlative colours:

Earth	*Wood*	*Metal*	*Fire*	*Water*
Yellow Emperor	Hsia/Xia	Shang	Chou/Zhou	—
Yellow	Green	White	Red	Black

The *Monthly Commands* connected the Five Agents more finely with the months of the year, with appropriate colours to be worn, and with the musical notes to be played. Climatic disasters would ensue if conformity to the patterns of the dominant Agent were disregarded. According to the *Hung Fan/Hongfan*, the *Grand Norm* or *Great Plan*, such cyclical changes in dynastic rule were the result of the waxing and waning of the cycle of Five Agents, and not, as was so prevalently thought entirely due to the morality and moral degeneration of rulers. Of the Five Agents, the *Hung Fan/Hongfan* states:

> The first is named water, the second fire, the third wood, the fourth metal, the fifth earth. The nature of water is to moisten and descend; of fire to burn and ascend; of wood, to be crooked and straight; of metal, to yield and to be modified; of earth, to provide for sowing and reaping. That which moistens and descends produces salt; that which burns and ascends becomes bitter; that which is crooked and straight becomes sour; that which yields and is modified becomes acrid; sowing and reaping produce sweetness.[62]

The cosmological cycles of the Five Agents were extended to directions, planets, deities, animals, emperors, mountains, musical tones and all kinds of phenomena, as we shall see below.

The individual responsible for these ideas was, again, Tsou Yen/Zou Yan, so Ssu-ma Ch'ien/Sima Qian's *Historical Records* tells us. While the *Yin–Yang* and Five Agents theories seem to have existed separately at first, it was Tsou Yen/Zou Yan who brought about a coalescing of the two, despite, as Rubin points out, the differences in nature between the two theories: "The *wu-hsing* concept, oriented on the static earthly space, is opposed by the Yin-yang concept, oriented on the heavenly movement of time."[63] What Tsou Yen/Zou Yan did was to introduce the movement integral to the *yin–yang* concept into the Five Agent theory. As Rubin says: "This concept created by Tsou Yen attained such significance that the *Wu-hsing* concept has come to be regarded exclusively as a concept of cyclic movement of elements, thus obliterating its basic, original difference from the *Yin-Yang* concept."[64] By Han times the *Yin–Yang* school and the Five Agents school were interchangeable names. It was an important correlation of two strands of thought that had an enormous impact. The interrelation of Heaven, Earth and human affairs became such that the seasons and the general welfare of humankind could be affected by the proper or improper actions of the ruler – he who embodied Chinese humanity. The coalescing of the two powerful theories of *yin* and *yang* and the Five Agents served to illustrate a direct correlation between the macrocosm of Heaven and the microcosm of the human.

The amalgamation of *yin* and *yang* and Tsou Yen/Zou Yan's Five Powers, as he called them, formed a formidable theory and philosophy of history centred around the influential school founded by Tsou Yen/Zou Yan in the state of Ch'i/Qi. As a result of Tsou Yen/Zou Yan's efforts, the idea that ruling powers followed the natural fixed sequences of the Five Powers was sufficient for the first Chinese Emperor Ch'in Shih Huang-ti/Qinshi Huangdi in 221 BCE to claim his right to rule in alliance with the ascendancy of the Power Water. Accordingly, he accepted black as his imperial colour. The succeeding Han dynasty then reverted to Earth and the colour yellow.

The function of the ruler came to be shifted towards aligning himself with the natural sequences of the Five Powers during the cycle of the year, and it was the proponents of Tsou Yen/Zou Yan's school that provided the expertise in interpreting the ways in which the ruler could align himself with natural forces. Given such knowledge it would be possible for a ruler to act in such a way that no misfortunes could occur in the natural, corporate life, or in his own personal life. It was in this context that the *Monthly Commands* provided explicit guidance. Here, the Five Powers are correlated with the seasons, Wood with spring; Fire with summer; Metal with autumn; Water with winter. And the actions of an emperor – from governing down to the colour of his clothes and what he may or may not eat – depended on the prevailing Power. The *Monthly Commands* tells us, for example, that if the ruler follows the regulations set out for summer at the wrong time rain will fall out of season, the leaves will fall from trees and plants too early, and the state will be uneasy and fearful. The balances of *yin* and *yang* throughout the year, combined with the Powers, regulated the life at court, the times when the ruler should reward or punish, the area of the palace in which to live, the colours to wear, the ritual to observe. While such practices declined subsequent to the Han dynasty, it is notable that even the last Emperor of China ousted by the Republic of China in 1911 was called "Emperor of [the Mandate] of Heaven and in accordance with the Movements [Five Agents]".

In later years some of Tsou Yen/Zou Yan's ideas were taken up by other thinkers. Tung Chung-shu/Dong Zhongshu mentioned earlier in this chapter was one. As a Confucian he was responsible for absorbing some of Tsou Yen/Zou Yan's ideas into official Confucian thought. Such was the importance of men like Tung/Dong that, belonging to what is known as the "New Text" school, they re-wrote the Confucian classics to interpret them in the light of *yin* and *yang* and Five Agent theories. Tung/Dong used the term *wu-hsing/wuxing* calling the Agents Five Movers. However, Tung/Dong's order of the Agents differs from that found in the *Grand Norm* and it is in the *Huai-nan-tzu/Huainanzi* that the definitive order is recorded. While the theory had wide appeal, it was also clearly excluded from certain texts like the *Appendices* to the *I Ching/Yijing*. On the other hand, Taoist schools such as the Shang-ch'ing/Shangqing school, for example, used the correlates of the Five Agents in the human body as focuses for meditation. The theory is also very much alive today in such aspects as Chinese medicine and the practice of martial arts and their derivatives.

The Five Agents as cosmological functions

The Five Agent theory depicts the rotation of the Agents in both a generating and a conquering cycle. In the generating or mutually producing cycle, Wood generates Fire; Fire generates Earth; Earth generates Metal; Metal generates Water; Water generates Wood. Here, the logical sequence is taken from ordinary observation of nature. Wood fuels a fire. Fire creates ashes and so forms earth. Earth provides the environment for metal that forms in its veins. Metal encourages underground waters or provides a surface for dew as a result of condensation. Waters encourage the growth of plants and trees – the wood that feeds fire. And so the cycle begins again. Here, the generating cycle is linked with the seasons, too. The wood of spring generates the fire of summer. Fire generates the earth itself. The earth generates the metal of autumn, and from autumn we pass to the water of winter.

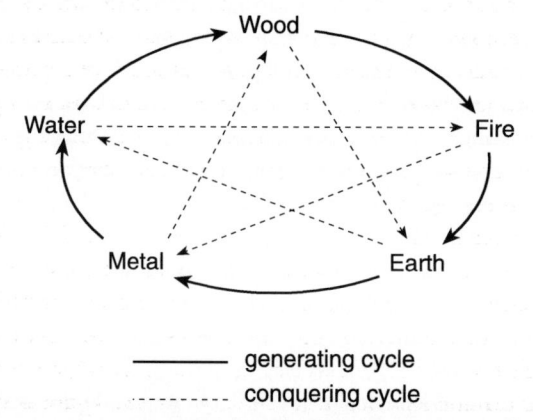

——— generating cycle
- - - - - conquering cycle

In the conquering or mutually overcoming cycle, where the Agents overcome each other, Wood overcomes Earth; Earth overcomes Water; Water overcomes Fire; Fire overcomes Metal; Metal overcomes Wood. Again, the sequence is taken from natural observation. Wood overcomes earth as the roots of trees and vegetation take over, or as the plough overcomes it. Earth overcomes water by obstructing its path, as in dams, or by filling rivers with mud and silt. Water overcomes fire by destroying it completely, and fire is the element that can melt metal. Metal then overcomes wood by chopping it. The logic of the order here in the context of ancient Chinese culture is noted by Graham: "Among Chinese proto-scientific concepts the conquest cycle stands out as independent of all correlations, and probably derives directly from observation of the five basic resources at the workman's disposal. Struggling with water, fire, metal, wood or soil, there is little room for disagreement as to which of the others is most required to dam, quench, melt, cut or dig the resisting material."[65]

The two different cycles diagrammatically are shown on the opposite page.

The *Huai-nan-tzu/Huainanzi* combines the generating and overcoming cycles to show that each of the Agents passes through a rising and declining cycle – the *yin* and *yang* of each Agent. When at its zenith, each Agent can generate the next one, but at the same time can overcome the Agent that is at its weakest. Throughout the cycles each Agent follows the one that it cannot overcome:

Birth	Wood	Fire	Earth	Metal	Water
Zenith	Water	Wood	Fire	Earth	Metal
Ageing	Metal	Water	Wood	Fire	Earth
Immobilization	Earth	Metal	Water	Wood	Fire
Death	Fire	Earth	Metal	Water	Wood

So at its most potent, each generates the one that begins its rise, and conquers the one that is in demise: each has an active and passive phase. Importantly, what this table shows is that there is continued interaction between the Agents. Since the Five Agents were the constituents of all phenomena, they were believed to be present in the three realms of Heaven, Earth and humanity. Their mutual interaction and balances and imbalances at any one time had a profound effect on human existence. Given the rise and decline of each individual Agent, it followed that the early cosmologists saw human and natural events as being dictated very much by the particular phases of the Five Agents. Such was the case not only on the larger canvas of historical dynasties, but also on the cyclical events of the days, months, seasons and years, even the human body. While one Agent might be predominant at a particular time of the day, month, season or year, the relative strengths and weaknesses of the others also had their effects.

In later alchemical texts the Agent that generates the following one is called the mother, and that which it generates is called the son. In the overcoming cycle, the Agent that overcomes is called the father, and that which is overcome, the wife. Additionally, each Agent has two sons. The interaction between sons themselves, between mother and son, father and wife are all symbols of the interaction of the forces that make the seasons, as well as such things as the relation between the different organs and parts of the body. Important, too, is the connecting of the Agents with the trigrams of the *I Ching/Yijing*. Thus we have:

Ch'ien/Qian	Metal	**Sun**	Wood
Tui/Dui	Metal	**K'an/Kan**	Water
Li	Fire	**Ken/Gen**	Earth
Chen/Zhen	Wood	**K'un/Kun**	Earth

The operation of *yin* and *yang* determines the seasons and the dominating Agent for that season. For some time the trigrams and hexagrams of the *I Ching/Yijing* stood independently as a cosmological scheme. The *Monthly Commands*, indeed, reflects such a separation.

However, by early Han times the process of applying the theories of *yin* and *yang* and the Five Agents in wider contexts was well in place. In the amalgamation of *yin* and *yang* with the Five Agents, the latter became the active Agents by which *yin* and *yang* could operate, and each Agent had its *yin* and *yang* cycle. Each of the Agents was assigned a *yin* or *yang* predominant force. Thus, Wood was lesser *yang*; Fire was great *yang*; Metal was lesser *yin*; Water was great *yin*. Earth, the central Agent, was the harmonizing point of them all. The fairly easy amalgamation of the different cosmological views was possible because of the Chinese view of an interdependent, interacting and interrelated universe that was ultimately a unity of its many parts.

The characteristics of the Agents

Wood (*Mu*) is the Agent associated with springtime when green leaves shoot out and vegetation revives from winter. It encompasses the ideas of expansion, of pushing upward, outward, budding forth and opening up. It is the Agent of beginnings, of youth, the sunrise, freshness and flowing energy. It balances with its opposite of Metal (*Chin/Jin*) the Agent of the autumn, when trees begin to lose their leaves, their branches becoming brittle, rigid and metallic. Metal suggests processes of binding, contraction, crystallization, restraint, withdrawal and inward movement. It is the beginning of *yin*. Fire (*Huo*) is clearly the Agent of summer. It is associated with vibrant growth and expansiveness to the point of maturity and accomplishment. Its warmth and heat are contrasted by the coldness and darkness of its opposite Agent of Water (*Shui*), the Agent of winter. Water is fluidity, dissolution, levelling, spreading, enveloping. It is *yin* at its fullest and oldest. Water was an important symbol in Taoist philosophy because of its naturalness, its ability to achieve its goal by gently wearing away its rocky banks, or adapting itself to fit any vessel. Water and Fire were always especially important, and became crucial to the processes of inner alchemy when linked with the *I Ching/Yijing*. We shall meet them again in chapter 6.

The Agent Earth (*Ti/Di*) is special in that it is central and pivotal to the other Agents. It is a preserving Agent. Since it is at the centre, it is the point of interaction for all the other Agents. Everything revolves around it and so it is balance and harmony, the point of change between the seasons, between *yin* and *yang*. It is worth noting here what Tung Chung-shu/Dong Zhongshu says about the central Agent of Earth: "Earth occupies the center, and is called the heavenly fructifier. . . . It is the assister of Heaven. Its power is abundant and good, and cannot be assigned to the affairs of a single season only. Therefore among the Five Elements and four seasons, earth embraces all. Although metal, wood, water, and fire each have their own particular duties, they could not stand were it not for earth."[66] Wood grows from earth, fire rises up from it, metals are found in it, and water is absorbed by it. Robinet commented:

> Earth is the center, providing cohesion to the whole. In the circle that makes up the round of the Five Agents, Earth controls transitions from one Agent to another, and it is located at the frontier that both joins and separates them: that is, Earth is where we cross from the areas of the Yang Agents (Wood and Fire) to those of the Yin Agents (Metal and Water), at the boundary of each of the sectors, the crossing points from one to another.[67]

In its central position, Earth is spatially at the centre of the four compass points and in terms of time is dominant at a point between summer and autumn. Earth lends to the theory a cosmologically *spatial* dimension.

The theory of correspondences

It was during the Han dynasty that the applications of the Five Agents begun by Tsou Yen/Zou Yan were extended not only to dynasties and historical cycles but to all manner of phenomena – the seasons, cardinal points, planets, bodily organs, calendrical signs, musical notes, colours, tastes, smells, numbers, and many other aspects. However, such correspondences necessitated the reduction of major phenomena also to five basic aspects. Sarah Allan suggests that the ancient Chinese division of the world into five geographical parts was the inspiration for the later significance of the number five.[68] Indeed, she points out that this geographical division amounted to four quarters and a central part, and that the number five was important in oracle bone inscriptions in Shang times. There were five major mountains and the deity Shang-ti/Shangdi had five ministers, perhaps thought to preside over the five geographical regions.[69] By Tsou Yen/Zou Yan's time the number five had become a sacred number and five Confucian virtues were the underpinning morality of the state. Categorizing all things in groups of fives was an attempt to unify and systematize the known universe. Bodde wrote: "This splitting up of the world into sets of fives is a typical manifestation of the rationalistic Chinese mind, which tries to find order and plan in all things, and which has therefore taken a particular delight in inventing numerical categories of all kinds, not only in fives, but in many other numbers."[70] For convenience, the correlates of the Five Agents are listed here:

	Wood	*Fire*	*Earth*	*Metal*	*Water*
Seasons	spring	summer	late summer	autumn	winter
Directions	East	South	centre	West	North
Time	morning	noon	—	evening	night
Month	1–2	4–5	3, 6, 9, 12	7–8	10–1
Weather	wind	heat	humidity	dryness	cold
Animal symbols	Blue Dragon	Red Bird	Yellow Dragon	White Tiger	Black Tortoise
Deities	Fu Hsi/ Fu Xi T'ai Hao/ Daihou	Shen-nung/ Shennong Yen Ti/ Yan Di	Huang-ti/ Huangdi	Shao Hao	Chüan-hsü/ Juan Xu
Divine ministers	Kou-mang/ Gou Mang	Chu-yung/ Zhu Yong	Hou Tu/ Hou Du	Ju-shou/ Ru Shou	Hsüan-ming/ Xuan Ming
Planets	Jupiter	Mars	Saturn	Venus	Mercury
Colours	blue-green	red	yellow	white	black
Stems	*chia/jia* & *i/yi*	*ping/bing* & *ting/ding*	*wu/mou* & *chi/ji*	*keng/geng* & *hsin/xin*	*jen/ren* & *kuei/gui*
Pitch-pipes	*chiao/jiao*	*chih/zhi*	*kung/gong*	*shang*	*yu/you*
Sacrifices	inner door	hearth	inner court	outer court	well

CREATIVE FORCES: *YIN* AND *YANG* AND THE FIVE AGENTS

Numbers	eight	seven	five	nine	six
Creatures	scaly	feathered	naked	furred, hairy	shelled
Domestic animals	sheep	fowl	ox	dog	pig
Wild animals	tiger	stag	bird	bear	monkey
Grains	wheat	millet	rye	rice	peas
Body organs	liver	heart	spleen	lung	kidneys[71]
Connected organs	gall-bladder	small intestine	stomach	large intestine	bladder
Sense organs	eye	tongue	mouth	nose	ear
Body parts	muscles; nails	pulse; complexion	flesh; lips	skin; body hair	bones; hair
Fluid	tears	sweat	lymph	mucus	saliva
Growth	germination	growth	transformation	reaping	storing
Emotions	anger	joy	worry	grief	fear
Energy	blood	psychic	physical	vital	volitional
Body sounds	crying	laughing	singing	sobbing	groaning
Tastes	sour	bitter	sweet	acrid	salty
Smells	"goatish"	burnt	fragrant	rank	rancid
Virtues	love	wisdom	faith	righteousness	propriety
Ministers	for Agriculture	for War	for Works	for the Interior	for Justice
Society	the people	the state	the prince	the vassal	products
Greatnesses	beginning	change	ultimate	simplicity	origin

The above table illustrates well how reflections on the balance between nature and human life, and beliefs in the interrelatedness of the entire cosmos, informed the Chinese psyche. The phenomenal world is portrayed as pulsating interchanges of different energies promoting and repelling each other in a multiplicity of combinations that result in what we view as life, both material and immaterial, and also spiritual. The Five Agents theory explained the way the whole world was perceived, from the macrocosmic deities to the bodily functions of the individual. The correlations posited between the transformations in nature and those of the human body illustrated the existing harmony between macrocosm and microcosm. Some, such as Tung Chung-shu/ Dong Zhongshu, correlated the parts of the body with the numerical categories of Heaven. Amongst these, he drew attention to the roundness of the human head, which was like the round shape of Heaven; to hair, which is like the stars; to ears and eyes, which are like the sun and moon; to nostrils and mouth, which are like the wind, and so on.[72]

The Five Agents cosmology is also an attempt to create an explanation for life in terms of perpetual rhythm and pattern. Linked with the theory of *yin* and *yang*, the springtime brought about by the Agent Wood is a time of generating, of birth, and the rising of the light of *yang* from the *yin* cold and darkness of the winter time. Cosmologically, it is the beginning of creation. Microcosmically, it is the dawn of the day, and the birthing process in living beings. As the warmth of Fire succeeds, *yang* strengthens to its fullest to permit the growth and development of all things. It is a time of great production and growth. Then, once again, *yin* begins to rise in *yang* and the fulfilment of processes is brought about through the Agent of Metal. As in the autumn, the time of fruitfulness, of bringing to an end the toiling on the land, nature comes to completion. Then comes the time of decay and death, the dark, the cold, brought about by Water. *Yin* is at its maximum, though the light of *yang* is now ready to begin once again its expansion to bring about rebirth. The medium for these changes is the Agent of Earth, which interacts with the other Agents assisting the transformations from one stage to the next.[73]

Wider influences

Along with *yin* and *yang* the Five Agents theory underpinned later theories in alchemy, medicine, science, astronomy, geomancy, and art, for example. In medicine, the *Huang-ti Nei-ching/Huangdi Neijing*, the *Yellow Emperor's Classic of Internal Medicine*, describes how the essential energy of the body, *ch'i/qi*, needed to be nourished by appropriate actions and living according to each of the four Phases and seasons of the year. What is interesting about the *Huang-ti Nei-ching/Huangdi Neijing* is the emphasis it places on a holistic view of life: outward activities thus affect the internal functioning of the body. The body is viewed as a whole, its parts interactive and delicately balanced between *yin* and *yang* energies. The internal organs of the body are hollow (*fu*) or solid (*tsang/zang*). The *yin* organs are the internal ones, like the liver, lungs, spleen, kidneys and heart. The *yang* organs are those concerned with externally manifested functions; they are organs such as the stomach, large and small intestines, bladder and gall-bladder. Each of the Five Agents has its *yin* and *yang* organs:

	Yin	*Yang*
Wood	liver	gall-bladder
Fire	heart; heart constrictor (pericardium)	small intestine; heat supply
Earth	spleen; pancreas	stomach
Metal	lungs	large intestine
Water	kidneys	bladder

The Five Agents are still used in modern Chinese medicine. In a standard textbook for modern-day practice of acupuncture and moxibustion, their function is clearly explained: "In traditional Chinese medicine the theory of the five elements is applied to generalise and explain the nature of the zang-fu organs, the inter-relationships between them, and the relation between human beings and the natural world. It thus serves to guide clinical diagnosis and treatment."[74] While recognizing the limitations of the theory and the need for greater development of it, the Five Agent theory is still retained as a useful tool: "When the theory of the five elements is applied in traditional Chinese medicine, the classification of phenomena according to the five elements and their interpromoting, interacting, overacting and counteracting relationships are used to explain both physiological and pathological phenomena, and to guide clinical diagnosis and treatment."[75] Then, too, the "mother–son" relationship, noted earlier, between the generating or promoting

Agent, and that Agent which it promotes, is still retained in clinical text books. In such medical practice the Five Agent theory and *yin* and *yang* are complementary to the extent that the use of one must include the other.

In alchemical breathing exercises, the Five Agents were linked to five breaths necessary to nourish the five vital organs of the body associated with each Agent. Such exercises were designed to suit each season of the year with its dominant Agent. In alchemy, too, five basic ingredients represented the Five Agents, Earth usually being the central power representing the intermediate place between all opposites. In geomancy, where the positioning of a temple, grave or important building needed to match the natural forces of the site, the Five Agent directions were also employed. From Han times on, the theory also penetrated the world of art in terms of the colours and animals representing the Agents. Cities were built directionally according to the principles of the Five Agents, and the family altar, likewise, was carefully constructed in line with the theory. In short, the concept and application of the theory of Five Agents, Elements, Powers or Phases, has been widespread in Chinese, and certainly Taoist, culture. Importantly, these integrated theories placed the human being on a cosmic map. Angus Graham thus made the point that the cosmic view is an anthropocentric one where the individual "still stands at the centre of things in interaction with the rest, and has only to contrast A and B to respond to them immediately as superior and inferior, better or worse".[76] Needless to say, individual consciousnesses vary, and perception of interrelation with the rest of the cosmos is not for all. Again, Graham said: "Man is in spontaneous interaction with things, but responds differently according to the degree of his understanding of their similarities and contrasts, connexion or isolation."[77]

With the trigrams and hexagrams of the *I Ching/Yijing*, *yin* and *yang*, and the Five Agents, we have a cosmological picture of the universe based on the interrelation of all things in the universe. Schirokauer points out that it was a very satisfying view of the world: "Not only did it explain everything, it enabled men to feel at home in the world, part of a temporal as well as spatial continuum. It provided both an impetus to the development of science and the basis for a sophisticated theoretical framework for explaining the world."[78] The three theories were not originally Taoist or Confucian, but were generically Chinese. However, they provided such a systematic view of the universe that both Confucianism and Taoism accepted them as their fundamental cosmology. They are theories that came to be embedded deeply in the subconscious of Taoist culture.

4

Tao and its Early Philosophers

Here, in this chapter, we are at the very essence of what many consider Taoism to be all about. The heartbeat of Taoism – its originating pulse and rhythm – is believed to be expressed in the thoughts of its ancient philosophers and in the seminal concepts of *Te/De*, *wu-wei*, naturalness, the sage and, above all, in the concept of *Tao* itself. Living in an age of savage warfare, of death, disease of the body and dis-ease of the inner being, two ancient thinkers stand out for the refreshing simplicity yet profundity of their thought. These men are Lao-tzu/Laozi and Chuang-tzu/Zhuangzi. Questionable facts about their historical existence, or the point that much of the works bearing their names, may not, indeed, have been written by them, need not concern us yet. Suffice it to say here that Lao-tzu/Laozi's *Tao Te Ching/Daodejing* and Chuang-tzu/Zhuangzi's book that bears his name, are the traditional foundations of Taoist belief regardless of how it has diverged into multiple paths. To these two sources, I want to add the later *Lieh-tzu/Liezi*, traditionally written by one who also gave his name to the book. It is these three sources that will provide the material for the present chapter. The three alleged authors did not set out to "found" a religion, and would not have thought of themselves as "Taoists" in any way. It was later Taoists who designated them as founders of their schools.

Except for short periods of time Confucianism was the orthodox "religion" accepted in China. As we have seen, it was a systematically rational, measured, moralist and conformist tradition that was expressed in exactitude, correctness and methodical practices. The thought found in the *Tao Te Ching/Daodejing*, the *Chuang-tzu/Zhuangzi* and the *Lieh-tzu/Liezi* is quite the opposite – free, spontaneous, non-conformist and challenging to orthodox thought. It resulted from a certain antagonism to the established order of societal and ethical life. The superficiality of Confucian existence is juxtaposed by these three thinkers' deeper insight into the spiritual depths of nature and the *raison d'être* of real existence as living in *Tao*. Theirs was the *yin* of feminine, receptive, yielding and mystical inner spirituality in contrast to the *yang* of the defined, rational rigidity of Confucian existence. The choice was between roaming beyond societal constrictions and conditionings or succumbing to existence within them. Our three philosophers chose the former route.

Lao-tzu/Laozi and the *Tao Te Ching/Daodejing*

Excluding the Bible, no other book has been translated so often as the *Tao Te Ching/Daodejing*. This is so despite the brevity of the text – a mere eighty-one very short chapters, many amounting to just a few lines. Needham referred to the book as "without exception the most profound and beautiful work in Chinese history".[1] And, indeed, it is an exquisite text, delightful in its simplicity and serenity, and yet tantalizing in its depth. The name of its traditional author, Lao-tzu/Laozi is a title meaning "Old Master", "Old Boy", "Old One" or "Old Fellow", where *Lao* means "old". However, Li Erh/Li Er is supposed to be his family and proper name. According to Paul Carus: "The plum-tree is the symbol of immortality, and the ear might signify the man who was willing to listen. Accordingly Lao-tzu's family name Li (plum) seems to be as much justified as his proper name Er (ear)."[2] It is this last name of Li Erh/Li Er that is generally accepted as the real name of Lao-tzu/Laozi. Confusion about the names of Lao-tzu/Laozi may have arisen because the ancient historian Ssu-ma Ch'ien/Sima Qian had great difficulty in writing a biography of Lao-tzu/Laozi – so much so that he possibly endorsed the connection of the historical person Li Erh/Li Er with a legendary Lao Tan/Lao Dan. Such is the view of sinologists such as Fung Yu-lan. He suggests that "Li Erh seized an opportunity to conceal his doctrines under the name of Lao Tan, thinking, in this way, to hide his own name, and at the same time gain for his principles the advanced reputation that goes with antiquity".[3] Ssu-ma Ch'ien/Sima Qian then recorded the connection. On the other hand, many consider Lao Tan/Lao Dan to have been a real person, the "Grand Historian" of Chou/Zhou in the fourth century BCE.[4] It is possible, too, that LaoTan/Lao Dan may also have been a name given the Old Master posthumously. All that can be said is that the *Shih Chi/Shiji*, *Historical Records*, of Ssu-ma Ch'ien/Sima Qian of the end of the second and beginning of the first century BCE, and our only source for the life of Lao-tzu/Laozi, cannot supply a clear account.[5] We are left with different theories about Lao-tzu/Laozi's identity and life. Indeed, Angus Graham described Ssu-ma Ch'ien/Sima Qian's biography of Lao-tzu/Laozi as a "puzzling litter of odds and ends".[6]

Ssu-ma Ch'ien/Sima Qian wrote not only the first biography of the life of Lao-tzu/Laozi but included some of the legends and myths that had grown up around the Old Master.[7] These include the tale of his mother's conception of Lao-tzu/Laozi after she had seen a shooting star. She did not, however, give birth to her "Old Boy" until sixty-two years later. Legend has it, too, that he was born a white-haired wise being. Ssu-ma Ch'ien/Sima Qian also recorded a visit to the Old Master from Confucius, the latter requesting advice on ritual. The visit is supposed to have taken place when Lao-tzu/Laozi was archivist in Chou/Zhou. Its historicity is very doubtful, but the record of the incident reveals Lao-tzu/Laozi's reputed impatience with Confucian knowledge, morality and pride. Then, it seems that Lao-tzu/Laozi, tired of the decadence at court and witnessing the deterioration of the Chou/Zhou dynasty, left for the western borders of China travelling on an oxcart, or the back of an ox. It was at the Western Gate, at the request of the gatekeeper of the border pass, that Lao-tzu/Laozi wrote down the content of the *Tao Te Ching/Daodejing* in five thousand Chinese characters, before disappearing into the West. This simple tale has been handed down into Taoist tradition and embellished further with all kinds of symbolism.[8] Legend has it that Lao-tzu/Laozi lived for more than a hundred and sixty years. So did he really exist? We have no idea. All that can be said is that the scant biographical details that we have concerning him are beset with problems at every point.[9] But by the middle of the third century BCE, Lao Tan was being referred to as the philosopher responsible for the *Tao Te Ching/Daodejing*. The second century BCE *Huai-nan-tzu/Huainanzi* cites the *Tao Te Ching/Daodejing* several times, so by that time the text must have been well known.

The *Tao Te Ching/Daodejing* was originally called the *Lao-tzu/Laozi* after the Old Master. Indeed, it was not for many centuries that it was given the former title.[10] The first two words of the later title *Tao Te Ching/Daodejing* reflect neatly the division of the book into two parts, one dealing with – or, rather beginning with – the word *Tao*, translated as "Way", and the other with *Te/De* "Virtue" or "Power". The addition of *Ching/Jing* came later. The word *ching/jing* means "prestigious book" or "classic", but the *Tao Te Ching/Daodejing* was only for a very short time, and at a much later date, placed on the same level as the Confucian classics. Despite the fact that the words contained in it are like the peaks of mountains that leave the reader to fill in the content of the valleys in between, the depth of image, and the ability of its words to stretch the limits of the mind are considerable. Jacob Needleman writes of it: "To read it is not only to see ourselves as we are but to glimpse a greatness extending far beyond our knowledge of ourselves and the universe we live in."[11] But while enigmatic and profound the *Tao Te Ching/Daodejing* has pragmatic advice to rulers, as we shall see. Yet it is clearly a text that aims to dislodge normal thought patterns. It challenges conventional knowledge and the narrowness of conditioned thought. In Graham's words it is "the masterpiece of a kind of intelligence at the opposite pole from the logical".[12]

Nevertheless, if the reader of the *Tao Te Ching/Daodejing* expects a sequentially constructed path to the deconditioning of belief and practice, he or she will find none of this in the text. The deeper meanings of the text are only hinted at, and this makes the words open to a variety of interpretations. The ambiguous nature of the terse statements permits literal, figurative or manipulative interpretation that itself challenges the mind. The ancient Chinese pictographic characters in which the text was written carry no grammatical indicators of tense, number, noun, verb or adjective, and no indicators of where a sentence might begin or end. Michael LaFargue and Julian Pas have demonstrated admirably the practical difficulties of translating a text like the *Tao Te Ching/Daodejing*.[13] Different translations are, therefore, legion and a definitive translation is impossible. Added to this are the textual errors that occurred through the copies made by generations of scribes. There were also changes made by those wishing to manipulate the text for political reasons. Then, too, out of a desire for unity, as one author puts it, a translator "often 'slants', 'tweaks', 'stretches', or 'bridges together' the meanings of the disparate sayings within a verse in a way that gives them some commonality".[14] According to LaFargue, the *Tao Te Ching/Daodejing* originated from a time when *oral*, rather than written transmission was prevalent. When "books" arose, they tended to be by composite, rather than single authors, and with the aim of collecting traditions pertinent to a particular school.[15] Repetitions and other stylistic oddities in the *Tao Te Ching/Daodejing* point to multiple authors.

Those who are familiar with the *Tao Te Ching/Daodejing* are accustomed to understanding it as a "mystical" text. But such has been the attraction of the *Tao Te Ching/Daodejing* and the *Chuang-tzu/Zhuangzi* in the West that they have been placed in what Clarke calls a "historical vacuum".[16] One problem emerging from this is that the *Tao Te Ching/Daodejing* especially has become so meaningful to individuals and groups, and to Taoism itself, that it is accepted as a "mystical" text without any attempt to analyse its origins. In what follows, I shall try to address a little of both its historical setting and its mystical tradition in an attempt to maintain some of the more modern scholastic attitudes alongside the popular and conventional ones.

So let us look first at some of the different ideas about the text. There are many academics who, with the vast majority of casual readers, understand the text as a mystical one underpinned by the concept of *Tao*. Some, like Toshihiko Izutsu, go as far as to depict *Tao* as an *Absolute, the* Absolute, and as a cosmic force and a personal god.[17] In his view, the *Tao Te Ching/Daodejing* is concerned with the "ultimate vision of the Absolute".[18] But it has to be said that there is no hint of *theistic* religious experience of a deity in the *Tao Te Ching/Daodejing* or the *Chuang-tzu/Zhuangzi*. If these are mystical texts, then it is because they suggest an inner reality that transcends both the self and the outer world. Julia Ching points out just how elusive definitions of mysticism must inevitably be.[19] But, as she says, peace and serenity, and the losing of oneself in nature, are part of the mystical experience associative specifically with Taoism. When the self dissolves in *Tao* and the dualities of existence fade into non-existence, it would be difficult to deny that mystical experience has occurred, despite a humanistic atheism or agnosticism in the *Tao Te Ching/Daodejing*. Yet there is, as Peerenboom has shown, considerable evidence in the text to posit *Tao* as a cosmogonic source, as eternal, and as continually sustaining the world.[20] While accepting that the *Tao Te Ching/Daodejing* is "multifaceted and endlessly adaptable to many-layered interpretations", Benjamin Schwartz is another who never undermines its mystical dimension.[21] To Schwartz, the real mysticism of the text is based in the "gnosis" of experience of *Tao* – "oneness or some kind of mystic union with the ultimate ground of reality" – that provides meaning for life.[22] Isabelle Robinet also accepted the mystical dimensions of the *Tao Te Ching/Daodejing*.[23]

Other scholastic views emphasize *Tao* as a vibrant force in life. Thus, Robert Henricks accepts *Tao* as a "cosmic reality" that existed before all things and gave rise to them,[24] but focuses on *Tao* as *present* in each individual thing as a kind of energy or force – the life force, perhaps", that encourages each thing to develop in its own special way.[25] It is *Tao* as *Te/De*, as we shall see later, that has this special function. Bryan Van Norden's view of the *Tao Te Ching/Daodejing* is similar in that he accepts the essential mystical element of the text but sees it as informing a "utopian social vision"[26] and the "soft primitivism" of a Golden Age.[27] He thinks the text calls for a return from a sophisticated societal life to a simpler one.

But there are an increasing number of scholars who reject the fundamental mysticism of the *Tao Te Ching/Daodejing* as rooted in a mystical metaphysical abstract of *Tao*. In this case it is the *experiences* of those responsible for the text in its historical setting that are the major focuses. Angus Graham was outstanding in the past as one who was always critical of those who tried to interpret the *Tao Te Ching/Daodejing* as centred around a mystical ultimate Reality, and believed that Chinese philosophy in general was never inclined to build metaphysical systems.[28] Michael LaFargue, whose views we shall revisit below, is one of the more recent writers who believes that the sayings of the *Tao Te Ching/Daodejing* are nothing but collections of wise words for different contexts.[29] Thus, there is no real need to suggest an overarching philosophical unity like *Tao* for the text. To a number of scholars today, the *Tao Te Ching/Daodejing* is all about "self-cultivation", "inner cultivation", and *Tao* in it refers not to a metaphysical principle, but to the inner experience that results from meditative praxis. Harold Roth, for example, believes that such inner cultivation is the "mystical praxis" that "is at the very heart of the Laozi".[30] Similar are the ideas of Mark Csikszentmihalyi, who argues that *Tao* is a term that linked together different groups as the term expressing the principles and goals of their practices. To him, *Tao* was a "common denominator" amongst a variety of different schools and groups, "a way of speaking about a unitary phenomenon that appeared in different guises once it was constructed in different traditions".[31] He therefore strips *Tao* of its mystical nature and makes it a phenomenon common to a number of intellectual and philosophical inquiries and praxis.

Regardless of the original historical setting of the *Tao Te Ching/Daodejing*, however, and important as such an analysis is, it cannot alter what the text has become, and what it has meant for Taoist religion. I do not think we can deprive it of its mystical associations and, with that mystical character, eschew the depth that has come to be associated with the text in a posited metaphysical and unifying principle of *Tao*. Thus, in what follows, I shall be leaning more towards the mystical dimensions of the text, but at times pointing out some of the different interpretations.

The earliest commentary on the *Tao Te Ching/Daodejung* was by Ho-shang-kung/Heshangong[32] in the second century BCE, followed by that of Wang Pi/Wang Bi in the third century CE. Wang Pi/Wang Bi included a copy of the text in his work, and that copy is likely to have been very old. It is Wang Pi/Wang Bi's text that has become the standard work.[33] However, there are notable other texts, including the Ma-wang-tui/Mawangdui texts that are dated as far back as the late second century BCE. They were discovered in 1973 and were hand written on silk. What is interesting about them is that they reverse the two halves of the text, putting the *Te/De* section first and the *Tao* section second. Texts were usually written on narrow slats of wood or bamboo and were held together by a thong. If the thong wore away or were broken, the slats became confused and could be put together in an altogether different order. Thus, one very old text that dates back to the late third century BCE does not have the eighty-one chapters, nor do the Ma-wang-tui/Mawangdui texts, though the order of the text is not far removed from the standard one we have today. An even more exciting discovery was made of what is called the "Bamboo Slip *Lao-tzu/Laozi*" in 1993 in a Chinese tomb at Guodian. It is a copy of the *Tao Te Ching/Daodejing* that has been dated back to before 300 BCE.[34] This text is thus older than the Ma-wang-tui/Mawangdui manuscripts.

Such complexities of the history of the text need not detain us much longer. Suffice it to say here that a pure transmission of the *Tao Te Ching/Daodejing* has not been possible through two and a half millennia, and present translations have been informed by a legion of past commentators and competing political and philosophical views. The choice of an appropriate text must be left to the reader, but the brevity of the text makes it possible to read a few. However, it is important to address two questions before moving on. These are the intricate questions of authorship and dating of the *Tao Te Ching/Daodejing*. Did Lao-tzu/Laozi write the book? Traditionally, the answer is yes; academically, we would have to say that it is very unlikely. Indeed, it is likely that the text is the result of multiple sources, some of which reflect ancient tradition, others being later additions. Hanson describes it as "an edited accumulation of fragments and bits drawn from a wide variety of sources – conventional wisdom, popular sayings, poems, perhaps even jokes",[35] and LaFargue favours such "artfully arranged collages of sayings, sometimes augmented by the comments of those who put the collages together",[36] but by those who found the ideas of the sayings especially meaningful in the light of their own philosophies.[37] Those like Schwartz, who finds in the *Tao Te Ching/Daodejing* "a coherence in multivalence, a unity in multiplicity",[38] suggestive of an underpinning harmony in the text, might indicate a single editor and compiler. Others prefer to see the text as a result of a group of like-minded people. The bottom line of this is that there may, in fact, be very little connection at all between a man called Lao-tzu/Laozi and the *Tao Te Ching/Daodejing* that he is alleged to have written.

The debate about authorship of the *Tao Te Ching/Daodejing* is an ongoing one. Michael LaFargue is of the opinion that the book stemmed from a "Laoist" group that he calls "alienated idealists", a small group of thinkers within the larger class of *shih/shi*. These latter were drawn from the upward mobile lower classes and the downward moving nobility forming "a cadre of men with specialized expertise necessary to foster and maintain the good socioeconomic order that formed each ruler's power base".[39] The *shih/shi* idealists rejected the normal conventions of socio-political life, but could render advice to rulers through a higher level of thinking. LaFargue considers that a number of small, informal schools, each grouped around a teacher, contributed to the text of the *Tao Te Ching/Daodejing*.[40] LaFargue believes that the material originated as oral sayings in the Laoist school. He identifies mainly two kinds of sayings, "proverb-like aphorisms" and sayings devoted to self-cultivation of mind.[41] The aphorisms, in particular, he believes, are relevant to the life-conditions of their own time.[42] As such, they would have related to certain situations and are "context bound" whose "meaning is exhausted in the point they make about a specific situation that they address".[43] Taking them together, and imposing on them an overarching philosophy of *Tao* is, according to LaFargue, misguided. Thus, LaFargue sees the purpose of the *Tao Te Ching/Daodejing* as pragmatic advice for the reform of society through self-cultivated leaders according to Laoist-style views. The aphorisms, he thinks, are pointers towards this process, but no more than that. "Organic harmony" rooted in the evolved consciousness of the individual and society as a whole is the aim.[44] The aphorisms, thus, relate to ways in which both the individual and society can evolve. The main focus according to LaFargue was inner, spiritual self-cultivation, and this, he believes, is the purpose behind the *Tao Te Ching/Daodejing*.

So if the *Tao Te Ching/Daodejing* were not written by Lao-tzu/Laozi, and arose from more diverse sources, the next question to ask is when was it written? Traditionally it is believed to have been written about 500 BCE in the Spring and Autumn stage of the Chou/Zhou dynasty. This would make its author as Lao-tzu/Laozi an older contemporary of Confucius. Both men are said to have met, and traditions concerning their meeting may well have been included by the historian Ssu-ma Ch'ien/Sima Qian from separate Confucian and Taoist sources,[45] though other sources also relate meetings between the two.[46] However, it is unlikely that any such meeting occurred and a date in the Warring States period is now the most favoured and appropriate setting for the *Tao Te Ching/Daodejing*. The Guodian text – despite not being as complete as the traditional version – shows that some form of the text must have been present before 300 BCE, and that would indicate a date of the fourth century BCE, but still within the Warring States period. Indeed, there may have been more than one line of transmission of the text.[47]

The *Tao Te Ching/Daodejing* utilizes the utmost brevity in its language. Commenting on its style, Robinet pointed out that its "poetic, metrical form suggests that it acquired an incantatory power through the kind of rhythmic, repetitive recitation that strenghthens a practice. It was intended to be sung and memorized, as it actually has been in certain religious sects".[48] Certainly, the style of the text makes it possible to learn much of it by heart. Nevertheless, given the complexities of authorship and compilations it is not unusual to find parts that simply do not fit their context. Some parts are clearly sayings that have been handed down orally by all sorts of people, some with perhaps slightly different versions from others. Some of these are very old. Typical of such a saying might be: "When a man lacks faith, others will have no faith in him" from chapter 23. Yet somehow, there has been an attempt to make the whole text into a unified whole. Palmer puts this rather well when he says that texts like the *Tao Te Ching/Daodejing* "arose from pieces of oral wisdom which were collected and then strung together rather like pearls on a cord. Each is distinct, rounded and polished by time and telling, yet together they give a sense of unity of purpose."[49] Such a description aptly suits the nature of the *Tao Te Ching/Daodejing*.

In the content of the *Tao Te Ching/Daodejing* we find many juxtaposed themes. Central is the concept of *Tao* that can only be vaguely depicted in negative terms as opposed to the power and potentiality of *Te/De*. Egoistic activity based on desires is balanced with egoless, spontaneous action. The soft and yielding nature is balanced with outward strength; inner power with external force; the feminine with the masculine; silence with verbosity; emptiness with fullness; the natural with the contrived; Non-Being with Being; oneness with plurality; ignorance with knowledge. The *Tao Te Ching/Daodejing* searches out the spaces not the forms, like the space that makes a door possible, and the emptiness within a pot that makes it what it is. The concepts of the sage, and rulership according to sage qualities, are central issues, yet these sections are balanced with those that praise the meditative life. The two, in fact, are seen as complementary. Opposition to the externalized values of Confucian virtue is present in the text. We find Lao-tzu/Laozi in chapter 19 advocating that people would be better off by abandoning so-called righteous behaviour – presumably of the Confucian type. The righteous virtues of Confucian ethics are portrayed as a degeneration from the experience of *Tao* and *Te/De* within all life. Lao-tzu/Laozi was against conventional living and the need to measure out the material world neatly and formalize righteous living. *Tao* is beyond language and conventional thought. Chad Hansen writes of Lao-tzu/Laozi here: "He shows that the entire process of learning language is a process of absorbing a conventional, social pattern of desires. Our moral attitudes are learned, not innate."[50] Returning to a *Tao*-orientated life ensures right action from inner naturalness, not from outward conformity. And the more Confucians stressed the need for moral action, the more evidence that would be of its decline!

In the centuries that followed, Lao-tzu/Laozi's disappearance to the West became synonymous with his ascension to a pure, heavenly realm: he became an immortal. Many myths grew up around his disappearance. One saw him travelling to India and conversing with the Buddha, teaching him the wisdom of *Tao*. Perhaps it is not too remarkable that, since so little is known of the man, and his disappearance became such a well-rehearsed legend, subsequent history created not only an outstanding life of sagacity for him, but also an afterlife of cosmic proportion. In the second century a shrine was set up in his honour by the emperor, with appropriate prescribed ceremonies for rendering reverence to him. This was the first of a number of shrines, and the deification of the Old Master. At the same time he became more anthropomorphized as a deity than he seemed in life. [51] As we shall see in chapter 5, Lao-tzu/Laozi became the chief deity in an important movement that began the process of Taoism as a real religion, and the anthropomorphic representation of *Tao*. In the seventh century the emperor gave him the title of the Great Supreme (T'ai-shang/Taishang), and in the eleventh century he gained the title Great Supreme One, the Ancient Master (T'ai-shang Lao-chün/ Taishang Laojun). In religious Taoism he became the greatest god in the Taoist pantheon.

Chuang-tzu/Zhuangzi

The work of Chuang-tzu/Zhuangzi, which has the same title as his name, is a delight to read. Instead of the terse depth of the *Tao Te Ching/Daodejing*, we find a plethora of stories, amusing incidents and anecdotes on which to feed the mind. Wilhelm called Chuang-tzu/Zhuangzi "a splendid figure in Chinese intellectual and spiritual life".[52] In contrast to the vague identity of Lao-tzu/Laozi, in Chuang-tzu/Zhuangzi we have a refreshingly vivid person, with an evolved sense of humour and wit, and the ability to convey profound thoughts through simple imagery. Burton Watson pointed out that humour is rare in Chinese philosophical literature, but in the *Chuang-tzu/Zhuangzi* "it is the single most potent device employed by the writer to jar the reader out of his mundane complacencies and waken him to the possibility of another realm of experience".[53] Yet his work has a somewhat elusive nature that challenges conventional thought, and he loved discourse and discussion – especially if there could be no right answer! Hansen writes of him: "Zhuangzi floats over the landscape of Chinese thought like a philosophical phantom shrouded in a self-created mist of elusive style and analytical skepticism."[54] From the fourth century onwards, his work was to remain highly important in the development and consolidation of the beliefs of Taoist religious groups. It was Kuo Hsiang/Guo Xiang of the beginning of the fourth century CE, who left the major edition of the *Chuang-tzu/Zhuangzi*, with revision and a commentary, which has lasted to the present day.

As in the case of Lao-tzu/Laozi, the second to first century BCE historian Ssu-ma Ch'ien/Sima Qian gives us a biography of Chuang-tzu/Zhuangzi in his *Historical Records*. He had a slightly easier task than was the case with Lao-tzu/Laozi, but we still know little of Chuang-tzu/Zhuangzi. He tells us that he was born in the town of Meng, located today in the province of Honan/Henan. His real name was Chuang Chou/Zhuang Zhou; *-tzu/zi*, the honorary title of "Master", was added later. He worked at the Lacquer Garden, though we are unsure what this was. Ssu-ma Ch'ien/Sima Qian tells us that he was offered an important post at the court. However, Chuang-tzu/Zhuangzi declined. He likened acceptance to the sacrificial ox that was well fed, well nourished and well decked. But at the moment of sacrifice the animal would certainly wish to be an ordinary creature of the field. Just so, Chuang-tzu/Zhuangzi saw no value in a privileged life at court. His reply was blunt: "Go away! Don't mess with me! I would rather enjoy myself in the mud than be a slave to the ruler of some kingdom. I shall never accept such an office, and so I shall remain free to do as I will."[55] Such freedom was essential to Chuang-tzu/Zhuangzi, and characterizes many of the debates and dialogues in the text between Chuang-tzu/Zhuangzi and his close friend Hui-tzu/Huizi.

From the *Chuang-tzu/Zhuangzi* we also know that Chuang-tzu/Zhuangzi was married and had children, and his wife's death is the subject of one discussion. He does not appear to have been wealthy, and was more concerned with inner riches of the self than outward materiality. While he shunned political life, he seemed to have had a good enough knowledge to be aptly critical of it. Living in the difficult age of the Warring States period of Chinese history, it is small wonder that the turbulence of the age drew forth his distaste of ruling parties of his day. However, while we know little about his life, it would have to be agreed, with Palmer, that "the figure who does emerge is one of the most intriguing, humorous, enjoyable personalities in the whole of Chinese thought and philosophy".[56] And if there is mockery in his words, and accounts of practical jokes and tricks, the humour that pervades the book has the purpose of breaking down the barriers of the mind, so that it becomes possible to laugh at the conventions of society. Hints of shamanism pepper descriptions of the holy sage, the perfected person that lives on air and dew, rides on the clouds and mists, and wanders freely on the back of a dragon.[57] Perhaps, too, the *Chuang-tzu/Zhuangzi* was influenced by the school of Yang Chu/Yangzhu, the "Yangists" who emphasized the nurturing of the body rather than worldly possessions.[58]

There are a number of translations of the *Chuang-tzu/Zhuangzi*. The main texts used here are those of Angus Graham,[59] and Martin Palmer[60] though Thomas Merton's work, for example, is intuitive and delightful to read.[61] But as Graham warns: "*Chuang-tzu* illustrates to perfection the kind of battering which a text may suffer between being written in one language and being transferred to another at the other end of the world some two thousand years later."[62]

If we turn to the authorship of the *Chuang-tzu/Zhuangzi* we find similar problems to those that beset the *Tao Te Ching/Daodejing*. The *Chuang-tzu/Zhuangzi* is a composite work, but though it may be divided differently, the first seven chapters, called the *Inner Chapters*, are fairly consistently ascribed to Chuang-tzu/Zhuangzi himself. At least in these chapters, we find some of the important concepts that are associated with Chuang-tzu/Zhuangzi. Some fragments assigned in later chapters to other authorship may also be attributed to him. As to the remaining twenty-four chapters, some have been ascribed to an author heavily influenced by the thought of Lao-tzu/Laozi, others to eclectic and syncretic Taoists of the early Han dynasty, disciples of Chuang-tzu/Zhuangzi and others.[63] Chapters 8–22 are generally recognized as the *Outer Chapters*, and the remaining Chapters 23–33 are sometimes set aside as *Mixed Chapters*.[64] The whole work, then, "is a catch-bag, an anthology of stories and incidents, thought and reflections which have gathered around the name of Chuang Tzu".[65] The dates of Chuang-tzu/Zhuangzi are fairly well established since he lived during the reigns of King Hui of Liang (370–319 BCE) and Hsüan/Xuan of Ch'i/Qi (319–301 BCE). Nevertheless, dates vary, and it is best to place him somewhere in the mid-fourth and early part of the third centuries BCE, traditionally 369–286 BCE. However, the other contributors of material to the *Chuang-tzu/Zhuangzi* lived much later, and it was centuries later that the text reached a full form.

The *Inner Chapters* deal with many topics – the need to transcend conventional knowledge and worldly concerns; the folly of definitive rights and wrongs; spontaneity in living one's life; problems of living an enlightened life in the working world and the advantages of being useless and unemployed; living by the innate power within the self rather than by outward conventions; death; statecraft and the ideal ruler. The content contains a rich mixture of tales about rich and poor, kings, sages, robbers, potters, butchers, carpenters and many others. And beggars and cripples are treated in exactly the same way as kings and sages. "It is a bag of tricks, knaves, sages, jokers, unbelievably named people and uptight Confucians! And through it strides the occasionally glimpsed figure of Chuang Tzu himself, leaving a trail of humour, bruised egos and damaged reputations."[66] It is no wonder that Maspero called Chuang-tzu/Zhuangzi the finest writer of ancient China. He wrote, too, of Chuang-tzu/Zhuangzi: "His style is brilliant, he has a marvellous sense of rhythm, and his wonderfully supple language lends itself to all sorts of nuances. His lively imagination gives to all the anecdotes with which he embroiders his tales an extraordinary colour and life. At the same time, he was probably the most profound thinker of his time."[67] Underlying all is the focus on *Tao* as that which makes possible the flight of the self to the unlimited freedom in the natural spontaneity of life lived within the reality that is *Tao*. Such spontaneity is reflected particularly and superbly in the spontaneous character of the content in the *Inner Chapters*. But the content of the *Chuang-tzu/Zhuangzi* as a whole has the kind of free-flowing easiness that Palmer likens to a travelogue that "meanders between continents, pauses to discuss diet, gives exchange rates, breaks off to speculate, offers a bus timetable, tells an amusing incident, quotes from poetry, relates a story, cites scripture".[68] Additionally, Chuang-tzu/Zhuangzi uses what has been described by some writers as a "dizzying array of literary techniques" in the *Inner Chapters*.[69] The term "dizzying" is a pertinent one, since it conjures up the desired effect of throwing the mind out of its logical and normal thought patterns.

While Chad Hansen adopts the view that *Tao*, as it is understood in Taoism, is not evident in an absolute sesnse in Chuang-tzu/Zhuangzi's *Inner Chapters*, Robinet saw a strong mystical element in the work of Chuang-tzu/Zhuangzi.[70] However, those who reject a metaphysical concept of *Tao* in the *Chuang-tzu/Zhuangzi*, as in the *Tao Te Ching/Daodejing*, take a much more individualized view of any mysticism that might be present in the texts. Self-cultivation is usually the tack that such writers take in viewing the texts in this way. Thus, for example, Allinson considers self-transformation to be the underlying theme of the *Inner Chapters* of the *Chuang-tzu/Zhuangzi*. As he sees it, Chuang-tzu/Zhuangzi's purpose is of "silencing the analytical thinking reflexes of the reader and simultaneously empowering the reader's dormant intuitive or holistic mental functions".[71] The transformation here is from the controlled mind "to the absolute freedom of the mind to move in any direction that it fancies" – the aim of the text, as Allinson understands it. In Allinson's view, this goal supplies coherence for the whole of the *Inner Chapters*.[72] He analyses the myths and metaphors of the text to demonstrate how important Chuang-tzu/Zhuangzi's choice of language and literary form are in the goal of self-transformation and the metamorphosis into "freedom, carefreeness and playfulness" that accompanies the change.[73]

How, then, should we assess Chuang-tzu/Zhuangzi as a philosopher? Thomas Merton brought Chuang-tzu/Zhuangzi's words into the modern perspective in a very pertinent way when he wrote: "But the whole teaching, the "way" contained in these anecdotes, poems, and meditations, is characteristic of a certain mentality found everywhere in the world, a certain taste for simplicity, for humility, self-effacement, silence, and in general a refusal to take seriously the aggressivity, the ambition, the push, and the self-importance which one must display in order to get along in society. This other is a "way" that prefers not to get anywhere in the world."[74] All things in life are such as they are. And what they are is masked by the conventions, conditionings, and over-shadowings that pervade the life condition.

Lieh-tzu/Liezi

We know very little about the life of Lieh-tzu/Liezi. He seemed to have lived his life in poverty and as a recluse. He lived in the principality of Cheng/Zheng for forty years before being forced to leave because of famine. It was then that his disciples are said to have written the book that bears his name, including a few scant details about the sage. Chuang-tzu/Zhuangzi refers to him so there must have been some prior tradition about him, perhaps a collection of his sayings. Chuang-tzu/Zhuangzi recounts the last years of Lieh-tzu/Liezi's life by including a charming tale of his transition from self-centredness to oneness with *Tao*.[75]

Despite the portrayal of Lieh-tzu/Liezi in the *Chuang-tzu/Zhuangzi* as a real person, we have no real evidence to suggest that he existed outside legend. The book that bears his name, the *Lieh-tzu/Liezi*, was probably compiled several centuries after his supposed lifetime. The practice of ascribing work to a legendary or traditionally famous person makes authorship of such texts difficult to ascertain. Many now date the text to around 300 CE, or later, though the first commentator was Chang Chan/Zhang Zhan in the second half of the fourth century CE. A percentage (about a quarter) of the text is found in other sources of the third and second centuries BCE. Angus Graham was one who accepted the later date for the work and, with the exception of chapter 7 – a rather hedonist chapter of differing tone to the rest – believed that it was even compiled by a single author.[76] Later, he suggested that the text was a "deliberate forgery", the original having been lost and another compiled based on some ideas about the original but with materials also directly lifted from elsewhere.[77] But he also points out that the dates suggested for the *Lieh-tzu/Liehzi* are separated by half a millennium![78]

So a good deal of the content of the *Lieh-tzu/Liezi* is gleaned from older sources like the *Chuang-tzu/Zhuangzi*. Also like the *Chuang-tzu/Zhuangzi*, the *Lieh-tzu/Liezi* contains tales and legends, parables and miracles, humorous anecdotes and jokes, but also a good deal of reflective philosophy, presented through the medium of prose and rhythmic verse.

Magic and mystery are interwoven. There are deep messages to be gleaned from episodes relating to life; dream and reality; knowledge and ignorance; the extraordinary; destiny and freedom; and morality. All these topics are dealt with in order to explain the nature of *Tao* in life. The *Lieh-tzu/Liezi* is less critical of Confucius the man than the *Chuang-tzu/Zhuangzi* is at times, but artfully uses words put into the mouth of Confucius himself to criticize Confucian values.

Such, then, is the philosophical foundation of Taoism, retrospectively cast back to three ancient sages and the works ascribed to them. We now need to turn to the heart of their philosophy and examine the concept of *Tao* as they understood it.

Tao

> Something formless, yet lacking nothing,
> There before Heaven and Earth.
> Silent and void,
> Standing alone and unchanging,
> Revolving, yet inexhaustible.
> Perhaps it is the mother of the universe.
> I do not know its name
> So I call it *Tao*.
> If pressed, I call it "Great".

Such is the description – or lack of it – of *Tao* in chapter 25 of the *Tao Te Ching/Daodejing*. The Chinese ideogram for *tao* contained the sign for moving on and a head. It indicated moving step by step, of walking feet, possibly in rhythmic movement.[79] The use of the character for the head combined with a foot suggests a "way", "path", "road", or even "method", with the head suggesting, perhaps, that it should be a thoughtful way forward. Thus it can be used in the sense of a political way, a social way, a religious way, or the way of Heaven. It can include the manner in which one goes along the way in the sense of "to lead" or "to guide". It can also mean "to speak", "to tell" or "to instruct".[80] It is a very old word that can obviously be used in a quite mundane sense. But from ancient times, it could be used in the sense of the way of humanity, with connotations of morality, virtue and righteousness. In more abstract meanings, and in a metaphysical sense, it can mean "Way" or "Truth" in the sense of a doctrine, or a principle.[81] Here, the meaning of the word is deepened, and it is in this sense that we shall need to look at the concept in Taoism, where the term was projected to its metaphysical ultimate. In Taoism, *Tao* represents ultimate Reality. Jonathan Star points out that since it can be both a noun and a verb: "It can represent the substance of the entire universe and the process by which the universe functions."[82] While the concept of *Tao* was integral to Taoism, it is important to remember that it was also used widely in other schools, its wide meanings enabling it to be used in a variety of different philosophical ways. Jacob Needleman encompasses the wide scope of the word in the following words: "Metaphysically, the term *Tao* refers to the way things are; psychologically, it refers to the way human nature is constituted, the deep, dynamic structure of our being; ethically, it means the way human beings must conduct themselves with others; spiritually, it refers to the guidance that is offered to us, the methods of searching for the truth that have been handed down by the great sages of the past – the way of inner work. Yet all these meanings of *Tao* are ultimately one."[83]

The Confucians used the term *Tao* in the sense of social order, and as a foundational ethical principle. Here, it is a right way in the political, social and moral activities of life. In this sense it could be furthered through knowledge, study, discipline and excellence in living. It could be nurtured in culture and propriety, and success in pursuing the Way would bring its rewards in life. It was an anthropocentric view of the human being as thoroughly capable of winning the support of Heaven by right societal behaviour. Such a conception of *Tao* has nothing of the metaphysical connotation that the Taoists gave it. In Taoism it is the Way of all nature, the deep naturalness that pervades all and makes everything such as it is. It is the ultimate Reality that informs all things. Yet, the ultimate Principle that is *Tao* in the pre-religious Taoist sense is essentially *impersonal*: it cannot reward or punish, favour the good or condemn the bad. *Tao* is a unifying ultimate principle, not a being. The Way of the Confucians is a describable Way; the Way of the Taoists is essentially metaphysical – the still, underlying, changeless unity that is the source of all motion, change and plurality in the universe, the point at which opposites meet and the harmony between them all.

In this book the Chinese term *Tao* will be retained rather than its translation of "Way". I want to avoid the tendency to project the concept of *Tao* to a transcendent Absolute in the sense of an indescribable divine entity, like the Hindu concept of *Brahman*. Certainly, there will be evidence later that such a move has taken place in the meanderings of Taoist evolution. But I want to avoid the link here, because I do not think there is much evidence for it in the books attributed to the Old Masters. Chad Hansen goes as far as to say that in the *Chuang-tzu/Zhuangzi* there are many *taos*. "The *Zhuangzi* contains references to great *dao*, extreme *dao*, mysterious *dao*, heavenly *dao*, the ancient king's *dao*, its, his or their *dao*, emperor's *dao*, human *dao*, sage's *dao*, the *dao* of governing, moral *dao*, the *dao* of long life, the master's *dao*, the *dao* you cannot (or do not) *dao*, the gentleman's *dao*, this *dao*, authentic *dao*, artificial *dao*, my *dao* . . ."[84] and so on. Hansen's point is that there is not just *one Tao* but many, and that it has been a mistake to understand one ultimate principle as the true meaning of *Tao*. It is an interesting point, but the wide used of the word *tao* in any text need not preclude one metaphysical principle being posited in addition. I do not want to oppose the concept of *Tao* as an ultimate principle in the same way as Hansen, though I accept the unlikelihood of a *divine* Absolute. But I want to keep the concept of *Tao* as open and fluid as possible at this juncture. Dropping the definite article *the Tao*, I think, aids in pulling the concept away from the embraces of a divine ultimate that so many wish it to have. It will be for the reader to draw his or her own conclusions as to the ultimate nature or non-nature of *Tao*.

An inexpressible ultimate principle

Tao is the undifferentiated Void and potentiality that underpins all creation, immutable, unchanging, without form and beyond all deities and even the idea of them. It is indescribable Reality, eternally nameless, but experience of it, and of its profound emptiness, is the goal of the Taoist. The opening of the *Tao Te Ching/Daodejing* has the words: "The *tao* that can be spoken of is not eternal *Tao*. The name that can be named is not the eternal Name." There are a variety of ways in which the Chinese characters can be translated here, but really, they all amount to the same thing, and that is to say that if you can speak about, tell of, or express *Tao*, then you do not really know what *Tao* is.[85] *Tao* is beyond human comprehension, and the term *Tao* is the best we can use to refer to it. *Tao* is a name that is not a name. Essentially, it has no name for it is beyond all language and thought. Giving it names, then, only suggests that it is not understood, and refers to something other than *Tao*.[86] The same is reiterated in the *Chuang-tzu/Zhuangzi*: "The great Way is not named" and "The Tao that is clear is not the Tao."[87]

In the same way that potentiality has to exist before things can come into being, so *Tao* is that which begins all things. In the words of Yung Fu-lan: "Since there are always things, *Tao* never ceases to be and the name of *Tao* also never ceases to be."[88] For Taoism, then, *Tao* is the unchanging "that", which underlies all things as their source, giving impulse, form, life and rhythm to the changing plurality of the cosmos – this last, depicted in the *Tao Te Ching/Daodejing* as the "ten-thousand things". So we are told in chapter 34 of the *Tao Te Ching/Daodejing*: "Great *Tao* flows everywhere, filling all to the left and to the right. The ten thousand things depend upon it for existence; it rejects none of them. It accomplishes its purpose silently and claims no fame." We find contrasted here the unchanging, unnameable absolute Reality that is *Tao* with the impermanent, changing world of names and forms, differentiation, opposites and dualities. But the two are not incompatible: the former is the unchanging Source, the latter the ever-changing world that proceeds from it. Chuang-tzu/Zhuangzi, particularly, associates *Tao* with the ebb and flow of change in the universe. And the inexplicable, rhythmic, pulsating, dynamism of *Tao* pervading life is the abstract principle that the sage needs to become in tune with in life. For Chuang-tzu/Zhuangzi *Tao* is the means by which the soul is nourished and is able to return to its source. But while the *Chuang-tzu/Zhuangzi* emphasizes that *Tao* transcends all language and thought it sees the immanence of *Tao* in all things down to a blade of grass.

While *Tao* was sometimes called T'ai Chi/Taiji "Supreme Ultimate", T'ien/Tian "Heaven", T'ai-hsu/Taixu "Great Void" and T'ai-i/Taiyi "Supreme Transformer", "Supreme Changer", it is its immanence in all existence, that lends *Tao* descriptors such as the mother of all things; the ancestor of all beings; the Non-Being from which Being comes; the shade of the valley; the naturalness of the Way of Heaven. Even in the *Tao Te Ching/Daodejing* there is what Lau referred to as "the feeling that the line is blurred between the *tao* as an entity and the *tao* as an abstract principle".[89] But in essence, *Tao* is that which makes things as they are, the flying of birds, the flowing of rivers to the sea, the blowing of the wind. But while *Tao* makes things what they are it is not itself a thing, and is *no-thing*, but experience of things as they are is also experience of *Tao*. Epithets used to describe *Tao* are enigmatic ones – vast, cool, shadowy, still, tranquil, hidden, mysterious, silent. It is the ultimate mystery, and as *no-thing* it would be useless to pray or sing praises to it, for it is completely impersonal, is without wilful intention, However, the *Tao Te Ching/Daodejing* tells us in chapter 79 that *Tao* remains with the good all the time. Perhaps what is meant by such statements is that *Tao* always flows the right way, and the "good" person is he or she that flows through life in the same, natural way. It is through working with *Tao* that goodness results. For *Tao* performs all things. It contains all, sustains all and permeates all and nothing can be separate from it. It is the "is-ness" of all things, all forces and all subtleties, the rhythms of existence, the patterns of nature, the order of the cosmos. Chuang-tzu/Zhuangzi tells us that: "The great Tao has both reality and expression, but it does nothing and has no form":[90] *Tao* simply operates, but it does so neutrally. It cannot control events; it simply is the transformations and changes that take place in existence as well as the source of them. The course that *Tao* takes is such as it is; nothing can alter it.

Such is *Tao* as a mystical principle, but it has to be remembered that there are completely different views and it is worth reiterating the opposite opinion of *Tao* by Michael LaFargue. He believes it is a mistake to see such a unifying and underpinning metaphysics in the *Tao Te Ching/Daodejing*. He strips *Tao*, and associated words like *Te/De*, stillness, emptiness and oneness, of their cosmic and metaphysical character and reduces them to the "concrete practice of self-cultivation".[91] Such terms, he believes, refer to a "hypostatized state of mind" of the experiencers, not to some principle or doctrine of *Tao* to which they conformed.[92] Perhaps he is right, but then it would still have to be claimed that *Tao* subsequently became something more than a quality of mind, and came to be accepted as a metaphysical principle underlying all creation. This was certainly the understanding of the term by Wang Pi/Wang Bi, the major early commentator on the *Tao Te Ching/Daodejing*. For Wang Pi/Wang Bi *Tao* was Non-Being (*wu*) in the sense that it is beyond form and all that exists.[93] It is the *evolved* conception of *Tao* with which Taoism became concerned.

Tao is Non-Being (*wu*) in the sense that it is beyond form and beyond all that exists and is *no-thing*. It is another way of saying that it is the indescribable Void and potentiality that underpins the world of forms and realized potential. In contrast, it is the changing world of things or "Being" (*yu*) that has names for this and that, and differentiates between matter. The ego becomes entangled in the world of matter, differentiation, and "Being", stimulated by desires for some things more than others. In the first chapter of the *Tao Te Ching/Daodejing* we find the words: "Always desireless you observe its mysteries. Always desiring, you observe its manifestations." Thus, "always desiring" one sees only Being, the world of matter. Only when desires are lost and the ego is stilled can Non-Being – *Tao* as the Great Void – be experienced. But *Tao* remains concealed like a mirror covered with dust to one full of desires. The same chapter tells us of the darkness of the Void, the "mystery within mystery" and of "the gateway to all mystery" that is hidden in the darkness of ignorant involvement with Being. Thus, the *Tao Te Ching/Daodejing* in chapter 40 also says: "Returning is the movement of *Tao*. Yielding is the means of *Tao*. The ten thousand things of the world are born of Being. Being is born from Non-Being." So Non-Being is not nothingness but, to use Wilhelm's expression, it is "something qualitatively different from existence".[94] It is the absence of the phenomenal forms of the cosmos. Being represents the process of differentiation and the multiplicity of phenomena that emerge: it is potentiality that has shifted into realized forms, the many from the One.

Creation

The source of all creation, then, is the mysterious depth and darkness of *Tao*. There are no distinctions between this and that or even between Non-Being and Being, or non-existence and existence. It is the potential for all things and that to which all things will return – the utter silence of the primordial Void. It is cosmic totality, Void, or chaos (*hun-tun/hundun*) that projects itself outward to form the whole of the universe and then reverts back to chaotic completeness.[95] In this sense *Tao* is beyond One, beyond unity, but always present throughout all creation, "deep and always enduring", chapter 4 of the *Tao Te Ching/Daodejing* tells us. The relational continuity between the primordial Void and the existent present is paramount. Not to know such is to misunderstand the nature of reality. The inactive stillness of potentiality in the Void exists alongside the spontaneous activity of *Tao* in life: Thus, chapter 37 of the *Tao Te Ching/Daodejing* says that: "*Tao* exists in non-action, yet nothing is left undone." The inseparability of these two aspects is critical to the understanding of the nature of *Tao*. *Tao* is the essence of potentiality that pervades creation at the same time as transcending it. The pervasion of *Tao* in all also includes its presence in the self – not only in the mind, but also in the body. Such presence of *Tao* within the self will be an important aspect of alchemy, as we shall see in a chapter 6.

The One

In chapter 42 of the *Tao Te Ching/Daodejing* we have the words: "*Tao* produced the One. The One produced the Two. Two produced Three. And Three produced the ten thousand things. The ten thousand things support *yin* and embrace *yang*. They achieve harmony by the interplay of these forces." It is important to note from these words that, at least from the evidence of the *Tao Te Ching/Daodejing*, *Tao* is beyond and prior to One – a factor that belies a monistic interpretation of Taoism. In Ho-shang-kung/Heshanggong's early commentary, he makes it absolutely clear that *Tao* precedes the One and that One is the vital essence that is created by *Tao*. All Heaven and Earth are produced from this essence, this energy that proceeds from *Tao*.[96] So from *Tao* comes One, the cosmic energy of *ch'i/qi*, a concentration of powerful creative potential. Graham described it as a "pool of energetic fluid".[97] Nothing will be able to exist without it, for it will permeate the universe in both *yin* forms and *yang* forms.

In the Neo-Taoism of the third century CE *Tao* and the One were merged by Wang Pi/Wang Bi, in particular, who saw the world as emerging from the One as *Tao*. Here, the One becomes the Supreme Ultimate, *T'ai Chi/Taiji*, the cause and essence of all. While *Tao* retains much of its original mystery, it moves closer to the realm of form in Wang Pi/Wang Bi's view of it. It becomes One as opposed to two, or One as opposed to many – a dualism of Non-Being and Being. Such deleting of the principle *Tao produced the One* was, thus, responsible for a radical change in the concept of *Tao* from the third century on. However, Girardot is suspicious about the *Tao Te Ching/Daodejing*'s statement of "*Tao* produced the One", since he thinks elsewhere in the text (chapters 10, 14, 22, 39) *Tao* is identified as the

One. What is more, the *Huai-nan-tzu/Huainanzi* omits the line. Girardot, in fact, prefers to accept the One as *Tao* in its pre-creative chaotic state.[98]

Two

From *ch'i/qi* comes the two, *yin* and *yang*. The spontaneous interaction between these two forces produces all in the universe. So there is no creator deity. Nor is there a creation in time and space. But at this point, the two are merely potentially present, not yet dynamically active. Nevertheless, we have to reckon with the fact that reference to *yin* and *yang* occurs only once in the *Tao Te Ching/Daodejing*, and that other interpretations of the two may be possible.[99] But if *yin* and *yang* are not specifically mentioned, the process of reversal by which opposites follow each other is a significant theme in the *Tao Te Ching/Daodejing* and amounts to the same principle as *yin* and *yang*.

The Three

The interplay between *yin* and *yang* produces the three. There are a variety of ways in which the "three" is interpreted. Some seem to think it is *yin* and *yang*, plus the results of their combination as the third.[100] Girardot points out that since *hun-tun/hundun* or chaos still obtains when the "three" are present, it is a state of cosmological unity in which the "two" are "mysteriously balanced by a third term that unites them perfectly". He suggests this is a paradisical form "associated with the undifferentiated or embryonic condition of wholeness at the beginning", a sort of "ordered chaos", as opposed to absolute chaos,[101] and a "paradise condition of the harmonious unity of the one and the two".[102] Girardot also thinks it possible that the "three" might refer to *ch'i/qi*, though the latter is usually seen to be the One.[103] Ho-shang-kung/Heshanggong's earliest commentary understood the three to be "the harmonious, the clear, and the turbid".[104] Frequently, the three are expressed as *great yin*, *great yang* and the *central harmony* that is represented by humanity. Heaven is *yang* and represents the abstract power of *Tao* in the cosmos. Earth is *yin* and the manifestation of *Tao*. Humanity is the equilibrium between the two, and is responsible for maintaining the balance and harmony of that equilibrium. However, we have to remember that at this point in the creative process, there is no humanity, only potentiality for all things, so while this view is popular it is hardly viable. The three on a microcosmic level came to be the *Three Treasures*. These are *ching/jing* "essence", *ch'i/qi* "vitality" and *shen* "spirit". It is these three energies that are the life-giving properties of all things in existence; they are the source of life and the means by which *Tao* sustains the universe.[105]

The ten thousand things

And so we come to the "ten thousand things" that emerge from the three. The expression is synonymous with all the phenomena that emerge in the universe. The sophisticated and complex combinations of varying degrees of *yin* and *yang* bring about the whole of the material world and all the ever-changing subtleties contained within it. It is beautifully described by Blofeld as a "perception of existence as a vast and timeless ocean of spotless purity upon which, through the interplay of dark and light, a myriad illusions play like ever-changing cloud formations or restless waves".[106] As we shall see below, it will be over-involvement with the myriad phenomena of the world that will obscure the reality behind them that is *Tao*.

Thus we have the concept of on-going creation as reflected in the *Tao Te Ching/Daodejing* and the *Chuang-tzu/Zhuangzi*. While *Tao* is nameless, and has no consciousness and volition, it represents all organic order – the patterns and rhythms of all cosmic existence. It is, therefore, essentially dynamic in that it informs the myriad patterns and created entities of existence, animate and inanimate, gross and subtle. It is such immanence that is experienceable to the Taoist, not by the intellect, logic or any kind of empirical knowledge, but by intuitive awareness of the essence of things. Such intuitive experience is the beginning of the return to *Tao*. The *Chuang-tzu/Zhuangzi* describes the whole creation process:

> At the great Origin there was nothing, nothing, no name.
> The One arose from it; there was One without form.
> In taking different forms, it brought life, and became known as Virtue.
> Before any shape was given, their roles were assigned,
> varied and diverse but all linked to one another.
> This was their lot.
> The forces worked on and things were created,
> they grew and took distinct shapes, and these were called 'bodies'.
> The bodies contained spirits,
> each distinct and mortal.
> This is what we call the innate nature.
> Train this innate nature and it will return to Virtue;
> Virtue at its best is identical with the Origin.
> Being of the One is to be ultimately formless, and this formlessness is vast.[107]

As far as the *Chuang-tzu/Zhuangzi* is concerned, the "ten thousand things" in creation are all equal. *Tao* runs through all things and unifies them all so that one thing is no more important than another. It was a principle for which Chuang-tzu/Zhuangzi became renowned. All things were also equal in that they were subject to transformation and change, and in that they would ultimately return to *Tao*. To be enlightened and experience that return to *Tao* in life was the ultimate goal of the sage. The return to *Tao* is by a process of transcending or "forgetting" the ten-thousand things – the dualities of life so wondrously worked with *yin* and *yang* variations; the self; and even the fact that one's self exists – until the unity of existence is experienced. Since the self becomes one with the eternal *Tao*, it, too, becomes eternal, immortal. The self can then "sit in forgetfulness" as the *Chuang-tzu/Zhuangzi* puts it, in the emptiness of the mind that is the emptiness of *Tao*, transcendent to all differentiation and dualities of existence. At the root of all the relativity, contingency and transience of life there is the eternal immobility of *Tao*, the point where *yin* and *yang* are harmoniously balanced potential.

Reversal and return

The Chinese term for "reversal, return" is *fan*. It suggests returning to the root, to the beginning, to the empty spirit, to nature, as far as the old commentators understood it.[108] The idea of return is part of a cyclical process that is reflected in the macrocosm and the microcosm. The unceasing activity of flux in all life as the work of *Tao* is accepted as proceeding in orderly cycles. Thus we have the perpetual cycles of seasons, days, nights, and patterns of stars and planets; as the interplay of *yin* and *yang* these are the active patterns of *Tao* within manifest existence. The process of manifestation, therefore, is not seen as an evolutionary forward movement, but as a cyclical movement of emanation and dissolution, of Being and Non-Being, of arising and decaying, of life and death. There is no beginning and no end, merely arising and dissolving in rhythmic patterns. Such is the state of manifest existence at both the macrocosmic and the microcosmic levels; the life of the human being is merely a miniature of the universe.

Creation in Taoism, therefore, is understood as a cosmic force that emanates beyond itself into the myriad manifestations of existence through a process that changes from void to spirit, spirit to vitality, vitality to essence and essence to form. In later times there were many other variations of pre-Taoist cosmology,[109] but this is essentially the view of the *Tao Te Ching/Daodejing* and the *Chuang-tzu/Zhuangzi*. All manifested existence is, then, like the energy radiated out from a centre that is ultimately formless, non-dual Reality, and it is only in relation to that centre that anything can obtain any level of reality. To return to the centre is to return to a state of non-differentiation and non-duality. The active vitality that emanates from the centre to the myriad phenomena is *Tao* manifest as *Te/De*, a concept that will be examined in detail below. In order to return to the source, to *Tao*, it is necessary to experience *Te/De* in every moment of life. This is "going with" the flow of existence and it is this that enables the Taoist sage to return to the source, the Void of *Tao*. The goal of the sage, then, "is to reach through order to the inner organism of the world, to its hub, its empty and vague center, which is Tao in its essence".[110] This, we would have to accept, is a mystical description of returning. LaFargue, however, would disagree. He thinks that "return", "turning back" is a process of self-cultivation to the still mind, not a return to a metaphysical cosmic source of *Tao*. In his view, returning is a reversal of the mind that is involved in the myriad events of life to an original stillness of mind.[111] As we have seen, he sees *Tao* as a convenient term to explain the inner experiences of the "self-cultivated". As such, it would be synonymous with *feelings* of stillness, oneness, equilibrium and the like.

The ultimate experience of enlightenment, however, is a mystical one, graphically portrayed by Livia Kohn:

> Mystics strive to go to the very center of the mind. They wish to free the spirit within and make it radiate through themselves, dissolving the conscious mind and the personal body. Thus they practice methods that lead ever farther inward, transforming ego and identity in favor of the spirit. Then, empowered by spirit radiance, the movement reverts to an expansion toward the outside, suffusing the body, now felt as an impersonal replica of the cosmos, with the energy of the Tao. As spirit merges with cosmic body, there is a return from darkness to light, from yin to yang, from enstasy to ecstasy, from duality to oneness, from earth

to heaven. The basic dichotomy of human existence is overcome as inner and outer are merged in an ascent toward the radiance of heaven.[112]

The *Chuang-tzu/Zhuangzi* speaks of a "Perfected Being" that could live on air, ride the winds, unite with the universe and be free from any constraints of individuality and egocentric involvement in the world. Chuang-tzu/Zhuangzi says of the enlightened being: "Such a person rides the clouds and mounts upon the sun and moon, and wanders across and beyond the four seas. Neither death nor life concern him, nor is he interested in what is good or bad."[113] This is surely a mystical experience.

The unity of the universe

From all that has been said above, it is clear that unity underpins the cosmos through the essence of *Tao*. Every entity has its own innate nature, but *Tao* unites all those natures into one. The multiplicity of the world is held in potentiality in the unformed *Tao*, and it makes no difference to the unity of all things whether they are in potential or realized form or part one and part other. In the end, all is *Tao*; multiplicity exists in unity, a unity that is itself beyond all duality yet that underpins all change.

We see the plurality of the world only because we cannot experience its underlying unity that is *Tao*. And yet, the multiplicity of phenomena are not regarded as unreal because of the hidden *Tao* that informs them. This leads Chad Hansen to oppose any sense of monism in the work of the Masters, and to favour a distinctly pluralistic system.[114] If all is one, he claims, then real distinctions can never be made,[115] and it would have to be admitted that distinctions are made because of the different innate potential and skills within each person.[116] In Hansen's analysis of *Tao* there are many *taos*, as was seen above. This suggests to him that there can only be different perspectives, different *taos*, of what is right or wrong, but no absolutes. In his view Chuang-tzu/Zhuangzi criticized those who adopted one perspective without being aware of the equally valid ones of others. He believes that we operate in contexts according to the *tao* specific to the context and not according to some monistic, underpinning *Tao* of *taos*. When we develop a skill to a level that becomes masterly, effortless, spontaneous and natural, we are experiencing a specific *tao* and not a unifying *Tao*.[117] Such a thesis, however, robs Taoism of its heart. Needham commented that: "If there was one idea which the Taoist philosophers stressed more than any other it was the unity of Nature, and the eternity and uncreatedness of the Tao."[118] Specifically, it is the unifying *ch'i/qi* that is the source of the plurality of existence, though it seems to permit individuation and differences in innate potential. There is a mutual arising and dependency of existence according to Taoism that demands a unifying principle that informs its interconnectedness, a *Tao* behind the *taos*.

While *Tao* underpins everything, it still permits the differences that make reality multifaceted and spontaneously expressed. There is a difference in the self-expression of all things, a "naturalness" (*tzu-jan/ziran*) in the way that things spontaneously are and act. Yet, the fact that *Tao* produces One, One, two and so on, means that the reverse process is possible: multiplicity ultimately returns to its common denominator that is One, and One merges in *Tao*. But the reality of external differences is not denied; it is just that their separateness is not as deep as we think. It is when we are involved with the dualities of life and forget the unity that informs them, that we have an incorrect perspective of reality. Chuang-tzu/Zhuangzi, especially, brings this point to the fore, with his challenges to the ways in which people normally think.

To return to an analogy used earlier, if we imagine a circle in which extreme opposites are either ends of diameters that cut through the centre, then it is only at the centre that opposites cancel each other out. And it is the energy of that central point as *Tao* that makes possible the dualities or opposites in life by which we come to know what things are. At the same time it is that point to which all returns, in the same way as a circle cannot exist without its centre. Opposites and dualities can only exist away from the centre, and the aim of the Taoist is to return to that central point where opposites cease to exist. The *Chuang-tzu/Zhuangzi* states: "The universe is the unity of all things. If we attain this unity and identify ourselves with it, then the members of our body are but so much dust and dirt, while life and death, end and beginning, are but as the succession of day and night, which cannot disturb our inner peace. How much less shall we be troubled by worldly gain and loss, good luck and bad luck!"[119] The moment we name something we differentiate it from everything else and, by so doing, place limitations on it. But at that point where opposites meet, which is neither this nor that, no limitations can be set at all because it is unnameable, indescribable and beyond the dualities and opposites that constitute normal knowledge. *Tao* is that centre point of rest, tranquillity, stillness. Perhaps this is what the *Tao Te Ching/Daodejing* means in chapter 45 when it says that: "Purity and stillness are the means for order in the world." And Chuang-tzu/Zhuangzi, too, said: "Tao is obscured when men understand only one of a pair of opposites, or concentrate only on a partial aspect of being. Then clear expression also becomes muddled by mere word-play, affirming this one aspect, and denying all the rest."[120]

It is the sage standing at the centre of the circle between all opposites, who has the correct view of things as neither this nor that, but as *Tao*. Experiencing *Tao* in this way is experiencing the essence and harmony of all the myriad things within existence – something that can be done only at that central point of *Tao* around which all revolves and from which all emanates. To use an analogy of Chuang-tzu/Zhuangzi's the sage at this central point of equilibrium is like a mirror that reflects all things but does not hang on to them when the image is gone. So must the mind become: the "I" of the self has to lose its "me". In such a state, or lack of it, rational forms of knowledge are left behind, emotions are stilled, definitions are abandoned, classifications are forgotten: "Fully at one with the flow of existence, with the Tao, one is able to enjoy everything as it is. This is 'free and easy wandering'; this is 'perfect happiness.' Attaining this, the true person fully realizes the spontaneity of the Tao."[121] The more complicated life becomes, the more one abandons simplicity and the more involvement there is with the dualities presented by the "ten-thousand things". So in the *Chuang-tzu/Zhuangzi* we find the words:

> The heart of the wise man is tranquil.
> It is the mirror of heaven and earth
> The glass of everything.
> Emptiness, stillness, tranquillity, tastelessness,
> Silence, non-action: this is the level of heaven and earth.

> This is perfect Tao. Wise men find here
> Their resting place.
> Resting, they are empty.[122]

In a condition of equilibrium there is no urge to interfere with the way things are in the natural order of the world. The tranquillity of stillness is the happiness of utter peace. And it has been beautifully depicted. Blofeld wrote: "The illusory ego falls away, yet nothing real is lost. Spirit, freed from its bonds, returns to Spirit, not as a dew-drop destined to form an insignificant particle of a vast ocean, but as the boundless returning to the boundless. The liberated consciousness expands to contain – to *be* – the entire universe! Could there ever, ever be a more glorious endeavour?"[123]

Te/De

The Chinese character for *Te/De* consists of three symbols, ten eyes and a curve, suggesting perfection (since ten eyes failed to see a curve), the heart, and a foot going forward. Combined, as Star comments, "Te is not so much "perfect-heartedness" but its *expression* and the action that gives rise to it".[124] This leaves us with a meaning of something like "perfect-hearted action", or "straightness of heart in action". Waley noted, too, the earlier connection of *te/de* with the idea of planting and potentiality, as in the planting of seeds. In this sense, it is the "latent power" or "virtue" in an entity.[125] Confucius used the term to signify virtue in the sense of correct living according to *Tao*, the right way. Later Confucians came to emphasize *te/de* as moral rectitude in living one's life, but especially in relation to the community, both politically and socially.

The usual translations of *Te/De* have retained the notion of "virtue", though it is sometimes translated as "power", or even as "nature" or "essence". But the Confucian sense of moral living is not the way in which we should see the word virtue. It is more like "virtuality", if ungrammatical, because in the Taoist sense of the word it is that power and potential in things that makes them what they are. It is the *Taoness* within, the true nature of something, that is activated exteriorly. As Needleman aptly depicts it: "*Te* refers to nothing less than the quality of human action that allows the central, creative power of the universe to manifest through it."[126] But that "central creative power" is not something that an entity may or may not have, for it is the force of life that flows from *Tao*. This is certainly the way in which Lao-tzu/Laozi understood the word – "something spontaneous, original or primal, that which is timeless and infinite in every individual living being".[127]

Te/De is the functioning of *Tao*. And it functions in the wind that blows; the soil that nurtures; the growth of the seed; the growth, and even the decomposition, of the human. Essentially, it is a *natural* and *spontaneous* potential, not a forced innate drive. Nor can such a potential be acquired from without; it exists naturally, instinctively, and is primal in all things. It is by means of *Te/De* that *Tao* can be experienced. The ability to be at one with the innate virtuality of what one is, is the ability to "go with" the flow and essence of things. It is the ability to experience *Tao* emanating out into the universe, and it will also be the means of experience of returning to *Tao*. Each entity is as it is by virtue of the specific nature manifested within it, but that unique energy will, eventually, return to its source.

To be able to experience the virtuality of something is to connect with the Source in different dimensions; it is to experience *Tao* in human, animal, plant and inanimate objects. It is an inward, mystical experience of the natural essences of things, a simple and natural experience that can be accomplished by "forgetting" conventional standards and conditioned ways of thinking and acting. Listening to the innate virtuality of the self, rather than directing energies to the outward ten thousand things, makes such "forgetting" possible. It will lead to an understanding of the nature of things such as they are, to a greater understanding of what life is and a concomitant freedom and happiness. In line with his view of *Tao* as an experience of the Laoist *shih/shi*, LaFargue believes *Te/De* to be the "charismatic power" that is aquired through the self-cultivation process advocated by the Laoists, which results in experiences of softness, oneness, harmony, and the like.[128] So LaFargue posits *Tao* and *Te/De* as "two names for the same personal quality taught to and developed by members of the Laoist school".[129] He does not, however, project either to the metaphysically cosmic level.

Outward perfection is not an indicator of *Te/De*. In chapter 4 of the *Chuang-tzu/Zhuangzi* it is pointed out that the crooked and gnarled tree is the one that is left standing, not the one whose straight trunk is useful for timber or whose fruit is plucked. Similarly, it is the hunchback who is too misshapen to be sent to war who escapes the misery of being a soldier. The particularization of *Tao* as *Te/De* in any thing does not suggest that it has to be perfect or even good. It is simply such as it is. And if we transfer such thought to the world of today, it is full of people who have always wished to develop a skill and potential that they know they have, but who have forced themselves, or have been forced, into doing other things at which they are not happy. In the *Chuang-tzu/Zhuangzi* we read so much of the craftsmanship of the highly skilled worker, whose skill is based on the naturalness that comes from inner experience. Similarly, it is often emptiness rather than materiality that reveals the *Te/De* of something, the empty space in a jar that provides its function, the empty spaces of doors and windows that make a home. Oshima believes operating from the heart rather than the mind brings about the pure awareness that allows one to "flow with" the wind, with *Tao*, and to feel at home with the direction in which *Tao* is taking one.[130]

Change

Te/De is not static but represents the processes of change and transformation in all things. Such cyclical process has been described by Roger Ames as "an endless spiral that evidences, on the one hand, persistent and continuing patterns and, on the other, novelty, with each moment having its own particular orbit and character".[131] This is an important point, because the change and transformation do not revert to old patterns but to new, unique formulations. This is why Chuang-tzu/Zhuangzi, for one, despised the fixed conventions that suggested there could always be one answer, one right way, in all situations of x or y. Going with the flow of life means understanding this shifting and dynamic nature of reality and moving with it, not against it.

Reversal is an important concept in the *Tao Te Ching/Daodejing*. For something to shrink, it must first expand, to fail it must first be strong, to be cast down it must first be raised, and for someone to receive, someone has to give. If anything, however, Lao-tzu/Laozi seems to favour humility, softness, weakness and the feminine. Similarly, the *Chuang-tzu/Zhuangzi* raises the crippled and the crooked to importance. But the aim is not to become weak and so on, but to adopt such characteristics in order to combat the opposite drives to succeed, do well, acquire skills, possessions, and the like. Equilibrium is still the ultimate aim. Lao-tzu/Laozi's advice to political and social problems, therefore, is one of reversal of conventional norms of political and social praxis. But such advice is not just an attempt to redress the imbalances in society, it is a statement of what is believed to be an invariable law of nature: reversal is the way things must be, just as hurricanes don't last forever or rain for eternity. So if we want to be strong we have to begin by recognizing that we are weak; whatever we want, we begin with its opposite – a point echoed again and again throughout the *Tao Te Ching/Daodejing*. While the *Tao Te Ching/Daodejing* barely uses the term *yin* and *yang*, the same principle of reversal, of the swing of the pendulum between opposites, is embodied in the *yin* and *yang* principle – the "two" that underpin all creation, and in the processes of change in the ancient *I Ching/Yijing*.

The *Chuang-tzu/Zhuangzi* reveals a different attitude to change from that of the *Tao Te Ching/Daodejing*. Whereas the *Tao Te Ching/Daodejing* idealizes a return to a "Golden Age", there can be no reversal to a Golden Age in the *Chuang-tzu/Zhuangzi*. Rather, there needs to be an acceptance of the "endless spiral" that Roger Ames wrote of, above. It is an ability to flow with such continuous change that is seen as essential in the *Chuang-tzu/Zhuangzi*. Hence, Chuang-tzu/Zhuangzi wished to turn the tables on conventions that crystallized and rigidified approaches to life that could never be natural, "life is followed by death; death is followed by life. The possible becomes impossible; the impossible becomes possible. Right turns into wrong and wrong into right – the flow of life alters circumstances and thus things themselves are altered in their turn. But disputants continue to affirm and to deny the same things they have always affirmed and denied, ignoring the new aspects of reality presented by the change in conditions".[132]

The ability to understand death alongside its opposite of life, and as part of the process of transformation and change, occupies considerable space in both the *Chuang-tzu/Zhuangzi* and the *Lieh-tzu/Liezi*. The latter is realistic about death: "That which is born is that which in principle must come to an end. Whatever ends cannot escape its end, just as whatever is born cannot escape birth; and to wish to live forever, and have no more of ending, is to be deluded about our lot."[133] Later, in the same chapter, Lieh-tzu/Liezi says: "Death is a return to where we set out from when we were born. So how do I know that when I die here I shall not be born somewhere else? How do I know that life and death are not as good as each other? How do I know that it is not a delusion to crave anxiously for life? How do I know that present death would not be better than my past life?"[134] To these words we might add the beautiful statement, again in the same chapter: "Dying is the virtue in us going to its destination."[135] The *Chuang-tzu/Zhuangzi*, too, accepts death as a necessary part of the natural processes of change, and an occasion when true belief in the natural laws must allow the passing away of one's closest without the usual lamenting and wailing. Like the *Lieh-tzu/Liezi*, Chuang-tzu/Zhuangzi was pragmatic about death: "That hugest of clumps of soil loads me with a body, has me toiling through a life, eases me with old age, rests me with death; therefore that I find it good to live is the very reason why I find it good to die."[136] Graham describes Chuang-tzu/Zhuangzi's view of death as a loss of self-identity through understanding *Tao*: what remains after death will be "identical with all the endlesly transforming phenomena of the universe".[137] Or, as Toshihiko Izutsu puts it, "Death is "nothing but one of the endless variegated forms of one eternal Reality".[138]

So can such *Te/De* be cultivated? As we have seen, many see self-cultivation as the essential ingredient of the *Tao Te Ching/Daodejing* and the *Chuang-tzu/Zhuangzi*. Tateno Masami is one, for example: "This *Dao*, which comes from within us, wherein the reality of the phenomenal world is embodied in the most profound regions of our understanding, is the practical and real knowledge that comes through earnest and disciplined *practice*."[139] *Tao* for Tateno Masami, then, is "the true reality of each of us"[140] experienced through cultivation of our inherent *Te/De*. The way to cultivate such awareness is through *tzu-jan/ziran* and *wu-wei*, as we shall see below.

Wu-wei: non-action

Broadly speaking, *wu-wei* means "not acting", though its specific meanings are wide and a little ambiguous. The word *wei* means "to be; to do; to make; to practise; to act out; to cause".[141] It can also have the nuance of meaning of acting out, as if on a stage, or to pose, make a show of. The addition of the negative *wu* means not to do these things. Paul Carus, therefore, suggested that *wu-wei* means "to do without ado", "to act without acting", "acting with non-assertion".[142] Such suggestions indicate admirably the sense in which the *Tao Te Ching/Daodejing* uses the term to mean acting without inner egoistic involvement with the action. It is action carried out externally from the still inactivity of the ego within. It is thus unforced and natural action of the kind that has no ulterior drives and motives behind it. It is the art of accomplishing much with the minimum of activity. That is why chapter 37 of the *Tao Te Ching/Daodejing* says that *Tao* is of the nature of *wu-wei*, of non-action, yet leaves nothing undone. *Wu-wei*, then, is the ability to act with minimum forced effort by going with the natural flow of things, in short, being in tune with *Tao* and its expression as *Te/De*. When heavy snow covers the branches of trees, the branch that can bend, like the willow, does not break. Just so, the art of taking the natural and softest path through life, with the minimum of show, force, assertion or parading of oneself, is acting according to *wu-wei*, and incurs less wear and tear.

Clearly, the *Tao Te Ching/Daodejing* does not suggest that *wu-wei* as inaction should be no action at all, total *laissez-faire*, since it states that nothing is left undone by *wu-wei*. And we have to remember that the *Tao Te Ching/Daodejing* is full of advice to rulers on the way to conduct statecraft and military affairs. It is *interference* that is wrong, the egoistic imposition of the will of a human being or human groups in a matter that can be better solved by more natural, moderate means. Water, for example, is weaker than stone, but in time will wear it away. *Wu-wei*, to quote Liu Xiaogan is, "the balance between minimal effort and best result".[143]

All this is in contrast to today's existence, where little is done dispassionately, unplanned and without being motivated by some kind of desire for an end product. Then, too, our actions are mostly conditioned by the societies in which we live, by education, religion, politics, and social, familial and peer groups. It is much the same in any age and any culture, and the Old Masters pointed out the folly of becoming entrapped in such life-patterns to the extent that naturalness in life was replaced with artifice, rigidity of thought and unnatural attitudes to life and its real meaning. Today, human beings get caught up in the multiple pressures of the challenging, postmodern world of home, work, family, finance, material improvement, and the host of proximate goals that propel people through a day's existence. *Wu-wei* today, no less than in the times of the *Tao Te Ching/Daodejing*, asks for a reassessment of the way things have become, and a return to the way they should be.

When actions are carried out in the *wu-wei* sense, they are harmoniously aligned to natural laws. They are not aggressive or forceful, violent or ego-motivated. Thus, they are usually right actions, and should reap harmonious results, even though they are not done with moral intent. Moreover, liberated from the constraints and conditionings of usual patterns of thought, there is a sense of freedom in natural, effortless action that is devoid of concern for selfish end products. Such freedom involves the letting go of normal response patterns, the ability to give way, yield, and be receptive. And all it is, is an ability not to go against the grain of things in the multiple situations life presents. And it is an ability to use the natural potential of one's own self, one's own *Te/De*, to fulfilment. Such living is far from passivity. The *Tao Te Ching/Daodejing* expected rulers to operate according to *wu-wei*, with sage-like qualities, but not to abrogate all activity: *wu-wei* is not a recipe for idleness. Much of the *Tao Te Ching/Daodejing* is a manual of how to govern well, how to maintain order amongst subjects, how to organize farming, trade, and the army. But to govern well the laws of nature cannot be disregarded, and the natural path – the more subtle way to look at things is the way of *wu-wei*.[144] *Wu-wei* is knowing, too, just the right amount to act and when to withdraw without being over-involved. It is relaxing into the action without the intensity of force, volition and tension. Most of us can do this when we drive a car, or ride a bicycle, for example. Chapter 19 of the *Chuang-tzu/Zhuangzi* includes the tale of a drunken man who falls off a cart. Because he is so relaxed he has no consciousness of falling out of the cart, any more than he knew he was riding in it! He is not worried about anything and so is not tense, rigid and fearful as he falls, which is exactly what would be expected had he had no wine. If wine can give this much security, the *Chuang-tzu/Zhuangzi* states, how much more is to be got from spontaneity?

The principle of *wu-wei* underlies the practice of T'ai Chi Ch'üan/Taijijuan, particularly as a martial art. Here, it is by yielding that strength is overcome. Benjamin Hoff gives the example of trying to strike a cork floating in water. The harder it is struck, the more it yields, and the more it yields, the harder it bounces back. The moral here is that it is better to neutralize force than use violence against it.[145] So the *Tao Te Ching/Daodejing* tells us that the softest thing in the universe will overcome the hardest (chapter 43). It is wiser to temper aggressive action, particularly when others suffer as a result. And it is wiser to temper the inner desires that lead to aggressive achievements of goals – on personal levels, and on national levels as in the case of aggressive war. Most importantly, there must be that inner inactivity of the egoistic self, of the drives and passions, the desires and aversions that are the usual motivators for action. The root of the understanding of *wu-wei* comes from this inner stillness of the ego. It is a crucial point that will be looked at in detail below.

The ultimate level of humanity is that of the sage. Much is said of the sage in the *Tao Te Ching/Daodejing*, especially in connection with *wu-wei*. The sage keeps in the background, but is always ahead, is detached, but at one with everything, acts selflessly, but is fulfilled (chapter 7). If kings and lords could act in this way, the *Tao Te Ching/Daodejing* says, then the ten thousand things would be able to evolve naturally, and everything would be peaceful (chapter 37). The foolish person is always busy, always doing things, always active, and the more he or she does, the more there will be to do. The sage refrains from acting and people are reformed. He enjoys peace and finds that people around him become honest. He does nothing and people become rich, and when he has no desires people revert to a more natural life (chapter 57). More than the *Tao Te Ching/Daodejing*, the *Chuang-tzu/Zhuangzi* expresses *wu-wei* as harmony with *Tao* and the dynamic powers of *Tao* as *Te/De*. But in the *Chuang-tzu/Zhuangzi* the sage is much more withdrawn from the world than in the *Tao Te Ching/Daodejing*: the *Chuang-tzu/Zhuangzi*, unlike the *Tao Te Ching/Daodejing*, sees *wu-wei* as non-involvement in politics.

Unlike the sage, the ordinary mortal is trapped in an active world. According to the *Chuang-tzu/Zhuangzi*, we pursue results, money, friends, changes, and become hopelessly caught up in complex activity:

> Those who are caught in the machinery of power take no joy except in activity and change – the whirring of the machine! Whenever an occasion for action presents itself, they are compelled to act; they cannot help themselves. They are inexorably moved, like the machine of which they are a part. Prisoners in the world of objects, they have no choice but to submit to the demands of matter! They are pressed down and crushed by external forces, fashion, the market, events, public opinion. Never in a whole lifetime do they recover their right mind! What a pity![146]

As far as the *Chuang-tzu/Zhuangzi* is concerned nature works perfectly without boasting, and its brilliant laws proceed without discourse. It simply operates naturally and spontaneously – a perfect model for humanity. And when at one with *Tao*, a sage like Lieh-tzu/Liezi, unobstructed by conventional goals, desires and ego rode on the winds, totally liberated in every dimension of being, not knowing whether it was the wind that he rode or whether the wind rode him.

Tzu-jan/ziran: naturalness and spontaneity

Chapter 76 of the *Tao Te Ching/Daodejing* points out that at birth we are weak and gentle, soft and supple. At death we are brittle and stiff. The same can be said of young tender plants that become withered and dry at death. So, to be stiff and unbending is to encourage death, but to be soft, yielding and flexible is to encourage life. To be flexible, adaptable, and to find ways around force and confrontation is to embody naturalness. This is living life according to *tzu-jan/ziran*.

Tzu-jan/ziran (*tzu/zi* "self" and *jan/ran* "such") means, adjectivally, "natural", "spontaneous", "so of itself", "so on its own", "just-so-ness" and, nominally, "naturalness", "spontaneity". It was a concept that was central to Ho-shang-kung/Heshanggong's interpretation of the *Tao Te Ching/Daodejing*. It is *Tao* that exhibits this and, indeed, *is* this, *par exellence*, and so all humanity needs to adopt the same principle in order to achieve harmony and oneness with *Tao*. Liu Xiaogan argues that naturalness is the "cardinal and central value of Taoism, while *wu-wei* is the essential method to realize it in social life".[147] So *wu-wei* is the means by which naturalness is actualized, because it is intimately involved with human behaviour.[148] Unlike *wu-wei*, Liu Xiaogan points out that: "'Naturalness' is a positive term used to describe the progression of a certain state of affairs or things, whereas '*wuwei*' is a negative term aimed at placing restrictions upon human activity."[149] In his view, a "reverence for 'naturalness' is the most distinguishing characteristic of the Daoist scheme of values."[150] And since *tzu-jan/ziran* and *wu-wei* are attributes of *Tao*, Liu Xiaogan thinks they are cosmological and ontological concepts.[151]

It is overdoing things, forcing life, lacking moderation in life, which are against naturalness. The *Tao Te Ching/Daodejing* advises one to stop short before filling things to the brim, over-sharpening the blade, amassing so much wealth that it cannot be protected, claiming great wealth and titles. It advises that it is better to retire when work is done rather than attempt to do that bit more. Such is naturalness and the way of *Tao* (chapter 9). But this can only be achieved by appreciating simplicity, realizing one's true nature and curbing selfishness and desire (chapter 19). It is not wrong occasionally to drift like the waves on the sea, or like the breeze and the wind (chapter 20). And it is essential to respect the naturalness that is part of the created universe. In chapter 29 we are told that we cannot control and improve the universe, and if we try to, we will ruin it. To gain naturalness in life, the *Tao Te Ching/Daodejing* tells us that we need to nourish *Te/De* in the body, the family, village, nation and the universe (chapter 54). Naturalness and *Te/De* go hand in hand.

The *Chuang-tzu/Zhuangzi*, too, endorses naturalness as the way to experience life. By getting rid of the conventional goals and drives of conditioned life, as Graham put it, "the focus of attention roams freely over the endless changing panorama, and responses spring directly from the energies inside us . . . this is an immense liberation, a launching out of the confines of self into a realm without limits".[152] So Chuang-tzu/Zhuangzi advises:

> Go side by side with the sun and moon,
> Do the rounds of Space and Time. . . .
> Be aligned along a myriad years, in oneness, wholeness, simplicity.
> All the myriad things are as they are,
> And as what they are make up totality.[153]

For Chuang-tzu/Zhuangzi, excess in living inhibited the experience of naturalness. A simple life engendered awareness and openness to the natural way of things. The *Lieh-tzu/Liezi*, too, extols naturalness: "If nothing within you stays rigid, outward things will disclose themselves. Moving, be like a mirror. Respond like an echo.[154] For some, naturalness led to the reclusive life, the simple life of the hermit; others became like the child, uninhibited by life's constraints and the conventions of society – an analogy that the *Tao Te Ching/Daodejing* frequently expresses. The simplicity of the child's knowledge, desires and even breathing are commended, and the sage is said to treat all like children. Girardot points out that *tzu-jan/ziran* is tantamount to the kind of freedom and completeness that obtained before creation and, moreso, to the naturalness and spontaneity of *Tao* in its creative mode.[155]

Naturalness, then, is that hidden undercurrent in life that we find when we set aside for a short time the normal constraints of living, the stresses and strains, the things for which we strive in long-term and short-term goals, and just stop. It is only when we are still, caught perhaps in a moment of warm sunshine, a smile, the song of a blackbird, a midnight sky full of stars, that the pendulum passes through the still point and permits a glimpse of another way of life:

> Be the stream of the universe!
> Being the stream of the universe
> Ever true and unswerving,
> Become as a child once more.[156]

Naturalness and spontaneity is acceptance of the moment as it is, and response and adaptation to that moment that is completely natural. Such, in fact, is the way the universe is, the way night follows day, and the seasons follow each other. Being assertive and purposeful about everything are inimical to balance and harmony in life. Such, indeed, was the message of the *Chuang-tzu/Zhuangzi*. Human beings have within them the natural spontaneity of *Tao* that they submerge, overshadow and forget, through conditioned conventions. Instead of living harmoniously and accepting the gifts nature offers, nature is harnessed, conquered and dominated, without anything being given back. Ultimately, nothing can be taken from the universe without necessitating serious debt; whatever we take we will have to repay.

The search for happiness that characterizes human living is a frenetic one built into the complexities of socio-economic drives. The urge to avoid death – albeit something that later Taoism adopted in the search for longevity, as we shall see in chapter 6 – is a wish to avoid the natural process of birth and decay in all things. The natural current of harmony runs through all things; few pause to experience it. But harmony is the key to life in all its manifestations. The spontaneous character of nature is indicative that there cannot be fixed principles in approaching life. Each moment is different, and it is the ability to correlate the self in harmony with the situational moment that is the key to spontaneous living. In achieving inner harmony through taking the softer paths through experience with minimum effort, then, maximum health, strength and benefit to others are achieved. For the individual acquires the ability to adjust in mutual response to the forces operating at a particular moment of time and space.

The uncarved block

In the *Tao Te Ching/Daodejing* we find an emphasis on what is natural, simple and in its original state. It is sometimes referred to as the *uncarved block*, that is to say, the natural state of something before it has been worked by an agent. Needham thought that the Chinese term *p'u/pu* meaning "simplicity", "wholeness", or "in the rough",[157] had political connotations in the *Tao Te Ching/Daodejing* and referred to the simplicity of earlier primitive collectivism. He cites chapter 15, for example, which certainly begins by talking about the ancient masters, and continues to extol their natural qualities.[158] The idea of rough, unhewn wood in its simplest state has now caused the term *p'u/pu* to be translated widely as "uncarved block". Its basic meaning is something like homogeneous simplicity, something not having been tampered with in any way and thus retaining its original, natural state, *like* an uncarved block. As such, then, it is a good analogy of that which is left in its natural state, be that a part of nature, a way of life, or whatever.

Concomitant with the concept of the uncarved block is the quietism that accompanies that which is left alone. Returning to *Tao* is stillness, chapter 16 of the *Tao Te Ching/Daodejing* tells us, and stillness is the way of nature in that its way is unchanging. All nature and all life have the stillness of *Tao* at their source. The uncarved block is the individual immersed in *Tao*, the one who has returned to the primordial state, what Girardot calls "the no-face of Hun-tun"[159] and "the chaotic matrix of fertility present in the earth".[160] Similarly, Roth believes that the uncarved block is the mystical experience of the still and desireless state by the practitioners of "inner cultivation".[161] He thinks that "unhewn" or "uncarved" like emptiness and tranquility "are technical terms that refer to various stages in the process of introvertive meditation leading to the experience of Union with the Way".[162] Human life rarely experiences such stillness, but should be able to be active externally while still within. Movement, action, speech, thought should stem from the silence and stillness of *Tao* within the self. While the *Tao Te Ching/Daodejing* does not recognize that withdrawal from the world is necessary for such experience, and active advice for statecraft is an important part of its message, the picture in the *Chuang-tzu/Zhuangzi* is very different. Here, it is withdrawal to solitude and the quiet life of the hermit that is the ideal: the solitude of a mountain retreat is what the *Chuang-tzu/Zhuangzi* recommends. The mind is allowed to turn meditatively inwards on itself to *Tao* and away from the anxieties and stresses that normal sense-stimuli bring.

While we cannot turn our backs on the world like the sage we can acquire wisdom that comes through patience. We do not have to know or say something on every subject, meddle in the affairs of others, have reasoned answers for all that we do. We intuitively know when we are doing too much, when we need to step back and be still. The *Tao Te Ching/Daodejing* tells its rulers to ease off, lessen aggression and ruling, and let people develop their own natural responses to life. But if we cannot control our own impulses to action, and we have no stillness and silence within, how can we expect governments to function with restraint, non-aggression and a more yielding politic? The answers, Lao-tzu/Laozi would have said, come from within, not from more injunctions from outside. The truly free person is liberated from the confines of over-activity and manipulative living and achieves goals naturally.

The functioning of *Tao* in life

As we have seen in a number of contexts already, according to the *Chuang-tzu/Zhuangzi*, *Tao* is experienced by the skilled craftsperson that is able to perform action with that extra ingredient that comes from within. It is intuitive relaxation into the activity that takes place when the individual is at one with the action. Then, no matter how complicated the activity is, it seems to happen naturally, effortlessly and smoothly. It is suggestive of experience of *Tao* in daily life, when we are at one with what we do. Conversely, according to the *Tao Te Ching/Daodejing*, when we become over-excited about things, over-desirous, over-emotional, because our senses are over-stimulated, we are unable to experience *Tao*. Whereas the craftsperson is open to the flow of *Tao* in life, the sense-bound person is only open to the stimuli of the material world. The goal of the Taoist is to experience the flow of *Tao* increasingly until it pervades all life, and when this happens, the individual is able to live life in the fullness of the moment. Happy, contended, serene, moderate and in harmony with all, those who achieve such a life-style attain to *Tao*.

Statecraft

In chapter 9 of the *Chuang-tzu/Zhuangzi* we find a description of a legendary Golden Age. It was a time when people lived simply, weaving their own clothes, and supplying their own food from the land. Communities were isolated and lived peacefully, not only amongst themselves, but also with the birds and beasts of the land. All people were equal because they followed their own intrinsic *Te/De*, living effortlessly and simply. They were in harmony with *Tao* and, therefore, one with another. It is perhaps such a belief in an ideal state that informed the way in which the Old Masters viewed the very different kind of society that had come about under the rule of manipulative kings. They saw the natural lives of the people altered by fixed laws and ways of life, and the natural spontaneity in life that came from living flexibly at one with *Tao* as inhibited by rulers. People were better off, therefore, living in ignorance, because it was an ignorance that enabled them to live a holistic life rooted in *Tao*. Chapter 18 of the *Tao Te Ching/Daodejing* describes how the decline in a life focused in *Tao* brought about the kind of sophistication in society that necessitated rules for order, piety and relationships. Chapter 80 deals with a social utopia that can be experienced when a sophisticated life-style is exchanged for a simpler one.

The exactitudes of centuries of incessant wars, power struggles and feudal aggression were the backdrop of the antagonism to the way in which the country was ruled. Yet the king was supposed to be the supreme mediator between Heaven and Earth. It was he who was responsible for right and appropriate action in life that would ensure the welfare of his people. The *Tao Te Ching/Daodejing* advocates a policy of *wu-wei* as much for the ruler as for the individual. Non-interference in people's lives permits them to develop their natural potentials, and the greatest rulers rule without making it obvious. The *Tao Te Ching/Daodejing*'s advice on how the ruler should manage his state is really geared to lack of constraint on people and allowing them a sense of freedom. If the people are well fed, well housed, healthy and happy, then they will not be dissatisfied. With such aims, war would be unnecessary. The ideal of small village communities seems to be what the *Tao Te Ching/Daodejing* recommends. The whole ideal is a return to what is natural. Smith's comments here are particularly pertinent about the *Tao Te Ching/Daodejing*: "It is scathing in its opposition to oppressive government, and the legal or moral attempts to make all men conform to a pattern. In its attempt to free men's minds from all man-made restraints and artificialities it taught conformity to nature, the relativity of good and evil, and the strength of non-action."[163]

According to the *Tao Te Ching/Daodejing*, ruling the country is like cooking a small fish (chapter 60): in other words it is a delicate operation that has to be in balance with the natural order of things. It also has to be like *Tao*, giving, but not possessing, benefiting, but not expecting gratitude, taking care of things but not exercising authority (chapter 51). Needless to say, the *Tao Te Ching/Daodejing* has a good deal to say about war. The lean years and land devastation that are the aftermath of war are mentioned in chapter 30, along with advice not to take advantage of power. And the following chapter depicts weapons as instruments of fear, only to be used when there are no alternatives. Rejoicing in victory is tantamount to rejoicing in killing. A victory should, rather, be mourned as a funeral. When a powerful country gives way to a small country it will truly conquer, and if a small country yields to a powerful one, it too will conquer in its own way (chapter 61). The moral, again, is that strength lies in apparent weakness. As to internal politics, a country ruled with a heavy hand will make the people cunning (chapter 58). People will starve through heavy taxes, rebel because rulers interfere in their lives too much, and think little of death because the rulers demand too much of them in life (chapter 75).

So the *Tao Te Ching/Daodejing* does not suggest that there should be no involvement in the political scene. But rulers should be sages; able to rule unobtrusively, and have the capacity to withdraw when a task is completed. Ivanhoe points out that possessing *Te/De* draws others towards that person,[164] particularly since the one with *Te/De* is humble, welcoming, accommodating and safe to be with.[165] Reaching stillness within, so characteristic of *Te/De*, automatically influences others. Hence the importance for the sage-ruler to possess *Te/De* himself, for when he does, strife in his lands will be minimal, and then he will be able to refrain from action. Thus, Ivanhoe sees an "intimate relationship" between *Te/De* and *wu-wei* in the ruler. Ivanhoe also concurs that a "simple agrarian utopia" is the ideal life advocated by the *Tao Te Ching/Daodejing*. The more the ruler does in laying down prohibitions and regulating society, the more problems will ensue. Doing less, and letting things be, will decrease them. Regulations make people poorer, as does private profit. The more ingenious inventions there are the more complicated life will become. The more laws there are, the more there will be thieves (chapter 57). Apart from being a book about *Tao*, then, the *Tao Te Ching/Daodejing* is also a manual for ruling, for *Tao* can act through the sage-ruler to make rulership as spontaneous and natural as *Tao* itself. LaFargue is of the opinion that the statecraft of the *Tao Te Ching/Daodejing* aims at "organic harmony" of the state through an ideal ruler who is "sensitive to the unique and shifting conditions in any social group, and will flexibly pursue policies designed to foster the kind of organic harmony appropriate to each unique situation".[166] He sees this as the unifying goal of the Laoist *shih/shi* school that he thinks was responsible for the *Tao Te Ching/Daodejing*.[167]

In the *Chuang-tzu/Zhuangzi* and the *Lieh-tzu/Liezi*, as noted above, we find far more antipathy to involvement with politics. If you have any wisdom then you steer clear of the court and anything to do with state officialdom. It is better to be useless and out of work so that no one interferes in your life. Chuang-tzu/Zhuangzi has much to say against the competitive nature of official life (chapter 4). However, if it *is* necessary to take on an official role, then the inevitable has to be accepted, though with caution in its undertaking (chapter 4). But, generally, the *Chuang-tzu/Zhuangzi* considers state institutions to be an imposition on individual freedom, particularly because they impose uniformity on society, allowing no room for individual differences. Such was his view of Confucian regularity that inhibited natural spontaneity and replaced what was natural with artificiality. A good ruler is a charismatic one that fulfils the needs of his people but wants nothing in return.

The ideal is a *sheng-jen/shengren*, a holy or perfected person. This is the person that can operate from a point of naturalness, not interfering with the just-so-ness of other things in creation. The Chinese character that makes up the word consists of three parts: a mouth, an ear and a person. The positioning of the ear and the mouth next to each other suggests the ability to hear directly.[168] This suggests an inner awareness of life. The sage is successful because he never strives; is modest, and thereby achieves greatness; accords respect to all, and so is honoured; asks for nothing, yet has the universe. In the *Tao Te Ching/Daodejing* the sage is the term used almost exclusively of the ideal ruler. It is the sage-ruler who is the ideal here, someone who has attained wisdom through ignorance, that is to say, through the ability to be unmoved by the passions that detract from *Tao* – through *ignore-ance*. Indeed, Fung Yu-lan notes a common Chinese saying that: "Great wisdom is like ignorance."[169] So the *Tao Te Ching/Daodejing* epitomizes the good sage-ruler as the complete opposite of the normal conceptions we would have of a president, prime-minister or king. Knowledge deep within is the key to understanding *Tao*.

For knowledge of *Tao* one does not have to seek it out, go anywhere, or study; it is simply there. With the deeper understanding that *real* knowledge of *Tao* brings, the ego is transcended, the emotions are controlled, and the self is not swayed by the this and that of existence. External modalities cease to have an effect, and equilibrium is maintained. True knowledge facilitates the adaptability to, and awareness of, the dynamic transformations of *Tao* in existence. It is, therefore, not static. True knowledge is that which transcends all opposites: it is, again, like the centre of a circle as the equilibrium between all opposites, between all dualities, from where there is the ability to experience all parts of the circle, all dimensions of *Tao*. Other kinds of knowledge are not balanced like this. They are viewpoints held from points away from the centre; they have their opposites, and thus their contradictions. Chuang-tzu/Zhuangzi dreamed he was a butterfly and, when he woke, wasn't sure whether he was Chuang-tzu/Zhuangzi who had dreamed he was a butterfly or whether he was a butterfly dreaming it was Chuang-tzu/Zhuangzi. Either way, he is as he is. The ultimate teaching about knowledge is encapsulated in chapter 2 of the *Chuang-tzu/Zhuangzi*, and that is that the highest knowledge sees everything in one; all is unified in *Tao*. Lesser knowledge breaks down that unity into multiple parts.

What inhibits the deeper knowledge of *Tao* are the desires that create the egocentricity of human beings. It is desires that inhibit the opposites of meekness, humility, contentment and moderation that characterize the natural life. And if we take a step behind desires, then it is sense-based, worldly consciousness that feeds them, in contrast to the inner, natural, spiritual consciousness of *Tao*. It is sense-based consciousness that encourages the anthropocentricity of viewing the world in terms of "I", "me" and "mine". Conditioning and habits then entrench the egocentric way in which we see the world, and deeper dimensions of it are lost. And since whatever we view in life is seen through the lens of our *own* desires, our own perspective of reality that is different from others, we become locked in "a maze of error":[170] According to chapter 12 of the *Tao Te Ching/Daodejing*: "The five colours make the eyes blind. The five notes make the ears deaf. The five tastes spoil the palate. Chasing and hunting excite the mind. Goods difficult to get hinder one's progress." Reducing desires will have the opposite effect and produce contentment and fulfilment in life. In short all egoistic involvement in the world is a movement away from *Tao*. Essentially, the ego is self-created: it is not permanent.

For the sage, in contrast, a complete lack of desire permits experience of the stillness within that is *Tao*. It is utter contentment and complete identification with *Tao* and the dynamism of its immanence in the universe. Livia Kohn writes of this state: "The ultimate oneness of existence is at work within and through oneself. By becoming fully one with all, the individual dissolves in the flow of life. He or she attains perfect oneness and harmony with the Tao. At this stage, a new sense of self emerges, a self no longer limited to the ego or defined by the body. The new self is identical with universal principle."[171] The desireless state when all dualities are transcended is the highest state: friends and enemies, good and harm, honour and disgrace, the *Tao Te Ching/Daodejing* tells us, are all the same (chapter 56). In a sensitively written passage Paul Wildish describes the enlightenment and immortality that are the ultimate state of the sage:

> At the moment of death the ego dies with the physical body and becomes pure spirit. Freed from all constraints the liberated consciousness then expands to encompass the universe. This is not a merging with the One as a mere rain droplet is returned to the ocean; one molecule amongst millions of molecules. This is to become the immense consciousness of the ocean itself, which simultaneously feels its waves beating on the shores of a thousand coasts and the pulsating rhythm of myriad organisms moving within its depths. This is the transcendent immortality that the adept seeks.[172]

The release of the self from the world of desire brings about the highest gain of all.

5

Taoism in Imperial China

With the end of the Chou/Zhou dynasty China passed into its imperial phase; kings became emperors and, apart from a few periods during its long history, imperial China lasted until the twentieth century. Minor feudal states of the Chou/Zhou had been increasingly absorbed by the more powerful states. Then the remaining powerful feudal lords fought over each other's dominions. By 221 BCE only one was left in power, the Ch'in/Qin which, in less than two decades, had unified all China into an empire. Imperial China is divided into three phases, Early, Middle and Late. Taking the Early period first, it is divided into four dynasties, the Ch'in/Qin, the Han, and the brief dynasties of the Hsin/Xin and Chin/Jin. Interspersed with and immediately following these dynasties are periods when the empire was disunited into a number of kingdoms or independent dynasties. The following chronological table should help to clarify these points, as well as indicating the main characteristics of each dynasty for the purposes of the present chapter. Let us just concentrate first on the Early period of imperial China.

Imperial China: Early period

Ch'in/Qin dynasty	*3rd century BCE (221–206 BCE)* Beginning of China's first empire China's first Emperor Ch'in Shih Huang-ti/Qinshi Huangdi (221–210 BCE) Centralized, bureaucratic government based on the precepts of the Legalists Building of the Great Wall of China Burning of books (213 BCE)
Han dynasty	*3rd century BCE–3rd century CE (206 BCE–220 CE)*
Former (Western) Han	*3rd century BCE–1st century CE (206 BCE–9 CE)* 3rd century BCE: beginnings of *fang-shih/fangshi* influence

129

2nd century BCE: Confucianism becomes the orthodox state doctrine
2nd century BCE: introduction of competitive examinations for government posts
2nd century BCE: Emperor Wu (140–86 BCE)
2nd century BCE: Huang-Lao Taoism
2nd century BCE: the *Huai-nan-tzu/Huainanzi*

Hsin/Xin dynasty — *1st century (9–23 CE)*
Later (Eastern) Han — *1st–3rd centuries CE (25–220)*
1st century: Buddhism introduced to China
1st century: Lao-tzu/Laozi deified
2nd century: *Scripture of Great Peace*
2nd century: Chang Tao-Ling/Zhang Daoling and Five Bushels of Rice Taoism
2nd century: the Chang/Zhang brothers and Way of Great Peace Taoism
2nd century: the Yellow Turbans rebellion

Then follows a period of division and disunity with the:

Three Kingdoms — *3rd century (220–280)*
Wei (220–64) Shu (Han) (221–63) and Wu (222–80) kingdoms
Celestial Masters school of Taoism
Rise of Neo-Taoism

The period of the Three Kingdoms was followed by a short dynasty:

Chin/Jin dynasty — *3rd–4th centuries (280–316)*

In 316 the Chin/Jin dynasty survived only in the South while the North came under the power of non-Chinese invaders. A series of dynasties arose in the succeeding years, generally known as the Six Dynasties period:

The Six Dynasties — *4th–6th centuries (316–581)*
Separation of Chinese states

Southern dynasties
(Chinese)
Western Chin/Jin 265–317: Ko Hung's *Pao-p'u-tzu/Baopuzi*
Eastern Chin/Jin 317–420: Shang-ch'ing/Shangqing Taoism; Ling-pao/Lingbao Taoism
Liu Sung/Liu Song 420–79: Lu Hsiu-ching/Lu Xiujing's first collection of Taoist scriptures
Southern Ch'i/Qi 479–502

                        Liang 502–57
                        Ch'en/Chen 557–87
                        Growth of Buddhism
                        Growth of Taoism

| **Northern dynasties** (non-Chinese) | **Northern Wei** 386–534: K'ou Ch'ien-chih/Kou Qianzhi begins new, reformed Celestial Masters Taoism, later is invested as Celestial Master by the emperor. Taoism spreads in the north. **Eastern Wei** 534–43 **Western Wei** 535–54 **Northern Ch'i/Qi** 550–77 **Northern Chou/Zhou** 577–81 |

The Ch'in/Qin dynasty

Trends under way in the Chou/Zhou and entrenched at the beginning of the Ch'in/Qin dynasty brought about a period of colossal change in Chinese life, a change that was to have an impact on the religious beliefs and practices. The old proliferation of feudal seignories ceased to exist and, instead, large principalities were set up, which were then subdivided into counties. It was in the new districts that the formal ceremony of religion was conducted, not in the old clan territories. As a result, the general populace was left without any formal participation in the imperial religious ceremony. It was inevitable that this new age brought about an increasing division between the wealthy with their organized, state religion, and the ordinary folk with their more colourful practices. In Shang and Chou/Zhou times, the peasants had had their religious ceremony meticulously undertaken on their behalf, but were observers. In Ch'in/Qin times, they became completely isolated from it. No wonder, then, that the more superstitious and shamanist practices of the past became more deeply rooted at a time when the closer knit feudal system had ended. In all, the more stable societal basis of family and clan was seriously undermined.

There were other important changes in societal life, too. In Maspero's words: "The increase of the population, the disappearance of cultivation by clearing and its replacement by irrigated fields, the invention of the drawn plow, the discovery of iron-working, the extension of the territory on all sides (especially its enormous expansion southward), as well as its growing links with the civilizations of the West and the development of commerce, all combined to transform the old society from top to bottom."[1] Then, too, the old feudal system was replaced by a draconian bureaucracy. Bureaucratic militarization, policing, taxation and standardization replaced the old feudal ethos. But on the positive side, weights and measures were standardized throughout the empire, as was the coinage and the Chinese characters that provided its system of writing. It is in the Ch'in/Qin dynasty that the Great Wall of China was built, not completely from scratch since many sections built previously by former independent states were simply linked together. Yet, the size of the undertaking, set up to ensure secure boundaries between China and the "barbarians", exemplifies well the burden of a powerful ruler on an oppressed people.[2] It is to Ch'in/Qin times, too, that the huge "terracotta army" belongs. Approximately eight thousand life-size soldiers – each with a different facial expression – were discovered in the tomb built for the first emperor of the dynasty.

The instigator of all these changes, and the first Emperor of the Ch'in/Qin, was Ch'in Shih Huang-ti/Qinshi Huangdi. The name Huang-ti/Huangdi was a shift from the old word "king" (*wang*) to the more powerful one of "emperor" (*huang-ti/huangdi*). Huang-ti/Huangdi was also the name of the legendary Yellow Emperor. By adding such a title, the Emperor probably hoped to appropriate some of the Yellow Emperor's divine status and prestige. Indeed, Ch'in Shih Huang-ti/Qinshi Huangdi's prestige was sufficient to hand down his name to posterity as the name of the empire – China.[3] He was a brutal and ruthless emperor, though an efficient one. Seeking to obliterate any rival philosophies from his own Legalist position, he ordered the burning of all books, writings and historical texts that did not conform to the imperial archives, and had any person seeking to hide such material put to death. It was the Confucian texts that particularly suffered here. However, since the *Classics* were known by heart, the burning of the books did not necessarily affect their transmission, though it was not until the Han dynasty that they could re-emerge. Some texts nevertheless survived, and texts connected with immortality were especially protected by the Emperor.

Fang-shih/fangshi adepts – of whom, more below – were prominent at his court with the aim of assisting the Emperor in becoming immortal. He was therefore supportive of alchemical practices carried out by the precursors of religious Taoism, the *fang-shih/fangshi*, but was to die on one of his many tours of his empire without immortality. *Fang-shih/fangshi* influence extended into the early Han period, as we shall see. The Legalist outlook was a harsh one. It was based on a strict enforcement of governing rules and regulations, with appropriate rewards and punishments for those that obeyed and transgressed its principles respectively. As Schirokauer points out, the Ch'in/Qin had a reputation for making people's lives so miserable in peace time that they were only too happy to go to war![4] Legalism underpinned and accompanied such harsh policies. Fortunately, it was a short dynasty of less than two decades.

The Han dynasty

With the Han dynasty we come to the end of the classical period in Chinese religion and philosophy. The Han dynasty spanned nearly four hundred years except for a short spell in the very early years of the first century CE, when Wang Mang interrupted the dynasty with his own short-lived Hsin/Xin rule. The period before this interregnum is known as the *Former* or *Western Han*, because the capital of the empire was in the West, and the period following it the *Later* or *Eastern Han*, since the capital was shifted to the East. The Han dynasty brought a number of important changes, especially since the Legalism of the Ch'in/Qin fell from favour and Confucianism rose to the fore. The most notable Han emperor was Wu (140–86 BCE), who ruled for nearly half a century. Although despotic, he set up an imperial university whose student numbers increased dramatically under the Later Han. One of his predecessors had also established an examination system for those chosen for government posts. Such a measure was to become important in later practice. It was Confucian texts that served as the basis of all learning, for Wu was a great patron of Confucianism, though not without encouraging aspects of Legalism and, also, a good deal of Taoism. Except for a few breaks, Confucianism was to become and remain the official doctrine of the empire down to the last century, and it is to Han times that it owes this legacy.

The seeds of religious Taoism were certainly sprouting under the Han. There was a considerable growth in what we might term magico-religious expression at the popular level – a legacy of the ancient shamanic and magical practices. Practitioners of these appealed to the continuing beliefs in magic and miracles, in the ability to see future events, and the superstitions that had been part of the Chinese psyche for generations. Martin Palmer comments:

> It is one of the most remarkable things about the Early Han period that it is in this era that we find the first major and popular manifestations of divination at a folk level, of physiognomy, of *feng shui* (geomancy) and other such practices. It is as if there were a great longing to know and to be in touch with the spiritual world. It is no exaggeration to say that during the period 208 BC to the end of the first century AD, there was a virtual explosion in religious practices, beliefs, gods, deities, magic, divination and the like.[5]

But it is likely, too, that some of these beliefs were still courted by a few intellectuals.[6] For the Han was a period of considerable eclecticism, and it is such eclecticism that blurs the boundaries of embryonic Taoism as much as Confucianism. As Creel commented concerning Confucianism: "It had triumphed, but at the cost of such transformation that one wonders whether it can still properly be called Confucianism."[7] It might have been the state doctrine, but a good many religious practices supporting belief in magic, miracles and the like, were added to Confucianism from the more popular beliefs of the time. Syncretism was also encouraged by the powerful Emperor Wu. He was fascinated with the supernatural and the spiritual beings that inhabited its realm, and hoped that the Taoists would procure the secret of immortality for him. The *fang-shih/fangshi*, especially, continued to promise the acquisition of wealth and immortality through their alchemical practices. The spirit of the time, then, was one of continuing belief in supernatural forces and varied alchemical praxis – with which Taoism was to be increasingly concerned – against a backdrop of Confucian political supremacy. As Needham commented: "So great was the heterodoxy of Taoism that even today there is apparently no good history of it after the period of the philosophers."[8]

The shared philosophies of the age included a view of the universe as an orderly, interconnected whole that was self-originating and self-generating. Each entity within it was an intimate part of the totality of the cosmos, whether that part was a physical and natural entity or a supernatural one. The interrelation of the many parts necessitated their interdependence. Energy, *ch'i/qi*, pulsated through the universe and gave rhythm and life to it, and the theories of *yin* and *yang* and the Five Agents, explored in Chou/Zhou times, explained the coming into being and passing away of all matter. No divine being needed to be postulated to explain the universe; it existed through its own natural processes. Concomitant with these theories, the acceptance of the Five Agents explained the qualities any existing entities possessed: they were the fundamental categories of reality, accounting for all things. The whole process of *yin* and *yang* and creation and destruction were felt to be reflected in the rise and fall of dynasties, of power, of seasons – in the natural rhythms of all life.

Thus, the ancient magico-religious expressions, and respect for, and awe of, nature, gained greater systematization from the Warring States period of the Chou/Zhou dynasty through the Ch'in/Qin and Han periods. Such trends, and the merging of ideas of nature with theories of the function of *ch'i/qi*, *yin* and *yang* and the Five Agents resulted in a developed philosophy of nature by the dawn of the common era.[9] Tomb manuscripts on wood, bamboo and silk from the Warring States, Ch'in/Qin and Early Han periods suggest that such beliefs pervaded the whole of society, not just the literati and court circles,[10] and that there was a thriving interest in the occult, ritual divination, magic, astrology, medicine, the planets, physiognomy, exorcism, dietetics, and demonology. As Harper comments: "For books on subjects related to natural philosophy and the occult to occur with such regularity in tombs is an indication of the ubiquity of this type of literature in their libraries."[11]

Fang-shih/fangshi

From the third century BCE until about the fifth century CE China witnessed the presence of a group of diverse men known as *fang-shih/fangshi*. They practised divination, medicine and magic in their early history and, later, astronomy, geomancy and music. Some were specialists in practices promoting longevity and immortality – two areas of specialism of particular interest to the court and higher classes. An excellent study of *fang-shih/fangshi* has been undertaken by Kenneth DeWoskin, who provides both a historical background to the group and, also, extremely interesting translations of biographies of *fang-shih/fangshi*.[12] They seem to have originated in Chou/Zhou times as rather unorthodox practitioners, but it is in the Han down to the Six Dynasties period that they really flourished, when they branched out into more scientific areas such as calendrics, pharmacology, biology, metallurgy and the like.[13] Some gained status at court as men of learning – as much for their science as for their knowledge of astrology, and their familiarity with magic, exorcism and the world of spirits and immortals. These more supernatural practices declined as the influence of the *fang-shih/fangshi* waxed in higher circles, though they could also be used at court as entertainers in magic. Their individual specialisms in many skills in Han times meant that their collective knowledge was very broad. Many *fang-shih/fangshi* were famous enough to have acquired the hagiographic state of immortality. Immortality was something that the emperors, especially, hoped to achieve, and this made the *fang-shih/fangshi* useful tools in that pursuit.

One such important skill of the *fang-shih/fangshi* lay in the ability to read omens for the future, to tell the way events would go. Here we see the continuing influence, though of a more subtle kind, of divination. De Woskin writes:

Concern with the future was obsessive, and the fang-shih were the pollsters of the day, enumerators who trained their eyes on heaven and earth, because heaven was understood to be the ultimate source of political authority. Heaven marked the passing of time for mankind in a predictable way. Heaven was as well the constant judge of human action, making signs of favor or disfavor in intelligible if not directly obvious ways. The signs were varied and numerous, subject to interpretation. In their role as advisors, fang-shih and others involved in divination and omen interpretation at court assured correct action and assured continuation of rule.[14]

Underlying such belief was, again, the perception of the universe as an interrelated Heaven and Earth. Harmony and rhythm were the norm of the universe and needed to be maintained in all aspects of life, but especially in that delicate balance between Heaven, the emperor who ruled by the Mandate of Heaven, and the subjects of the empire. The balances and rhythms of *yin* and *yang* and the explanation of all things through the Five Agents were accepted by *fang-shih* but often reinterpreted. *Yin* and *yang* and the Five Agents were particularly involved in the biological interpretation of the human body, which was seen as a microcosm that reflected the macrocosm of the universe. The same interactive energies charged both, and it was essential that the energies of the human body were harmonized with the external, but interrelated, cosmos. The *I Ching/Yijing* remained one of the most important means of divination. The rise of *fang-shih/fangshi* coincided with the beginning of the Han dynasty when everything possible was done to give legitimacy to the new Han rule. The correlation of macrocosmic Heaven with microcosmic Earth was reflected in the correlation between aspects of the cosmos and the state bureaucracy. Attempts were made to set up bureaucratic units that corresponded with aspects of the human body, directions of space and heavenly constellations, for example.

Fang-shih/fangshi are important because they are connected with the older shamanism that we saw in Shang times, though they lacked the ecstatic practices of their forebears. Later, we shall see some of the influences of *fang-shih/fangshi* on Taoism, not only in practices, but also in the continuing belief in immortality of the physical self. They were, in short, the precursors of Taoists. Robinet commented: "The affinity between the subjects studied by the *fangshi* and those of interest to the Taoists was so great and lasted for so long that the distinction between these thinkers and the Taoists is not easy to make – to the point that many treatises on geomancy and divination that derive from *fangshi* practices have been incorporated into the *Daozang*, the Taoist canon."[15] Interest in immortals, in longevity and alchemy, in particular, are common to both Taoism and the *fang-shih/fangshi*.

What the phenomenon of *fang-shih/fangshi* also implies is that there must have been a good deal of such activity amongst the poorer class. As noted before, there was a considerable gap between the official religion of the state and the more localized religion of the general populace. Not being part of the state religion, such practices would have been regarded as heterodox, to say the least, and this is where formative religious Taoism had its appeal. Local shrines were multiple, and supplied the means for the ordinary folk to propitiate the gods and local spirits for help. Early Chinese historians have recorded for posterity the inscriptions that were engraved on shrine stones.[16] At the level of the ordinary peasant the needs for rain, for stable crops, and a healthy family, were expressed by the *fang-shih/fangshi* by the magical use of talismanic scripts and symbols – both features that were to characterize later Taoism. *Fang-shih/fangshi* evolved into the *tao-shih/daoshi*, "specialists of *Tao*", who became part of the stock of clientele in religious Taoism.

Religious Taoism really began in Later Han times amidst the backdrop of all that has been described so far. Its overriding aim was the achievement of immortality, and a variety of means were adopted to secure this. The search for means to immortality had been a feature of some strands of Chou/Zhou times, but it was clear that, whatever methods adopted to achieve it, immortality still eluded its protagonists. The Han answer came from *fang-shih/fangshi* who posited the development in the self of an immortal, invisible "embryo". Essentially, this indestructible spirit soul had to be cultivated and its growth nourished by all sorts of practices – meditation, drugs, breathing exercises, sexual practices, trance, gymnastics, special diets, and bodily postures. If such an embryo could be nourished and developed, when death occurred, it would simply rise from the body as the true self, metamorphosed like the butterfly that emerges from the chrysalis. Instead of death, a wonderful life with other immortals would await the soul, or it would have the freedom to wander the universe. In the Han dynasty the practice of alchemy became important for producing the elixirs that could promote longevity and immortality, and in an inner sense could help nourish the spirit embryo that would ensure immortality. The whole realm of alchemical practices that so attracted Taoism is important enough to need separate treatment in chapter 6. Here, it needs to be noted how Han times encouraged alchemical practices. It was the *fang-shih/fangshi*, especially, who united the many different ideas of alchemy, immortality, the Five Agents, *yin* and *yang*, and the nourishing of a spirit embryo into a primitive religious Taoism.

Huang-Lao Taoism

A number of other movements of the Han period also require mention as part of the building blocks in the development of Taoism. The Huang-Lao school of the second century BCE is one, for it was another factor that led to the emergence of religious Taoism. It was the main school of Taoism in its time.[17] Originating in eastern China, it spread widely amongst political and learned circles. The Huang-Lao school was nearer to the precepts of Lao-tzu/Laozi and Chuang-tzu/Zhuangzi than the magico-religious expressions of the likes of the *fang-shih/fangshi*, though it was Lao-tzu/Laozi who was the main influence on the school. The name of the school may be derived from Huang-Lao Chün/Huanglaojun, the name given to the deified Lao-tzu/Laozi.[18] On the other hand, it may be a composite of Huang-ti/Huangdi, the Yellow Emperor, and Lao-tzu/Laozi. Both the Yellow Emperor and Lao-tzu/Laozi epitomized the very best in government praxis, the former because he ruled in a Golden Age, and the latter because much of his terse *Tao Te Ching/Daodejing* advocated non-interference of the state in ordinary life, and simplicity of rule. Huang-Lao Taoism was a religious messianic movement with a concern also for longevity. Seidel and Strickmann wrote of the adherents of the movement, "their ensemble of teachings concerning both ideal government and practices for prolonging life continued to evoke considerable interest and is perhaps the earliest truly Taoist movement of which there is clear historical evidence".[19]

The Huai-nan-tzu/Huainanzi

Influenced by Huang-Lao Taoism and reflecting the eclectic spirit of the times was the *Huai-nan-tzu/Huainanzi*. It was a very important text that came together through the efforts of Liu An, the Prince or minor King of Huai-nan. His dates are approximately 179–122 BCE, and he was the grandson of Liu Pang/Liu Bang, the founder of the Han dynasty. The text consists of twenty-one essays, each a chapter, and was presented to Emperor Wu in 139 BCE. Three major works were written under the auspices of Liu An, but it is only the *Huai-nan-tzu/Huainanzi* that has survived. Of the three, this is the "Inner Book" and is more Taoist in character. The *Huai-nan-tzu/Huainanzi* covers a wide variety of topics – myth, government praxis, philosophy, military concerns, astronomy, cosmology, history, geography, society. In Roth's words: "The breadth of these topics indicates that the compilers of the book were attempting to create a comprehensive work that would present their understanding of the nature and functioning of the universe and all the phenomena that exist within it."[20] The text seems to have been influenced by the *Tao Te Ching/Daodejing*: its metaphysics project the beginnings of reality beyond all form or potential for it, rather as the *Tao Te Ching/Daodejing* projects ultimate Reality beyond even One: "There was a beginning. There was a time before that beginning. There was a time before the time which was before the beginning. There was being. There was non-being. There was a time before that non-being. There was a time before the time which was before that non-being."[21] The eclectic nature of the text draws on theories of *yin* and *yang* and the Five Agents, Confucian, Legalist, Taoist and Huang-Lao thought. Charles Le Blanc says of the work: "We may characterize the basic intent of the *Huai nan tzu* as a political utopianism and the work as a handbook for the instruction of an enlightened ruler and his court".[22]

So did Liu An write the text? Since he gathered together eminent specialists at his court, it is likely that he did not. But authorship is disputed and arguments for stylistic diversity on the one hand suggest many authors, while consistency in editing on the other suggests unitary authorship. Perhaps it is the syncretistic ideas that create the former, as Roth suggests.[23] He favours multiple authors, but a single editor.[24] He writes: "The *Huai-nan Tzu* is not simply an incoherent string of unrelated essays, nor is it the creation of Liu An alone. Its philosophical diversity is more the result of early-Han Taoist syncretism than random eclecticism. There is simply too much diversity in style and subject matter for the work to have been the product of one hand. There is, however, a definite organization to the book that would indicate that there must have been an overall directing and editing force."[25] The texts we have today are the result of numerous changes so that an authentic text is impossible to retrieve. They were also transmitted in two very different textual lines from Han times with a confusing composite edition at a later date.[26] Falling out of favour with the Emperor in 122 BCE, perhaps because of an antipathy to Huang-Lao Taoism at court, Liu An is believed to have committed suicide. Traditionally, it is believed he ascended to the Heavens as a Taoist immortal.

Another major factor in the origins of religious Taoism was the infiltration of Buddhism in China at the end of the Han. Buddhism had much to offer an oppressed people, with a doctrine of compassion, salvation for all, and its deified beings who vowed to help all people on the path to salvation. Its doctrine of *karmic* justice and concept of rebirth also helped to make sense of the injustices of life. Buddhism entered China through the trade routes, the earliest evidence of its presence being a Buddhist community at the court of the King of Ch'u/Chu.[27] A text called the *Hua-hu Ching/Huahujing*, "Scripture of the Conversion of the Barbarians", in 166 CE claimed that Lao-tzu/Laozi had visited the lands in the West as the Buddha for the purpose of converting the "barbarians".

As the Han dynasty declined, the adverse conditions and misery of the populace increased. Organized, institutionalized religious Taoism grew out of the vicissitudes of life at the time. It was also a reaction against political and Legalist thought. Individuals and groups in society had no personalized religion to combat such difficult times. It was the need for a warmth of religious experience, in contrast to the arid bureaucracy of the Confucians and Legalists, which created the seeds that would develop into a more organized religious Taoism rooted in the lives of ordinary people.

Five Bushels of Rice Taoism: the beginnings of Celestial Masters Taoism

The beginnings of a truly organized religious Taoism occurred in the early second century CE, in north-west China. Lao-tzu/Laozi was believed to have appeared to a Taoist at his mountain retreat. He was called Chang Lin/Zhang Lin, later to be called Chang Tao-ling/Zhang Daoling. Chang Tao-ling/Zhang Daoling was said to have had magical powers, and was able to cure diseases and sickness. The movement he began was, thus, a healing cult. Lao-tzu/Laozi told Chang Tao-ling/Zhang Daoling that he was to become a "Celestial" or "Heavenly Master", a *T'ien-shih/Tianshi*. The Mandate of Heaven had been withdrawn from the Han, and the people needed to be delivered from the evil of the dynasty. Such an injunction, however, was probably not interpreted as a call to overthrow the Han – despite the militaristic nature of the priest-soldiers of the movement – but as one to restore a more religious and spiritual rule. Adherents of the sect paid an annual tax of five bushels of rice, hence the sect became known as Five Bushels of Rice Taoism. Needless to say, Lao-tzu/Laozi, the "Great Lord on High" (T'ai-shang Lao-chün/Taishang Laojun), the source of the revelation to Chang Tao-ling/Zhang Daoling, became the chief deity of the sect. So Chang Tao-ling/Zhang Daoling became head priest of the first real Taoist organized religion characterized by a priesthood, rituals, ceremonies and scriptures. The movement was crucial for the development of Taoism, not least in the person of its leader. The very term "Celestial Master" was indicative of the powers Chang Tao-ling/Zhang Daoling had in Heaven, including the ability to transfer those powers for the purpose of those on Earth.

As to practices, the Five Bushels of Rice sect turned against animal sacrifices, though they continued to use cooked vegetable offerings in their worship of spirits. The healing of illnesses and the confession of sins were important features of the sect from the beginning. Official registers were kept of the progress made by adherents. Members of the sect meditated on their sins in a "quiet room", then had their sins written down. These written confessions were offered to the "Three Officials", "Three Rulers" or "Three Agents". These three were the forces that ruled Heaven, Earth, and the Waters beneath the Earth. Each had his own appropriate festival, and each festival was a time of reckoning of the good and evil deeds done by each mortal. So people took the record of their sins to the tops of mountains to the ruler of Heaven, buried them in the ground for the ruler of Earth, and immersed them in rivers for expiation from the ruler of Water. Such ritual later became embodied in the Festival of the Three Agents, a festival that was universally accepted in China in the third and fourth centuries. As well as such communal confessions of sins, there were also communal ceremonies to mark the beginnings of the seasons in festivals that were bequeathed to modern Taoism. Solstices and equinoxes were also marked by festivals.

Chang Tao-ling/Zhang Daoling was reputed to be a great exorcist, and talismans for such, and for healing, are still used today.[28] Talismanic water healed the sick. A talismanic script bearing the names of spirits and deities was burnt and its ashes mixed with water, thus passing the potency of the divine beings into the water. Once drunk or sprinkled on a sick person, the divine power would ward off the evil spirits that caused ill health.[29] The use of talismans was to remain a prevalent feature of the Taoist religion. Similar practices included the ingesting of elixirs to promote longevity. The sect also adopted the chanting of scriptures and incantations, but it was as a healing cult that it gained popularity. Sickness was looked on as a punishment for sins committed in the past: prisons, therefore, were full of sick people reflecting on their sins, not with those who had committed societal offences – their sins would catch them up later in some form of illness.

Through missionary activity the sect's influence spread considerably, its numbers absorbing many other Taoist adherents. Such was Chang Tao-ling/Zhang Daoling's organization that the foundations of a theocratic state were well under way. It was Chang Lu/Zhang Lu, the grandson of Chang Tao-ling/Zhang Daoling, who consolidated his grandfather's work. He appointed "libationers" to head the twenty-four districts into which he divided the fully established theocratic "state". They were responsible for the religious welfare of the people, but were also socially and politically active. The weakened Han dynasty had little control over this particular, rather secluded, area around Hanchung/Hanzhong. When the Han fell, and the Three Kingdoms emerged, Chang Lu/Zhang Lu had the sense to submit to the powerful military rule of the Wei general and was greatly rewarded for doing so. It was a strategic act that allowed the school to flourish. So when the Han dynasty came to an end, the successors of Chang Tao-ling/Zhang Daoling became titled at the court of the kingdom of Wei. Henceforth, Lao-tzu/Laozi's representative on Earth was recognized as Chang Tao-ling/Zhang Daoling and, thereafter, his hereditary successors were to be called officially Celestial Masters, in charge of what became known as the Central Orthodox School of Taoism, Way of Orthodox Unity (Cheng-i Meng-wei Tao/Zhengyi Mengweidao) or Celestial Masters Taoism. The impact of Chang Tao-ling/Zhang Daoling and the resulting rise of Taoism as a religious organization was such that royal sacrifices began officially to Lao-tzu/Laozi in 165. We shall need to look at this school in more detail below, for it was an important part of the growth of religious Taoism, of which Chang Tao-ling/Zhang Daoling is usually regarded as the founder: *institutional* Taoism began with him. The Celestial Masters school was to become the major Taoist school to the present day.

Way of Great Peace Taoism: the Yellow Turbans

Another, very similar, Taoist movement of interest was *Way of Great Peace Taoism* or T'ai-p'ing Tao/Taipingdao, of the second century CE, in eastern China. It was a considerable messianic movement that grew out of the misery of the turbulent political and military instability of the time. To those disenchanted with poverty and hardship, the movement offered return to a Golden Age and security in a future paradise. It was founded by Chang Chüeh/Zhang Jue and his two brothers, Chang Liang/Zhang Liang and Chang Pao/Zhang Bao, who claimed to represent Heaven, Earth and humankind – indicative of the entire universe. Perhaps the three were related to the Changs/Zhangs of the West.[30] Faith healing accompanied by confession and repentance of sins were the major practices of this Taoist movement, as well as meditation and the chanting of sacred texts. Chang Chüeh/Zhang Jue became the "Heavenly General" of an intense missionary and charismatic religious movement, which attracted large public gatherings in many areas of eastern China. As in Chang Lu/Zhang Lu's movement in the West, adherents were organized into districts in a theocratic state with a distinct military character. Huang-Lao became the major deity of the movement and the *Tao Te Ching/Daodejing* the major scripture. A Taoist priesthood was established for the movement in conjunction with its missionary activities. The movement incorporated already existing Taoist beliefs – the search for means to longevity, and breathing, dietetics and fasting to promote it. The Five Agents explained the mechanics of life, and sexual practices were added to enhance longevity.

Chang Chüeh/Zhang Jue's influence covered nearly two-thirds of China, each of the thirty-six districts therein being headed by a kind of "general". Each controlled about ten thousand people, but minor "generals" existed to look after lesser numbers of six to eight thousand. Such numbers give us a good idea of the extent and popularity of the movement. Smaller units also facilitated administration of the adherents. The success of the three brothers may have had a good deal to do with the fact that the ideas of their movement were consonant with those of other Taoists. According to Maspero: "Taoism was so widespread in all classes of Chinese society in the second century A.D. that the sudden expansion of the Yellow Turbans sect seems to me to have been due less to the conversion of non-Taoist outsiders than to the attraction which the new sect exerted upon numerous Taoists".[31] The sheer size of the gatherings, coupled with the politically activist nature of the movement, alarmed the Han rulers, who set out to suppress it. The adherents of the movement chose to wear yellow turbans as a defiant symbol against the Han. The colour symbolizing the Han was blue/green. Yellow was the colour associated with Earth, the Yellow Emperor, and a very different Golden Age type of rulership. Their yellow turbans were, thus, tantamount to heralding an overthrow of Han rule. They rose in rebellion in 184 CE and their sheer numbers and geographical spread gave the Han a hard time in overcoming them.

The Scripture of Great Peace

The similarities between the movements founded by Chang Tao-ling/Zhang Daoling in the West and the Chang/Zhang brothers in the East are probably accounted for by the fact that both drew on the same Taoist *Scripture of Great Peace*, the *T'ai-p'ing Ching/Taipingjing*. This was a messianic text that told of a Celestial Master who would bring peace. It was presented to the emperor in the first half of the second century and became an influential scripture that led to a number of new Taoist movements. The *T'ai-ping Ching/Taipingjing* dates in part to Han times, or even before, and was to be extended with different titles in later centuries. It is important because it was the earliest Taoist scripture. Its main emphases were on the peace and harmony of a paradisical world that could be brought about by moral living of all people, and of a Celestial Master that would be sent to inaugurate such a peace in all the world. Medicinal herbs and plants were thought to be of assistance in promoting the well-balanced person, as well as acupuncture, and the burning of dried leaves of a special plant close to the skin. For harmony to ensue, the ruler needed to be a sage, and the wise needed to share their spirituality and wisdom with others. The rich should share with the poor. Only then could *Tao* be experienced in all aspects of life, and peace reign in the world. The *T'ai-ping Ching/Taipingjing* also has sections on meditation and immortality. Thus, Pas rightly points out that it is important because, on the one hand it reaches back to the older philosophical Taoism and, on the other, it pre-empts later developments in Taoism. He writes: "Classical ideas are the yin-yang structure of the universe and the triad of heaven, earth and man. But above all, it is the Tao that controls all changes in the universe. This universe, as macrocosm, is inherent in human beings and society, the microcosm. Great Peace (and Equality) can only be achieved if these two worlds interact through the mediation of an enlightened and virtuous ruler."[32] Clearly, the ancient shamanistic thought of the interaction and interdependence of the material and spiritual worlds is still evident in formative Taoism. Given the sacred nature of the *T'ai-ping Ching/Taipingjing* – believed to be a gift from the ruler of Heaven – it had immense talismanic power.

The Yellow Turban uprising quickened the demise of the Han dynasty, and other rebellions were to follow. The generals that were engaged in crushing the Yellow Turbans themselves turned on the Han. The closing years of the dynasty were immensely turbulent, though they were to end an important era in Chinese history. In Schirokauer's words: "What was coming to an end was more than a political dynasty – an entire epoch of Chinese civilization was drawing to a close. The end of the Han was one of the great watersheds in the history of Chinese civilization."[33] Under the Han, China had become a great imperial power, one to compare with imperial Rome.

The period of the Three Kingdoms

After the fall of the Han three generals emerged as contenders to the empire. However, none was powerful enough to control the others so a tripartite system emerged with three kingdoms, one in the North, one in the south-east and one in the south-west – hence the name given to the period, the Three Kingdoms. Wei ruled the North and north-west, Wu ruled the South and south-east and Han the south-west. Han considered himself the legitimate successor of the Han, hence the name, to which he had changed from Shu. It will be mainly the Taoist movements that need to be mentioned in the context of this particular period of Chinese history.

Consolidation of the Celestial Masters school

It is with the rise of the Celestial Masters school of Taoism, and its widespread popularity, that we first find a fully formulated and well-organized, if ongoing and expanding, expression of Taoism. It is the Celestial Masters school, too, that provides us with the earliest texts of religious Taoism. The origins of the school lay in the Five Bushels of Rice sect that emerged towards the end of the Han dynasty, as was seen above. It is perhaps with some justification that many scholars see the rise of this school as the proper beginnings of religious Taoism. One reason for seeing the Celestial Masters school as the real foundation of religious Taoism is its meticulous organization of followers and their practices. Male and female priests acted as intermediaries between the people and the many spirits of the "other side". Regions were organized into religious districts to facilitate this. It was an attempt at a systematization that the looser fringe adherents of Taoism could hardly withstand, and many became absorbed into the developing Celestial Masters school. Where absorption proved difficult, the school capitulated to include local gods like those of the earth and hearth into its own pantheon of deities. Characteristically Chinese, the spirit world was still viewed as a hierarchy that matched its earthly counterpart in the organization of the sect, but the deities and spirits were now formulated into an *official* hierarchy. While there were vestiges of shamanistic practices in the school, the Celestial Masters did not approve of the cults of the ordinary people, and sought to get rid of the non-official gods and spirits, and the host of charlatans who plied their trade in all kinds of ways. However, despite being outspoken against popular religion, the Celestial Masters adepts became experts at exorcising the hosts of demons as the shamans had done, though they sought to dissociate themselves with any such sorcerers, *wu*. Thus, despite overt antagonism to popular beliefs, there was much in the official tenets and practices of the school that was rooted in popular belief itself. But since the school gained state recognition, it had to align itself with state dissociation from the practices of the general populace. The stellar, celestial deities of the Celestial Masters school were believed to be reflected in the human body, and were very different from the mundane, terrestrial deities.[34] There were, then, both differences and similarities in the beliefs and practices between the Celestial Masters school and popular religion. No doubt it was the more deeply embedded beliefs – the need for long life, the reverence for ancestors, divination, belief in miracles, exorcism for example – that were common to both.

The sect established a meritocracy between lay people, libationers and chief libationers. The merit of officials and of lay people was determined three times in the year. Regulation of merit guarded the carefully graded hierarchy. From childhood to adulthood, increasing "registers" of spirits and immortals, who would assist in the well-being of the individual, were divulged. The more registers an individual obtained, the higher his or her rank in the sect. Each register gave control over specific deities and spirits, so others outside the sect were contracted out, and adherents were forbidden to worship them. This is what Orthodox Unity, the later name of the school, implied – a unity of specific spirits and gods, and forswearing of any not in the registers. As part of the systematic and bureaucratic organization of the sect, registers of members were kept along with a record of their merits and their status. For effective requests to the gods, these records of good and evil deeds had to be thoroughly accurate and updated regularly, for the gods kept their own records, and a mismatch between them would result in denial of requests by the gods. The gods kept their eye on all people; thus, the local earth, house and hearth gods were retained to fulfil such a role. Those individuals found to be wanting in good behaviour were expected to reflect on their sins. Sickness, especially, as we have seen, was regarded as divine punishment of sins. Moral behaviour resulted in a lengthening of life, sin in a shortening of it. Such moral behaviour was prescriptively clarified, especially through allegorized interpretation of the *Tao Te Ching/Daodejing*, but included a good deal of Confucian values.

The talismanic registers that were to influence Taoism down the centuries were very important.[35] When kings gave nobles land in feudal China, they also gave them a list of people for whom they were responsible, but who were their subordinates. The same principle underlies the registers of the Celestial Masters school. Chang Tao-ling/Zhang Daoling entered into a contract with Lao-tzu/Laozi and was given control over certain deities and spirits – these latter then entered into the unity of the Celestial Masters sect. In particular, the three divine forces of Heaven, Earth and Water came into the unity of the school. A circular diagram composed of eight points of the compass, eight trigrams and divisions of calendrical and cosmic energies, encompassed the different "essences" or *fu* of the cosmos.[36] It is this diagram that libationers would have received. Each libationer was matched to a particular *fu*, and this became his or her protective essence and that by which he or she wielded authority. Along with the *fu*, the libationer was given a register of the deities and forces associative with his or her personal energy. So the libationer had a talismanic sign, a *fu*, and a register or *lu*. Today, the *fu* are textual, and are recited.[37] *Fu-lu*, then, are "spirit registers" that list the name of official Taoists and their spirits, deities and immortals in Heaven, who would obey them.

Buddhism was also developing in these early centuries of the first millennium, and its influence was felt on the Celestial Masters school in time. Buddhist practices like the circumambulation of shrines and deities and the chanting of texts came to be adopted by the sect, especially the chanting of the *Tao Te Ching/Taodejing*. Buddhism perhaps influenced the sect's belief in ultimate salvation of the soul in immortality. The Celestial Masters' belief in *Tao* as the indescribable origin of all things, spontaneously giving rise to them and immanent in and around them, shows the basic philosophy as that reflected in the *Tao Te Ching/Daodejing*. But a huge pantheon of deities and spirits was added with whom there was a more pragmatic dialogue in terms of divine involvement in human existence.

The practices of the sect crystallized some of the wider Taoist beliefs. A major belief was in rhythmic breathing to encourage the spirit embryo, the nourishment of which, as was seen earlier, enabled the soul to survive death and become immortal. Sexual ceremony in which male and female engaged in a ritual dance before copulation was part of the meticulous ritual that began the birth of the spirit embryo. Major calendrical times like the equinoxes were celebrated with special ceremonies and communal meals, the latter also being characteristic of the main life-cycle events such as birth and death. One very important practice in terms of its later development in Taoism was the ritual involved with the "purity chamber". Robinet described it as a kind of chapel that was meticulously and precisely designed and built, not only publicly, but also in the home. The ritual involved with it was also very precise, for its intent was to communicate with divine powers for the benefit of the adherent.[38] As Robinet pointed out, this ritual is an outline of what was to become accepted Taoist liturgy centuries later.[39] What the ritual also exemplifies is how adept the Celestial Masters school was in delineating ritual down to the last detail.

The Celestial Masters school of Taoism reached its height in the first half of the fifth century, and then lost some of its impetus in competition with other schools. But it survived, and still does so today, with a line of hereditary Masters. In the fourth to fifth centuries K'ou Ch'ien-chih/Kou Qianzhi reformed the movement in the North. He was both a Taoist and a shrewd politician at the time of the Northern Wei dynasty. He claimed that he had had a visitation from the divine Lao-tzu/Laozi who instructed him to embark on reform. In the South, too, another splinter group of Celestial Masters Taoism was begun by Lu Hsiu-ching/Lu Xiujing – of whom we shall hear more later in the context of the Taoist canon – and he, also, reformed some of the practices and teachings of the Celestial Masters school. In the T'ang/Tang dynasty the school moved its centre to Mount Lung-hu/Longhu, and the Celestial Masters school sometimes was referred to by this name. Later, in the Yüan/Yuan dynasty, Khubilai Khan put the thirty-sixth Master in charge of all the Taoist schools in the South, giving him the title by which all future Masters would be known – *chen-jen/zhenren* "perfected being". In 1304 the emperor of the Yüan/Yuan dynasty gave the title *Cheng-i Chiao-chu/Zhengyi Jiaozhu* "Master of Orthodox Unity" to the thirty-eighth Master of the Lung-hu/Longhu school of Taoism, and "Orthodox Unity" became the preferred name for the school from Yüan/Yuan times on. Clearly, the school flourished under the Mongol emperors of the Yüan/Yuan dynasty. In more recent times, ousted by the People's Republic in 1949, the school was forced to move its headquarters to Taiwan.

The Chin/Jin dynasty

Despite the fact that the northern kingdom of Wei was the strongest of the Three Kingdoms, the Wei rulership was internally challenged by the Chin/Jin clan in 265, and in 280 the Chin/Jin succeeded in unifying China once again. But the success was shortlived and in 316 the Chin/Jin had to flee south in the face of non-Chinese invaders of the North. From that time on, until 581, China was divided into two with a succession of dynasties in the North and another succession of dynasties in the South, both independent of each other. Because there was no central controlling power, it was a time when local regions could flourish though it was a time, also, of admixing of ideas. Buddhism, particularly, seemed to fulfil the needs of the people in these decades, but Taoism, too, continued to flourish.

Ko Hung/Ge Hong

In the fourth century the great naturalist and alchemist Ko Hung/Ge Hong gave his literary name Pao-p'u-tzu/Baopuzi, "the Master who embraces simplicity", to a major work with the same title, completing it in 317. While he wrote many books, and possessed a considerable library, his *Pao-p'u-tzu/Baopuzi* gathered together all previous theories concerning immortals and alchemy, as well as discussing some major philosophical tenets of Taoism. Needham described him as "the greatest alchemist in Chinese history".[40] Most accept him as a Taoist, though some have reservations about this, considering his leanings towards, and erudition in, Confucianism.[41] The "outer chapters" or exoteric chapters of the *Pao-p'u-tzu/Baopuzi*, that is to say those dealing with the outward things of life, show Ko Hung/Ge Hong to have accepted Confucian morality and virtue in social and political living. But he seems to have been a Taoist at heart. The "inner chapters" of the *Pao-p'u-tzu/Baopuzi*, the *Nei-p'ien/Neipian*, are the esoteric chapters. They deal with the inner being, and are dedicated to the study of immortals, immortality, the nourishing and lengthening of life, and the means by which this can be brought about – alchemical elixirs, medicines, drugs, breathing exercises, dietetics, sexual practices, and talismans. In his own words: "My *Nei p'ien*, telling of gods and genii, prescriptions and medicines, ghosts and marvels, transformations, maintenance of life, extension of years, exorcising evils, and banishing misfortune, belongs to the Taoist school. My *Wai p'ien*, giving an account of success and failure in human affairs and of good and evil in public affairs, belongs to the Confucian school."[42]

If his outward life displayed deep respect for Confucianism, Ko Hung/Ge Hong's inner spirit was Taoist. In his autobiography he stated: "I confess to being the most miserable of Confucianists,"[43] and "Taoism is lord over all the other schools of thought; the original progenitor of the human ideal and propriety. So much for the question of the differences between it and Confucianism. There can be no interchanging of head and tail; the one is exalted, the other soiled".[44] The dual loyalties caused him to have great respect for the teaching of the ancient Taoist philosophers, but not so far as to exclude societal intercourse as they had done. He was sufficiently Confucian to see the relevance of societal interaction, but of a kind that was promoted by an inner sense of *Tao*, what he called the "Mystery". If human existence were governed only by the natural harmony that ensued from being at one with *Tao*, then there would be no need to impose prescriptive codes of behaviour on society. The conception of *Tao* was, then, very similar to that of Lao-tzu/Laozi and Chuang-tzu/Zhuangzi. The following beautiful translation of the opening part of his *Pao-p'u-tzu/Baopuzi* shows this well:

> The mystery is the first ancestor of the Spontaneous,
> the root of the many diversities.
> Unfathomable and murky in its depths, it is also called imperceivable;
> stretching far into the distance; it is also called wonderful;
> so high that it covers the nine empyreans,
> so wide that it encompasses the eight cardinal points;
> shining beyond the sun and moon,
> speedy beyond the rapid light;
> it both suddenly shines forth and disappears like a shadow,
> it both surges up in a whirlwind and streaks away like a comet; . . . [45]

Ko Hung/Ge Hong's words give nothing away about *Tao*; in fact he deepens the mystery of it. But for Ko Hung/Ge Hong, acceptance of *Tao* and living one's life with it within would be pointless were it not for the goal of immortality. Since nature itself shows us that radical change and metamorphosis are natural to life, there seemed no reason why human life, too, could not be metamorphosed to a state of immortality. Death is but the pathology of wrong living; if living could be harmonious, healthy and moral, then life could be extended to the point of immortality. Such transformation from physical life to physical immortality was hierarchized; some ascended to the skies and heavens, others remained on Earth. Some were destined never to become immortal.

As to the means to immortality, Ko Hung/Ge Hong believed that self-effort was essential, as well as moderation in all things in life, and assistance from a Master and the gods. Being able to control the gods and spirits to keep evil at bay was essential. Those wishing to tread the path to immortality would gain by retreating from life to great mountains to live tranquilly, or from meditation in a purity chapel or chamber – those introduced by the Celestial Masters. Diet was important: meat and cereals were coarse and gross foods to be avoided, though wine was not a deterrent to immortality: indeed, the sages were believed to be able to consume wine without getting intoxicated. Essential to immortality was to "feed" on the *ch'i/qi*, the vital energy of life.

What we have with Ko Hung/Ge Hong is a much closer link with the earlier philosophical Taoism of Lao-tzu/Laozi and Chuang-tzu/Zhuangzi. Where he departed from his two predecessors was in the *fang-shih/fangshi* Taoist inheritance that bequeathed to him an alchemical background and a fair measure of magico-spiritual beliefs and practices. Despite a veil of fatalism about human life, he encouraged self-effort in the pursuit of a moral, healthy and harmonious life that might aid longevity or end in immortality. As Pas writes of Kung Ho/Ge Hong: "He transformed Taoism from being a movement for the masses to one of individual practice and personal choice in the search for immortality."[46]

Neo-Taoism

During the Three Kingdoms period and the Chin/Qin dynasty, we find the rise of what has been called Neo-Taoism. Alongside the religious Taoism attractive to many ordinary people, it was a revival of Taoist philosophy and a metaphysical analysis of it. Neo-Taoists sought to dissociate themselves from the political arena in order to live a more natural and simple existence. Smith put this well: "It was a protest against the arid scholasticism of Han dynasty Confucianism, and an attempt to promote critical study, free inquiry and independent thinking. It was an attempt to escape from conventional value, and to seek for oneself the meaning of ultimate reality."[47]

While being basically Taoist, however, Neo-Taoism could not escape being coloured by Buddhism and Confucianism, especially the latter, since there was less a sense of withdrawal from the world than a spontaneous engagement within it. There was also a tendency to regard Confucius as pre-eminent over Taoist sages.[48] The three major names associated with Neo-Taoism are Wang Pi/Wang Bi (226–49), Ho Yen/He Yan, who died in 249, and Kuo Hsiang/Guo Xiang, who died in 312. Seidel and Strickmann believed the term "Neo Taoism" to be misleading when applied to these men. They wrote: "Their primary aim was to harmonize *Tao-te Ching* and *Chuang-tzu* with their own conception of a practical life devoted to affairs of state."[49] Wang Pi/Wang Bi commented on the *Tao Te Ching/Daodejing* and the *I Ching/Yijing*. His metaphysical view of *Tao* was as Non-Being (*wu*), that is to say *Tao* was the unmanifest origin, the ultimate Reality, from which all Being, or manifest existence, came into being. He used the terms *t'i/ti* to depict *Tao* as the substance or latent and unmanifest foundation from which all *yung/yong*, function, sprang, and reason or principle, *li*, to depict *Tao* as that in total conformity with it. *Li* was an important concept to the Wei-Chin/Wei-Qin scholars. Essentially, Wang Pi/Wang Bi stressed the unity of all things in the one ultimate Reality.

From a different point of view, Ho Yen/He Yan taught of the necessity of transcending all words and forms in order to experience *Tao* that is beyond all categories. Different again was the other major erudite philosopher, Kuo Hsiang/Guo Xiang, who wrote a commentary on the *Chuang-tzu/Zhuangzi*. But he did not share Chuang-tzu/Zhuangzi's rejection of social and political life. Instead he believed that one could follow one's own nature and still engage in societal life: naturalness did not exclude social interaction. Naturalness to Kuo Hsiang/Guo Xiang was defined as the harmony of the non-personal force of spontaneity of the self; the limitations placed on an individual by his or her life span, position in society and personal makeup; and the constant change that characterizes human beings. Such views were more obviously a blend of Taoism and Confucianism. Unlike Wang Pi/Wang Bi, Kuo Hsiang/Guo Xiang did not accept the concept of *wu*, Non-Being. He was decidedly humanist in his acceptance of a universe that transformed itself without the need of divine agency or ultimate Reality. *Li*, principle, was the important concept to Kuo Hsiang/Guo Xiang, for each entity had its own *li* and, therefore, its own natural pattern of transformation. He did not lift *li* to a cosmic level as did Wang Pi/Wang Bi, so he had to accept a fatalistic view of an individual's existence, as bound by his or her own *li*.

Two major movements characterized Neo-Taoism. The School of Pure or Light Conversation, *Ch'ing-t'an/Qingtan*, was one, the best known example of which were the Seven Sages of the Bamboo Grove. These lived in Honan and defied the usual societal and Confucian norms in their meetings together. They conversed, ate, drank, enjoyed nature, wrote poetry, and played the lute, relying solely on the kind of spontaneity in life of which Chuang-tzu/Zhuangzi had been fond, and the sensitivity to nature, the moment and silences characterized by the way of Lao-tzu/Laozi. "The whole outlook was a romantic wandering over the universe... and an intimate union with ultimate reality."[50] Overlapping the Pure Conversation school were the Metaphysical Schools or Hsüan-hsüeh/Xuanxue, "Mystery Learning", who also searched for reality in the more metaphysical philosophies that posited non-being as the ultimate Reality from which all originated. "Mystery Learning" based its premises on the *I Ching/Yijing*, the *Tao Te Ching/Daodejing* and the *Chuang-tzu/Zhuangzi*, and was the inspiration for later movements. Alongside the development of religious Taoism at the popular level, these Neo-Taoist movements provided a more philosophical parallel that retained and re-emphasized the classical inheritance – albeit a syncretic one. But we should not view such syncretism in a pejorative manner, for the integration of ideas proved both stimulating and enriching for Taoism as much as for Buddhism.

The period of disunity: the Six Dynasties

From 316 to 581 China was divided between non-Chinese rulers in the North, and six successive Chinese dynasties in the South – Western Chin/Jin, Eastern Chin/Jin, Liu Sung/Liu Song, Southern Ch'i/Qi, Liang and Ch'en/Chen. Two important Taoist movements rose up in the southern dynasties, and they deserve attention here. These were the Shang-ch'ing/Shangqing school and the Ling-pao/Lingbao school.

The Shang-ch'ing/Shangqing *school*

According to tradition, between 364 and about 370, and in the time of the Eastern Chin, Lady Wei Hua-ts'un/Wei Huacun, a deceased libationer of the Celestial Masters school, and other perfected or immortal beings from the "Heaven of Supreme Clarity", appeared to Yang Hsi/Yang Xi. Sacred scriptures from gods, immortals and ancient saints were revealed to him. The content of the material consisted of biographies of the different immortals, meditation techniques and ideas about stellar forces. The resultant scriptures were commended for the excellence of their calligraphy and poetic style, and were soon copied and circulated widely, forming the basis of the Shang-ch'ing/Shangqing school. The name *Shang-ch'ing/Shangqing* is that of the second of three Heavens, the "Heaven of Supreme Clarity". This Heaven and the Shang-ch'ing/Shangqing scriptures were hailed as superior to those of Celestial Masters Taoism. The texts were also dictated to two others, Hsü Mi/Xu Mi (303–373), a court official, and his youngest son Hsü Hui/Xu Hui. The latter left his family and retired to the hills of Mao Shan, Mount Shan. Between them, Yang Hsi/Yang Xi, Hsü Mi/Xu Mi and Hsü Hui/Xu Hui account for all the revelations to be found in the Shang-ch'ing/Shangqing corpus of texts. A century later, T'ao Hung-ching/Tao Hongjing managed to retrieve the original manuscripts and form an organized school, centred on Mao Shan, which became the first real Taoist spiritual centre – a prototype of the monasteries to follow. Following the move to Mao Shan, the school is sometimes called Mao Shan Taoism. Mao Shan became an important focus. Shang-ch'ing/Shangqing Taoism was a messianic teaching that believed the world was being cleansed by demonic forces. Underneath the great mountain the good would go at the end of the world, purifying themselves further until a new age dawned with the arrival of the messianic figure of Li Hung/Li Hong. As a result of the growth and prestige of the school, other monastic communities were established and these monasteries became centres of pilgrimage.

Robinet considered Shang-ch'ing/Shangqing Taoism to be the first proper school of Taoism, in that it was "solidly based on canonical texts that make up a coherent whole following strictly enforced rules of transmission."[51] These scriptures attracted highly educated proponents, a factor that also increased the status of the sect. The ritual, meditation and talismans connected with the movement, and the reciting or copying of its texts were deemed exceptionally powerful tools with intensely potent outcomes. What the Shang-ch'ing/Shangqing professed to have in its possession were words handed down for aeons all the way from *Tao* itself through the gods to the succession of Masters of the school. It was a precious and prestigious heritage.

The teachings of the school seem to have been a blend of Ko Hung/Ge Hong's Taoism with some elements from the Celestial Masters school; in particular the latter's use of purity chambers. The influence of the Celestial Masters school came about because the capture of the northern capital of Loyang/Luoyang by foreigners caused an exodus to the South. These northerners took with them Celestial Masters Taoism, which many in the South also came to adopt. But after the Shang-ch'ing/Shangqing revelations, an amalgam of Celestial Masters and Shang-ch'ing/Shangqing ideas occurred. One important change from this fusion, however, was the connection of sickness with physiological imbalances rather than sins, and this led to an emphasis on drugs, gymnastics and diet as essential for balanced health. Confession of sins as in Celestial Masters Taoism was, therefore, no longer important. But if the Celestial Masters school had its influence, so did popular custom in the South. Seidel and Strickmann described Shang-ch'ing/Shangqing Taoism as the "most brilliant synthesis of the Way of the Celestial Masters with the indigenous traditions of the Southeast".[52] Lagerwey, too, points out that the Shang-ch'ing/Shangqing literature "completely transformed the methods of the traditional Taoism of the South... by incorporating them into a complex system revealed in ecstatic prose and poetry by a kind of automatic writing during séances. Recitation of these sacred texts and visualization of the spirits described in them became the high roads to spiritual realization in this movement".[53]

While influenced by some of the ideas of Ko Hung/Ge Hong, the school had much less interest in immortals. Instead, its adherents hoped for life in Heaven, in Shang-ch'ing/Shangqing. The school also had its own gods that it believed were superior to those of other schools. These gods were instrumental in the pursuit of salvation, but the means to salvation were more mystical and inward rather than being ritualistic. Inner visualization of the images that would bring salvation was an essential ingredient of Shang-ch'ing/Shangqing practice. When such visualization was at the level of the sage it was believed possible to fly to paradises and mingle with the gods, to the stars and planets, especially to the Big Dipper, and to the sun and the moon. Livia Kohn points out that: "The aim of their visionary and ecstatic practices is to reorganize their consciousness. From ordinary people, practitioners develop into cosmic beings."[54] But for those who were unable to match the heights of consciousness of the sage, Shang-ch'ing/Shangqing Taoism offered more personal approaches.

The means to salvation were, therefore, prescriptive but thoroughly individual. Each had to work out his or her own salvation. And what prevented salvation was not just an individual's own sins, but the sins of the fathers too. The unbreakable bond with ancestors was emphasized in the belief that the sins of ancestors of several generations past still affected the individual of today. However, reciprocally, the relative sin or merit of a living individual could also affect that of past ancestors. And if that living individual were to achieve salvation, then so would the ancestors. The gods were thought to visit Earth regularly to assess the various merits and demerits of individuals so that they could be recorded in the heavenly registers, and one's lifespan continued to be adjusted accordingly. Recitation of the sacred texts as a major means of salvation was central to the practice of adherents of the school. Important, too, was the visualizing of the many gods of the inner body as being unified with the gods of Heaven. The goal was unity – "The ultimate goal is to arrive at Oneness through the diversity and the multiplicity of forms of the life that animates our body. The human being is conceived as a plurality that must be harmonized, a totality that must be overcome, a oneness that must be constructed while retaining complexity."[55]

Alongside the emphasis on interiorized development of the self, the Shang-ch'ing/Shangqing school also advocated *tao-yin/daoyin*, "gymnastic exercises", for the benefit of good health. Such exercises were ancient and long known, and were thought to promote the circulation of essential energy, *ch'i/qi*, in the body. T'ao Hung-ching/Tao Hongjing wrote extensively on alchemy and divination, and was interested in martial arts, medicine and herbology. But, from a different view, the meditative emphasis, and the simple and reclusive lifestyle advocated by T'ao Hung-ching/Tao Hongjing, was reminiscent of the *wu-wei*, the non-action of the philosophical strands of earlier Taoism. It was Taoism devoid of excessive ritual, stressing the need to focus calmly without the intrusion of the mind's usual proliferation of thoughts.

Overall, the Shang-ch'ing/Shangqing school of Taoism was important because of its role in the development of an inner, interiorizing process of discovering *Tao*, because of its scriptural foundation, and its highly organized character. While the school developed into the foremost of Taoist movements by the end of the fifth century, and flowered under the T'ang/Tang, it declined thereafter though survived until the nineteenth century. But in the T'ang/Tang dynasty, especially, the Mao Shan tradition became the main expression of Taoism, "the most powerful Taoist order during the T'ang, when its primacy was virtually unchallenged".[56] Its scriptures are extant and incorporated in the Taoist canon.

The Ling-pao/Lingbao *school*

Not long after the Shang-ch'ing/Shangqing revelations, new scriptures, the *Ling-pao/Lingbao*, " sacred" or "mystical treasure", scriptures were written by Ko Ch'ao-fu/Ge Chaofu at the end of the fourth or beginning of the fifth century in south-east China. Ko Ch'ao-fu/Ge Chaofu gleaned material from his famed relative Ko Hung/Ge Hong, as well as from a number of Mahayana Buddhist texts, from which he wrote the "revelations".[57] The texts reveal a concern for universal salvation in celestial Heavens that were considered superior to the Shang-ch'ing/Shangqing Heaven. Such a belief in universal salvation was an open borrowing from Mahayana Buddhism, and reflected the Buddhist tradition of *boddhisattvas* – those enlightened beings who remained in the world to aid all others, alive and dead, in attaining perfection, the aim being universal salvation. Robinet points out that such a theory of salvation combines three traditions. First is the Buddhist idea of universal salvation. Then, there is Chinese ancestor worship in that the dead are affected by the *karma* of the living, and are also included in salvation. The third is the old idea of the perfected being, the sage, the enlightened one, being the ultimate goal of human striving.[58] To reach the perfected state, the Confucian values were first essential. Only then could possession of a sacred text be granted in order for the adept to engage in the appropriate ritual and, especially, the ritual chanting of the text.

Whereas Shang-ch'ing/Shangqing Taoism emphasized an internalized journey of the individual self, liturgical ritual was the main emphasis of Ling-pao/Lingbao Taoism. Importantly, the liturgical ritual laid down in the scriptures formed the basis of future

Taoist liturgy down to the present day. It was Lu Hsiu-ching/Lu Xiujing (406–77), a great traveller and recluse, who gathered together all Taoist texts and standardized Taoist rituals, drawing heavily on the Ling-pao/Lingbao scriptures for this dimension of his work. It was the first collection and systematized collation of Taoist scriptures, the beginning of the *Tao-tsang/Daozang*, the Taoist canon. It was he who drafted a good deal of Buddhist beliefs onto the Ling-pao/Lingbao tradition through his textual editing. Thus, through his efforts, Taoism came to accept a doctrine of compassion, reincarnation and the doctrine of *karma*, and concepts of heaven and hell – hell being absent in Shang-ch'ing/Shangqing and other Taoist beliefs of the time. The doctrine of *karma*, the idea that one's good and bad actions reap appropriate merit and demerit for oneself, was aligned with the registers of good and evil deeds held by the gods. However, only males could achieve the kind of merit that would bring perfection. Again, this was probably a sign of Buddhist influence. The Buddha had great difficulty in accepting that women could be perfected beings in human life. Lu Hsiu-ching/Lu Xiujing was not a Ling-pao/Lingbao Taoist Master, for he was the seventh patriarch of Shang-ch'ing/Shangqing Taoism.[59] So a good deal found in earlier traditions is present, though developed, in the codified texts he produced – beliefs and practices from the Celestial Masters school, from Shang-ch'ing/Shangqing Taoism, Buddhism and also Confucianism. But it is the liturgy of Ling-pao/Lingbao Taoism that is its greatest legacy to modern-day Taoism. It *externalized* the interiorized, meditative ritual of the Shang-ch'ing/Shangqing school, and this necessitated a developed priesthood on the one hand and highly complex, symbolic, dramatic and vivid ritual on the other, the latter characterized by colour, music, dance and chants and based on ancient praxis. The ritual symbolizes the unity of Heaven, Earth and the interior organs of man. While at first sufficiently organized to command greater popularity in the South than Shang-ch'ing/Shangqing Taoism, and despite its legacy of ritual praxis to the present day, by T'ang/Tang times Ling-pao/Lingbao Taoism had become absorbed by the Shang-ch'ing/Shangqing school.

The Taoist canon[60]

The Taoist canon is called the *Tao-tsang/Daozang*. It is the collected scriptures from different strands and schools of Taoism. It was Lu Hsiu-ching/Lu Xiujing of Shang-ch'ing/Shangqing Taoism, and from south-east China, who compiled the first canon, collecting and collating the different texts as a response to imperial demand. Other compilations were to ensue, the latest, other than twentieth-century texts, being a product of the Ming dynasty. The content of the numerous volumes of the *Tao-tsang/Daozang* ranges from lengthy scriptural texts of the schools to extracts from popular religion, divination texts, and incantations – a very heterogeneous mixture of contents. Just as Theravada Buddhism divided its scriptures into three "baskets" so Lu Hsiu-ching/Lu Xiujing divided the Taoist canon into three sections, sometimes called "caverns", or "grottoes", though the division may have been earlier and a product of the Shang-ch'ing/Shangqing school.[61] It was a division that was to remain a feature of the canon to the present day. However, unlike the Buddhist division according to types of literature the Taoist one represents three different schools.

The three caverns were hierarchized. The most important are the Shang-ch'ing/Shangqing scriptures and other Mao Shan material. The second cavern is devoted to the Ling-pao/Lingbao scriptures and associative texts, and then the *Scripture of the Three Sovereigns*, the *San-huang Ching/Sanhuangjing* makes up the third cavern. In this last, the three sovereigns refer to Heaven, Earth and humanity, but though the third text was traditionally handed down from Ko Hung/Ge Hong to Lu Hsiu-ching/Lu Xiujing, and so included in the canon, its authorship is unknown. Judging from the minute sections of it that remain, the texts were more concerned with exorcism and talismanic magic. The hierarchized three sections correspond to similarly hierarchized three supreme deities:

- Yüan-shih T'ien-tsun/Yuanshi Tianzun   Shang-ch'ing/Shangqing scriptures
- Ling-pao T'ien-tsun/Lingbao Tianzun   Ling-pao/Lingbao scriptures
- Tao-te T'ien-tsun/Daode Tianzun   San-huang scriptures

Celestial Masters literature is not included, perhaps because of the distaste some felt for its sexual practices, or because some material was already absorbed by the Shang-ch'ing/Shangqing and Ling-pao/Lingbao schools. On the other hand, Pas makes the point that, when the three-tiered Taoist canon was composed, the Celestial Masters texts may not have been included because they were associated with "lower class" Taoism.[62] Later, other material was added to the canon, including the *Tao Te Ching/Daodejing*, the *Chuang-tzu/Zhuangzi*, the *Scripture of Great Peace* (*T'ai-p'ing Ching/Taipingjing*), some texts from the Celestial Masters school and some texts on alchemy, medicine and meditation. It also has guides to moral virtue and collections of hymns. These supplements are ancillary to the different caverns. It is, thus, an all-embracing collection, complex, largely undated, confusingly intricate and disparate, and often written in an esoteric style that makes understanding of the content very difficult. As Lagerwey comments: "The Three Caverns constituted a complete and self-contained canon of exorcistic, liturgical, and meditational texts: together they met every religious need, from that of a sick peasant requiring an exorcism to that of the refined aristocrat seeking sublime spiritual union."[63] All the texts were believed to be divinely inspired, and so were, and are, regarded as sacred. Lu Hsiu-ching/Lu Xiujing is also remembered for revising and adapting the Celestial Masters ritual and magical praxis to accommodate it in southern China.

At the end of the period of disunity, then, a number of more organized Taoist schools had emerged. Rather than being loosely grouped or individualized, Taoists in the sixth century were members of organized movements with specific rituals, fasts, festivals and ceremonies. These movements had retained much of earlier traditions but had borrowed extensively during their development. Buddhism by this time was very much an established religion in China, but so was Taoism and, as we shall see, was to develop to its historical heights in the imperial dynasties to follow.

The Sui dynasty

As was noted above, China was divided between North and South, the South having the Six Dynasties under discussion. In the North, the non-Chinese unified state of the Wei weakened, and from 534 a number of states existed in the North. In 577 one of these states, the Northern Chou/Zhou succeeded in unifying the whole of the North and set up a new Sui dynasty. In 581 the whole of the South was also brought under Sui power, creating once more, an imperial China. At this point, we begin the Middle Period of imperial China that stretched from 581 to 907. A chronological outline of these years is as follows:

Imperial China: Middle Period

Sui dynasty	*6th–7th centuries (581–617)* China is reunited Important Buddhist schools
T'ang/Tang dynasty	*7th–10th centuries (617–907)* 7th–8th centuries: Buddhism at its height 8th–9th centuries: great period of poetry 9th century: persecution of Buddhism (845)

The Sui dynasty was short-lived: its end came when revolution broke out in 617 and a new dynastic family came to power, inaugurating the rule of the T'ang/Tang.

The T'ang/Tang dynasty

The T'ang/Tang period was one of relative stability, of cultural flowering, and successful bureaucratic control. It was an important time for the growth of Taoism. To begin with the Taoists told Li Shih-min/Li Shimin, the founder of the dynasty, that he was a descendant of Lao-tzu/Laozi, for Lao-tzu/Laozi had had the same family name of Li. Such a diplomatic action gave the Taoists a good deal of favour from the Emperor. It was also a time of considerable literary activity, and Needham notes that many poets and writers were "deeply affected" by Taoism.[64] Like earlier periods, it was a time of great eclecticism, and the early T'ang/Tang rulers supported both Taoism and Buddhism alongside Confucianism: there was a good deal of influence from each to the others. The ancient indigenous nature of Confucianism and Taoism meant that there was much of mutual interest to both, and the moral virtues of Confucianism were accepted by most Taoists. But there were fundamental differences. Marcel Granet put this point very well when he wrote: "It was less by the ideological base than by the direction taken by practical speculation that Taoism and orthodoxy were distinguished: they represented twin streams of doctrine springing from ancient national beliefs."[65] It was Buddhism, however, that was more of a rival to Taoism, gaining in strength and self-identity in a way that Taoism did not. However, many people probably found little to differentiate between Taoist and Buddhist sects and the three strands of belief interacted with and influenced one another. Confucianism donated an emphasis on ethics and morality and the practicalities of life; Buddhism encouraged concepts of rebirth and compassion; while Taoism affected attitudes to nature and the cyclical phases of life. Saso describes this intermingling of essential ideas rather well: "Confucianism is called the warp, and Taoism the woof of Chinese religion. It is precisely in the Taoist woof that creativity, color, and variable meaning are woven. The golden threads of Buddhism are blended into this tapestry . . . the Confucian threads, which run in a perpendicular manner from the top to the bottom of Chinese society, define the ethical norms of Chinese behaviour."[66] Taoism always remained closest to the popular folk religion of the everyday individual past and present, mainly because it could embrace so many facets, and because it had its roots in the nature religions and shamanic practices of ancient times.

Under the T'ang/Tang the main characteristics of Taoism were allowed to surface as a result of imperial support. After all, a dynasty founded by descendants of the deified Lao-tzu/Laozi could not persecute the religion that grew from him. In fact, the T'ang/Tang family was more foreign than Chinese, and therefore needed the legitimacy that Taoism had given it with a celebrated and deified ancestor. Emperor Kao-tsung/Gaozong, who reigned from 649 to 683, had some leanings towards Taoism at the end of his reign. He had Buddhist and Taoist temples established in each district, and honoured Lao-tzu/Laozi with great titles. But it was particularly Emperor Hsüan-tsung/Xuanzong, who reigned from 712 until 756, who promoted Taoism, especially the cult surrounding Lao-tzu/Laozi. Barrett considers that such patronage was likely to have been a mere exploitation of Taoism, rather than a preference for it and a genuine desire to see it developed.[67] If it were exploitation, then it was considerable, and took the form of encouragement of the worship of the deified Lao-tzu/Laozi and, also, of using Taoist texts instead of Confucian ones for examinations for government service. As Charles Benn comments, Taoism "had never before received official patronage on the scale that Hsüan-tsung accorded it nor had it been as thoroughly integrated with state institutions and ideology as it was in the T'ien-pao era".[68]

Benn points out that an important result of Hsüan-tsung/Xuanzong's policies was that Taoism was projected *nationally* through his conscious effort to encourage localized worship of ancestor Lao-tzu/Laozi, alongside devotion to himself. The monarchy was popularized through the means of wider religious allegiance. According to Benn: "The cult of Lao Tzu provided Hsüan-tsung with an opportunity, unparalleled in previous or subsequent dynasties, for unifying diverse rituals to secure spiritual protection for the dynasty and the monarchy from a single deity whose power was recognized by the family, the state, and the masses and whose image was both particular and universal, private and public."[69]

It was in Hsüan-tsung/Xuanzong's reign, then, that the first temple to Lao-tzu/Laozi was erected. The temple where Lao-tzu/Laozi was reputedly born received such patronage from Hsüan-tsung/Xuanzong that it was extended to immense proportions and incorporated a massive number of personnel, even five hundred guards.[70] Lao-tzu/Laozi was believed to have visited a number of people and to have spoken to the Emperor himself in a dream, acknowledging the Emperor as his direct descendant. The importance given to the cult of Lao-tzu/Laozi was sufficient to make him the dominant deity in the Taoist pantheon in T'ang/Tang times. Lao-tzu/Laozi's *Tao Te Ching/Daodejing* became the pre-eminent classic for study, and a separate Taoist examination was instituted. Additionally, a College of Taoist Studies was set up and, soon after, similar schools were established in the different districts of the empire. New temples occurred in all the cities, and necessitated a greater number of Taoist priests. Since priests could marry they lived in their communities and reinforced Taoism at the popular level. Taoist monasteries increased and Taoist nuns as much as monks gained considerable respect. Hsüan-tsung/Xuanzong also decreed that a copy of the *Tao Te Ching/Daodejing* should be in every home, and ordered an imperial commentary on it to be undertaken. In 721 the text of the *Tao Te Ching/Daodejing* was inscribed on a stele in the capital in three calligraphic styles, and more such engravings of the text took place in following years. The Taoist canon was also extended at his behest.

Successors to Hsüan-tsung/Xuanzong also took advantage of Taoist connections to strengthen their ancestral ties, but not to the extent that Hsüan-tsung/Xuanzong did. Indeed, his immediate successor favoured Buddhism, and Taoism, though not weakened, was not significantly encouraged further. Imperial patronage of Taoism under succeeding emperors of the T'ang/Tang waxed and waned – the Empress Wu, for example, demoted Lao-tzu/Laozi and the *Tao Te Ching/Daodejing* in favour of Buddhism – though, generally, sufficient support of the Taoists was maintained for political purposes. It is thus in the T'ang/Tang dynasty times that Taoism became a major force in China, reaching its zenith, its high-water mark, having been aided clearly by Hsüan-tsung/Xuanzong. Although Confucianism always remained the orthodox doctrine, Taoism under the T'ang/Tang, far succeeded Buddhism in popularity.

In accordance with the pattern of previous dynasties the greatness of the T'ang/Tang declined. Political machinations eventually destroyed it in the same way that they had earlier dynasties. The central bureaucracy broke down, allowing the rise of separate states that virtually became autonomous. In 906, the T'ang/Tang dynasty finally came to an end. In the ensuing hiatus in imperial history, disunion occurred for almost half a century until reunification brought about the Late Period of imperial China. Some important dates and a list of the dynasties succeeding the T'ang/Tang are as follows:

Five Dynasties *10th century (907–60)*
Period of disunion
Five Northern Dynasties – Later Liang; Later T'ang/Tang; Later Chin/Qin; Later Han; Later Chou/Zhou
Ten Southern Kingdoms
Printing introduced

Imperial China: Late Period

Sung/Song dynasty *10th–13th centuries (960–1279)*
Rise of Neo-Confucianism

	Decline of Buddhism
	Period of division with separate dynasties, the Northern Sung/Song (960–1127); Southern Sung/Song (1127–79); Chin/Qin (1115–1234); and Liao (907–1119).
Northern Sung/Song	*10th–12th centuries (960–1127)*
	Introduction of new Taoist rituals
	Taoist inner alchemy
	11th century: revival of Confucianism
	12th–13th centuries: Northern China under Jurchen rule (1115–1234)
	Jurchen Chin/Qin dynasty falls under the rulership of Khubilai Khan
Southern Sung/Song	*12th–13th centuries (1127–1279)*
	13th century: Southern Sung Dynasty falls to Khubilai Khan (1279)
Yüan/Yuan dynasty	*13th–14th centuries (1279–1367)*
	Mongol rule, the first period of foreign rule. Khubilai Khan is Emperor of China (1279–1294)
Ming dynasty	*14th–17th centuries (1368–1644)*
	Restoration of Chinese rule
Ch'ing/Qing dynasty	*17th–20th centuries (1644–1911)*
	Second period of rule by foreigners, the Manchus

The period of the Five Dynasties

After the fall of the T'ang/Tang a succession of five dynasties occurred in the North of China, not all of which were ethnically Chinese. In fact, there were more than five dynasties since a good many independent states also existed during this turbulent period. There is little that needs to be said concerning Taoism in this period, except for one significant point, and that was the development of printing. Such a catalyst enabled the printing and wider distribution of Confucian classics as well as Taoist and Buddhist texts.

The Sung/Song dynasty

When the Sung/Song dynasty began in 960, it was to last for over three hundred years. The centuries of Sung/Song rule were characterized by considerable instability, as well as military pressures from non-Chinese states eager to expand their territories into China. It was a time when bureaucracy extended to religious life, and deities were expected to be state approved. There was, thus, a systematization of popular gods, and a fusion of them with the major Taoist pantheon took place. New deities were added, too, commensurate with the growth of cities. Printing was widespread and enabled another compilation of the Taoist canon to be undertaken in the early eleventh century. During the Sung/Song dynasty, some Taoists began to turn away from the more outward alchemical practices to what is called "inner alchemy" – a more mystical approach to transformation of the self than chemical elixirs manufactured in laboratories.

There was altogether a much closer blending of Taoist ideas with Confucianism and Buddhism during Sung/Song times. The Confucian emphasis on moral virtue remained the mainstay of ethical behaviour and was supported and upheld by the Taoists, too. A *Book of Rewards and Punishments* was circulated widely, setting down the kinds of sins that would be punished, and delineating the kind of behaviour that would lead to immortality.[71] There was an intimate involvement of the gods in human activity. As in earlier times, longevity was the reward for virtue, and lessening of life the punishment for transgression. And no one could get away from the observation of good and evil action in the face of the Kitchen God, so strategically placed to know all! While the Emperor Hui-tsung/Huizong, who reigned from 1101–25, supported Taoism and was the patron behind the new Sung/Song Taoist canon, he forced a number of Buddhist temples to become Taoist, and prevented any expansion of Buddhist monastic territory. Hui-tsung/Huizong created new high-ranking positions for Taoist priests and nuns and encouraged study of the *Tao Te Ching/Daodejing*, the *Chuang-tzu/Zhuangzi*, the *Lieh-tzu/Liezi* and an inner alchemy text, by setting up doctorates for these fields.

By the Sung/Song dynasty, Taoism had evolved more or less to its fully established character, and not too many changes ensued in the succeeding dynasties. The main deity of the Taoists had become the Jade Emperor, and an image of him was to be found in most Taoist temples. As noted above, there was a move by the Sung/Song to bring popular gods into the officially recognized pantheon and official titles were given to many. As Ebrey and Gregory note, such a move was politically motivated: "Government recognition of gods, like patronage of Buddhism and Taoism, harnessed the spiritual resources of the land for the protection of the Dynasty."[72] It was a measure that helped the state to keep control of local areas. But for local people, too, it was worthwhile having a deity officially recognized and listed by the state as being able to receive sacrifices, since some costs for maintaining the god's temple would be met by the state. Communication with such deities was still through methods of divination and oracles: the ancient practices had not been abandoned, only changed and elaborated. Many Taoists had turned away from popular rituals that involved animal sacrifice, though the practice continued despite criticism. Just as in times past the gods had to be notified about human activities, so as not to offend them, so they had to be cared for with human necessities of food and drink. The greater the offerings, the more likely the god would be to respond favourably with miracles or responses to questions. The status of a deity was matched by the splendour, or lack of it, of its temple, and the amount of offerings. Some Taoist Masters, too, adopted the state policy of incorporating popular deities – meat sacrifices as well – into the official Taoist pantheon of deities. Thus there were the greater and purer deities of Taoism to whom no animal sacrifice was offered and the lesser deities incorporated from popular religion, for whom bloody sacrifices were normal.

Ancestor reverence also became more elaborate under the Sung/Song. Such was the case at the popular level, as well as for establishing ancient ancestry at the level of the emperor. As in centuries past the veneration of ancestors held a family together, bringing its members together for ritual and creating and maintaining depth with the past as much as links with the future. It was still a reciprocal arrangement of care of ancestors through ongoing offerings and care for the living through ongoing support. Linked with the religious rites of popular cults there was a certain stability of traditions, even if the times were politically and militarily unstable. Household gods remained popular and the older practices of divination, exorcism, and use of spirit mediums were continued alongside beliefs in ghosts, magic and miracles. Judith Magee Boltz has shown how much in demand Taoist exorcists were in ascertaining where offence to the local spirits had occurred and how to appease them.[73] Such was the importance of exorcism at the time that many of the gentry who held official posts were also experts in Taoist ritual exorcism.[74] Sorcery, too, continued to be practised at the popular level, but not by Taoists it seems, for the Taoist exorcist was different from the ordinary sorcerer. [75] Nevertheless, the roots of official Taoist exorcism and sorcery lay in the same shamanic traditions of the ancient past.

In the final decades of the Sung/Song dynasty the Mongols to the North were becoming increasingly more powerful and eventually engaged the Sung/Song empire itself in a contest that lasted nearly half a century. Eventually, the Sung/Song was forced to flee to the South, where the Southern Sung/Song dynasty was established. Here, Taoism was less popular. But in the North, three new schools were established at this time – Complete (or Perfect) Reality (or Realization, Perfection) Taoism, which has survived to the present day; Grand Unity Taoism; and Great Way Taoism.

The Yüan/Yuan, Ming and Ch'ing/Qing dynasties

The Sung/Song was extinguished in 1279 by Chinghiz Khan. A few years later, Khubilai Khan became the first Yüan/Yuan emperor of China, which was ruled by foreign Mongols for almost a century. By the end of the Sung/Song Taoism had virtually reached its finalized forms of ritual and beliefs. The remaining dynasties, therefore, need not detain us too long. During the Yüan/Yuan dynasty, China became more open to Western influence, and it is a measure of the successful empire of Khubilai Khan that many Westerners know of his name, even if they know little or nothing about him. It was under Khubilai Khan that Marco Polo claimed that he served from 1271 to 1292. The Mongols made their capital Peking, which it has been to present times. Khubilai Khan made Buddhism the state religion, and Taoism was suppressed and many of its texts destroyed. Once again, however, internal weaknesses and rebellions brought about the downfall of the Yüan/Yuan dynasty, though not with a complete overhaul of its institutions.

The Ming dynasty was founded in 1368 and lasted until 1644. It was a despotic and autocratic dynasty, though it was characterized by prosperity and increased commercialism. Its first emperor was an ordinary man, an orphan, who had once been a mendicant monk. As leader of a rebel group he successfully overthrew the Yüan/Yuan, and began the long Ming dynasty. Under the Ming, Taoism was allowed to consolidate and prosper through the favour of the Ming emperors, and Taoist Masters were bestowed with high ranks. The number of Taoist sects grew considerably, perhaps fired by the popularity of talismanic magic, sorcery and efforts to cultivate an indestructible, immortal body. These were characteristics of the Ming dynasty that came under considerable criticism from the following, and last, Chinese dynasty.

In 1644 the Ming dynasty was itself overthrown by foreigners, the Manchus, who established the Ch'ing/Qing dynasty that was to last right down to the twentieth century. It was the last dynasty of China – at least as far as our present experience can say, though who knows what awaits the future of China, given the pattern of the past. Where the Ming emperors bestowed their favour on Taoism, the Ch'ing/Qing removed it. It was not a time when Taoism or Buddhism could flourish. However, despite being under foreign rule, no radical break with indigenous Chinese traditions seems to have occurred. By the Ch'ing/Qing dynasty, Confucian, Buddhist and Taoist beliefs and practices had thoroughly infiltrated Chinese religious life. Buddhas and *bodhhisattvas* were accepted as Taoist deities, Lao-tzu/Laozi could be identified as a buddha, and Confucian protocol was imbued in religious praxis. While there are purist elements in Taoism, Confucianism and Buddhism, which separate them from one another and from popular Chinese religion *per se*, it is futile to try to isolate any strand completely – mutual influence has been endemic.

The weaknesses of the Ch'ing/Qing lay in a new and disturbing factor – demographic trends. Ebrey writes:

> By 1850 the population reached about 400 million. This demographic change affected many other aspects of life. By the beginning of the nineteenth century, the pressure of population on available land resources was becoming acute. All the land which could profitably be exploited using traditional methods was already under cultivation, so any increase in food supply had to come from less and less rewarding additions of labor or marginal land. As a consequence, the prospect of widespread suffering became very real, especially in times of drought or flood. The government structure did not keep pace with the population's growth; in fact, it remained static in size during the Ch'ing period, so that government services and control became weaker, stretched thin to cover two or three times as large a population as before.[76]

The expansion of population was not helped by the custom of a man having a number of wives and concubines, in addition to slave-girls, at his disposal. Needless to say, the suffering of the people made rebellion epidemic. In the nineteenth century the Opium War with Britain resulted in Chinese defeat and foreigners on Chinese soil who dictated commercial policies. It was after this war that Britain obtained some Chinese territories, including Hong Kong. Under the Ch'ing/Qing, education was widened to the villages in the nineteenth century, and those who could afford it could send their children to school for three or four years. Then, in 1911, the Ch'ing/Qing dynasty was brought to an end by a totally new phenomenon for China, a republic.

6

Alchemy

What is alchemy?

Like so many other cultures and religions, the dream of immortality, of the continued existence of the self beyond the grave, was no less featured in the Chinese search to make sense of the life that preceded death. For many Chinese, and certainly for Taoists, immortality became the goal of life. And this was not really a strictly *religious* goal, for it had nothing to do with communication with a divine being in an afterlife, or the metaphysical fusion with a divine force. It was more a sense of a long bodily life, *ch'ang-sheng/changsheng*, which stretched so far into the future that it became eternal. Thus, there is a continuum of existence without the break from life to death, albeit that death appeared to happen. The goal came to be the replacement of the physical, mortal, perishable body with an equally physical, but immortal and imperishable body that developed gradually within the body framework. It was alchemy that provided the means for such transformation.

While alchemy was inextricably linked to Taoism, it was a broadly accepted phenomenon in Chinese upper-class life and, therefore, not limited to Taoism *per se*. But what the Taoists did, was to work towards a quantifiable, qualifiable and immutable *Tao* that could be replicated in the human body. Needless to say, such a goal was far removed from the masses of Chinese people, who were more interested in the simpler goal of a long and happy life before inevitable death. While tales of those who had become immortals always remained popular with the ordinary folk, alchemical processes to procure such a prestigious goal, as we shall see below, not only demanded infinite patience, but also great financial resources. Moreover, the ingredients used by the alchemist were difficult to obtain, some of them being rather rare, and this, too, made alchemical practice possible only for those who were supported by the wealthy nobility, including many emperors. Thus, as Maspero put it: "Human life is short, and the search for Immortality is long."[1] Few had the means or the tenacity to pursue such a goal.

As the forerunner of metallurgy and chemistry, alchemy was the process by which base metals were transmuted into gold. In a physical sense, too, it was the transmutation of the mortal body into an immortal one. Since gold was an immutable substance, turning the bones to gold and the flesh to jade were believed to be ways in which the physical body could also become immutable. Taoists adopted both these pathways. The Chinese use the word *tan/dan*, which means "cinnabar" "elixir" or "pill", to refer to alchemy in its widest sense. Cinnabar is a red mineral from which we get mercury and, like gold, it was believed to be a *Tao*-like substance, that is to say, a basic substance in the universe. To use Schipper's words, "these minerals and metals are the products of the interaction of cosmic energies and time and thus constitute the quintessence of our planet".[2] Sometimes, the two words "gold-cinnabar", *chin-tan/jindan*, are combined as the term for alchemy. Chinese distinguishes between alchemical practices that are conducted in the laboratory, and are concerned with the transmutation of metals and minerals as "outer", "external", *wai*, alchemy, and the "inner", "internal" transformations of the body as *nei*.[3] In the pages that follow, then, I shall be referring to outer alchemy or *wai-tan/waidan* and inner alchemy or *nei-tan/neidan*.

While turning base metals into gold was certainly a goal in itself both outer and inner alchemists sought to promote good health, longevity and eternal life. It was simply the interpretation of the means that differed. Both sought purification and perfection, one of metals and the other of the body, though many great alchemists of the outer alchemy schools were also dedicated to the perfection and immortality of the body through the ingestion of substances perfected in the laboratory. In this sense, both outer and inner alchemists conducted *physiological* alchemy, as it is sometimes referred to. But pure inner alchemy did not need the external aids of ingested substances mixed in the furnaces of the laboratory to gain immortality. Here, the path was thoroughly internalized by concentration on the inner body itself in order to transform it into *Tao*.

Needless to say, there were many different streams that informed the general ocean of secretive traditions and texts that promised the best pathways to longevity and immortality. Meticulous preparation of utensils in the laboratory was essential for results in outer alchemy and the range of methods for inner alchemy was prolific. John Lagerwey writes of the breadth of the latter: "Internal alchemical methods ranged from the relatively empirical, scarcely distinguishable from the more ordinary techniques of breath circulation, to the extremely abstract and symbolic, virtually indistinguishable from traditional cosmological speculation."[4] Joseph Needham, too, commented that unity and simplicity were altogether absent from the many inner alchemy traditions. He wrote: "The *nei tan* palace was in fact a house of many mansions, and over the two millennia of its existence there grew up a multiplicity of teachers, schools and sects, embodying the traditions of a number of Taoist centres. Each of these had a favourite terminology of its own, and specialised in particular techniques."[5] What follows in this chapter, then, can only generalize a very complex web of traditions and practices in the way of an introduction to the intricacies of Taoist and Chinese alchemy.

Despite the very different approaches of outer and inner alchemy, it has to be remembered that both were informed by the same goal of searching for purification to the point of perfection and, while immortality was the aim of the latter, it was frequently the aim of the former, too. A duality and complementarity of the material and the physical pervades the two – not least because the Chinese never separated the physical body from the spiritual self or the mind, as we shall see. In the three aspects of the universe – Heaven, Earth and humanity – only humanity is perishable. This may have led to the belief that, since all emanates from *Tao*, there must be some aspect of the human self that also has the same immutability and permanence of *Tao*: it merely has to be recreated. Secrets of the creation of an immortal self were, however, carefully guarded, and the language of the texts was deliberately partial, symbolic, misleading and only for initiates. Traditions were oral before being committed to esoteric language that today is difficult to decipher without the aid of good commentaries. Consider, for example, the following, very beautiful poem, *The Moon Cave* by a thirteenth century Taoist Master:

> The Moon Cave is clear and deep,
> The environment most beautiful;
> The one who dwells there
> Makes a living upside down,
> Refining the gold potion
> In the jade furnace,
> Cooking white snow sprouts
> In the gold cauldron.
> Operating the cosmic cycle,
> Turning the handle of the Big Dipper,
> Alternately passive and active,
> Conveying the flow of energy,
> Having passed through all barriers
> He freely sails the silver river in peace.[6]

That this is nothing to do with alchemical practices in the laboratory will become clear as this chapter proceeds. Suffice it here to say that, while esoteric language pervaded inner alchemy, and outer alchemy was so secretive that, for example, where ingredients were mentioned the proportions of usage often were not, the result was a contrived attempt to avoid the dangers of the information being understood by the uninitiated. Jean Cooper points out, too, that there were times when alchemy was not in imperial favour and there was a necessity to couch its practices in allegorical terms.[7] Important, too, is the point that many alchemical terms can only be interpreted in their specific contexts, beyond which, they can have widely different meanings.[8]

While outer and inner alchemy had the same goals, there was also much similarity in practice and language, especially in their earliest phases. Outer alchemists might concentrate also on inner meditative practices and inner alchemists on an alchemical "Golden Pill" to finalize their process of immortalization. Some alchemists were both outer and inner at the same time, and many alchemical texts reflect the same *wai-tan/waidan nei-tan/neidan* character. However, the great flowering of outer alchemy in the T'ang/Tang dynasty was to mark its demise thereafter; particularly in Sung/Song times, the complementary nature of the two gave way to the precedence of inner alchemy. However, the legacy of outer alchemy to its inner counterpart, was a commonality of language, so that inner alchemists used the language of the laboratory to depict the inner transformations of the body into an immortal self. One further point here should also be noted. Alchemy was only one means to longevity. Some engaged in such practices as meditation, dietetics, gymnastic exercises, respiration techniques or sexual practices. These were methods that were also adopted as complements to alchemical routes to longevity by some, though each could stand alone as an independent pathway. Nevertheless, later, we shall need to touch on their nature in so far as each is seen as complementary to Taoist alchemy.

The origins of alchemical ideas

The origins of alchemy reach far back into the distant shamanic practices that obtained well before Taoism. It is to the ancient practices of the shamans – the workers of magic that could enhance life through spells to ward off illness, disease and malevolent spirits – that alchemy owes its beginnings. In addition, there are the tales of great sages who could ride the clouds on the backs of dragons, defy the ageing process and death, and enjoy immortality. Here we have the ideas of magical extension of life beyond its normal years. But in a more technical sense Bertschinger notes that alchemy arose from three main sources: experimentation with plants, herbs, animals, minerals and potions to aid health; experimentation to create gold; and the use of inorganic materials to promote health.[9] Certainly, by the fourth century BCE there seems to have been what Daniel Overmyer terms an "active quest for immortality" in a variety of ways.[10] But on a more philosophical level, innate in the Chinese psyche was also – as we have seen in earlier chapters – a sense not only of the interrelation of microcosmic Earth with macrocosmic Heaven, but also belief in what Needham described as an "organist conception in which every phenomenon was connected with every other according to a hierarchical order".[11] Such a view led to the replication of the macrocosm of the universe within the microcosm of the human body, even with the same hierarchical distinctions. Such a concept is at the root of inner alchemy. And in the same way that Heaven and Earth are characterized by the rhythmic changes of *Tao* so, also, is the energy and breath of all life. Sivin illustrated the point admirably:

> In China the earliest and in the long run the most influential scientific explanations were in terms of time. They made sense of the momentary event by fitting it into the cyclical rhythms of natural process. The life cycle of every individual organism – its birth, growth, maturity, decay, and death – went on eternally and in regular order: the cycle of day and night, which regulated the changes of light and darkness, and the cycle of the year, which regulated heat and cold, activity and quiescence, growth and stasis. It was the nested and intermeshed cycles of the celestial bodies that governed the seasonal rhythms and, through them, the vast symphony of individual life courses.[12]

Alchemy was sensitive to such pulsating and rhythmic forces in the macrocosm, and saw them as no different in the laboratory furnace or the human body. Thus, all alchemy was conducted in conjunction with the phases of the cosmos – the moon the sun, the stars, the time of year, month, week, day. Harmonizing the microcosm of the body – whether with a Golden Pill or through inner meditation and visualization – with the macrocosm and dynamism of *Tao* was the philosophical idea that informed alchemy.

The first Chinese alchemists were traditionally the legendary emperors Huang-ti/Huangdi and Yü/Yu. Emperor Huang-ti/Huangdi was taught about *Tao* and such topics as medicinal substances and meditation by a number of immortals. Legend has it that, after ruling for more than a hundred years, he rose to Heaven on the back of a dragon along with some of his court. The legendary Emperor Yü/Yu was credited with the smelting of metals and the differentiating of them into *yin* and *yang* categories. But the earliest real alchemists date back to perhaps as early as the fourth, but certainly the first, century BCE. Indeed, in the mid-second century BCE, the Emperor forbade attempts to make counterfeit gold. Chapter 10 of the *Tao Te Ching/Daodejing* opens with the suggestion that keeping the various souls united in the body, thus holding fast to oneness, was essential for the enlightened sage. Since separation of the souls – a point to be explored later in the section on the anatomy of the body – was tantamount to death, then their unity bespoke maintaining life. Such views were crucial to the understanding of inner alchemy in particular as, also, the repeated motifs in the *Tao Te Ching/Daodejing* concerning the return to childlike innocence, naturalness and freshness. Chuang-tzu/Zhuangzi, on the other hand, spoke out against the prolongation of life and its concomitant avoidance of death, but he also saw life as the concentration of energy and death as the dispersal of it. Then, too, Chuang-tzu/Zhuangzi used the term "Nourishing the Vital Principle". Generally, this became the art of maintaining the mental and physical health of the body by control of its vital energies – *ching/jing* and *ch'i/qi*. By the second and first centuries BCE alchemical practices seem to have been well in place.[13] Notable was the discovery of the remains of Lady Tai/Dai in a tomb at Ma-wang-tui/Mawangdui dated to mid-second century BCE Han times. Her body, which revealed high traces of mercury and lead, was remarkably well preserved. Sivin comments: "These elements were distributed in a way consistent with ingestion before death. Traces in the intestines include native cinnabar, frequently prescribed by physicians as an immortality drug, rather than an artificial elixir."[14]

But it was particularly with the widely skilled *fang-shih/fangshi* that alchemical practices were obvious. Their skills in magical healing and attempts to prolong life through herbs and minerals were to have a significant impact on Taoism. Those who were healing practitioners influenced the development of the later Celestial Masters school of Taoism. Those interested in longevity and immortality were the forerunners of the great alchemists. They occupy a long span of historical time from the early centuries BCE to well into the early centuries of the first millennium. They created potions for immortality from plant, mineral and animal sources. They advocated breathing techniques, gymnastic exercises, dietetics, and sexual practices for the promotion of longevity, and kept alive the notion of the spirit world that invaded the human realm. Indeed, Robinet considers that inner alchemy derived "in direct lineage" from the *fang-shih/fangshi*.[15] One well-known *fang-shih/fangshi* of the second century BCE was Li Shao-chün/Li Shaojun, who won the favour of Emperor Wu for his experiments in making gold, and for his medical practices. He later became one of the famous Taoist Immortals and is recognized today as the first Chinese alchemist.

Needless to say, recipes for immortality were varied and legion, and fed the basic Chinese thought that a good life was a long life, and sagehood an eternal one. Had the Chinese accepted a *spiritual* immortality and not a *physical* corporeal one, there would have been no need for the alchemists. The need to replace the physical organs of the body with everlasting ones, the bones with gold and the flesh with jade – all to create a new and permanent body – were ideas that fed both outer and inner alchemy. Thus, the whole personal self would survive death, or avoid it entirely. Tales abound of those who seemingly died, only to have left no other trace in their coffins than a walking stick, a cloak, or the like. Li Shao-chün/Li Shaojun's coffin, for example, was found to contain only his gown and his hat. While making gold (aurifaction) and making artificial gold (aurifiction) were the precursors of bodily alchemy, it was probably the third century BCE Tsou Yen/Zou Yan of the *Yin–Yang* and Five Agent school who first linked the transmutation of metals into gold with the ingestion of gold for longevity and immortality.[16] Clearly, the desire of emperors to rule indefinitely promoted the search for the elixir of life. However, an inscription on what seems to have been the jade knob of a staff, which Needham dates to as early as the sixth century BCE, gives evidence of breathing exercises and the circulation of *ch'i/qi* in the body – clear links with later inner alchemical practices.[17] This might indicate that the prototype of inner alchemical practices predates experiments with external elixirs or, at the very least, was contemporaneous. However, the inscription may be later, perhaps third or fourth centuries BCE. Although many different schools emerged, and external alchemy flowered in T'ang/Tang times, by the thirteenth century a sharp division had occurred between the outer and inner schools, and it was the latter that were destined to survive.

Textual sources are far too numerous to deal with here. But the textual origins of alchemy stem from the fourth century BCE work *The Yellow Emperor's Classic of Internal Medicine*, the first chapter of which is concerned with longevity and immortality. Another very important text, the *Ts'an-t'ung Ch'i/Cantongqi*, *The Union of the Three*, or *Triple* or *Triplex Unity* as it is sometimes called,[18] is dated in part to the mid-second century. The text is a revision of, and commentary on, an earlier work that was considered ancient even in the times of the alleged author of the *Triple Unity*, Wei Po-yang/Wei Boyang. However, as an immortal, Wei Po-yang/Wei Boyang may well have been purely legendary. Robinet thought so, and considered an early date unlikely for the text attributed to him.[19] While the author's purpose was to create a clear presentation of alchemical processes in the light of the morass of complex and misinformed teachings on alchemy of his time, his own text is plagued with obscurity. Thus, inner or outer alchemists could interpret it in whatever way they wished. Much of the elusive language of alchemy stems from his text – the toad of the sun, the hare of the moon, the black mercury that contains the golden flower, for example[20] – and notable emphasis on the *I Ching/Yijing* and Five Agents. Legend has it that one day, Wei took his dog and three students to the mountains to refine his elixir. When ready, he gave it to his dog, who immediately died! Wei then decided to take the potion himself, whereupon he, too, died straight away. One of his students decided to follow his Master even in death, and he, too, took the potion and died, but the remaining two chose to live and left the scene. After they had gone, Wei, his dog and his student awoke, rose up into Heaven, and became immortals.

I do not want to dwell on the wealth of texts on alchemy, and the interested reader can glean more information elsewhere.[21] However, of immense importance is the work of Ko Hung/Ge Hong of the third to fourth centuries, and I shall have occasion to refer to him and to his work many times in the following pages. His *Book of the Master Who Embraces*

Simplicity: Inner chapters or *Pao-p'u-tzu Nei-p'ien/Baopuzi Neipian* is a major work that deals with the preparation of potions for long life and immortality: how to still the mind; lists of ingredients for potions; techniques for exercises and respiration; the benefits of sexual arts; talismans for warding off evil spirits in the mountains; and how to gain unity within the self. The canvas is encyclopedic, with discussion of herbs and minerals and all kinds of miscellaneous information. The work shows how broad the definition of alchemy could be for some practitioners of it, but its aim seems to have been to gather together the many recipes and practices that led to immortality. There are two parts to Ko Hung/Ge Hong's *Pao-p'u-tzu/Baopuzi*, the *Wei-p'ien/Weipian*, which deals with much that is listed above and is more Taoist in character, and the *Nei-p'ien/Neipian*, which deals more with Confucian ideas of morality in the social and public sphere. While his work by no means excludes inner alchemy, the tone of it is mainly concerned with outer alchemy. Indeed, Ko Hung/Ge Hong believed that only by partaking of the "Golden Elixir", the "Pill" of Immortality, could one become an immortal. Thus, his work lays down meticulous instructions for the collection of materials, the preparation of utensils, the appropriate timing of the process, and so on.

The Golden Elixir

The foundation of much alchemical practice was the belief in the possibility of creating a drug, a pill or an elixir that would prolong life indefinitely, reverse the ageing process and permit an immortal existence. As one author puts it: "Procreation may be nature's necessity, but immortality would be mankind's masterpiece."[22] The modern term for such is *macrobiotics*, albeit one that has more natural connotations in today's world. Substances used to make the ultimate of pills, *the* Elixir, varied from herbs and plants to minerals and animals. Some believed in a specific plant of immortality to be obtained from the elusive islands in the ocean in the East. But while emperors sent expeditions to procure it, the islands and the plant were never found. While such an aim might seem to be a worldly one, Sivin points out that it was an aim that still had "self-cultivation, a means toward transcendence"[23] as its informing goal. The Elixir is identified with the butterfly's transformation from its chrysalis; the transformation of the yolk of an egg into a baby chick; a fish resting in still water; the moon rising in the evening across a still lake; the morning mists on green hills. It is the naturalness that is the expression of *Tao* in the universe. For outer alchemy, the Elixir is an ingested, purified substance. For inner alchemy it is the stilling of the mind to the point of emptiness, to singleness and unity of mind – a gathering of inner energy that begins the process of the formation of an inner Elixir. Here, the Elixir is seen as an internal essence, a pure, spiritual energy that has been refined to perfection, "the unfragmented original essence" as Liu I-ming/Liu Yiming called it.[24] However, ordinarily, it remains unrefined and lost in the desires and enticements of worldly living. What we need to do now is examine just how both outer and inner processes were believed to have brought to fruition the Elixir of Immortality.

Outer alchemy

We have seen that the making of drugs to prolong life was an early phenomenon in China, and that it was the tenth century before the demise of such practices. Since substances like gold, jade and mercury were seen to be imperishable, it seemed logical that if one ingested them – tiny particles over long periods – then the internal body would change its structure from impermanent decaying organs, flesh and bones, to permanent ones. Apart from this rather naïve conception there was a more metaphysical one that translated into physical laboratory praxis, and that was to speed up the processes observed in the universe in the furnaces of the laboratory. It was an attempt to emulate *Tao* in its processes of change in a more concentrated form. Whereas it might take thousands of years to return to the natural state of *Tao*, the laboratory was seen as the means by which cosmic time could be encapsulated into a relatively minute gestation period. Sivin puts this clearly: "They constructed in their laboratories working models of the cosmic order as manifested time. They not only shrank the dimensions of the universe to fit their four walls but also compressed time to make the duration of their manipulations feasible. Thus through point-by-point correspondence the artificial circumstances of the laboratory were made profoundly natural and responsive to the operation of the cosmic *Tao*, to the rhythms of the great order outside."[25] To do this meant that laboratory praxis had also to conform to the patterns of *yin* and *yang*, the cosmology set out in the *I Ching/Yijing*, and to the workings of the Five Agents. The *yin* and *yang* forces had to be returned to a state of balance.

While some outer alchemists sought to prolong life through the ingestion of herbs, fungi, or animals that lived long like tortoises, turtles, cicadas and cranes, particularly the eggs of this last,[26] others maintained the idea of metals and minerals as the best ingredients. For such alchemists, mercury, lead, cinnabar and silver were the main ingredients, and were fired in a cauldron with the strictest and most meticulous observations of timing, heating, blowing with the bellows and cooling. The alternating heating and cooling processes represented the seasons. Prayers, meditations, the correct orientation of the cauldron, the dimensions of the cauldron, and the positions of the sun, moon and stars were essential for correct results. The five main ingredients of the outer alchemist were cinnabar, realgar (a mineral of arsenic sulphide), kalenite, malachite and magnetite.

Many alchemists believed that, though herbs, gymnastic and respiratory exercises might aid in prolonging life, immortality could only be procured by taking the Elixir: only that would enable one to rise up on the clouds and ride through the skies on the back of a dragon. Many compounds were lethal. Ingestion of compounds composed from cinnabar (called red sand), gold, jade, silver, pearl, sulphide of arsenic (called cock-yellow), mica (called mother of the clouds), quartz (called mineral flower) and sometimes with combinations of plant extracts like pine needles, plants from the sesame family and fungis, all became appropriate materials for the alchemists. Each school had its own particular well-guarded secret recipes so that the variations in the lists of ingredients, the amounts to be used and so on, made any consensus of opinion out of the question. Then, too, many of the ingredients were given wonderfully poetic names as part of a coded means to prevent discovery.

ALCHEMY

But the ultimate metals for the alchemists were gold or cinnabar. Ko Hung/Ge Hong said of these:

> By taking these two substances we refine our bodies, so that we neither grow old nor die. I suggest that this seeking of external substances to fortify ourselves may well be compared with a fire that does not die as long as the fuel maintains it, or with feet smeared with verdigris so that they will not decay in water because the strength of the copper serves to protect the underlying flesh. On entering the body, however, gold and cinnabar permeate the blood and breath circulatory systems; it is not a case of mere external help, such as verdigris provides.[27]

Gold was the "true lead" epitomized as the *yang* line between two *yin* ones in the trigram *K'an/Kan* ☵ that is Water. It is the interaction of this trigram with *Li* Fire ☲ that is replicated in the heating and cooling processes of the furnace. The combining of the *yang* line in the middle of *K'an/Kan* with the *yin* line in the middle of *Li* produces the desired result, the Golden Elixir. This is an important aspect that we shall explore in more detail in the context of inner alchemy. Gold, like cinnabar, becomes brighter and more wondrous with the application of heat, suggesting the apparent perfecting of the fusion of the two trigrams to produce pure, balanced and united *yin* and *yang*. Ko Hung/Ge Hong made artificial gold as the ultimate Elixir. It is not clear to what extent he was an inner alchemist, and reading his work one comes away with a clearer impression of his acceptance of laboratory praxis as essential, though his *Pao-p'u-tzu/Baopuzi* is not at all devoid of language that must only be construed as that of inner alchemy. As a graphic example of his belief in external alchemy, the following is a good example:

> In T'ai-I's elixir for Summoning Gross and Ethereal Breaths the five minerals [cinnabar, realgar, arsenolite, malachite, and magnetite] are used and sealed with Six-One lute as in Nine-crucible cinnabars.... It is particularly effective for raising those who have died of a stroke. In cases where the corpse has been dead less than four days, force open the corpse's mouth and insert a pill of this elixir and one of sulphur, washing them down its gullet with water. The corpse will immediately come to life. In every case the resurrected remark that they have seen a messenger with a baton of authority summoning them.[28]

Such an extract shows clearly the extent to which Ko Hung/Ge Hong advocated laboratory techniques, and there are innumerable examples of such in the *Pao-p'u-tzu/Baopuzi*. If Ko Hung/Ge Hong advocated inner alchemy at all, it was only right up to the final point of the brink of immortality. Then, the Golden Elixir, the Pill of Immortality, was the only means by which final immortality could be procured. If this were so, however, Ko Hung/Ge Hong was sufficiently eclectic to accept the use of sexual practices, talismans, herbs and all kinds of concoctions as an aid to the prolongation of life.[29] Fungi, in particular, were considered by Ko Hung/Ge Hong to be highly powerful in promoting longevity.[30] From the third century on, however, cruder drugs were displaced by cinnabar elixir as the ultimate pill for immortality.[31]

Cinnabar was connected with vitality and immortality. Crystals of cinnabar are red, blood-like and, therefore, connected with the life force. It was a *yang*, fiery, substance. Schipper writes of it: "Found in the depths of the earth's crust, cinnabar is, so to speak, a highly concentrated form of solar energy which makes all things live and can heal any form of decay."[32] As mercuric sulphide, cinnabar is transformed into mercury, and that must have been a dramatic change from red to silver for the alchemists. It was the purely *yang* cinnabar that was believed to have the properties for the highest kind of immortality. To reach this potency, we learn from the *Pao-p'u-tzu/Baopuzi* that the cinnabar had to be refined nine times – synonymous with the gestation period of the child in the womb. Each time it rendered the Elixir more powerful and made the time in which immortality could be achieved less. Thus, for just one transmutation it would take three years to become an immortal. After nine transmutations, it would only take three days. But each of the nine transmutations brought different powers, different visions, and different heightened consciousness, though any one of the nine transmutation processes was thought to bring about immortality. However, while gold and cinnabar were the central metals for immortality, Ko Hung/Ge Hong's work includes a host of elixirs from other means, all of which were designed to bring about heightened powers – invisibility; having whatever one asks for; knowing the future; exorcizing ghosts, for example.

By T'ang/Tang times, outer alchemy had reached its zenith. And with its development had come intricate and meticulous praxis. The quality of utensils, and of ingredients, and the preparation and composure of the alchemist, were all absolutely necessary for success. Ko Hung/Ge Hong had earlier stressed that only those of the highest calibre should attempt to make the Elixir, and then only after a hundred days of purification processes. He mentions a number of rituals that should precede the preparation of the Elixir.[33] The "laboratory" should not be thought of as wholly confined to a building; in fact, the best places to prepare Elixirs were mountains. Secrecy was essential, and the mountains formed an ideal retreat for such practices. Ko Hong/Ge Hong stipulated that no more than three companions should witness the process. The deities of the mountains would make the preparation more auspicious and, according to Ko Hung/Ge Hong earthly immortals also dwelt there. The mountains also supplied magical herbs and fungi. And, on a more pragmatic note according to Ko Hung/Ge Hong: "They are good places in which to sit out war and catastrophe."[34] By T'ang/Tang times the cult of immortality was of considerable importance in the court of the emperor and the outer alchemists had a hey-day.

The firing process was critical to the supposed success of the experiment. The natural process by which metals and lead were transmuted into cinnabar and, eventually, gold took thousands of years, with rhythmic alterations of the *yin* coolness of moonlight and the *yang* warmth of sunshine. It was exactly this that the alchemists tried to emulate in their meticulously designed furnaces, and T'ang/Tang times are notable for the attempt to build furnaces that would replicate perfectly the *yin* and *yang* rhythms of the universe, in condensed format, as we have seen. The sixty-four hexagrams of the *I Ching/Yijing* were used as a basis for the cycles of heating and cooling. The combining of *yin* and *yang* metals in such a way that they became one, as in pre-creation times, was what was created by the transmutation of metals. It was a return of the substances to their original state, their original oneness. The end result after ingesting the Elixir was also a return to the timeless state of primordial *Tao*, the transcending of the mind constraints of ordinary mortality, and equality of essence with both Heaven and Earth, along with the immortality that these possess.

Outer alchemy obviously did not achieve its aims! And it was clear by late T'ang/Tang times that such was the case. Nevertheless, tombs like that of Lady Tai/Dai have subsequently been discovered with remarkably well-preserved bodies within them, probably the result of ingesting mercury and lead. It also has to be said that alchemical experimentation brought about discoveries in all kinds of preliminary sciences – botany, herbology, medicine, zoology, metallurgy, for example. But we have to remember that the goal of any experimentation was immortality, and discoveries in any of these fields would not have been given great prominence. Many discoveries were accidental or unconscious ones. Yet physicians, in particular, were to learn a good deal from the alchemists. Despite such advances, it could not go unnoticed that chronic pain, illness and death awaited those who ingested deadly poisons. Five T'ang/Tang dynasty emperors died in such attempts to gain immortality. The alchemists themselves blamed such deaths on the lack of appropriate preparation of the recipient, or considered the ravings of an agonized body and mind as experience of wondrous things! In fact, the more radical the effect, the more the alchemists believed the drug to have worked! And when death occurred, this seemed to be a premature summoning of the person to the Land of the Immortals. Michel Strickmann cited the following example of the devastating effects of a "White Powder of the Perfected of the Grand Bourne for abandoning the waistband":

> When you have taken a spateful of it, you will feel an intense pain in your heart, as if you had been stabbed there with a knife. After three days you will want to drink, and when you have drunk a full *hu* your breath will be cut off. When that happens, it will mean that you are dead. When your body has been laid out, it will suddenly disappear, and only your clothing will remain. Thus you will be an immortal released in broad daylight by means of his waistband.[35]

It was small wonder, then, that people came to view elixirs with distrust. Then, too, despite numerous deaths, there were no innovations to the well-worn theory and practice of outer alchemy by late T'ang/Tang times. It was, therefore, the inner alchemists who survived to point the way to different means of becoming immortal. It is to these and their beliefs and practices that we must turn shortly, but before doing so, it is essential to have some idea of how Taoists viewed the internal body.

The Taoist anatomy of the body

The Taoist view of the inside of the body is one of a microcosm that reflects in its entirety the macrocosm of the universe. Imagine a journey through your own body that is like a journey through the earth, the stars, the planets and the whole universe. Inside the body are the mountains, lakes, oceans and plains of the earth, the spirits and deities that inhabit the heavens, and the primordial essences that are the stuff of the universe before it ever came into being. The outcome of such a belief is that the body is an expression of *Tao*. The physical being is not that which has to be denied in the search for a subtle self that transcends it as a soul. The physical being *itself* has the answers to the problems of life. It, itself, is capable of reversing the attitudes of mind that connect it with the materialism of the world, back to the primordial *Tao-ness* that it really is. It has to be said that the Taoists bent any current theories of the anatomy of the body to their own particular perspectives of a microcosmic body that paralleled the macrocosm of Heaven. To analyse such views, we must begin with concepts of the soul, the spirit of the human being, and how this was related to the concept of death.

The ancient idea of spirits and natural forces affecting the lives of individuals might well have informed such a belief that the inner body reflects the macrocosm of the world around. But we need to look closely at the ways in which the inner being connected with the outer macrocosm. Early texts tell us *hsien/xian* or "souls" could soar up into the skies like birds. Such souls were to become the immortals. But this was not the fate of all. Two kinds of souls were identified, the *yang*, *hun* souls that could rise up after death and become a *shen*, a spirit, and the *yin*, *p'o/po* souls that descended into the grave of the earth, where they disintegrated with the corpse. Tu Wei-ming points out the unique nature of such a theory that gives human beings not one, unique and isolated soul, but numerous souls that link the individual inseparably with the cosmos, and with other deceased souls. He writes: "The biological nature of our existence is such that we do not exist as discrete temporal and spatial entities. Rather, we are part of the cosmic flow that makes us inevitably and fruitfully linked to an ever-expanding network of relationships."[36] In the earliest times, only nobility was expected to rise to Heaven. While the idea of *hsien/xian*, "immortals", who could survive mortal death, sip jade, dwell in the clouds and exist in the islands of the East in the Realms of Immortals was evident in early Han times,[37] for most, the fate was the netherworld – both for *hun* and *p'o/po* souls.

The *hun* souls are the deeper innate souls of the self, the inner nature. There are three of them, and they are the spiritual dimensions of the self that lean towards Heaven, towards goodness and discernment. They are expanding and evolving in character and are the rationalizing aspects of the self. They are *yang* in nature. The *hun* can rise to Heaven and become *shen*, like deities and kindly spirits. But they are also the medium for reincarnation. Becoming a *shen*, that is to say rising to the status of a benevolent spirit, is the fulfilling in part of the highest spiritual nature of the individual. While the numerous souls posited by the Chinese and the Taoists are by no means clear cut in nature, function and ultimate end, Livia Kohn notes that each of the three *hun* souls is related to Heaven, the Five Agents and Earth, respectively, and are also called "Womb Radiance", "Numen Guide" and "Gloomy Essence", respectively. "The first spirit soul always strives for the purity of man; the second always wishes him involved in manifold affairs; the third, finally, produces his desire for comfortable living."[38] The *shen* had widely different meanings for the Chinese and, indeed, for many Taoists. But, generally, the Taoists accepted the *shen* as material, and as that which was formed when the first breath of life was taken, when the primordial Breath of the universe, *ch'i/qi*, combined with the innate Essence, *ching/jing*, of the individual. Breath and Essence made life possible; separation of them meant death.

P'o/po souls have more to do with the outward life and emotions of a person, with desires and aversions. Hence they are the inner aspects of the self that are involved in the world. There are seven of them, and they are fundamentally inimical to the health and spiritual progress of the individual, for they belong with ghosts, with death, and with demons, and they are contracting and involuting in nature. The *p'o/po* souls will divide and decay with the corpse after death, or will exist physically in the underworld of hells. However, if a violent death has occurred, the *p'o/po* will almost certainly become a malevolent ghost, a *kuei/gui*. Tu Wei-ming suggests that the *p'o/po* spirits, being the negative *yin* spirits of the self, are in any case, equated with *kuei/gui*,[39] the more malevolent ghosts and spirits that are bent on harming human beings.

Since the *hun* souls are of the nature of Heaven, and the *p'o/po* souls of Earth, they orientate towards their natural origins. Robinet aptly commented on this battle within the human being: "Here again are two dynamic principles that pull human beings upward and downward and that we must harmonize and maintain within our bodies, because they are the source of life. When these souls tear apart and escape, that is death."[40] Keeping all the spirits together in the body was, therefore, essential to the continuance of life. Such a theory of multiple souls of different natures, and differently *yin* or *yang*, informed a remarkably complex number of ideas concerning the fate of the soul after death, not least because of the influence of Buddhism with its many heavens and hells, and its theories of *karma* and rebirth. Suffice it to say for our purposes here that retaining *all* the souls in the body was necessary for continued life. In a wider context, Tu Wei-ming emphasizes superbly the importance of the Chinese concepts of souls in such aspects as ancestor veneration:

> To the Chinese, souls are neither figments of the mind nor wishful thoughts of the heart. They have a right to exist, like stones, plants and animals, in the creative transformation of the cosmos. The malevolent, negative souls can harm people, haunting the weak and upsetting the harmonious state of the human community. However, by and large, human beings benefit from positive aspects of the soul, for through the "soul force" they are in touch with the dead and with the highest spiritual realm, Heaven."[41]

We need to bear in mind such ideas in the understanding of the control of the inner body and being that is necessary in inner alchemy.

Working for the death of the body are three major cadavers or worms lodged within. Each is appropriated to one of three "cinnabar fields" of the body, one called "Old Blue" in the head, "White Maiden" in the thorax and "Bloody Corpse" in the abdomen. They reside at three "gates". At certain times of the year, they report to the Jade Emperor of the Heavens on the good or evil deeds and thoughts of the individual. The worms create illness, since the more they hasten the death of the body, the sooner they can be free of it. Their reports to the Jade Emperor are, therefore, of evil deeds rather than good ones, since the life of their hosts will be shortened by the Jade Emperor for any misdemeanours they have committed. Other worms reside in cavities along the spine, and prevent the flow of *yang* energy up through the spine, as do the three cadavers who have control of the gates. The cadavers sap vitality in their respective fields. Destruction of the cadavers and worms is essential for avoiding death, returning to *Tao* and, thus, for immortality. Since they love meat, cereals, alcohol and pungent flavours like onions and garlic, avoiding these was believed to weaken them. Moreover, the same substances are those loathed by the *good* spirits and deities in the body, who will leave it if they are exposed to them too much.

We all know that emotions affect our energies in life. The mind is difficult to still, the heartbeat is affected by fear, emotional upset, sex, anxiety, excessive happiness or sorrow. Leakage of energy in the body leads to tiredness, sometimes exhaustion and illness and contributes to ageing. One of the aims of internal alchemy was to prevent such leakage of energy. Even the loss of saliva and, as we shall see below, semen, from the body, represented a leakage of essential energy. And, like the rhythm of *yin* and *yang* in the cosmos, the body develops its *yang*-evolving energies during the first part of its life, before the declining, ageing *yin* takes over and gradually increases until the point of death, when *yang* is minimized. *Yang*, too, is representative of the subtle and spiritual aspects of the self, *yin* of the grosser, physical self, just as Heaven was formed from cosmic *yang* energy and Earth from cosmic *yin*.

The body also has energy channels that convey energy throughout, as well as crucial "openings". When blocked, illness occurs through imbalance. Such a theory lies at the heart of the practice of acupuncture. There are special circulations of energy that we shall look at later in more detail, but here we need merely to note that the flow of energy without blockage was essential for the development of the body that could become immortal. The flow of energy, *ch'i/qi*, in the body was believed to match the flow of cosmic energy when it operated without impediment. Some was *yin*, passive and descending, and some was *yang*, active and rising.

The cosmic energy of the universe is, then, mirrored in the whole body as, indeed, are all the other features of the universe. Kohn writes: "Every single part of the body corresponds to a celestial or geographical feature of the world – the body is the world. Vice versa, the world is also in the body."[42] The five essential organs, for example, match the Five Agents. There are forces of good and forces of evil, and the tensions between them are as evident in the body as in the universe. In short, the universe has what Robinet termed "a sequence of nested enclosures in time and space",[43] which were to be found on a microcosmic scale in the human body. In the same way that the universe is a unity of both physical and subtle matter, so the physicality of the body alongside its subtle energies and aspects are seen as a unity. There is no dualism of spirit and matter in the Taoist, or Chinese, concept of the self: immortality would be as much of the body as of the spiritual essence.

The whole landscape of Earth, then, is to be found within the body. It is a view of the body that lasted from the early centuries CE to the present day.[44] I do not want to dwell on the intricacies of depicting such a bodily landscape, but an example should suffice here from the *Jade Calendar*:

> The landscape of the head consists of a high mountain, or rather a series of peaks around a central lake. The lake lies midway between the back of the skull and the point between the eyebrows (the Pole Star and mirror). In the middle of the lake stands a palatial building, where there are eight rooms surrounding a ninth, central one. This is the Hall of Light (*ming-t'ang*), the house of the calendar of the kings of ancient China. In front of this palace and the lake around it, lies a valley (the nose). The entrance to the valley is guarded by two towers (the ears). Inside one, hangs a bell and inside the other, a stone chime. Whenever someone passes, they are struck – something we perceive as the ringing of the ears. At the far end of the valley runs a stream bringing water from the big lake into a smaller one at the other end . . .[45]

And so the descriptions continue. In terms of meditation and inner alchemy I need only mention some of the more important aspects of the body here. The three cinnabar fields, noted earlier, are the most important. They are the *tan-t'ien/dantian*, also called the "elixir fields". While texts differ as to the exact locations within the body, the lowest of the three fields is generally said to begin between one and three inches below the navel, depending on the source. Ko Hung/Ge Hong, for example, cited it as two and four-tenths inches below. This really places it between the kidneys, a space, Robinet stated that "symbolizes the mid-point between Yin and Yang, the equivalent of the Supreme Pinnacle, the Center, and the highest point of the world that encloses Yin and Yang. It is both the primordial couple and the place of their union, and at the same time the child born of them."[46] It is here that a Spirit Embryo is conceived and nourished and is thus the place where energy is generated. It is also called the "Sea of Breath" (*Ch'i-hai/Qihai*), and is the most important of the three fields. The middle field, often referred to as the "Yellow Court", the "Crimson Palace" or "Golden Palace", is in the area of the "Golden Gate Towers" below the heart and spleen. The uppermost field is about three inches within the head from the point between the eyebrows, and is sometimes referred to as the "Mud Pill Court", or the "Palace of Ni-wan".[47] Names, terms and locations are, however, not consistent. Each of the regions is an area of heat, suggested by the word *tan/dan* – these are the cauldrons of the body that will replace those of outer alchemy.

Also in the body are three important "gates" or "passes" through which energy flows. Such gates are to be found along the spine, and control entry into the cinnabar fields. The lowest is situated at the coccyx, or between the kidneys. The second is in a vertebra of the chest, between the shoulder blades. The top one, also called the "House of Wind", is at the occiput, where the spine joins the skull. These gates or passes will be important in the process of inner alchemy, as we shall see. Then there are nine orifices, which are the three fields, the three "gates" and three others in the head. These nine are crucial to the circuit of energy, *ch'i/qi*, through the appropriate meridians. There are also "bridges", which serve the purpose of linking the major meridians.[48]

Most important within the body are its inhabitants – the deities. Livia Kohn writes: "The body, as much as the larger universe, is ruled and lived in by the gods – the multi-faceted manifestations of spirit, the visible and accessible aspect of the Tao on earth. The body as a residence of the gods, as a network of divine halls and palaces, as a replica of the universe is the true body of the Tao, the way in which the Tao is found in everyone and everywhere."[49] Thus, the way to the gods is within. And there is a multiplicity of deities within the body for they are responsible for every joint and organ, some of the more important parts of the body having a number of deities responsible for them.[50] Controlling and regulating the body was much like regulating a state. Ko Hung/Ge Hong thus said:

> The body of an individual can be pictured as a state. The diaphragm may be compared with the palace, the arms and legs, with the suburbs and frontiers. The bones and joints are like officials; the inner gods like the sovereign; the blood like ministers of state; the breath like the population. Therefore, anyone able to regulate his own body can regulate a state. To take good care of the population is the best way to make your state secure; by the same token, to nurture the breaths is the way to keep the body whole, for when the population scatters, a state goes to ruin; when the breaths are exhausted, the body dies.[51]

Here, then, is part of the rationale behind inner alchemy, for it sees the nurturing of the harmony and unity of the body as essential to avoid the separation of souls that result in death. The body is divine, for it has the divine expressions of *Tao* within it. Realizing that divinity, the *Tao* from which one emerged and which one is, is what inner alchemy is all about.

Three major deities reside in each of the cinnabar fields or the three palaces. They are the important *Three Ones*. T'ai-i/Taiyi "Supreme One" resides in the uppermost field (though as the "Supreme One", and therefore the One that unifies all, it may also be found in the lower fields[52]), T'ien-i/Tianyi "Heavenly One" in the middle, and Ti-i/Diyi "Earthly One" in the lowest. The Three Ones are also equated with the Three Treasures – *shen*, *ch'i/qi* and *ching/jing*, respectively (to be examined immediately below). All the deities of the body – and some texts put them at thirty-six thousand[53] – were not just abstract ideas, but were important in meditational visualization. Each had its own particular attire, its particular residence, its special days, and specific function or functions in the body. The female deity, the Mother, features in many aspects of the body. She is the Jade Maiden of Obscure Brilliance. She is a *yin* energy that can take on many different roles. She has six female attendants, Jade Maidens of the kidneys, who report the misdemeanours of their host.[54] The art of visualizing such deities and spirits – who could, if they wished, depart from the body – kept them happily retained in the body on the one hand, and unified and harmonized them all on the other. There were also ministers, offices, and governing bureaus to be kept happily content within the body by the pure and good life lived by their host.

In being host to the deities of the universe, the body is host to *Tao*. The entanglements with the world obscure this reality, and the inner body is neither known nor nourished. The deities of the inner self that nourish the inner energies and nature are what keep it alive, keep it functioning. When they depart, there can be no life at all. In a wonderfully expressive statement of the goal here, Robinet wrote of the adept:

> By contemplating himself and by locating himself in a correctly aligned geometric schema that represents the cosmos as a sort of mandala, he finally identifies himself correctly and ritually in relationship to the axis of the world. Further, by rediscovering the Prime Mover, he rediscovers the order of the world and his own relationship to it. The two movements go together. He must impose order on the world to reconcile it to himself and to reconcile himself with himself.[55]

Such an alignment is brought about by contemplation of the inner nature of the self that is ultimately *Tao*. But *Tao* that is experienced in its totality within is concomitant with the development of a new body that is *Tao*, a new spiritual body of cosmic unity, a spiritual self that merges with the cosmos. We must turn now to examine how that comes about.

The Three Treasures

Critical to the understanding of the body, to the experience of *Tao* and to the attaining of immortality through the development of a new spiritual self, a spiritual Embryo that develops into an immortal body, are the Three Treasures – *ching/jing*, *ch'i/qi* and *shen*. They are sometimes called Three Flowers, Herbs or Jewels. It is these Treasures that make life possible. Cosmically, they are the functioning of the energies of *Tao* in the universe, just as they are responsible for the life-giving essences of the body. While the first two of these may have been rather undifferentiated in earliest times, they all came to have different, yet interrelated functions in the cosmos as much as the human body. They are energies within the body, but energies that were once pure *Tao*. Restoring the original purity of each, and their primordial nature and unity, is the aim of inner alchemy. Each obtains both inwardly, in each individual life, and cosmically, in the universe itself. *Ching/jing* is the vital essence, vitality, sometimes equated with semen, though it has wider meanings; *ch'i/qi* is vital breath and energy; *shen* is spirit. The importance of the Three is illustrated in the following extract from the *Secret Instructions of the Holy Lord on the Scripture of Great Peace*:

> To pursue long life you must guard energy and harmonize spirit and essence. Never let them leave your body, but continue to think of them as joined in one. With prolonged practice your perception will become finer and subtler. Quite naturally you will be able to see within your body. The physical body will become gradually lighter, the essence more brilliant, and the light more concentrated. In your mind you will feel greatly restful, delighted and full of joy. You will go along with the energy of Great Peace. By then cultivating yourself, you can turn around and go along with all without. Within there will be perfect longevity; without there will be perfect accordance with the order of the universe. Without the exertion of any muscle you naturally attain Great Peace.[56]

Such is a description of the effects of harmonizing these three essential components of existence. The greater the degree of harmony, the greater the strength and longer the life of the individual. Leakage of any essence or energy from the body is, as was noted above, inimical to health and long life, and leakage occurs through engagement in the world in such a way that stress, anxiety, emotion, sorrow, excessive eating, drinking, desires, aversions – all contribute to loss of the Three Treasures. Conversely, maintaining the Three Treasures and refining them into one energized unity, results in immortality, for the primordial essence of all life that is *Tao* becomes the very essence of the self.

Ching/jing

Ching/jing is *yin* vital essence, that which generates all life. It provides us with our state, or lack of, well-being, depending on its levels and quality. At its coarsest level, it is bodily male and female sexual fluids, that which generates new life, and resides in the lowest cinnabar field. But it can, in addition, refer to wider secretions of the body,[57] and hence to substances like saliva that should not be leaked from the body any more than sexual fluid. It is also the vital essence that creates forms, both on the worldly level, and on the cosmic level of the creative energy that brings about the cosmos from the primordial Void that is *Tao*. It is the essence in the seed that makes things what they are, as much as the essence in the Void that makes the universe what it is. It is also that which permits the wisdom of the sage:

> The vital essence of all things:
> It is this that brings them to life.
> It generates the five grains below
> And becomes the constellated stars above.

> When flowing amid the heavens and the earth
> We call it ghostly and numinous.
> When stored within the chests of human beings,
> We call them sages.[58]

The storage of this essence in our chests, that is to say, in the middle cinnabar field, and not in the lowest cinnnabar field where it is normally concentrated, is necessary for the enlightenment that the sage attains. Increasing it, then, brings health and longevity; decreasing it, illness and death. It is decreased by the involvement of the mind in the world.

Ch'i/qi

Ch'i/qi has wide meanings – anything from the subtle breath of life itself to abdominal wind.[59] Originally, it referred to the steam arising from cooked rice. But its importance lies in the fact that it is the emanation of *Tao* in all aspects of life from the cosmos at large to its expression in the human body itself. As such it has multiple forms, so there are many *ch'i/qi*s that can be both energy and matter. It is cause and effect in the changing rhythms of all that exists. Livia Kohn puts this admirably: "It is a continuously changing, forever flowing force, an energy that can appear and disappear, can be strong and weak, can be controlled and overwhelming. *Qi* is what moves on in the changing rhythm of the seasons; *qi* shines in the rays of the sun; *qi* is what constitutes health or sickness; *qi* is how we live, move, eat, sleep."[60] So while it can mean the air that we breath, and the breath itself, it can also be indicative of energy and vitality. Michael Page likens it to a cut diamond that reflects different lights, yet is the same diamond.[61]

The cosmic importance of *ch'i/qi* cannot be overestimated. It is the *One* in the Taoist process of creation, the first subtle entity that emerges from *Tao*. As such it is also *Te*, the expression of *Tao* in the whole cosmos. Divided it is *yin* and *yang*, and therefore informs the rhythms of rise and fall, ascent and descent, advance and retreat and the swing of all things between polarities. It is what makes possible all the changes and transformations in the universe and what, at the same time, interrelates and unites all the changing phenomena. It is also the causative nature of the Five Agents, that which makes Wood the Agent of spring, Fire of summer, Metal of autumn, and Water of winter. It is what gives each of the "ten thousand things" its special nature; and the particular nature of it in each individual, makes you what you are and I what I am. Ultimately it is the subtle link between all things and *Tao*.

Medics of ancient China were less interested in the organs of the body than in the fluids and energies that pervaded it: healing the *ch'i/qi* energy was the most important facet of restoring health.[62] For health and longevity it is essential, but can only be stirred, nourished and stored when the body is diverted from external emotions and over-involvement with the world. In inner alchemy it will be the crucial link between *ching/jing* and *shen* and is located mainly in the middle cinnabar field between the *ching/jing* in the lowest and *shen* in the uppermost, though T'ang/Tang alchemists believed it to be in the lowest field.[63] Breathed into the body it is *yang* and embodies the energies of the sun and fire. Breathed out it is *yin*, and embodies the energies of the moon and water. It circulates in the meridians of the body and is affected by emotions, temperature, rest, exhaustion, so that being over-animated disperses it, and getting tired and exhausted wastes it. Here, it is in its subtle form in the body, but it also condenses into more solid tangible forms such as the vital organs, and even more condensed forms as the skeleton, muscles and flesh. In the same way it can be subtle cosmic air or condense to form huge mountains.

While its presence in the body can only be inferred through imbalances, energy loss and gain, and the like, the physical act of breathing, and the necessity of breath for life meant that respiration was the most observable facet of *ch'i/qi* in human existence. It was an observation that prompted breathing techniques as a means of nourishing the *ch'i/qi* in the body. Since health, and life itself, depended on *ch'i/qi*, then it was also thought to be important not to let much of the air out – from any part of the body (hence the need for attention to diet!). Retaining the air that was inhaled and letting as little out as possible, became a means to store and nourish *ch'i/qi*, and the Taoist adept was expected to feed on it, and nourish it within the body.

Shen

Shen is spirit, the soul, the psyche, the spiritual aspect in the self. Cosmically, it is the Void, the undifferentiated *Tao* of primordial chaos. In the body, *shen* is associated with the heart, the seat of emotions; with the mind; the deepest consciousness; and with the nervous system. However, though connected with the heart, it functions through other organs also. The *Huai-nan-tzu/Huainanzi* recognized that it was important to lose desires and still the emotions in order to nourish the *shen*, for it was considered to be the means of mystical knowledge, should that be possible. In Roth's words: "So the *shen* seems to act as the essential directing agent in human experience. It is a core element of consciousness, inherently tranquil, which is disturbed and injured by emotions, desires, excessive thinking. The harm that these do seems to involve tying up the attention of the *shen* so that it is not clear and cannot direct cognition."[64] To counter such harm inner alchemy produces refined *shen* by purifying, nourishishing and transmuting *ch'ing/jing* and *ch'i/qi* into *shen*. *Shen* is the part of us that is intimately *Tao* and the means by which we can experience *Tao*. It is the means of return to the primordial state of *Tao* from whence we sprang. Located in the uppermost field of the body, in the head, it is the flower that needs to develop from the roots of *ching/jing* and the stem of *ch'i/qi*.

The Spirit Embryo

At the beginning of his classic *Understanding Reality* the eleventh century Taoist Chang Po-tuan/Zhang Boduan began his teaching with the following words:

> If you do not seek the great way to leave the path of delusion, even if you are intelligent and talented you are not great. A hundred years is like a spark, a lifetime is like a bubble. If you only crave material gain and prominence, without considering the deterioration of your body, I ask you, even if you accumulate a mountain of gold can you buy off impermanence?[65]

The creation of a *new* and *physically spiritual* body was the ultimate aim of the inner alchemists. It was as early as Han times that the belief arose in the possibility of developing an immortal foetus, an embryo, within the body. It was thought to be subtle, light, and yet physical. It was given many names – the Golden Embryo; the Holy Embryo; the Immortal Embryo; Golden Elixir; the True Person Cinnabar of the North; the Golden Pill; the Pearl. It is formed after a long period of inward concentration. Chang San-feng/Zhang Sanfeng is reputed to have written: "At this time a point of absolutely positive vitality crystallizes within the centre. It is stored in the time when desires are cleared and emotions are stilled, yet it has appearance and form. When you get to this stage, the breath stays in the 'womb'. Incubation inside and out with unerring timing is called the ten months' work."[66] It is the True Self and is formed when *shen* is purified and unified with *ch'i/qi* and *ching/jing*, the three being indistinguishable and united. The proper circulation of energies in the body feed and nourish it until, when fully developed, it is able to leave the body like the butterfly that leaves the chrysalis.

The point at which the Spirit Embryo is formed is synonymous with the opening of what is called the *Mysterious Pass* or *Gate*. For this to occur there must be an emptying of the self in the sense of a cessation of egoistic involvement with the world. Such a state is sometimes also called the *Mysterious Female*, the imagery being of the emptiness of the womb into which the embryo is planted. It is described, too, as the "centre", but not so much as the centre of the body as the central equilibrium of the self, "an undefined opening anywhere in the eternity of time and the infinity of space".[67] As such it is the central "point" of the universe – the same axis as the *Tao* that is centripetal to all life. But it is an opening that has to be worked for:

> Nourish yourself thus within,
> Tranquil and still in the void,
> While at source concealing brilliance
> Which illuminates within your whole body.
> Shut and close up the mouth,
> Repressing within the spiritual trunk,
> The senses all swallowed up
> To gently support that pearl so young.
> Observe it there, the unobvious –
> So close by and easy to seek.[68]

The whole process of creating then nourishing the Spirit Embryo through its "conception", its growth, and its release into the Void is what inner alchemy entails.

Sexual alchemy

Sometimes separated from inner alchemy, but sometimes included in its broad remit, are sexual practices. The idea that sex diminished energy and length of life was an ancient one in China. The pre-pubescent male, "green dragon", and female, "white tiger", were believed to have their generative energies intact, with healthy *yang* energy, since there were no menstrual or seminal emissions. Thus, regulation of sexual practice seems to have been advocated by early medical texts. However, judging by five texts on sexual techniques found at the Ma-wang-tui/Mawangdui tombs dated to second century BCE Han times, the "art of the bedchamber" seems to have rivalled medical and *yogic* sexual restraint since late Chou/Zhou times.[69] If sexual intercourse were harmful to health and longevity, it was nevertheless the natural union of *yin* and *yang* that brought about procreation of new life, as it had with the creation of the universe and the division of cosmic *ch'i/qi* into *yin* and *yang*. Legend has it that the "art of the bedchamber" was first taught to Huang-ti/Huangdi, the Yellow Emperor, by a maiden goddess. There were also other legends of goddesses that taught sexual arts to men who, as a result, lived long and healthy lives. Perhaps, too, the spring festivals of ancient Chinese origin, where copulation was part of the marking of the end of the long winter, had some influence on the way Chinese viewed sexuality.

But the important idea that gained ground was the art of intercourse without male ejaculation. Such a view was concomitant with the medical view that loss of coarse *ching/jing* was to be avoided if one wished to be healthy, live a long a life, or for those adepts who pursued ideas of immortality. It is because of this idea that there is a close link between sexual practices and inner alchemy. Indeed, representations of alchemical praxis in visual form were frequently sexual.[70] But it is also possible that inner alchemy used the language of sex to explain the union of *yin* and *yang* within that brings about the birth of the Spirit Embryo.[71] Cleary and Aziz note that sexual symbolism came to be a mode of expression in inner alchemy, providing a dramatic means to define the creation of the Spirit Embryo. The union of the trigrams Heaven and Earth, the union of Fire and Water, and of the Agents Wood and Metal, are frequently written of as a "wedding" in the firing process of inner alchemy.[72]

The aim of sexual alchemy, then, was to gather and conserve the coarse *ching/jing* in the form of semen, and change or transmute it into *ch'i/qi*. It was the gathering of energy from a sexual partner in order to enhance one's own levels of vital energy. Thus, it is sometimes referred to as "paired practice", or "dual cultivation". While the act did not preclude benefits to women, it has to be said that it was men who practised sexual alchemy – and not without criticism from many quarters. It was sexual arousal that generated energy, and orgasm or ejaculation that depleted it. The aim, therefore, was to absorb energy at the moment of orgasm or ejaculation, but withdraw at that point to absorb the energy of the partner. Needless to say, this was not a reciprocal, two-way process: only one of the two could benefit, the woman preventing orgasm but receiving male semen, or – and more frequently – the male preventing ejaculation[73] and receiving energy from the woman's orgasm. Love, passion and desire do not enter into the contract, for if they do, energy is lost, not gained. The aim is purely pragmatic in generating *ching/jing*, and considerable training has to be undergone in order to make the sexual act free of ego and desire. The more partners one has, the greater the acquisition of energy gained. The younger and healthier the partner, the better the quality of energy obtained. As Wile comments on this point: "Partners are chosen then on the criteria of looks, feel, freshness, and taste – like fruit in the marketplace."[74]

In sexual alchemy, the female essence is regarded as *yin* cinnabar, and the male essence as *yang* mercury. Combining *yin* and *yang* in the furnace of the receiving body is representative of the union of Heaven and Earth. The energy gained is stored in the lowest cinnabar field. The trigram *K'an/Kan* ☵, in which the male, *yang* line is in the centre, represents the generative energy of the woman. Here, the hidden *yang* is the Tiger and lead in the watery female. The male generative energy is the reverse, with the *yin* line hidden between two *yang* lines in the trigram *Li* ☲ . The *yin* line here is the Dragon, and mercury or cinnabar, and is hidden in the fiery male. The whole point of the union of male and female, as of inner alchemy, is the fusion of the *middle yin* and *yang* concealed lines in the *K'an/Kan* and *Li* trigrams. Through the Fire of the donor, and the Water of the receiver, the liquid *ching/jing* is obtained and stored in the lowest cinnabar field, where *ch'i/qi* and *shen* separate the coarse *ching/jing* from the subtle. Subtle *ching/jing* is then transmuted to the upper fields to become the Elixir of Immortality,[75] with the creation of a Spirit Embryo. The two trigrams *K'an/Kan* and *Li* are the closest one can get to the pure *yang* of Heaven and the pure *yin* of Earth. The uniting of Heaven and Earth produced the multiplicity of phenomena in the universe. What the extraction of the middle *yin* and *yang* lines of *K'an/Kan* and *Li* do is to reverse that process to *yin* and *yang* in total primordial equilibrium. This is the whole point of inner alchemy.

The relation between sexual alchemy and inner alchemy was often a very close one. But there also seems to have been an independent school of sexual alchemy at the time of Ko Hung/Ge Hong.[76] It seems, too, that many regarded sexual alchemy as a means to longevity, but not to immortality itself. Ko Hung/Ge Hong would certainly have stressed the need for the final Elixir of Immortality. According to him: "Sometimes, narrow-minded processors try to observe solely the recipes regarding sexual intercourse in order to control the gods and genii without utilizing the great medicines of gold and cinnabar. This is the height of folly!"[77] Communal ritual sex was a pronounced feature of the Celestial Masters religious sect of Taoism and, also, of the later Southern branch of the Complete Reality school of Sung/Song times. While authorship and dating are doubtful, three texts, *Summary of the Golden Elixir*, *Secrets of Gathering the True Essence* and *Rootless Tree*, have been attributed to Chang San-feng/Zhang Sanfeng, the alleged founder of T'ai Chi Ch'üan/Taijiquan. All, but particularly the first two of these, accept sexual alchemy praxis.[78] Some practices were private and others communal, the latter designed to absolve sins and ward off misfortunes.[79]

While sexual alchemy might seem to open the door for all kinds of malpractice, in fact, the conditions for it – time of day, the woman's cycle, the lunar phase, weather, diet, degree of tiredness, the physical nature of the woman – all conspired against treating the process lightly. Indeed, there were considerable prohibitions as to inappropriate times. These factors, together with the extensive training necessary, meant that genuine adepts certainly existed, despite critics. Needham pointed out that such practices were an "amplification" of other practices like meditation, and an extension of the contemplative life.[80]

Inner alchemical praxis

Inner alchemy is the process of successive refinement of *ch'ing/jing*, *ch'i/qi* and *shen* in the furnace of the body. It is an inner path to enlightenment and immortality, in which nothing extraneous to the body itself is necessary. Since there were many different schools of *nei-tan/neidan*, there was considerable variation in practice and emphasis on different aspects. But, in the main, we should understand inner alchemy as a process that is usually supported by a basic theoretical framework, a dependence on the theories of the *Yin/Yang* school, the *I Ching/Yijing* and the Five Agents theory.

The harmony of the inner body, a calm inner state, a still mind, and freedom from extraneous influences, are general characteristics of inner alchemy that are reminiscent of the *Tao Te Ching/Daodejing* and the *Chuang-tzu/Zhuangzi*. Chapter 10 of the *Tao Te Ching/Daodejing* talks of keeping the spirits within, and keeping the One, the unity of all the deities within. It talks about making breathing as soft and gentle as an infant's, a purified vision of the inner self, of realizing the feminine through control of the "gates", and of the mysterious white light that penetrates all within. These are concepts highly akin to the practices of inner alchemy. The harmony advocated by texts such as the *Tao Te Ching/Daodejing* is brought about in the body by the union of opposites, creating utter equilibrium. The goal is to preserve, restore and transmute the energies within into their natural state that existed at conception, to their natural primordial state of *Tao* that existed before awareness of the world dissipated them. It is a spiritual refinement that aims to produce from such purified energies, an immortal, spiritual body within the physical outer frame.

Complementary techniques

While there were many proponents of inner alchemy that dissociated themselves from what they regarded as extraneous techniques such as breathing, gymnastics and dietetics, others saw such practices as essential in the process of refining the self and creating an immortal body. Robinet made a neat distinction between the two, however, by pointing out that inner alchemy texts *always* use chemical terminology to depict its processes, while texts on respiration and gymnastics, as in *chi-kung/qigong*, do not.[81] On the other hand, Needham certainly associated gymnastic exercises with inner alchemy,[82] and today's practice of T'ai Chi Ch'üan/Taijiquan, in which respiration is critical to the movements, seems to embody much of the inner alchemical tradition. This suggests that breathing techniques and gymnastic exercises were not too far removed from inner alchemy. However, breathing exercises are not specifically Taoist, but belong to the wider context of Chinese interest in health and longevity.

The importance of breath in promoting inner stability is a long-established concept in China. Breath breathed into the body gave health, while expelled breath got rid of what was impure. In the process of inner alchemy, the breath was the means by which the "firing process" was effectuated, with fast *yang* and slow *yin* breathing. Alchemically, breath was capable of unifying the whole body, and building inner harmony. Catherine Despeux writes: "Since breathing is a constant exchange of the inner and the outer, it also plays an important role in setting the inner circulation of *qi* in motion and in eliminating eventual blockages on the way. It also serves to harmonize the movements into a proper rhythm and to maintain a given posture."[83] To attain immortality, impure breaths had to be replaced with pure, cosmic *ch'i/qi*. It became important in inner alchemy to retain the pure breath in the lowest cinnabar field where, combined with pure Essence, the Spirit Embryo could form. A text like *Inward Training*, dated to about the early or mid-fourth century BCE, emphasizes the need to develop the vital Breath within in order to calm the mind and cultivate the inner self. While not concerned with immortality, but with the mystical return to *Tao* more in line with the philosophy of Lao-tzu/Laozi and Chuang-tzu/Zhuangzi, it contains much about the combination of breathing and inward meditation.[84]

In T'ang/Tang times and thereafter breathing practices became more physically internalized. The breath was "guided" internally. Guiding the breath meant moving it at the behest of the adept to whatever part of the body was desired. The whole process was called "womb breathing" or "embryonic breathing", though the term was wide enough to include different practices. "Womb breathing", from the idea of the foetus "breathing" in the womb, was also thought to be through the umbilical cord, the space between the kidneys or the whole body, and the *Chuang-tzu/Zhuangzi* even mentions through the heels. In womb breathing the breath was particularly guided to the region of the lower abdomen; there, the attention of the mind was also settled, so that mind and breath became one.[85]

Outer alchemy referred to the bellows that fanned the fires of the furnace, regulating the temperature in line with the seasons and the *yin* and *yang* of the year. In inner alchemy, breath became the bellows, the means by which the Elixir of life could be formulated in the inner furnace of the body. The "vapour" produced by inner alchemical practice was the Primordial Breath that existed before creation, and its circulation in the body was necessary in the creation, nurture and maturing of the Spirit Embryo.

While gymnastic exercises were less associated with innner alchemy *per se*, the association between breathing and gymnastic exercise, *tao-yin/daoyin*, is also a firm one. But, as Despeux notes, gymnastic movements ranked fairly low in the ultimate aim of longevity and immortality. They were useful at preliminary stages and for ongoing support for the higher goals, but not in themselves as a means to immortality.[86] The advantages, however, were clear to Ko Hung/Ge Hong: "Ability to writhe like a dragon, stretch like a tiger, waddle like a bear, swallow like a tortoise, fly like a swallow, twist like a snake, dilate like a bird, look heavenward and earthward" would enable one to hear well![87]

As to dietetics a strict dietary regime was more of a preparatory practice for inner alchemy than an essential part of it. It was expected to promote harmony in the body and mind, and it would be difficult to accept that a glutton, or one who did not respect the deities within the body and feed them appropriately, would be a serious adept on the road to immortality. Then, too, so many foods were considered harmful to the good deities within. Indeed, immortals, the *hsien/xian*, are traditionally represented as living on a diet of herbs, dew and roots in the mountains.[88] Ko Hung/Ge Hong recommended moderation – not so much wine as to gain the opinion that people couldn't wait to hear one singing!

Returning to Tao

The major philosophy underpinning inner alchemy is the idea of *return* to *Tao* by *reversal* of the process of creation. It is a reversal that starts with the state of the human self as it is, and refines it back to its state in the Void, as *Tao*. The idea is adapted and reversed from the conception, gestation and birth of the child. Before a child is conceived, it is the undifferentiated *Tao* existing only in potential. At conception, it is no longer undifferentiated, but becomes a manifestation of *Tao*, and from that point on the separation of that embryo from *Tao* becomes accentuated. At birth, it faces the world for the first time, and its energies are separated from its mother – it has its own *ch'ing/jing*, *ch'i/qi* and *shen*. As the ability to understand the world grows and the multitude of stimuli affect the mind, the child's emotions develop and, gradually, the energies of the body are weakened and lost. Sexual activity, anger, desire, aversion – all cause the weakening of the internal energies and lead to ill health. Sickness, ageing and, eventually, death are the results of the leakage of energy. The process of return sets out to reverse this.

The goal of returning, then, is a return to the Source that one really is. To do this one has to become empty like the depth of a valley, pure *yin*, devoid of ego and differentiation of dualities, still, silent and at the point into which all pours – microcosmically the valley, macrocosmically, *Tao*. It is a return from some point on a circle to the centre of it. As opposed to evolution from the Void and from subtle to gross manifestation in the ten thousand things, and the generative cycle of the Five Agents, *involution* occurs. This is back from the gross to the subtle and the Void, and the reverse, destructive order of the Five Agents. So, just as the gestation of *Tao* produces the One, the Two and the Three, and then the ten thousand things, there is a gestation within the self in the sense of a rebirth that reverses the process and returns to *Tao*.

Meditation

The earliest form of meditation goes back to Han times and was called the "ingestion of the five sprouts" and was connected with visualization of the Five Agents within the body.[89] The early, or mid-fourth century BCE text *Inward Training* also points to early mystical practices,[90] particularly circulating the breath as a meditative practice,[91] as well as the circulation of vital energy.[92] A text like *Inward Training* illustrates rather well how the holistic nature of practices of breathing, exercises, diet and meditation inform the journey back to the Source and, at the same time, stresses the stilling of the mind as the crux of all meditation. Chapter 16 of the *Tao Te Ching/Daodejing* spoke of emptying the mind in the same way: " Create emptiness to the utmost. Carefully keep complete stillness. The ten thousand things come and go. The self concentrates on return."

Chuang-tzu/Zhuangzi, too, spoke of sitting and forgetting, of listening with the breath and not the ears, of abandoning consciousness of the outer world, and of guarding the One – a practice that will be examined more closely below. Essentially, it is the "I" forgetting its "me". It was necessary for inner alchemists to employ meditative techniques in the internal processes of transmutation of the Three Treasures, for the "me" that is enmeshed in the world is too egocentric to bring about those processes. There is a transcendence of ordinary subjective consciousness, a forgetting of who the self is in the world. In the words of the *Huai-nan-tzu/Huainanzi*:

> When the mind does not worry or rejoice,
> This is the perfection of inner power.
> When it is absorbed and does not alter,
> This is the perfection of stillness.
> When lusts and desires do not fill it up,

> This is perfection of emptiness.
> When there is nothing liked or disliked,
> This is the perfection of equanimity.
> When it is not confused by external things,
> This is the perfection of purity.[93]

Since the inner body is seen as mirroring the macrocosm, meditation and visualization of its inward nature are tantamount to understanding of the cosmos itself. Inner stillness, quietude and tranquillity are necessary to nourish inner health, power, unobstructed pure energy and essence that are of the nature of *Tao* and *Te*. The well-being and harmony of the inner self need to be brought in line with the harmony of the universe. Then, all objects cease to be objects that are separate from the self, the interrelation of all is experienced and all is seen as a movement of *Tao* in life and interfused with it as the Source of all. Transcending the senses is the key to such inner harmony. The senses involve the individual in ordinary consciousness that is subject–object, "I–that" orientated. *Real consciousness* is of the reality of *Tao*. In Ishida's study of body and mind in Chinese thought, he states that the mind was seen as fluid, "part of the eternally moving flux of the human physis". It was not a static aspect of the self, but could pervade the whole body, function with it and, therefore, affect any part of it. The normal mind has a tendency to be distracted by things outside the body, and hence to leave it. Thus, the inner self, the inner deities are not cared for.[94] Seduced by worldly concerns, the inner nature is forgotten. The beginnings of inner alchemy, therefore, consist of governing the mind, controlling the desires and emotions that pervade it. The transmutation process can only occur when the mind is still, empty and serene.

Visualization is a key aspect of meditation, particularly of the deities within the body, and this is not just a visualization of the form of the deities but a dialogue with them and confession of any misdemeanours. Since these deities are essential for the life of the individual, "maintaining", "keeping", or "holding on" to them, termed *shou*, is essential. Visualization could also be of the sun or moon, with their light descending and circulating in the body. The sun, moon and stars as the first creations of *Tao* were felt to have purer energy. The Big Dipper, the *Pei-tou/Beidou* was particularly important in such visualization.

Of the deities visualized in the body, the "Three Ones", *san-i/sanyi*, or the Three Primordial", *san-yüan/sanyuan*, noted earlier, are the most important. They represent the Three Primordial energies that emerged from *Tao*. In inner alchemy the Three in creation are defined as *yin* and *yang* and the combination of these two in wholeness. Since the Three emerged from the unity of *Tao* essentially, they are One. In the body they are also the Three Treasures, and the three cinnabar fields, and they are also indicative of other threefold aspects of the universe. But it is their Oneness that is important. Separately, *yin* and *yang* are two, combined they create the third aspect of a whole, a separate Oneness that is at the same time a unity. Such Oneness emerges from the primordial *Tao*, and it is such Oneness that needs to be experienced in the self as indicative of return to *Tao*. The Three are, at the same time, the three celestial deities that represent the Oneness of *Tao* in the cosmos *and* reside also in the microcosm of the human body. If they can be harmonized within, then the Oneness of the body will become identical to the Oneness of the cosmic Three: such is the goal. Andersen describes the method of holding the Three Ones:

> One fixates the seven stars of The Big Dipper and brings it down to a position directly above the head. The Three Ones emerge from the bowl of The Dipper, each accompanied by a minister. Three times one breathes in very deeply, and each time one of the Three Ones, accompanied by his minister, follows with the breath and enters into his proper place in one of the three cinnabar-fields of the body. After this has been accomplished one meditates to ascertain that The Ones are at rest in their respective palaces.[95]

If the mind is truly emptied and concentration on the Three deities is sufficient, their light will fill the body and the adept will be able to leave the body and roam with them in the cosmos. Such practices were a particular development of the Shang-ching/Shangqing school of Taoism.

Guarding the One

Harmonizing the Three Ones as One in the body is *shou-i/shouyi*. It means Guarding, Preserving or Keeping the One, a term that was used by both Lao-tzu/Laozi and Chuang-tzu/Zhuangzi. Since it is, however, a general term for meditation, and dates back to pre-Han times, it covers a variety of practices.[96] In inner alchemy, this method of meditation was mainly concerned with the particular balance and nature of the Three Treasures, though "Nourishing the Body/Breath/Spirits" or "Nourishing the Vital Principle" were often concomitant practices of keeping the inner body harmonious, the many deities in their appropriate places, and the breaths circulated. But, specifically, Guarding the One in inner alchemy concentrates on the transmutation of *ching/jing*, *ch'i/qi* and *shen*. In this process, the heart, which is considered to be the Agent Fire, the trigram *Li*, the South, and *yang*, and the kidneys, which are Water, the trigram *K'an/Kan*, the North, and *yin*, are what transmute the Three Treasures by their interaction in the body. Guarding the One is indicative of the interplay between the Three.

The One is cosmic centrality. Kohn depicts it thus: "The One as a god within or without the human body is a personification of the central power of life and the universe".[97] It can signify both the primordial chaos that preceded the emanation of *Tao* that begot the world, or the One that emerged from *Tao*. It can also represent the One from which Heaven and Earth emerged in the sense of the *I Ching/Yijing* trigrams, as well as to the holistic Oneness that results from the union of *yin* and *yang*. In an anthropomorphic sense, the One became the major deity of the body as "The Perfect Great One of the Yellow Centre of Great Purity", and this One, like the cosmic One, multiplied into numerous other deities in the body as much as their counterparts in the universe, though ultimately all these are One. But, however it is used, to "guard" that Oneness is to return to it, experience it, equate with it. It is to transcend the world of egocentric desires and attain the stillness from which one emerged. It is a return to Source. So Guarding and Keeping the One also means being at home with *Tao* and not permitting the senses to stir into worldly involvement, when Oneness is lost. It is the search for, and, finally the experience of, Oneness and the unified essence that lies at the root of multiplicity. It is a return to the centre and the attainment of immortality.

The firing process

Inner alchemy uses the language of outer alchemy to express the transmutation of *ching/jing* to *ch'i/qi* and *ch'i/qi* to *shen* in order to produce the Spirit Embryo. Instead of refining metal to produce gold, there is an internal refinement of the artificial self into a real and pure self. Such language, then, is symbolic language, and this factor, together with the secretive nature of the schools, oral tradition, the complex anatomy of the body with its many symbolic names, and the variety of traditions, serves to make the "firing process" a complicated area. The firing process is the term used for the means, the process, of transmutation. The outward nature of the trigrams *Li* as Fire, and *K'an/Kan*, Water, were described in chapter 2 on the *I Ching/Yijing*. But it is not the outward, overall trigram that is important in inner alchemy as much as the *middle line* of the trigrams, as noted earlier. In the firing process, then, we have the interchange of the Dragon, which is the middle *yang* line of the trigram *Li*, with the Tiger, the middle *yin* line of the trigram *K'an/Kan*. A point worth remembering is that ordinarily, water sinks and fire rises up. However, given the aim of reversal in inner alchemy, fire will need to *descend* and water *rise up*. The four alchemical necessities, then, are the Dragon and Tiger (the ingredients), and the Cauldron and Furnace (the means). Their equivalents are as follows:[98]

Dragon: The trigram *Li* is predominantly *yang*, but the important middle line is *yin* and so the Dragon is female. It is the *yin* essence in *yang*, Water in Fire, the female in the male, the moon in the sun. It is referred to as Green Dragon, Cinnabar, True Mercury, the Golden Raven in the Sun, the Golden Flower, the Jade Maiden, amongst others. It is water that rises, being heated, and is therefore fiery but yielding, rising to Heaven.

Tiger: The trigram *K'an/Kan* is Water and predominantly *yin* and female. But the middle line is *yang* and alchemically is the *yang* in the *yin*, the White Tiger, the Red Raven, or the Jade Rabbit in the moon. It is associated with True Lead and its function is to descend to Earth when fire reacts with it. It is the Fire in Water.

Cauldron: The cauldron or crucible is the mind, the head, and the space between the kidneys. Liu I-ming/Liu Yiming equated the cauldron with Heaven. In this case the trigram *Ch'ien/Qian*, symbolized by the three *yang* lines, suggested firmness, strength and stability or, at a deeper level, "single-minded concentration of will, by which one can bear the Tao".[99] The lowest cinnabar field is a cauldron for *ching/jing*, the middle one for *ch'i/qi* and the uppermost one for *shen*, but the lowest one is the place where the Spirit Embryo is "conceived".

Furnace: The furnace is the stove, the body, the abdomen, and *ch'i/qi*. Liu I-ming/Liu Yiming equated the furnace with Earth and, therefore, with the trigram *K'un/Kun* and its three, broken *yin* lines, representing the warmth, flexibility, evenness and peace of the "Jade Furnace", that is able to effectuate gradual change.[100]

With language like: "Knock on bamboo to call the tortoise to ingest jade mushroom"; "Strum the lute to call the phoenix to drink from the medicinal spoon"; "the yellow woman"; "the metal man"; "single cavity of the mysterious gate" and so on, it is no wonder that interpretations could be wide.

The *I Ching/Yijing* is of immense importance in the understanding of inner alchemy. As Robinet commented: "Diverted from their divinatory uses, the trigrams are taken as stylized, abstract forms of fundamental truths, as ways of speaking concisely, of bringing together several levels of truth in one single sign."[101] Harmonizing *yin* and *yang* was the key to the formation of the Spirit Embryo. Liu I-ming/Liu Yiming depicted such harmony of the two in the following language of inner alchemy:

> On the peak of Sacred-Flower Mountain, the male tiger roars;
> At the bottom of Sun-Mulberry Ocean, the female dragon howls.
> The matchmaker of the center spontaneously knows how to join them together;
> They become husband and wife, sharing the same core.[102]

In the firing process, the middle *yin* and *yang* lines in the trigrams of *Li* and *K'an/Kan* respectively are interacted with each other to effectuate the restoration of the new, pure *yin* and *yang* trigrams of Heaven and Earth. The process is sometimes referred to as the "immersion of Fire in Water". It is through such interaction that transmutation of the Three Treasures takes place. All the *yin* and *yang* balances in the body must first be harmonized – the back (*yang*) with the front (*yin*); the left (*yang*) with the right (*yin*); the upper (*yang*) with the lower (*yin*). When the *yin* and *yang* energies combine in the lowest cinnabar field, they are referred to as the "dragon and tiger swirling in the winding river". When they combine in the middle field "the sun and moon reflecting on each other in the Yellow Palace" and in the uppermost cinnabar field, "the union of husband and wife in the bedchamber".[103] The Spirit Embryo that is produced is sometimes called the "Dragon-Tiger Pill", and the total harmony of *yin* and *yang* the "Valley Spirit". However, since the human being is a blend of Heaven and Earth in makeup, and since he or she leans towards the earthly stimuli rather than the spiritual heavenly ones, there has to be a certain *yangization* of the self in the process of inner alchemy. That is to say, there has to be a focus on the spiritual, heavenly *yang* and the stilling of the earthly desires and passions, the *yin*.

If we cast our minds back to the two *Pa-kua/Bagua* diagrams that were examined in chapter two, the first was an arrangement of trigrams in the original, primal "Yellow River Map" (*ho-t'u/hetu*) of Fu Hsi/Fu Xi. The second was King Wen's arrangement that represented the motion of change throughout the cycle of the year. In inner alchemy, the earlier arrangement is regarded as the state of purity that needs to be brought about by the alchemical process. The later one represents the pattern of life as it is, the process of ageing. Changing from the latter to the former is what the process of reversal is all about. In the earlier arrangement, *Ch'ien/Qian* is at the top of the circle in, to the Chinese, the South and *K'un/Kun* at the bottom, in the North. *K'an/Kan* is in the West and *Li* in the East, *Li* is the sun and *K'an/Kan* is the moon. The later arrangement has *Li* and *K'an/Kan* on the

South–North axis with *K'un/Kun* following *Li* and *Ch'ien/Qian* preceding *K'an/Kan*. The aim of inner alchemy is to transform the later arrangement to the primal one by the extraction of the middle *yin* and *yang* lines of *K'an/Kan* and *Li* respectively and the use of them to recreate pure *Ch'ien/Qian* and *K'un/Kun* but on a reversed North–South axis. The process was, thus, one of separation and restoration. A new, *yang*, *Ch'ien/Qian* has to be generated as the means to allow the immortal to rise to Heaven.[104] Put in another way, the *yang* in the middle of Water is taken to fill the *yin* in the middle of Fire, so reproducing Heaven. The *yang* in Water is the ultimate vitality within the body; the *yin* in Fire is the energy of mind. In the transmutation process, the *yang* vitality is what is changed into subtle form. Of course, the other trigrams also have to be transformed until the primal arrangement of the *Pa-kua/Bagua* is achieved.[105] In alchemical terms, the process is expressed by Eva Wong as follows:

> the alchemical interaction is between the yang in the yin (White Tiger) and the yin in the yang (the Green Dragon). In this interaction, the White Tiger and the Green Dragon are transformed into numinous energy and united to form the Golden Elixir. The yang component in k'an moves into li to occupy the middle position, and the yin component in li is drawn into the center of k'an. The first process is described as using k'an to fill li, refining the silver in the lead, extracting the white metal from the water of the north, and returning the essence of the sun to the empty hollow of the moon. The second process is described as playing with the Red Raven, extracting the mercury from the fire, and refining mercury from cinnabar. The interaction itself is referred to as the Green Dragon copulating with the White Tiger, or the soul of the moon embracing the spirit of the sun.[106]

Li and *K'an/Kan* are the products of the union of *Ch'ien/Qian* and *K'un/Kun*. That union causes the middle lines of the trigrams *Li* and *K'an/Kan*. The *yin* in the middle of the trigram *Li* is called "True Lead", or the Jade Rabbit, and is descending. The *yang* in the middle of *K'an/Kan* is "True Mercury" and is rising. They are dynamic representations of the original, primal *yin* and *yang* in the pure trigrams of Heaven and Earth. Ordinarily, the *yang* has the tendency to rise towards Heaven, or the head in the human body, and the *yin* is striving to descend to pure Earth and to the lowest cinnabar field of the body. Bringing the two together in a central place of the body is the goal. In the alchemical process, the *yang* in the Water is used to settle the *yin* in Fire: the Water rises and the Fire descends, inverting their normal functions. Thus, the solid *yang* line is taken out of the Water to replace the middle *yin* line in Fire, thus producing Heaven. The *yang* being within the *yin* represents the enlightened real consciousness being entrapped in worldly consciousness. Extracting it and replacing the middle *yin* line of *Li* restores the ultimate reality of Heaven.

Ch'ien/Qian and *K'un/Kun* are the cauldron and furnace within. *Li* and *K'an/Kan* are the ingredients that are brought together within them. All the other trigrams and the hexagrams indicate the firing times in the process of transmutation.[107] For example, two upper *yang* lines and a lowest *yin* one indicates two parts *yang* to one part *yin* in terms of the blend of heat and cold.[108] Being a key factor in the firing process, Fire has to be carefully controlled. Whereas in outer alchemy this was done with the bellows, in inner alchemy the breath – its pace and depth – provides the same role.

ALCHEMY

The Five Agents were also fitted into the inner alchemical scheme of things. Since they are related to the seasons, they, too, conformed to the firing times. But it was also important to align the Agents with the four major trigrams. The means to such was the central Agent of Earth, the "Central Palace" or the "Yellow Woman". Then, too, the five major organs of the body – heart, liver, lungs, kidneys and spleen – were also associated each with one of the Five Agents. Just as the *Pa-kua/Bagua* was reversed into its original form, so the Agents, too, are reversed from their generative to their mutually overcoming order. Such reversal of the Agents enables the interaction of the energies of the three cinnabar fields, allowing the transmutation process.

In the transmutation process, *ch'ing/jing*, *ch'i/qi* and *shen* become one. There are a number of stages in this process:

Conservation of *ching/jing* As was seen above, retention of coarse *ching/jing* is essential to prevent leakage and dissipation of energy. Essentially, it meant not only preventing ejaculation, but also controlling the senses in general, so that the mind is beginning to be anchored in itself and not world orientated. To this end, eating the right foods, breathing and gymnastic exercises, and keeping the mind quiet help to collect and restore *ching/jing*. Moderation, naturalness and lack of over-stimulating the body and mind are essential at this stage.

Transmutation of *ching/jing* Refinement of coarse *ching/jing* into subtle *ching/jing* is the next stage. The latter is needed for the transmutation of *ch'i/qi*. Subtle *ching/jing* is the Water trigram, and rises when it becomes subtle. Subtle *ching/jing* is a transformation from the coarse form in semen and blood, for example, to a formless state rather like the cosmic *ching/jing* that obtained before creation. The transmuted *ching/jing* passes to the middle cinnabar field, the middle cauldron, where it is ready to assist in the transmutation of *ch'i/qi*.

Nourishing of *ch'i/qi* Subtle *ch'i/qi* is nourished through stillness of mind, aided by breathing. It is important that breathing remains calm, so the emotions that alter breathing must be quelled. The mind must remain detached from external stimuli that might be harmful to the store of *ch'i/qi*: equanimity of mind is critical to the process. But coarse *ch'i/qi* must also be collected and nourished for it is the means by which subtle *ch'i/qi* can be taken around the body. Breathing in coarse *ch'i/qi* stirs the subtle *ch'i/qi* of the body.

Transmutation of *ch'i/qi* Refinement of coarse *ch'i/qi* is brought about by subtle *ching/jing* in the middle cinnabar field. The "winds" or breaths of *ch'i/qi* help to bring about this transmutation. Combined with subtle *ching/jing* the vapour that is subtle *ch'i/qi* emerges. The vapour rises and ascends to the gate at the entry of the uppermost cinnabar field. Subtle *ch'i/qi*, like subtle *ching/jing*, has a great affinity with the primordial cosmic *ch'i/qi*. Both subtle *ching/jing* and subtle *ch'i/qi* merged are needed for the transmutation of *shen*.

Nourishment of *shen* Coarse *shen* is the animating spirit of the mind, but in its subtle state, it is the primordial cosmic spark of the Void that exists potentially within the mind. It is, thus, like Mind within mind, and it is this fusion of a purified mind with the

Mind of Void that must ultimately take place. For such fusion the ordinary mind has to be totally calm, the "I" lost, and the mind of form changed to the formless mind. Such is nourishing of *shen*. When *shen* is nourished in this way it aids subtle *ch'i/qi* which, in turn, nourishes subtle *ching/jing*.

Transmutation of *shen* Subtle *ching/jing* and subtle *ch'i/qi* are usually prerequisites for the transmutation of coarse *shen* into its subtle state when the mind is stilled. When subtle *shen* becomes pure spirit ordinary knowledge ceases and real consciousness occurs, that is to say, consciousness of absolute reality. The mind no longer exists, but has become Mind, in utter harmony and equivalence with primordial Void.

Transmutation of Void *shen* When the subtle states of all Three Treasures merge as one, the *shen* that results is pure *yang* and is transmuted into Void. It is at this point that the Spirit Embryo is created, an Embryo which, after a period of gestation, will become the immortal body, able to leave the body at will, and finally at death. Such is immortality, prefaced by youthful skin and body, keen vision, radiance, youthful vigour and robust health, until the old body is shed and the metamorphosis is complete. Then, return to the Source, to *Tao*, is complete.

The whole process of refinement or transmutation reverses the evolution of creation, Void > spirit > vitality > essence > form, to one of involution, form > essence > vitality > spirit > Void.

The "fire" of the firing process is supplied by the breath. Collecting and nourishing the Three Treasures requires *yin* fire, that is to say, slow, warm breathing. Transmutation, however, requires a heavier, faster and hotter *yang* fire. The furnace of the body is the lowest cinnabar field, but the cauldrons, one in each of the cinnabar fields, are the places where the Three Treasures are collected, nourished and transmuted, *ching/jing* in the lowest, *ch'i/qi* in the middle and *shen* in the uppermost. The firing process involves six stages:

1 The birth of *yang*

This is the point when *yang* appears as the bottom line of an otherwise wholly *yin* hexagram, the hexagram *fu*. It is the first sign of *yang* and life energy. It is the time at which the furnace can be generated in the cauldrons in each of the cinnabar fields. The initial process takes place in the lowest cinnabar field, and the fires of the furnace are "lit" here. Water acts as the generator. The cauldron is then set up. The lowest gate on the spinal column is opened to give access to the lowest cauldron. Breath regulates the heat in the process while the transmutation of *ching/jing* takes place. After the coarse *ching/jing* has become subtle, it rises to pass through the middle gate on the spine into the middle cinnabar field. The same process of transmutation of *ch'i/qi* takes place in the middle field, and its subtle form then passes through the third gate into the uppermost cinnabar field for the transmutation of *shen*. Now, all the gates are open, and subtle *ch'i/qi* is able to move to all three fields uninterrupted. It does this in two orbits or circuits, a microcosmic, lesser one and a macrocosmic or greater one.

2 The emergence of the Herbs or Flowers

The Herbs or Flowers are the purified, transmuted Three Treasures that have

ALCHEMY

become subtle and combine as pure spiritual energy, the *yang-shen*, in the uppermost cinnabar field. It is a stage called the "Blossoming of the Golden Flower", or "Three Flowers gathering at the top of the head".

3 Collecting the Herbs

This is a period of consolidation, when the mind has to be still so that the subtle forms of the Three Treasures can be gathered from all parts of the body. The pure vapour or energy is circulated around the body to collect the three energies and unite them. The Spirit Embryo is formed after the pure energy circulates once around the body and gathers the three Herbs, the subtle Three Treasures. The combined and undifferentiated pure energy of the Three is then drawn down into the lowest cinnabar field as the subtle spirit from which the Embryo is created.

4 Closing and containing

The senses now have to be closed off from egoistic contact with the external world, from desires and attachments that will only serve to lose the pure energy gained and lose the immortal Embryo.

5 The microcosmic circuit

The microcosmic circuit is the circulation of *ching/jing*, *ch'i/qi* and *shen* through the *tu/du* and *jen/ren* meridians. It feeds the Embryo during its ten months of incubation, just as the mortal baby is fed in the womb.

6 Cleansing

Circulation of the energies is continued in order to purify the inner body as much as hold the mind in stillness. It is this process that regenerates youthfulness.

When the Embryo is fully mature, it rises to the middle cinnabar field and then to the uppermost, and leaves the body at the top of the head – an immortal. Just as a young child, it leaves the body for only short distances at first, then further and further until, when the body dies, it is liberated into the undifferentiated *Tao*.[109]

The microcosmic and macrocosmic circuits[110]

The microcosmic orbit or circuit is the direction of energy around the body through the power of breathing. The route starts with a *yang* half-circuit beginning in the abdomen, in the lowest cinnabar field at the base of the spine. It runs along the *tu/du yang* meridian. The energy is directed along this meridian to the perineum, then up the back to the coccyx, up the spine to the thorax, then to the occiput from where it feeds the brain, to a point between the eyebrows, then to the mouth where it is mixed with saliva. At this point, half the circuit is completed and the *tu/du* meridian ends. Then, the *yin* begins its increase by descending, as is its nature, to the throat, down past the heart and to the stomach. The journey of the energy runs along the *jen/ren yin* meridian at the front of the body until it joins the *tu/du*. When unblocked flow occurs, energy is circulated through this orbit, creating what is sometimes called the "waterwheel". Connecting the two meridians enables the water of *K'an/Kan* in the *yin* lowest cinnabar field to meet the fire of *Li* in the *yang* of the head. The fusion of the two produces the original Heaven and Earth trigrams.[111] One complete circuit is said to take three and three-quarter hours, and can be either clockwise or anti-clockwise, with different benefits. The clockwise direction is necessary for the transmutation process above. The anti-clockwise direction nurtures and stimulates *ch'i/qi*, which in turn nurtures and stimulates *ching/jing*. The circuits generate heat. The *tu/du* and *jen/ren* meridians, respectively, control all the *yang* and *yin* channels of the body.

The macrocosmic orbit of energy extends beyond the *tu/du* and *jen/ren* meridians to the limbs. It begins at the base of the spine, and travels right up the back of the body through the spine to the *ni-wan* cavity in the head before descending down the front of the body to what is called the cavity of the Bubbling Spring at the bottom of the feet from where it returns up the legs to the spine again. One circuit takes nine hours to complete. Timing of the microcosmic and macrocosmic circuits is an important factor.

Becoming the Void

> In the quiet room I open the mirror of mind;
> In the vacant hall I light the lamp of wisdom.
> Outside is clear and bright,
> Inside is effulgent light.
> A tiny grain appears in the glow,
> The silver moon is clear in the water.
> In the gold crucible, suspended in space,
> A grain of great elixir crystallizes.[112]

Such is the description of the birth of the Spirit Embryo. It is a time of harmony within the self, and with the outer cosmos. The adept "dissolves the imperfect coagulations of the soul, reduces the latter to its *materia*, and crystallizes it anew in a nobler form. But he can accomplish this work only in unison with Nature, by means of a natural vibration of the soul which awakens during the course of the work and links the human and cosmic domains".[113] The "tiny pearl" of the Spirit Embryo is itself the formless and undifferentiated reality that is *Tao*. It is the original energy of pre-creation. Nourished by equanimity, harmony, balance, and stillness of mind it develops. The perception of the self as *Tao* pervades the self and maintains such equilibrium. Once fully developed and able to leave the body, the body remains in the world of the human, but the spirit is liberated to roam in the cosmos, until the body sheds its life. Here, there is what Blofeld called a "relaxation in the totality of being", and "a state of consciousness in which all sense of self and other, of heaven and earth, has vanished; there is naught but pure void, a limitless ocean of *ch'i* resembling a panorama of ever-changing cloud-forms".[114]

Experience of *Tao* is experience of the Void, of utter emptiness and yet utter fullness, because *Tao* is the unity of all opposites. There is at once both unconsciousness – of the world as a separate entity from the self – and yet real consciousness of *Tao* as and in all things. It is a return home, a return to the Source, a return to the centre of the circle, the central point between all dualities. The pure energy created in the self returns to the primordial energy of the cosmos.

7

Life Beyond Earth: Ancestors, Deities, Immortals and Sages

The mythologies that enrich the Taoist religion have to be seen against the wider setting of Chinese tradition and culture. Traditions about ancestors, deities, immortals and sages have been handed down for generations not only by the Taoists themselves, but also by Confucians, Buddhists and ordinary folk, and with considerable overlap between them. Indeed, just as it is impossible to draw out the various strands informing Taoism from the other traditions, so the myths and legends of ancient historical and legendary personages of human or divine form have been embellished down the centuries with contributions from wider Chinese contexts than Taoism itself. Then, too, Confucianism as the dominant and accepted state doctrine of China lent its refining processes to official ancient personages who should be worshipped. What we are left with, then, are legends that have undergone considerable change, that vary from one cultural microcosm to another, and that often bear the traces of all kinds of influences beyond Taoism. Thus, the boundaries are blurred in depicting a myth or legend as specifically Taoist, for the syncretistic borrowing and influence between the cultural microcosms in China provided a good deal of the warp and weft of the tales and legends that were spun. Naturally, such a rich blend of ideas also resulted in a hazy distinction between history and myth.

In what follows, then, I have tried to present a range of legends and stories surrounding characters that pervade Taoist belief and practice past and present. At the same time, I have strayed into territory encompassed by the broader spectrum of Chinese traditions that would be acceptable to the ordinary Taoist, whose beliefs and practices are more syncretistic. An important point to note about what follows, however, is that there is also an overlap between the categories in which I have chosen to present the material. For famed ancestors were mostly deified. Many were also sages, particularly ancient kings. Sages like Lao-tzu/Laozi, too, were deified, and all were thought to be immortal.

Ancestors

The veneration of ancestors was essential to Chinese culture. It provided the link between the living and the dead that made sense of life, and it accentuated the role of the family unit by encouraging respect of the younger for the elder and for the deceased, entrenched by customary rites. With justification, considering its influence, Thompson describes the presence of the veneration of ancestors in China as "the very warp of a high culture throughout millennia of time".[1] I have used the term "veneration" to avoid the pitfalls that the more frequently used expression "worshipped" suggests. For in fact, while ancestors of the great emperors frequently found themselves deified and ritually approached as such, in the wider context of family life, ancestors were respected and venerated, but hardly worshipped, though reciprocal aid might be expected between the living and the dead. Such a concept was the foundation of much Chinese belief and practice from ancient times, and remained so throughout its long history. Ancestor veneration provided a continuum between life and death on the one hand, and kept the dead in the context of life in the world on the other. Stephen Teiser puts the position succinctly:

> If the system works well, then the younger generations support the senior ones, and the ancestors bestow fortune, longevity, and the birth of sons upon the living. As each son fulfills his duty, he progresses up the family scale, eventually assuming his status as revered ancestor. The attitude toward the dead ... is simply a continuation of one's attitude towards one's parents while they were living. In all cases, the theory goes, one treats them with respect and veneration by fulfilling their personal wishes and acting according to the dictates of ritual tradition.[2]

This succinct statement of the nature of the case shows very clearly that worship is not an appropriate term for the relationship between the living and their ancestors.

While the lineage of the ordinary folk was maintained through the veneration of its immediate ancestors, the lineage of kings was essential to the credibility of their ruling power. Here, founding ancestors *were* important, essential enough to be deified, and remembered in an official way through religious ritual. Here, too, it was not just the immediate ancestors who were remembered, but the whole patrilinear line, represented by wooden tablets in the official temple. It is around such ancestors, who were believed to found monarchical lines, that myths grew. These were the ancestors that became deified, who dwelt in the lands of the gods, and who could intercede with the gods on behalf of their descendants. In ancient times it was sacrifices to such deified ancestors that procured their blessings. For an emperor, the legitimization of his rule, and the whole fabric of political, economic and social life that came from it, were authenticated by the reciprocal interaction of ancestors with the living.

Much has already been said about the importance of ancestors in Shang times in chapter 1 and I do not want to repeat such information here. However, it needs to be remembered that the ritual and cyclical honouring of royal ancestors, and the informing of ancestors before important royal undertakings, was essential in the ancient cult. It is uncertain whether the highest god of Shang times, Shang-ti/Shangdi, was of the nature of a deity

LIFE BEYOND EARTH: ANCESTORS, DEITIES, IMMORTALS AND SAGES

or a great ancestor,[3] but it was later tradition that projected the earliest ancestors to pre-Shang times. Purely mythical, such ancestors were often depicted as part animal and part human, and the distinction between their status as ancestors and deities is a blurred one. We shall now examine some of these major ancestors and the myths associated with them.

P'an-ku/Pangu

When *yin* and *yang* divided at the beginning of creation, *yang* became Heaven, and *yin* gradually solidified to form Earth. But as *yin* and *yang* separated P'an-ku/Pangu was born and occupied the space between the developing Heaven and Earth. For thousands of years he hammered and chiselled the basis of the world until he became exhausted and died. It was then that his body was divided up to add the refined characteristics of the world – the mountains, rivers, lakes, winds, clouds, rain, soil and all things. And humans? Well, according to some versions of the myth, they were formed from the bugs on his body! The creative idea here, according to Girardot, is one of slow change and "continuous transformation and regeneration of the world"[4] that resembles the concept of slow evolution rather than creation at a point in time.

The Three August Ones

Three ancient figures are depicted as the ancestors of the human race, though they are semi-divine at the same time. They are called the Three August Ones, and are Fu Hsi/Fu Xi, Nü-kua/Nügua and Shen-nung/Shennong. The three were facilitators of human civilization. Shen-nung/Shennong was human in form, but the other two were part animal. Palmer and Xiaomin point out that, in the latter case, these two represent the evolutionary shift that humans had to make as a distinct species.[5] Together, they were the creators of agriculture, farming, weaving, music and writing.

Fu Hsi/Fu Xi and Nü-kua/Nügua were brother and sister. They, too, were believed to have been born at the time of the division of *yin* and *yang*. They had human faces, but snake tails. Nü-kua/Nügua is credited with the creation of humans, some whom she fashioned from the yellow soil, and others from the droplets of a string that she dragged through wet clay or through water. Those she fashioned herself from clay were thought to be the nobility, her quicker method producing the commoners. According to another myth the brother and sister were the progenitors of the human race. They sought the advice of the gods for their union, asking the gods to give them a sign. If the smoke lingered over their sacrifice to the gods, they would know that it would be wrong. But if it rose as, indeed, it did, then they would know that the gods sanctioned their union. So the pair ensured the continuation of life. Fu Hsi/Fu Xi, as was noted in chapter 1, was the one who was alleged to have created the eight trigrams, fashioning them from his experience of his own body and the different aspects of Heaven and Earth. Shen-nung/Shennong was the founder of farming, with great knowledge of the nature of seeds, plants and fruits, of the best kinds of soils, and the correct places from which to draw water. He made the first plough, and agricultural implements were believed to have been introduced by him.

Such, then, is the role of semi-divine ancestors in the ongoing regeneration and creation of the world. Although not one of the Three August Ones, the legendary Yü/Yu the Great might be mentioned here as an example of others who were believed to have inaugurated aspects of civilization. Yü/Yu gave knowledge of mining, the *yin* and *yang* of metals and the nature of the cauldrons used for their smelting. For emperors, as noted above, the necessity of having a Great Ancestor, the first of the lineage, was urgent in order to claim legitimate rule. But, also, such an Ancestor represented the decree of Heaven by which the king or ruler could rule. In Chou/Zhou times, the ruler adopted Hou Tse/Houze, the Lord of Millet as the Great Ancestor of the ruling house. Appropriate rites and particular times were set aside for veneration of such an important personage, for if offended the Mandate of Heaven by which the king ruled could certainly be withdrawn.

But famous ancestors were not only confined to mythical people of the past. They could also be real personages that appeared in historical settings. Lü Yen/Lü Yan, or Ancestor Lü as he was called, was a historical person dated to the T'ang/Tang dynasty, who became the forerunner of the Complete Reality school of Taoism. We shall meet him again below as the Immortal Lü Tung-pin/Lü Dongbin. He was a renowned scholar, and author of the *Hundred Character Tablet* in the Taoist canon. It is only great ancestors such as these for whom the distinctions between deity, ancestor, immortal and sage become blurred. The introduction of Buddhist ideas of reincarnation into China brought about a belief that an ancestor resided in the Taoist heavens or hells for some time but was reincarnated back into the world. Veneration of that ancestor is then no longer required.

Deities

While religious Taoism itself did not have a plethora of deities, it is popular Taoism that has built up and collected a numerous variety of deities of all kinds, deities that have been gleaned from traditions, local stories of heroes, of magical places, and ancient legends. The whole gamut of nature, officialdom, history, legend, fact, shamanism and fame, has contributed to an enormous pantheon of gods and spirits. Some are celestial, some stellar. Some are connected to mountains, streams and the like, some are historical people who have become immortal. Some incarnate on Earth, some are human, and others are not. Even Taoist Masters have been deified. Providing the credibility of the deity is maintained by a belief in its power, then that deity is recognized through ritual practice. Conversely, where such power appears to have waned, the deity becomes obsolete. As far as practical ritual is concerned, Robinet divided deities into those on whom demands are made in ritual, and the great celestial gods to whom obeisance should be given.[6] Thompson, too, comments:

> It is this specialization in power, rather than origins or titles, that identifies the deities as individuals. They are not personifications of abstract virtues or passions or activities like Greek gods but rather are more like human officials who have the power to grant or withhold favors within the limits of their own jurisdiction. Many of them are indeed designated as officials in the spiritual hierarchy, counterparts to the bureaucrats in the old imperial tables of organization.[7]

LIFE BEYOND EARTH: ANCESTORS, DEITIES, IMMORTALS AND SAGES

Thus, a conglomeration of deities developed more as a result of imaginative needs than logical theology. Unlike the ancient semi-divine ancestors noted above, there are often no legends at all to accompany many of the deities. Others, however, have notably a variety of colourful tales attached to them.

There is a certain pragmatism attached to the polytheistic worship of deities that has characterized Chinese religion in general from its ancient past. Early belief in the deities and spirits associated with natural forces, along with localized gods of the earth, locality, city, district and home, indicate well how much deities were associated with the ongoing lives of the people. Given the emphasis on the family and importance of territorial safety, each area had its own traditions about gods so that consistency in legends is impossible to find. Yet, at a deeper level, it has to be said that however much pragmatism informs the worship of many deities, philosophically they are all united by *Tao*, emanate from *Tao*, and are infused by *Tao*: the kaleidoscope of myriad divinities must, ultimately, be united as one. However, in some ways philosophical and mystical Taoism was an intrusion into a world of polytheistic animism, which has never really left the ordinary folk. The old shamanic view of the necessity of placating and not offending the spirit world made the assistance of deities crucial. Belief in a plurality of deities rather than more philosophical contemplation of a mystical unity that underpins them was, therefore, pragmatic. In Palmer and Xiaomin's words: "Believing in the Taoist deities is a little like playing the lottery. You just never know when you might be blessed!"[8]

Since deities could arise from all sorts of sources, many were once humans. But if they were not, then many are usually found to have been anthropomorphized to the extent that humanized legends can be ascribed to them. Those who were previously humans and posthumously raised to the status of god had sometimes met their deaths unjustly or prematurely. Then, too, there were famous men like General K'uan/Kuan, who became a famous deity. We shall meet him again below. Not all gods were immortal: this was a status characterizing only the greatest deities. Many of the lesser ones were subject to *karmic* rebirth in the same way as mortals.[9] It is easier for the human mind to relate to all such beings than to the mysterious *Tao* and, thus, it was such deities that fired the human imagination more than a metaphysical principle.

The earliest concepts of deity have been dealt with already in the context of the Shang and Chou/Zhou dynasties in chapter 1. Suffice it to say here, that even in these ancient times the gods and goddesses were exceptional human beings, superior to the ordinary human through their greater power. They were colourful characters and subject to the kinds of emotions as humans, and they were not far removed from the context of human life given their responsibility for locations, agriculture, the home and natural forces, for example. Only Shang-ti/Shangdi, the great god of Shang times, was an impersonal, inscrutable and distant deity that was amalgamated into a more personal great deity in Ti/Di or T'ien/Tian of Chou/Zhou times. As Bishop points out in this context, the change was one from a tribal concept in Shang times to a universal and anthropomorphized deity in the Chou/Zhou, though a more impersonal and philosophical conception emerged in late Chou/Zhou times.[10]

Before we look at some of the most interesting deities it needs to be noted that there was much interchange between Taoist and Buddhist concepts of deity. Nowhere is this more apparent than with the lavish concept of Buddhist hells that became part of Taoist belief, each hell with its own special administrator. The Buddhist concept of *bodhisattvas* was also influential. Here, an individual with an enormous amount of merit became deified, but delayed passing into enlightenment in order to assist all other beings through the means of his or her accumulated merit. Such a belief was bound to perpetuate the petitioning of deities for all kinds of well-being. Then, too, the Celestial Venerables – of whom, more below – are very similar to Buddhas, and Buddhas and *bodhisattvas* were to be depicted as immortals.[11] The mixture of Taoist and Buddhist concepts of deity is exemplified well in the iconography of their respective temples.

While Taoism has a vast array of deities, belief in them is not essential to the designation of a person as a Taoist. Blofeld commented: "The fact is that deities entered the body of Taoism more or less accidentally and may be regarded or disregarded at will."[12] While the first part of this statement is debatable given the deep shamanistic influence on Taoist thought and its natural division of human and supernatural, the second part is certainly valid. Indeed, those attracted to Taoism in the West, for example Masters or practitioners of T'ai Chi Ch'üan/Taijiquan, and those inspired by philosophical Taoism, have little knowledge or awareness of the deities that proliferate religious and popular Taoism past and present. But the statement still stands that deities can be accepted or disregarded entirely. Given theories like the transforming changes of the *I Ching/Yijing*, the theories of *yin* and *yang* and the Five Agents, there was no need for a creator deity, and the world could operate in unending change quite by itself. Where they were important, however, was in the revelations they were believed to give humankind. This was especially so with the sacred texts of the different schools of religious Taoism, each being associated with a particular divine patron. At the popular level, nevertheless, ordinary Taoists would propitiate a number of deities – earth, local, district or city, for example – and would pay their respects to different deities on special days throughout the year.

We must turn now to the ancient emperors who became deities. And the one person who facilitated their ongoing presence in China was Confucius, for it was he who cast back onto ancient emperors an excellence of character that presented them as models for all future rulers. So when Confucianism became the official state doctrine of China, the ancient emperors of legendary nature were incorporated into the state religion and became inseparably bound with Confucian moral principles. Out of the dark mists of the past came whitewashed deities. The Three August Ones were part of this process, but in addition to them were the Five August Emperors – the Yellow Emperor, Huang-ti/Huangdi; Chuan Hsü/Zhuanxu; Yü/Yu or K'ao-hsin/Kaoxin; Yao; and Shun. Space does not permit a detailed analysis of each, though the Yellow Emperor is important enough to be the exception. Yao and Shun were humans; the remainder were divine beings. Chuan-hsü/Zhuanxu was the grandson of the Yellow Emperor, but he has never been a prominent figure. Yao was famous for the benevolence of his rule. He passed his rulership on to Shun who, in turn, made Yü/Yu his successor. Emperor Yü/Yu is credited with having stemmed the floods of the Yellow River by redirecting its flow to the ocean. This he did by boring holes through the mountains. His energies being depleted with his irrigation of the land and extensive travelling, he began to walk with a limp. This gait was copied by Taoists in a shamanic dance called the "steps of Yü/Yu", which is still performed in Taoist liturgy.

LIFE BEYOND EARTH: ANCESTORS, DEITIES, IMMORTALS AND SAGES

The Yellow Emperor

The Yellow Emperor deserves special attention. He was hailed as the first ruler of China from about the end of the second century BCE[13] and as founder of the Hsia/Xia rule. In the Taoist tradition he is the greatest Ancestor of all, and was believed to have been adept at longevity and the arts of immortality. He was, therefore, considered the founder of alchemy. *The Yellow Emperor's Classic of Internal Medicine*, written in about the fourth century BCE incorporates some of his alleged ideas on immortality and long life, but it was compiled by a number of writers. Other texts, too, have been attributed to this legendary Emperor. In the "Biographies of the Immortals", the *Lieh-hsien Chuan/Liexian Zhuan*, it is said that he could speak when only a small child, that he could foretell the future, and that he had the qualities of a sage. He knew the innate nature of all things, and was highly respected by the gods. Following his death and burial, a landslide on the mountain opened his coffin. Inside, there were only his sword and his slippers. But the same text also recounts how a dragon descended to take Huang-ti/Huangdi to Heaven. He strode onto the back of the dragon and was lifted up into the sky. His courtiers hung on to the whiskers of the dragon, hoping to accompany him, but were dropped when the whiskers became loose.[14]

Other texts reveal that he was taught the "art of the bedchamber" by goddesses. He was also alleged to have been taught military strategy. The word *huang* means "yellow", the symbol for Earth, and the centre: this would link Huang-ti/Huangdi with the later alchemists. Anna Seidel noted that the word also means "radiant" and found some indication of the myth of a sun god connected with the name. She also noted that the name can mean "august, sovereign" and pointed to a possible connection with Shang-ti/Shangdi.[15] The Yellow Emperor is also credited with the founding of the Chinese calendar, rites of sacrifice and funerals, the compass and musical scales, among other things. He is often depicted as wearing a crown with a flat board on top and tassels of jade hanging from the front and back of it.[16] His august presence is such that great respect is accorded him, unlike, for example, some of the tales surrounding the Jade Emperor, whom we shall meet later. His interest in, and protection of, humanity earned him the reputation of a benevolent, moral ruler, and tales about him show his wisdom and sagacity, as well as his fight for justice as much against the gods as unjust humans. The *Chuang-tzu/Zhuangzi*, however, is sometimes critical of him. Legend tells us that his wisdom was learned in the mountains in the ninetieth year of his reign from a sage dedicated to *Tao*. But he surely began life as a localized, tribal figure, before being projected to the great Ancestor of Taoists and of China itself. Cosmologically, he represents the centre, the *axis mundi* from which access to the divine world can occur. This point is discussed by Girardot, who sees the Emperor's ascension to Heaven from Mount K'un-lun/Kunlun as resembling the flight of a bird. This is significant, Girardot points out, since the colour yellow is linked with birds like the owl, crane, swan, crow and pelican.[17] The Yellow Emperor is, thus, symbolically associated with perfect transformation into immortality. Today, the Yellow Emperor has been the inspiration of a new religion founded in the twentieth century in Taiwan. Under a new name Hsüan-yüan chiao/Xuanyuan jiao, "Yellow Emperor Religion", its adherents have combined aspects of Taoism with Confucianism and Mohism, and seek to return to former Chinese values. Politically, they hope for the reunification of the Chinese empire.[18]

The Yellow Emperor divided the earth into four regions, North, South, East and West. He himself was the centre with his magnificent earthly palace on the peak of Mount K'unlun/Kunlun. Each area had its own ruler. The Grand Emperor of the East, Lord King of the East, Tai Hou/Dai Hou, is a *yang* deity, and is associated with the Agent Wood, and with springtime. He is, therefore, the Green Emperor. He lives on Mount T'ai Shan/Taishan, and was especially the deity of the Chou/Zhou. He is one of the foremost gods since it is he who records the length of time an individual should live, the times of their births and of their deaths. He also has a host of ministers to assist him. Then, too, he also controls the passing of the deceased to the next stage of their existence in the underworld. It is here that judgement is passed on them and their fate in the afterlife decided. Some tales suggest that he had the body of a snake. He is also credited with giving humanity the gifts of fire and fishing, according to some legends.

The Emperor or King of the South is associated with the Agent Fire. He was sometimes called the Red Emperor, God of the Sun, or Divine Peasant, and seems to have been half-brother of the Yellow Emperor, with a human body and the head of an ox.[19] He was called the Divine Peasant since he was said to have given humanity the gift of five cereals, along with advice on how to cultivate them. He was also associated with markets, agriculture and medicinal plants. The Emperor of the West is the White Emperor, whose associative season is Autumn, and the Emperor of the North is the Black Emperor, whose Agent is Water and season Winter. His name was Chuan-hsü/Zhuan Xu, and he was the great-grandson of the Yellow Emperor and one of the Five August Emperors. Legend tells that he cut the ladder between Heaven and Earth so that it would be difficult for humans to reach Heaven and for heavenly beings to descend to Earth. His actions were believed to prevent the gods from inciting rebellion amongst the people. He survived as a Taoist god under various names – in China as Chen-wu Ta-ti/Zhenwu Dadi, "Truly Martial Great Emperor", and in Taiwan, where he is very popular, as Hsüan-t'ien Shang-ti/Xuantian Shangdi "Emperor on High of the Dark Quarter". Iconographically, he is portrayed as sitting on the back of a tortoise that is encircled by a serpent, and surrounded by water.

The Taoist pantheon

It would be impossible here to give even the slightest coverage of the deities that cluster the Taoist pantheon. However, since they are modelled on the official bureaucratic structure of the empire, they are hierarchically arranged, though without any one definitive hierarchy! While there are subtle and highly celestial deities, there are also innumerable deities that fit into the administrative scheme of things, responsible for tasks from the most menial to the more prestigious. Moreover, "Heaven" has eighty-one levels filled with divine officials of all kinds. But we should remember that alongside this complex bureaucracy runs the theory that rhythmic transformation and change takes place irrespective of any divine interference. Deities have prescribed functions, but *Tao* operates impersonally and independently of all. Nevertheless, for the individual who needs an anthropomorphic conception of what divinity is, for those needy times of assistance, for help with illness and sickness, for safety in the home and success in business, there are the deities. For everything in nature – the wind, the lakes, the clouds, the stars the flowers – and in the locality

LIFE BEYOND EARTH: ANCESTORS, DEITIES, IMMORTALS AND SAGES

– the home, the place of work, the city – there are protective deities. Indeed, we have the same principle of spirits mirroring all earthly phenomena that we saw at the outset, in ancient China.

Out of this great complexity of deities only a few would be relevant to each individual. There would be no need to contemplate the entire host of them. Deities possess what is called *ling*, "power", and their power to assist is the pragmatic criterion that informs the choice of deities that any individual might wish to observe. The home is crucial to the integrated life of its inhabitants, so house gods and gods of the wider locality would be important. Students would favour the god of literature, and professions, too, have their associative deities, as we shall see. But power, *ling*, is the key to understanding the hierarchy of deities: the more power a deity has, the higher in the pantheon it is placed. Having said that, the deities pertinent to certain sects are given prominence by their adherents. Generally, the Celestial Lords, the *t'ien-tsun/tianzun*, head the pantheon. Of these, there are three, though there are variations as to who these are, as we shall see. Below the Celestial Lords or Celestial Venerables are the great Emperors like Huang-ti/Huangdi and the Jade Emperor. Kings and Queens, themselves also sometimes called emperors and empresses, like the Lord King or Emperor of the East, and the Queen Mother of the West, come next. These two, specifically, are the *yang* and *yin* of the divine hierarchy, the polar complements. Then there are the immortals, followed by the lowest rank of a multitude of spirits. The emperors and kings have their respective palaces, containing innumerable deities, immortals and attendant divine ministers.[20] The status of a spirit, immortal or deity is not static. Just as in earthly bureaucratic systems one can rise from lowly status to the higher echelons, in the divine world too it would be possible over a great length of time for a spirit to rise to divine status. Such would occur by the meticulous fulfilling of one's allotted functional role.

The highest deity

The highest deity is Tai-i/Tai-yi, "The Great One", "Supreme Unity" or "Supreme Oneness", introduced in Han times. It came to be the unity, the One, of the *Tao Te Ching/Daodejing*, the One that produces the two. It is the formless beginning of all things, the cosmic unity that is generated by *Tao*, the energy by which all is created and sustained. By late Han times it had become personalized, a personification of *Tao*, and was thought to reside in the Pole Star. But it retained its formless state in inner alchemy, where it remained the ultimate Void into which the adept was eventually liberated. It was, however, diversified into a triad of three deities, the highest deities in the Taoist pantheon.

The Triad

Three Celestial Venerables form the official triad of deities in religious Taoism. They are all *t'ien-tsun/tianzun*. *T'ien/tian* means "Heaven" and *tsun/zun* "venerable", "honoured" or "worthy". The whole expression, then, means " Celestial" (or "Heavenly") "Venerables" (or "Worthies"). Their creation was a contribution to Taoism of the Ling-pao/Lingbao school of Taoism, perhaps influenced by the Buddhist *trikaya* doctrine of the three *kaya*, or bodies, of the Buddha. The Celestial Venerable of the Primordial Beginning, is also called the Celestial Venerable of Jade Clarity (Yü-ching/Yujing), and Tao of Majestic Vacuity. His name, Yüan-shih T'ien-tsun/Yuanshi Tianzun has survived from T'ang/Tang times. As the leading deity of the Three Pure Ones, the *san-ch'ing/sanqing*, he is without limit, eternal and imperishable, yet he is also characterized as compassionate. In the Celestial Masters tradition, however, he was anthropomorphized sufficiently for his garments to be vividly described.[21] He rules over the Heaven of Jade Purity, Yü-ch'ing/Yuqing, the highest level of Heavens. While he was not always placed at the very top of the hierarchy of deities, he has become the supreme abstract deity. As such, he still exists through the cycles of manifestation and dissolution of the universe, revealing *Tao* to humankind at the beginning of each cycle through the medium of the lesser deities. It is only in his palace that immortals can exist through the cycles of the universe: all else ceases to be. In some cases, however, his place has been usurped by the much more popular Jade Emperor. Indeed, some Taoist sources suggest that the Celestial Venerable of the Primordial Beginning placed the Jade Emperor in charge, and resigned from his illustrious position.

The Celestial Venerable of the Numinous Treasure, or Magic Jewel, is also called the Mysterious Majesty of the Jade Aurora, the Eminent Saint of Supreme Purity. His name is Ling-pao T'ien-tsun/Lingbao Tianzun, though he is sometimes referred to as T'ai-shang Tao-chün/Taishang Daozun "Supreme Lord of Tao". As the second of the Three Pure Ones, he rules over the Heavens of Supreme Purity, Shang-ch'ing/Shangqing. He is particularly associated with the rhythms of *yin* and *yang* in the universe, the rhythms of time and, also, with magical texts. This deity, like the other two, was pre-eminent amongst the three at one time, but was demoted by the Shang-ch'ing/Shangqing and Ling-pao/Lingbao schools. The third of the Three Pure Ones is Celestial Venerable of *Tao* and *Te*, Tao-te T'ien-tsun/Daode Tianzun. In T'ang/Tang times he was known as T'ai-shang Lao-chün/Taishang Laojun, "Supreme Lord Lao-tzu/Laozi". Thus, he was the deified Lao-tzu/Laozi and, like him, is depicted as white-haired and white-bearded, and with clearly human features. He rules over the Heavens of Great or Supreme Purity, T'ai-ch'ing/Taiqing.

By Sung/Song times, the Three Pure Ones had come to represent time past, present and future. They are also of considerable importance in Taoist alchemy for they are located in the three cinnabar fields of the body. Here, they represent the primordial energies of *ching/jing*, *ch'i/qi* and *shen* and the unifying of the three that results in return to *Tao*.[22] There are, however other deities representing the same triad. Palmer warns: "This triad has taken many different shapes and forms over the centuries, and to this day is capable of different sets of deities."[23] Thus, we might certainly find the Jade Emperor included, especially in more recent times, as well as the Yellow Emperor.

The Three Agents or Rulers

The Three Rulers, Officers or Agents, *san-kuan/sanguan* are much more closely appropriate to the daily lives of ordinary Taoists than the Three Pure Ones. They have been venerated since early times, and featured in the Celestial Masters' rite that we saw in chapter 5, by which people confessed their sins to the three. T'ien-kuan/Tianguan is the Agent of Heaven, and is responsible for the prosperity and good fortune of people. He is the Agent of happiness. In the Celestial Masters school, those who had sinned wrote their misdemeanours on a strip of paper and burnt it on the peak of a mountain to represent their confessions to T'ien-kuan/Tianguan. Ti-kuan/Diguan is the Agent of Earth, and was especially concerned with absolving peoples' transgressions. They buried their strips of paper in the earth for him. Shui-kuan/Shuiguan is the Agent of Water, and is particularly associated with the overcoming of people's difficulties. He is the Agent that removes misfortune. For him, the pieces of paper were thrown into the river. Since the Celestial Masters school believed that sickness was concomitant with sins, these three Rulers were the medium by which illnesses could be cured. Their association with morality made them the holders of the registers of good and evil actions, and they are still venerated at specific festivals, especially the Festival of Lanterns. Each also has his own festival. The Agent of Heaven is the usual one to be found represented iconographically, particularly on New Year cards, and in the not too distant past, used to present himself to theatre audiences before performances in order to bestow good wishes on the spectators.[24]

Three Gods of Happiness

Even more revered popularly are the three stellar gods of longevity, health and blessing – happiness in general. These are Fu, Lu and Shou. They are found in Chinese homes, on the roofs of temples, in the workplace, in Chinese restaurants, and are to be found, too, in some shops and garden centres in the West. They are three very characterful individuals. Shou is the one who appears most in Chinese art. He is the God of Longevity, and is easily recognized by his bald, highly-domed head. There is a bulge on the front of his head, accentuating the domed shape. It is indicative of the *ch'i/qi* that he has transmuted. The same can be said about his bulging belly. In one hand he holds a peach of immortality, and in the other, a long, gnarled branch of a tree, often as a staff and sometimes showing one or two gourds on it. He is the oldest of the three, has a long white beard, and is the strangest looking of them, though he is usually portrayed with a happy smile and rosy cheeks that belie his great age. When seated, he is on a crane, one of the many symbols of longevity. Lu, the God of Official Position or Dignitaries, and, therefore, of wealth, happiness and honour, is dressed very regally. Fu, who has a kindly face, is the God of Blessings. He is often depicted carrying a child, for it is he who grants children, particularly sons.

The Jade Emperor

We come now to a highly important personage, the Jade Emperor, Yü-huang Shang-ti/Yühuang Shangdi, a colourful figure that is prolific in Chinese and Taoist legends. The Celestial Venerables are considered to be prior to the creation of the world, so the Jade Emperor belongs to time itself, and not to primordial time. In fact, he appears on the official scene rather late, at the beginning of the second millennium, though his cult had been developing for centuries before.[25] He is the present, supreme ruler of all Heaven and Earth, "the One, the axis, the mediator, and the centre toward which everything converges".[26] At a philosophical level this is an apt comment, but pragmatically and anthropomorphically, his task is a difficult one, for he has to deal with all kinds of problems. Very often he is unsuccessful, and is even ridiculed and cheated. One tale tells of his inviting all creatures to his birthday party. But few of them bothered to go – only twelve in fact. It was these animals that were rewarded by being the twelve animals of the Chinese calendar. All mortals, deities, spirits of the underworld, and even buddhas and *bodhisattvas*, are inferior to him. It is the Jade Emperor who presides over the Heavenly courts and to whom deities, ministers and officials of all kinds report on events in their jurisdiction, and on the misdemeanours of all others. Everyone is tried by him, and lives are shortened or lengthened according to merit and demerit. He is assisted by his nephew, Ehr-ling/Erling, a powerful militarist and magician, who chases away evil with the aid of his dog, T'ien-kou/Tiangou. The Emperor is also assisted by his messenger, Wang, who is the gatekeeper to the highest Heaven. It is here that the Emperor dwells and conducts his rule. Wang is also to be found at the entrance of temples. The Jade Emperor is a thoroughly masculine, *yang*, deity. Palmer and Xiaomin describe him as "the ultimate masculine symbol of perfection".[27] Pictorially, he is portrayed sitting on his throne and clothed in a dragon-embroidered long robe. His traditional head covering is topped with a square-shaped board. His face is stern – an appropriate expression considering his role. He has remained the highest deity of popular, religious Taoism as well as of wider Chinese religion. Popularly, he is known as T'ien-kung/Tiangong, "King Heaven" or "Master Heaven".

The influence of Taoist schools

The development of the Taoist pantheon of deities was concomitant with the rise of the Taoist schools. The Celestial Masters school, for example, had an extensive pantheon.[28] It was the founder of Taoism, Chang Tao-ling/Zhang Daoling, later deified, who received scriptures from the gods and founded the Five Pecks of Rice school. His title, T'ien-shih/Tianshi, "Celestial Master" is used to the present day. For him, Lao-tzu/Laozi was the supreme deity. The Shang-ching/Shangqing scriptures were believed to have been revealed by the highest deities, a fact that accounted for the prestige and success of the school in its early days. For this school, with its heavy influence on meditation, inner visualization, and inner alchemy, the Three Originals or Primordials – each residing in one of the cinnabar fields of the body – were the most important gods in the pantheon. The mystical concentration on the Three as One was essential to the tenets of the school. The later Ling-pao/Lingbao school has influenced Taoist liturgy down to present times, and ensured the survival of certain deities, while adding others. It was this school that elevated the Celestial Venerable of the Primordial Beginning to the head of the Three Pure Ones. For all the schools partnership between the divine beings, past sages, immortals, and the adepts who were striving for immortality, was essential. Those who dwelt beyond Earth were the only medium that could procure the liberation of the self into the immortal state.

The deified Lao-tzu/Laozi

During the Han and Six Dynasties periods, Lao-tzu/Laozi was deified as Lord Lao, and was important enough in many cases to be worshipped alongside the Yellow Emperor, particularly in the cult in the early Han, known as Huang-lao Taoism – a name that combines the two personages. By the mid-second century the Huang-lao school had thoroughly combined the characters of the Yellow Emperor and Lao-tzu/Laozi as the deity Lord Huang-Lao,[29] and the school was well established in the first century.[30] In his deified status Lao-tzu/Laozi is independently known as T'ai-shang Lao-chün/Taishang Laojun, Supreme Master Lao. He is probably important enough to rival the status of the Jade Emperor himself.

In his deified form, Lao-tzu/Laozi incarnates or communicates with humankind, bestowing scriptures and guidance. As Kohn says, for the *fang-shih/fangshi* he was a master thinker and practitioner of the art of longevity and immortality. But it was in official circles that he was to become the great cosmic deity, and the personification of *Tao*. For messianic sects of Taoism, too, he became the ultimate saviour.[31] In his cosmic divine dimensions, Lao-tzu/Laozi was believed to exist before the cosmos, preceding creation, but appearing to sage-kings in various ages.[32] An inscription dated to the end of the Han dynasty depicts Lao-tzu/Laozi as a cosmic deity, dwelling in the centre of Heaven in the Big Dipper, and being coexistent with the primordial *Tao*. The *Transformations of Lao-tzu Scripture (Lao-tzu pien-hua ching/Laozi bianhuajing)*, dated to the early second century, describes the transformations or incarnations of Lao-tzu/Laozi.

Female deities: The Queen Mother of the West

Hsi Wang-mu/Xiwangmu "The Queen Mother of the West" is the most significant goddess to have emerged in Taoism, reaching her most popular status in T'ang/Tang times. She is an interesting goddess because her origins reach back into antiquity, and her portrayal in T'ang/Tang times, where she is mainly associated with the Shang-ch'ing/Shangqing school of Taoism, retains much of her ancient character. She is the dark, *yin*, female force that is representative of the cosmic feminine in creation. Suzanne Cahill says of her: "As a ruler, she controlled creation, transcendence, and divine passion. As a woman, she was mother, teacher, and lover. Her western association links her in traditional Chinese cosmology with autumn, death, the afterlife, and paradise. Further connections with the west, important in poetry, include the color white, the Agent Metal, and the emotion of melancholy."[33] She was instrumental in assisting the transcendence of desires and egoism that impeded immortality, and was the major mediator between Earth and Heaven.

The Queen Mother of the West features widely in the literature of the T'ang/Tang dynasty, but particularly in the lengthy account of Tu Kuang-t'ing/Du Guangting in his *Yung-ch'eng Chi-hsien lu/Yongcheng Jixianlu*, "Records of the Assembled Transcendents of the Fortified Walled City", as well as in a number of poems. Earliest references to her are perhaps on Shang oracle bones[34] and, much later, in the *Chuang-tzu/Zhuangzi*. Later still, in the time of the Warring States, there seem to have been a number of different traditions that suggest a plurality of goddesses by the same name. But by T'ang/Tang times, all these had been subsumed under one title for one goddess,[35] and she headed the list of female goddesses in Shang-ch'ing/Shangqing Taoism. Here, she was given the official title of The Ninefold Numinous Grand and Realized Primal Ruler of the Purple Tenuity from the White Jade Tortoise Terrace, though she had many other names.

There is a superiority about this goddess that lends distinction to her legends and iconography. Perhaps her success lay in the fact that she would commune with humans, teach them, and provide them with means to immortality. She also arranged divine marriages between evolved mortals and celestial beings. Rather like the Hindu goddess Kali, or Durga, she had both a terrifying and benign form, for she was sometimes depicted as part tiger, and was perhaps associated with animal sacrifices.[36] Such duality is, as Cahill portrays, exemplified well in her associations with weaving on the one hand, and with the destructive tiger on the other.[37] Thus, this goddess is a symbol of both creation and destruction. Cahill also notes that there is much that is shamanic in her appearance – teeth like a tiger, tail like a leopard, dishevelled hair, roaring and whistling, and the ability to ascend to Heaven from the tops of mountains, and travel to the stars. Her association with the West – the unknown realm where immortals lived, but feared as the symbol of death – also brings out the duality associated with her personality. Wonderful descriptions of her home on Mount K'un-lun/Kunlun, her magnificent palace, the gardens where she keeps the peaches of immortality (said to ripen only once in three thousand years), the servants and attendants, and her personal being and attire are found in T'ang/Tang sacred and secular literature. In meditative visualization, and in the nurturing of the inner alchemical Spirit Embryo, she plays a prominent role. Her power is immense. One text says of her:

> The Queen Mother embodies the deepest foundation of the weak and yielding: she represents the origin of the ultimate yin. Therefore she rules over the direction of the west. She mothers and nourishes all kinds of beings, whether in heaven above or on the earth below, whether in any of the three worlds or in any of the ten directions. Especially all women who ascend to immortality and attain the Tao are her dependents.[38]

The Han concepts of *yin* and *yang* and the Five Agents were woven into her hagiographical legends. Her *yang* consort is in the East, appropriately, The King Father of the East, whom she visits once a year. Their union perpetuates the created universe, after which she sustains it by maintaining the balances between *yin* and *yang*. Of her many roles, Cahill writes:

> She legitimizes divine and worldly power. She transmits texts, talismans, and practices associated with the Shang ch'ing school and the cult of transcendents. She bestows the word of the sacred scriptures; the word is the intermediary between gods and humans. She sanctions ascents to transcendence by men and women, registering the new immortals. She serves as matchmaker in Taoist divine marriages. In short, she controls access to immortality and relations between humans and deities.[39]

But apart from these important roles, The Queen Mother of the West champions women, nuns, the recluses, female Taoist adepts, and is the Queen of female immortals especially. She is worshipped at many shrines and immortalized archaeologically on stone inscriptions, having become a respectable, aristocratic goddess, though she never seems to have lost some of her more primal character.

The Queen of Heaven

A prominent female deity is the Empress or Queen of Heaven, Ma-tsu/Mazu or T'ien-shang Sheng-mu/Tianshang Shengmu, "Holy Mother in Heaven". She is a beautiful goddess, a true mother figure, who takes care of sailors, travellers, women and children. As a young girl she was devoted to meditation and holy texts. She came from a fishing family and, one day, her father and brothers were out at sea in a terrible storm. She meditated, and her *hun* souls left her body. As they were about to lose their lives, her father and brothers saw her white figure gliding to their boat. She began to tug them back to safety. However, her mother came into the room and, finding her still, shook her. Her souls returned, but before she could drag her family to safety. Only two brothers survived to tell the tale. Ma-tsu/Mazu died young and celibate, a woman with great spiritual power. Her mummified body was entombed in her native village in a temple built for her that lasted right up until the time of the Cultural Revolution in the last century. Her cult began in a small way, but in the centuries after her death (which probably occurred in the tenth century), and when many miracles were attributed to her, she rose in the official list of deities. She became a national deity, and was eventually given status in one of the stars of the Big Dipper. She became Queen of Heaven in the seventeenth century and is widely worshipped, but she has remained the patron saint of sailors and commerce to this day. Sailors in the area where she lived, and those wider afield, sometimes carry her picture on their boats. Pictorially she is to be seen seated on waves or on clouds, dressed in a long gown, with an imperial cap on her head.

Another female deity is the mother of Lao-tzu/Laozi. She had a number of different aspects. Before the incarnation of *Tao* as Lao-tzu/Laozi, she is the virginal Jade Maiden of Mystery and Wonder. As the mother of Lao-tzu/Laozi she is Mother Li and the incarnation of *Tao*, and as the teacher of her son, she is T'ai-i Yüan-chün/Taiyi Yuanjun, "Goddess of the Great One". She is also Great Queen of the Former Heaven.[40]

An important goddess that spans both popular Taoism and Buddhism – indeed, all China – is Kuan-yin/Guanyin. She is an exquisitely beautiful goddess and images of her can be found frequently in garden centres in the West. She is the Goddess of Mercy and Compassion. In the Mahayana strands of Buddhism she is Avalokitesvara, who is often portrayed as male. She is his female counterpart in esoteric, *tantric* sects. He, too, is the Buddha of Compassion. Kuan-yin/Guanyin must be the most popular of deities, since she is a perfect motherly figure who aids all who need her. She grants sons to childless women, and heals illnesses. She is usually portrayed as covered in a white veil and holding a child in her arms. She sits on a lotus, the symbol of enlightenment. While she is rarely seen in temples, she is almost always to be found in the home.

Major, professional and personal deities

In the development of the complex Taoist pantheon the prominence given to ordinary mortals who had become deities was considerable, particularly in the context of popular religion. Immortals, too, as we shall see below, were ranked high, while the nature divinities more and more came to be recognized as *karmic* individuals who would have to rise to higher statuses by increasing their store of merit. In Sung/Song times, the Emperor Chen-ts'ung/Zhencong added many new deities and immortals to the official pantheon and, therefore, expanded the number of temples and shrines to accommodate their worship.

Kuan-ti/Guandi (also known as Kuan-kung/Guangong),[41] the God of War and patron of military arts, is an important deity. He, too, was a historical person, Kuan Yü/Guan Yu, a third century general in the state of Shu. He was executed by his enemies in 220 despite his complete fidelity and honour, and became a great hero. As the God of War, he leads the armies of Heaven against evil, but he is also the defender of officials. These twin roles are depicted in his iconography, the former reflected in his image as a man of huge size, clad in the armour of war, with his horse at his side, and the latter in official dress without military trappings. He is expected to protect the country from invasion. In his less military role, he is a patron of literature and commerce. He has a red face – a feature of his character in theatre performances – a magnificent beard and legendary eyebrows that look like silkworms. A fourteenth century novel, *The Romance of the Three Kingdoms*, tells his story and blends Confucian morality with supernatural and magical events. It is a work that has helped to maintain the popular nature of the god since its contents have been adopted so much for the popular theatre. Kuan-ti/Guandi is directly responsible to the Jade Emperor, for it is he who keeps the Heavenly host in order. Thus, he is sometimes called Emperor, for such is the might of this god who can allay all demons and evil spirits. He is also associated with automatic spirit writing and is believed to be a frequent visitor at seances. Perhaps such skills stem from the legendary events after his death. For when his enemy was about to receive royal reward, Kuan-ti/Guandi's spirit took possession of his enemy's body causing him to hurl a string of insults at the king! There are many such tales of him in his mortal life as well as his afterlife.[42] He is sufficiently popular to be found in homes, restaurants and shops, and martial arts halls, in addition to temples; in Taiwan, he has become the head of the Taoist pantheon in some sects, dislodging the Jade Emperor himself.

The God of Wealth is an important one for those in business, as well as for ordinary families. He is Ts'ai-shen/Caishen. His form is to be found in many homes and even on bank statements. He is frequently to be found on Chinese calendars, especially since, at New Year, it is hoped that he will bless the family with financial gain in the year to come. He is dressed impressively as a high-status official and carries a scroll bearing his name. Naturally, he heads the Ministry of Wealth in the divine bureaucracy with many accompanying officials in his department.

Some of the other deities need only be mentioned here. A god of longevity and a god of immortality are often to be found on almanacs as symbols of good luck. They are perhaps not so much worshipped for longevity or immortality – the average person would be fully aware that neither would be his or her fate – but as "representations of an idea".[43] There are deities representing professions and trades – even gambling and prostitution! Lu Pan/Lu Ban is the god of carpenters, joiners, blacksmiths and potters: each trade will have its patron.[44] Hou-chi/Houji is the god of agriculture, and She-chi/Sheji the god of the land, the soil and grain. In Taiwan, multiple deities called Wang-yeh/Wangye are the patrons of the immigrants who fled from the island of Fukien to

Taiwan after World War Two.[45] In the Taiwanese pantheon, too, is the "Great Emperor Who Preserves Life", Pao-sheng Ta-ti/Baosheng Dadi. He, like so many other deities, had once been human, a medical practitioner called Wu Chen-jen/Wu Zhenren. As Thompson points out, since *chen-jen/zhenren* is a term for a perfected person, a true person, or a sage that will become an immortal, the term is an indicator of the skills and character of the man.[46]

Nature deities

If we cast our minds back to chapter 1 of this book, we can recall that natural phenomena were thought to be animated with spiritual forces from the earliest times, and certainly before Taoism came on the scene in any form. I said then that such a view of nature was part of the Chinese psyche. While no longer ranking so highly in the hierarchy of those who exist beyond Earth, the continued belief in nature deities is part of that ingrained psyche. Popular, are gods of the weather – thunder, lightning (Tien-mu/Dianmu, female), rain (Yü-shih/Yushi), and wind (Feng-po/Fengbo), for instance. Lei-kung/Leigong, the god of thunder is the chief, and the most popular of these, as well as being the most ferocious looking. He carries a string of drums and a wooden mallet with which to beat them and create the sound of thunder. He was important enough to be divided up into a whole bureau of thunder ministers. The goddess of lightning created its streaks by holding up two mirrors. The god of wind kept winds imprisoned in leather bags, ready to open them when he wished to create storms, but just a little for soft breezes.

Mountains and rivers were also assigned their respective deities and spirits. Mountains were always important in the history of Taoism. Immortals frequented their slopes, and departed for immortality from their peaks. Sages retreated to them to begin their journeys to *Tao* and deities had their palaces on their peaks, like the Emperors of the North, South, East and West, and the Yellow Emperor – each with his palace on one of the five sacred mountains in his associative area.

Another colourful nature deity is the Old Woman Who Sweeps Heaven Clear. She cleans the skies and the Heavens after rain.[47] Water spirits also feature in Taoist popular belief. Towards the end of the Chinese year in the tenth month, the birthday of the God of Water is celebrated until the end of the year. A banquet is held on his birthday to celebrate the release of souls from their abode in the underworld. Rain spirits are associated with dragons. Since rain is so essential for crops, it is important that it arrives at the right time. Dragon ceremonies, therefore, are a colourful feature of the requests to the spirit world for rain. There are four Dragon Kings, each responsible for one of the four seas that were believed to envelop the earth, and for sending rain in the appropriate season that matched each direction. Dragons have immense powers, being able to traverse the underworld, or soar to Heaven. Dragon Kings abound in folklore and theatre. Additionally, they inhabit lakes, rivers and pools. They can be kind, but also antagonistic, and are the medium of much exciting legend.

Deities of the earth, of locations, and of the home

The concept of earth deities is an ancient one in China, as we saw in chapter 1. But it is now part of Taoist belief. Homage to the earth god in the form of the god of the home or the flat is the first action of the day. Just as in ancient times, when the earth god was notified before major events like harvesting, so in the home today the earth god is notified about activities in the home. The hierarchy of gods is evident at this level, too, for the house god is responsible to the local god, he to the district god, and the district god to the city god, and he to the god of the province. Many of the earth gods have been mortals who have died in tragic circumstances – females who have died as virgins, for example, or those who have committed suicide. It is as if their destiny were cut off, and they were held to the localities in which they lived by being prevented from moving on. Others are former local heroes, whose wisdom, bravery, sagacity or outstanding qualities make them good candidates for the status of localized earth gods.

The deities connected to cities have been termed in the past the gods of walls and ditches or wall-and-moat deities. These are terms that replaced the old one of earth gods, though the latter describes rather well their function today. Gods of walls and moats, *ch'eng-huang-shen/chenghuangshen*, or city gods, originated in T'ang/Tang times when walls and moats surrounded the cities, and their shrines or temples were therefore built on the perimeter of the city.[48] The city deity is responsible for the care of the city – protecting it from harmful flooding, disease or drought, so it has some function in providing rain. Each city deity has its special temple and is honoured on its particular festival day. Some of these city gods are famous, like the City God of Hsin-ch'u/Xinzchu in Taiwan.[49]

The deities specific to a locality, to small areas like a street, a district, hamlet, a piece of land, a bridge, a building, a temple, and also the home, are *t'u-ti/tudi*. It is these deities that are the closest to the inhabitants, and their relatively meagre-looking shrines belie their importance in daily life. It is to these deities that people turn in difficult times, when there are problems at home or in the locality, at work, or on farmland. The *t'u-ti/tudi* of these small areas are different from the *t'u-ti/tudi* of the home, the latter being even more intimately associated with the family. It is these deities right at the bottom of the hierarchical structure of earth gods that really know the woes and joys of the home they protect. The small images that represent these deities are placed on the ground, next to the earth near the altar, thus effectuating closer control of the space on which the home is built. In Taiwan, shrines to the district deities are prolific.

It is the deities associated with the home itself that are carefully respected. There are door gods who stand either side of the entrance to a home, and whose function is to drive away evil spirits. They sometimes take the form of scrolls, but more often pictures of warriors in remembrance of two warriors who guarded the entrance to an emperor's bedroom, preventing disturbing demons from harming him. After he saw they lacked sufficient sleep, he had portraits made of them instead. They are to be found either side of the entrance to temples. The Kitchen, Hearth or Stove God, is a colourful character. While being low in the hierarchy of earth gods, his role is such that he is given great respect. Situated in the kitchen, at the hearth of the home, he is strategically placed to pick up all the gossip, and to note all the little good and bad things done by the family. At the end of the year, he leaves the home to report all he has seen and heard to the Jade Emperor. He is represented by a picture on the kitchen wall, or sometimes by a piece of paper on which an invocation is written. This is burnt, to send him on his way, and a new piece is put up to herald his return in the New Year. Since the fortune of the family in the coming year will depend on his report, before he leaves he may be sweetened up by sweet food, or he may be given a very glutinous rice to seal his mouth together so that he cannot report anything! Fireworks often herald his departure and his arrival back is an occasion for ceremony and offerings. But at least the revelries of New Year can be enjoyed while he is away. The Kitchen God is sometimes to be found with his wife, and six domestic animals. While the Kitchen God is the key deity of the home, there are a number of others, like the Lady of the Toilet and Bathroom, an old deity who was formerly the Goddess of the Latrine-Ditch, and the Lord and Lady of the Bed.

The Kitchen God is sometimes connected with the stellar god and director of destiny, Ssu-ming/Siming. The latter is certainly very ancient going well back to several centuries BCE. He had connections with alchemy, and in inner alchemy was visualized in the uppermost cinnabar field. It was he who kept the registers of life and death, of merits and demerits for each person, and requested the Great One, the highest deity, to lengthen or shorten an individual's life accordingly.[50] In popular legend, however, the origin of the Kitchen God is much later, and less widely associated with Ssu-ming/Siming. There are many stories about his origins, but popularly, he was said to have once been a poor man who had to sell his wife in marriage to someone else. Years later, while he was begging in an area, he recognized her, felt ashamed, and hid himself in the cooking stove, in which he was accidentally burnt. It would be stories like this that are more likely to be associated with the Kitchen God rather than an ancestry of the nature of Ssu-ming/Suming.

The city and district deities keep records of all their inhabitants, their births and their deaths, and when someone dies, it is the responsibility of these gods or goddesses to escort the soul to their senior, so that they eventually reach the city god. It is the city god who conducts the soul to the hells for judgement, assisted by two characters called Oxhead and Horseface, and two others called White Old Gentleman and Black Old Gentleman. These judge the soul, weighing up its respective merits and demerits before taking it to an appropriate hell. Earth Gods are highly significant in the context of the vision we have of religious practice. While remote celestials hardly enter into daily life, these localized deities are the intimate mediums by which humans engage with divinity. Angela Zito makes the point that these gods are indicative of the way in which, in the past, people shaped their social world, "a world that combined the family, the imperial domain, and the cosmos into an interactive whole".[51] This connective tissue that links the heart of the home with the wider cosmic reality is no less evident in present day belief. What takes place is, to borrow Zito's phrase, a "sacralization of place in the universe".[52]

Stellar deities

The position of the stars in the sky was felt to influence human life, particularly since the stars overlooked Earth. The sun, moon and stars all had their respective deities, and many groupings of stars were connected with the Five Agents, along with major planets.[53] In addition to the three stellar Gods of Happiness noted earlier, and Ssu-ming/Siming above, there are other stellar deities. The God of Literature, Wen Ch'ang/Wen Chang dwells in six stars near the Great Bear. If his constellation shines brightly, then it will be a time of literary prosperity. He is a deity favoured particularly by scholars, and is invoked especially before examinations. He is also believed to be the author of many tracts written through the medium of the divination brush. It was Wen Ch'ang/Wen Chang who was the God of the civil service examinations instituted by the state centuries ago in Sung/Song times. He ran the divine intelligence corps, but also had power over the elements.[54] His skills are wide, from creating thunder, to establishing justice, curing illnesses and granting children. He is believed to incarnate as a scholar many times[55] and many temples dedicated to him can be found in Taiwan.

A very important group of stars is the Big Dipper (*Ursa Major*), as well as the Pole star. The Mother of the Northern Dipper is Tou-mu/Doumu, who seems to have been influenced by both Hindu and Buddhist ideas. She is rather like Kuan-yin/Guanyin, being a compassionate goddess. She is sometimes called T'ien-mu/Tianmu "Mother of Heaven" and also Tao-mu/Daomu, "Mother of *Tao*", with a full title of Yüan-ming Tou-lao yüan-chün/Yuanming Doulao Yuanjun.[56] With her Indian spouse she had nine sons, seven of whom form the stars of the Big Dipper, the other two being the gods of the North and South Poles. The seven stars of the Dipper dictate the fate of all those below, for all humans are born under the guardianship of one or another of the stars. Her iconography is strongly suggestive of Buddhist influence, with her many arms and three eyes.

Ch'ang'o/Chango, Goddess of the Moon, is exquisitely beautiful, with long dark hair. She and her husband lost their divine status and had been banished to Earth. She became Goddess of the Moon by drinking an elixir of immortality that had been given to her husband by the Queen Mother of the West. He didn't take the elixir straight away, but hid it, intending for them both to take it a few days hence. There was only sufficient for both of them to have eternal life, but not enough for them to have immortality. However, Ch'ang'o/Chango found the elixir, and took the lot, so that she rose up immediately to the Heavens. But rather than rise to Heaven, where the gods might chide her for her actions, she decided instead to reside in the moon.

Deities of the underworld

The Taoist pantheon extends not just upwards into the heavens, but downwards, too, into the hells. These are hierarchically graded with gods and ministers who mete out punishments to those who have sinned. There are ten hells, each for different types of sinners, each ruled by a king and judge, and each having many sub-departments. Such a proliferation of hells was adopted from Buddhism. The God of them all is Hou-tu/Houdu, who is directly responsible to the Jade Emperor. The innocent return to a reincarnated life; others face their punishment in an allotted hell, where punishments exceed any kind of creative writing one might wish to use to describe them![57]

In addition to all the deities and good spirits, there are also demons, devils and evil spirits. They are pests that create havoc for deities and mortals, causing sickness, hardship, droughts, fires, and natural, elemental phenomena like typhoons. The demon and evil spirit world is swelled by those whose deaths have been particularly violent or unhappy, and by those who have no family to accept them as ancestors. These are "orphan souls", hungry ghosts. Some houses have "devil walls" a few feet from the door in order to keep out unwanted spirits. The belief in such spirits has been a part of Chinese pre-history and history to the present day, and the old shamanic practices to get rid of them have evolved into all kinds of superstitious ritual.

Thus we have the range of Taoist deities, from the great celestial divinities down to the gods of the home. Sometimes, in the stories and legends surrounding the multiplicity of divine, semi-divine and demonic beings it appears that we have come a long way from the mystical conception of *Tao* that is, and that emanates forth to be, the ten-thousand things in the universe. But Taoism has the ability to cater for all minds, for all stages in the evolutionary path of returning to *Tao*. We now have to turn our attention to those who have made that journey, the immortals.

Immortals

In its long history, Taoism courted a number of theories about immortality and the means to procure it. The *Tao Te Ching/Daodejing* does not seem to contain immortality as a major theme of its text. The *Chuang-tzu/Zhuangzi*, too, regards death as a balance of life, part of the natural rhythm and order of things, and an unavoidable end to life that only the enlightened sage can take in his stride. But the text also refers to *shen-jen/shenren*, "divine" or "spirit beings". Alchemical Taoism, as we saw in an earlier chapter, had an altogether different view. Longevity was the aim of the alchemists and, by extension, eternal life in immortality, accomplished through return to *Tao* by the means of a Spirit Embryo that would mature within. Then, too, the ordinary mortal, the ordinary Taoist, would not contemplate everlasting life. Rather, he or she would hope for a good and blessed present one. To these ideas must be added the concept of life as very anthropomorphic immortals, in tune with *Tao* but able to live a colourful life on Earth or in the heavens. Of these, eight are especially famous, and we shall return to look at them below. First, however, we need to note a few points about the origin of the idea of immortality.

Origins and early nature

The idea of immortality in China is an ancient one, with legends of those who have transcended death to live in heavenly realms, or of those who live in lonely parts of mountains and forests. Some were believed to have had apparent rather than real deaths. Such concepts were widespread in Chinese thought in the third century BCE. But, according to Robinet, the belief in physical immortality is witnessed on Shang bronze inscriptions dated to as early as the eighth century BCE, and talk of the isles where plants for immortality grew was present in court circles in the fourth century BCE.[58] In time, the status of immortals rose to exceed that of the earth gods. It came to be believed that, through excessively good merit, some mortals could by-pass the hells after death, and take their place in the ranks of heavenly beings, from where they would be able to rise in status, eventually becoming full immortals.

The Chinese character for immortal is *hsien/xian*, which is usually translated as "immortal", even as "genie". It can also mean "perfected" or "transcendent". It refers to a person who has lived such a holy and spiritual life that he or she has transcended normal patterns of existence and has taken on the nature of a saint. The Chinese character *hsien/xian* is itself composed of two characters, one for "human being" and the other for "mountain". Put together, the image is of a mortal being who dwells in the mountains, or of one who transcends. Thus, as Schipper points out: "Phonologically, the word *hsien/xian* derives from the root meaning 'to change, evolve, go up,' or even 'to dance.' This recalls the themes of transformation, of ascension to heaven, and of dance which, in the ritual, allows one to take possession of a sacred space."[59] Schipper's words here are reminiscent of the shamanic dances and flights of the shaman to the realms of the spirits and gods. But one characteristic seems to pervade the concept of an immortal, and that is the easy-going, free and spontaneous nature of those who realize such a level of spirituality. A variant form of the character for *hsien/xian* in the *Book of Songs* means "to dance with flying sleeves", a superb picture of the free immortal. Kohn notes that, according to the commentary on the *Book of Songs*, the combination of the human being and the mountain in the Chinese character can mean "to reach old age and not to die". Thus, Kohn comments: "The obvious basic implication of the term *xian* is therefore twofold. It connotes, first, the idea of a take-off, a separation from normal life, be it in an ecstatic dance or by going into the mountains; and, second, the notion of longevity and the complete avoidance of death."[60]

In particularly graphic words, Robinet described the immortals thus:

> Immortals prefer to live in hiding, far from the world, withdrawn into the mountains and often living in caves. . . . They are masters of the rain and the wind, like the wu sorcerers, and . . . they can pass through fire without burning and through water without getting wet. These are the signs that they know how to control Yin and Yang (water and rain, fire and wind). They move up and down with the clouds, as they please. They have wings, on which feathers grow, and they ride either cranes or fish (air-yang and water-yin). They know the future. They are masters of time and space. They can, at will, reduce the world to the size of a gourd, or turn a gourd into a world as vast as the universe. They are evanescent, disappearing and appearing in the wink of an eye.[61]

These are words that portray many of the characteristics of the early shamans, and immortals combine the skills of the latter in healing and magical practices. They are usually portrayed as being eternally youthful, with soft skin, shining eyes, square pupils, elongated head, long ears, a luminous body, and with movement as swift, nimble and fleet as a deer. Their figures cast no shadow, though they can exist disguised as ordinary mortals. They seem to be astride the human and divine realms and able to function in either. But at a deeper level they are at one with the universe, with *Tao*.

The early immortals were believed to reside in beautiful countries, but in later times they took up residence in the bureaucratic range of heavens, themselves graded according to their immortal status, like the divine beings that also inhabited the heavens. The overlap between immortals and sages is seen, particularly, in the nature of the Taoist adept who has achieved the level of holy status as a being of *Tao*, *tao-jen/daoren*; spirit being, *shen-jen/shenren*; or true, perfected man, *chen-jen/zhenren*. It is these that feature in the *Tao Te Ching/Daodejing* and the *Chuang-tzu/Zhuangzi*, but in the latter it is the sage that rises in equanimity beyond fear of death, who features prominently. However, the short step between the sage and the full-blown immortal was an easy concept for Taoists to take on board.

Much literature supported the belief in immortals. The *Shen-hsien chuan/Shenxian zhuan* "Biographies of Spirit Immortals" was one important post-Han text written by Ko Hung/Ge Hong in the fourth century.[62] The literature concerned with immortals gives not only an account of their lives, but also some description of the method by which immortality was achieved in each case. These methods, as Schipper notes, are not uniform: "There are as many ways to become immortal as there are Immortals, and there is nothing systematic about it."[63] Some of the literature connected with immortals clearly points to the legendary nature of many of them. On the other hand, some were historical figures, as we shall see. Some of the latter obviously died naturally, but are believed to have had their physical being and spirit reunited after death.

Not all immortals are portrayed as secretive, mystical beings. They might ride the winds and sip dew, but many are depicted as colourful characters. It is especially in the popular mind that these more accessible immortals are held dear. These are the immortals that engage in earthly events, appearing to uphold justice and defend the weak. It is these who are artistically portrayed in art and iconography, and who take on profoundly anthropomorphic personalities. They may sip dew, which might also, on occasion, be wine, or be seen playing the lute. They are merry people, at ease with each other and with themselves, existing in perfect contentment. Unlike deities and ancestors, they are not confined to particular locations like temples, for their "free and easy wandering" is a major facet of their nature. Blofeld noted that immortals are often likened to floating clouds that *are* without making any effort to *be*: "The filmy lightness of an idling summer cloud is suggestive of the sensation of weightlessness that characterises immortals, a sensation born of absolute freedom from care and anxiety."[64] Immortals thus epitomized the ultimate goal for mortals – in whatever way that goal was visualized. Physical contentment in a physical body could be the end product of one's spiritual efforts, as much as life in the abodes of the immortals, or passage into the ultimate non-being of *Tao*: it was simply a matter of degree. But the path was not an easy one, and this point is reflected in the portrayal of some immortals as old men, representing the years of arduous pursuit of the spiritual goal.

The Eight Immortals (*Pa-hsien/Baxian*)

Of all the immortals, eight are particularly special. They are found in a prominent position in most Taoist temples, where they have the special function of warding off evil. They are to be seen in the home, at celebrations like weddings and anniversaries, or represented in dance at the beginning of theatrical performances. They are depicted on paintings, vases, plates, teapots, and can be found in craft shops and garden centres in the West. Such is their importance that they are not just a Taoist phenomenon, but are popular in the wider context of Chinese religious life as a whole. Since these Eight Immortals defend the weak and uphold justice they illustrate that the life-condition of the truly good person can be turned from one of poverty to riches or from oppression to joy. In short, they provide hope, and the Immortals are always ready to intervene in the human situation to turn hope into reality. Given the hardship of the peasants and lowest strata of Chinese society, the tales of the Eight Immortals were welcomed as illustrations of how persecutors could themselves be punished and how the rich could be brought low. The tales of the Immortals are ones in which happiness follows sadness for those who are virtuous.

The Eight Immortals are examples of those who have reached the ultimate goal but who have remained in the world, or returned to it, to help others, rather like the Buddhist concept of *bodhisattvas*. They participate in the lives of ordinary folk, disguising themselves to perpetrate justice. They have very different characters, but generally they are funny, happy, free, and often drunk. Their purpose in the many tales and anecdotes about them is manifold. Apart from championing justice, sometimes, for example, they provide an explanation for a geographical feature like the grottoes of Ching Ling/Jingling, explained by their digging and burrowing through the mountain in search of a precious pearl.[65] But they are champions of Taoism, helping people to understand the functioning of *Tao* in the world. Then, too, the characters in the stories reflect the daily life of ordinary people – the oil seller, woodcutter, beggar, local commissioner, for example. Of the Eight, however, some have always been more popular than others: Lü Tung-pin/Lü Dongbin, Ti Kuai-li/Diguaili and Chang Kuo-lao/Zhang Guolao, the first three, are far more important than the rest. Some of the Eight only occur in the context of the others in their group, but the important ones are portrayed in tales individually. Their characters span social boundaries of rich and poor, official and peasant, male and female, old and young, the healthy and the sick. The origins of the tales of the Eight Immortals date back to T'ang/Tang times, though the tales about them were developed more significantly in Sung/Song times. But it was not until Ming times that the official legends about the Immortals were finalized. We now need to look more closely at each of these characters.

Lü Tung-pin/Lü Dongbin

The most famous and most popular of the Immortals, Lü Tung-pin/Lü Dongbin "Lü the Cavern Guest" (also called Lü Yen/Lü Yan), was a bright student, and is believed to have been a historical person living in the early ninth century. He is symbolic of intelligence, wealth and literacy, though he failed his examinations! One day, when he was journeying to the capital to take his doctorate, he stopped at an inn. There he met the Immortal Chung-li Ch'üan/Zhongli Quan in disguise. After a chat while mulled wine and cooked millet were being prepared, Lü Tung-pin/Lü Dongbin fell asleep. He dreamed of his life ahead, successful for many years – passing his exam, marrying a beautiful and influential woman, acquiring great wealth. But then his life changed, and he witnessed the unfaithfulness of his wife, his family being disgraced, scattered and executed, he himself banished and eventually killed at the hands of a brigand. When he woke he felt as though he had lived his whole life – all the years stretched out before him – before even the millet was cooked! He then understood that worldly affairs would be his ruin, and he turned to *Tao*, taught by Chung-li Ch'üan/Zhongli Quan.[66] But he was not a model Immortal, and on one occasion was stripped of his status for getting a young woman pregnant! He had to work hard to be reinstated. Being young, he was impetuous and some tales tell of his vengeance, his pride, and his arrogance.[67] The other Immortals could also be argumentative and difficult, and could easily take offence. Their love of wine and frequent inebriety are well known!

Yet Lü Tung-pin/Lü Dongbin's good deeds are told in many tales. He tested people and rewarded the good, teaching those that were worthy about *Tao*, and wandering far and wide healing the sick, even leaving beautiful poems on walls and stones.[68] He is represented as a handsome, bearded, young man in a scholar's dress. He is associated with charms, and with healing and medicine, particularly herbal remedies. But he is especially the healer for the poor, his remedies being ascertained by divination.[69] His emblem is a sword, which he carries on his back, and also a fly-whisk. His sword is used to expel evil spirits but it also symbolizes the destruction of the ego, through the transcending of desires and aversions. The popularity of this Immortal makes statues of him ubiquitous, and at his shrines and temple images people worship to be cured of their illnesses.[70] He is the only Immortal to whom temples have been erected in present-day Taiwan. Those who practice divination through automatic writing also venerate Lü Tung-pin/Lü Dongbin. Importantly, too, he is Ancestor Lü, the ancestor of the Complete Reality school of Taoism, as well as of other sects, and is an ancestor, too, of inner alchemy. He is also the author of the *Hundred Character Tablet* in the Taoist canon, and works attributed to him are to be found in the *Lü-tsu ch'üan-shu/ Lüzu Quanshu*.

Li T'ieh-kuai /Li Tieguai

Li T'ieh-kuai /Li Tieguai, "Li with the Iron Crutch" is perhaps the next most popular of the Immortals. He is also called Li Hsüan/Li Xuan. He has the appearance of a beggar and, appropriately, his symbol is a crutch as well as a gourd. Since he is mainly associated with medicine the gourd contains medicines and potions for the relief and cure of disease. In some tales he carries peaches of immortality in his gourd. These he obtained from the Queen Mother of the West. Apothecaries used to have his symbol or figure outside their practices. He is a somewhat eccentric character, and rather a cross one, but he defends the weak and cures their illnesses. According to one legend, he was a handsome youthful man who used to leave his body for days at a time. Once, when he left for six days he asked his disciple to take care of his body during his absence, with the directive that, should he not return by the seventh day, his disciple should burn it. When the six days were almost up, the disciple's mother was taken seriously ill and, torn between loyalty to his master and his mother, he prematurely burned his master's body. When the spirit of his master returned it had no body, and had to make do with the ugly, old body of a crippled beggar who had just died. This accounts for the ugly, dark face and protruding eyes of the Immortal. But Lao-tzu/Laozi, who is said to have been his teacher, gave him a gold ring to hold back the remaining dishevelled strands of hair on his, almost bald, head.

In the tales surrounding Li T'ieh-kuai/Li Tieguai he is often depicted as being taught by, or having meetings with, Lao-tzu/Laozi. At one such meeting, Lao-tzu/Laozi gave him a pill that enabled him to walk faster than a swallow, and to fly through the air. According to one legend, it was Lao-tzu/Laozi, too, that gave Li T'ieh-kuai/Li Tieguai the gift of immortality, along with a bottle of medicine that would never empty and that could be used to cure any illness. It could also restore the dead to life, as could the contents of his magical gourd. In one tale, we find Li T'ieh-kuai/Li Tieguai leaving his fellow Immortals and living amongst ordinary people as a lame healer.[71] At night, however, legend tells that he hung up his gourd, leapt into it and slept in it.[72] There are other tales of how he became an Immortal. One says he changed his form into a dragon and flew up to Heaven. Another says he asked a disciple to stand on a leaf floating on a pond. The disciple, weighed down with the burdens of the ego and the material world, would not do so. But Li T'ieh-kuai/Li Tieguai did, and instantly disappeared, not into the water, but into immortality. He represents the poor, the deformed and oppressed. But, while popular, and occasionally jolly since he is fond of wine, he is also a crotchety old man.

Chang Kuo-lao/Zhang Guolao

Chang Kuo-lao/Zhang Guolao, "Old Chang Kuo/Zhang Guo", is the magician of the group. He is said to have been a historical individual during the T'ang/Tang dynasty, and head of the imperial academy. When he retired, he became a hermit in search of *Tao*. However, tales about him state that he was born into poverty, so poor that his parents had to send him to a cruel farmer to live and work. It was at the hands of this farmer that, according to one account, he eventually met his death. He has a magical and rather wonderful white donkey, which he sometimes rides backwards. It can travel a thousand miles a day. After riding his donkey he folds it up like a piece of paper and keeps it in a little box until needed again. Then, he spits cold water on the paper and the donkey resumes its form. According to another tale, he used to carry the produce from his poor farming parents for sale in the market, riding on a donkey. One day, he stopped at his usual resting-place at an abandoned temple. There, he smelt the most wonderful stew cooking, so wonderful that he could not help devouring it, though he gave some to his donkey, too. But, unknown to him, the stew was a special brew of herbs that would grant immortality, and the Taoist who had made it returned for the precious contents only to see Chang Kuo-lao/Zhang Guolao looking remarkably well fed. The donkey started to run off, as did Chang Kuo-lao/Zhang Guolao. He leapt on his donkey, but backwards, and smacking the donkey to get it going, off the two went. To his amazement, Chang Kuo-lao/Zhang Guolao found that the ride became incredibly smooth. And then he realized they were flying! Not only had he become an Immortal, but his donkey had been immortalized too.[73]

Chang Kuo-lao/Zhang Guolao's symbol looks like a musical instrument consisting of a long piece of bamboo with smaller pipes at the top. However, it could be the quiver for arrows since, as Maspero noted, he is sometimes depicted as drawing a bow or crossbow and aiming it at the dog star Sirius who is harmful to children.[74] He is also found with a phoenix feather. He is believed to grant male children, and so is popular with couples who want children. In this case, pictures of him will be found in such homes. He was also believed to be able to raise the dead. His image is that of an elderly man with a long beard,

219

and he is a good example of how fate can be kind for, in a way, his immortality came about by sheer chance and good fortune! He led the life of a wanderer and recluse, refusing all invitations or summons to the imperial court. Eventually, he succumbed to the requests of the Empress Wu, but dropped dead when he got there. According to legend, he was seen shortly afterwards in the mountains, having feigned his own death and a decaying corpse. Eventually, he disappeared to the Land of the Immortals.

Ts'ao Kuo-chiu/Cao Guojiu

The other Immortals are less popular and usually feature only in the context of the whole group. Ts'ao Kuo-chiu/Cao Guojiu, "Ts'ao, the Country's Maternal Uncle", is said to have been the brother of a Sung/Song dynasty queen mother empress, in the eleventh century, and thus "maternal uncle" of the emperor. As the judge in the group, and a member of the nobility, his symbol is an imperial tablet granting audience with the emperor, though he sometimes carries castanets. He is mature in appearance and dressed in official robes. He seems to have been a ruthless character and not the least appropriate as an Immortal. Legend has it that he and his family abused their royal rank as brothers-in-law to the emperor through all sorts of means, including robbery and murder. Indeed, he was lucky to escape the death sentence – a fate that brought him to his senses and a reformed life in search of *Tao*.[75] He represents aristocrats and nobility. He was the last to join the Eight Immortals. It is said that he was asked by them to point to *Tao* and he pointed to Heaven. When asked again, he pointed to his own heart. Delighted, the other Immortals accepted him in their group.

Han Hsiang-tzu/Han Xiangzi

"Han, the boy from the Hsiang/Xiang River" is the artistic member of the group, being both a poet and a musician, though he also had considerable magical powers. He was the nephew of a great ninth century scholar, statesman and poet. His symbol is a jade flute, though he sometimes carries a basket of flowers or peaches, and has the ability to produce instantaneous beautiful blooms in the dead of winter. Primarily, he is the patron of musicians. His image is a child-like one and a very beautiful one. Kwok Man Ho and O'Brien write of this Immortal: "A great poet and musician, a lover of the solitude and beauty of the mountains, he represents the idea of a contented person, dwelling in bliss with the basic harmony of the universe and appreciating the beauty of its solitary places. He is, in fact, a true Taoist mountain man."[76] Indeed, he belonged in remote caves, hidden in mists, where he sipped dew at midnight, feasted on the glow of the clouds in the dawn sun, and dissolved pearls with the sound of his flute. On the other hand, one tale tells of his trying to climb a tree in the Queen Mother of the West's garden in order to steal the peaches of immortality. Instead, he fell out of the tree, but achieved true immortality all the same. Thus, he has both the beauty of youth and its spontaneity and impishness. He epitomizes the naturalness of a free-flowing spirit.

THE EIGHT IMMORTALS (PA-HSIEN/BAXIAN)

Chung-li Ch'üan/Zhongli Quan

Old, scantily clad, rather fat, and dressed in a large untidily donned cloak, Chung-li Ch'üan/Zhongli Quan, "Powerful Chung-li/Zhongli", also known as Han Chung-li/Han Zhongli, is traditionally believed to be a historical figure, though there is no real evidence to suggest so. He was said to have been a general in Han times, or perhaps governor of a province, and would be the earliest of the Immortals. His symbol is a plumed fan, or fly-whisk by which he calms storms at sea, or creates favourable winds. Occasionally, too, he is featured carrying a two-edged sword and the peach of immortality. He was a great alchemist and was reputed to have transmuted metals into silver during periods of famine, so that he could give it to the poor. But his greatest claim to fame seems as the teacher of the famous Immortal Lü Tung-pin/Lü Dongbin, and the medium by which the latter dreamed of his whole life in the space of seconds. There are lots of different tales about his becoming an Immortal. One suggests that while he was meditating a jade container containing instructions on how to make the pill of immortality appeared in his hut. When he produced the pill he rose to Heaven on a cloud. Other tales say that he rose to Heaven on a stork or a crane. He represents the powerful and the criminal in society.

Lan Ts'ai-ho/Lan Caihe

This member of the group sometimes appears to be a man, and sometimes a woman. But perhaps the feminine appearance is indicated by the hair worn in bunches like a girl or a child. He (or she) is "Lan, The One in Harmony with All" but harmony is not part of this Immortal's appearance. Maspero described him as "an ill-dressed adolescent, with one foot bare and the other shod",[77] but perhaps his appearance is indicative of being partly in this world and partly in the divine one.[78] He seems rather eccentric and a little insane, and thus represents the oddities, the lunatics and those on the fringes of societal life. Blofeld described him as "the original flower-child or hippy".[79] Perhaps he represents, too, the transvestite or homosexual. In winter he wore little, and in summer was heavily clad, but his general dress was as a beggar, for in life he was a poor street singer, a wandering minstrel, clothed in rags. The coins he earned he strung on a long cord that trailed behind him wherever he went. He used them to help the poor, but also to indulge in wine in the places where he sang. Stopping at an inn one day, he is said to have stripped off his clothes and risen to immortality on the back of a crane. His symbol is a magic flower basket that is brimming over with flowers, and it seems that he liked to collect flowers and herbs of every kind that was known.[80]

Ho Hsien-ku/He Xiangu

Ho Hsien-ku/He Xiangu, "Ho/He The Immortal Maiden", is the only woman of the group. She is young and dressed elegantly. Her emblem is a lotus flower, representing her purity and wisdom, and sometimes a peach or a bamboo ladle. She is believed to have lived in the seventh century, and was a great ascetic and follower of *Tao*. She went long distances to gather herbs to feed her sick mother. According to one story, it was on one

221

such journey that she was given a stone to grind into a powder of immortality; according to another, an immortality-conferring peach from Lü Tung-pin/Lü Dongbin. She was then able to fly far away to gather herbs for her mother, she herself not requiring food at all. Another tale tells of her being the last to join the other Immortals. She was being severely ill-treated by the old woman for whom she worked. One day, when the old woman was away, the seven Immortals disguised as starving beggars came and asked her for food. She took pity on them and cooked rice for them. When the old woman returned she was furious and beat the girl, accusing her of stealing the food. However, Ho Hsien-ku/He Xiangu managed to break free and run after the beggars, pleading with them to return and bear witness to the old woman that she had stolen nothing. When the beggars returned with Ho Hsien-ku/He Xiangu, the old woman scolded them all and demanded that they should vomit what they had eaten immediately. When they did so, she commanded Ho Hsien-ku/He Xiangu to eat every scrap as punishment. Just as the terrified girl put the first piece into her mouth, she felt herself rise in the air, getting lighter and lighter. She, and the beggars, rose into the heavens.[81] Yet another tale tells of sexual dual cultivation between Ho Hsien-ku/He Xiangu and Lü Tung-pin/Lü Dongbin, whereby Ho Hsien-ku/He Xiangu skilfully managed to achieve immortality through the semen of her partner. But other stories point to her chastity. In one, when she was being forced into marriage, she is said to have risen to immortality leaving only her slippers behind.

Thus, we have the Eight Immortals of Taoism. Each is associated with one of the trigrams of the *Pa-kua/Bagua*. In a clockwise direction, and in the later arrangement:

Ch'ien/Qian	Lan Ts'ai-ho/Lan Caihe	North-west
Sun	Han Hsiang-tzu/Han Xiangzi	South-east
K'an/Kan	Chang Kuo-lao/Zhang Guolao	North
Ken/Gen	Ts'ao Kuo-chiu/Cao Guojiu	North-east
K'un/Kun	Ho Hsien-ku/He Xiangu	South-west
Chen/Zhen	Chung-li Ch'üan/Zhongli Quan	East
Li	Li T'ieh-kuai/Li Tieguai	South
Tui/Dui	Lü Tung-pin/Lü Dongbin	West

As we have seen, there were different ways in which one might become an Immortal, and this was the case with other immortals, too. And just as each member of the Eight had a different personality, so too there are different kinds of immortals in general. Some are heavenly, some are earthly, some spirits, some ghosts. Some are mythical, and some had had mortal lives. Some are thought to have always been immortals, dwelling in islands and distant paradises. In all, there are many kinds of grades and ranks of immortals, generally depending on the different lives of individuals in their pre-immortal status.[82] But the heavenly immortals are superior to any others, their status being signified by their rising up to Heaven in broad daylight at their moment of immortality, accompanied by celestial chariots drawn by dragons. These heavenly immortals live among the stars. Less prestigiously, others simply rise into the air and vanish. In Han times whole princely households were believed to rise into immortality. Earthly immortals live their existence in the earthly realm, in the mountains, caves and forests. Some become immortals posthumously, and undergo an ordinary death. These are "delivered from the corpse", so that when their coffins are opened, nothing other than perhaps their sandals, a bamboo staff or the like, are to be found, or their bodies remain perfectly healthy. Others take the root of inner alchemy to immortality, with the creation and nourishment of a Spirit Embryo.

Apart from the Eight Immortals, then, there were many others around whom legends of immortality grew. Master Fu-chü/Fuju, a mirror-polisher and great healer, was one.[83] Then there was the famous Lady Wei who became an immortal and revealed sacred scriptures of Shang-ch'ing/Shangqing Taoism to Yang Hsi/Yang Xi. Ko Hung/Ge Hong was believed to have been "delivered from the corpse", and his coffin was found to contain only his clothes. The Lands of the Immortals are graphically depicted. They are vast, stretching to continents, with two major paradises at the edge of the world and bathed in light. The mythical Mount K'un-lun/Kunlun, home of the Queen Mother of the West, Queen of the immortals, was the ultimate paradise. Such places are a source of imaginative inspiration to Chinese artists, and a glittering world of spectacular beauty. The immortals themselves wear wonderful attire, flying robes of light texture in radiant colours.[84] But, again, the realms of immortals are hierarchical and each immortal has to work his or her way up, or down, in merit, rank, and power.

The Taoist adept is able to leave his or her body for flights to Heaven, to the stars, or to ride on the winds. Ultimately, however, there is a final transcendence of all worldly life and the passage into full immortality. Those who remain in contact with the earthly sphere are a constant reminder of the spontaneity and naturalness of the liberated person, and of the necessity for turning away from worldly conventions to lose the self in nature, and the spirit in *Tao*. The message of the immortals is put remarkably well by Schipper, who writes:

> Every human being, whether big or small, humble or great, young woman or old man, musician, herbalist, clown, or scholar, may – on the sole condition of finding his or her own mountain – quit the treadmill of progress towards death and discover the return towards life. It is not even necessary to act intentionally: luck and a certain predisposition may sometimes be the only needed conditions, but nothing is guaranteed. It is necessary, however, to at all times be open and prepared to recognize, at a given moment of one's life, the mountain or the initiating Immortal, which some day is to be found on everyone's life path. It is in this readiness and openness that we find all possible latitude for individual free will and faith.[85]

Sages

So much has been written about the sage in previous chapters that it is my purpose here simply to draw together the various strands. Indeed, the Taoist sage is the culmination of years of effort by the adept, and is the concluding phase of life on Earth that culminates in immortal life beyond it. There are many terms used for the sage, as we have seen – *sheng-jen/shengren*, "sage" or "saint", the term used in the *Tao Te Ching/Daodejing*; *chen-jen/zhenren*, "true", "real" or "perfect being";[86] *shen-jen/shenren*, "spirit being"; *chih-jen/zhiren*, "perfect being",[87] the terms found in the *Chuang-tzu/Zhuangzi*.[88] While inhabiting Earth, the sage has the means to traverse beyond it in the same way as immortals. He is at one with *Tao*, but his involvement in human affairs can range from the rule of the sage-king of early texts like the *Tao Te Ching/Daodejing* to instruction of disciples on lonely mountainsides. This two-fold nature of the sage epitomizes the distinction between those involved in life, and those who withdrew from it to solitude. The term "sage" is, therefore, an all-embracing one, though it encompasses for all sages the status of imminent immortality, and the ability to be both this-worldly and other-worldly, the perfect pivot between Heaven and Earth.

It is the ability to be astride this and the other world beyond ordinary life that links sages with the shamans of the ancient past. With the sage we find none of the ecstatic and wilder activities of the shaman, but the thread of continuity between the two is not that difficult to see. Indeed, when they become immortals they will have all the skills of shamans, many of which they acquire in pre-immortal state. They acquire power over nature and time, and act in unconventional ways. So, in a way, we have come full circle from the shamans of ancient times to the sage as the ultimate goal of the Taoist adept, and to immortals, especially, who bear so many of the characteristics of shamanic practices.[89]

Inner stillness

The sage is the culmination of earthly life and the medium for transcendence to the heavenly one. He is at the same time in the world and beyond it at the pinnacle of reality, *Tao* itself, and he has the freedom to wander at will from one to the other. His egoistic self has vanished, and he is ageless like the sun and moon. Like the shamans of old, the Taoist sages leave the confines of the world for the splendours of the heavens. Such wandering in the universe "leads out of the entanglements of given laws into a freedom in which the rules of tradition no longer prevail".[90] The sage journeys beyond the ordinary self, and even the transcendent self. It is a journey that ultimately loses the self in utter tranquillity and serenity, stillness and emptiness.

Because the sage has become empty of individual personality and selfhood, he is like a pure tube through which the light of *Tao* pours into his being. The rhythm of the universe floods through him, linking him to the ten thousand things with which he is in total harmony. Perfect simplicity and innocence to all things pervades the mind and being of the sage. Thus, he conforms to the transformations of *Tao* as they occur in the universe, knowing that they will take their own courses in an orderly rhythm: and he is totally harmonized with such rhythm. All conventional knowledge is dispelled for a state of ignorance that, paradoxically, opens the mind to the entire universe. It is a process of "forgetting the forgetting", that is to say, forgetting all conventional knowledge even to the extent that you have forgotten that you have forgotten it. Thus, the mind becomes truly empty and freed from its own volition. It is in this state of no-self, of utter emptiness and Void, that *Tao* is found. "The Tao takes over the identity that once was the individual's alone."[91] Gazing out into the vastness of the universe with its myriad stars and galaxies, the sage is an atom of that whole being, flowing with it, feeling its cosmic energy in his whole being. It is a return to one's cosmic beginnings and tuning of the self to the ongoing pulses of creation.

The sage has the perfect balance between *yang* outer activity and *yin* inner passivity. The English poet Wordsworth captured this when he wrote: "With an eye made quiet by the power of harmony and the deep power of joy, we see into the heart of things". And with inner serenity, the sage is able to act in the world without ever losing the calm serenity and stillness within. For the sage is at the centre of the circle, he is at that point where dualities cease to exist. He is the equipoise, the balance between the this and that of all opposites and all things, and between *yin* and *yang*. The sage has not *found Tao* for he had never really lost it. He simply experiences it as himself and all things. It is in the living, breathing and eating of the day, in the clouds, the moon, the winds, the morning mists, the song of the bird. *Living* is *Tao* and is experience of the interconnectedness and unity of all.

The sage offers the example that stillness and quietude, serenity, calmness and harmony are the qualities that we should develop in the self. To nourish the inner being, to enable it to grow, to reach its full spiritual potential, we have to nurture these qualities. We suffer only when we move away from harmony; we suffer only when we strengthen our likes and dislikes, when we forget that we are part of the wholeness of the universe. Taoism is a process of the evolution of the individual's consciousness, a refining of consciousness throughout life so that the real self, the self devoid of ego and desire is free. In the rather poignant words of John Blofeld:

> A mind fed on words such as heaven, earth, dew, essence, cinnabar, moonlight, stillness, jade, pearl, cedar, and winter-plum is likely to have a serenity not to be found in minds ringing with the vocabulary of the present age – computer, tractor, jumbo jet, speedball, pop, dollar, liquidation, napalm, overkill! . . . And how full of wisdom is a philosophy that draws man away from the rat race, from the tooth-and-claw struggle for status, wealth, power or fame, to live frugally and contentedly in harmony with nature, reaching effortlessly for the tranquillity that flowers in a heart nurtured in stillness![92]

And yes, the dream seems impossible, but as the *Tao Te Ching/Daodejing* says, the tree as large as a person's embrace starts only from a small shoot, and a nine-storied terrace begins with a small pile of earth. The journey of a thousand miles starts under one's feet: the first footstep can always be taken. The path to harmony is the path to peace, the path to experience of *Tao* on Earth.

8

Religious Taoism

The eclectic nature of religious Taoism

Religious Taoism embraces many beliefs that have filtered down from antiquity through centuries of trends, turbulence, superstitions, philosophies and traditional and locational practices. Touched deeply in its many twists and turns by Buddhism and Confucianism, it has also remained close to popular experiences, needs and customs, even though, at the same time, it was important to the higher echelons of society. Taoist religious praxis is characterized by the kind of pragmatic pluralism that enables the worshipper to approach Buddhist deities as much as Taoist ones when the occasion arises. The choice of deity is determined by the needs of the moment, not by any conformity to specific religious institutional praxis. Despite such diversity, however, there is an underlying rationale that seems to be present in any aspect of Taoism or Chinese religion in general, and that is to create, or restore, and maintain the balances and harmonies that exist between Heaven, Hell and the human realm. Many Taoist practitioners are the mediums by which such balance and harmony is effectuated. Just as in ancient times, the theories of *yin* and *yang* and the Five Agents underpin the ritual of religious Taoism in the search for that harmony. But the seriousness of the goal of harmony does not inhibit the means by which it is brought about. For Taoist religion is replete with ritualistic expression that surfaces in colour, music, rhythm, dance, symbols and imagery while, at the same time, it maintains a certain amount of structure through centuries of lineage and meticulous transmission of traditions. All this serves the purpose of bringing the world of humanity in balance with the supernatural forces of the cosmos.

There have been many that have seen this more colourful and religious aspect of Taoism as a degenerate form of the earlier mystical philosophy so well expressed in the texts of the *Tao Te Ching/Daodejing* and the *Chuang-tzu/Zhuangzi*. The view, however, is a myopic one; for religious Taoism does not depart radically from some of the foundational ideas of philosophical Taoism; it is just that it is more social, more communal, more group-orientated than the latter. It supplies, in fact, the emotional and spiritual expressions of religion that permit the warmth of theistic belief, thus catering for the ordinary human being as opposed to the mystic recluse. It makes more sense, therefore, to view philosophical and religious Taoism as complementary rather than disparate, both supplying different needs within the same conceptual framework of creating harmony and balance between the self, the community of those alive and those dead, and *Tao*. The legacy of religious Taoism is, in fact, considerable. In Donald Bishop's words: "It made the present more bearable by providing people solace in periods of distress and hope in times of despair. It provided a religious impetus and sanction for social protest movements. It upheld a high ethical standard insisting on inner purity and virtuous deeds. It advocated meditation as a means of attaining a right view of one's self and the world. It emphasized bodily and spiritual health and continued the theme of living simply and naturally or in conformity with nature."[1] Thus, the contribution of religious Taoism is as positive as its more philosophical counterpart. And when all is said and done, the goal of a healthy, happy and long life underpins both, however mystical or practical one would want to view that goal.

The origins of religious Taoism might be said to begin with certain movements of the early first millennium, but the practices that characterize it reach right back to antiquity, to times well before the advent of Lao-tzu/Laozi and Chuang-tzu/Zhuangzi – divination, sorcery, magic, shamanism, mediums, healing, and so on. Then, too, the varied practices of the *fang-shih/fangshi* that we looked at in chapter 5 were especially contributive to the nature of religious Taoism. In terms of specific movements, we would have to look to the second century of the Common Era and the rise of institutional movements like the healing cults, in particular that of Chang Tao-ling/Zhang Daoling, who is the father of religious Taoism or *Tao-chiao/Daojiao*. Such cults provided a source of considerable solace for a society that was enduring immense suffering in the degenerate phase of the declining Han dynasty. In its appeal to the masses, religious Taoism gave the Chinese populace a religious focus that answered immediate needs. However, in the centuries that followed, religious Taoism became enmeshed in popular practice that was both Taoist and more broadly Chinese. This admixture of beliefs and practices has remained characteristic, and it is really impossible to extract religious Taoism in the modern and post-modern world from popular Chinese practices. Strictly Taoist praxis is only for priests: for the rest of the populace the blurring of the distinctions between Buddhist, Confucian and Taoist practices has been endemic.

Influenced by Buddhism, religious Taoism has a doctrine of salvation for all. Hitherto, the goal had been immortality for the few, but in religious Taoism existence after death could be influenced by the way in which life was lived in the present. Since the afterlife was modelled on the earthly one – albeit that it was believed to be the other way around – there were many places to be filled in the hierarchies of the heavens and hells in the post-death experience while awaiting rebirth. This is just one good example of the fusion of Buddhist and Taoist ideas. Since popular Taoism is so all-embracing and syncretic, there is no set doctrine prescribed by a particular religious institution to follow: there is a compass point through life, but no ordnance map to dictate the pathways. There are, then, considerable local variations in ritualistic praxis. It may well be that a Taoist or even Buddhist specialist may conduct ritual, as we shall see, in which case, the longstanding formalities of strict tradition will be followed. Nevertheless, such specialists are not always necessary, and a master of ceremonies who is neither may well preside over ritual. And even where such specialism is employed, Maspero noted, long ago, that the Taoist or Buddhist priest or monk was closer to the needs of the ordinary people than to the ritualistic tradition in which each may stand – a point, he wrote, that keeps specialists close to the laity.[2] Indeed, Taoism, more than Buddhism or Confucianism, was closest to the people.

Ordinary folk would find it difficult to designate themselves as Taoist or Buddhist, and would certainly not be at pains to differentiate between the two. It is a matter of pragmatism that at one time a particular Buddha or Buddhist *bodhisattva* may be more appropriate to approach than a Taoist deity. Since those in the divine world have different functions it always makes sense to take one's problems to the divine being who specializes in that area. Ultimately, the goal is the same. Asking what the goal of Taoist practice is, Bill Porter encountered the following response from the abbot of a monastery in Loukuantai in China:

> Man's nature is the same as the nature of heaven. Heaven gives birth to all creatures, and they all go different directions. But sooner or later they return to the same place. The goal of this universe, its highest goal, is nothingness. Nothingness is the body of the Tao. Not only man, but plants and animals and all living things are part of this body, are made of this body, this body of nothingness. Everything is one with nothingness. There aren't two things in this universe. To realize this is the goal not only of Taoism but also of Buddhism. Everything in this world changes. Taoists and Buddhists seek that which doesn't change. This is why they don't seek fame or fortune. They only seek Tao, which is the nothingness of which we are all created and to which we all return. Our goal is to be one with this natural process.[3]

Despite the homogeneity of aims here, Buddhism and Taoism remained historical rivals. But to ordinary folk, the blend of beliefs and practices of the two helped them to make sense of their world. To such obvious syncretism must be added the influence of Confucianism in the expression of a sense of order and careful arrangement in ritual praxis.

Common to all such variety is the overriding belief in the supernatural power of spirits and gods to aid or deter humans in their passage through life and, indeed, through death. It is this question of the power of supernatural forces to affect life, and the power of certain individuals to tap in to, divert, expel, or use that supernatural power, that informs religious Taoism. Essentially, it is involved with the perfection of a potency that creates harmony and balance in life and society. Thus, practice is a critical aspect of religious Taoism, and it is the special powers of a person, geared to a specific problem – childlessness, illness, difficulties in business, for example – that would attract a temporary adherent, not the underpinning beliefs. Indeed, an individual is free to visit any temple or shrine for specific needs, irrespective of his or her overriding beliefs – if these are present at all. If Taoism in an official form has any role to play here, it is in providing more intensive structure at times of communal importance, particularly on festivals for the birthdays of deities, for example. What more established canonical Taoism provides here is ritual steeped in ancient texts, liturgy, and symbols, adding efficacy to religious praxis on special occasions. The Taoist specialist, then, is what Michael Saso terms "the mandarin of the spirits, and of nature", one who "penetrated to the very core of the Tao's working in the cosmos".[4]

So Taoism in the past has been an eclectic phenomenon that, consequently, has denied definition. And it is no less so in the present. Kenneth Dean makes the point that despite the contradictions that must surely abound in so diverse a phenomenon as Taoism it is the very fact that there is a lack of set doctrine and dogma that allows it to unite all the different facets in some kind of loose pantheism.[5] Commenting on the interchange between specialist Taoist ritual and popular Taoism in south-east China today, Dean writes: "The interaction between Taoist liturgy and cult observances generates a rich, constantly changing, play of forces embedded in powerfully charged cosmological symbols".[6]

As we shall see later, the vicissitudes of politics banished religion from China, and it is only now that a resurgence of religion is taking place and many of the old religious customs and beliefs are being, and have been, revived. However, there are places where there has been greater continuity of practice. It is to Taiwan that we shall turn for perhaps the most authentic Taoist practices to be found in China today. Taiwan is a long island off the coast of south-east China. It has always been part of China, but was taken by Japan in 1895, and remained in Japanese hands until 1945, after which it was returned to China. Many of the customs that will be mentioned below will be Taiwanese. Another significant area where Taoist customs are to be found is Hong Kong. Given the wide variety of religious practices, it is well beyond the scope of this chapter to cover ritual in any kind of detail. My purpose is more to express the scope of its dimensions than to deliver factual fineness. Inevitably, there will be an overlap between Taoism, popular Taoism and Chinese customs, but it would seem an injustice to the brief of this book to omit so much of the richness of popular belief that encircles and spirals through Taoist practices. In the main, I want to confine the material to more present-day praxis, with touches of tradition here and there. Let us begin, then, with a look at the different Taoist schools to be found today.

Schools of Taoism

Two major schools of Taoism are extant today, Complete Reality and the Celestial Masters, or Cheng-i/Zhengyi, Orthodox Unity, school, to give it the name by which it was known after the fourteenth century. From these two schools a large number of sub-schools have emerged. Differences between them are characterized by differences in the texts that they transmit.

The Complete Reality school

The Complete Reality, Complete Realization, Complete Perfection, Realization of Truth or Perfect Truth, Ch'üan-chen/Quanzhen school has many branches, the most important of which is the Lung-men/Longmen school. Complete Reality Taoism was founded by the Confucian Wang Che/Wang Zhe, who adopted Taoism and took the name Wang Ch'ung-yang/Wang Chongyang in the twelfth century. It is a tradition that was predominant in northern China, but it spread throughout the country during the sixteenth and seventeenth centuries, and can be found in all parts of mainland China today. The Complete Reality school is monastic in tradition, its best-known monastery being the famous White Cloud Monastery in Peking. Its monastic traditions in the Wu-tang/Wudang mountains have also earned the school the name of Wu-tang/Wudang Taoists. Some monasteries are hereditary, others are public.[7] It is a syncretic school that amalgamates Confucian ethics with Buddhist meditation practices, the Buddhist concept of emptiness of mind, and Taoist inner alchemy. In ways reminiscent of the *Chuang-tzu/Zhuangzi*, adherents retreat from the world to practise austere means of quelling desires. Concomitant with the still mind is the infiltration of it with goodness. Thus, charitable acts are part of Complete Reality teaching. Today, its priests are still celibate and vegetarian, and their practice is meditative, rather like Zen Buddhism. Since their practices lack the kind of ritual associated with what the Chinese authorities consider to be "superstitious", the priests are tolerated in today's China.

Following the death of Wang Ch'ung-yang/Wang Chongyang, the Complete Reality school sprouted a number of important branches. A northern branch was founded by Ch'iu Ch'u-chi/Qiu Chuji, and this developed into the Lung-men/Longmen or Dragon Gate school. A southern branch, the Tzu-yang/Ziyang or Purple Yang school, was founded by Chang Po-tuan/Zhang Boduan, the great inner alchemist, but this was not destined to last in the way the northern branch did. The Lung-men/Longmen school, named after the mountain on which the earliest proponents of the school meditated, is today the most well-known branch of the Complete Reality school of Taoism. They are, like their predecessors, monastic in character, but they also have a following of lay people who attempt to live by some of their tenets, albeit in the context of everyday life. Their chief monastery is that of the Complete Reality school of past centuries, the White Cloud Monastery. It is here that the founder of the school was buried.

The Celestial Masters school

It is the Way of Celestial Masters school, T'ien-shih Tao/Tianshi Dao, that is expert in colourful and complex rituals for funerals, festivals, exorcisms, healing, and the use of charms and talismans, and so is involved with the populace. It has been predominantly associated with southern China, and is to be found in present-day Fujian. Its priesthood is a hereditary one, so there is a direct transmission of liturgical tradition from its founder, Chang Tao-ling/Zhang Daoling, himself. The present Celestial Master is the sixty-fourth in succession, and resides in Taiwan. Such succession means the passing on from generation to generation of the liturgical texts, the secrets of mastery of spirits and gods, the talismans in words and in diagrams, and the minutiae of ritual praxis. The receipt of such is tantamount to having control over, and the aid of, specific forces in the cosmos.

The efficacy of the Masters and priests of this school comes from the protection and aid of their founder, Chang Tao-ling/Zhang Daoling, and from the deities who assisted him and his descendants. The talismans and charms revealed by such deities are still used to ward off danger, to ask for rain, protection and blessings, for example. They are also used in funeral rites to guide the soul to its life in the underworld. Only one Master will be ordained in each generation. Part of the responsibility of the Celestial Master is to appoint the priests, or *tao-shih/daoshi*, also hereditary, who officiate at local level. Given the importance of transmission of tradition, priests are allowed to marry and live in local communities, and monastic life is minimal. Despite the prestigious nature of such priests and of the Masters, they are not members of an institutional body that dictates lay practice. Quite the opposite: their services are only used when requested by the laity, and they work from their own homes, disappearing back into ordinary society when their priestly functions on an occasion are fulfilled. Often, they are withdrawn a little from the other inhabitants of their locality. Something of the old, philosophical ideas we met in the *Tao Te Ching/Daodejing* is reflected in the following words of Michael Saso in depicting a Taoist *tao-shih/daoshi* in Taiwan: "'The man who claims expertise of Taoist magic is an impostor, and the man who denies knowledge is an expert,' is the attitude taught to the disciples in the master's entourage. The villager's image of a Taoist is usually that of a strange man who talks to spirits, who drinks heartily, and who comes and goes as he wills. There is something sinister about his magic, his exorcism of demons, that sets him apart from the rest of his community. His friends are few and his presence is feared."[8]

Mao-shan Taoists

Amongst the ranks of the magicians and sorcerers who still pervade Taoism are Mao-shan Taoists.[9] They are sorcerers who are adept at exorcism, or at preventing disaster. It is their role to ward off the evils from the spirit world that intrude into the daily life of ordinary people. Less involved with the greater deities, they are inclined to be involved with lower supernatural powers. Eva Wong writes of them: "Mao-shan sorcerers use talismans and objects of power such as mirrors, bells and coin-swords. They are especially adept at calling deities and spirits to enter their bodies to enhance their personal power. Practitioners from other sects will invoke only certain deities, but Mao-shan sorcerers are pragmatic, and will muster anything that will help them."[10] As Wong points out, they are a secretive, closed and highly selective sect of Taoism. One special function that they contribute is protection of the souls of the deceased.

Three-in-One Taoism

Another attempt to combine Buddhism and Confucianism with Taoism is found in the ideas of Lin Chao-en/Lin Zhaoen in the sixteenth century. He emphasized meditation and inner alchemy in bringing about the unity of mind exemplified by the mind of Confucius, Lao-tzu/Laozi and the Buddha. His ideas have survived until today in the Three-in-One sect of Taoism, particularly in Taiwan.

Unity Taoism

Again uniting Taoist, Buddhist and Confucian tenets, Pervading Unity Taoism, or the Unity school, has become very popular at the level of the ordinary folk, especially because its basic belief is universal salvation. Salvation can be achieved only through initiation into the sect, and results when an adherent's name is removed from the divine register for Hell to the one for Heaven. Thus, the sect also has a strong ethical and moral emphasis. Like other aspects of Taoism, meditation is important, as is ritual chanting of the scriptures, exercises like T'ai Chi/Taiji, and abstention from meat. Particularly prominent is the veneration of a mother goddess. In Jordan and Overmyer's case study of the Unity sect in Taiwan, they note the "dash of romance" that might well have been the means for the success of this sect, since its foundation and growth was forced underground by the Chinese authorities: what is forbidden so often appears attractive![11] The sect is a late one, apparently having been founded early in the twentieth century.[12] In this sect we find an emphasis on spirit writing, a phenomenon that we shall need to look at closely below. Spirit writing enables new sects to arise. Overmyer comments that many new scriptures have been revealed by such communications from deities through the medium of the pen since the late nineteenth century. Thus, many new Taoist sects have arisen in Taiwan in recent times.[13]

Shen-hsiao/Shenxiao Taoism

Shen-hsiao/Shenxiao Taoism stretches back in origin to the twelfth century and was founded by Lin Ling-su. It is particularly popular in northern Taiwan and southern Fujian in mainland China. The specialists of the sect are "Red-head" Taoists, of whom we shall learn more in the section below on priests. The school is particularly known for its use of talismans combined with inner alchemy, and for "thunder magic". It is the practices of this school that have survived rather than the school *per se*.

Lü Shan San-nai Taoism

Also associated with "Red-head" priests, the priests in the Lü Shan tradition are well known for their participation in exorcism, specifically for healing sickness. They are associated with mediums, for whom they act as interpreters. The means by which they call deities to their services or dispel them is an ox horn.[14] The sect is to be found mainly in Fukian and Taiwan. According to Saso, the term Lü Shan is associated with the "Gate of Hell", a gate in the cosmos through which demons pass to attack the human realm. Lü Shan priests use their ritual to capture and return the demons. The term San-nai refers to "Three Sisters" who were exorcists and mediums.[15]

Acton and Karma Taoism

Not a sect in itself, but spanning many schools and sects, and very popular with ordinary folk, Action and *Karma* Taoism probably originated in the twelfth century with a text entitled *T'ai-shang kan-ying p'ien/Taishang Ganyingpian* by Li Ying-chang/Li Yingzhang. As its name suggests, Action and *Karma* Taoism believes in good, moral actions that will accrue good *karma*. Simply, goodness is close to *Tao*; evil deeds are not. And good *karma*, in all sorts of charitable acts, means rewards from the deities; evil *karma* means retribution. Like shadows, then, rewards are the appropriate response from *Tao* for good actions, bringing success, longevity and health; the converse is so for bad actions. It is the Jade

Emperor, whom we met in chapter 7, that is the final arbiter of one's rewards and punishments. He is aided in his decision by deities such as the Kitchen God, by each individual's astral deity, which is his or her guardian star at birth, and by the malevolent Worms in the human body. An added impetus is given to morality in that the actions and thoughts of an individual are not just effective for him or her, but for the whole family including ancestors and descendants.[16] The tally of good or evil deeds became prescriptively established: three hundred good deeds, for example, would procure immortality on Earth, while thirteen hundred would bring immortality in Heaven.

K'un-lun/Kunlun Taoism

Originating in western China, this sect was exposed to Tibetan Buddhist traditions. It is now to be found in south-east Asia, Hong Kong and Taiwan, as well as China. Its priests are experts in the use of magic and, like Buddhists, use *mudras*, hand gestures, as well as talismans to procure blessings for the populace. The deities invoked by this sect to bless and protect, or ward off evil are as much Buddhist as Taoist.

Throughout the ritual that characterizes many of the branches of Taoism is an immense amount of colour and ceremonial devotion – all designed to cement the ties between Earth and Heaven, between inhabitants of the human world and the divine one. The destiny of human beings is tied up with the honour and respect that they show to the hidden powers of the universe. Harmony between the two is the ultimate goal.

Priests

Any examination of the functions of priests in Taoism today cannot fail to note the similarities with the ancient shamans, and the old *fang-shih/fangshi*, the healers and sorcerers, magicians and early alchemists, to depict just a few of their varied skills. But it is especially the ability to communicate with the spirits and deities of the supernatural world that underpins the similarities of distant past and present. Nevertheless, Taoist "priests", as we call them, are, strictly speaking, specialists in ritual, and some of the more overt shamanistic skills are provided by others such as mediums and diviners. Some priests, however, belong to the monastic tradition like that of the Complete Reality school and have little involvement in ritual in the lay community. These priests do not marry, though they are not numerous. Outside the monastic schools are priests who do marry – "fire-dwellers" as they are called, to depict their family life. They live in the community, and perform important services for the lay people. They are divided into two groups, *Black-heads* and *Red-heads*, though the distinction between the two is more academic than practical, for the functions of the two often overlap.

Black-head priests

Black-head priests, so called because of the formal black caps they wear on their heads as part of their ritual attire, belong to the Celestial Masters school of Taoism. They are orthodox, in that they have the skills to conduct specialist festivals and celebrations like the *chiao/jiao* festival (of which, more below), in the traditional manner, and have to be literate to do so. However, they are also known to heal and perform exorcisms. Their functions are to perform rituals for the dead as well as the living, and it is mostly from funerals that they can earn any kind of salary at all. They also heal sickness, are called upon to perform rituals for blessings during life-cycle rites, and perform rituals for rain and burial of the dead, accompanying the soul on its journey into the afterlife. But it is at the more important *chiao/jiao* festivals that their expertise is particularly needed. They are ranked as the highest kind of priest and are *tao-shih/daoshi*, "gentlemen" or "dignitaries" of *Tao*. Lagerway writes of this functionary:

> The Taoist is completely self-possessed: the forces he uses in the war against evil are not those of a medium but his own. His chief function, in fact, is not that of an exorcist, a warrior, but that of a civil official in the court of the Tao. He has risen beyond mastery of methods to mastery of the "system" as a whole. According to that system, the Tao is a vast womb containing within it three pure energies that, over time, give birth to all things. The Taoist's real contribution to the war against evil results from his capacity, by means of ritual, to transform his own body into the body of the Tao and then to conduct all things back to their origin in purity.[17]

Such words encapsulate very well this true Taoist priest as he who has the power within himself to call upon divine forces for blessing and protection of the community. Since the position of *tao-shih/daoshi* is hereditary, the Black-head priest inherits the talismans, texts and traditions of ritual, along with the skills to use them, which are jealously kept secret by each family. Thus, when the rituals are performed, it is only the priest who knows what is happening. Many operate from a room in their own home in an office called the "altar of *Tao*". Here, they provide for those who come to see them the kind of talismans that are able to grant blessings or dispel problems.[18] Indeed, Jordan has described the role of such priests in Taiwan as a "private practice", since there are no real Taoist temples, only folk temples.[19]

Red-head priests

Red-head priests are not as skilled as the Black-heads. They are so called because they wrap red cloths around their heads or waists during ritual. They are far more involved with the populace, for it is they who are called upon to cure illnesses and to exorcise demons. Their rituals are varied and colourful, and they have strong connections with the shamanistic heritage in China. It is their very limited performing of rituals for the dead that differentiates them from the more orthodox Black-heads. Red-heads are more associated with medium divination. "Masters of method" (*fa-shih/fashi*), or exorcists, they interpret the words of the local gods when these possess individuals. The Red-heads carry a cow-horn that they use in ritual, and often a sword, a whip and a hand bell. It is usually the Black-heads that conduct the specialist *chiao/jiao* festivals, though Red-heads also do so, but without the excellence of ritual offered by Black-heads. Shen-hsiao/Shenxiao and Lü-shan Taoists, in particular, are Red-heads.

Generally, then, Taoist priests and other such functionaries are ranked according to power; that is to say, the power they have to command the forces of Heaven and Earth. In more empirical terms, they will be graded according to the number of "registers" or liturgical texts that they know and can use.[20] At a much deeper level, the rank of a priest will depend on the ability to practise the kind of inner alchemy that transmutes the inner self to the primordial emptiness that allows *Tao* to pervade his entire being. But it is only in their vocational capacities that they are accorded any respect and value. However, when their services are required, their status is reflected in the exquisite ritual garments, especially those worn by the *tao-shih/daoshi* during ritual celebration. Every aspect of colour and decoration on these vestments symbolizes some aspect of the Taoist cosmos and Taoist belief,[21] though robes of monastic priests are comparatively simple. When their services are over, the priests merge back into nonentity or even into a "despised and lowly" status.[22] Those who call on the services of a Taoist priest may well not be Taoists themselves, but the power of the priest in effectuating blessings and protection for the community is such that his services are essential. In many ways, when we use the term "Taoist" in today's world, it is the *tao-shih/daoshi* to whom we are referring. Amongst the populace, few would see themselves as specifically "Taoist".

Few priests that operate in China today are of the Complete Reality, Ch'üanchen/Quanzhen school. Rather, it is the Celestial Masters, or Cheng-i/Zhengyi school, that provides the ritual specialism according to field studies such as in Fujian,[23] but they share their work with Buddhist monks – a point that demonstrates well the lack of any firm demarcation of religious affiliation amongst the populace. However, in the process of reviving religion in China, Taoist priests are important, indeed indispensable, in consecrating renovated temples and the images of deities within them.[24] There is considerable variation of ritual, depending on the lineage of the priests and their respective localities, but whatever the ritual, it is the Taoist priests that carry the long tradition of knowledge of the way each intricate aspect of it is to be conducted. It is especially at funerals that the Taoist priest has the knowledge to guide the deceased soul through the various levels of hells, aided by bribes of artificial money for the officers of the hells, as we shall see later. Thus, he is essential in the final life-cycle rite of all individuals. But it is at the *chiao/jiao* rituals that the expertise of the Taoist priest is specifically required. Again, we shall look at this in a little more detail below.

What makes the *tao-shih/daoshi*, the orthodox priest, so indispensable is what takes place in the inner alchemical processes within his own body, particularly at the *chiao/jiao* festivals. I have mentioned this briefly above. Essentially, the body of the priest is the microcosm in which alchemical changes take place. These changes are mirrored in the macrocosm of the universe, where the highest gods, the Three Pure Ones, are called to assist. In Dean's words, the priest "telescopes time and space by constructing a universe, then speeds up cosmic cycles through the recitation and oblation of divine texts and the dispersal of the sacred space in order to generate merit for himself, the community representatives, the village, and for all the beings and spirits along the Great Chain of Being. Every being is promoted upward on the cosmic scale".[25] Immense merit ensues from the priest's inner ritual.

The training necessary for a priest to reach expertise at such a level is highly demanding. And, considering that such a position is a hereditary one, few make it to such a level. Those who do not, will supply supporting roles in ritual. But for those who become experts, music, dance, chanting, recitation, rhythm, knowledge of texts, meditation and minutiae of ritual have all to be perfected.[26] The training is hierarchical, with menial tasks being undertaken at first and then, as the years go by, the possibility of acquiring more senior positions arise. Given the lengthy lacuna in religious practice in China, there are very few old priests available today to teach new generations of novices over lengthy periods of time: they are hardly likely to survive to complete the task. Those who reach the stage of ordination are special members of *tao-shih/daoshi* families who are prepared to undertake the long training and to whom are entrusted the registers of ritual, and knowledge of the divine forces that will be at their command. Calligraphy is essential, since the ordained priest will have to copy the traditional texts that have been handed down to him. Such ordained priests can be recognized by their traditional top-knot, for they grow their hair in the ancient tradition, and tie it up on their heads. Some are affiliated to a particular Taoist Master, who will train the novice as a disciple. Here, too, few reach outstanding ranks, opting for a shorter period of training. And as far as Taoist monks are concerned, again, there are few old monks who can train the younger novices. Authentic ordination of monks in China today is probably non-existent, given such absence of proper training.[27] While there seems to be an increasing number of peripatetic Taoist monks and priests who provide a variety of services for the people, such as getting rid of unwanted ghosts or providing charms for protection, their numbers are still few in comparison to their Buddhist counterparts.

Spirit mediums

Mediums are a very different phenomenon from priests. They may not even be Taoists, though they will be involved with the same rituals as the more orthodox priests. Whereas the priest has total control over events, and over the divine forces that he summons both within his own body and the cosmos, the medium has no control at all over events that take place. The medium's body is taken over by a god, and he becomes a tool, a puppet, a child, or a "divining youth" of the god, and the means by which that deity conveys a message. Mediums are thus possessed, and are used as oracles. In their trance states they are known to push skewers through their cheeks, arms and calves, or cut themselves in some way to illustrate their entranced imperviousness to pain. In Taiwan, they are often attached to small temples or shrines though, equally so, many are not. However, it is a temple area that usually provides the environment for their trances. Traditionally, such mediums are believed to loathe being required to take up their calling, for being selected by a particular deity to be his mouthpiece makes their lives not their own, and short. Some, however, enter the local temple to train in the art.

According to Jordan, apart from being an oracle, the medium "is also a spectacle or perhaps, one might say, a miracle",[28] given the severe mortification of the flesh which he undergoes during his trance states. This serves two purposes: on the one hand, it shows possession since, ostensibly, the medium feels no pain when possessed and, on the other, it shows that he is still a member of the human world. When special local celebrations take place, these mediums are sent from other localities for the occasion. On a smaller scale, mediums are often used for private seances in which they may be used to contact the dead, for example. Whereas *tao-shih/daoshi* and "divining youths" are all male, such smaller-scale mediums may be women, and old or young. In fact there are many different kinds of mediums. In some cases mediums become the voice of the dead. Other mediums claim to be able to journey afar in their trances. Still others use divination to convey their message – spirit writing, or the divining chair, for example – but it is always through the power of a deity particular to the medium that his or her skills are exercised. In Taiwan, such general mediums may have "offices" where they can be consulted in times of personal difficulty. Importantly, it is communication with the spirit world, or the world of the dead, that renders the mediums essential in the lives of individuals and communities. This is shamanistic practice in the present day. While it is more folk practice than specifically Taoist, links between Taoism and popular religion are cemented by the Red-head Taoists, who are experts in medium oracle interpretation.[29]

Exorcists

Tao-shih/daoshi are often called upon as exorcists to cure illness, and it is they who undertake the more intensive ritual for exorcism like the attack on Hell, which we shall look at later, and which liberates a deceased soul.[30] But it is to less highly-ranked exorcists that the purification of homes, villages, or curing of illness is often charged. These are the *fa-shih/fashi*, the masters of method, and it is they who interpret the words or divination writing of the mediums who are attached to them, and who are masters of the mediums. They are Red-head Taoists and in true shaman style have to walk on red-hot coals and climb a ladder of sharp knives in order to demonstrate their powers and be accepted as Red-head priests. Climbing the ladder is tantamount to ascending to the court of the Jade Emperor himself, where the assistance of the gods is procured. Like the shamans of old these exorcists can travel to any part of the world, to the underworld, or to the heavens where they acquire their knowledge. The interaction between priest and medium and the colourful, dramatic and theatrical ritual adds to the otherwise solemn nature of such occasions. These magical rites are, in foundation, performed for the same reasons as those of the ancient shamans – anything from rain-making to healing. The exorcist is often like a magician, or sorcerer, who has acquired skill in the procuring of power from the gods and the ability to use it. The power of the god may be used to enhance his own power or the god himself may be summoned to assist – a more dangerous scenario since the power of the god is independent and more potent. Even more dangerous is the use of the medium of the priest's own body by the god. Power is also invested in talismans, mirrors, swords, gourds, bells, and the like, in order to assist the priest. It is the Mao-shan school of Taoism that is particularly known for their skills in exorcism.

Divination

We saw in the early chapters of this book that divination was a prominent feature of ancient Chinese practice, and it is still practised today, albeit in wider format. The use of moon blocks, as they are called,[31] is reminiscent of the *yin* and *yang* negative or positive responses, and is underpinned by such. They are so called because they are shaped like a pair of quarter moons. They can be quite small when used in the home, but are larger when used in temples. The curved, outer sides of the blocks symbolize *yang* while the flat inner sides are *yin*. When a request is made to a deity, the petitioner casts the blocks onto the ground. If they land unevenly, and so one flat and one curved surface are seen, then the answer is favourable. If, however they both land flat sides down, or curved sides down, the answer of the gods is negative.[32] (Flat sides upwards indicates that the god is laughing, and the inquirer should try again!). It is a form of divination that is very popular in Taiwan,[33] as well as Hong Kong. For more elaborate responses, divination slips are found at the larger temples. A slip of paper on which is a number is drawn at random and then matched with a bamboo slip on which is a short verse supplying the answer to a question or problem. Since the responses on the slips are difficult to understand, an interpreter is often at hand in the temple. Some questions are profound, others are mundane: "Why is our child doing poorly in school? Why is my husband always tired? What can be done about the pain in my left arm? Should we build a new wing on the east side of our house or the west side?" [34] Complementary or separate is *ch'ien/qian* divination with the use of bamboo sticks, individually numbered and held in a bamboo container. This is then shaken until one stick falls out, its number being matched to a printed response.[35]

Spirit writing is another form of divination known from Sung/Song times. One form of it is the use of divination chairs. These are small sedan chairs carried by two mediums by its legs. A deity is invoked to sit in the chair and the mediums in trance reflect the animation of the deity by the jerking of the chair. From time to time the chair appears to write in Chinese characters in sand that has been placed on a platform or specially prepared table. It is this message from the god that is divined by the experts. Sometimes, the deity conveys its message by means of the medium, who writes in the sand with a willow or peach-tree stick, the traditional tool used for the divination. Illiteracy was once required of the mediums who engaged in such divinatory writing. Such spirit writing is not just a means to request advice of a deity; it is also a means of revelation of whole texts. Jordan and Overmyer note the importance and popularity of possession and divination in Taiwanese culture, where it is practised by all classes.[36]

Additionally, the calendar itself is an important medium of divination. For the position of the stars and planets, in conjunction with the time of one's conception will be indicative of the ways in which changes in time and space in its ever-flowing cycles are having an effect on the life of an individual at a given point in time. And there are no set patterns, which suggests that an individual's life can be adapted and changed in accordance with the tenor of the present cosmic pattern of events. Creating harmony and balance is the key here in understanding why divination is important. Divination is a way of putting oneself back on the cosmic track by making the right choices and changes. It can take many forms – the observation of the stars; the way in which the energies of the earth are presently aligned; the configuration of energies at a given moment; the reading of natural phenomena like the flight of birds, the configuration of clouds or mists; the reading of omens; the casting of *joss* sticks on which are hexagrams. However, the concept of regaining or maintaining harmony between Heaven and Earth, macrocosm and microcosm, lies at the root of all such divination. The ancient ideas of change according to the interplay of *yin* and *yang* and the interaction of the Five Agents informs the concept of divination as a means to ascertain the way in which events are moving. So requests of moon blocks, the use of divination chairs or slips are attempts to interpret this pattern of events or, more pertinently, the way in which adverse events in personal life are out of line with cosmic change. Divination has been a Chinese phenomenon from ancient times, but it became a Taoist art, too, and while diviners are not always Taoist, it is Taoist art that has been the medium for praxis.

Temples

A Taoist temple resembling a monastery or abbey is a *kuan/guan* or *kung/gong*. Some are great public centres of Taoism, *tao-kuan/daoguan*, to which Taoist priests from any locality go to practise Taoism. Others are smaller, hereditary temples that are the focus of a particular line of hereditary priests.[37] A smaller temple is called a *miao*, and a shrine a *tz'u/ci* or *ko*. But, by and large, there is little to distinguish between the organization and administration of Taoist and Buddhist temples, and the same terminology for the smaller temples can apply to both. There are three famous temples, T'ai Shan/Taishan of the eastern Peak in Shantung/Shandong province, one in Shansi province, and Yung-le Kung/Yonlegong in southernmost Shansi.

While such centres of Taoist activity exist, local temples are the responsibility of the laity and are independent of each other. It is the laity that funds their building and maintenance, and each temple will act as a community meeting place, a chess club, a school, playground, or business conference place, and so on. It would not be unusual for such temples to be devoid of any resident priest, for their affairs are run entirely by a lay committee, and it would be up to that committee to invite a priest for any special religious occasions. Thus, there is a limited role for Taoist priests of any kind in the local temples.

Since temples are the responsibility of the laity, and often funded by wealthier citizens, architecturally they are usually the most prestigious buildings in a locality. They are palaces of the deity, and are built so that the major deity within, and the main door, faces South, which is *yang*. Thus, they are constructed on a North–South axis, like the emperor's palace through history. Space does not permit detailed description here of the symbolism to be found in the construction of a Taoist temple both within and without, but the cosmology of Heaven and Earth and the energies between them underpin the careful design.[38] The whole design of the temple is based on the theories of *yin* and *yang* and the Five Agents. It is worth mentioning the profound links with Taoist cosmology and philosophy exemplified in the following words of Michael Saso:

> In the development of Chinese liturgical architecture, the very structure of the village temple, household altar, as well as the Taoist sacred area, are modeled on the structure of the triple cosmos. Thus, the incense burner in the center of the temple, the alchemical furnace from which the elixir of life and precious metals are refined, and the "Yellow Court" or the center of gravity inside the human body, are centers from which the meditator comes in contact with the Transcendent Wu-wei chih Tao. On the ceiling above the spot where the incense burner is placed is inscribed the eight trigrams, symbolizing the Tao's presence.[39]

Inside the temple, then, the incense burner or brazier, whose smoke symbolizes rising *ch'i/qi*, is an essential item, for it is by means of it that ritual is performed to the gods. Care of it is essential and often local families take the responsibility of such care for it in turn. Ashes from one burner will be used to begin a new temple. The worshipper also burns incense or *joss* sticks on the central brazier as part of his or her private ritual, for temples are always open, and individuals can present their pleas to a deity at any time. The most frequent images to be found inside are of the Three Pure Ones, the God of War, as well as city deities. Local temples will have their own central deity which, at special festivals, will be moved to the side to accommodate the Three Pure Ones, as well as other high-ranking deities. On occasions of special ritual, when the temple is filled with ritual specialists and surrounded outside by devotees, the atmosphere is particularly charged: "The blaze of votive lamps and candles, the swirling clouds of perfumed smoke and the richly coloured garb of the officiants sometimes produce a powerful effect, especially if the voices are good and the sweet music of flutes replaces the rather harsh music of clarinet, drum, cymbals and 'wooden-fish drum', although this, too, may be impressive."[40]

Altars, too, are constructed in such a way that they are representative of the triple world of Heaven, Earth and humanity. An altar is a *t'an/tan*, a "sacred place", and wherever it is set up, its symbolism is evident. Its core represents *Tao*, and the space around, or further away from the centre, is increasingly less sacred, like waves of decreasing energy. There are, however, various traditions as to how an altar should be constructed. The intricacies of altar construction are too detailed to mention here, and the interested reader should look elsewhere for a close analysis,[41] but a few points are worth noting. The first is that the altar is a moveable device, whether that is in a home or in a temple. The second point is that, on very special occasions involving the highest priestly ritual, the proceedings at the altar within the temple are conducted secretly, with few personnel present. The deities of the temple are arranged as guests during such ritual. Family shrines will have pictures or images of their own deities, as well as tablets of the immediate ancestors, though the latter may be housed in a separate shrine. But, again, it is the incense burner that is the central feature of practical worship. It is never empty, and incense sticks are burnt on it whenever any act of reverence takes place in the day.

Ritual

Throughout China's prehistory and history, the proper conduct of ritual in all its dimensions was a carefully handed down tradition. Known as *li*, appropriate conduct was exigent on all occasions of religious ceremony, for by it the harmony and balance between

Heaven, Earth and humanity were maintained, the seasons followed each other in the right order, the rivers flowed, and the stars followed their correct courses. The same is true for ritual today, because the efficacy of the ritual depends on correctness in practice. At large festivals sound and colour vibrate and dazzle the senses, while the smell of incense intoxicates and firecrackers startle. It is a charged and emotional atmosphere.

It is the Ling-pao/Lingbao scriptures that provided the base for ritual praxis right up to the present day. Despite the variety that ensued and that is evident today, there is a unified philosophy that underpins ritual praxis in the concept of bringing about oneness with *Tao* and of reaping the benefits and protection for the individual and community that ensues from such oneness. It is the uniting of microcosm and macrocosm that ensures the mutual harmony of both. And since the Ling-pao/Lingbao tradition preached the concept of universal salvation, the legacy of its ritual is the ultimate return of all to *Tao*. The more elaborate rituals can last for hours or days. Here, I can only mention a few of the aspects that are common to different ones. Purification ritual is important before commencing any ritual, and is repeated throughout. Not only does it purify the participants but also the whole ceremonial area in order to identify it as a special sacred place suitable for divine presence. The invocation of the deities that are the spectators of the ritual is also a central part of ritual. The installation of the sacred area of the altar and its consecration represents the world in microcosm, symbolizing the creation of the world emanating from *Tao*. Offerings to the deities are an essential part of the ritual, too. For special ceremonies these may not be items of food, but sacred writings, which are burned in offering. In communal ritual like the *chiao/jiao*, families set up tables of offerings to the deities outside the temple. But the final, important part is the merit to the recipients that is then bestowed by the deities, the representatives of *Tao*. Recitation of sacred texts has always been important in ritual. The *Tao Te Ching/Daodejing* was ritually chanted as early as Han times and was believed to have magical powers when repeatedly chanted.[42] It was especially the Celestial Masters school that saw recitation of the *Tao Te Ching/Daodejing* as the key to well-being and immortality.

In addition to the ritual conducted by priests, are the activities of the lay community. Temple processions are beloved by festival participants.[43] The young men of the area display their skills in choreographed martial arts. Part of the ritual programme are the theatrical performances or puppet shows that are themselves entertainment and offerings to the deities. Puppets, moreover, are believed to aid in dispelling evil forces by chanting and dancing. This is because they are supported by the deities who observe and enjoy their performance. Another feature of ritualistic theatrical performance is opera. While it is far less widespread today than in imperial times, music and dance feature prominently. Chanting, incantation and hymns may be accompanied by music, though also occur without accompaniment. Musical instruments like a bowl-shaped bell that is struck, a hand bell, a gong, cymbals, drums, a lute, a two-stringed instrument and a buffalo horn are traditional ritualistic musical instruments, each with symbolic religious meaning.[44] There has always been a strong connection between temples and drama, but while religious ritual could be conducted in the temple, so too could religious drama or secular shows – the latter even "raucous and spectacular".[45]

Dance is especially important and symbolic. The priests engage in meticulously choreographed ritualistic dance. Particularly important is the dance known as the Steps of

Yü/Yu, a very ancient rite[46] in which the priest drags his feet through nine paces, resembling the walk of the ancient ancestor Yü/Yu, the legendary founder of the oldest Chinese dynasty. He wandered the nine provinces of the land preventing floods and overcoming chaos until he became lame through weariness. The steps are symbolic of the "magic square", a three-by-three square containing nine numbers which, when added horizontally, vertically or diagonally, always add up to nine. The dance summons spirits that engage in battle against evil. So the outward movements of the priest are only bare glimpses of the power that he is gathering and controlling within himself and in the cosmos. In true shamanic form, the power enables the priest to meet with the three highest deities within his own being and transmit merit and blessing to the community and to the souls in the underworld as a result. It is a salvific formula that serves to assist evolution to *Tao*. Only the highest priests can achieve such meditative heights when the whole inner being is emptied of its spirit world to be one with the Void of *Tao*.

We should remember that, aside from communal ritual, there is the personal ritual of ancestor veneration that has been referred to so often in this work. While the main focus of family life would be the deities, a smaller part of the family altar would be used for ancestors. Wealthier families, however, may have a separate hall or place for ancestor tablets. The ritual involved here is aimed at ensuring that the dead are comfortable in their post-life abode. For those in living memory, the ritual is individualized. For those long passed into general ancestry, a collective ritual takes place at special festivals. The more immediate ancestors are enlivened by a ritual by which a red colour is daubed on their ancestor tablets, usually by a priest. A brush is dipped in red ink or blood, and then marks representing eyes, heart and so on are put on the long, narrow strip of wood that is the ancestor tablet. This animates the tablet, making it officially able to be placed on the family altar and able to be the recipient of offerings, requests, announcements, and so on.[47] The spirit of the deceased is then in contact with the family and, if properly cared for, should be able to progress easier through the hells to a new rebirth. In return for such care, the deceased spirit watches over the family's interests.

It is sons, and mainly the eldest, who have the responsibility of creating the ancestor tablet and of maintaining the offerings to the deceased. Not to do so would bring hostile fortune to the family through an unhappy ghost. If a man has no sons to undertake such a task, such is the importance of ritual for ancestors that a foster son may be acquired by adoption from a family who has several sons, or a daughter's husband or first son is adopted.[48] Whoever the adopted person is, he has to agree to set up an ancestral tablet for his foster father and conduct the required ritual at the appropriate times. There is no hope for a soul that has no one to care for it after death, and the greater the care, the easier the path in the existence after death. Some families ask priests to conduct ritual that assists the passage to Heaven. Such ritual involves informing deities of the soul's departure and need of help, and reading of texts that will speed the passage of the soul through the hells. Wine and incense are the usual offerings to ancestors, along with some words about the plans for the day, or a request for a good day. Birthdays of ancestors require more elaborate ritual.[49]

One important aspect of ancestor ritual is the use of "spirit money" to aid the journey in the hereafter. Such is the belief that beings in the other world – whether gods or deceased souls – have the same kinds of needs as humans that artificial money is ritually burned to assist them. In Taiwan, deities are given gold paper money in this way, ancestors silver-coloured money, and ghosts, copper coloured. The paper for the gods is yellowish-gold with a square of aluminium foil on which are the three Gods of Happiness, Success and Longevity. Many temples provide braziers for the burning of such spirit money. Wads of it can be bought in the markets. Adler notes an interesting custom in Taiwan: "Every fifteen days business owners in Taiwan burn spirit money in red braziers and set out offering tables on the sidewalk for both gods and ghosts. . . . Some of the offering tables are quite elaborate; for example a restaurant may offer an entire meal, complete with beer or wine."[50] The point is that happy and pleased gods protect and bless people, angry ones cause havoc.

Another aspect of spirit money is the depositing of money in the Banks of Hell or the Celestial Treasury – money that is owed purely by living life. Anna Seidel explained: "To be born is to receive an advance payment, to die is to have exhausted one's loan from the Celestial Treasury. Although logically one should assume it to be more beneficial to settle the overdraft of one's celestial account during one's own lifetime, 'Repaying the Debt' refers to the money offerings made during the traditional funeral rites performed by one's descendants."[51] Black-head priests are able to transfer the money on behalf of someone by a writ. Red-head priests, however, use a medium, who will take the money to the appropriate bank while in trance. But spirit money is also used to bribe the officials of Hell, or to offset stolen or defective money; it is even sent as pocket money! And to make certain that the money can be extracted only by the right individual a document is sent (burnt) to the bank, with a copy to the deceased. Both copies will be placed alongside each other and one seal placed by the priest over the two copies. Thus, there can be no problems when the deceased and the bank match the two together.[52] As we shall see later, there are festivals for the dead at which the burning of such spirit money will be important. Such ritual of ceremonies is designed to bring comfort and deliverance from harm for both the living and the dead and to release the latter from suffering in Hell.

The *chiao/jiao* ceremonies

The most prestigious of rituals is the *chiao/jiao* or "offering", which may last several days, and is held for a variety of reasons. While a *chiao/jiao* can be a small affair – even a simple family offering – the scale of some of the more important of these means that they are likely to be held every so many years, as when a temple needs to be consecrated. These larger *chiao/jiaos* are grand-scale ceremonies to which people travel from considerable distances, and are occasions when the services of the highest priests are needed. Ritual, as was seen above, is the symbolic and outward expression of Taoist cosmology, and the *chiao/jiao* is the prime example of such. Strictly speaking, two rituals, *chai/zhai* and *chiao/jiao*, separate in the past, are now combined in the festival. The former is more concerned with individuals, with the liberation of souls from Hell, fasting and purification, and the latter, with blessing for the community and union with *Tao*. The *chiao/jiao* festivals today combine the two like a "great symphony in which two melodic themes are developed"[53] as elements of a festival of cosmic renewal, with the aim of the regeneration of the creative forces that make all things possible. The term *chiao/jiao* means "pure sacrifice" and refers to the offerings that are given – wine, incense and tea. These are offered to the Three Pure Ones, who are the major divine guests at the ceremony. In the *chai/zhai* rituals for the dead, however, blood sacrifices are offered to the souls in Hell.[54] It is popular deities that are offered blood sacrifices, but not at the *chiao/jiao*. Here, these deities are placed to one side to make way for the great Three Pure Ones at the main altar, and other great deities. The Three Pure Ones are representatives of *Tao* that gives birth to the ten thousand things, through creating the One, Two, Three and all things. They also represent Heaven Earth and humanity, and the alchemical *ch'i/qi*, *ching/jing* and *shen*. Thus, as the guests of the *chiao/jiao*, they represent all things – from the Void of *Tao* to all its animated forms. Lagerwey justifiably calls the *chiao/jiao* "the combined density of Chinese mythology and cosmology".[55]

The pageant of ritual that makes up a *chiao/jiao* is too lengthy to describe in full here.[56] Suffice it to say that it is full of dramatic representation and symbolism, frenzied beatings on drums and the bangs of firecrackers, creating a spectacular scene. There is firewalking, possessed mediums, great processions, drama, puppet shows, and a throng of people who have come from far and wide, and even from overseas for the occasion. One custom is the procession to the river where people float paper or bamboo rafts to invite souls that have drowned to their feast. Thus, there are a host of activities in which to participate and to watch outside the temple. Needless to say, it is an expensive occasion for all concerned – and all *are* concerned. Cosmic renewal *chiao/jiaos* occur at regular intervals of three, five, twelve, or even sixty years. They last from three to nine days (these days usually the former), though in the past, they could last several weeks. Ritual that takes place outside the temple is to do with offerings that members of the community are able to see. But the serious meditative and recitative ritual is done by the *tao-shih/daoshi* in the inner sanctum of the altar area where, as noted earlier, only certain people are allowed. It is this specialized ritual that liberates souls from Hell, and secures blessing from, and union with, *Tao*. To make a mistake in this ritual, however small, is to render the whole proceedings invalid: yet it is not a ceremony that the highest of *tao-shih/daoshis* perform very frequently.

While there is considerable variety in the respective traditions, underscoring the proceedings is a homogeneous harmony and interconnection of events both within and without the temple. Dean writes:

> The ritual, the procession, the offerings, and the theatre are intimately interrelated. There is a rhythm and a flow of intensities throughout the course of the entire community performance. Each performance by the priests of a ritual text is unique. Each community brings its own desires to bear upon the selection of elements from the regional culture and the ritual tradition. Unique connections between different sectors occur at each ritual, criss-crossing the structural unity.[57]

It is especially at the sixty-year *chiao/jiao*, the end of a cycle, and the need for renewal of the whole community into a new cycle of time, that such interrelation of ritual has to be carefully planned. For years previous to the festival, the temple is renovated, and it is a matter of prestige to donate the necessary finance for this. The intensity of the occasion is prefaced with purificatory acts of the whole community – fasting, repentance of sins, repayment of debts, special diets and clothes, for example. The sixty-year *chiao/jiao* is indicative of the renewal of life, the restoration of *yang*, and the blessings of the highest deities to ensure the continuation of harmonious living. Needless to say, the expelling of all evil forces is necessary to ensure such security and harmony.[58]

The *chiao/jiao* ceremonies are times for the whole community to participate, not only inwardly through purification of mind and body, but also in wider customs. For a long space of time any religious activity such as this was forbidden in China. Today, under the more relaxed, though watchful, eyes of the authorities, many villages in China have begun to hold their *chiao/jiao* festivals once again.

Worship

From what has been said above regarding the functions of Taoist priests, it is obvious that they are far from religious leaders of their respective communities. Quite the contrary, their services are very much at the beck and call of the laity. Neither does the laity focus too narrowly on the local deity. In day-to-day life, and influenced over the centuries by Buddhism, the acquisition of merit is the all-important concern. And given the point that good and evil deeds are recorded in the registers of Heaven, actual quotas of good deeds are prescribed for prolonging or lessening one's life. Thus, at festival times like those noted above, each individual has the opportunity to donate what he or she can and, in return, receive a quota of merit. The wealthier individuals are able to contribute to the building of hospitals or homes for the elderly, and the like. Then, too, there is the easy way of acquiring merit by the burning of spirit money, noted above. Such an action deposits money in the Bank of Hell and offsets the sins of ancestors for which the present descendants may suffer. It is a means of creating balance between the living and the dead, and between the living and the living, cementing familial ties through the generations alive in each family.

Lighting candles and burning incense at the family altar and ancestor shrine in the home are central acts of worship. The most important factors in life are health, wealth and longevity to enjoy both. These are the immediate aims of ordinary people who know that they are a long way from immortality. Yet there is, too, as noted earlier, an idea of ultimately universal salvation, a concept for which the average individual has the influence of Buddhism to thank. But, apart from offerings to gods and ancestors, meditation, breathing exercises, the slow exercise of T'ai Chi Ch'üan/Taijiquan or the similar *ch'i-kung/qigong* are Taoist practices that are adopted as part of the lay attitude to religious life. Keeping oneself healthy in body and mind is a facet of the religious quest.

Religious Taoism encompasses the overt theism that characterizes popular religion in most cultures. It is the anthropomorphized *Tao* that enables us to speak of *the Tao*. This *Tao* is not the abstract Void, but a *Tao* with a personality, one to whom requests can be made, to whom one can pray, chant and offer worship. As to other deities, many have a Taoist/Buddhist character that involves both Taoist and Buddhist worship.[59] Deities are *yang*, unlike *yin* spirits of the dead and ancestors. As *yang* entities, deities have much to offer humankind in terms of receiving their prayers, requests, hymns and the like, and providing a focus for celebrations on the festivals held at their birthdays. It is these deities that can be found in the form of images (called *josses* in Taiwan), in both temples and homes. Such temple images are owned by the lay people of a locality, not by priests, though some families may have their own images. For those who do not, pictorial representations suffice. Jordan makes the point that possession of an image of a deity is tantamount to a contract between the two, the deity supplying welfare and blessings for the family, and the family supplying care for the deity.[60] While a number of deities might be worshipped, apparently it is not wise to have too many. If one deity out of many is requested for help it might well take the attitude that, since the worshipper usually worships "Old So-and-so", why should it bother to respond![61]

There are many popular deities, and the worship of them is fairly fluid, with their popularity waxing and waning according to fashion. A deity such as Kuo Ch'ung-fu/Guo Chongfu, for example, has become very popular in Fujian with admixtures of Taoist, Confucian and Buddhist worship.[62] Wu Tao/Wu Dao the Divine Physician (also called Pao-sheng Tati/Baosheng Dadi, Ta-tao Kung/Dadao Gong and Wu Chen-jen/Wu Zhenren) is popular in south-east China, in Fujian and Taiwan. This deity, too, is part Buddhist and part Taoist. One very popular deity who we have already met, is Ma-tsu/Mazu, the Queen of Heaven. She is especially popular in Taiwan, but also in Hong Kong and right along the southern coast of China itself. Her 1,001st birthday was celebrated with a particularly colourful festival in Taiwan.[63] Her temples in Taiwan have become grandiose, and are often surrounded by smaller temples for the goddess. Most localities will elevate one deity to take on the role of protector of the village or area.

Despite the presence of so many temples, collective worship is minimal in comparison to worship at home at the family altar. This structure is usually simply a long table on which the deities are placed, and is to be found in the main room of the home. The ancestor tablets are on the far left, the *yin* side, and the deities on the larger right-hand, *yang*, side. Of these deities, those protecting the home, particularly the earth god, are especially important. This large altar is something sufficiently sacred not to be moved. However, a smaller, square table placed in front of it is one that, apart from being functional for secular purposes, is also used as a portable altar that can be carried outside. Pictures of deities hang behind the altar, and talismans or charms are pasted beside them. On the altar are also the memorabilia acquired from festivals or visits to other temples, which are believed to be effective in maintaining the harmony and health of the home and its inhabitants. The absence of a priestly focus in the religion and the lack of institutionalization means that it is up to the individual to maintain any format of worship. However, it is usually the mother of the home that presents the offerings to the ancestors and deities, performing this function for her family twice a day. However, for special ceremonies for ancestors, the male head of the home is the one who conducts the ritual. Despite such traditional praxis the more industrial cultures like Hong Kong have abandoned the local, community earth god, though he is still to be found protecting the home in less urban areas. In Hong Kong, too, the economically dispersed families have resulted in a distinct lack of family unity in home worship.[64] In all, worship and religion are informal. A special problem might occasion a visit to a temple, or the employment of a Taoist or Buddhist specialist, but if one is a Taoist, neither of these actions is necessary. Spontaneity of religion is as much evident in modern praxis as in the ancient philosophy.

The calendar

Religious events are mainly determined by the lunar rather than the solar calendar. A lunar month, the time it takes the moon to revolve around the earth, is about twenty-nine to thirty days. The first of the month occurs at the new moon, and the middle of the month is the time of the full moon. Of course, this means that the New Year would never be fixed in terms of the seasons. To ensure that is was fixed, and to keep in line, too, with solar time, the time it takes the earth to revolve around the sun, extra months had to be added to the lunar year now and then. In the time of the legendary Yellow Emperor, in the year 2637 BCE, the calendar was begun, and time was mapped out in cycles of sixty years. Indeed, the sixty-year cycle is still important today, for one's sixtieth birthday is a time for special celebration. The year is also divided into periods of solar fortnights that reflect changes in climate. These periods are named according to their nature – awakening of the insects; clear and bright; a little warm; great heat; frost descends; a lot of snow.

Each cycle of sixty years is informed by the cycle of Five Agents, and since each Agent has a *yin* and *yang* nature, altogether these amount to "Ten Heavenly Stems". Additionally, the Ten Heavenly Stems are combined with "Twelve Earthly Branches",[65] and it is these that are associated with the twelve animals – Rat, Ox, Tiger, Hare, Dragon, Snake, Horse, Goat, Monkey, Rooster, Dog, Pig.[66] Since each of the Stems is associated with a particular colour, a year might be described both with its Stem colour and its animal. Each year, then, will have its special characteristics. The year 1990, for example, was Metal, *yang*, and the year of the horse. It will take sixty years for the same Stem, colour and Branch to match once again those at birth: so anyone born in 1990 will not find the same Metal, *yang*, horse combination until he or she reaches the age of sixty in 2050. As I write these words in 2004, I am in the year of the Monkey, the Agent of Wood, and a *yang* year.[67] The year in which one is born will naturally dictate the kind of personality one has, so horoscopes are taken seriously by the Chinese. In chapter 7 we saw that, according to one legend, the twelve animals were the only ones to turn up at the Jade Emperor's birthday party. Another legend tells that the Jade Emperor, in order to create a calendar, invited all the animals to cross a wide, swiftly running river. The first to arrive would give its name to the first year, the second to the second, and so on. The machinations of the animals and how they crossed the river in the order shown above, make a delightful story.[68]

The meticulous divisions of the calendar to reflect the Five Agents, *yin* and *yang*, the Stems and Branches, the position of the planets and stars, and the nature of change, permitted some forecast of the way things might be on a given day and, also, the way things *should* be on a given day. Maintaining harmony in one's daily life necessitates knowledge of each hour, day, and greater period of time. Here, the almanac provided in the past, as in the present, a forecast of what might be auspicious or inauspicious on a particular day. In late imperial China, the almanac was surely the most widely circulated book. It gave not only the nature of a particular day, but broke down the day into the best and worst times at which to do something, thus informing times for marriage, business arrangements, agriculture, visits, and so on. Indeed, the almanac was a veritable encyclopedia for daily life, even explaining dreams, the right charms to use and divination methods, and is very evident in many Chinese homes today.

Festivals

Festivals pepper the calendar year, providing times for communal celebration in localities and households. Some celebrations are universal; others, like the birthdays of village deities, are local. Generally, there is considerable variety in the ways in which festivals are celebrated from one community to another for, again, it is the laity that decides how things should be done according to local needs. Local historical publications, the *Gazetteer* of each locality, announced when and how festivals were to be celebrated. The festivals celebrated today are too numerous to detail, and in what follows I shall only highlight the more important and popular festivals, while briefly mentioning others. Festivals are part of the *yin* and *yang* pattern of creating harmony between the community and the cosmos, and of channelling the blessings of the gods into the community and the home. It is often a time when the specialist functions of priest – both Taoist and Buddhist – are called upon, as well as the mediums and diviners who provide supporting roles. Let us look first at the traditional and universal festival of New Year, which falls roughly at the end of our January or early February.

Chinese New Year

Chinese New Year occurs at the second new moon after the winter solstice. It is a highly auspicious time, for it heralds the time at which *yang* begins to rise again in the cosmos. While the winter solstice marks the solar New Year, the lunar New Year, which is the beginning of spring, is so much more important that preparations for it begin on the twenty-fourth day of the last lunar month. On this day, the household deities leave the home to report to the Jade Emperor on the good and evil deeds of the members of the family during the year. In particular, the Kitchen God is given a banquet and bribed with offerings of sweet foods before he leaves. Traditionally, these offerings to him have been done by males, for women have to keep away at the time. Out of respect, too, they were not expected to wash their hands or comb their hair in front of the Kitchen God. While the deities are away, the home is thoroughly cleaned to purify it of the dark *yin* forces, and prepare it for the arrival of the heavenly deities, the household deities not returning until the fourth day, when they are also greeted with food.

Celebrations begin on the eve before the first day. The women prepare the food for the banquet the following day. When the preparations are over, five talismans representing the Five Agents, and auspicious verses on red paper requesting blessings for the coming year are pasted over the lintels of the main door into the home, and the door is sealed from visitors. The exact time of the arrival of the heavenly deities is not specified, so each family decides for itself when that is. To welcome them, candles are lit, incense is burned and offerings of sweet rice cakes, turnip cake, oranges, wine and spirit money are presented, when possible in sets of five, to represent the Five Agents. Then, too, a banquet is offered to the ancestors, who share in the festivities with their living descendants. In order to know when the divine and ancestor guests have finished eating the divining moon blocks are cast. If they fall in the same manner three times this is indicative that the family is able to partake of the "remainder". But before doing so, offerings are made to any wandering spirits who may have some past connection with the home. In some places today the banquet is set out in the temple and the festivities include the carrying of lanterns to guide the heavenly gods, as well as a dragon procession.

Everyone tries to return home for New Year, and if they cannot, then an empty chair with an article of clothing replaces the absent person at the banquet. Traditionally in China, people retired into their homes for several days at New Year. All businesses closed, and the streets were empty. For women, especially, it was considered bad luck to leave the home. Were they to do so, they would take the good luck of the home out with them.[69] The custom in general is reminiscent of ancient China when the populace used to seal themselves in their homes for the winter months. Today, however, only some families seal themselves in on New Year's Eve, awaiting the arrival of the New Year, but businesses remain closed for several days, and one is not expected to do any work until the household deities return on the fourth day. It is customary in many areas for women to return to their native homes on the second day of the New Year. Many marriages take place at New Year when the extravagances of celebration can be shared between the two functions. After the New Year has arrived, the seals are taken off the door during the night to let in its blessings. Firecrackers are set off to rid the area outside of any remaining evil forces.

New fire is important at the festivities. It represents new life, rather like the new fire that was started in the springtime in ancient times. The main fire in the kitchen is extinguished when the Kitchen God is burned to indicate his departure. Using the embers of the fire, a small stove is lit, and is placed under the banquet table. These days, red paper is put into it to symbolize fire. Red is the colour of the festival – red posters on the doors, red flowers in the women's hair, red envelopes containing money for the children. On the first day of the New Year, everyone bathes and dons new clothes before visiting the temple, relatives and friends, and exchanging presents. In each home there will be five kinds of sweets for visitors, symbolic of the Five Agents, and sweetened tea. It is a time for pleasant behaviour, pleasant words and lucky sayings. Everyone tries to laugh and be happy, and avoid fractious interchange. The whole tenor of New Year is a time for the neutralizing of evil forces so that the New Year can be started afresh.

The other festivals in the Chinese lunar year can be dealt with briefly.

First month
9th: Birthday of the Jade Emperor

Festivals for the birthdays of deities are particularly colourful affairs, rather like the *chiao/jiaos* described above, though they are mainly lay occasions and may not involve the functions of priests. It will be around the major temple dedicated to the deity that the festival will take place, attracting people from far and wide, if the deity is a major one. The main part of the festivities is the processing of the deity on a palanquin or open truck around the town, accompanied by musicians, dancers and firecrackers. Some participants may have brought other deities to honour the celebrated god or goddess. This kind of festival is called a *tan/dan*. The most important deities, the Three Pure Ones, have their birthday celebrated on New Year's Day, but the prestigious Jade Emperor's birthday also falls within the New Year period. It used to be only men who celebrated his birthday at the temple or in the home, but today the whole family joins in, except perhaps for menstruating women or women who have just given birth. Bands of musicians travel from house to house playing special music.

> *13th: Festival of Kuan Yü/Guanyu God of War*
> *15th: Beginning of three stages and Lantern festival*

The calendar year is divided into three unequal parts. The first part begins on the fifteenth of the first month and is the Period of the Heavenly Spirits, and lasts for six months. It is this day that marks the end of the New Year period. It is, therefore, the time to bid farewell to the spirits of ancestors who have been invited for the New Year festivities. This is done in the Lantern Festival, when lanterns of all kinds are hung up to light the souls' journey away from their families. The lanterns, too, represent the renewal of the *yang* energies in the cosmos. Another feature of this festival is the dragon-lantern processions, when an immensely long and grotesque-looking dragon is animated by many men (and sometimes women) underneath, who act as its feet. Those who participate here are martial arts youths who practise the choreographed movements of the twisting dragon for many weeks previously. On the dragon are candles and, representing clouds, it chases a symbolic sun, a small red ball, heralding the spring rains to come. Interpreted in a specifically Taoist way, according to Saso, the dragon represents the force of *yin* that searches for the immortal pill, the pure *yang* that is the red ball. When swallowed, the blessing of immortality is procured.[70] The time is also one when "the transcendent Tao has implanted a new charge of primordial breath in the center of the cosmos",[71] and the red ball symbolizes that breath. Eventually, the dragon catches and swallows the red ball, becomes tame, and allows people to pass underneath to secure the blessings of *Tao*. Many minor traditions accompany these major celebrations on the fifteenth of the first month.[72]

Second lunar month
> *2nd: Birthday of the God of the Soil*

The God or Marquis of the Soil is honoured twice a month (1st and 15th or 2nd and 16th). The second of the second month, a double *yin* day, is also the first offering that is made to him in the new year. The God of the Soil is a heavenly deity that comes down to earth like water. Lagerwey writes: "He gathers in underground cisterns, forms subterranean rivulets, and springs unexpectedly, mysteriously, to the surface. Underground, he circulates, a hidden treasure of untapped – potential – energy; above ground, the community, by rendering him a cult, taps this limitless source of heaven-sent, but earth-derived life."[73] As Lagerwey also points out, he is associated, too, with virtue and power, and with wealth.[74] As the God of the Soil, he is able to make the earth prosper or withhold its blessings. He is responsible for the wealth and blessing of the whole community, and reports to the Jade Emperor on good and evil deeds. Merchants, especially, honour him on this day, hoping for prosperity in their professions. Another function he has is of maintaining the divisions between the living and the dead.

3rd: Birthday of the Patron of Scholars

The Patron of Scholars is a stellar constellation of six stars representing six individual deities. Two we already know, the immortal Lü Tung-pin/Lü Dongbin, and Ssu-ming/Siming, the controller of life, who keeps the register of life and death. Another is a deity so ugly that he frightened all that saw him, though such ugliness proved exceptional in frightening away demons! Another controlled wealth, and another disasters.

15th: Birthday of Lao-tzu/Laozi

Lao-tzu/Laozi's birthday is found in the heart of the springtime.

19th: Birthday of Kuan-yin/Guanyin

Kuan-yin/Guanyin, as we saw in chapter 7, is a female deity that is popular with Buddhists and Taoists and with Chinese people in general. As a merciful goddess, she is invoked in order to free those suffering in Hell, and is renowned for her great mercy and compassion.

22nd: Birthday of Kuo Hsing-wang/Guo Xingwang

Kuo Hsing-wang/Guo Xingwang is popular with geomancers and practitioners of Chinese medicine.

Third lunar month

3rd: Birthday of Hsüan-t'ien Shang-ti/Xuantian Shangdi

The birthday of this god is celebrated especially by butchers and barbers, of whom he is the patron. He is associated with the Pole Star and with the capabilities of bringing both fortune and misfortune.

3rd: Ch'ing-ming/Qingming

Traditionally the third of the third month is the time of Ch'ing-ming/Qingming, "Bright and Clean". Despite the connotations of springtime in the name, the festival is a time for the cleaning of graves. Perhaps the two aspects were separated in the past. It is one of the major three festivals for the dead and, like the other two, was probably influenced by Buddhism. Cemeteries did not exist in China, and people set up their own graveyards outside the village or town and planted trees around the graves until the Communist regime ploughed many of the areas. The whole family joins together to visit the graveside for the cleaning ritual. This usually takes place early in the morning when the spirits are "at home" in their tombs after their night's rest. After offering food as a sacrifice to the ancestors, the family combines the occasion with a picnic nearby. Red rice and long noodles for longevity are a special feature of the foods. Talismans and charms are placed on the graves, as well as offerings like a peeled egg, or egg shells. Firecrackers are set off, and paper money burned. The God of the Soil, who keeps the *yin* spirits from harming the living members of the family, is always invited as a guest; since he guards graveyards it is wise to present offerings to him.

This day is also a time to honour young girls, some of whom have the chance to choose a possible marriage partner. Since it is not a lunar, but a solar festival, the date is fixed as the 106th day after the winter solstice. The day before the festival is traditionally a time for eating only cold food. Such a custom arose from the practice of putting out the old fire and eating cold food for twenty-four hours before lighting the new fire at Ch'ing-ming/Qingming. Again, such a practice is reminiscent of ancient times and "bringing out the fire" when the old fire was taken out of the home in springtime, and a new one made to burn the winter growth before ploughing. What we have in today's festival is perhaps a remainder of the old agrarian fertility festival that we looked at in chapter 1.

15th: Birthday of Pao-sheng Ta-ti/Baosheng Dadi

To the people of Taiwan, Pao-sheng Ta-ti/Baosheng Dadi is the patron of medicine. Like many divinities he was once a mortal of the Sung/Song dynasty, and lived a life dedicated to curing people of their illnesses through supernaturally revealed recipes for his medicines.

23rd: Birthday of Ma-tsu/Mazu

Since Ma-tsu/Mazu is associated with seafaring people and is the protectress of sailors, it is the provinces on the coast of south-east China who celebrate her birthday and, particularly, the Taiwanese. In Taiwan, Lukang is the centre of festivities on her birthday, and people come from far and wide to celebrate the occasion, though many celebrate in their own homes. In the afternoon, people set up small altars in their doorways with offerings for her. According to tradition, it always rains on Ma-tsu/Mazu's birthday, because she did not turn up for her wedding to a deity. The rain is a punishment from the bridegroom.

26th: Birthday of Chang Tao-ling/Zhang Daoling

Chang Tao-ling/Zhang Daoling is important to all aspects of religious Taoism, having been the first Celestial Master of the school by the same name, and the father of religious Taoism.

Fourth lunar month

14th: Birthday of Lü Tung-pin/ Lü Dongbin

Lü Tung-pin/Lü Dongbin, is one of the Eight Immortals, whom we encountered in chapter 7. Those dedicated to internal alchemy particularly revere him, and he is associated with pure *yang*.

26th: Birthday of Shen-nung/Shennong God of Medicine

Shen-nung/Shennong is the ancient legendary ancestor of the Chinese who is reputed to have given them grains for agriculture, the herbs that are used for medicine, and pottery. He is a god of the summertime, and so is linked with the colour red and the Agent Fire. His face is sometimes red, but may be found painted black or white, representative of his ingestion of many different kinds of herbs.

Fifth lunar month
5th: Dragon Boat festival

The fifth of the fifth is the beginning of summer, and close to the solstice. It is a time of intense heat often without cool breezes. Torrential rain falls periodically, things turn mouldy, and diseases can spread. So, while the light of summer is all too evident, the darkness of death threatens, too. It is a time devoted to the health of children, especially boys, and a time for wishing people good health. Herbal baths are taken, and charms worn to protect people from the five poisonous creatures – spiders, centipedes, snakes, lizards, toads and scorpions. Children can be seen with such charms or bags of incense hung around their necks and red amulets tied around their wrists. In Taiwan, people tie herbs, leaves and twigs over their doorposts with a red ribbon to dispel evil. Wine made from flowers of sulphur is believed to be especially good for averting evil. Heat necessitates rituals to dispel the forces of sickness and harm, so the days surrounding the solstice are a time of needy purification in the form of *chiao/jiaos*.

Also at this time are the Dragon Boat races, when youths race their boats on rivers or seas. These boats are narrow, very long, and brightly coloured, with prows displaying the heads of the dragons. Given the dangers of illness at this time of the year, and the torrential rains and floods, the festival may be the remains of an offering to the river – perhaps of a human victim, for the races can be dangerous enough even today for young men to lose their lives. In ancient times, as we noted in chapter 1, a young girl was floated down the river tied to a light raft that eventually sank, representing her marriage to, and appeasement of, the god of the river. There must be some association, too, between the rain and the dragons, who are usually accepted as responsible for it. The festival also remembers Ch'ü Yüan/Quyuan, an ancient poet of the third century BCE, who drowned himself in the river.[75] The dragon boats are often regarded as like those that searched for him. A special food of sweet triangular-shaped rice dumplings wrapped in bamboo leaves is eaten to commemorate offerings to him of the same, in the distant past.

13th: Birthday of Kuan-sheng Ta-ti/Guansheng Dadi

Once a great third century CE general, Kuan-sheng Ta-ti/Guansheng Dadi became the deity whose protection stretched to the entire empire. In Taiwan, there are great processions on the days leading up to the festival, and some dress up as the god's soldiers, though as his servants they are barefooted, shoddy looking and wear a yoke around their necks.

Sixth lunar month
1st –15th: Summer solstice

The first half of the year is now complete. It is not a time that is particularly celebrated, though it is a time of house cleaning for some. It is time to get rid of the mould that has settled during the heat and rains of the spring and early summer. Kuan-yin/Guanyin is popular on this day, since it is the time when she is believed to have ascended to Heaven.

Seventh lunar month
1st: Opening of Hell

At the beginning of autumn the Gates of Hell are opened and souls are allowed to go free. Those who have no one to honour them roam listlessly from place to place for the whole month. It is a time when they can visit the living in ways that are not really welcome. So merit can be acquired through the offerings made to these lonely, orphaned and hungry souls while, at the same time, the offerings afford the souls some release from their plight, and a means of coaxing them not to plague and take revenge on the living. A strong Buddhist influence informs the beliefs here. In Taiwan, these lost souls are called "the good brothers", even though, or especially since, some of them are believed to be in Hell for crimes they have committed – all the more reason to placate them! It is the responsibility of the whole community to assist these lost souls for the safety and security of everyone. Rites to appease the hungry souls occur throughout the month, beginning on the first and occurring throughout the month. The fifteenth of the month is particularly important. It is a time to appease but beware! And it is not a time when one would want to open a business, get married, move house or go to the dentist!

7th: The Festival of Seven Ladies

The maidens of the Seven Sisters constellation (*Pleiades*) came down to Earth to bathe. A cowherd fell in love with the seventh and married her, so she was unable to return to the skies. The Jade Emperor was furious and banished the maiden to the spinning-maiden star, and the cowherd to another star, separating them both by the Milky Way. Once a year, on the seventh of the seventh, the two are permitted to meet when magpies form a bridge across the Milky Way for them to meet. Dramatic performances of the tale are popular, and the time is an auspicious one for young women who, if they can thread a needle by moonlight, will marry a good man. Tradition holds, too, that it is a day when a woman has the right to propose to a man. The seven maidens are believed to protect children.

15th: Festival of Earth Spirits

On the fifteenth day of the seventh month, the Rule of the Earth Spirits begins, the second of the three periods into which the year is divided. It is a time in which forgiveness of sins is possible, especially for the souls in the hells. The Festival of the Earth is thus a major one, dwarfed only by the New Year. It is a time when the souls, freed from the hells, are invited to a sumptuous communal banquet. Saso explains: "The summer harvest is soon to begin, and the earth, like the fertile womb of a mother, is about to yield its blessings for human life. Therefore those who are lodged in the depths of the earth and under the waters are released and sent off to the heavens, lest any offenses and forgotten misdeeds of the past hinder the harvesting of nature's bounty."[76] So this is a time when people return home if they can, and join in the ritual undertaken to help all those souls from Hell to cross over to Heaven and salvation. It is a concept thoroughly influenced by Buddhism's view of universal salvation. Such ritual is important enough to require the skills of the specialist priests, both Taoist and Buddhist.

The souls are attracted to the feast by lanterns and beacons to light their way and lanterns are floated on rivers in order to assist those that have drowned. Each home sets up an altar at the main doorway with offerings and incense sticks, and spirit money is burned. But it is the communal rites performed by the priests that are the focus, when all kinds of things are offered through burning to the dead – paper clothes, cars, model houses, gardens, furniture. The priests chant through the day and night. At the end of the festival, lanterns are also floated on the rivers to light the souls on their way to Heaven. The fifteenth is also the birthday of the Second Primordial who is the Lord of the Earth. At the end of the month the Gates of Hell are once again closed, though according to some traditions they are closed on the thirteenth of the month, and those souls that have nowhere to go have to return before that date.

Eighth lunar month
3rd: Birthday of the Kitchen God
15th: Mid-Autumn Festival of Moon

The harvest full moon is the occasion for inviting blessings to the home, and for a banquet in the open air under the stars in the brightness of the moon and the light from lanterns that are hung around the garden. Since the harvest has been gathered it is a time when luscious fruits are enjoyed, and also sweet moon cakes, that are shaped like the moon. Fruits, candles and incense sticks adorn the outside altar. It is a time of softness, stillness, for reading poetry, gazing at the moon, and moonlight walks. Women, particularly, are linked with this festival since the moon is *yin* and feminine. The story of Ch'ang-o/Chang-o, she who stole the pill of immortality from her husband and rose up to the moon, is special at this time. The moon is cool like jade, and Ch'ang-o/Chang-o's palace in the moon is made of pure jade. Chinese see the western "man in the moon" as a hare sitting under a tree grinding together the ingredients of the pills of longevity. But there is also an Old Man in the Moon who is responsible for arranging marriages and recording the names of new-born babies.

Ninth lunar month
9th: Full or Double Yang and the Birthday of T'ai-tzu Yeh/Taiziye

The ninth of the ninth finds youngsters flying kites in celebration of, and offerings to, the spirits of the Pole Star at this minor festival. It is also a time for walking and hiking in the hills. People drink rice wine with yellow chrysanthemum petals. *Yang* is at its height and will soon give way to the rise of *yin*. T'ai-tzu Yeh/Taizi Ye also has his birthday on the ninth of the ninth. He is a deity favoured by the Three Sisters, Lü Shan, sect of Taoism and is a child deity honoured by mediums.

Tenth lunar month
1st: Garments for the Dead

The first of the tenth is the third occasion in the year when the dead are the focus of the festival. It is not a major festival, but is a time when offerings to ancestors are made at the graves. The offerings include paper clothes for the coming winter. These are burned in order to send them on to the ancestors.

10th: Birthday of Yü/Yu the Great
15th: Birthday of the God of Water, beginning of the Rule of Water Spirits

Water dominates the time from this date until the Reign of Spirits begins again. It is the beginning of the third period into which the year is divided. Winter places the earth in full stasis and the renewal of the cosmic energies of the universe is imminent. It is the cosmic renewal festival of the *chiao/jiao* that will release the new energies to dispel the darkness of winter, herald the light of spring, and the rise of *yang*. A communal banquet to free the souls who have drowned is also part of the activities of this day.

Eleventh month
Solstice, the Solar New Year

At this point, *yin* is at its maximum and *yang* once more begins its ascendancy. It is a time of renewal of the cosmos. It is a family festival symbolized by making round rice balls that have red paste in the middle – the beginnings of *yang* in the surrounding *yin*. These are placed all around the home – even in the toilet – to mark those things that are blessings in life. Offerings of rice cakes are made to the ancestors on the previous day and then cooked in a sweet soup with red and white rice dumplings for the family.

Twelfth lunar month
12th: Last festival of the God of the Soil

On the first and fifteenth days of the month, offerings are made to the important God or Marquis of the Soil, who is the patron of businesses amongst his many roles. Since the New Year celebrations will begin shortly, bonuses are given to employees so that they can celebrate the New Year well. In the past, they were given banquets.

Apart from the more general festivals outlined above in which Taoism might be said to have some contribution in the past or present, there are numerous festivals pertinent to localities as well as considerable local variation in more widely celebrated festivals. One aspect that is common to all such celebrations is the offering of food to deities and ancestors. In local cults and for lesser deities, blood sacrifices are usual, but higher deities are not usually offered meat. For each festival there is a special food, and it is an occasion when people can indulge in the kind of diet that is not readily affordable at other times. Schipper goes as far as to say that, "the cycle of festivals is part of the alimentary cycle".[77] Ritualistically, food is the medium by which the community communicates with the deities and spirits of the other world, with the domains of the dead, and how families share their lives with their ancestors.

Symbols

Taoism, as Chinese religion and culture in general, abounds with the use of symbols to convey abstract ideas. Many, like the well-known *yin* and *yang* symbol, have been discussed in earlier chapters. Here, one or two others need some mention. Gazing out at the stars, constellations like the Big Dipper, or Bushel (*Ursa Major*) fired the imagination. This particular constellation features, as we have seen, in the heart of ritualistic symbolism, and the heart of the alchemical body, while the Pole Star is symbolized in the flaming pearl that is atop the headdress of the highest priests. In Schipper's words: "The bushel stands symbolically for an exact measure, a closed space, and a perfect standard; transposed in the sky as a constellation, the Bushel (Big Dipper) is a heavenly clock marking the cycle of the seasons by its rotation."[78] The Dipper is also symbolic of the oneness of *yin* and *yang*, and is considered to be the centre point between the sun (*yang*) and the moon (*yin*) and, thus, unity that is *Tao*.

Returning to Earth, the majesty of the land itself rendered fodder for natural symbols. Nowhere is this more evident than in the symbolism connected with mountains. There are five great mountain peaks, corresponding to the Five Agents and the five directions: T'ai-shan/Taishan in the East, Heng-shan in the South, another Heng-shan (which reads the same in transliteration but is really a different Chinese name) in the North. Hua-shan is in the West, and Sung-shan/Songshan is in the centre. T'ai-shan/Taishan is the mountain of the East that symbolizes birth, like the rising of the sun, and yet the Chinese believed that it was the abode of death, too. The god T'ai-shan/Taishan, who is the anthropomorphized force of the mountain, sustains all life, and rewards the good and punishes the evil. But it is for his role as the one who presides over Hell for which he is mostly known. Such is the importance of T'ai-shan/Taishan that his temples are prolific. Additionally, a cult has grown up around the daughter of T'ai-shan/Taishan.[79] The southern deity of Heng-shan controls the movements of the stars, dragons, and creatures of the waters. Hua-shan presides over watercourses, marshes, and canals, but also hills, mountains and forests. The northern deity Heng-shan is responsible for metals and their interaction, as well as birds and creatures with hair. Sung-shan/Songshan presides over the larger rivers, tigers and leopards and similar speedy animals, as well as reptiles. One famous mountain is the Mao-shan range, which is the perfect environment for the reclusive sage, the meditative monk, or glimpses of the legendary earthly immortals. Monasteries, shrines and temples once covered its pine peaks – all, like so many others, destroyed by the Japanese and the Red Army in the twentieth century, though monastic and temple life there is now being restored and attracts many pilgrims. Many other mountains are specially associated with Taoism.[80] Dragon-Tiger Mountain, Lung-hu-shan/Longhushan, for example, is home to the Celestial Masters school.[81]

Much has been said in earlier chapters about talismans. In the past, a talisman (*fu*) was energized by a Master in such a way that something of the power of the Master passed into a diagram or text, providing protection for the recipient that could be released by certain ritualistic words. Texts, in particular, are invested with incredible powers, particularly those known to the elite priesthood of Taoism. But even in the home, having one of the *Classics* is considered to bring blessings to the family. Ancient diagrams like the *lo-shu* (magic square), and the *ho-t'u/hetu* are believed to have immense powers, but simpler talismans are often made by Taoist medics or priests in order to cure illnesses or banish problems. Here, special symbols are written and empowered to effect the cure, with incantations to summon the correct spirits who will assist in the cure, and adjure those who might harm the individual to stay away. The final script is then wrapped and given to the recipient. The more powerful priests summon the spirits under their control, and within their own bodies, to empower the talisman. A more shamanistic practice involves the symbol of blood, where the priest cuts himself and uses his own blood to seal the talisman. Talismans are often used as amulets, but amulets are also made from such things as peach stones. Peaches, we should remember, are associated with immortality, and so are particularly lucky in life. Others might favour a small figure of one of the immortals. Colours, too, have their symbolic meaning, with red and yellow being especially lucky.

Animal symbolism is prolific in Taoist and Chinese culture. The crane is a symbol of wisdom and longevity, particularly the black crane. It was the mythical mount of immortals and of Lao-tzu/Laozi. Since the pine tree also survives for a long time, the crane is often pictured with it. The crane is also a symbol of wisdom. Dragons (*lung/long*) are important enough to be deified animals. Some live in the skies and are responsible for rains. Others live in the oceans. They can be very small – the size of a silkworm – or as large as the space between Heaven and Earth. They play in the sky with a ball or pearl causing rain and thunder, or live in the seas and preside over springs, lakes and rivers. Some have the responsibility of guarding treasure.[82] The dragon is the symbol of masculine strength and is, therefore, *yang*. According to Wilhelm, "the dragon stands for a purifying breakthrough, a liberating thunderstorm; it is the supreme symbol of temporal power assigned to the Son of Heaven".[83] The Son of Heaven, the Emperor, was also symbolized by the dragon, had dragon designs on his robes, particularly dragon's claws, and sat on a dragon throne.[84] As early as Shang times the dragon was a symbol of awesome power that struck terror in people and could cause destruction. On the other hand, it symbolized beneficence by granting life-giving fertility and essential rains. The coalescence of these dualities of character is seen in the might and power of great storms.

The phoenix (*feng-huang*) symbolizes all things female and so is *yin*. It is an ancient symbol, and was associated with just emperors. Whereas the dragon is a symbol of the emperor, the phoenix symbolizes the empress. It is linked with the wind and with feathered creatures. Sometimes it is portrayed as both *yin* and *yang*, representing union, and occasionally is said to be *yang* not *yin*.[85] Its *yin* and *yang* character may have something to do with, on the one hand its association with fire and the sun, which are *yang*, and on the other, with its three-day death and association with the moon, which are *yin*. Cooper points out that its composition is also *yin* and *yang*. Its eyes, for example, are *yang* and solar, while its beak is *yin* and the crescent moon.[86] From ancient times the tortoise and turtle were special creatures that were honoured for their longevity. The domed shell of the creature represents Heaven, and its lower plastron Earth, so it is a symbol of the cosmos and of immutability. Its upper surface was used for divination in the distant past of antiquity, and it is also eaten to cure illnesses. The cicada, too, was always an important symbol. It is an insect whose mature larva survives underground for a long period until it finally becomes fully-grown. Because it then emerges and soars up into the sky, it is reminiscent of the idea of immortality. It is associated with rebirth and life that begins anew in a new form.

There are numerous other symbols from the plant world that are also important in Taoist and Chinese culture. Amongst the most important are the pine, which has already been mentioned as a symbol of longevity: its seeds were eaten by Taoist adepts. Gourds feature in much of Taoist folklore, and are sometimes found as a joined pair, symbolic of the union of *yin* and *yang*.[87] The peach was noted above, too. But, apart from the association of its fruit with immortality, the wood is *yang* and is used in exorcisms. The flowering apricot is a symbol of Taoism itself. It is a special tree that blossoms in the middle of winter: "At dawn, its flowers catch exactly the pink of first light on gathering storm clouds. At night, the flowers bring the moon down: white rays direct to the earth."[88] In the realm of

Life-cycle rites

Birth

In a culture that accepts the presence of unseen forces, it is important to take good care of the unborn baby, as well as the baby's health after birth. The foetus is looked after by a spirit called T'ai-shen/Taishen, who lives in a variety of places in the house, in the wardrobe, or under the bed, for example, and so it is imprudent to disturb the spirit by moving the furniture around or by cleaning out cupboards.[89] If the pregnant woman's in-laws cause her any problems, the spirit may become angry. It is a sensible arrangement for, with variations from culture to culture, the pregnant woman is protected from moving heavy objects herself, or from an accident by others doing so. Additionally, she is not expected to tie heavy bundles, use large knives, bore holes, burn things, lead buffalo by a rope, empty buckets, attend funerals or carry a coffin, or go out late at night. She is unable to visit the temples, reach for things that are high up, quarrel, go on long journeys, visit crowded places or eat certain foods. In short, her duties are minimalized so that she and her baby are safe.

While she cannot visit temples, the pregnant woman may make offerings at the family shrine in the hope of a safe delivery of her baby. If the woman is pregnant at the time of the Lantern Festival she may try to determine the sex of the child. After offering incense at the home shrine, she goes outside and listens for the first words spoken. If the topics overheard are feminine ones – flowers, clothes, for example – then the baby will be a girl. If the words are to do with sport, fighting or lanterns (since the word for lantern in Chinese also means a boy), then she will have a boy.[90] Another method of determining the sex of the unborn child which is popular today is the following. Seven sevens are forty-nine: add the conception month, subtract the mother's age, and add nineteen. Odd is a boy, and even is a girl.[91] Alternatively, a diviner might be consulted to determine the sex. Birth is at conception not at the actual delivery from the womb, so a child at delivery, assuming that gestation is normal, is nearly a year old, ten moons.

Considering the emphasis that has always been placed on family life in Chinese tradition, children are important in continuing the family line, but sons have always been more favoured than daughters. Far more fuss occurs when a boy is born and elaborate presents are given. Birth is a woman's world and local women's customs dictate the rituals and traditions that surround the birth, leading to considerable variation in them. Female spirits are responsible for taking care of the new-born baby and his or her mother. One, in particular, is responsible for the birth itself, along with several attendants. After the birth, the mother gives offerings of things like baby clothes to these female spirits at their shrines. A godparent may be chosen to help in the harmony of the child's future.

After the birth, local customs dictate that special foods are fed to the mother. These are usually highly nutritious foods that will strengthen her. She is thus well cared for until the end of the first month, when restrictions are lifted. For the first month, then, the mother is "sitting the month", resting, eating well, eating warm *yang* foods and nourishing herbs, and generally being waited on. At the end of the month, the baby's hair is shaved, and it is given symbolic offerings. From this time on, the baby is able to go outside. At four months the baby's life is celebrated with presents of clothes from relatives and friends, and peach cakes are traditionally made. Another celebration takes place when the baby is a year old and is given its first solid food. Traditionally, at this time, the baby is presented with a tray of items symbolizing assets it needs in life such as health, intelligence, wealth, and industriousness.

Name-giving is a complicated affair. To begin with children are often given unpleasant names like "little animal", "naughty child", "pig" or "stupid", so that evil spirits will not envy the child and harm it. Later, the child is given its other names, many of which are changed during the phases of its life. The real name of all these is given just after birth. The clan or family name, however, will be the most important element in it. This will be attached to a *yang*-natured object like a mountain, dragon or tiger, for a boy and to a *yin*-natured object like jade, a flower or a tree for a girl.[92] The family name comes first and the personal name second, but the first part of the latter is usually the same character as the rest of the family. It is to this that the second, more distinctive part is added. Another name, suited to the character of the child, is given at about the age of ten, and this name is based on the child's personality.[93]

As a child grows, another spirit takes over its welfare and takes care of it until it is sixteen years old. If the child becomes ill or upset, then offerings are made to this spirit to cure the child. Children in Taoist homes will learn about the basic teachings of Taoism. This may take the form of chanting the *Tao Te Ching/Daodejing* or learning meditation techniques, perhaps learning to play ritual instruments. In traditional China there used to be a capping ceremony as an initiation ceremony for a boy at age sixteen, and a hairdo for the girl. The former was a very formal rite in which the boy was capped or crowned, and the latter, a less formal rite, in which the girl was given an adult hairdo.

Marriage

Since character is determined by one's time of birth, horoscopes are essential in ascertaining whether a possible marriage is auspicious or inauspicious. Strictly speaking, traditionally, marriage is for life, since the family line of ancestors would get into dreadful complications were divorce and remarriage endemic. In today's world, however, widow remarriage in China is widespread. In some communities, so important is marriage that if a girl dies unmarried a "spirit marriage" takes place whereby a groom accepts – usually by way of a considerable monetary bribe – to go through a marriage ceremony in which the bride is represented by her ancestral tablet.[94] Such a marriage allows a daughter's ancestral tablet to take its place in the family home; without the marriage it can have no place, and the ghost will be an unhappy one. Sometimes a nominal marriage takes place between a deceased girl and a deceased male, their places at the wedding being taken by their respective ancestor tablets.

The ancient formal wedding is a rare sight these days,[95] when a much simpler process occurs. Letting the ancestors know of the proceedings on the day of the wedding is the first priority. Then, the bride's hair is done and she is dressed in her wedding attire. The formal ritual begins when she is given wine and then she bows four times. She is asked to be a good wife, daughter-in-law and mother, to which she silently assents. Then she awaits the arrival of the groom at a banquet prepared for the wedding. The groom, meantime, is going through a similar ritual at the ancestor shrine in his own home, where he too is asked to be a good husband. The procession to the bride's house is the next major event where he meets his veiled bride. The bride removes her veil and everyone sits down to the feast. Both the bride and the groom then drink wine from the wedding cup, sign the wedding document and enjoy the feast. It is not until the following day that the bride traditionally leaves her own home for that of her husband where she offers gifts at her husband's family ancestor shrine. The next time she visits her parents' home, it will be as a visitor three days after her marriage. In effect, she has been transferred to another ancestral home to which she will contribute with her own children.

The security and blessing of the family, its cohesion and vision for the future, as well as its links to its past ancestral line, depended on the children who were born. However, in the past century, China's population growth was colossal. A rigorous policy by the state has sought to limit families to just one child each. Even so, the population continues to expand. But, aside from the problems of economy with an enormous population, the curtailing of family life – particularly the bearing of a son, should the first child be a daughter – has broken down the old family ties and ancestral traditions. Such is so at least on the surface, and more so in the towns and cities, than in the countryside.[96]

Death

The end of earthly life is only the beginning of a new journey – and rather an unpleasant one. As a result of Buddhist influence, Taoist and Chinese belief in general came to accept that the soul had to spend a period of time in hells appropriate to its sins, before reincarnation in a new form.[97] Alternatively, some believe that souls live a shadowy existence, invisible to us, but with the same needs. Either way, it is necessary for living descendants to supply all kinds of commodities for use in the afterlife. Paper houses filled with all kinds of things are burned for the deceased. Jordan writes: "Indeed, the artistry of these paper houses, equipped as they are with furnishings, gardens, and a staff of servants, easily surpasses the level of many a folk art that has received more attention as art."[98] And if such comforts are not provided, trouble will ensue for the living; hence the communal need to provide for "good brothers", those who have no descendants to care for them. It is "the good brothers" who are blamed for any run of bad luck in the family, and were such a case to occur, they would have to be ritually removed. It is fear of such a kind that provides one reason for the extensive rituals surrounding death. The other main reason for death rituals is concerned with the Confucian-influenced concept of filial respect. To neglect the correct rituals is a shameful thing to do and would bring a family into disgrace. David Johnson points out that both priests and exorcists are present at a funeral to respond to these two main needs: the priest performs the correct and respectful ritual, and the exorcist makes sure the deceased departs and does not hang around to pester the family.[99]

To ensure that the deceased person really does depart, a funeral rite known as *The Attack on Hell* is performed. Here, a paper and bamboo fortress is built and the family of the deceased crouch in a semi-circle around it. Each one puts a hand on it and shakes it now and then. It represents Hell, and the ritual is enacted to release the soul of the deceased from there. At the same time, it is the ritual at which the living really say farewell to the dead, so it is a cathartic and moving experience for the immediate family.[100] Ritual such as that found at funerals is ancient, and while there are always variations, it is usually detailed and protracted – a fact that emphasizes its immense importance.[101]

While funeral proceedings may seem laboriously long, they provide full expression for mourning, for assuring the living that the dead are well cared for, and assuring them, too, that blessings will be reaped for the living through their time and care. Lack of respect for such a goal by not performing ritual for the dead is tantamount to being ostracized by the family and community. At the same time there are fears of the "contagion" of death, and neighbours may put red paper or cloth over their front doors to act as protection. Red, as we have seen, is a symbol of life, and serves to prevent any malign influence from the dead. The whole process is a vivid reminder of the closeness between the living and the dead in Chinese culture. The end product is the release of the soul after as short as possible a time in Hell and a raising of its status to Heaven. The bridge is crossed between the world of the living and the world of the dead and, finally, between the world of Hell and the world of Heaven. And those bridges can only be crossed by the interaction of the living with the dead – albeit at a safe distance for most of the time. It is interesting that authorities in China prevented such funerals from taking place and encouraged cremation. However, with the relaxing of the bans on religious praxis there, traditional funerals have become something of a status symbol.[102] It is this revival of Taoism in China after a long demise that will occupy some space in the final chapter.

9

Taoism Today

Communist China

In the last centuries of imperial rule in China, religious life was pervasive with a proliferation of temples, shrines, door gods and protective house deities. The beauty of the mountains boasted splendid monasteries and temples to which pilgrims flocked, and life-cycle rites and festivals peppered the ordinary lives of individuals. But, despite the presence of Taoist priests at many rites, Taoism had lost the impetus that it had had many centuries before. As was noted in chapter 8, lay people could perform their own ceremonies, and did not always have the occasion to call upon the services of true Taoists. As to ordinary individuals their "Taoism" was mixed so much with Buddhist and Confucian beliefs and practices that they could in no way be called Taoists, despite intensely religious-orientated lives. Their religion was too familial and communal to be individualistically Taoist. Neither Taoism nor Buddhism had much organizational power and Taoism had been only minimally an institutional facet of Chinese religion. And yet it is Taoism that has influenced popular beliefs and practices. It is there in the roots – if not by name, then in the beliefs. But alongside the proliferation of religious beliefs came Western influence in the nineteenth century, and the decline of both Taoist and Buddhist monasteries and temples.

Politically, the Ch'ing/Qing dynasty was crumbling and China was humiliated by her defeat at the hands of the Japanese in 1895 and, in the wake of the Boxer Rebellion of 1900, by the allied Japanese and Western powers. Apart from famines and natural disasters, there was considerable public unrest and a number of revolutionary groups sprang up. The last dynasty of China, the Ch'ing/Qing dynasty, ended in 1911 after a successful rebellion led by Sun Yat-sen's Nationalist Party, and China became a Republic. The emperor abdicated the following year. Sun Yat-sen died in 1925, a few years after the formation of the Communist Party in 1921. The successor to Sun Yat-sen was Chiang Kai-shek, who attempted to consolidate his power in the early new Republic. However, political disorder remained throughout the rule of the Nationalist government that he led. War with the Japanese from 1937 to 1945 brought further political disaster.

Changes in outlook in the urban towns and cities produced a new kind of Chinese intellectual, one not held so much by traditional values, but who questioned economic, political and social balances, and who was ripe for radical change. Such intellectuals, many of whom had studied abroad, began to see China as underdeveloped in an otherwise modern world. Students objected to having their education dominated by the old classical language that restricted the use of modern concepts and prevented wider literacy for all people. Exposed to Western ideas, they were hampered in their visions forward by their cultural identities, and their attitudes to religion became indifferent. As people moved from country areas to the factories in the towns for work, their old familial ties were broken, creating a vacuum that nothing seemed to fill.

All this was changed under the leader of the Communists, Mao Tse-tung/Mao Zedong who, in 1949, led a successful revolution against the Nationalist government, forced it to retire to Taiwan, and instituted the People's Republic of China. Mao Tse-tung/Mao Zedong fostered not familial but nationalistic identity, and a more thorough rebuttal of traditional ideas. Initial thought was that with modernization old religious ideas would become obsolete and a move to atheism would be a natural path. When this did not occur, there was an overt attempt to prevent superstitious practices. And such practices, as we have seen, have much that is Taoist in character. It was the Communist Red Guards who perpetrated the worst horrors against religious praxis – killing and maiming, forcing religious individuals into acts against their beliefs, invading their homes to destroy any vestiges of religion. In these turbulent years, what replaced religion was allegiance to Mao Tse-tung/Mao Zedong in what must be regarded as a deification of him. A doctrine of propaganda to make Chairman Mao the focus of every individual's attention was adopted. In homes, schools, the workplace, cinemas, parks, streets, there were posters of Chairman Mao, and quotations from his *Quotations from Chairman Mao* were ubiquitous. Lucy Jen Huang wrote:

> While the Communists attacked religion as the opiate of the people, Maoism seemed to have similar euphoric influence on the masses, chanting and reciting Mao's quotations at every important occasion and believing it could perform feats and miracles. The unification of the nation is more effectively achieved if the masses possess religious zeal and dauntless faith in Maoism. At the same time, through the worship of Mao, the insecure and the alienated find a sense of identity, belonging and esprit de corps in the common struggle and dedication of a common course.[1]

Under Mao, improvement in education, industry, health care, land distribution, new occupations and the vision of a vibrant future helped to foster the kind of Maoism found in the words above in some constructive ways. But Mao also wanted grass, flowers and pets eliminated.[2] Even today cats and dogs are rarely found in the cities. Inevitably, young people grew up with allegiance not to their family, but to the state. In the words of a popular song of the time: "Father is close, Mother is close, but neither is as close as Chairman Mao".[3] Young students had no objection to the destruction of religious objects during the Cultural Revolution from 1966 until Mao's death in 1976. It was a time of systematic destruction of temples, and local committees saw to it that ancestral tablets and altars in all homes were burned. Thousands of volumes of religious texts were destroyed – either burned or made into pulp at a paper factory. The fate of Taoism in particular during this period was disastrous. As soon as the old empire fell and China became a Republic, state support for Taoist temples ceased. Many monasteries and temples that remained fell into disrepair. When the Japanese armies invaded in 1937, the destruction of such buildings had already been devastating. Under the Communists, monks and nuns were persecuted, forced from their monasteries, and put to work in labour gangs where many died. Religion was all but obliterated.

With the post-Mao years came changes in policy with regard to religion. After a few unsettled years, Teng Hsiao-p'ing/Deng Xiaoping took over the Communist leadership in 1979, and opened China to greater Western influence and greater freedom of religion. Five religions were accepted as official – Buddhism, Taoism, Protestant Christianity, Roman Catholic Christianity and Islam, though Taoism is not now regarded as having any eminent position in China.[4] Confucianism came under great persecution in the twentieth century, and was blamed for the antiquated ideas of the Chinese more than other religions, so it is absent from the list. It is tolerated only as a subject for scholastic study. What is not tolerated is superstition and, therefore, popular religion continues to be regarded as illegal. Yet, popular religion is thriving! It is springing up wherever a loophole can be found for it to emerge.

The revival of Taoism and other religions in China is permitted politically mainly because of the tourist attraction of the old temples and monasteries, so the state is investing in their rebuilding and refurbishment as prudent economy, despite underlying inhibition and much prohibition. Yet, there is a good deal of support from outside China to reinstate religious practices once again, and encouragement for the training of priests, monks and nuns. The number of Taoist priests in China is now increasing. Field studies in Fujian have revealed that Taoist rituals were again being performed in restored temples in the mid-1980s and large-scale processions were evident there in the early 1990s, though restoration of practices is slower elsewhere.[5] However, the number of Taoist monks and nuns is far fewer than the personnel of the other four official religions.[6]

Limited tolerance of religion is giving support to the setting up of religious seminaries, some religious ceremonies and salaried religious personnel. However, there is still careful control and monitoring of religious movements and bodies, and a Religious Affairs Bureau sanctions practices. Local Taoist (or Buddhist, Muslim and so on) Religious Associations control the practices in a locality, making sure that they are not out of line with state policies. The Taoism that the party line wants is an official version that is devoid of any mystery, awe and myth. A festival like the *chiao/jiao* would now need special permission to take place, though religious ritual for life-cycle rites is acceptable. Celebration of festivals is now very much in evidence. Yet it has to be said that China's youth has grown up without any form of religion. It is difficult to see how socialist-orientated youths and, indeed, those in middle age, can adopt a religious culture without which they have grown up and matured. Some of these continue to revere the long deceased Chairman Mao's portraits at Chinese New Year, and taxi drivers have been known to carry portraits of him to protect them from traffic accidents.[7] To be a member of the Communist Party itself, one *has* to be an atheist, a fact that suggests to the Chinese that religious belief is inferior.

TAOISM TODAY

The two major Taoist sects to be found in China today are Celestial Master Taoism and the Cheng-i/Zhengyi, Complete Reality, monastic order. Taoism has survived, and perhaps has done so better than is thought, considering its amorphous nature that defies categorization.[8] In Pas' words, "the Chinese people are very tenacious and resilient; like the loyalists of early times, when the Tao prevails in the country, they come forward; when the Tao is in darkness, they go into hiding".[9] While a number of young men and women want to be trained to be Taoists and can, for example, take a one-year study course in Beijing, they are hardly likely to be commensurate with the early Taoists who undertook a lifetime of study. Those who train in the monasteries themselves do little better in terms of commitment and knowledge. Any visitor to China today is unlikely to see a profusion of Taoist temples, and perhaps more tourists than pilgrims on the mountain slopes leading to the major temples and monasteries. But great temples like the White Cloud Monastery, the largest in North China, are now up and running and training monks. Thus, Taoism is far from dead in China, as was once thought it would be. As Schipper poignantly remarks about culture in China, "one only has to scratch the surface in order to find living Taoism".[10]

From the field studies undertaken in recent years, it can certainly be claimed that Taoism is alive in China, particularly so in the coastal provinces of Fujian and Canton in the South.[11] The cult of Ma-tsu/Mazu is especially popular now in south-east China. Slowly, old texts that survived the purges are being copied, and vestments and temple hangings are being restored where possible. Any vestiges of shamanism, including *feng-shui* now popular in the West, as will be seen below, are strictly regarded as superstitious and, therefore, are illegal. Such a policy excludes much that might be considered as Taoist praxis, but research today demonstrates that popular religion in China is thriving in rural areas.[12] Apparently, many homes have reinstated their family altars and the old funeral rites have been revived with all the extravagance of the past. Even young people are fascinated enough with religion to go on pilgrimages to temples.[13] One researcher estimated that, in southern Szechuan/Sichuan in 1988, as many as 80 percent of homes had a traditional altar dedicated to Heaven first and then the country, as well as ancestors, the Kitchen God and the earth god. However, daily rituals seem to have been abandoned, and incense is only burned at the altars on festival days.[14] But door gods have returned to guard the entrances of homes, usually two at the front door and one at the rear. Julian Pas remarked on the "amazing and fascinating" variety of door gods that he saw in China decades ago in 1985.[15] Religious drama and marionette theatre have re-emerged also, in conjunction with the old priestly rites in the temples.

Elsewhere, Taoism has always been allowed to thrive outside China. Especially in Taiwan, its traditions have been relatively undisturbed. It also thrives in Hong Kong and Singapore and in Chinese communities in the United States and elsewhere where Chinese immigrants have settled. While world wide there are perhaps no more than thirty million Taoists, religious belief is a tenacious phenomenon. Thompson aptly remarks that: "Religious forms, like certain plants, can remain dormant for a very long time, only to spring up again when the environment becomes favourable."[16]

Taoism in the West

We live in a time of considerable excitement and interesting challenges on the one hand, and heightened stresses and conflict at so many levels on the other. More and more today, people are turning towards non-institutional spiritual pathways in order to ease the dis-ease of mind and body, and a diminished state of well-being that seems to plague our times. Such factors are surely behind the attraction of eastern concepts and practices. The *Tao Te Ching/Daodejing*, unknown to the vast majority of people half a century ago, is now easily found in bookshops. Indeed, Clarke remarks that: "The long slow decline of Daoism in China is synchronous with its long slow rise in Western consciousness."[17] Many Westerners now believe in *karma* and reincarnation, and many seek alternative eastern therapies when they are ill or ill at ease. I was surprised recently to be sent for acupuncture treatment under the National Health Service, and to find that training for it is now possible for National Health staff. Those wanting alternative medical therapy do not have to search far to find it in their local area. To embark on an analysis of all such influences that have stemmed from Taoism is beyond the scope of this chapter. But I want to single out two practices that are now part of Western culture, T'ai Chi Ch'üan/Taijiquan, and *feng-shui*.

T'ai Chi Ch'üan/Taijiquan[18]

Most people today are familiar with the visual expression of T'ai Chi Ch'üan/Taijiquan, or simply T'ai Chi/Taiji, as it is more familiarly known. It is a practice, in fact, that is multi-layered and multi-faceted, but that ultimately unifies all its elements into a wholeness that mirrors the unified fabric and rhythms of the universe. While we do not see groups of people practising T'ai Chi/Taiji in the parks and town or city squares of the West – a common sight in China – classes in T'ai Chi/Taiji are now very popular in leisure centres of the western world. In the busy and somewhat stressful lives that we seem to live in the West, even the sight of people practising T'ai Chi/Taiji offers an immediate contrast to abnormally tense lives that have come to see stress and hectic living as normal. Few people realize when watching or practising T'ai Chi/Taiji that there is a wealth of Chinese and Taoist culture and traditions that have contributed to its present expression. Paul Crompton makes the apt point that "the world of Tai Chi today is like an enormous warehouse in which the past has accumulated".[19] Multiple strands inform its practice, strands that reach back into the distant past of ideas and practices that were concomitant with the evolution of Taoism – alchemy, meditation, spiritual development and martial arts. Like Taoism, too, it is concerned with the holistic evolution of body and mind, the evolution of the physical and the spiritual.

T'ai Chi/Taiji has been termed "China's cultural ambassador to the world" by Douglas Wile. He writes, too: "Touching the lives of more Westerners, and perhaps more deeply, than books, films, museums, or college courses, T'ai-chi Ch'üan is often the entrée to Chinese philosophy, medicine, meditation, and even language."[20] Those who know nothing of Chinese thought will almost certainly be familiar with the symbol of *yin* and *yang* and with the graceful movements of the T'ai Chi/Taiji *form*. In fact, in Britain today, the BBC is currently using a brief caption of the movements as the interlude between some of its programmes. Paul Crompton's words, written long before the adoption of such, describe rather well what BBC viewers now witness: "Moving slowly, under the trees, breathing, it seems, in time with a gentle breeze; merging with Nature itself in a healing rhythm. Head, shoulders, arms, trunk, legs and feet moving as one; continuously, smoothly and restfully; as if swimming into a new, all pervading element; a different time, a different space . . .".[21]

The word *t'ai/tai* in Chinese has a number of meanings. It can mean "high", "great", "supreme" or "remote", and in Taoism the highest or greatest level of achievement is to be in complete balance with *Tao*. Thus, the word *t'ai/tai* incorporates ideas that represent the highest goal of Taoists. *Chi/ji* in Chinese means the "ultimate", the "utmost point", "ridge-pole", this last as in the highest point of a building. In Taoism it is *Tao* that becomes the ridge-pole; *Tao* is the central point to which everything connects and from which everything comes. In the human body, the ridge-pole is the spinal column through which passes the essential energy of the body. Understanding the workings of *yin* and *yang* and reproducing their cosmic balance in the inner self helps to achieve that "supreme" goal of harmony with *Tao*. *Yin* and *yang* are the balancing agents that keep opposites in harmony, and T'ai Chi/Taiji aims to create the kind of harmony of them – their perfect balance – that results in experience of the Supreme Ultimate *Tao*. Philosophically, T'ai Chi/Taiji is a unifying principle, a oneness, and the totality and unity of all. The word *ch'üan/quan* in Chinese means "fist", or "boxing". It is a word normally associated with more aggressive martial arts such as Shao-lin Ch'üan/Quan, the boxing of the Shao-lin tradition. Perhaps, as Sophia Delza interprets the term, *ch'üan/quan* is a metaphor for action, a symbol of the power and control over one's own mind and movements.[22] Putting the words together, then, we have a meaning of "Supreme Ultimate boxing" or "Supreme Ultimate fist". However, the whole term T'ai Chi Ch'üan/Taijiquan is a late one, and its practice was probably not known by this name until as late as the early twentieth century.[23]

T'ai Chi/Taiji has its roots in many practices of the ancient past. Gymnastic exercises were popular, for example, in the time of Chuang-tzu/Zhuangzi, and we have evidence for their existence in chapter 15 of his text. It seems, too, that gymnastic exercises were widely used for therapy in the third and second centuries BCE.[24] Throughout the following centuries many variations on these exercises, postures and movements developed. But we can go back even earlier than these gymnastic exercises, to the dances of the shamans. These dances were important to remedy lack of rain, illnesses, aberrations of climate and the like. The dances facilitated the flow of energy on earth as much as in the human body. Despeux writes: "The dances are therefore conceived of as a means of resolving the congestion and stagnation of vital energy, to ensure its healthy circulation within human beings, as much as they are used to help the flow of the rivers on the earth."[25] The idea of harmonizing energies, of creating the correct balances in nature and in the human self are clear from these words. So the idea of movement to create harmony is a very old one in Chinese culture. Then, too, shamanic dances often imitated the movements of creatures, a feature that has also inspired some of the movements in T'ai Chi/Taiji. The Han silk manuscripts found at Ma-wang-tui/Mawangdui, which date back to about the second century BCE, have drawings of people of all ages and both sexes engaged in physical exercises, rather like today's practices of T'ai Chi/Taiji.

Many different strands of belief and practice inform the practice of T'ai Chi Ch'üan/Taijiquan in today's world. So there are great variations in the movements, in their nature, their speed, the degree to which the martial side is evident, and the extent to which Taoist philosophy underpins practice. Whether the emphasis is on the martial aspect or not, the underlying philosophy of Taoism is clearly evident. In texts belonging to one of the T'ai Chi Ch'üan/Taijiquan traditions, the Yang family, we find the words: "Finally, we can speak of the martial and the spiritual, sagehood and immortality. If one speaks of the body and mind from the point of view of the martial arts and applies these principles to the cultivation of power, it must be in the context of the essence of the *tao*. It is a mistake to focus exclusively on physical skills."[26] The best practitioners of T'ai Chi/Taiji, therefore, do not neglect the spiritual for the sake of the physical. It is a holistic practice that combines meditation with movement, mind with body, the spiritual with the physical. The circulation of energy in the body is essential for sound health. But in T'ai Chi/Taiji as a martial art it is the awareness of that energy, and how it is about to be used in an opponent's body, which is at the root of each movement.

All the martial arts like T'ai Chi/Taiji will have a *form* that is composed of a number of choreographed postures. In Crompton's words: "The postures can be thought of as places on a map that one passes through, and the movements as the roads that connect the postures together. So a form is a kind of moving map".[27] While the postures may have the same names, there are variations in how they appear in the different styles, traditions or schools.[28] The names of the postures are ancient and are taken from nature, from observance of actions, and from the movements of birds and animals, or the interaction of human and animal. Thus we have postures called *High Pat on Horse, Play the Lute, White Crane Spreads Wings, Snake Creeps Down, Rooster Stands on One Leg*, for example.

The links to Taoist philosophy are numerous. The *form* is based on circular patterns that reflect the rhythmic cycles of *Tao*, rather like the well-known *yin/yang* symbol. Sophia Delza of the Wu tradition puts this point superbly when she writes: "The body in action is a small universe of multiple movements and synchronized Forms, moving on itself and in space, duplicating, as it were, the composite rotation of the planets, where each, turning in its own rhythm, is in perfect co-ordination with the others in orbit."[29] The movements of T'ai Chi/Taiji reflect the fact that nothing in nature has straight lines, only arcs and curves, and that everything is subject to change. So in the *form*, as Delza puts it: "You are sensitized to the dynamics of change, to intricacies of pattern, to the weaving of space. You can experience the moment of synchronized stillness and the dovetailing process of movement."[30] Ultimately, the aim is to create the same kind of harmony that obtained at the beginning of the universe.

There are other strong links, too, between T'ai Chi/Taiji and philosophical Taoism. Important, is the idea of the soft and weak overcoming the hard and seemingly strong, in the same way that water wears away the hardest surface as it bends around it. The concepts of balance, the goal of equilibrium, and the need for harmony in the self are also very akin to philosophical Taoism. One profound feature of early philosophical Taoism was the idea of returning to the origin, returning to the source of all, *Tao*, and that is the ultimate aim of serious students of T'ai Chi/Taiji. In all life there is an ebb and flow, a fullness and emptiness – a rhythmic swing between two polar opposites. Indeed, a *form* is designed on the rhythmic alterations of the ancient concept of *yin* and *yang*. The ideas of naturalness, of "going with the flow", of yielding, are also common to ancient, philosophical Taoism and T'ai Chi/Taiji. But, though T'ai Chi/Taiji is rooted in Taoism, at the same time it has become part of the wider Chinese tradition. Given the difficulties of overt religious praxis in the past in China, it was wise for many to dissociate T'ai Chi/Taiji from its religious background in order for it to survive. But, despite such a veneer of secularization, true Masters do not separate it from its religious roots and aims.

The benefits to be gained from the practice of T'ai Chi/Taiji are considerable, both in the long term and the short term. Physiologically, the blood circulation is improved, leading to greater energy and alertness of mind. Breathing is altered: it becomes deeper, and this, too, stimulates energy. Muscles are more relaxed and supple and the skeleton is more flexible. Mentally, the mind becomes more focused, is able to concentrate better, and the balance between body and mind is heightened, so relieving stress and tension and creating a more harmonious and calm state of being that begins to pervade all aspects of life. So the balance between mind, emotions and body becomes harmonized, promoting an integrated, unified personality. An individual does not have to be young and strong to practice T'ai Chi/Taiji: it can be taken up in any state of health, at any age. It can assist in the cure of physical illnesses and it can enable the mind to use energy in the right way, without causing anxiety, stress, tension, and nervousness. Every part of the body is exercised in the practice of T'ai Chi/Taiji, but in such a way that no part is repetitively under stress: the carefully choreographed movements ensure that the whole body is equally used, softening muscles, stretching tendons and articulating joints. Even in China today, where religious practice had long been suppressed, the practice of T'ai Chi/Taiji is compulsory in schools, and is now a national way of exercise. As a soft form, it has mainly dropped its martial-art emphasis and has become a means to restore and nurture sound health of body and mind. According to Galante, "for the body it is an exercise; for the mind it is a study in concentration, will power and visualization; and for the soul, it is a system of spiritual meditation".[31]

Stuart Olson makes the pertinent point that in the West we treat our bodies like a car, not bothering with it too much until it breaks down, and then we see a mechanic. We wait until we get ill before we help our bodies. The Chinese, he says, treat the body more like a garden, weeding it, nourishing it, caring for it, and strengthening it against illness from the inside.[32] As we saw in chapter 4, *Tao* is that which cannot really be explained. Neither, ultimately, can T'ai Chi/Taiji. It is only by practice that its inexplicable subtleties can be experienced.

Feng-shui

The art of divination, so long a facet of Chinese and Taoist philosophy and practice, was extended also to the patterns of the earth itself in the form of *geomancy*, or *feng-shui* (pronounced *fung-shway*), a practice that is at least three thousand years old. The Chinese term means "wind and water" and, just as wind and water shape the contours of the earth, refers to the vibrant and changing energies of the land itself. The science of it predated Taoism by many centuries, though many strands seem to have contributed to its present expression. It perhaps stemmed originally from the idea that ancestors had to be comfortable in their graves. Later the idea was influenced by the concepts of the *I Ching/Yijing*, *yin* and *yang* and the Five Agents. By the early T'ang/Tang dynasty, there were many different schools of geomancy.[33]

Running through the whole of the earth is the power, the energy, of *ch'i/qi*, which is the creative force behind all the earth's patterns, and which comes from Heaven. It mingles with the *yin ch'i/qi* energy of Earth to form veins of energy in the land, often called "dragon vapours" or "dragon veins". Sometimes it twists and turns, rises and falls, creating mountains and valleys, or it suddenly surges upward causing volcanic reaction. All its formations can be negative or positive, *yin* or *yang*. Building a temple, monastery, home, grave, or any kind of building at places where there are negative forces can only serve to bring misfortune to the occupants, who will be affected by those energies. Quite the contrary is the case when buildings are placed where there are positive energies, for here, success, health and harmony will ensue from the beneficial forces that pervade the environment. But energy, like the cosmos itself, is constantly undergoing change and experts have always been needed in the past, as in the present, to determine the lie of the land's energies.

Calculations of the land's energies are made according to the readings of a geomantic compass of varying complexity, depending on the practitioner. At its centre are the needle points that align North and South and it also includes the eight trigrams, the Five Agents and the Nine Palaces. The last are the *lo-shu*, the magic square composed of nine smaller squares. Each square has a number from one to nine, arranged in such a way that they add up to the same number diagonally, horizontally or vertically (the number fifteen, which is the number of days it takes for the moon to wax or wane).[34] The mythical ancestor Yü/Yu is said to have seen this magic square on the back of a turtle coming out of the River Lo. The numbers on the turtle were represented by black and white dots, which came to be featured in the *lo-shu* diagram. The sequence of the numbers is the same as the Later Arrangement of the eight trigrams. There are four main schools of *feng-shui* in the West, divided according to their methods, the Eight Directions school, the Eight House school, the Flying Star school, and the Form school. The last school makes the least use of the geomantic compass. Needless to say, it was the Chinese practitioners of *feng-shui* that invented the compass.

There are certain visual characteristics of the land that are more obvious markers of beneficial energies – softness of the landforms, for example. Conversely, sharpness and harshness of the land will produce negative energies. Eva Wong writes:

> Roads, rivers, and valleys are pathways along which energy flows. Energy that flows down steep roads, gorges, or slopes is destructive; energy that meanders is beneficial. The most undesirable places to build a house or erect a grave are at the end of a T-junction and in the fork of a Y-junction in a road. At a T-junction, energy rushes straight at the house, as waves crash against the shore. In a Y-junction, the dwelling is squeezed between two roads.[35]

Visually, too, a building that is exposed and not nestled with higher ground behind for protection is likely to be in a disadvantageous location. Yet the peaks of mountains are especially known to be places that emit an immense amount of vital energy, like massive power stations. Also emitting powerful positive energies are the many grottoes or caves on mountainsides, perhaps because they were attractive to the Taoist recluses, and were said to be the dwellings of deities and spirits. Old monasteries were, therefore, often built in places of natural perfection on a mountainside. Flowing water is a special medium for the carriage of energy, but if it is flowing away from a place it will take energy away with it, though it can bring it if it flows towards a place. Wind sweeps *ch'i/qi* away, so no home should be in a windswept place.[36] Straight lines are especially inauspicious, particularly if they point directly to the site of a home or garden. Where they occur, they are usually diverted or blocked, perhaps by a pool or pond, a cluster of trees, or some rounded and smooth boulders. Nature is happier running in curved lines rather than straight ones, and the best kind of *ch'i/qi* runs like the contours and twists of a dragon.

But, apart from these obvious visual determinants of the nature of the land's energies, there are far less obvious and far subtler aspects of the energy forces that only experts can understand. All in all, there should be three-fifths *yang* and two-fifths *yin* at site. Such calculations are for Taoist specialists, or *hsien-sheng/xiansheng*, to determine. And in Jack Potter's words: "Handling *fung shui* is like dealing with a high voltage electric current; the benefit one receives from its power is directly proportional to the technical skill employed."[37] The energy forces are sufficiently crucial, too, for the well-being of a whole village. Moreover, if a grave were to be placed in the wrong way – just, perhaps, a few inches amiss – the well-being of all the descendants of the deceased would be adversely affected.

Ch'i/qi has different kinds of energies, which are dependent on the direction from which it flows. The four cardinal points of the compass each has an animal to symbolize the character of its energy. South is the Red Phoenix, and when *ch'i/qi* comes from this direction it is a symbol of fame, and good fortune. It is the source of goodness and beauty. South is associated with the summertime, as is the *yang* Red Phoenix, and is a time of energy and invigorating strength. Having the front of one's home or business facing this direction will bring these qualities. This was the direction in which all monasteries and temples faced. The North is associated with the *yin* Black Tortoise, with long life and endurance. If *ch'i/qi* comes from this direction it is, like the tortoise, slow, sluggish and sleepy. The North and the Tortoise are connected with winter, so having one's home facing North is to invite tiredness and sluggish energy into the home. West is associated with the White Tiger, a *yin* and unpredictable animal that might snooze quietly one moment and bring roaring change the next. Having one's house facing in this direction invites adventure, disruption to routine, and surprise events from the *ch'i/qi* that flows to it. To the East is the Green/Blue/Azure Dragon, from which flows protective *ch'i/qi* and the kind of *yang* energy that promotes wisdom and educational enhancement, which is what the occupants of a home will acquire if the home faces East. East is associated with springtime and new growth. Richard Craze summarizes the best location for any home in the light of such data:

> Ideally you would have low hills to the west to lessen the power of the White Tiger and good sloping Dragon hills to the east to get as much wise Ch'i as possible flowing down towards the house. To the south there should be a flat open view, preferably with a stream, to encourage all that invigorating Ch'i. And to the north more hills – even mountains – to protect and nurture.[38]

The Dragon is the left-hand side when looking out of a home, not facing it. The Green Dragon should always be a little higher than, and predominant over, the White Tiger in order to keep it in check, so high hills, or forests to the East and low hills or treeless terrain to the West are important in maintaining the harmony of energies. Additionally, there can be good, auspicious *ch'i/qi*, which is called *sheng ch'i/qi*, or bad, inauspicious *ch'i/qi*, called *shar ch'i/qi*. The former is known as the dragon's cosmic breath, and the latter the dragon's killing breath. Simple devices such as wind chimes or a mirror surrounded by the *Pa-kua/Bagua* are used to deflect any adverse energies.

Kwok Man-ho and Joanne O'Brien note the interesting case of the building of the greatest banks in Hong Kong according to *feng-shui* praxis. When the Hong Kong and Shanghai Bank was built in Hong Kong, it faced North, was in a favourable position according to *feng-shui* experts, and was the tallest building in the city. The Bank of China also intended to build a bank nearby, but waited until the Hong Kong and Shanghai Bank was finished. Then, they built their bank taller and in such a way that adverse *feng-shui* would affect the business of the Hong Kong and Shanghai Bank. Kwok Man-ho and Joanne O'Brien take up the tale of rivalry in the following words:

> The construction of the bank also adversely affected the feng shui of other nearby businesses – the reflective windows of the Bank of China turned bad fortune back on to its neighbours and the sharp corners of the buildings acted like daggers, slicing through neighbouring businesses. To avert further bad luck, and to protect clients and staff, the managing directors of neighbouring office blocks hung ba-gua mirrors or small tridents on the outside walls of their offices to stave off the ill-effects of the sharp corners. A third office block, known as the Central Plaza, has been built on Honk Kong Island – it is the tallest building in the area, and has symbolic financial dominance over all the surrounding businesses.[39]

The machinations of the bankers illustrate rather well the interconnectedness of energies that underpins the theory of *feng-shui* – albeit here, that it was used in the context of economic skulduggery.

Today, *feng-shui* is becoming popular in the West, where home designers ascertain the best lay-out of a room, the right situation for a study, a bedroom, a kitchen and so on, and also the best places in which to put furniture. The layout of a garden, especially, is becoming influenced by the principles of *feng-shui*. Michael Page writes sensitively of the traditional plan of a *feng-shui* home and garden:

> A house or a room is like a body, having its own metabolism. Its occupants are its organs, to be nourished by a healthy and balanced flow of ch'i. Traditional houses ... were built around a central court: it was believed that, no matter how far from the country, the residents should never lose touch with the elemental universe. So they kept Nature just outside in the central courtyard, where there would be rocks, bonsai and water. The garden was seen as a reflection of the macrocosm, so that every opportunity was taken to encourage the interplay of yin and yang.[40]

In the ancient texts a house might be described as "Baby dragon looking at its mother" – a most auspicious place, with excellent influences. Conversely, the site might be "Tiger in waiting" – not the place where one would want to live or build a temple.

At its heart, *feng-shui* seeks to align the individual self, the home, room, or garden with the energies of the land. It is underpinned by the belief of creating harmony with the environment, so that the individual's energies flow with those of the land and, hence, with cosmic changes. Even deeper, it harmonizes the microcosm of Earth, the macrocosm of Heaven, and humanity as the middle element between the two. While expert practices are needed to facilitate such harmony, the ideal is no different from the ancient ideas of Lao-tzu/Laozi and Chuang-tzu/Zhuangzi of spontaneous flow between the self and nature, of a oneness between the self and *Tao* and its expressions as *Te*. Ultimately, *feng-shui* is concerned with the harmonious interrelation of, and concomitant changing interaction with, the ten thousand things in all existence. Where *ch'i/qi* runs freely just below the surface of the earth, nature responds well, with verdant grass, lush vegetation and large numbers of trees. When humankind destroys what is natural, the energy goes much deeper, deserting the surface of the earth, and leaving it a desert.

The contours of energies and rhythms that pulsate in the earth are reflected in Chinese landscape painting, as well as gardens. Jean Cooper points out that the energy of *ch'i/qi* pervades the end product of all the arts – music, painting, poetry or landscape gardening. All remain true to nature, she says: "In a well-designed garden", for example, "it should be difficult to distinguish between the work of man and Nature."[41] Chinese art, therefore, usually reflects the simplicity of nature and, especially, space. The Chinese were the inventors of watercolour painting, and watercolours are the best medium for achieving a fluidity that permits a certain unity in the painting. Chinese painting is concerned with capturing the energies of a scene – the *ch'i/qi* and the balances of *yin* and *yang*. Outward forms are less important; it is the *essence* of the subject matter that is the focus. The inter-relation of all things in life means that a bird or butterfly in a painting is seen as part of the unity of the whole and not in isolation. Space is essential: it suggests infinity, and sets the subject matter against such a philosophical backdrop through intentional statement. Two-thirds of a Chinese painting is usually given over to space, while the remaining third contains the subject matter. The space is usually above the subject, suggesting the vastness of Heaven. John Blofeld described the influence of Taoism in paintings admirably in the following words:

> The voidness of the non-void is hinted at by vague expanses of ocean, snow, cloud and mist, and by solid objects which seem just on the point of emerging from or melting into the void. Man's triviality in relation to heaven's vastness is suggested by rolling landscapes in which mortals and their dwellings appear insignificant against the grandeur of their surroundings. Mountains appear cloud-like; clouds resemble mountains; rocks and tree trunks seem strangely animated, as though peering at the viewer or smiling; or the contours of men and animals are so united with those of natural objects that they appear to be of a single substance.[42]

In gardens, too, the changing rhythms of light in the day, of the seasons, of the weather are reflected in the freedom and softness of space, simplicity and curves. The mind is moved forward into space and infinity by carefully positioned boulders, shrubs and trees. The features of the wider landscape – mountains, valleys, rivers, lakes – are portrayed in the microcosm of the garden. Mountains are represented by rocks surrounded by a lake or pool of water – the *yang* of Heaven surrounded by the *yin* of Earth. Water is particularly symbolic of the weakness and adaptability that overcomes the hard and the rigid.

The art of *feng-shui* is one that harmonizes human life into its environment – an aim that is perhaps all too exigent given today's concerns for the state of our planet. In Eva Wong's words: "By cultivating intuition and sensitivity to the environment, we can become aware of the energy that flows through the universe and catch a glimpse of the fleeting moments of transformations and the underlying reality of all things."[43] Whether or not we would want to adopt the practices of *feng-shui* into our personal lives, engendering deeper sensitivities to the environment on individual levels is surely the way forward to regaining respect for the planet on which each individual lives for such a very short period of time. Gill Hale reiterates:

> We have reached a stage where the human race has become capable of the most amazing feats on the one hand and the most amazing follies on the other. We have the capacity to cure hereditary diseases but also to let genetically-engineered organisms loose into the environment in the most dangerous form of warfare humankind has ever known. We send people into space to collect information never dreamed of half a century ago, yet at the same time we allow the planet we inhabit to become increasingly polluted and less able to sustain the life forms on which we depend for our survival.[44]

If Taoism can offer anything to the twenty-first century, it is certainly the ideas of balance and harmony in the many dimensions of human existence. It offers, too, the idea of an interrelatedness in life's energies that makes one action, one thought, part of a wider matrix. It calls for stillness and calm in the midst of activity in life.

The influence of Taoism is considerable today. Robinet said that "Taoism is a complete world and its history is a complete human history, containing everything since the emergence of human beings on earth and their desire for transcendence. It is a history that through the centuries has preserved a single identity".[45] It is perhaps a travesty to such Taoist identity that practices like T'ai Chi Ch'üan/Taijiquan, so prevalent in the West today, have been separated in Western minds from the richness of their Taoist roots, particularly since such practices are informed by much ancient and very valuable philosophy. As to its philosophy *per se*, while we might want to reject the mythological traditions, there is much that is gentle and wise in the words of Lao-tzu/Laozi and Chuang-tzu/Zhuangzi that we can take with us on the day-to-day journey through life. Clarke has a very positive view of the present impact of Taoism in the West. He believes, "we cannot easily ignore the fact that Daoism is emerging as a reticent yet increasingly visible player in contemporary culture, and has become a site of cultural transformation and spiritual creativity that is beginning to operate globally at many levels".[46] Taoism's timeless philosophy still has much to offer, perhaps because it forges fluid links between humankind and nature, and accepts change as a facet of existence and not something to be resisted. It is interesting that the religious identity of Taoism is reaffirming itself in China, and the deep-rooted facets of the Chinese psyche are re-emerging.

Notes

Introduction

1. Lama Anagarika Govinda, *The Inner Structure of the I Ching: The Book of Transformations* (Tokyo and New York: Weatherhill, 1981), p. 10.
2. James R. Ware, translator and ed., *Alchemy, Medicine, & Religion in the China of A.D. 320: The Nei P'ien of Ko Hung (Pao-p'u-tzu)* (New York: Dover Publications, 1982, first published 1966), p. 25.
3. Charles A. Moore in the Foreword to Wing-tsit Chan, *A Source Book in Chinese Philosophy* (Princeton, New Jersey: Princeton University Press and London: Oxford University Press, 1963), p. vii.
4. *Peoples Republic of China: Administrative Atlas* (Washington D.C.: Central Intelligence Agency, 1975), pp. 46–7.

Chapter 1   The Origins of Taosim: Ancient China

1. Julia Ching, *Chinese Religions* (Basingstoke, Hampshire and London: The Macmillan Press, 1993), p. 85
2. Joseph Wu, "Taoism" in Donald H. Bishop (ed.), *Chinese Thought: An introduction* (Delhi: Motilal Banarsidass, 2001, first published 1985), p. 39.
3. *Ibid.*, p. 55.
4. Donald H. Bishop, "Introduction" in Bishop (ed.), *Chinese Thought, ibid.*, p. 165.
5. Isabelle Robinet, *Taoism: Growth of a religion* translated from French by Phyllis Brooks (Stanford, California: Stanford University Press, 1997, first published as *Histoire du Taoïsme des origines au XIVe siècle*, in 1992), p. 1.
6. *Ibid.*, pp. 2–3.
7. Translator Wu Yao-yü, *The Taoist Tradition in Chinese Thought*, translated by Laurence G. Thompson, edited by Gary Seaman. *San Chiao Li Ts'e, Part 1* (Los Angeles: Ethnographics Press, University of Southern California, 1991), pp. 1–2.
8. Robert E. Allinson, "An Overview of the Chinese Mind" in Robert E. Allinson (ed.), *Understanding the Chinese Mind: The philosophical roots* (Oxford, New York and Hong Kong: Oxford University Press, 1989), p. 15.
9. Michael Saso, *Blue Dragon White Tiger: Taoist rites of passage* (Washington, D.C.: The Taoist Center, 1990), p. 1.
10. Robinet, *Taoism*, p. 261.
11. *Ibid.*, p. 20.
12. Timothy H. Barrett, *Taoism under the T'ang: Religion and empire during the Golden Age of Chinese history* (London: Wellsweep, 1996), p. 17.

13 Buddhism, having been introduced from India, was a very different phenomenon.
14 Derk Bodde, *Essays on Chinese Civilization*, edited and introduced by Charles Le Blanc and Dorothy Borei (Princeton, New Jersey and Guilford, Surrey: Princeton University Press, 1981), p. 133.
15 Bodde, "Dominant Ideas in the Formation of the Chinese Culture" in Bodde, *Essays on Chinese Civilization*, p. 132.
16 Bodde, "Harmony and Conflict in Chinese Philosophy", *ibid.*, pp. 262–3.
17 Marcel Granet, *The Religion of the Chinese People*, translated and edited by Maurice Freedman (Oxford: Basil Blackwell, 1975), p. 46.
18 David N. Keightley, "Late Shang Divination: The Magico-Religious Legacy" in Henry Rosemont Jr., (ed.), *Explorations in Early Chinese Cosmology*. Journal of the American Academy of Religion Studies vol. 50 no. 2 (Chicago, California: Scholars Press), p. 25.
19 Allinson, "An Overview of the Chinese Mind", p. 8.
20 Martin Palmer, *The Elements of Taoism* (Shaftesbury, Dorset and Rockport, Massachusetts: Element, 1991), p. 14.
21 The word "shaman" may have some connection with the Sanskrit word *sramana*, a word that is associated with ascetic wanderers, and with the Chinese term *hsien-men/xianmen*. See Joseph Needham, *Science and Civilization in China, Vol. 2: History of scientific thought* (Cambridge: Cambridge University Press, 1956), p. 133.
22 Palmer, *The Elements of Taoism*, pp. 17–18.
23 The synonymy between shamans and sorcerers is variously asserted and denied. Eva Wong considers them to be separate because the shaman invites a spirit to enter his or her body at will, whereas sorcerers are possessed by the spirit. Eva Wong, *The Shambhala Guide to Taoism* (Boston and London: Shambhala, 1997), pp. 14–15.
24 Ching, *Chinese Religions*, p. 49.
25 Bishop, "Introduction" in Bishop (ed.), *Chinese Thought*, p. 174.
26 Bodde, "Dominant Ideas in the Formation of Chinese Culture", p. 133.
27 See Conrad Schirokauer, *A Brief History of Chinese Civilization* (San Diego, New York, Chicago, Austin, Washington, D.C., London, Sydney, Tokyo, Toronto: Harcourt Brace, 1991), p. 5.
28 Kwang-chih Chang, *Shang Civilization* (New Haven and London: Yale University Press, 1980), pp. 284–5.
29 *Ibid.*, p. 338.
30 *Ibid.*, p. 339.
31 *Ibid.*, p. 340.
32 *Ibid.*, p. 349.
33 *Ibid.*, p. 361.
34 John Blofeld, *Taoism: The quest for immortality* (London, Boston, Sydney, Wellington: Unwin, 1989, first published 1979), p. 19.
35 The material relating to the Shang is to be found in *Yin-pen-chi/Yinbenji*, an important chapter in the *Shih Chi/Shiji* of Ssu-ma Ch'ien/Sima Qian.
36 Joseph Needham, *Science and Civilisation in China, Vol. 1: Introductory orientations* (Cambridge, New York, New Rochelle, Melbourne, Sydney: Cambridge University Press, 1988 reprint of 1961 edn, first published 1954), p. 89.
37 *Ibid.*, p. 84.
38 Sarah Allan, *The Shape of the Turtle: Myth, art and cosmos in early China* (Albany, New York: State University of New York Press, 1991), p. 1.
39 For the full range of topics used, see David N. Keightley, "Shang Oracle-Bone Inscriptions" in Edward L. Shaughnessy (ed.), *New Sources of Early Chinese History: An introduction to the reading*

40 Allan, *The Shape of the Turtle*, p. 113.
41 Keightley, "Late Shang Divination", pp. 13–14.
42 *Ibid.*, p. 20.
43 Richard J. Smith, *Fortune-Tellers and Philosophers: Divination in traditional Chinese society* (Boulder, San Francisco, Oxford: Westview Press, 1991), p. 14.
44 Keightley, "Shang Oracle-Bone Inscriptions", p. 53.
45 Keightley, "Late Shang Divination", p. 22.
46 *Ibid.*, p. 16.
47 *Ibid.*, p. 19.
48 Schirokauer, *A Brief History of Chinese Civilization*, p. 12.
49 Allan, *The Shape of the Turtle*, p. 46.
50 Donald Bishop, "Chinese Thought before Confucius" in Bishop (ed.), *Chinese Thought*, p. 7.
51 *Ibid.*
52 See Allan, *The Shape of the Turtle*, p. 20.
53 Henri Maspero, *Taoism and Chinese Religion*, translated by Frank A. Kierman, Jr. (Amherst: University of Massachusetts Press, 1981, first published as *Le Taoïsme et les religions chinoises* in 1971), p. 12.
54 *Ibid.*, p. 4.
55 D. Howard Smith, *Chinese Religions* (New York, Chicago, San Francisco: Holt, Rinehart and Winston, 1970 reprint of 1968 edn), p. 4.
56 Henri Maspero, *China in Antiquity*, translated by Frank A. Kierman, Jr. (Folkestone, Kent: Dawson, 1978, first published in 1927 as *La Chine Antique*), p. 162.
57 Needham, *Science and Civilization, Vol 2*, p. 134.
58 Maspero, *China in Antiquity*. p. 132.
59 *Ibid.*, p. 133.
60 Marcel Granet from *Festivals and Songs of Ancient China* translated by E. D. Edwards in Laurence G. Thompson (ed.), *The Chinese Way in Religion* (Belmont, California: Wadsworth Publishing Company, 1973), p. 28.
61 Peter Hessler, "The New Story of China's Ancient Past" in *National Geographic* (Washington D.C.: National Geographic Society, July, 2003), p. 64.
62 *Ibid.*, p. 71.
63 See Keightley, "Late Shang Divination", p. 13.
64 *Ibid.*, p. 26.
65 Edward L. Shaugnessy, "Western Zhou Bronze Inscriptions" in Shaughnessy (ed.), *New Sources of Early Chinese History*, p. 84.
66 Gilbert L. Mattos, "Eastern Zhou Bronze Inscritions" in Shaughnessy (ed.), *New Sources of Early Chinese History, ibid.*, p. 86.
67 *Ibid.*, p. 88.
68 Named after the chronicle of these years, the *Spring and Autumn Annals*.
69 Needham, *Science and Civilization in China, Vol. 1*, p. 96.
70 Maspero, *Taoism and Chinese Religion*, p. 16.
71 Smith, *Chinese Religions*, p. 80.
72 John S. Major, "Shang-ti" in Mircea Eliade (ed.), *Encyclopedia of Religion* (hereafter *ER*, New York and London: Macmillan Publishing Company, 1987), vol. 13, p. 223.
73 *Ibid.*, pp. 223–4.
74 *Shu*: Kao Tsung 3, translator Smith, *Chinese Religions*, page 19. It is easy to see from words such

as these how a later Buddhist doctrine of *karma* could be incorporated into the Chinese psyche.

75 The prevalence of an ongoing belief in demons, for example, is reflected in more recent fears. When Mildred Cable and Francesca French were preparing for an expedition into the Gobi Desert in the early part of the last century, the local people of then Kiayükwan were terrified of the demons of the desert. "They call out", said one young man of the desert demons, "just as a man would shout if he wanted help, but those who turn away from the track to answer them never find anyone, and the next call is always a little farther from the path, for those voices will lead a man on, but they will never call him back to the right way." Mildred Cable with Francesca French, *The Gobi Desert* (London: Landsborough Publications, 1958, first published 1943), p. 12.

76 Female *wu* were still prevalent in the second century when they were employed in the performance of ancestral sacrifices. By the end of the T'ang/Tang dynasty, however, they no longer featured in state praxis and became a persecuted, though persistent, sector of social and religious life, branching out into all sorts of practices.

77 Smith, *Fortune-Tellers and Philosophers*, pp. 17–18.

78 *Ibid.*, p. 18.

79 The year was based on the cycles of the moon, with the addition of an extra lunar period from time to time in order to harmonize with the solar year.

80 Maspero, *China in Antiquity*, p. 107.

81 Matthias Eder, *Chinese Religion*, Asian Folklore Studies Mongraph no. 6 (Tokyo: The Society for Asian Folklore, 1973), p. 19.

82 *Ibid.*, p. 37.

83 Smith, *Chinese Religions*, p. 33.

84 Confucius *Analects* 16:9 translator Deborah Sommer (ed.), *Chinese Religion: An anthology of sources* (New York and Oxford: Oxford University Press, 1995), p. 43.

85 *Ibid.*, 14:29, translator Sommer, p. 43.

86 *Ibid.*, 15:20, translator Sommer, p. 44.

87 Herrlee G. Creel, *Chinese Thought: From Confucius to Mao Tsê-Tung* (London: Methuen, 1962, first published 1954), p. 43.

88 Smith, *Chinese Religions*, p. 42.

89 Creel, *Chinese Thought*, p. 52.

90 Palmer, *The Elements of Taoism*, p. 71.

Chapter 2 *The Interconnected Cosmos: The I Ching/Yijing*

1 Richard Wilhelm, translator, *I Ching or Book of Changes*, translated into English by Cary F. Baynes (London: Penguin, Arkana, 1989 third edn, first published 1950).

2 *Ibid.*, p. xlvii.

3 Fung Yu-lan, *A History of Chinese Philosophy, Vol. 2: The period of classical learning (from the second century B.C. to the twentieth century A.D.)*, translated by Derk Bodde (Princeton: Princeton University Press, 1983 reprint, first published in English in 1953, first published in Chinese 1934), pp. 88–9.

4 John Blofeld, translator, *I Ching: The Book of Change* (London, Sydney, Wellington: Unwin Paperbacks), translator's *Foreword*, p. 7.

5 See Wilhelm, *I Ching or Book of Changes*, p. 4.

6 Deborah Sommer (ed.), *Chinese Religion: An anthology of sources* (New York and Oxford: Oxford University Press, 1995), p. 4.

7. Fritjof Capra, *The Tao of Physics: An exploration of the parallels between modern physics and eastern mysticism* (1990 reprint of 1983 edn, first published 1975), p. 121.
8. Fung Yu-lan, *A History of Chinese Philosophy, Vol. 1: The period of the philosophers (from the beginnings to circa 100 B.C.)*, translated by Derk Bodde (Princeton, New Jersey: Princeton University Press, 1983 reprint of second English edn 1952, first published in Chinese in 1931), p. 390.
9. Carl Jung, from the *Foreword*, Wilhelm, *I Ching or Book of Changes*, p. xxxix.
10. Jou, Tsung Hwa, *The Tao of I Ching: Way to divination* (Scottsdale, AZ: Tai Chi Foundation, 2000 reprint of 1983 edn), p. 8.
11. *Ta-chuan/Dazhuan* 8:1, translator Wilhelm, *I Ching or Book of Changes*, p. 304.
12. Richard J. Smith, *Fortune-tellers and Philosophers: Divination in traditional Chinese society* (Boulder, San Francisco, Oxford: Westview Press, 1991), p. 15.
13. Richard Rutt, *The Book of Changes (Zhouyi): A Bronze Age Document translated with introduction and notes*. Durham East-Asia Series no. 1 (London: RoutledgeCurzon, 2002 reprint of 1996 edn), pp. 30–1.
14. Edward L. Shaughnessy, "I ching", in Michael Loewe (ed.), *Early Chinese Texts: A bibliographical guide* (Berkeley, California: The Society for the Study of Early China, and The Institute of East Asian Studies, University of California, 1993), p. 218.
15. Rutt, *The Book of Changes (Zhouyi)*, *passim*.
16. *Ibid.*, p. 24.
17. *Shuo-kua/Shuogua* 1:1, translator Wilhelm, *I Ching or Book of Changes*, p. 262.
18. In other words he took some ideas from his own body and others from things extraneous to his body.
19. *Ta-chuan/Dazhuan* 2:1, translator Wilhelm, *I Ching or Book of Changes*, p. 328.
20. Wilhelm, *I Ching or Book of Changes*, p. liii.
21. Shaughnessy, "I ching", p. 219.
22. Rutt, *The Book of Changes (Zhouyi)*, p. 29.
23. *Ibid.*, p. 34.
24. Henri Maspero, *Taoism and Chinese Religion*, translated from French by Frank A. Kierman, Jr. (Amherst: The University of Massachusetts Press, 1981, first published 1971 as *Le Taoïsme et les religions chinoises*), p. 59.
25. Rutt, *The Book of Changes (Zhouyi)*, p. 45.
26. *Ibid.*
27. Hellmut Wilhelm, *Change: Eight lectures on the I Ching*, translated from German by Cary F. Baynes (London: Routledge & Kegan Paul, 1975 reprint of 1961 edn, first German edn 1944), p. 67.
28. Rutt, *The Book of Changes (Zhouyi)*, p. 46.
29. *Ibid.*, p. 45.
30. Xinzhong Yao and Helene McMurtrie, "History and Wisdom of The Book of Changes: New Scholarship and Richard Rutt's Translation", *Journal of Contemporary Religion*, 14 (1999), p. 137.
31. For the ways in which the *I Ching/Yijing* was differently interpreted by eminent Sung/Song thinkers see Kidder Smith Jr., Peter K. Bol, Joseph A. Adler and Don J. Wyatt, *Sung Dynasty Uses of the I Ching* (Princeton, New Jersey: Princeton University Press, 1990), *passim*.
32. Martin Palmer, Joanne O'Brien and Kwok Man Ho, *The Fortune Teller's I Ching* (London: Wordsworth Editions, 1993, first published 1986, also published in 1989 as *The Contemporary I Ching*), pp. 28–9.
33. Hellmut Willhelm, *Change*, p. 68.
34. Thomas Cleary, translator, in Cheng Yi, *The Tao of Organization: The I Ching for group dynamics* (Boston, Massachusetts and London: Shambhala, 1995 reprint of 1988 edn), p. 217.
35. *Ibid.*, p. 218.

36 *Ibid.*, p. 217.
37 Smith, *Fortune-tellers and Philosophers*, p. 108.
38 Blofeld, *I Ching*, pp. 31–2.
39 Thomas Cleary, translator, *The Taoist I Ching* (Boston, Massachusetts and London: Shambhala, 1986), p. 7.
40 Hellmut Wilhelm, *Change*, p. 38.
41 A particularly good analysis of the concept of change in the "Great Treatise" appended to the *I Ching/Yijing* can be found in an article by Gerald Swanson, "The Concept of Change in the Great Treatise", in Henry Rosemont, Jr. (ed.), *Explorations in Early Chinese Cosmology*, Journal of the American Academy of Religion Studies, vol. 50 no. 2 (Chicago, California: Scholars Press, 1984), pp. 67–93.
42 Hellmut Wilhelm, *Heaven, Earth and Man in the Book of Changes* (Seattle: University of Washington Press, 1977), p. 100.
43 For an altogether different origin of the word as "lizard", and the association of the lizard's mobility and changeability with transformation and change, as well as wider meanings of *i/yi* in antiquity, see Hellmut Wilhelm, *Change*, p. 14.
44 Stephen Karcher, *Total I Ching: Myths for change* (London: Time Warner Books, 2003), p. ix.
45 Blofeld, *I Ching*, p. 39.
46 Hellmut Wilhelm, *Change*, p. 23.
47 Lama Anagarika Govinda, *The Inner Structure of the I Ching: The Book of Transformations* (Tokyo and New York: John Weatherhill in association with Wheelwright Press, San Francisco, 1981), p. 26.
48 Wu Yao-yü, *The Taoist Tradition in Chinese Thought*, translated by Laurence G. Thompson, edited by Gary Seaman. *San Chiao Li Ts'ê, Part 2* (Los Angeles: Ethnographics Press, University of California, 1991), p. 26.
49 Wilhelm, *I Ching or Book of Changes*, p. 283.
50 *Ibid.*, p. lv.
51 *Ta-chuan/Dazhuan* 6:1, translator Wilhelm, *ibid.*, p. 301.
52 Rutt, *The Book of Changes (Zhouyi)*, p. 88.
53 See Hellmut Wilhelm, *Change*, p. 33.
54 See Joseph Needham, *Science and Civilization in China, Vol. 2: History of scientific thought* (Cambridge: Cambridge University Press, 1956), p. 313, and Lama Anagarika Govinda, *The Inner Structure of the I Ching*, pp. 46–7.
55 *Shuo-kua/Shuogua* 2:11.
56 Smith, *Fortune-Tellers and Philosophers*, p. 101.
57 *Shuo-kua/Shuogua* 2:3, translator Wilhelm, *I Ching or Book of Changes*, p. 265. See also verses 4 and 6, and Wilhelm's comments on these verses.
58 Adapted from Cleary, *The Taoist I Ching*, p. 22.
59 Translator Cleary, *ibid.*, p. 11.
60 Cleary, *ibid.*
61 Actually the word "*Ch'ien/Qian*" is exclusive to the *I Ching/Yijing* and its *Appendices*; it occurs nowhere else in the Chinese language.
62 *Ta-chuan/Dazhuan* 2:3, translator Wilhelm, *I Ching or Book of Changes*, pp. 322–3.
63 Wilhelm, *ibid.*, p. lvi.
64 See Rutt, *The Book of Changes (Zhouyi)*, pp. 97–8.
65 See Shaughnessy, "I ching", p. 217.
66 Xinzhong Yao and McMurtrie, "History and Wisdom of the *Book of Changes*", p. 135.
67 Rutt, *The Book of Changes (Zhouyi)*, p. 122.

68 Karcher, *Total I Ching*, p. xi.
69 Rutt, *The Book of Changes (Zhouyi)*, p. 87.
70 *Ibid.*
71 A word that may have some connection with pigs, see Rutt, *The Book of Changes (Zhouyi)*, pp. 122–3.
72 *Ibid.*, p. 123.
73 For further explanation and a full table of these hexagrams, see Shaughnessy, "I ching", pp. 17–18 and 28–9.
74 Interestingly, the only one of the *Ten Wings* to be incorporated in the text is the *Hsi-tz'u/Xici*, the "Appended Statements".
75 Karcher, *Total I Ching*, pp. 54–64.
76 Jung in Wilhelm, *I Ching or Book of Changes*, p. xxiv.
77 Blofeld, *I Ching*, p. 68.
78 Rutt, *The Book of Changes (Zhouyi)*, p. 166.
79 For a fuller description of the lines of hexagrams see Smith, *Fortune-Tellers and Philosophers*, pp. 99–100.
80 See Smith, *ibid.*, for a fuller discussion of the relationships between lines.
81 The six lines have also been applied to the human body and the head, for example, see Jou, *The Tao of I Ching*, pp. 50–4.
82 Cleary, *The Tao of Organization*, p. xii.
83 See Cleary, *ibid.*
84 Cheng Yi, translator Cleary, *ibid.*, p. xvii.
85 Within a hexagram there are also "ruling" lines. The "governing" ruler is the one that sets the whole tone of the hexagram. It is usually in the fifth place, but not always. There is also a "constituting" ruler to add meaning to the hexagram. Sometimes, both governing and constituting ruling lines are in the same place – a most auspicious and favourable occurrence. It is particularly when either ruling line is a moving one that their importance is considerable. See Smith, *Fortune-Tellers and Philosophers*, pp. 100–1.
86 *Achillea sibirica*, a Chinese yarrow that was regarded as being particularly sacred. See Richard Herne, *Magick, Shamanism & Taoism: The I Ching in ritual and meditation* (St Paul, Minnesota: Llewellyn Publications, 2001), p. 16. It is "a common aromatic perennial herb of the Compositae family, related to chamomile, chrysanthemum, tarragon and ladslove" according to Rutt, *The Book of Changes (Zhouyi)*, pp. 151–2.
87 For a full account of how this is done, see Wilhelm, *I Ching or Book of Changes*, pp. 311 and 721–2, Jou, *The Tao of I Ching*, pp. 62–9, and Rutt, *ibid.*, pp. 158–66.
88 For detailed historical accounts of *I Ching/Yijing* divination by individuals, see Smith, *Fortune-Tellers and Philosophers*, pp. 112–17.
89 Palmer, O'Brien and Kwok Man Ho, *The Fortune Teller's I Ching*, pp. 37–8.
90 Rutt, *The Book of Changes (Zhouyi)*, p. 166.
91 However, Rutt is definitive that the inscribed side (heads) is *yin* and the reverse (tails) is *yang*, *ibid.*, p. 167.
92 See Palmer, O'Brien and Kwok Man Ho, *The Fortune Teller's I Ching*, pp. 40–4.
93 *Ibid.*, p. 41.
94 See Blofeld, *I Ching*, pp. 61–2 and 79–80, and Jou, *The Tao of I Ching*, pp. 62–9.
95 Iulian K. Shchutskii, *Researches on the I Ching*, translated by William L. MacDonald and Tsuyoshi Hasegawa with Hellmut Wilhelm (Princeton: Princeton University Press, 1979, first published in Britain 1980, London: Routledge and Kegan Paul), p. 226.
96 Wilhelm, *I Ching or Book of Changes*, p. lvii.

97 Helmutt Wilhelm, *Heaven, Earth and Man in the Book of Changes: Seven Eranos lectures* (Seattle and London: University of Washington Press, 1977), p. 31.
98 Raymond Van Over (ed.), *I Ching*. Based on the translation by James Legge. New York, Scarborough Ontario and London: Mentor, 1971), p. 127.
99 Blofeld, *I Ching*, p. 24.
100 Shchutskii, *Researches on the I Ching*, p. 221.
101 *Ibid.*, p. 228.
102 Smith, *Fortune-Tellers and Philosophers*, p. 120.
103 *Ibid.*, p. 121.
104 Liu I-ming/ Liu Yiming, *The Book of Balance and Harmony*, translator Cleary, *The Taoist I Ching*, p. 17.
105 Needham, *Science and Civilization in China, Vol. 2*, p. 337.
106 *Ibid.*, p. 336.
107 Raymond Van Over, *I Ching*, p. 14.
108 Hellmut Wilhelm, *Change*, p. 9.

Chapter 3 *Creative Forces: Yin and Yang and the Five Agents*

1 Laurence G. Thompson, *Chinese Religion: An Introduction* (Belmont, California: Wadsworth Publishing Company, 1989 reprint of 1979 edn), p. 3.
2 Jean C. Cooper, *Taoism: The Way of the mystic* (Wellingborough, Northamptonshire: Crucible, 1990 revised edn, first published 1972), p. 35.
3 Sarah Allan, *The Shape of the Turtle: Myth, art, and cosmos in early China* (Albany, New York: State University of New York Press, 1991), p. 17.
4 *Ibid.*, p. 73.
5 *Ibid.*, p. 176.
6 See Richard Wilhelm, *I Ching or Book of Changes*, translated from German by Cary F. Baynes (London: Arkana, 1989 first published in Great Britain in 1951), p. lvi.
7 Henri Maspero, *China in Antiquity*, translated by Frank A. Kierman Jr. (London: Dawson, 1978. Originally published in French as *La Chine Antique*, vol. 4 of *Histoire du Monde*, Paris 1927), pp. 165–6.
8 See Julian F. Pas in cooperation with Man Kam Leung, *Historical Dictionary of Taoism* (Lanham, Middlesex and London: The Scarecrow Press, 1998), pp. 371–2.
9 Fung Yu-lan, *A History of Chinese Philosophy, Vol. 2: The period of classical learning (from the second century B.C. to the twentieth century A.D.)*, translated by Derk Bodde (Princeton, New Jersey: Princeton University Press, 1983 reprint, first published in English in 1953. First published in Chinese in 1934), p. 88.
10 A. C. Graham, *Yin-Yang and the Nature of Correlative Thinking*. Occasional Paper and Monograph Series no. 6 (Singapore: The Institute of East Asian Philosophies, 1989 reprint of 1986 edn), p. 73.
11 See Fung Yu-lan, *A History of Chinese Philosophy, Vol. 1: The period of the philosophers (from the beginnings to circa 100 B.C.)*, translated by Derk Bodde (Princeton, New Jersey: Princeton University Press, 1983 reprint of second English edn 1952), p. 163.
12 See Vitaly A. Rubin, "The Concepts of *Wu-Hsing* and *Yin-Yang*", *Journal of Chinese Philosophy*, 17 (1982), pp. 131–58.
13 See Graham, *Yin-Yang and the Nature of Correlative Thinking*, pp. 12–13.
14 See Fung Yu-lan, *A History of Chinese Philosophy, Vol. 2*, p. 9.
15 Translator Fung Yu-lan, *A History of Chinese Philosophy, Vol. 1*, p. 160.

16 For a full account of the beliefs of Tung Chung-shu/Dong Zhongshu, and Chu Hsi/Zhu Xi, see Henri Maspero, *Taoism and Chinese Religion*, translated by Frank A. Kierman, Jr. (Amherst: The University of Massachusetts Press, 1981. Originally published as *Le Taoïsme et les religions chinoises*, 1971), pp. 71–4.
17 Cooper, *Taoism*, p. 40.
18 From Liu I-ming/Liu Yiming, *Eight Elements of the Spiritual House*, translator Thomas Cleary, *The Taoist I Ching* (Boston, Massachusetts and London: Shambhala, 1986), p. 20.
19 From Huang Yüan-ch'i/Huang Yuanqi, *Annals of the Hall of Blissful Development*, translator Cleary, *ibid.*, pp. 15–16.
20 From Liu I-ming/Liu Yiming, *Eight Elements of the Spiritual House*, translator Cleary, *ibid.*, p. 20.
21 A term favoured by Rubin, "The Concepts of *Wu-Hsing* and *Yin-Yang*", p. 141.
22 *Tao Te Ching/Daodejing* 2.
23 Chung-Ying Cheng, "Chinese Metaphysics as Non-metaphysics: Confucian and Taoist Insights into the Nature of Reality", in Robert Allinson (ed.), *Understanding the Chinese Mind: The philosophical roots* (Oxford, New York and Hong Kong: Oxford University Press, 1989), p. 177.
24 Translator Fung Yu-lan, *A Short History of Chinese Philosophy* (London: Collier Macmillan and New York: The Free Press, 1948), p. 134.
25 Fritjof Capra, *The Tao of Physics: An exploration of the parallels bewteen modern physics and eastern mysticism* (London: Flamingo, 1990 impression of 1983 edn, first published 1975), p. 157.
26 *Tao Te Ching/Daodejing* 36.
27 Jean Cooper, *Yin and Yang: The Taoist harmony of opposites* (Wellingborough, Northamptonshire: The Aquarian Press, 1981), p. 17.
28 *Tao Te Ching/Daodejing* 22.
29 Derk Bodde, *Essays on Chinese Civilization*, edited and translated by Charles Le Blanc and Dorothy Borei (Princeton, New Jersey: Princeton University Press, 1981), p. 239.
30 Isabelle Robinet, *Taoism: Growth of a religion*, translated from French by Phyllis Brooks (Stanford, California: Stanford University Press, 1997, first published in Paris, 1992 as *Histoire du Taoïsme des origine au XIVe siècle*), p. 10.
31 See Graham, *Yin-Yang and the Nature of Correlative Thinking*, pp. 27–8.
32 See Thompson, *Chinese Religion*, p. 32.
33 Bodde, *Essays on Chinese Civilization*, p. 279.
34 *Ibid.*, p. 280.
35 Stephen S. Teiser, "Introduction" in Donald S. Lopez, Jr., *Religions of China in Practice*. Princeton Readings in Religion (Princeton, New Jersey: Princeton University Press, 1996), p. 33.
36 Julian F. Pas, "Yin-yang Polarity: A Binocular Vision of the World", *Asian Thought and Society* 8 (1983), p. 199.
37 *Ibid.*, p. 189.
38 Chung-Ying Cheng, "Chinese Metaphysics as Non-metaphysics", p. 188.
39 *Ibid.*, pp. 188–9.
40 Examples here are "albino members of a species; beings that are part-animal, part-human; women who die before marriage and turn into ghosts receiving no care; people who die in unusual ways like suicide or on battlefields far from home; and people whose bodies fail to decompose or emit strange signs after death". See Teiser, "Introduction", p. 35.
41 Cooper, *Taoism*, p. 37.
42 *Huai-nan-tzu/Huainanzi* 3, translator Graham, *Yin-Yang and the Nature of Correlative Thinking*, p. 31.
43 *Ibid.*
44 Robinet, *Taoism*, pp. 8–9.

45 Fung Yu-lan, *A History of Chinese Philosophy*, Vol. 2, p. 131.
46 *Ibid.*, p. 132.
47 Cheng Xinnong, (ed.), *Chinese Acupuncture and Moxibustion* (Beijing: Foreign Languages Press, 1999 revised edn, first published 1987), p. 14.
48 From the *Yellow Emperor's Classic of Medicine*, translated by Mark Coyle, "The Interaction of Yin and Yang", in Patricia Buckley Ebrey (ed.), *Chinese Civilization and Society: A sourcebook* (New York: The Free Press and London: Collier Macmillan, 1981), p. 37.
49 See Graham, *Yin-Yang and the Nature of Correlative Thinking*, p. 15.
50 Maspero, *Taoism and Chinese Religion*, p. 254.
51 Robinet, *Taoism*, p. 14.
52 *Ibid.*, p. 9.
53 Moderation, harmony, equilibrium in human nature that reflects the same qualities in the universe.
54 Wing-tsit Chan, translator and compiler, *A Source Book in Chinese Philosophy* (Princeton, New Jersey: Princeton University Press, and London: Oxford University Press, 1963), p. 246.
55 Robinet, *Taoism*, p. 11.
56 See R. H. Mathews, *Mathew's Chinese–English Dictionary* (Cambridge, Massachusetts: Harvard University Press, Revised American Version 2000, first published 1931), pp. 409–10.
57 See Graham, *Yin-Yang and the Nature of Correlative Thinking*, p. 47.
58 *Ibid.*, p. 74.
59 Some, however, much prefer the translation "Elements". See, for example, Rubin, "The Concepts of *Wu-Hsing* and *Yin-Yang*", p. 132.
60 See Graham, *Yin-Yang and the Nature of Correlative Thinking*, pp. 84–5.
61 Richard J. Smith, *Fortune-tellers and Philosophers: Divination in traditional Chinese society* (Boulder, San Francisco, Oxford: Westview Press, 1991), p. 15.
62 Translator Fung Yu-lan, *A History of Chinese Philosophy*, Vol. 1, p. 163.
63 Rubin, "The Concepts of *Wu-Hsing* and *Yin-Yang*", p. 151.
64 *Ibid.*
65 Graham, *Yin-Yang and the Nature of Correlative Thinking*, p. 52.
66 Tung Chung-shu/Dong Zhongshu, *Ch'un-ch'iu/Chunqiu* 11: 3: 5, translator Fung Yu-lan, *A History of Chinese Philosophy*, Vol. 2, p. 21.
67 Robinet, *Taoism*, p. 11.
68 Allan, *The Shape of the Turtle*, p. 102.
69 *Ibid.*, p. 101.
70. Bodde, *Essays on Chinese Civilization*, p. 135.
71 In some texts, the organs are assigned differently – **Wood** spleen; **Fire** lungs; **Earth** heart; **Metal** liver; **Water** kidneys. See, for example, the order in the list given by Conrad Schirokauer, *A Brief History of Chinese Civilization* (San Diego, New York, Chicago, Austin, Washington, D.C., London, Sydney, Tokyo, Toronto: Harcourt Brace Gap College Publishers, 1991), p. 74, and Rubin, "The Concepts of *Wu-Hsing* and *Yin-Yang*", p. 136. The order in the chart in the present book is to be found in the *Huang-ti Nei-ching/Huangdi Neijing*, the prestigious medical *Yellow Emperor's Classic of Internal Medicine*, and is that accepted in modern Chinese medical practice.
72 See Fung Yu-lan, *A History of Chinese Philosophy*, Vol. 2, pp. 30–1.
73 Not all were enamoured by the extensive theories applied to the Five Agents. Wang Ch'ung/Wang Chong in the first century was one who applied rationalism to the theories of his day. In his essay *Wu-shih/Wushi The Nature of Things*, he pointed out that there were many anomalies in the Five Agents correlates. Animals associated with the Agents did not have the same characteristic power to overcome. Thus Water, for example, may overcome Fire, but the

rat, which is associated with Water, cannot chase away a horse associated with Fire. Nature, he showed, does not in fact support the Five Agent theory. Then, too, Chia K'uei/Jia Kui, also in the first century, pointed out that irregularity and not harmony characterized the heavens, and that the future could not be predicted by aligning oneself to the unbalanced macrocosm. A little later, Ch'ang Heng/Chang Heng suggested that the earth was round and not square, and that natural disasters were more to do with earthly irregularities than imbalances between Earth and Heaven. So we must not think that the Five Agents theory was unchallenged. Yet it passed into Chinese belief and practice and very much into Taoism.

74 Xinnong (ed.), *Chinese Acupuncture and Moxibustion*, p. 20.
75 *Ibid.*, p. 24.
76 Angus C. Graham, *Disputers of the Tao: Philosophical argument in ancient China* (La Salle, Illinois: Open Court, 1991 reprint of 1989 edn), p. 350.
77 *Ibid.*, p. 355.
78 Schirokauer, *A Brief History of Chinese Civilization*, p. 73.

Chapter 4 Tao and its Early Philosophers

1 Joseph Needham, *Science and Civilisation in China, Vol. 2: History of Scientific Thought* (Cambridge: Cambridge University Press, 1956), p. 35.
2 Paul Carus, translator, *The Teachings of Lao-tzu: The Tao Te Ching* (London, Sydney, Auckland, Johannesburg: Rider, 1999 revised edn, first published 1913), p. 14.
3 Fung Yu-lan, *A History of Chinese Philosophy, Vol. 1: The period of the philosophers (from the beginnings to circa 100 B.C.)*, translated by Derk Bodde (Princeton, New Jersey: Princeton University Press, 1983 reprint of second English edn 1952, first published in Chinese in 1931), p. 172. However, the Li family name might have been cast back in time to Lao-tzu/Laozi in order to enhance the Li family status through the connection.
4 See Robert G. Henricks, *Lao Tzu's Tao Te Ching: A translation of the startling new documents found at Guodian* (New York: Columbia University Press, 2000), pp. 134–5.
5 Notable in Ssu-ma Ch'ien/Sima Qian's account is his uncertainty about the facts that he is giving about his subject. He frequently shows the tenuous nature of his material by saying "it is said that" or "some say that", even indicating that his information cannot be verified.
6 Angus C. Graham, "The Origins of the Legend of Lao Tan" in Livia Kohn and Michael Lafargue (eds), *Lao-tzu and the Tao-te-ching* (Albany, New York: State University of New York Press, 1998), p. 24.
7 According to LaFargue, Ssu-ma T'an (died 110 BCE) was the earliest biographer. The dates, however, are close and most commentators accept Ssu-ma-Ch'ien/Sima Qian as the major, and earliest biographer. See Michael LaFargue, *Tao and Method: A reasoned approach to the Tao-te-ching* (Albany, New York: State University of New York Press, 1994), p. 302.
8 See, for example, the account given by Jonathan Star, translator and commentator, *Lao Tzu Tao Te Ching: The definitive edition* (New York: Jeremy P. Tarcher, 2001), pp. 1–2.
9 See Arthur Waley, *The Way and Its power: The Tao Tĕ Ching and its place in Chinese thought* (London, Sydney and Wellington: Unwin Paperbacks, 1987 reissue of 1977 edn, first published 1934), pp. 106–8.
10 The *Tao Te Ching/Daodejing* is also called the *Wu-ch'ien-wen/Wuqianwen* the "Five Thousand Character Classic".
11 Jacob Needleman "Introduction" in *Lao Tsu Tao Te Ching* translated by Gia-fu Feng and Jane English (New York: Vintage Books, 1989, first published 1972), p. v.
12 Angus C. Graham, *Disputers of the Tao: Philosophical Argument in Ancient China* (La Salle, Illinois:

Open Court, 1991 reprint of 1989 edn), p. 218.
13. Michael LaFargue and Julian Pas, "On Translating the *Tao-te-ching*" in Kohn and Lafargue (eds), *Lao-tzu and the* Tao-te-ching, pp. 277–301.
14. Star, *Lao Tzu Tao Te Ching*, p. 6.
15. LaFargue, *Tao and Method*, p. 303.
16. J. J. Clarke, *The Tao of the West: Western transformations of Taoist thought* (London and New York: Routledge, 2000), p. 28.
17. Toshihiko Izutsu, *Sufism and Taoism: A comparative study of key philosophical concepts* (Berkeley, Los Angeles, London: University of California Press, 1983), p. 372.
18. *Ibid.*, p. 376.
19. Julia Ching, "The Mirror Symbol Revisited: Confucian and Taoist Mysticism" in Steven T. Katz (ed.), *Mysticism and Religious Traditions* (Oxford, New York, Toronto, Melbourne: Oxford University Press, 1983), p. 227.
20. This last description he uses as evidence of an anthropomorphic *Tao*, though this may be stretching interpretation too far. R. Peerenboom, "Cosmogony: The Taoist Way" in *Journal of Chinese Philosophy* 17 (1990), pp. 158–60.
21. Benjamin Schwartz, "The Thought of the *Tao-te-ching*" in Kohn and LaFargue (eds), *Lao-tzu and the* Tao-te-ching, p. 189.
22. *Ibid.*, p. 190.
23. Isabelle Robinet, "The Diverse Interpretations of the Laozi" in Mark Csikszentmihalyi and Philip J. Ivanhoe (eds), *Religious and Philosophical Aspects of the* Laozi (Albany, New York: State University of New York Press, 1999), pp. 127–60.
24. Robert G. Henricks, "Re-exploring the Analogy of the Dao and the Field" in Csikszentmihalyi and Ivanhoe (eds), *Religious and Philosophical Aspects of the* Laozi, p. 161.
25. *Ibid.*, p. 162.
26. Bryan W. Van Norden, "Method in the Madness of Laozi" in Csikszentmihalyi and Ivanhoe (eds), *Religious and Philosophical Aspects of the* Laozi, p. 187.
27. *Ibid.*, p. 193.
28. Graham, *Disputers of the Tao*, p. 204.
29. Michael LaFargue, "Recovering the *Tao-te-ching*'s Original Meaning: Some Remarks on Historical Hermeneutics" in Kohn and LaFargue (eds), *Lao-tzu and the* Tao-te-ching, p. 266.
30. Harold D. Roth, "The *Laozi* in the Context of early Daoist Mystical Praxis" in Csikszentmihalyi and Ivanhoe (eds), *Religious and Philosophical Aspects of the* Laozi, p. 60.
31. Mark Csikszentmihalyi, "Mysticism and Apophatic Discourse in the *Laozi*" in Csikszentmihalyi and Ivanhoe (eds), *Religious and Philosophical Aspects of the* Laozi, p. 53.
32. The name, however, may be purely fictional, see William Boltz, "Lao tzu Tao te ching" in Michael Loewe (ed.), *Early Chinese texts: A bibliographical guide*. Early China Special Monograph Series, no. 2 (Berkeley, California: The Institute of East Asian Studies and The Society for the Study of Early China, University of California, 1993), p. 273.
33. For a full list and discussion of commentaries see Isabelle Robinet, "Later Commentaries: Textual Polysemy and Syncretistic Interpretations" in Kohn and LaFargue (eds), *Lao-tzu and the* Tao-te-ching, pp. 119–42.
34. Henricks, *Lao Tzu's Tao Te Ching*, p. 3.
35. Chad Hansen, *A Daoist Theory of Chinese Thought: A philosophical interpretation* (Oxford: Oxford University Press, 1992), p. 201.
36. LaFargue, *Tao and Method*, pp. 333–4.
37. *Ibid.*, p. 335.

38 Schwartz, "The Thought of the *Tao-te-ching*", p. 209.
39 Michael LaFargue, *The Tao of the Tao Te Ching: A translation and commentary* (Albany, New York: State University of New York Press), p. 191.
40 *Ibid.*, p. 195.
41 LaFargue, *Tao and Method*, p. 127.
42 *Ibid.*, p. 127.
43 *Ibid.*, p. 158.
44 *Ibid.*, p. 164.
45 For a full discussion of the problem of dating and authorship see *Lau Tzu Tao Te Ching* translated by D. C. Lau (London: Penguin, 1963), pp. 147–62.
46 The "Taoist" *Chuang-tzu/Zhuangzi* and the Confucian *Li Chi/Liji* "The Book of Rites".
47 See Henricks, *Lao Tzu's Tao Te Ching*, p. 22.
48 Isabelle Robinet, *Taoism: Growth of a religion* translated from French by Phyllis Brooks (Stanford, California: Stanford University Press, 1997, first published in France in 1992 as *Histoire du Taoïsme des origines au XIVe siècle*), p. 29.
49 Martin Palmer, *The Elements of Taoism* (Shaftesbury, Dorset and Rockport, Massachusetts: Element, 1991), p. 42.
50 Hansen, *A Daoist Theory of Chinese Thought*, pp. 229–30.
51 See Robinet, *Taoism*, p. 50.
52 *Lao Tzu Tao Te Ching: The book of meaning and life*, translation and commentary by Richard Wilhelm, translated into English by H. G. Ostwald (London, New York, Ontario, Toronto, Auckland: Arkana,1990 reprint of 1985 edn), p. 98.
53 Burton Watson in the *Foreword* to Victor H. Mair (ed.), *Experimental Essays on Chuang-tzu*. Centre for Asian and Pacific Studies (University of Hawaii: University of Hawaii Press, 1983).
54 Hansen, *A Daoist Theory of Chinese Thought*, p. 265.
55 Martin Palmer, translator, with Elizabeth Breuilly, Chang Wai Ming and Jay Ramsay, *The Book of Chuang Tzu* (London, New York, Ontario, Toronto, Auckland: Penguin, Arkana, 1996), p. xv.
56 Palmer, *The Book of Chuang Tzu*, p. xiii.
57 See Ching, *Chinese Religions*, 94.
58 See Angus Graham, *Chuang-Tzu: The Inner Chapters* (London, Boston, Sydney, New Zealand: Unwin Paperbacks, 1989, first published 1981), p. 117.
59 *Ibid.*
60 Palmer, *The Book of Chuang Tzu*.
61 Thomas Merton, *The Way of Chuang Tzu* (New York: New Directions, 1965).
62 Graham, *Chuang-Tzu*, p. 27.
63 For a more detailed account of authorship, see Harold Roth "Who Compiled the *Chuang Tzu*" in Henry Rosemont Jr. (ed.), *Chinese Texts and Philosophical Contexts: Essays dedicated to Angus C. Graham* (La Salle, Illinois: Open Court, 1991), pp. 80–128.
64 Such was Angus Graham's division of the text, though there are others. There is some evidence of a longer version of the text – some 52 chapters – that existed before Kuo Hsiang/Guo Xiang edited the text and reduced the chapters to 33. See Graham, *Chuang-Tzu*, p. 27.
65 Palmer, *The Book of Chuang Tzu*, pp. xix–xx.
66 Palmer, *The Book of Chuang Tzu*, p. xv.
67 Henri Maspero, *China in Antiquity*, translated by Frank A. Kierman Jr. (Folkestone, Kent: Dawson and Massachusetts: University of Massachusetts, 1978. Originally published in French as *La Chine Antique*, vol. 4 of *Histoire du Monde* by E. De Boccard (ed.), Paris 1927 and revised in 1965 as part of the *Annales du Musée Guiment Biblioteque d'Études*), p. 306.

68 Palmer, *The Book of Chuang Tzu*, p. xx.
69 Sam Hamill and J. P. Seaton, translators and eds, *The Essential Chuang Tzu* (Boston, Massachusetts: Shambhala, 1998), p. xix.
70 Robinet, *Taoism*, p. 33.
71 Robert E. Allinson, *Chuang-Tzu for Spiritual Transformation: An analysis of the inner chapters* (Albany, New York: State University of New York Press, 1989), p. 7.
72 *Ibid.*, p. 11.
73 *Ibid.*, p. 77.
74 Merton, *The Way of Chuang Tzu*, p. 11.
75 See *Chuang-tzu/Zhuangzi* chapter 7.
76 Angus C. Graham, translator, *The Book of Lieh-tzû: A classic of the Tao* (New York: Columbia University Press, 1990, first published 1960), p. 12.
77 Angus C. Graham, *Studies in Chinese Philosophy and Philosophical Literature* (Albany, New York: State University of New York Press, 1990 reprint, first published 1981), pp. 281–2.
78 *Ibid.*, p. 219.
79 Alan Watts, *Tao: The watercourse Way* (London, New York, Victoria, Ontario, Auckland: Penguin, 1975), p. 39. Watts likened the movement to going (*yang*) and pausing (*yin*).
80 R. H. Mathews, *Mathews' Chinese–English Dictionary* (Cambridge, Massachusetts: Harvard University Press, revised American edn 2000, first published 1931), p. 884.
81 *Ibid.*, p. 882.
82 Star, *Lao Tzu Tao Te Ching*, p. 272.
83 Jacob Needleman, "Introduction" in Gia-fu Feng and English, *Lao Tsu Tao Te Ching*, p. viii.
84 Hansen, *A Daoist Theory of Chinese Thought*, p. 268.
85 The word *tao* occurs three times in the first line, and in the second case is normally translated as "told", "spoken of", "expressed".
86 It is the word for "eternal" here that lends some force to the concept of Absolute. By short extension of the meanings of the Chinese term for it, *ch'ang/chang*, which has all the qualities of an "Absolute", it refers to *Eternal Tao*, thus shifting the emphasis from a strictly undefined *Tao* to a metaphysical Absolute Reality. Jonathan Star seems to have taken this route, *Lao Tzu Tao Te Ching*, pp. 273ff.
87 *Chuang-tzu/Zhuangzi* chapter 2, translator Graham.
88 Fung Yu-lan, *A Short History of Chinese Philosophy* edited by Derk Bodde (New York: The Free Press and London: Collier Macmillan, 1966, first published 1948), p. 95.
89 Lau, *Lao Tzu Tao Te Ching*, p. 23.
90 *Chuang-tzu/Zhuangzi*, chapter 6, translator Palmer.
91 LaFargue, *Tao and Method*, p. 177.
92 *Ibid.*, p. 257.
93 For an analysis of Wang Pi/Wang Bi's commentary on the *Tao Te Ching/Daodejing*, see Alan K. L. Chan, "A Tale of Two Commentaries: Ho-shang-kung and Wang Pi on the *Lao-tzu*" in Kohn and LaFargue (eds), *Lao-tzu and the* Tao-te-ching, pp. 100–17.
94 Wilhelm, translator *Lao Tzu Tao Te Ching*, p. 19.
95 See Norman J. Girardot, *Myth and Meaning in Early Taoism: The theme of chaos (hun-tun)* (Berkeley, Los Angeles, London: University of California Press, 1988 reprint of 1983 edn), p. 55.
96 For an analysis of Ho-shang-kung/Heshanggong's commentary on the cosmogony of *Tao*, One, Two, Three and ten thousand things, see Chan, "A Tale of Two Commentaries", pp. 91–4.
97 Graham, *Chuang-Tzu*, p. 18.

98 Girardot, *Myth and Meaning in Early Taoism*, pp. 57–8.
99 They could refer to the primordial *Tao* that is inexplicable and inscrutable and the *Tao* that is active energy as *ch'i/qi*. The usual interpretation is, however, as *yin* and *yang*.
100 See Livia Kohn, *Early Chinese Mysticism: Philosophy and soteriology in the Taoist tradition* (Princeton, New Jersey: Princeton University Press, 1992), p. 47, and Terry F. Kleeman "Daoism and the Quest for Order", in Norman J. Girardot, James Miller and Liu Xiaogan (eds), *Daoism and Ecology: Ways within a cosmic landscape* (Cambridge, Massachusetts: Harvard University Press, 2001), p. 62.
101 Girardot, *Myth and Meaning in Early Taoism*, p. 59.
102 *Ibid.*, p. 62.
103 Julian Pas has noted the awkwardness of *yin* and *yang* blending with *t'ai chi/taiji* to produce the three, see "Yin-Yang Polarity: A binocular vision" in *Asian Thought and Society* 8 (1983), p. 195.
104 See Chan, "A Tale of Two Commentaries", p. 92.
105 On a very different tack, Wilhelm understood the three to be the upper and lower *I Ching/Yijing* trigrams of Heaven, the Creative, and Earth, the Receptive, with their combinations making up the whole world in the eight trigrams – the three. See Wilhelm, *Lao Tzu Tao Te Ching*, p. 66.
106 John Blofeld, *Taoism: The quest for immortality* (London, Boston, Sydney, Wellington: Mandala, 1989, first published 1979), p. 1.
107 *Chuang-tzu/Zhuangzi*, chapter 12, translator Palmer, *The Book of Chuang Tzu*, p. 97.
108 Isabelle Robinet, "The Diverse Interpretations of the *Laozi*" in Csikszentmihalyi and Ivanhoe (eds), *Religious and Philosophical Aspects of the* Laozi, p. 145.
109 See, for example, the outline of Han cosmology from the *Huai-nan-tzu/Huainanzi* given by Pas, *Historical Dictionary of Taoism*, pp. 168–70, and the section on creation in chapter 5.
110 Kohn, *Early Chinese Mysticism*, p. 163.
111 LaFargue, *Tao and Method*, pp. 227–8.
112 Kohn, *Early Chinese Mysticism*, pp. 163–4.
113 *Chuang-tzu/Zhuangzi* chapter 2, translator Graham, *Chuang-Tzu*, p. 18.
114 Hansen, *A Daoist Theory of Chinese Thought*, p. 269.
115 *Ibid.*, p. 285.
116 *Ibid.*, p. 288.
117 *Ibid.*, pp. 292–303 *passim*.
118 Needham, *Science and Civilisation in China, Vol. 2*, p. 46.
119 *Chuang-tzu/Zhuangzi* chapter 20, translator Fung Yu-lan, *A Short History of Chinese Philosophy*, pp. 114–15.
120 *Chuang-tzu/Zhuangzi* chapter 2:3, translator Merton, *The Way of Chuang Tzu*, p. 42.
121 Kohn, *Early Chinese Mysticism*, p. 56.
122 *Chuang-tzu/Zhuangzi* chapter 13:1, translator Merton, *The Way of Chuang Tzu*, p. 80.
123 Blofeld, *Taoism*, p. 15.
124 Star, *Lao Tzu Tao Te Ching*, p. 260.
125 Waley, *The Way and Its Power*, pp. 31–2.
126 Needleman, "Introduction" in Gia-fu Feng and English, *Lao Tsu Tao Te Ching*, p. x.
127 Wilhelm, *Lao Tzu Tao Te Ching*, p. 84.
128 LaFargue, *Tao and Method*, p. 225.
129 *Ibid.*, p. 226.
130 Harold H. Oshima, "A Metaphysical Analysis of the Concept of Mind in the *Chuang-tzu*" in Mair (ed.), *Experimental Essays on Chuang-tzu*, p. 69.
131 Roger T. Ames, "The Local and the Focal in Realizing a Daoist World" in Girardot, Miller and Xiaogan (eds), *Daoism and Ecology*, p. 278.

132 *Chuang-tzu/Zhuangzi*, chapter 2:3, translator Merton, *The Way of Chuang Tzu*, p. 42.
133 *Lieh-tzu/Liezi* 1, translator Graham, *The Book of Lieh-tzu*, p. 23.
134 *Ibid.*, p. 25.
135 *Ibid.*, p. 26.
136 *Chuang-tzu/Zhuangzi*, chapter 6, translator Graham, *Chuang-Tzu*, p. 86.
137 Graham, *Disputers of the Tao*, p. 202.
138 Toshihiko Izutsu, *Sufism and Taoism: A Comparative Study of Key Philosophical Concepts* (Berkeley, Los Angeles, London: University of California Press, 1983), p. 315.
139 Tateno Masami, "A Philosophical Analysis of the *Laozi* from an Ontological Perspective" in Csikszentmihalyi and Ivanhoe (editors), *Religious and Philosophical Aspects of the Laozi*', pp. 179–80.
140 *Ibid.*, p. 181.
141 Mathews, *Mathews' Chinese–English Dictionary*, p. 1048.
142 Carus, translator, *The Teachings of Lao-tzu*, p. 22.
143 Liu Xiaogan, "Non-Action and the Environment Today" in Girardot, Miller and Xiaogan (eds), *Daoism and Ecology*, p. 334.
144 As a modern example of the unnatural path, consider the following: "One of the main reasons for the continued rain forest conflagration in Indonesia is 'industrialized burning' set by plantation owners and subcontractors, which has devoured at least two million hectares of the world's second-largest region of rain forest. For every hectare of burned land, one hundred hectares is engulfed in smoke stretching from Thailand to the Philippines to New Guinea and the northern coast of Australia. Smoke has affected people's health right across the region. An estimated forty thousand Indonesians have suffered respiratory problems, and up to one million have suffered eye irritations. Smoke has been blamed for ship and air crashes that killed about three hundred people." Liu Xiaogan, *ibid.*, p. 318.
145 Benjamin Hoff, *The Tao of Pooh & The Te of Piglet* (London: Methuen, 1995 reprint of 1982 edn), p. 96.
146 Merton, *The Way of Chuang Tzu*, p. 142
147 Liu Xiaogan, "Naturalness (*Tzu-jan*), the Core Value in Taoism: Its Ancient Meaning and its Significance Today" in Kohn and LaFargue (eds), *Lao-tzu and the Tao-te-ching*, p. 211.
148 *Ibid.*, pp. 217–18.
149 Liu Xiaogan, "An Inquiry into the Core Value of Laozi's Philosophy", in Csikszentmihalyi and Ivanhoe, *Religious and Philosophical Aspects of the* Laozi, p. 215.
150 *Ibid.*, p. 211.
151 *Ibid.*, p. 212.
152 Graham, *Chuang-Tzu*, p. 8.
153 *Chuang-tzu/Zhuangzi* chapter 2, translator Graham, *ibid.*, p. 59.
154 *Lieh-tzu/Liezi* chapter 4, translator Graham, *The Book of Lieh-tzu*, p. 90.
155 Girardot, *Myth and Meaning in Early Taoism*, p. 56.
156 *Tao Te Ching/Daodejing* 28, translators Gia-fu Feng and English, *Lao Tsu Tao Te Ching*.
157 For a full analysis of the term, see Pas, *Historical Dictionary of Taoism*, pp. 351–2.
158 Needham, *Science and Civilization in China*, Vol. 2, pp. 114–15.
159 Girardot, *Myth and Meaning in Early Taoism*, p. 71.
160 *Ibid.*, p. 75.
161 Harold D. Roth, "The *Laozi* in the Context of Early Daoist Mystical Praxis" in Csikszentmihalyi and Ivanhoe, *Religious and Philosophical Aspects of the* Laozi, p. 75.
162 *Ibid.*, p. 78.

163 D. Howard Smith, *Chinese Religions* (New York, Chicago, San Francisco: Holt, Rinehart and Winston, 1968, pp. 70–1.
164 Philip J. Ivanhoe, "The Concept of *de* ("Virtue") in the *Laozi*" in Csikszentmihalyi and Ivanhoe (eds), *Religious and Philosophical Aspects of the* Laozi, p. 242.
165 *Ibid.*, pp. 242–3.
166 LaFargue, *Tao and Method*, p. 168.
167 *Ibid.*, p. 171.
168 See Star, *Lao Tzu Tao Te Ching*, p. 256.
169 Fung Yu-lan, *A Short History of Chinese Philosophy*, p. 103.
170 Wilhelm, *Lao Tzu Tao Te Ching*, p. 76.
171 Kohn, *Early Chinese Mysticism*, p. 75.
172 Paul Wildish, *Principles of Taoism* (London: Thorsons, 2000), pp. 22–3.

Chapter 5 Taoism in Imperial China

1 Henri Maspero, *Taoism and Chinese Religion*, translated by Frank A. Kierman, Jr. (Amherst: The University of Massachusetts Press, 1981), pp. 20–1.
2 The present Great Wall of China is a much later, fifteenth century, edifice.
3 However, China has generally been the non-Chinese term. Chinese themselves have called their country Chung kuo/Zhongguo, "Central Country", or refer to themselves as the "Han people".
4 Conrad Schirokauer, *A Brief History of Chinese Civilization* (San Diego, New York, Chicago, Austin, Washington, D.C., London, Sydney, Tokyo, Toronto: Harcourt Brace Gap College, 1991), p. 49.
5 Martin Palmer, *The Elements of Taoism* (Shaftesbury, Dorset and Rockport Massachusetts: Element, 1991), p. 71.
6 See D. Howard Smith, *Chinese Religions* (New York, Chicago, San Francisco: Holt, Rinehart and Winston, 1968), pp. 96–7.
7 Herrlee G. Creel, *Chinese Thought: From Confucius to Mao Tsê-Tung* (London: Methuen, 1962, first published 1954), p. 192.
8 Joseph Needham, *Science and Civilisation in China, Vol. 2: History of scientific thought* (Cambridge: Cambridge University Press, 1956), p. 432.
9 Donald Harper, "Warring States, Qin and Han Manuscripts Related to Natural Philosophy and the Occult" in Edward L. Shaughnessy (ed.), *New Sources of Early Chinese History: An introduction to the reading of inscriptions and manuscripts* (Berkeley, California: Society for the Study of Early China, and The Institute of East Asian Studies, University of California, 1997), p. 223.
10 *Ibid.*, p. 224.
11 *Ibid.*, p. 228.
12 Kenneth J. DeWoskin, *Doctors, Diviners, and Magicians of Ancient China: Biographies of Fang-shih* (New York: Columbia University Press, 1983).
13 *Ibid.*, p. 2.
14 *Ibid.*, p. 10.
15 Isabelle Robinet, *Taoism: Growth of a religion*, translated from French by Phyllis Brooks (Stanford, California: Stanford University Press, 1997, first published as *Histoire du Taoïsme des origines au XIVe siècle* in 1992), p. 43.
16 For examples of these see Patricia Ebrey, translator, "Local Cults" in Patricia Buckley Ebrey (ed.), *Chinese Civilization and Society: A source book* (New York: The Free Press, and London: Collier Macmillan, 1981), pp. 38–40.
17 For a full analysis of the movement see R. P. Peerenboom, *Law and Morality in Ancient China:*

The Silk Manuscripts of Huang-Lao (Albany, New York: State University of New York Press, 1993).

18 Julian F. Pas in cooperation with Man Kam Leung, *Historical Dictionary of Taoism* (Lanham, Middlesex and London: The Scarecrow Press, 1998), pp. 170–1.

19 Anna Seidel and Michel Strickmann (eds), "Taoism", in *Encyclopedia Britannica, Macropedia*, vol. 28 (Chicago: University of Chicago, 1992, 15th edn), p. 400.

20 Harold David Roth, *The Textual History of the Huai-nan Tzu*. Monographs for the Association for Asian Studies, no. 46 (Ann Arbor, Michigan: The Association for Asian Studies, University of Michigan, 1992), p. 12.

21 *Huai-nan-tzu/Huainanzi* 2, translator and compiler Wing-Tsit Chan, *A Source Book in Chinese Philosophy* (New Jersey: Princeton University Press, and London: Oxford University Press, 1963), p. 306.

22 Charles Le Blanc, "*Huai nan tzu*" in Michael Loewe (ed.), *Early Chinese Texts: A bibliographical guide* (Berkeley, California: The Society for the Study of Early China, and The Institute of East Asian Studies, University of California), p. 189.

23 Roth, *The Textual History of the Huai-nan Tzu*, p. 19.

24 *Ibid.*, p. 20.

25 *Ibid.*, p. 22.

26 *Ibid.*, pp. 58 and 79–82.

27 Maspero, *Taoism and Chinese Religion*, p. 38.

28 See Pas, *Historical Dictionary of Taoism*, p. 73.

29 Eva Wong, *The Shambhala Guide to Taoism* (Boston, Massachusetts and London: Shambhala, 1997), p. 35.

30 Needham, *Science and Civilisation in China, Vol. 2*, p. 156.

31 Maspero, *Taoism and Chinese Religion*, p. 430.

32 Pas, *Historical Dictionary of Taoism*, p. 143.

33 Schirokauer, *A Brief History of Chinese Civilization*, p. 64.

34 Patricia Buckley Ebrey and Peter Gregory, "The Religious and Historical Landscape" in Patricia Buckley Ebrey and Peter N. Gregory (eds), *Religion and Society in T'ang and Sung China* (Honolulu: University of Hawaii Press, 1993), pp. 24–5.

35 For a full account of the nature of registers, see Kristofer Schipper, *The Taoist Body* (Berkeley, Los Angeles, London: University of California Press, 1993, first published in 1982 as *Le corps taoïste*), pp. 60–71.

36 *Ibid.*, p. 62.

37 *Ibid.*, p. 67.

38 Robinet, *Taoism*, p. 62.

39 *Ibid.*

40 Needham, *Science and Civilization in China, Vol. 2*, p. 437.

41 See, for example, Pas, *Historical Dictionary of Taoism*, p. 187.

42 *Pao-p'u tzu/Baopuzi* 50:96, translator and ed. James R. Ware, *Alchemy, Medicine & Religion in the China of A.D. 320: The Nei P'ien of Ko Hung (Pao-p'u-tzu)* (Cambridge, Massachusetts: Massachusetts Institute of Technology Press, 1966, and New York: Dover Publications, 1981).

43 *Ibid.*, 50:4b.

44 *Ibid.*, 10:5a.

45 Opening lines of Ko Hung/Ge Hong's *Pao-p'u-tzu/Baopuzi*, translated by Robinet, *Taoism*, p. 82.

46 Pas, *Historical Dictionary of Taoism*, pp. 188–9.

47 Smith, *Chinese Religions*, p. 106.

48 See Needham, *Science and Civilization in China*, Vol. 2, p. 433.
49 Seidel and Strickmann, "Taoism", p. 401.
50 Wing-tsit Chan, *A Source Book in Chinese Philosophy*, p. 315.
51 Robinet, *Taoism*, p. 115.
52 Seidel and Strickmann, "Taoism", p. 402.
53 John Lagerwey, "The Taoist Religious Community" in *ER*, 14: p. 309.
54 Livia Kohn, *Early Chinese Mysticism: Philosophy and soteriology in the Taoist tradition* (Princeton, New Jersey: Princeton University Press, 1992), p. 112.
55 Robinet,. *Taoism*, p. 134.
56 Michel Strickmann, "On the Alchemy of T'ao Hung-ching" in Holmes Welch and Anna Seidel (eds), *Facets of Taoism: Essays in Chinese religion* (New Haven and London: Yale University Press, 1979), p. 127.
57 Anna Seidel, "Chronicle of Taoist Studies in the West 1950–1990" in *Cahiers d'Extrême-Asie* 5: 1989–90, p. 240.
58 Robinet, *Taoism*, p. 155.
59 See Pas, *Historical Dictionary of Taoism*, p. 214.
60 For a complete survey of Taoist literature see Judith Magee Boltz, *A Survey of Taoist Literature: Tenth to seventeenth centuries* (Berkeley, California: Institute of East Asian Studies, Center for Chinese Studies, University of California, 1987), pp. 4–7, and by the same author, "Taoist Literature" in *ER*, 14: pp. 317–29. A thorough survey of religious texts is also to be found by Stephen Bokenkamp, "Taoist Literature Part I: Through the T'ang Dynasty", and Judith Magee Boltz, "Taoist Literature Part II: Five Dynasties to the Ming" in William H. Nienhauser, Jr. (ed. and compiler), *The Indiana Companion to Traditional Chinese Literature* (Bloomington: University Press, pp. 9–22 and 152–74 respectively.
61 Pas, *Historical Dictionary of Taoism*, p. 326.
62 *Ibid.*, p. 327.
63 Lagerwey, "The Taoist Religious Community" in *ER*, 14: p. 309.
64 Joseph Needham, *Science and Civilisation in China Vol. 1: Introductory Orientations* (Cambridge, New York, New Rochelle, Melbourne, Sydney: Cambridge University Press, 1988 reprint of 1961 edn, first published 1954), p. 127.
65 Marcel Granet, *The Religion of the Chinese People*, translated, edited and with an Introduction by Maurice Freedman (Oxford: Basil Blackwell, 1975, first published in 1922 as *La religion des Chinois*), p. 120.
66 Michael Saso, *Blue Dragon White Tiger: Taoist rites of passage* (Washington, D.C.: The Taoist Center, 1990), p. 16.
67 Timothy H. Barrett, *Taoism under the T'ang: Religion and empire during the golden age of Chinese history* (London: WellSweep, 1996), p. 61.
68 Charles Benn, "Religious Aspects of Emperor Hsüan-tsung's Taoist Ideology" in David W. Chappell, *Buddhist and Taoist Practice in Medieval Society: Buddhist and Taoist Studies II*. Asian Studies at Hawaii no. 34 (University of Hawaii: University of Hawaii Press, 1987), p. 128.
69 *Ibid.*, p. 140.
70 *Ibid.*, p. 131.
71 For extracts, see Mark Coyle, translator, *Book of Rewards and Punishments*, in Ebrey, *Chinese Civilization and Society*, p. 71.
72 Ebrey and Gregory, "The Religious and Historical Landscape", p. 29.
73 Judith Magee Boltz, "Not by the Seal of Office Alone" in Ebrey and Gregory (eds), *Religion and Society in T'ang and Sung China*, pp. 255–6.
74 *Ibid.*, pp. 264–5.

75   *Ibid.*, p. 270.
76   Ebrey, *Chinese Civilization and Society*, pp. 177–8.

Chapter 6 *Alchemy*

1   Henri Maspero, *Taoism and Chinese Religion* translated by Frank A. Kierman, Jr. (Amherst: The University of Massachusetts Press, 1981. First published as *Le Taoïsme et les religions chinoises*, 1971), p. 271.
2   Kristofer Schipper, *The Taoist Body*, translated by Karen C. Duval (Berkeley, Los Angeles, London: University of California Press, 1993. First published as *Le corps taoïste*, Paris 1982), p. 175.
3   Both words *wai* and *nei* are used very differently depending on the contexts in which they are found; see Isabelle Robinet "Original Contributions of *Neidan* to Taoism and Chinese Thought" in Livia Kohn (ed.) in cooperation with Yoshinobu Sakade, *Taoist Meditation and Longevity Techniques*. Michigan Monographs in Chinese Studies, vol. 61 (Ann Arbour: Centre for Chinese Studies, The University of Michigan, 1989), p. 297 n. 1.
4   John Lagerwey, "Worship and Cultic Life: Taoist Cultic Life" in Mircea Eliade (ed.), *The Encyclopedia of Religion* (hereafter *ER*, New York: Macmillan Publishing Company and London: Collier Macmillan Publishers, 1987), vol. 4, p. 485.
5   Joseph Needham with the collaboration of Lu Gwei-djen, *Science and Civilisation in China, Volume 5 Chemistry and Chemical Technology: Part V Spagyrical discovery and invention: physiological alchemy* (Cambridge, London, New York, New Rochelle, Melbourne, Sydney: Cambridge University Press, 1983), p. 34. However, there seems to have been a fairly homogeneous development of alchemical schools up to and during the Six Dynasties period, see Michel Strickmann, "On the Alchemy of T'ao Hung-ching" in Holmes Welch and Anna Seidel, *Facets of Taoism: Essays in Chinese religion* (New Haven and London: Yale University Press, 1979), p. 192.
6   Translator Thomas Cleary, *The Book of Balance and Harmony* (London, Sydney, Auckland, Johannesburg: Rider, 1989), p. 132.
7   Jean C. Cooper, *Chinese Alchemy: The Taoist Quest for Immortality* (Wellingborough, Northamptonshire: The Aquarian Press, 1984), p. 138.
8   Isabelle Robinet, *Taoism: Growth of a religion*, translated by Phyllis Brooks (Stanford, California: Stanford University Press, 1997, first published in Paris as *Histoire du Taoïsme des origines au XIVe siècle* in 1992), p. 231.
9   Richard Bertschinger, *The Secret of Everlasting Life: The first translation of the ancient Chinese text on immortality* (London: Vega, 2002, first published 1994), p. 12.
10 Daniel Overmyer "Chinese Religion: An Overview" in *ER*, 3 p. 264.
11 Joseph Needham, *Science in Traditional China* (Cambridge, Massachusetts: Harvard University Press, and Hong Kong: The Chinese University Press, 1982 reprint of 1981 edn), p. 14.
12 Nathan Sivin, "Chinese Alchemy and the Manipulation of Time" in Nathan Sivin (ed.), *Science and Technology in East Asia* (New York: Science History Publications, 1977), p. 110.
13 See Maspero, *Taoism and Chinese Religion*, p. 427.
14 Nathan Sivin, "Alchemy: Chinese Alchemy" in *ER*, 1 pp. 188–9.
15 Robinet, "Original Contributions of *Neidan* to Taoism and Chinese Thought", pp. 300–1.
16 See Joseph Needham, *The Refiner's Fire: The enigma of alchemy in East and West*. The second J. D. Bernal Lecture (London: Birkbeck College, 1971), pp. 6–7.
17 Needham, *Science and Civilisation in China, Vol 5, Part 5*, p. 129.
18 The title is difficult to translate and appears in a variety of forms.
19 Robinet, *Taoism*, p. 220.

20 Robinet, "Original Contributions of *Neidan* to Taoism and Chinese Thought", p. 303.
21 See, for example, Robinet, *ibid.*, pp. 303–6 for important inner alchemy texts, and Needham, *Science and Civilisation, Vol. 5, Part 5*, pp. 75–122 for an extensive analysis of all major texts.
22 Douglas Wile, *Art of the Bedchamber: The Chinese Yoga Classics including women's solo meditation texts* (Albany, New York: State University of New York Press, 1992), p. 10.
23 Sivin, "Chinese Alchemy and the Manipulation of Time", p. 121.
24 Liu I-ming commentary on Chang Po-tuan *Understanding Reality* 1:3, translated by Thomas Cleary, *The Taoist Classics: The collected translations of Thomas Cleary, Vol. 2* (Boston, Massachusetts: Shambhala, 2003, first published 1986), p. 38.
25 Sivin, "Chinese Alchemy and the Manipulation of Time", pp. 113–14.
26 See Cooper, *Chinese Alchemy*, pp. 48–9 for a succinct list of such ingredients.
27 Ko Hung/Ge Hong, *Pao P'u-tzu/Baopuzi* 4:2b, translator and ed. James R. Ware, *Alchemy, Medicine & Religion in the China of A.D. 320: The Nei P'ien of Ko Hung (Pao-p'u tzu)* (New York: Dover Publications Inc., 1966), p. 71.
28 Ko Hung/Ge Hong, *Pao P'u-tzu/Baopuzi* 4:12b, *ibid.*, p. 87.
29 See Timothy H. Barrett, "Ko Hung" in *ER*, 8 p. 358.
30 Akahori, "Drug Taking and Immortality" in Kohn (ed.), *Taoist Meditation and Longevity Techniques*, pp. 78–9.
31 *Ibid.*, p. 90.
32 Schipper, *The Taoist Body*, p. 176.
33 Ko Hung/Ge Hong, *Pao P'u-tzu/Baopuzi* 4:5b.
34 *Ibid.*, 4:16b.
35 Translator Strickmann, "On the Alchemy of T'ao Hung-ching", p. 137.
36 Tu Wei-ming, "Soul: Chinese Concepts" in *ER*, 13: 449.
37 Norman J. Girardot, "Hsien" in *ER*, 6: pp. 475–7.
38 Livia Kohn, "Taoist Insight Meditation: The Tang Practice of *Neiguan*" in Kohn (ed.), *Taoist Meditation and Longevity Techniques*, p. 205 n. 7, following the *Yunji qiqian* 54.
39 Tu Wei-ming, "Soul: Chinese Concepts" in *ER*, 13: 448.
40 Robinet, *Taoism*, p.14.
41 Tu Wei-ming, "Soul: Chinese Concepts" in *ER*, 13: 449.
42 Livia Kohn (ed.), *The Taoist Experience: An anthology* (Albany, New York: State University of New York Press, 1993), p. 162.
43 Robinet, *Taoism*, p. 14.
44 Schipper, *The Taoist Body*, p. 104.
45 *Ibid.*, pp. 105–6. See also Maspero, *Taoism and Chinese Religion*, pp. 325–9, and for an excellent analysis Schipper, *ibid.*, chapter 6, pp. 100–12.
46 Robinet, *Taoism*, pp. 108–9.
47 A term that is synonymous with Buddhist *nirvana*.
48 For a good summary of the most important points of the anatomy of the body, see Wile, *Art of the Bedchamber*, pp. 36–9.
49 Kohn, *The Taoist Experience*, p. 162.
50 See Maspero, *Taoism and Chinese Religion* pp. 279–82 and 346–52 for a comprehensive account of these.
51 Ko Hung/Ge Hong *Pao P'u-tzu/Baopuzi* 18:4b, translator Ware, *Alchemy, Medicine & Religion in the China of A.D. 320*, pp. 307–8.
52 Schipper, *The Taoist Body*, p. 111.
53 The number of deities corresponded to the number of days in the year, to twenty-four solar half-months, and so on. See Maspero, *Taoism and Chinese Religion*, pp. 347–48.

54 See Schipper, *The Taoist Body*, pp. 111–12.
55 Robinet, *Taoism*, p. 17.
56 Cited in Sommer (ed.), *Chinese Religion*, p. 147.
57 See Pas, *Historical Dictionary of Taoism*, p. 80.
58 From *Inward Training* 1, translator Harold D. Roth, *Original Tao: Inward Training and the foundations of Taoist mysticism* (New York and Chichester, West Sussex: Columbia University Press, 1999), p. 46.
59 For its chemical and medical meanings see Nathan Sivin, *Chinese Alchemy: Preliminary Studies* (Cambridge, Massachusetts: Harvard University Press, 1968), p. xviii.
60 Kohn, *The Taoist Experience*, p. 133.
61 Michael Page, *The Power of Ch'i: An introduction to Chinese mysticism and philosophy* (Wellingborough, Northamptonshire: The Aquarian Press, 1988), p. 11.
62 Hidemi Ishida, "Body and Mind: The Chinese Perspective" in Kohn (ed.), *Taoist Meditation and Longevity Techniques*, p. 45.
63 Livia Kohn, *Taoist Mystical Philosophy: The Scripture of Western Ascension* (Albany, New York: State University of New York Press, 1991), p. 94.
64 Harold Roth, "The Early Taoist Concept of *Shen*: A Ghost in the Machine?" in Kidder Smith Jr. (ed.), *Sagehood and Systematizing Thought in Warring States and Han China* (Brunswick, Maine: Breckinridge Public Centre Asian Studies Program, 24, Bowdoin College, 1990), p. 21.
65 Chang Po-tuan/Zhang Boduan, *Understanding Reality* 1:1, translator Cleary, *The Taoist Classics, Vol. 2*, p. 35.
66 Chang San-feng/Zhang Sanfeng, "Zhang Sanfeng's Taiji Alchemy Secrets: The Alchemical Process", translated by Thomas Cleary, *Taoist Meditation: Methods for cultivating a healthy mind and body* (Boston, Massachusetts: Shambhala, 2000), p. 120.
67 Robinet, "Original Contributions of *Neidan* to Taoism and Chinese Thought", p. 322.
68 Wei Po-yang/Wei Boyang, *Ts'an-t'ung Ch'i/Cantonqi*, translator Bertschinger, *The Secret of Everlasting Life*, p. 104.
69 Wile, *Art of the Bedchamber*, p. 19.
70 See Philip Rawson and Laszlo Legeza, *Tao: The Chinese philosophy of time and change* (London: Thames and Hudson, 1973), pp. 121–4.
71 See, for example, the lengthy example Schipper supplies, along with his comments, *The Taoist Body*, pp. 153–4.
72 See the extensive discussion of this point in Thomas Cleary and Sartaz Aziz, *Twilight Goddess: Spiritual feminism and feminine spirituality* (Boston, Mass. and London: Shambhala, 2000), pp. 87–9.
73 This was achieved by applying pressure to a point in the perineal region in order to block the urethra. See Needham, *Science and Civilisation in Ancient China, Vol. 5, Part 5*, p. 197. As Needham pointed out, whereas it was believed that the semen could pass up through the cinnabar fields to the brain, in fact it would have been passed to the bladder.
74 Wile, *Art of the Bedchamber*, p. 7.
75 For a summary of this process in relation to the *Dragon-Tiger Classic* see Eva Wong, *Harmonizing Yin and Yang: The Dragon-Tiger Classic* (Boston, Massachusetts and London: Shambhala, 1997), pp. 5–8. See also Wile, *Art of the Bedchamber*, pp. 29–30.
76 *Ibid.*, p. 25.
77 Ko Hung/Ge Hong, *Pao P'u-tzu/Baopuzi* 8:4a, translator Ware, *Alchemy, Medicine & Religion in the China of A.D. 320*, p. 141.
78 Wile, *Art of the Bedchamber*, p. 146.
79 Maspero, *Taoism and Chinese Religion*, p. 533.
80 Needham, *Science and Civilisation in Ancient China, Vol. 5, Part 5*, p. 217.

81 Robinet, "Original Contributions of *Neidan* to Taoism and Chinese Thought", p. 301.
82 Needham, *Science and Civilisation in China, Vol. 5, Part 5*, pp. 155–81.
83 Catherine Despeux, "Gymnastics: The Ancient Tradition" in Kohn, *Taoist Meditation and Longevity Techniques*, p. 257.
84 Roth, *Inward Training, passim*.
85 For an extensive analysis of breathing techniques, see Maspero, *Taoism and Chinese Religion*, pp. 459–517.
86 Despeux, "Gymnastics: The ancient tradition", pp. 245–6.
87 Ko Hung/Ge Hong, *Pao P'u-tzu/Baopuzi* 15:9b, translator Ware, *Alchemy, Medicine & Religion in the China of A.D. 320*, p. 257.
88 In the modern context, it is difficult to see what is left for a Taoist to eat! Michael Page lists prohibited foods as "processed grain foods, deep fried food, coffee, alcohol, tobacco, chocolate and other sweets, spices, rock salt, mustard, pepper, vinegar, pickles, curry, red meats, salmon, tuna, mackerel, shark, swordfish or whale, sugar, ice cream, jellies, synthetic fruit juices, potatoes, tomatoes, aubergines, rhubarb, spinach, meat extracts, soups or gravies, cheese, milk, butter, boiled or fried eggs, lard or dripping from animals, and any fat birds or fish"! *The Power of Ch'i*, p. 71.
89 Kohn (ed.), *The Taoist Experience*, p. 193.
90 Roth, *Original Tao*, p. 2.
91 *Ibid.*, pp. 110–11.
92 *Ibid.*, pp. 120–2.
93 From the *Huai-nan-tzu/Huainanzi*, translator Harold D. Roth, "The Inner Cultivation Tradition of early Daoism" in Donald S. Lopez (ed.), *Religions of China in Practice* (Princeton, New Jersey: Princeton University Press, 1996), p. 138.
94 Hidemi Ishida, "Body and Mind: The Chinese Perspective" in Kohn (ed.), *Taoist Meditation and Longevity Techniques*, pp. 71–2.
95 Poul Andersen, *The Method of Holding the Three Ones: A Taoist manual of meditation of the fourth century A.D.* (Copenhagen: Scandinavian Institute of Asian Studies, 1980), p. 23. For a more detailed account see pp. 46–8 in Andersen's work.
96 Livia Kohn, "Guarding the One: Concentrative Meditation in Taoism" in Kohn (ed.), *Taoist Meditation and Longevity Techniques*, p. 125. See also in the same source pp. 155–6 for a list and description of the different representative methods of Guarding the One in Taoism.
97 *Ibid.*, p. 154.
98 Equivalent terms are widely (and wildly) at variance. I have, therefore, only given those that appear to be consistently held.
99 Liu I-ming/Liu Yiming's commentary on Chang Po-tuan/Zhang Boduan's *The Inner Teachings of Taoism*, translator Cleary, p. 83.
100 *Ibid.*
101 Robinet, *Taoism*, p. 232.
102 Liu I-ming/Liu Yiming, translator Kohn, *The Taoist Experience*, p. 319.
103 Eva Wong, *The Shambhala Guide to Taoism: A complete introduction to the history, philosophy, and practice of an ancient Chinese spiritual tradition* (Boston, Massachusetts and London: Shambhala, 1997), pp. 175–6.
104 For a detailed description of such processes, see Needham, *Science and Civilisation in China, Vol. 5, Part 5*, pp. 52–67.
105 For a very concise and clear description of these changes see Eva Wong, translator, *Cultivating Stillness: A Taoist manual for transforming body and mind* (Boston, Massachusetts and London: Shambhala, 1992), p. 133–4.

106 Wong, *Harmonizing Yin and Yang*, p. 14. See also pp. 17–20 for a list of alchemical interactions found in the *Dragon-Tiger Classic*.
107 For the numerology associated with the *Pa-kua/Bagua* see Cleary, *The Book of Balance and Harmony*, pp. 26–8, and for a clear chart of these Wong, *ibid.*, p. 135, with explanations on pp. 132–3.
108 See Wong, *Harmonizing Yin and Yang*, pp. 20–9 for further discussion on this point in connection with the *Dragon-Tiger Classic*.
109 Wong, *The Shambhala Guide to Taoism*, pp. 179–83.
110 Texts are remarkably contradictory on this area, and even the same author will give different accounts in different books. I can only give some general indications as to the approximate meanings of these terms, which are likely to have varied meaning in different schools of thought.
111 Wong, *Cultivating Stillness*, p. xxiii.
112 From the *Book of Balance and Harmony*, translator Cleary, p. 144.
113 Titus Burckhardt, *Alchemy* (Shaftesbury, Dorset: Element Books, 1987 impression of 1986 edn, first published 1960), p. 123.
114 Blofeld, *Taoism*, p. 153.

Chapter 7 *Life beyond Earth: Ancestors, Deities, Immortals and Sages*

1 Laurence G. Thompson, *Chinese Religion: An introduction* (Belmont, California: Wadsworth Publishing Company, 1989 fourth edn, first published 1979), p. 36.
2 Stephen F. Teiser, "Introduction" in Donald S. Lopez, Jr. (ed.), *Religions of China in Practice* (Princeton, New Jersey: Princeton University Press, 1996), pp. 26–7.
3 See Robert Eno, "Deities and Ancestors in Early Oracle Inscriptions" in Lopez, *ibid.* pp. 44–5.
4 Norman J. Girardot, *Myth and Meaning in Early Taoism: The theme of chaos (hun-tun)* (Berkeley, Los Angeles, London: University of California Press, 1983), p. 204.
5 Martin Palmer and Zhao Xiaomin, *Essential Chinese Mythology: Stories that change the world* (London: Thorsons, 1997), pp. 8–9.
6 Isabelle Robinet, *Taoism: Growth of a Religion* translated by Phyllis Brooks (Stanford, California: Stanford University Press, 1997, first published in French as *Histoire du Taoïsme des origines au XIVe siècle* in 1992), p. 19.
7 Thompson, *Chinese Religion*, p. 63.
8 Palmer and Xiaomin, *Essential Chinese Mythology*, p. 30.
9 See Henri Maspero, *Taoism and Chinese Religion* translated by Frank A. Kierman, Jr. (Amherst: The University of Massachusetts Press, 1981, first published in 1971 as *Le Taoïsme et les Religions Chinoises*), pp. 86–7.
10 Donald H. Bishop, "Introduction" in Donald H. Bishop (ed.), *Chinese Thought: An introduction* (Delhi: Motilal Banarsidass Publishers Private Limited, 2001 reprint of 1985 edn), pp. 175–6.
11 Maspero, *Taoism and Chinese Religion*, pp. 84–5.
12 John Blofeld, *Taoism: The quest for immortality* (London, Boston, Sydney, Wellington: Mandala, 1989 reissue of 1979 edn), p. 90.
13 Sarah Allen, *The Shape of the Turtle: Myth, Art, and Cosmos in Early China* (Albany, New York: State University of New York Press, 1991), p. 64.
14 Livia Kohn (ed.), *The Taoist Experience: An anthology* (Albany, New York: State University of New York Press, 1993), pp. 351–2.
15 Anna Seidel, "Huang-ti" in Mircea Eliade (ed.), *The Encyclopedia of Religion* (hereafter *ER*, New

York: Macmillan Publishing Company and London: Collier Macmillan Publishers, 1987), vol. 6, p. 484.
16 Laurence G. Thompson, "Taoist Iconography", in *ER*, 7, p. 51.
17 Girardot, *Myth and Meaning in Early Taoism*, p. 201.
18 Seidel, "Huang-ti", in *ER*, 6, p. 485.
19 Yuan Ke, *Dragons and Dynasties: An introduction to Chinese mythology*, selected and translated by Kim Echlin and Nie Zhixiong (London, New York, Victoria, Auckland, Harmondsworth: Penguin Books, 1993 reprint of 1991 edn), p. 27.
20 A Taoist monk of the fifth to sixth centuries attempted a classification of the deities, immortals and sages in a work called "Table of the Hierarchy of the Real Transcendents of the Sacred Jewel of the Mystery among the Arcana". For a description of the hierarchy it contains, see Maspero, *Taoism and Chinese Religion*, pp. 358–60.
21 See extracts from the *Fafu kejie wen*, "*Rules and Precepts Regarding Ritual Garb*" in Kohn, *The Taoist Experience*, p. 337.
22 See the *Jinque dijun sanyuan zhenyi jing* "*The Scripture of the Three Primordial Realized Ones by the Lord of the Golden Tower*", in Kohn, *ibid.*, p. 204.
23 Martin Palmer, *The Elements of Taoism* (Shaftesbury, Dorset and Rockport, Massachusetts: Element, 1991), p. 114.
24 Maspero, *Taoism and Chinese Religion*, p. 159.
25 See Anna Seidel, "Yü-huang" in *ER*, 15, p. 541.
26 Kristofer Schipper, *The Taoist Body* translated by Karen C. Duval (Berkeley, Los Angeles, London: University of California Press, 1993, first published in 1982 as *Le corps taoïste*), p. 87.
27 Palmer and Xiaomin, *Essential Chinese Mythology*, p. 27.
28 See Robinet, *Taoism*, pp. 69–70.
29 See Harold D. Roth, "Huang-lao Chün" in *ER*, 6, p. 484.
30 David C. Yu, translator, *History of Chinese Daoism, Vol. 1* (Lanham, New York and Oxford: University Press of America, Inc., 2000), pp. 58–61.
31 Livia Kohn, "The Lao-tzu Myth", in Livia Kohn and Michael LaFargue (eds), *Lao-tzu and the Tao-te-ching*" (Albany, New York: State University of New York Press, 1998), pp. 41–50.
32 See Charles Benn, "Religious Aspects of Emperor Hsüan-tsung's Taoist Ideology", in David W. Chappell (ed.), *Buddhist and Taoist Practice in Medieval Chinese Society: Buddhist and Taoist studies II* (Asian Studies at Hawaii no. 34, University of Hawaii: University of Hawaii Press, 1987), p. 130.
33 Suzanne E. Cahill, *Transcendence & Divine Passion: The Queen Mother of the West in Medieval China* (Stanford, California: Stanford University Press, 1993), p. 3.
34 But see Cahill, *ibid.*, p. 13.
35 *Ibid.*, pp. 13–14.
36 *Ibid.*, p. 81.
37 *Ibid.*, p. 17.
38 "The Queen Mother of the West" (Xiwang mu), from *Yong-cheng jixian lu* ("Record of the Assembled Immortals of the Heavenly Walled City") in Kohn, *The Taoist Experience*, p. 57.
39 Cahill, *Transcendence & Divine Passion*, pp. 42–3.
40 Kohn, *The Taoist Experience*, p. 116. See also Livia Kohn, "The Lao-tzu Myth" pp. 51–3 for an account of the three births of Lao-tzu/Laozi.
41 He has a number of other names, too: Kuan-sheng Ti-chün/Guansheng Dijun, "Holy Emperor Lord Kuan/Guan" is perhaps the main one, but he is also called Wen-heng Ti-chün/Wenhen Dijun, Fu-mo Ta-ti/Fumo Dadi, Hsieh-t'ien Ta-ti/Xietian Dadi and En-chu kung/Enzhu Gong.

42 See Palmer and Xiaomin, *Essential Chinese Mythology*, pp. 126–39.
43 Kwok Man Ho and Joanne O'Brien, translators and eds, *The Eight Immortals of Taoism: Legends and fables of popular Taoism* (London, Sydney, Auckland, Johannesburg: Rider, 1990), pp. 22–3.
44 For a full account of these see Maspero, *Taoism and Chinese Religion*, pp. 147–9.
45 Thompson, *Chinese Religion*, p. 63.
46 *Ibid.*, p. 67. Thompson also notes that there are two distinct historical traditions about the origins of this man that has become a god, though they are dated widely apart.
47 For a detailed description of nature deities, see Maspero, *Taoism and Chinese Religion*, pp. 96–101.
48 Valerie Hansen, "Gods on Walls: A Case of Indian Influence on Chinese Lay Religion" in Patricia Buckley Ebrey and Peter Gregory (eds), *Religion and Society in T'ang and Sung China* (Honolulu: University of Hawaii Press, 1993), pp. 75–6.
49 See Angela Zito, "City Gods and their Magistrates" in Lopez (ed.), *Religions of China in Practice*, pp. 74–6 for a detailed discussion of this god, and the story surrounding his investiture.
50 Julian F. Pas in cooperation with Man Kam Leung, *Historical Dictionary of Taoism* (Lanham, Middlesex and London: The Scarecrow Press, Inc.,1998), pp. 109–10.
51 Zito, "City Gods and their Magistrates", p. 72.
52 *Ibid.*
53 See Pas, *Historical Dictionary of Taoism*, pp. 292–4.
54 Terry F. Kleeman, "The Expansion of the Wen-ch'ang Cult" in Ebrey and Gregory (eds), *Religion and Society in T'ang and Sung China*, p. 47.
55 *Ibid.*, p. 48.
56 Pas, *Historical Dictionary of Taoism*, p. 346.
57 See Maspero, *Taoism and Chinese Religion*, pp. 176–81.
58 Robinet, *Taoism*, pp. 37–8.
59 Schipper, *The Taoist Body*, p. 164.
60 Livia Kohn, *Early Chinese Mysticism: Philosophy and soteriology in the Taoist tradition* (Princeton, New Jersey: Princeton University Press, 1992), p. 84.
61 Robinet, *Taoism*, p. 49.
62 The text was later lost, and reconstructed in the sixth century. For other literature concerning immortals, including extracts from texts, see Kohn, *The Taoist Experience*, pp. 325–32 and 335.
63 Schipper, *The Taoist Body*, p. 164.
64 Blofeld, *Taoism*, p. 60.
65 For the full tale, see Kwok Man Ho and O'Brien, *The Eight Immortals of Taoism*, pp. 61–3.
66 For a full translation of the tale see "Lü Dongbin" from the *Zengxian liexian zhuan* ("Illustrated Immortals' Biographies") in Kohn, *The Taoist Experience*, pp. 126–32.
67 See for example the story of his sojourn at the Ou River in Palmer and Xiamin, *Essential Chinese Mythology*, pp. 112–16.
68 See Schipper, *The Taoist Body*, p. 160.
69 See Kwok Man Ho and O'Brien, *The Eight Immortals of Taoism*, p. 23.
70 *Ibid.*, p. 25.
71 For the full story, see *ibid.*, pp. 109–12.
72 For other tales of Li T'ieh-kuai /Li Tieguai see Palmer and Xiaomin, *Essential Chinese Mythology*, pp. 102–12 and 117–22.
73 For this, and other tales about Chang Kuo-lao/Zhang Guolao see Kwok Man Ho and O'Brien, *The Eight Immortals of Taoism*, pp. 115–27.
74 Maspero, *Taoism and Chinese Religion*, pp. 172–3.
75 The full account is in Kwok Man Ho and O'Brien, *The Eight Immortals of Taoism*, pp. 128–9.
76 *Ibid.*, p. 28.

NOTES TO PP.221-31

77 Maspero, *Taoism and Chinese Religion*, p. 163.
78 Richard Herne, *Magick, Shamanism & Taoism: The I Ching in ritual and meditation* (St. Paul, Minnesota: Llewellyn Publications, 2001), p. 312.
79 Blofeld, *Taoism*, p. 98.
80 See "The Flower Basket Epiphany" in Kwok Man Ho and O'Brien, *The Eight Immortals of Taoism*, pp. 142–7.
81 For this and other tales of Ho Hsien-ku/He Xiangu, see *ibid.*, pp. 130–6.
82 See Michel Strickmann, "On the Alchemy of T'ao Hung-ching" in Holmes Welch and Anna Seidel (eds), *Facets of Taoism: Essays in Chinese Religion* (New Haven and London: Yale University Press, 1979), pp. 181–2.
83 See John Lagerway, "Chen-jen", in *ER*, 3, p. 232.
84 See *Fafu kejie wen* ("Rules and Precepts Regarding Ritual Garb") in Kohn, *The Taoist Experience*, pp. 336–43.
85 Schipper, *The Taoist Body*, pp. 164–5.
86 A term, according to Benn, that had many characteristics similar to those of deities. "Religious Aspects of Emperor Hsüan-tsung's Taoist Ideology", p. 130.
87 Strictly speaking the word "being" should be translated as "man". I have avoided genderized language where possible, but it needs to be remembered that the sage was almost invariably male.
88 For distinction between the different terms, see Isabelle Robinet, *Taoist Meditation: The Mao-Shan Tradition of Great Purity*, translated by Julian F. Pas and Norman J. Girardot (Albany, New York: State University of New York Press, 1993, first published in French in 1979 as *Méditation taoïste*), pp. 42–8.
89 See Kohn, *The Taoist Experience*, pp. 280–1.
90 Hellmut Wilhelm, *Heaven, Earth, and Man in the Book of Changes: Seven Eranos Lectures* (Seattle and London: University of Washington Press, 1977), p. 179.
91 Livia Kohn, *Taoist Mystical Philosophy: The Scripture of Western Ascension* (Albany, New York: State University of New York Press, 1991), p. 142.
92 Blofeld, *Taoism*, p. 40.

Chapter 8 *Religious Taoism*

1 Donald H. Bishop, "Introduction" in Donald H. Bishop ed., *Chinese Thought: An introduction* (Delhi: Motilal Banarsidass, 2001 reprint of 1995 edn, first published 1985), p. 169.
2 Henri Maspero, *Taoism and Chinese Religion*, translated by Frank A. Kierman, Jr. (Amherst: The University of Massachusetts Press, 1981, first published as *Le Taoïsme et les religions chinoises* in 1971), pp. 78–9.
3 Master Jen Fa-jung, quoted in Bill Porter, *Road to Heaven: Encounters with Chinese hermits* (San Francisco: Mercury House, 1993), pp. 56–8.
4 Michael Saso, *Blue Dragon White Tiger: Taoist rites of passage* (Washington D.C.: The Taoist Center, 1990), p. 21.
5 Kenneth Dean, *Taoist Ritual and Popular Cults of South-east China* (Princeton, New Jersey: Princeton University Press, 1993), pp. 13–14.
6 *Ibid.*, p. 17.
7 See Yoshitoyo Yoshioka, "Taoist Monastic Life" in Holmes Welch and Anna Seidel (eds), *Facets of Taoism: Essays in Chinese Religion* (New Haven and London: Yale University Press, 1979), pp. 230–1.

8 Michael Saso, *Taoist Master Chuang* (Eldorado Springs, Colorado: Sacred Mountain Press, 2000), p. 86.
9 There is no connection here with the old Shang-ch'ing/Shangqing school of Taoism, which is sometimes called the Mao-shan school.
10 Eva Wong, *The Shambhala Guide to Taoism* (Boston, Massachusetts and London: Shambhala, 1977), p. 116.
11 See David K. Jordan and Daniel L. Overmyer, *The Flying Phoenix: Aspects of Chinese sectarianism in Taiwan* (Princeton, New Jersey: Princeton University Press, 1986), pp. 213–14 and *passim*.
12 *Ibid.*, p. 216.
13 Daniel L. Overmyer, "Chinese Religion: An Overview" in Mircea Eliade (ed.), *Encyclopedia of Religion*, hereafter *ER* (New York: Macmillan Publishing Company and London: Collier Macmillan Publishers), 1987, vol. 3, p. 283.
14 See Saso, *Blue Dragon White Tiger*, p. 53.
15 Saso, *Taoist Master Chuang*, p. 60.
16 See Wong, *The Shambhala Guide to Taoism*, pp. 190–4.
17 John Lagerwey, "Taoist Priesthood" *ER*, 11, p. 547.
18 For a full account of such personal services supplied by priests, see Kristofer Schipper, *The Taoist Body*, translated by Karen C. Duval (Berkeley, Los Angeles, London: University of California Press, 1993, first published in 1982 as *Le corps taoïste*), pp. 73–4.
19 David K. Jordan, *Gods, Ghosts and Ancestors: The folk religion of a Taiwanese village* (Berkeley, Los Angeles, and London: University of California Press, 1972), p. 29.
20 For these grades, see Saso, *Taoist Master Chuang*, p. 198.
21 See John E. Vollmer, "Clothing: Religious Clothing in the East" in *ER*, 3, pp. 537–8.
22 Michael Saso, *Taoism and the Rite of Cosmic Renewal* (Pullman, Washington: Washington State University Press, 1990 reprint of 1989 edn), p. 23.
23 Kenneth Dean, "Revival of Religious Practices in Fujian: A Case Study" in Julian F. Pas (ed.), *The Turning of the Tide: Religion in China today* (Oxford, Hong Kong, New York: Hong Kong Branch Royal Asiatic Society in association with Oxford University Press, 1989), p. 51.
24 Dean, *Taoist Ritual and Popular Cults of South-east China*, p. 7.
25 *Ibid.*, p. 47.
26 For a full account of the training of a *tao-shih/taoshi* see Schipper, *The Taoist Body*, pp. 82–8.
27 See Thomas H. Hahn, "New Developments Concerning Buddhist and Taoist Monasteries" in Pas *The Turning of the Tide*, p. 91.
28 Jordan, *Gods, Ghosts, and Ancestors*, p. 78.
29 For a detailed account of traditional Chinese spirit divination see Richard J. Smith, *Fortune-tellers and Philosophers: Divination in traditional Chinese Society* (Boulder, San Francisco, Oxford: Westview Press, 1991), chapter 6, pp. 221–57.
30 For a full account of this ritual see John Lagerwey, *Taoist Ritual in Chinese Society and History* (New York: Macmillan Publishing Company and London: Collier Macmillan, 1987), chapter 13.
31 Called *chiao/jiao*, *pei/bei*, *pei-chiao/beijiao* or *chiao-kua/jiaogua*, see Smith, *Fortune-tellers and Philosophers* pp. 234 and 234–5 for a full description of their use.
32 See Wei Yi-min and Suzanne Coutanceau, *Wine for the Gods: An account of the religious traditions and beliefs of Taiwan* (Taiwan: Ch'eng Wen Publishing Company, 1976), pp. 26–7.
33 See Jordan, *Gods, Ghosts, and Ancestors*, pp. 61–2.
34 Jordan and Overmyer, *The Flying Phoenix*, p. 125.
35 Smith gives a colourful account of such practice in Hong Kong, *Fortune-tellers and Philosophers*, pp. 1–3.
36 *Ibid.*, pp. 13 and 36.

37 Yoshioka, "Taoist Monastic Life", p. 229.
38 For a full description see Schipper, *The Taoist Body* pp. 20–23, and Laurence G. Thompson, *Chinese Religion: An introduction* (Belmont, California: Wadsworth Publishing Company, 1989 reprint of 1979 edn), pp. 68–74.
39 Saso, *Blue Dragon White Tiger*, p. 10.
40 John Blofeld, *Taoism: The quest for immortality* (London, Boston, Sydney, Wellington: Mandala, Unwin Paperbacks), pp. 98–9.
41 See, for example, Lagerwey, *Taoist Ritual in Chinese Society and History*, pp. 25–48.
42 Livia Kohn, "The *Tao-te-ching* in Ritual" in Livia Kohn and Michael LaFargue (eds), *Lao-tzu and the* Tao-te-ching (Albany, New York: State University of New York Press, 1998), pp. 143–9.
43 For an account of these in Taiwan, see Avron A. Boretz, "Righteous Brothers and Demon Slayers: Subjectivities and Collective Identities in Taiwanese Temple Processions", in Paul R. Katz and Murray A. Rubinstein (eds), *Religion and the Formation of Taiwanese Identities* (New York and Basingstoke: Palgrave Macmillan, 2003), pp. 219–52.
44 See Isabelle Wong, "Music and Religion in China, Korea and Tibet" in *ER*, 10, p. 198.
45 Stephen H. West, "Drama" in William H. Nieuhauser, Jr. (ed. and compiler), *The Indiana Companion to Traditional Chinese Literature* (Bloomington: Indiana University Press, 1986), p. 14.
46 Dated by Harper to Warring States or early imperial China, see Donald Harper, "Warring States, Qin, and Han Manuscripts Related to Natural Philosophy and the Occult" in Edward L. Shaughnessy (ed.), *New Sources of Early Chinese History: An introduction to the reading of inscriptions and manuscripts* (Berkeley, California: Society for the Study of Early China, and The Institute of East Asian Studies, University of California, 1997), p. 241.
47 Schipper, *The Taoist Body*, p. 37.
48 See Jordan, *Gods, Ghosts, and Ancestor*, p. 91.
49 For a full account of ancestor offerings and ritual at special times, see Saso, *Blue Dragon White Tiger*, pp. 153–6.
50 Joseph A. Adler, *Chinese Religions* (London and New York: Routledge, 2002), p. 117.
51 Anna Seidel, "Buying One's Way to Heaven: The Celestial Treasury in Chinese Religions" in *History of Religions*, 17 (1978), p. 421.
52 *Ibid.*, p. 427.
53 Saso, *Taoist Master Chuang*, p. 195.
54 *Ibid.*
55 Lagerwey, *Taoist Ritual in Chinese Society and History*, p. 51.
56 There are a number of excellent contemporary case studies of the *chiao/jiao* in south-east Asia particularly. See, for example, Dean's work, *Taoist Ritual and Popular Cults of South-east Asia*, and the descriptions of a *chiao/jiao* on the occasion of the birthday of a god, chapter 2, pp. 61–98. See also Saso's work, *Taoism and the Rite of Cosmic Renewal, passim*. For a very vivid and warm account, that captures the atmosphere more than other works, see Lagerwey, *Taoist Ritual in Chinese Society and History*, chapter 4. For celebration in Hong Kong, see Tanaka Issei, "The Jaio Festival in Hong Kong and the New Territories" in Pas, *The Turning of the Tide*, pp. 271–98.
57 Dean, *Taoist Ritual and Popular Cults of South-east China*, p. 17.
58 For a full account of the sixty-year *chiao/jiao*, see Saso, *Taoism and the Rite of Cosmic Renewal*, pp. 43–57.
59 See, for example Dean's comments on the Patriarch of the Clear Stream whose birthday is celebrated inside the temple by Buddhist priests and outside by Taoist ones, in *Taoist Ritual and Popular Cults of South-east China*, pp. 128–9.
60 Jordan, *Gods, Ghosts, and Ancestors*, p. 104.

61 *Ibid.*, p. 103.
62 See Kenneth Dean, "Daoist Ritual in Contemporary South-east China", pp. 306–11.
63 For a full account of this festival in Peikang, Taiwan, see Christian Jochim, *Chinese Religions* (New Jersey: Prentice-Hall, 1986), pp. 152–6.
64 See David Faure, "Folk Religion in Hong Kong and the New Territories Today" in Pas, *The Turning of the Tide*, p. 259.
65 These seem to have been current in ancient times, see Harper, "Warring States, Qin, and Han Manuscripts Related to Natural Philosophy", pp. 233–4. According to Kwang-chih Chang, as early as Shang times, all the names of kings contained one or another of the Ten Stems, *Shang Civilization* (New Haven and London: Yale University Press, 1980), p. 5. The Shang also used the Ten Stems as a unit of time – ten days.
66 These are sometimes given different names: the Rat is sometimes the Mouse; the Ox, Bull or Buffalo; the Hare, a Rabbit; the Goat, a Sheep or Ram; the Rooster, Chicken or Fowl; the Pig, Boar.
67 Since the Chinese New Year does not begin until 22 January, anyone born before, between 1 February, 2003 and that date, would have been born in the year of the Goat, a Water and *yin* year.
68 See Yin-lien C. Chin, Yetta S. Center and Mildred Ross, *Chinese Folktales: An anthology* (Armonk, New York and London: North Castle Books, 1996), pp. 157–67.
69 Wolfram Eberhard, *Chinese Festivals* (New York: Henry Schuman, 1952), p. 49.
70 Saso, *Taoism and the Rite of Cosmic Renewal*, pp. 27–8.
71 Saso, *Blue Dragon White Tiger*, p. 173.
72 For these, see Wei and Coutanceau, *Wine for the Gods*, pp. 9–15.
73 Lagerwey, *Taoist Ritual in Chinese Society and History*, p. 22.
74 *Ibid.*, pp. 22–3.
75 For a full account of the story surrounding this hero, see Kwok Man Ho and Joanne O'Brien, *The Eight Immortals of Taoism: Legends and Fables of Popular Taoism* (London, Sydney, Auckland, Johannesburg: Rider, 1990), pp. 36–8.
76 Saso, *Blue Dragon White Tiger*, pp. 180–1.
77 Schipper, *The Taoist Body*, p. 31.
78 *Ibid.*, p. 72.
79 See Laurence G. Thompson, *The Chinese Way in Religion* (Belmont, California: Wadsworth Publishing Company, 1973), pp. 183–5 and for the cult of T'ai Shan/Taishan pp. 178–85 *passim*.
80 Ch'ing-ch'eng Shan/Qingchenshan, Chung-nan Shan/Zhongnanshan, Ho-ming Shan/Hemingshan, Huang-shan, Ko-tsao Shan/Gezaoshan, K'un-lun/Kunlun, Lou-fu Shan, Lung-hu Shan/Longhushan, Wu-tang Shan/Wudangshan. See Pas, *Historical Dictionary of Taoism*, pp. 224–31.
81 For a list of mountains and literature related to them, see Judith Magee Boltz, *A Survey of Taoist Literature: Tenth to seventeenth centuries* (Berkeley, California: Institute of East Asian Studies, Center for Chinese Studies, University of California, 1987), pp. 101–21.
82 Wolfram Eberhard, *A Dictionary of Chinese Symbols: Hidden symbols in Chinese life and thought* (London and New York: Routledge, 1988), pp. 84–6.
83 Hellmut Wilhelm, *Change: Eight Lectures on the I Ching*, translated from German by Cary F. Baynes (London: Routledge and Kegan Paul, 1975 reprint of 1961 edn), p. 28.
84 Tao Tao Liu Sanders: *Dragons and Spirits from Chinese Mythology* (Peter Lowe, 1980), p. 48.
85 See Eberhard, *A Dictionary of Chinese Symbols*, pp. 234–6.
86 Jean C. Cooper, *Chinese Alchemy: The Taoist quest for immortality* (Wellingborough, Northamptonshire: The Aquarian Press, 1984), p. 135.

87 Pas, *Historical Dictionary of Taoism*, p. 253.
88 E. N. Anderson, "Flowering Apricot: Environmental Practice, Folk Religion, and Daoism" in Norman J. Girardot, James Miller, and Liu Xiaogan (eds), *Daoism and Ecology: Ways within a cosmic landscape* (Cambridge, Massachusetts: Harvard University Press, 2001), p. 158.
89 Most of the information here and in what follows in this section is based on the research of Michael Saso, *Blue Dragon White Tiger*, pp. 121–39.
90 *Ibid.*, p. 125.
91 Charles Windridge, *Tong Sing: The Chinese Book of Wisdom* (Leicester: Silverdale Books, 2002, first published 1999), p. 259. See also the use of a conception chart, pp. 260–2.
92 Saso, *Blue Dragon White Tiger*, pp. 129–30.
93 See Eberhard, *A Dictionary of Chinese Symbols*, pp. 203–4.
94 For the custom in Taiwan, see Jordan, *Gods, Ghosts, and Ancestors*, pp. 140–55.
95 For the full ritual ceremony, see Saso, *Blue Dragon White Tiger*, pp. 99–120.
96 Conrad Schirokauer, *A Brief History of Chinese Civilization* (San Diego, New York, Chicago, Austin, Washington D.C., London, Sydney, Tokyo, Toronto: Harcourt Brace & Company, 1991), p. 371.
97 However, the tension between reincarnation and a life in Heaven that haunts other religions does so also in Chinese-Taoist traditions.
98 Jordan, *Gods, Ghosts, and Ancestors*, p. 33.
99 David Johnson, "Popular Beliefs and Values" in William Theodore de Bary and Richard Lufrano, compilers and eds., *Sources of Chinese Tradition: Vol. 2 from 1600 through the twentieth century* (New York: Columbia University Press, second edn 2000), pp. 85–6.
100 See Johnson, *ibid.*, and Lagerwey, *Taoist Ritual in Chinese Society and History*, pp. 216–37.
101 For a full account see Thompson, *The Chinese Way in Religion*, pp. 140–53.
102 Donald E. MacInnis, *Religion in China Today: Policy and Practice* (Maryknoll, New York: Orbis Books, 1989), p. 370.

Chapter 7 Taoism Today

1 Lucy Jen Huang, "The role of Religion in Communist Chinese Society" in Laurence G. Thompson, *The Chinese Way in Religion* (Belmont, California: Wadsworth Publishing Company, 1973), p. 241.
2 See the biography of Jung Chang cited in Deborah Summer (ed.), *Chinese Religion: An anthology of sources* (New York and Oxford: Oxford University Press, 1995), p. 315.
3 *Ibid.*, p. 313.
4 1982 Policy Paper on religion cited in Julian F. Pas, "Introduction: Chinese Religion in Transition" in Julian F. Pas (ed.), *The Turning of the Tide: Religion in China today* (Oxford, New York and Hong Kong: Hong Kong Branch Royal Asiatic Society in association with Oxford University Press, 1989), p. 11.
5 Kenneth Dean, "Daoist Ritual in Contemporary South-east China", in Donald S. Lopez (ed.), *Religions of China in Practice* (Princeton, New Jersey: Princeton University Press, 1996), p. 310.
6 For these statistics, see Pas, "Introduction: Chinese Religion in Transition", pp. 8–9.
7 Julia Ching, *Chinese Religions* (Basingstoke, Hampshire: Macmillan, 1993), pp. 211–12.
8 Restoration of temples, for example, has to be with official sanction, but there is some evidence to suggest that local people build temples anyway, and flout state requirements if they can. See Thomas A. Hahn, "New Developments Concerning Buddhist and Taoist Monasteries" in Pas, *The Turning of the Tide*, p. 88.
9 Pas, "Introduction: Chinese Religion in Transition", p. 20.

10 Kristofer Schipper, *The Taoist Body* translated by Karen C. Duval (Berkeley, Los Angeles and London: University of California Press, 1993, first published in 1982 as *Le corps taoïste*), p. 19.
11 For detail of today's Taoist practices in Fujian, see Kenneth Dean, "Revival of Religious Practices in Fujian: A Case Study" in Pas, *The Turning of the Tide*, pp. 51–78 and, also Dean, *Daoist Ritual and Popular Cults of South-east China* (Princeton, New Jersey: Princeton University Press, 1993).
12 See Donald E. MacInnis, *Religion in China Today: Policy and practice* (Maryknoll, New York: Orbis Books, 1989), pp. 367–8.
13 See the excerpt from Helen F. Siu's *Reforming Tradition: Politics and popular rituals in contemporary China*, in MacInnis, *ibid.*, pp. 368–72.
14 Stevan Harrell in a private letter to Donald MacInnis, *ibid.*, p. 373.
15 Julian F. Pas, "Revival of Temple Worship and Popular Religious Traditions" in Pas, *The Turning of the Tide*, pp. 176–7.
16 Laurence G. Thompson, *Chinese Religion: An introduction* (Belmont, California: Wadsworth Publishing Company, 1989 reprint of 1979 edn), p. 145.
17 J. J. Clarke, *The Tao of the West: Western transformations of Taoist thought* (London and New York: Routledge, 2000), p. 37.
18 For a comprehensive study of T'ai Chi Ch'üan/Taijiquan see Jeaneane Fowler and Keith Ewers, *T'ai Chi Ch'üan: Harmonizing Taoist belief and practice* (Brighton: Sussex Academic Press, 2005).
19 Paul Crompton, *Tai Chi: An introductory guide to the Chinese art of movement* (Shaftesbury, Dorset and Boston, Massachusetts: Element, 2000, first published in different format in 1990), p. 119.
20 Douglas Wile, *Lost T'ai-chi Classics from the Late Ch'ing Dynasty* (Albany, New York: State University of New York Press, 1996), p. xv.
21 Paul Crompton, *Tai Chi: An introductory guide to the Chinese art of movement* (Shaftesbury, Dorset, Boston, Massachusetts and Melbourne, Victoria: Element, 2000, first published in different format in 1990 as *The Elements of Tai Chi* also by Element), p. 7.
22 Sophia Delza, *T'ai Chi Ch'üan Body and Mind in Harmony: The integration of meaning and method* (Albany, New York: State University of New York Press, revised edn 1985, first published 1965), p. 14.
23 Stuart Alve Olson, *T'ai Chi According to the I Ching: Embodying the principles of the Book of Changes* (Rochester, Vermont: Inner Traditions, 2001), p. 38
24 Catherine Despeux, "Gymnastics: The Ancient Tradition" in Livia Kohn (ed.) in cooperation with Yoshinobu Sakade, *Taoist Meditation and Longevity Techniques*. Michigan Monographs in Chinese Studies, vol. 61 (Michigan: Center for Chinese Studies, The University of Michigan 1989), p. 241.
25 *Ibid.*, p. 239.
26 "An Explanation of the Essence and Application of T'ai-chi" from the *Yang Family Forty Chapters*, translator Wile, *Lost T'ai-chi Classics from the Late Ch'ing Dynasty*, p. 70.
27 Crompton, *Tai Chi*, p. 18.
28 The *form* usually refers to the whole series of movements, though in some schools the plural, *forms*, is used to depict the whole series. See for example Delza's use of the term in *T'ai-chi Ch'üan*, *passim*.
29 Delza, *ibid.*, p. 21.
30 *Ibid.*, p. 22.
31 Lawrence Galante, *Tai Chi: The Supreme Ultimate* (York Beach, Maine: Samuel Weiser, Inc., 1981), p. 13.

32 Olson, *T'ai Chi According to the I Ching*, pp. 11–12.
33 Patricia Buckley Ebrey, "The Response of the Sung State to Popular Funeral Practices" in Patricia Buckley Ebrey and Peter N. Gregory (eds), *Religion and Society in T'ang and Sung China* (Honolulu: University of Hawaii Press, 1993), p. 215.
34 See Eva Wong, *The Shambhala Guide to Taoism* (Boston, Massachusetts and London: Shambhala, 1997), pp. 139–40.
35 *Ibid.*, p. 138.
36 Without any knowledge of *feng-shui* when we bought our home, I now find it to be in a perfect spot! It is protected from high winds by hills behind it in the north. It is a place where a stream meanders slowly, and it nestles in the embrace of hills that provide protection, rather like an armchair, with a sloping view to the south. See Michael Page, *The Power of Ch'i: An introduction to Chinese Mysticism and Philosophy* (Wellingborough, Northamptonshire: The Aquarian Press, 1988), p. 80.
37 Jack Potter, "Wind, Water, Bones and Souls: The Religious World of the Cantonese Peasant", *Journal of Oriental Studies* 8 (1970), cited in Laurence G. Thompson, *The Chinese Way in Religion* (Belmont, California: Wadsworth Publishing Company, 1973), p. 221. Potter's research was based on his study of the village of Ping Shan in the New Territories of Hong Kong in 1961–3. It makes interesting reading, particularly concerning the lengths to which the villagers would go to adopt the principles of *feng-shui* – even to the extent of growing a moustache to change the energies in one's face! See pp. 218–30 in the same source.
38 Richard Craze, *Practical Feng Shui: The Chinese art of living in harmony with your surroundings* (London, New York, Sydney, Bath: Lorenz Books, 1997), p. 15.
39 Kwok Man-ho with Joanne O'Brien, *Feng Shui: An introductory guide to the Chinese way to harmony* (Shaftesbury, Dorset, Boston, Massachusetts and Melbourne, Victoria: Element, 1999, first published in different format in 1991), pp. 11–12.
40 Page, *The Power of Ch'i*, p. 78.
41 Jean Cooper, *Yin and Yang: The Taoist Harmony of Opposites* (Wellingborough, Northamptonshire: The Aquarian Press, 1981), p. 43.
42 John Blofeld, *Taoism: The quest for immortality* (London, Boston, Sydney, Wellington: Mandala, Unwin Paperbacks, 1989, first published 1979), p. 7.
43 Eva Wong, *Feng-shui: The ancient wisdom of harmonious living for modern times* (Boston, Massachusetts and London: Shambhala, 1996), p. 255.
44 Gill Hale, *The Practical Encyclopedia of Feng Shui* (London: Hermes House, 2001, first published 1999), p. 7.
45 Isabelle Robinet, *Taoism: Growth of a Religion*, translated by Phyllis Brooks (Stanford, California: Stanford University Press, 1997, first published as *Histoire du Taoïsme des origines au XIVe siècle* in 1992), p. 260.
46 Clarke, *The Tao of the West*, p. 196.

Glossary of Chinese Names and Terms

Chang Chan/Zhang Zhan	fourth century author of a commentary on the *Chuang-tzu/Zhuangzi*.
Chang Chüeh/Zhang Jue	one of the three Chang/Zhang brothers who founded Way of Great Peace Taoism and led the Yellow Turbans against the Han in 184.
Chang Kuo-lao/Zhang Guolao	one of the eight Taoist Immortals.
Chang Liang/Zhang Liang	one of the three Chang/Zhang brothers who founded Way of Great Peace Taoism and led the Yellow Turbans against the Han in 184.
Chang Lu/Zhang Lu	grandson of the founder of Five Bushels of Rice and Celestial Masters Taoism, who consolidated his grandfather's work.
Chang Pao/Zhang Bao	one of the three Chang/Zhang brothers who founded Way of Great Peace Taoism and led the Yellow Turbans against the Han in 184.
Chang Po-tuan/Zhang Boduan	tenth to eleventh century Taoist and inner alchemist; traditional founder of the Southern branch of inner alchemy.
Chang San-feng/ Zhang Sanfeng	the traditional founder of T'ai Chi Ch'üan/Taijiquan.
Chang Tao-ling/Zhang Daoling	founder of Five Bushels of Rice and Celestial Masters Taoism in the early second century.
Ch'eng I/Cheng Yi	eleventh century commentator on the *I Ching/Yijing*.
Cheng-i chiao-chu/ Zhengyi Jiaozhu	"Master of Orthodox Unity".
Cheng-i Meng-wei Tao/ Zhengyi Mengweidao	Way of Orthodox Unity Taoism (Celestial Masters).
chen-jen/zhenren	"perfected, true, real, being".
chi/ji	"ultimate", "utmost point", "ridge-pole".
ch'i/qi	energies within and surrounding all things; vitality.
chiao/jiao	pure sacrifice ceremonial offerings.

GLOSSARY OF CHINESE NAMES AND TERMS

chih-jen/zhiren	"perfect being".
chi-kung/qigong	energy circulation through bodily movement.
ching/jing	essence; the liquid element of the body, including saliva, sweat, semen and gastric juices.
Ch'ing-t'an/Qingtan	Pure or Light Conversation school.
Ch'in Shih Huang-ti/ Qinshi Huangdi	the first Emperor of China.
Chou I/Zhouyi	*The Changes of the Chou/Zhou*, the early name for the *I Ching/Yijing*.
ch'üan	"boxing", "fist".
Ch'üan-chen/Quanzhen	Complete Reality school of Taoism.
Chuang-tzu/Zhuangzi	a Taoist classic, said to have been written by Chuang-tzu/Zhuangzi.
Chuang-tzu/Zhuangzi	an early sage, traditional author of the *Chuang-tzu/Zhuangzi*.
Chuan-hsü/Zhuanxu	one of the mythical Five August Emperors.
Chung-li Ch'üan/ Zhongli Quan	one of the Eight Taoist Immortals.
chün-tzu/junzi	Confucian term for a superior person, a gentleman.
fang-shih/fangshi	an early diverse group of people who practised divination, magic, medicine, and the like, and who promoted ideas of immortality.
fa-shih/fashi	Red-head Taoist priests.
feng-shui	"earth magic", geomancy.
fu	a talismanic, symbolic and magical sign.
Fu Hsi/Fu Xi	mythical Emperor, the founder of hunting and animal husbandry; reputed founder of the eight trigrams.
Han Hsiang-tzu/ Han Xiangzi	one of the Eight Taoist Immortals.
Ho Hsien-ku/ He Xiangu	one of the Eight Taoist Immortals.
Ho-po/Hebo	the god, Count of the River.
Ho-shang-kung/ Heshanggong	second century BCE author of the earliest commentary on the *Tao Te Ching/Daodejing*.
ho-t'u/hetu	"Yellow River Map", the primal arrangement of the eight trigrams, traditionally discovered by Fu Hsi/Fu Xi.
Ho Yen/He Yan	third century Neo-Taoist.
Hsiang Chuan/Xiangzhuan	*Commentary on the Images*, one of the *Ten Wings* of the *I Ching/Yijing*.
hsien/xian	an immortal.
Hsi Wang-mu/ Xiwangmu	the Queen Mother of the West.
Hsüan-hsüeh/Xuanxue	"Mystery Learning" metaphysical school of Taoism.

GLOSSARY OF CHINESE NAMES AND TERMS

Hsüan-tsung/Xuanzong	eighth century Emperor of the T'ang/Tang dynasty.
Hsüan-yüan chaio/Xuanyuan jiao	recently founded "Yellow Emperor Religion" in Taiwan.
Hsü Hui/Xu Hui and Hsü Mi/Xu Mi	two persons to whom the Shang-ch'ing/Shangqing scriptures were revealed.
Hsü-kua/Xugua	*Sequence of Hexagrams*, one of the *Ten Wings* of the *I Ching/Yijing*.
Huai-nan-tzu/Huainanzi	second century text.
Huang-Lao Chün/Huanglaojun	name given to the deified Lao-tzu/Laozi.
Huang-ti/Huangdi	the Yellow Emperor.
Huang-ti Nei-ching/Huangdi Neijing	the *Yellow Emperor's Classic of Internal Medicine*.
hun	the spirit that survives the body at death and that transforms into a *shen*.
hun-tun/hundun	chaos.
i/yi	"intention".
I Ching/Yijing	*Book of Changes*, the ancient Chinese *Classic* concerning change and transformation in the universe.
jen/ren	love
Ko Ch'ao-fu/Ge Chaofu	founder of the Ling-pao/Lingbao tradition of Taoism.
Ko Hung/Ge Hong	fourth century CE naturalist and alchemist, author of the *Pao-p'u-tzu/Baopuzi*.
K'ou Ch'ien-chih/Kou Qianzhi	reformer of the Celestial Masters school.
kua/gua	"trigrams", yarrow-stick divination.
kuan/guan (or *kung/gong*)	a monastery or abbey.
Kuan-ti/Guandi	God of War
kuei/gui	physical forms or ghosts after death.
kung/gong (or *kuan/guan*)	a monastery or abbey.
Kuo Hsiang/Guo Xiang	third to fourth century Neo-Taoist.
Lan Ts'ai-ho/Lan Caihe	one of the Eight Taoist Immortals.
Lao-tzu/Laozi	early sage, traditionally the founder of Taoism and author of the *Tao Te Ching/Daodejing*.
Lao-tzu pien-hua ching/Laozi bianhuajing	"Transformations of Lao-tzu Scripture".
li	propriety; reason; principle.
Li Chi/Liji	*Book of Rites* or *Rituals* from the Chou/Zhou dynasty.
Lieh-hsien Chuan/Liexian Zhuan	"Biography of the Immortals".
Lieh-tzu/Liezi	early Taoist sage, traditional author of the text that bears his name.

GLOSSARY OF CHINESE NAMES AND TERMS

Li Erh/Li Er	traditionally the real name of Lao-tzu/Laozi.
Li Hung/Li Hong	messianic figure who will herald a Golden Age.
ling	power.
Ling-pao/ Lingbao Taoism	influential school of Taoism in the Six Dynasties period.
Ling-pao T'ien-tsun/ Lingbao Tianzun	also called T'ai-shang Tao-chün/Taishang Daozun, the second of the three highest deities in the Taoist pantheon.
Li Shao-chün/Li Shaojun	one of the Eight Taoist Immortals.
Li T'ieh-kuai/Li Tieguai	one of the Eight Taoist Immortals.
Liu An	second century Prince or minor King of Huai-nan, editor of the *Huai-nan-tzu/Huainanzi*.
lu	a register of spirits and deities at the command of an earthly master.
Lu Hsiu-ching/ Lu Xiujing	compiler of the first collection of Taoist scriptures in the fifth century, and founder of a splinter group of Celestial Masters Taoism in the South of China.
Lü-shih Ch'un-ch'iu/ Lüshi Chunqiu	*Annals of Spring and Autumn from the state of Lü* dated to Chou/Zhou dynasty times.
Lü Tung-pin/ Lü Dongbin	one of the Eight Taoist Immortals.
Lü Yen/Lü Yan	Ancestor Lü, reputed forerunner of the Complete Reality school of Taoism and one of the Eight Taoist Immortals, also known as Lü Tung-pin/Lü Dongbin.
Ma-tsu/Mazu	Empress or Queen of Heaven, also called T'ien-shang Sheng-mu/Tianshang Shengmu.
miao	a small temple.
Nei-p'ien/Neipian	the esoteric chapters of Ko Hung/Ge Hong's *Pao-p'u-tzu/Baopuzi* dealing with Taoism.
nei-tan/neidan	inner or internal alchemy, the alchemy of the body.
Nü-kua/Nügua	one of the Three August Ones, a mythical ancestor credited with the creation of humans.
Pa-hsien/Baxian	the Eight Immortals.
Pa-kua/Bagua	the basic eight trigrams of the *I Ching/Yijing* arranged in a circular system.
P'an-ku/Pangu	a mythical ancestor and source of the world according to one legend; also one of the Three August Ones.
Pao-p'u-tzu/Baopuzi	literally, "the Master that embraces simplicity", the literary name of the fourth century CE naturalist and alchemist Ko Hung/Ge Hong, and the name of a text that he wrote.
Pao-sheng Ta-ti/ Baosheng Dadi	the Divine Physician.

GLOSSARY OF CHINESE NAMES AND TERMS

Pei-tou/Beidou	the Big Dipper.
p'o/po	the physical *yin* spirit that survives after death and returns to the earth.
san-ch'ing/sanqing	the Three Pure Ones.
San-huang Ching/ Sanhuangjing	*Scripture of the Three Sovereigns*, one of the three "caverns" of the Taoist canon.
san-i/sanyi	the "Three Primordials" or "Originals".
san-kuan/sanguan	the Three Agents or Rulers.
san-yüan/sanyuan	the "Three Ones".
Shang-ch'ing/ Shangqing Taoism	influential school of Taoism in the Six Dynasties period.
Shang-ti/Shangdi	"Lord on High", the major deity of the Shang dynasty.
shen	spirit; the spiritual essence of the body.
sheng-jen/shengren	"sage", "saint".
Shen-hsien Chuan/ Shenxian Zhuan	*Biographies of Spirit Immortals*.
shen-jen/shenren	"divine" or "spirit" beings.
Shen-nung/Shennong	ox-headed, mythical Emperor who founded agriculture and medicine.
shen spirits	*yang* spirits that rise from the body at death and that are capable of rebirth.
Shih Chi/Shiji	*Records of the Grand Historian* composed by Ssu-ma Ch'ien/Sima Qian in the second to first centuries BCE.
Shih Ching/Shijing	*Book of Poetry* or *Songs* from the Chou/Zhou dynasty.
Shih-i/Shiyi	the *Ten Wings*, the *Appendices* to the *I Ching/Yijing*.
Shu Ching/Shujing	*Book of Documents* from the Chou/Zhou dynasty.
Shui-kuan/Shuiguan	the Agent of Water.
Shun	one of the mythical Five August Emperors.
Shuo-kua/Shuogua	*Discussion of Trigrams*, one of the *Ten Wings* of the *I Ching/Yijing*.
Ssu-ma Ch'ien/ Sima Qian	second to first century historian, author of the *Records of the Grand Historian*, the *Shih Chi/Shiji*.
Ta-chuan/Dazhuan	*The Great Treatise*, one of the *Ten Wings* of the *I Ching/Yijing*.
t'ai/tai	"high", "great", "supreme", "remote".
T'ai-chi/Taiji	"Supreme Ultimate".
T'ai-hsü/Taixu	"Great Void".
T'ai-i/Taiyi	"Supreme One/Changer/Transformer", the major deity of the Three Ones.
T'ai-ping Ching/ Taipingjing	*Scripture of Great Peace*.
T'ai-p'ing Tao/ Taipingdao	Way of Great Peace Taoism.

GLOSSARY OF CHINESE NAMES AND TERMS

T'ai-shang Lao-chün/ Taishang Laojun	"Supreme Lord on High", or "Supreme Lord Lao-tzu/Laozi", an early name for the deified Lao-tzu/Laozi.
T'ai-shang Tao-chün/ Taishang Daozun	"Supreme Lord of Tao" the second of the triad of highest deities in Taoism, also called Ling-pao T'ien-tsun/Lingbao Tianzun.
tan-t'ien/dantian	a term in inner alchemy for three "cauldrons", three important areas of the body – upper middle and lower – which are important in the circulation and transmutation of energy in internal alchemy.
Tao	the non-manifest and manifest essence of the universe.
Tao-chia/Daojia	philosophical and mystical Taoism.
Tao-chiao/Daojiao	religious Taoism.
T'ao Hung-ching/ Tao Hongjing	founder of the Shang-ch'ing/Shangqing school of Taoism.
tao-jen/daoren	"being" or "person" of *Tao*.
tao-kuan/daoguan	a large public centre of Taoism.
tao-shih/daoshi	"specialists of Tao", or Black-head priests.
Tao Te Ching/Daodejing	text of eighty-one short chapters attributed to Lao-tzu/Laozi.
Tao-te T'ien-tsun/ Daode Tianzun	"celestial Venerable of *Tao* and *Te*", one of the titles of Lao-tzu/Laozi as the third member of the triad of highest deities.
Tao-tsang/Daozang	the Taoist canon.
tao-yin/daoyin	gymnastic exercises.
Te/De	the spontaneous, natural and rhythmic expression of *Tao* in the universe.
ti/di	ancestors and personal gods.
T'ien/Tian	Heaven.
T'ien-i/Tianyi	"Heavenly One", one deity of the Three Ones.
T'ien-kuan/Tianguan	the Agent of Heaven.
T'ien-shang Sheng-mu/ Tianshang Shengmu	Empress or Queen of Heaven, also called Ma-tsu/Mazu.
T'ien-shih/Tianshi	"Celestial" or "Heavenly Master".
T'ien-shih Tao/ Tianshi Dao	the Celestial Masters school of Taoism.
T'ien-tsun/Tianzun	the Three Celestial, Heavenly Lords or Venerables at the head of the Taoist pantheon of deities.
T'ien-tzu/Tianzi	Son of Heaven.
Ti I/Tiyi	"Earthly One", one deity of the Three Ones.
Ti-kuan/Diguan	the Agent of Earth.
Ts'ai Shen/Caishen	God of Wealth.
Tsa-kua/Zagua	one of the *Ten Wings* of the *I Ching/Yijing* containing miscellaneous comments on hexagrams.
Ts'an-t'ung Ch'i/ Cantongqi	the *Triplex Unity*, a mid-second century internal alchemy text, said to have been composed by Wei Po-yang/Wei Boyang.

GLOSSARY OF CHINESE NAMES AND TERMS

Ts'ao Kuo-chiu/Cao Guojiu	one of the Eight Immortals of Taoism.
Tsou Yen/Zou Yan	founder of the combined school of *Yin-Yang* and the Five Agents.
tz'u/ci	a shrine.
tzu-jan/ziran	naturalness, spontaneity.
Wai-p'ien/Waipian	the exoteric chapters of Ko Hung/Ge Hong's *Pao-p'u-tzu/Baopuzi*.
wai-tan/waidan	outer or external alchemy, the alchemy of the laboratory.
Wang Pi/Wang Bi	third century Neo-Taoist and author of a commentary on the *Tao Te Ching/Daodejing*.
Wei Po-yang/Wei Boyang	second century author of the *Triplex Unity*.
Wen Ch'ang/Wen Chang	God of Literature.
Wen-yen/Wenyan	*Commentary on the Words*, one of the *Ten Wings* of the *I Ching/Yijing*.
Wu-chi/Wuji	the undifferentiated Void; absolute nothingness that exists before creation.
wu-hsing/wuxing	the Five Agents, Elements or Phases.
wu-wei	non-action.
Yang Hsi/Yang Xi	fourth century revealer of the scriptures of the Shang-ch'ing/Shangqing school of Taoism.
Yao	one of the mythical Five August Emperors.
yin and *yang*	the two complementary forces in all existence.
Yü/Yu	mythical founder of the Hsia/Xia dynasty according to some traditions, and one of the Five August Emperors, also known as K'ao-hsin/Kaoxin.
Yüan-shih T'ien-tsun/Yuanshi Tianzun	Celestial Venerable of the Primordial Beginning, the head of the triad of Taoist deities.
Yü-huang Shang-ti/Yuhuang Shangdi	the Jade Emperor.

Bibliography

The bibliography is select and confined to sources in English.

Eliade, Mircea (ed.) 1987: *Encyclopedia of Religion*. New York: Macmillan Publishing Company is abbreviated throughout as *ER*.

General sources on Taoism

Baldrian, Farzeen 1987: "Taoism: An Overview". In *ER*, 14: pp. 288–306.
Barrett, Timothy H. 1987: "Taoism: History of Study". In *ER*, 14: 329–32.
Blofeld, John 1978: *Taoism: The Road to Immortality*. London, Boston, Sydney, Wellington: Mandala. Published also by Shambhala in 2000, including John Eaton and Calthorpe Blofeld as authors.
—— 1973: *The Secret and Sublime: Taoist mysteries and magic*. London: George Allen & Unwin.
Bokenkamp, Stephen 1986: "Taoist Literature Part I: Through the T'ang Dynasty". In William H. Nienhauser, Jr. (ed. and compiler), *The Indiana Companion to Traditional Chinese Literature*. Bloomington: Indiana University Press, pp. 9–22.
—— 1987: *A Survey of Taoist Literature, Tenth to Seventeenth Centuries*. Berkeley: Institute of East Asian Studies.
Boltz, Judith Magee 1987: "Taoism: Taoist Literature". In *ER*, 14: pp. 317–29.
—— 1986: "Taoist Literature Part II: Five Dynasties to the Ming". In William H. Nienhauser, Jr. (ed. and compiler), *The Indiana Comapnion to Traditional Chinese Literature*. Bloomington: Indiana University Press, pp. 152–74.
Chryssides, George 1983: "God and the Tao". *Religious Studies* 19: pp. 1–11.
Cooper, Jean C. 1990 reprint of 1972 edn: *Taoism: The Way of the mystic*. Wellingborough, Northamptonshire: The Aquarian Press.
Creel, Herrlee. G. 1982 reprint of 1970 edn: *What is Taoism? And Other Studies in Chinese Cultural History*. Chicago and London: University of Chicago Press.
Fischer-Schreiber, Ingrid 1996: *The Shambhala Dictionary of Taoism*, translated from German by Werner Wünsche. Boston: Shambhala.
Forstater, Mark 2001: *The Spiritual Teachings of the Tao*. London: Hodder and Stoughton.
Girardot, Norman J., James Miller and Liu Xiaogan (eds.) 2001: *Daoism and Ecology: Ways within a cosmic landscape*. Cambridge, Massachusetts: Harvard University Press.
Hanson, Chad 1992: *A Daoist Theory of Chinese Thought: A philosophical interpretation*. Oxford, New York et al.: Oxford University Press.
Hartz, Paula R. 1993: *Taoism: World religions*. New York: Facts on File, Inc.
Izutsu, Toshihika 1984: *Sufism and Taoism: A comparative study of key philosophical concepts*. Berkeley, Los Angeles, London: University of California Press.
Kirkland, Russell 2004: *Taoism: The enduring tradition*. New York and London: Routledge.

Kohn, Livia 1992: *Early Chinese Mysticism: Philosophy and soteriology in the Taoist tradition*. Princeton, New Jersey: Princeton University Press.
—— 1989: "The Mother of the Tao". *Taoist Resources* 1.2: pp. 37–113.
—— 2000: *Daoism Handbook*. Leiden: Brill.
—— and Harold Roth (eds.) 2002: *Daoist Identity: History, lineage and ritual*. Honolulu: University of Hawaii Press.
Major, John S. 1981: *Taoism and Chinese Religion*. Translated from French by Frank A. Kierman Jr. Amherst: University of Massachusetts Press.
Maspéro, Henri 1981: *Taoism and Chinese Religion*, translated from French by Frank A. Kierman Jr. Amherst: University of Massachusetts Press. Originally published as *Le Taoïsme et les religions chinoises*, 1971.
Palmer, Martin 1991: *The Elements of Taoism*. Shaftesbury, Dorset and Rockport, Massachusetts: Element.
Pas, Julian F. 1988: *A Select Bibliography on Taoism*. New York: Stony Brook, Institute for Advanced Studies of World Religions.
—— in cooperation with Man Kam Leung 1998: *Historical Dictionary of Taoism*. Lanham, Maryland and London: The Scarecrow Press, Inc.
Peerenboom, R. P. 1990: "Cosmogony, the Taoist Way". In *Journal of Chinese Philosophy* 17: pp. 157–74.
Pregadio, Fabrizio (ed.), 2004: *The Encyclopedia of Taoism*, 2 vols. New York: RoutledgeCurzon.
Rawson, Phillip and Laszlo Legeza 1991, first published 1973: *Tao: The Chinese philosophy of time and change*. London: Thames and Hudson.
Robinet, Isabelle 1997: *Taoism: Growth of a religion*. Translated from French by Phyllis Brooks. Stanford, California: Stanford University Press. First published in 1992 as *Histoire du Taoïsme des origines au XIVe siècle*.
Seidel, Anna 1989–1990: "Chronicle of Taoist Studies in the West 1950–1990". *Cahiers d'Extrême-Asie* 5: 223–347.
—— and Michel Strickmann (eds) 1992 15th edn: "Taoism". In *Encyclopaedia Britannica, Macropedia*, vol. 28. Chicago: University of Chicago, pp. 394–407.
Thompson, Laurence 1993: "What is Taoism? (With Apologies to H. G. Creel)". *Taoist Resources* 4.2: pp. 9–22.
Verellen, Franciscus 1995: "Taoism". In "Chinese Religions: The state of the field (Part II). Living Religious Traditions: Taoism, Confucianism, Buddhism, Islam and Popular Religion". *Journal of Asian Studies* 54: pp. 322–46.
Watts, Alan 2000: *What is Tao?* Novato, California: New World Library.
—— with the collaboration of Al Chung-Liang Huang 1975: *Tao: The Watercourse Way*. London: Penguin.
—— and Mark Watts (ed.) 1999: *Taoism: Way beyond seeking*. San Francisco: Harper Collins.
Welch, Holmes and Anna Seidel (eds) 1979: *Facets of Taoism: Essays in Chinese religion*. New Haven and London: Yale University Press.
Wildish, Paul 2000: *Principles of Taoism*. London: Thorsons.
Wong, Eva 1997: *Taoism: A complete introduction to the history, philosophy, and practice of an ancient Chinese spiritual tradition*. Boston, Massachusetts and London: Shambhala.
Wu, Joseph 2001 reprint of 1985 edn: "Taoism". In Donald H. Bishop (ed.), *Chinese Thought: An introduction*. Delhi: Motilal Banarsidass, pp. 32–58.
Wu, Yao-yü 1991: *The Taoist Tradition in Chinese Thought*. Translated by Laurence G. Thompson, edited by Gary Seaman. *San Chiao Li Ts'ê, Part 1*. Los Angeles: Ethnographics Press, University of Southern California.

—— 1995: *The Literati Tradition in Chinese Thought*. Translated by Laurence G. Thompson, edited by Gary Seaman. *San Chiao Li Ts'e, Part 2*. Los Angeles: Ethnographics Press, University of California.

Yu, David C. (translator) 2000: *History of Chinese Daoism, Vol. 1*. Lanham, New York, Oxford: University Press of America.

Van de Weyer, Robert (ed.) 2001: *366 Readings from Taoism and Confucianism*. New Alresford, UK: Arthur James, and Cleveland, Ohio: The Pilgrim Press.

Chinese History, philosophy and religion

Primary sources

Blanc, Charles Le 1985: *Huai-nan-tzu: Philosophical Synthesis in Early Han Thought*. Hong Kong: Hong Kong University Press.

de Bary, William Theodore and Irene Bloom (compilers), with the collaboration of Wing-tsit Chan 1999 revised, second edn first published 1960: *Sources of Chinese Tradition Vol. 1: From earliest times to 1600*. New York: Columbia University Press.

de Bary, William Theodore and Richard Lufrano (compilers) 1999 revised edn first published 1960: *Sources of Chinese Tradition Vol. 2: From 1600 through to the twentieth century*. New York and Chichester, West Sussex: Columbia University Press.

Chan, Wing-tsit (translator and compiler) 1963: *A Source Book in Chinese Philosophy*. Princeton, New Jersey: Princeton University Press, and London: Oxford University Press.

DeWoskin, Kenneth J. (translator) 1983: *Doctors, Diviners, and Magicians of Ancient China: Biographies of the Fang-shih*. New York: Columbia University Press.

Ebrey, Patricia Buckley (ed.) 1981: *Chinese Civilization and Society: A sourcebook*. New York: The Free Press, and London: Collier Macmillan.

Major, John S. 1993: *Heaven and Earth in Early Han Thought: Chapters Three, Four and Five of the Huainanzi*. Albany, New York: State University of New York Press.

Sommer, Deborah (ed.) 1995: *Chinese Religion: An anthology of sources*. New York and Oxford: Oxford University Press.

Thompson, Laurence G. 1973: *The Chinese Way in Religion*. Belmont, California: Wadsworth Publishing Company.

Waley, Arthur (translator) 1955: *Nine Songs: A study of shamanism in ancient China*. London: Allen & Unwin.

Secondary sources

Adler, Joseph A. 2002: *Chinese Religions*. London and New York: Routledge.

Allan, S. 1991: *The Shape of the Turtle: Myth, art, and cosmos in early China*. Albany, New York: State University of New York Press.

Allinson, Robert (ed.) 1989: *Understanding the Chinese Mind: The philosophical roots*. Oxford, New York and Hong Kong: Oxford University Press.

—— 1989: "An Overview of the Chinese Mind". In Robert Allinson (ed.), *Understanding the Chinese Mind: The philosophical roots*. Oxford, New York and Hong Kong: Oxford University Press, pp. 1–25.

Ames, Roger T. 1983: *The Art of Rulership. A study in ancient Chinese political thought*. Honolulu: University of Hawaii Press.

Barrett, Timothy H. 1996: *Taoism under the T'ang: Religion and empire during the golden age of Chinese history*. London: WellSweep.

Benn, Charles 1987: "Religious Aspects of Emperor Hsüan-tsung's Taoist Ideology". In David W.

BIBLIOGRAPHY

Chappell (ed.) 1987: *Buddhist and Taoist Practice in Medieval Chinese Society: Buddhist and Taoist Studies 2*. Asian Studies at Hawaii no. 34. Honolulu: University of Hawaii Press, pp. 127–45.
Bishop, Donald H. (ed.) 2001 reprint of 1985 edn: *Chinese Thought: An introduction*. Delhi: Motilal Banarsidass.
—— 2001 reprint of 1985 edn: "Chinese Thought before Confucius". In Donald H. Bishop (ed.), *Chinese Thought: An introduction*. Delhi: Motilal Banarsidass, pp. 3–13.
—— 2001 reprint of 1985 edn: "Introduction to Medieval Period". In Donald H. Bishop (ed.), *Chinese Thought: An introduction*. Delhi: Motilal Banarsidass, pp. 153–83.
—— 2001 reprint of 1985 edn: "Introduction to Modern Period". In Donald H. Bishop (ed.), *Chinese Thought: An introduction*. Delhi: Motilal Banarsidass, pp. 305–10.
Blanc, Charles Le 1993: "*Huai nan tzu*". In Michael Loewe (ed.), *Early Chinese Texts: A bibliographical guide*. Berkeley, California: The Society for the Study of Early China and The Institute of East Asian Studies, University of California.
Bodde, Derk. 1981: *Essays on Chinese Civilization*. Edited and translated by Charles Le Blanc and Dorothy Borei. Princeton: Princeton University Press.
Chang Kwang-chih 1980: *Shang Civilization*. New Haven and London: Yale University Press.
Chilson, Clark and Peter Knecht (eds) 2003: *Shamans in Asia*. New York: RoutledgeCurzon.
Ching, Julia 1993: *Chinese Religions*. Basingstoke, Hampshire and London: Macmillan.
Creel, Herrlee G. 1962 first published 1954: *Chinese Thought: From Confucius to Mao Tsê-tung*. London: Methuen.
Cua, Antonio S. (ed.) 2003: *Encyclopedia of Chinese Philosophy*. New York: RoutledgeCurzon.
Dawson, Raymond. (ed.) 1964: *The Legacy of China*. Oxford: Clarendon Press.
de Bary, William. Theodore and the Conference on Ming Thought 1970: *Self and Society in Ming Thought*. Studies in Oriental Culture no. 4. New York and London: Columbia University Press.
——1983: *The Liberal Tradition in China*, Ch'ien Mu Lectures, 1982. Hong Kong: Chinese University Press.
Ebrey, Patricia Buckley and Peter N. Gregory (eds) 1993: *Religion and Society in T'ang and Sung China*. Honolulu: University of Hawaii Press.
Eder, Matthias 1973: *Chinese Religion*. Asian Folklore Studies Monograph no. 6. Tokyo: The Society for Asian Folklore.
Edwards, Mike, photography by O. Louis Mazzatenta 2004: "Han Dynasty". In *National Geographic*, vol. 205, no. 2, February, pp. 2–29.
Eliade, Mircea 1964: *Shamanism*. Translated by W. R. Trask. London: Routledge & Kegan Paul.
Fu, Charles Wei-hsun and Wing-tsit Chan 1978: *Guide to Chinese Philosophy*. The Asian Philosophies and Religions Resource Guides. Boston, Massachusetts: G. K. Hall, and London: George Prior.
Fung Yu-lan 1983 reprint of second English edn 1952, first published in Chinese in 1931: *A History of Chinese Philosophy, Vol. 1: The period of the philosophers (from the beginnings to circa 100 B.C.)*, translated by Derk Bodde. Princeton, New Jersey: Princeton University Press.
—— 1983 reprint, first published in English in 1953, first published in Chinese in 1934: *A History of Chinese Philosophy, Vol. 2: The period of classical learning (from the second century B.C. to the twentieth century A.D.)*, translated by Derk Bodde. Princeton, New Jersey: Princeton University Press.
—— 1966 reprint of 1948 edn: *A Short History of Chinese Philosophy*. Edited by Derk Bodde. New York: The Free Press and London: Collier Macmillan.
Gernet, Jacques 1999 reprint of 1982 edn: *A History of Chinese Civilization*. Translated by J. R. Foster and Charles Hartman. First published in French as *Le Monde Chinois*. Cambridge: Cambridge University Press.
Graham, Angus C. 1990, first published 1986: *Studies in Chinese Philosophy and Philosophical Literature*.

State University of New York Series in Chinese Philosophy and Culture. Albany, New York: State University of New York Press.

—— 1992 second edn, first published 1958: *Two Chinese Philosophers: The metaphysics of the brothers Ch'êng*. La Salle, Illinois: Open Court.

—— 1991 reprint of 1989 edn: *Disputers of the Tao: Philosophical argument in ancient China*. La Salle, Illinois: Open Court.

—— 1990 reprint, first published 1981: *Studies in Chinese Philosophy and Philosophical Literature*. Albany: State University of New York Press.

Granet, Marcel 1995: *The Religion of the Chinese People*. Edited and translated with an introduction by M. Freedman. Oxford: Basil Blackwell, and 1977 New York: Harper & Row.

Henderson, John B. 1984: *The Development and Decline of Chinese Cosmology*. New York: Columbia University Press.

Harper, Donald 1997: "Warring States, Qin, and Han Manuscripts Related to Natural Philosophy and the Occult". In Edward L. Shaughnessy (ed.), *New Sources of Early Chinese History: An introduction to the reading of inscriptions and manuscripts*. Berkeley, California: Society for the Study of Early China, and The Institute of East Asian Studies, University of California, pp. 223–52.

Hessler, Peter, photography by O. Louis Mazzatenta 2003: "The New Story of China's Ancient Past". In *National Geographic*, vol. 204, no. 1, July, pp. 56–81.

Howard, Jeffrey A. 1984: "Concepts of Comprehensiveness and Historical Change in the *Huai-nan-tzu*". In Henry Rosemont Jr. (ed.), *Explorations in Early Chinese Cosmology*. Journal of the American Academy of Religion Studies, vol. 50 no. 2. Chicago, California: Scholars Press, pp. 119–132.

Ivanhoe, Philip. J. (ed.) 1996: *Chinese Language, Thought and Culture: Nivison and his critics*. Chicago and La Salle Illinois: Open Court.

Jochim, Christian 1986: *Chinese Religions: A cultural perspective*. Upper Saddle River, New Jersey: Prentice-Hall.

Keightley, David N. 1984: "Late Shang Divination: The Magico-Religious Legacy". In Henry Rosemont Jr. (ed.), *Explorations in Early Chinese Cosmology*. Journal of the American Academy of Religion Studies, vol. 50, no. 2. Chicago, California: Scholars Press, pp. 11–34.

—— 1997: "Shang Oracle-Bone Inscriptions". In Edward L. Shaughnessy (ed.), *New Sources of Early Chinese History: An introduction to the reading of inscriptions and manuscripts*. Berkeley, California: Society for the Study of Early China, and The Institute of East Asian Studies, University of California, pp. 15–56.

Kardos, Michael A. 1998: "Western Language Publications on Religions in China 1990–1994", *Journal of Chinese Religions* 26, pp. 67–134.

Lin Tongqi, Henry Rosemont Jr., and Roger T. Ames 1995: "Chinese Philosophy: A Philosophical Essay on the 'State of the Art'". *The Journal of Asian Studies* 54 (3): pp. 727–58.

Loewe, Michael (ed.) 1993: *Early Chinese Texts: A bibliographical guide*. Early China Special Monograph Series, no. 2. Berkeley, California: The Institute of East Asian Studies and The Society for the Study of Early China, University of California.

—— 1997: "Wood and Bamboo Administrative Documents of the Han Period". In Edward L. Shaughnessy (ed.), *New Sources of Early Chinese History: An introduction to the reading of inscriptions and manuscripts*. Berkeley, California: Society for the Study of Early China, and The Institute of East Asian Studies, University of California, pp. 161–92.

Major, John S. 1987: "Shang-ti". In *ER*, 13: pp. 223–4.

Maspéro, Henri 1978: *China in Antiquity*, translated by F. A. Kierman, Jr. Folkestone, Kent: Dawson, and Massachusetts: University of Massachusetts Press. Originally published in French as *La Chine Antique*, vol. 4 of *Histoire du monde*, Paris 1927, revised edn 1965.

Mattos, Gilbert L. 1997: "Eastern Zhou Bronze Inscriptions". In Edward L. Shaughnessy (ed.), *New Sources of Early Chinese History: An introduction to the reading of inscriptions and manuscripts*. Berkeley, California: Society for the Study of Early China, and The Institute of East Asian Studies, University of California, pp. 85–124.

Needham, Joseph 1988 reprint of 1961 edn, first published 1954: *Science and Civilization in China, Vol. 1: Introductory orientations*. Cambridge, New York, New Rochelle, Melbourne, Sydney: Cambridge University Press.

—— 1956: *Science and Civilization in China, Vol. 2: History of scientific thought*. Cambridge: Cambridge University Press.

Nienhauser, William H. Jr. (ed. and compiler) 1986: *The Indiana Companion to Traditional Chinese Literature*. Bloomington: Indiana University Press.

Overmyer, Daniel L. 1986: *Religions of China: The world as a living system*. San Francisco: Harper & Row.

—— 1987: "Chinese Religion: An Overview". In *ER*, 3: pp. 257–89.

Peerenboom, R. P. 1993: *Law and Morality in Ancient China: The Silk Manuscripts of Huang-Lao*. State University of New York Series in Chinese Philosophy and Culture. Albany, New York: State University of New York Press.

Roth, Harold 1987: "Fang-shih". In *ER*, 5: pp. 282–4.

—— 1992: *The Textual History of the Huai-nan Tzu*. Monograph Series no. 46. Ann Arbor, Michigan: The Association for Asian Studies.

Schirokauer, Conrad 1991: *A Brief History of Chinese Civilization*. San Diego, New York, Chicago, Austin, Washington D.C., London, Sydney, Tokyo, Toronto: Harcourt Brace Gap College.

Schwartz, Benjamin 1985: *The World of Thought in Ancient China*. Cambridge, Massachusetts: Harvard University Press.

Shaughnessy, Edward L. (ed.) 1997: *New Sources of Early Chinese History: An introduction to the reading of inscriptions and manuscripts*. Berkeley, California: Society for the Study of Early China, and The Institute of East Asian Studies, University of California.

—— 1997: "Western Zhou Bronze Inscriptions". In Edward L. Shaughnessy (ed.), *New Sources of Early Chinese History: An introduction to the reading of inscriptions and manuscripts*. Berkeley, California: Society for the Study of Early China, and The Institute of East Asian Studies, University of California, pp. 57–84.

Smith, D. Howard 1970 reprint of 1968 edn: *Chinese Religions*. New York, Chicago, San Francisco: Holt, Rinehart and Winston.

Thompson, Laurence G. fourth edn 1989, first published 1979: *Chinese Religion: An introduction*. Belmont, California: Wadsworth Publishing Company.

—— 1985: *Chinese Religion in Western Languages: A comprehensive and classified bibliography of publications in English, French and German through 1980*. The Association for Asian Studies. Tucson, Arizona: The University of Arizona Press.

—— (compiler) 1993: *Chinese Religions: Publications in western languages 1981 through 1990*. Ann Arbor, Michigan: Association of Asian Studies.

Vittinghoff, Helmolt (ed.) 2001: "Recent Bibliography in Classical Chinese Philosophy". *Journal of Chinese Philosophy* 28, pp. 1–208.

Weber, Max 1964, first published 1951: *The Religion of China: Confucianism and Taoism*, translated and edited by Hans H. Gerth, with an introduction by C. K. Yang. New York: The Macmillan Company, and London: Collier Macmillan.

Wieger Leon 1988: *Philosophy and Religion in China* edited by Derek Bryce. Felinfach, Lampeter: Llanerch Enterprises.

Wu, Laurence C. 1986: *Fundamentals of Chinese Philosophy*. Social Philosophy Research Institute Book

Series no. 3. Lanham, Maryland, New York, London: University Press of America.
Yu, David C. 1985: *Guide to Chinese Religion*. Boston, Massachusetts: G. K. Hall.

The *I Ching/Yijing*

Primary sources

Blofeld, John, 1989 reprint of 1984 edn, first published 1965: *I Ching: The Book of Change*. London, Sydney, Wellington: Unwin, Mandala.

Cheng Yi 1995 reprint of 1988 edn: *The Tao of Organization: The I Ching for group dynamics*, translated by Thomas Cleary. Boston, Massachusetts and London: Shambhala.

Cleary, T. (translator) 1986: *The Taoist I-ching*. Boston, Massachusetts and London: Shambhala.

—— 2003, first published 1986 and 1989 *The Taoist Classics: The collected translations of Thomas Cleary, Vol. 4: The Taoist I Ching, I Ching Mandalas*. Boston, Massachusetts and London: Shambhala.

Govinda, Lama Anagarika 1981: *The Inner Structure of the I Ching: The Book of transformations*. Tokyo and New York: Weatherhill.

Jou, Tsung Hwa 2000 reprint of 1983 edn: *The Tao of the I Ching: Way to divination*. Scottsdale AZ: Tai Chi Foundation.

Karcher, Stephen 2003: *Total I Ching: Myths for Change*. London: Time Warner Books.

Kunst, Richard Alan 1985: *The Original 'Yijing': A text, phonetic transcription, translation, and indexes, with sample glosses*. Unpublished Ph.D. dissertation, Ann Arbour, Michigan: University Microfilms International.

Legge, James (translator) 1988 reprint: *The Sacred Books of China: The texts of Confucianism. Part II: The Yi King*. The Sacred Books of the East, no. 16. Delhi: Motilal Banarsidass.

Over Raymond van (ed.) 1971: *I Ching*. Based on the translation by James Legge. New York, Scarborough, Ontario and London: Mentor.

Palmer, Martin, Kwok Man Ho and Joanne O'Brien, 1993, first published 1989: *The Fortune Teller's I Ching*. Ware, Hertfordshire: Wordsworth Editions. Also published under the title *The Contemporary I Ching*.

—— Jay Ramsay and Xiaomin Zhao 1995: *I Ching: Shamanic oracle of change*. London: Thorsons.

Ritsema, Rudolph and Stephen Karcher (translators) 1994: *I Ching: The classic Chinese oracle of change*. Shaftesbury: Element.

Rutt, Richard 2002: *The Book of Changes (Zhouyi): A Bronze Age document translated with introduction and notes*. Durham East-Asia Series no. 1. London and New York: Routledge Curzon, first published in 1966 as *Zhouyi, the Book of Changes: A new translation with commentary*. Richmond: Curzon Press.

Shaughnessy, Edward (translator) 1996: *I Ching: The classic of changes*. New York: Ballantine.

Wilhelm, Richard (translator) 1989, first published 1951: *I Ching or Book of Changes*. Translated from German by Cary. F. Baynes. London: Arkana.

—— 1990 reprint of 1985 edn: *The Pocket I Ching: The Richard Wilhelm translation*, translated from German by Cary F. Baynes and simplified by W. S. Boardman. London: Arkana, Penguin.

Wu, Jing-Nuan 1991: *Yi King*. Honolulu: University of Hawaii Press.

Secondary sources

Cheng, Chung-ying and E. Johnson 1987: "A Bibliography of the *I-ching* in Western Languages". *Journal of Chinese Philosophy* 14:1: pp. 73–90.

Shaughnessy, Edward L. 1993: "I ching". In Michael Loewe (ed.), *Early Chinese Texts: A bibliographical guide*. Berkeley, California: The Society for the Study of Early China, and The Institute of East Asian Studies, University of California, pp. 216–28.

Shchutskii, Iulian 1979: *Researches on the I Ching*. Translated by William L. MacDonald and Tsuyoshi Hasegawa with Hellmut Wilhelm. Bollingen Series 62. Princeton, New Jersey: Princeton University Press, first published in Britain in 1980: London: Routledge & Kegan Paul.

Smith, Kidder Jr., Peter K. Bol, Joseph A. Adler and Don J. Wyatt 1990: *Sung Dynasty Uses of the I Ching*. Princeton, New Jersey: Princeton University Press.

Swanson, Gerald 1984: "The Concept of Change in the *Great Treatise*". In Henry Rosemont, Jr. (ed.), *Explorations in Early Chinese Cosmology*. Journal of American Academy of Religion Studies, vol. 50, no. 2. Chicago, California: Scholars Press, pp. 67–93.

Wilhelm, Hellmut. 1977: *Heaven, Earth, and Man in the Book of Changes: Seven Eranos Lectures*. Seattle: University of Washington Press.

—— 1975 reprint of 1961 edn, original German edn 1944: *Change: Eight Lectures on the I Ching*. Translated from German by Cary. F. Baynes. London: Routledge & Kegan Paul.

—— 1975: *The Book of Changes in the Western Tradition: A selective bibliography*. Seattle: Institute for Comparative and Foreign Area Studies University of Washington.

Yao, Xinzhong and Helene McMurtrie 1999: "History and Wisdom of the Book of Changes: New Scholarship and Richard Rutt's Translation". In *Journal of Contemporary Religion* 14: 1, pp. 133–7.

Yin and *yang* and the Five Agents

Primary sources

Homann, Rolf (translator) 1976: *Pai wen p'ien or The Hundred Questions: A dialogue between two Taoists on the macrocosmic and microcosmic system of correspondences*. Religious Texts Translation Series, Nisaba no. 4. Leiden: E. J. Brill.

Wong, Eva. 1997: *Harmonizing Yin and Yang: The Dragon-tiger Classic*. Boston, Massachusetts and London: Shambhala.

Secondary sources

Cheng, Chung-Ying 1989: "Chinese Metaphysics as Non-metaphysics: Confucian and Taoist Insights into the Nature of Reality". In Robert Allinson, *Understanding the Chinese Mind: The philosophical roots*. Oxford, New York and Hong Kong: Oxford University Press, pp. 167–208.

Cooper, Jean C. 1981: *Yin and Yang. The Taoist Harmony of Opposites*. Wellingborough: The Aquarian Press.

Graham, Angus C. 1989 reprint of 1986 edn: *Yin-Yang and the Nature of Correlative Thinking*. Occasional Paper and Monograph Series no. 6. Singapore: Institute of East Asian Philosophies.

—— *Disputers of the Tao: Philosophical argument in ancient China*. La Salle, Illinois: Open Court, chapter 4, pp. 313–58.

Harper, Donald 1997: "Warring States, Qin, and Han Manuscripts Related to Natural Philosophy and the Occult". In Edward L. Shaughnessy (ed.), *New Sources of Early Chinese History: An introduction to the reading of inscriptions and manuscripts*. Berkeley, California: Society for the Study of Early China, and The Institute of East Asian Studies, University of California, pp. 223–42.

Louton, John 1984: "Concepts of Comprehensiveness and Historical Change in the *Lü-shih ch'un-ch'iu*". In Henry Rosemont Jr. (ed), *Explorations in Early Chinese Cosmology*. Journal of the American Academy of Religion Studies, vol. 50, no. 2. Chicago, California: Scholars Press, pp. 105–17.

Major, John S. 1984: "The Five Phases, Magic Squares, and Schematic Cosmography". In Henry Rosemont Jr. (ed.), *Explorations in Early Chinese Cosmology*. Journal of the American Academy of Religion Studies, vol. 50 no. 2. Chicago, California: Scholars Press, pp. 133–66.

Morgan, Carole 1990/1991: "T'ang Geomancy: The Wu-hsing ("Five Names") Theory and its Legacy". In *Tang Studies* 8–9: pp. 45–76.

Pas, Julian F. 1983: "Yin-yang Polarity: A Binocular Vision of the World". *Asian Thought and Society* 8: pp. 188–201.
Rosemont, Henry Jr. (ed.) 1984: *Explorations in Early Chinese Cosmology*. Journal of the American Academy of Religion Studies, vol. 50, no. 2. Chicago, California: Scholars Press.
Rubin, Vitaly A. 1982: "The Concepts of *Wu-Hsing* and *Yin-Yang*". *Journal of Chinese Philosophy* 9: pp. 131–58.
—— 1984: "Ancient Chinese Cosmology and *Fa-chia* Theory". In Henry Rosemont Jr. (ed.) *Explorations in Early Chinese Cosmology*. Journal of the American Academy of Religion Studies, vol. 50, no. 2. Chicago, California: Scholars Press, pp. 95–104.

Lao-tzu and the *Tao Te Ching*

Primary sources

Translations of the *Tao Te Ching/Daodejing* are too numerous to list here. Those found below are among the more well known, are well translated, and mostly easily available.
Addiss, S and S. Lombardo (translators) 1993: *Lao-Tzu Tao Te Ching*. (Ink paintings by S. Addiss). Indianapolis and Cambridge: Hackett Publishing Co.
Carus, Paul (translator) 2000: *The Teachings of Lao-tzu: The Tao Te Ching* London, Sydney, Auckland, Johannesburg: Rider.
Chan, A. K. L. 1991: *Two Visions of the Way: A study of the Wang Pi and the Ho-shang-kung Commentaries on the Lao-tzu*. Albany, New York: State University of New York Press.
Cleary, Thomas (translator) 1991: *The Essential Tao: An initiation into the heart of Taoism through the authentic* Tao Te ching *and the Inner Teachings of Chuang Tzu*. San Francisco: HarperSanFrancisco.
Feng, Gia Fu and Jane English (translators) 1989, first published 1972: *Lao Tsu: Tao Te Ching*. New York: Vintage.
Henricks, Robert G. (translator) 2000, first published 1989: *Lao-tzu: Te-tao Ching*. New York: Ballantine Books.
—— 2000: *Lao Tzu's Tao Te Ching: A translation of the startling new documents found at Guodian*. New York: Columbia University Press.
Hoff, Benjamin 1981: *The Way to Life. At the Heart of the Tao Te Ching*. New York and Tokyo: Weatherhill.
LaFargue, Michael 1992: *The Tao of the Tao Te Ching: A translation and commentary*. Albany, New York: State University of New York Press.
—— 1994: *Tao and Method: A reasoned approach to the Tao-te-ching*. Albany, New York: State University of New York Press.
Lao Tzu 1990: *Tao Te Ching*. Boston, Massachusetts: Shambhala.
—— 1993: *Tao Te Ching*. Translated from the Chinese by Kwok Man Ho, Martin Palmer & Jay Ramsay; calligraphy by Kwok-lap Chan. Shaftesbury, Dorset, Rockport, Massachusetts, Brisbane, Queensland: Element.
Lau, D. C. (translator) 1963: *Lao Tzu: Tao Te Ching*. Baltimore: Penguin Books.
Le Guin, Ursula K. (translator) 1997: *Lao Tzu: Tao Te Ching*. Boston, Massachusetts: Shambhala.
Legge, James (translator) 1989, first published 1891: *The Texts of Taoism: Part 1 The Tao Te Ching of Lao Tzu (Books I–XVII)*. Scotland: Tynron Press.
Mair, Victor H. (translator) 1990: *Tao Te Ching: The classic book of integrity and the Way*. New York: Bantam Books.
Maurer, Herrymoon (translator) 1986, first published 1982: *Tao: The Way of Ways*. Aldershot, Hants: Wildwood House.

Rump, Ariane and Wing-tsit Chan (translators) 1987 reprint of 1979 edn: *Commentary on the Lao-tzu by Wang Pi*. Monographs of the Society for Asian and Comparative Philosophy no. 6. Honolulu: University of Hawaii Press.

Star, Jonathan (translator) 2001: *Tao Te Ching: The definitive edition*. New York: Jeremy P. Tarcher.

Waley, Arthur (translator) 1987 reissue, first published 1934: *The Way and its Power: The Tao Tê Ching and its place in Chinese thought*. London and Sydney: Unwin Paperbacks.

Wilhelm, Richard (translator and commentator) 1990 reprint of 1985 edn: *Lao Tzu Tao Te Ching: The book of meaning and life*. Translated from the German by H. G. Oswald. London: Arkana.

Wu, John C. H. (translator) 1963: *Lao Tzu*. New York: St John's University Press.

Secondary sources

Allan, Sarah and Crispin Williams (eds.) 2000: *The Guodian Laozi: Proceedings of the International Conference*. Berkeley: Society for the Study of Early China.

Baxter, William H. 1998: "Situating the Language of the *Lao-tzu*: The Probable Dating of the *Tao-te-ching*". In Livia Kohn and Michael LaFargue, *Lao-tzu and the* Tao Te Ching. Albany, New York: State University of New York Press, pp. 231–54.

Boltz, Judith 1987: "Lao-tzu". In *ER*, vol. 8: pp. 454–9.

Boltz, William G. 1982: "The Religious and Philosophical Significance of the 'Hsiang erh' *Lao tzu* in the Light of the Ma wang tui Silk Manuscripts". *Bulletin of the School of Oriental and African Studies*, 45: pp. 95–117.

—— 1984: "Textual Criticism and the Ma wang tui *Lao tzu*". *Harvard Journal of Asiatic Studies* 44: pp. 185–224.

—— 1985: "The *Lao tzu* Text that Wang Pi and Ho-shang Kung Never Saw". *Bulletin of the School of Oriental and African Studies*, 48: pp. 493–501.

—— 1993: "Lao tzu Tao te ching". In Michael Loewe (ed.), *Early Chinese Texts: A bibliographical guide*. Berkeley, California: The Society for the Study of Early China and The Institute of East Asian Studies, University of California, pp. 269–92.

Chan, Alan K. L. 1998: "A Tale of Two Commentaries: Ho-shang-kung and Wang Pi on the *Lao-tzu*. In Livia Kohn and Michael LaFargue (eds), *Lao-tzu and the* Tao Te Ching. Albany: New York: State University of New York Press, pp. 89–118.

Csikszentmihalyi, Mark 1999: "Mysticism and Apophatic Discourse in the *Laozi*". In Mark Csikszentmihalyi and Philip J. Ivanhoe (eds), *Religious and Philosophical Aspects of the* Laozi. Albany, New York: State University of New York Press, pp. 33–58.

—— and Philip J. Ivanhoe (eds), 1999: *Religious and Philosophical Aspects of the Laozi*. Albany, New York: State University of New York Press.

Finazzo, Giancarlo 1981 reprint of 1968 edn: *The Notion of Tao in Lao Tzu and Chuang Tzu*. Taiwan: Taipei: Mei Ya Publications.

Girardot, Norman J. 1988 reprint of 1983 edn: *Myth and meaning in Early Taoism: The theme of chaos (hun-tun)*. Berkeley, Los Angeles, London: University of California Press.

Graham Angus C. 1998: "The Origins of the Legend of Lao Tan". In Livia Kohn and Michael LaFargue (eds), *Lao-tzu and the* Tao Te Ching. Albany: New York: State University of New York Press, pp. 23–40.

Henricks, Robert G. 1999: "Re-exploring the Analogy of the *Dao* and the Field". In Mark Csikszentmihalyi and Philip J. Ivanhoe (eds), *Religious and Philosophical Aspects of the* Laozi. Albany, New York: State University of New York Press, pp. 161–74.

Hoff, Benjamin 1994, first published 1982 and 1992: *The Tao of Pooh & The Te of Piglet*. London: Methuen.

Ivanhoe, Philip J. 1999: "The Concept of *de* ("Virtue") in the *Laozi*". In Mark Csikszentmihalyi and

BIBLIOGRAPHY

Philip J. Ivanhoe (eds), *Religious and Philosophical Aspects of the Laozi*. Albany, New York: State University of New York Press, pp. 239–58.

Kaltenmark, Max 1969, first published 1965: *Lao Tzu and Taoism*. Translated by Roger Greaves. Stanford, California: Stanford University Press.

Kohn, Livia 1998: "The Lao-tzu Myth". In Livia Kohn and Michael LaFargue (eds), *Lao-tzu and the Tao Te Ching*. Albany, New York: State University of New York Press, pp. 41–62.

—— 1998: *God of the Dao: Laozi in history and myth*. Ann Arbor: University of Michigan Center for Chinese Studies.

—— and Michael LaFargue (eds) 1998: *Lao-tzu and the Tao Te Ching*. Albany: New York: State University of New York Press.

LaFargue, Michael 1998: "Recovering the *Tao-te-ching*'s Original Meaning: Some Remarks on Historical Hermeneutics". In Livia Kohn and Michael LaFargue (eds), *Lao-tzu and the Tao Te Ching*. Albany, New York: State University of New York Press, pp. 255–76.

—— and Julian Pas 1998: "On Translating the *Tao-te-ching*". In Livia Kohn and Michael LaFargue (eds), *Lao-tzu and the Tao Te Ching*. Albany: New York: State University of New York Press, pp. 277–302.

Liu Xiaogan 1991: "Wu-wei (non-action) from Laozi to Huainan-zi". *Taoist Resources* 3: 1, pp. 41–56.

—— 1999: "An Inquiry into the Core Value of Laozi's Philosophy". In Mark Csikszentmihalyi and Philip J. Ivanhoe (eds), *Religious and Philosophical Aspects of the* Laozi. Albany, New York: State University of New York Press, pp. 211–38.

—— 1998: "Naturalness (*Tzu-jan*), the Core Value in Taoism: Its Ancient Meaning and its Significance Today". In Livia Kohn and Michael LaFargue (eds), *Lao-tzu and the Tao Te Ching*. Albany, New York: State University of New York Press, pp. 211–29.

Robinet, Isabelle 1999: "The Diverse Interpretations of the *Laozi*". In Mark Csikszentmihalyi and Philip J. Ivanhoe (eds), *Religious and Philosophical Aspects of the* Laozi. Albany, New York: State University of New York Press, pp. 127–60.

—— 1998: "Later Commentaries: Textual Polysemy and Syncretistic Interpretations". In Livia Kohn and Michael LaFargue (eds), *Lao-tzu and the Tao Te Ching*. Albany, New York: State University of New York Press, pp. 119–42.

Roth, Harold D. 1999: "The *Laozi* in the Context of Early Daoist Mystical Praxis". In Mark Csikszentmihalyi and Philip J. Ivanhoe (eds), *Religious and Philosophical Aspects of the* Laozi. Albany, New York: State University of New York Press, pp. 59–96.

Schwartz, Benjamin 1998: "The Thought of the *Tao-te-ching*". In Livia Kohn and Michael LaFargue (eds), *Lao-tzu and the Tao Te Ching*. Albany, New York: State University of New York Press, pp. 189–211.

Tateno Masami 1999: "A Philosophical Analysis of the *Laozi* from an Ontological Perspective". In Mark Csikszentmihalyi and Philip J. Ivanhoe (eds), *Religious and Philosophical Aspects of the* Laozi. Albany, New York: State University of New York Press, pp. 175–86.

Van Norden, Bryan W. 1999: "Method in the Madness of the *Laozi*". In Mark Csikszentmihalyi and Philip J. Ivanhoe (eds), *Religious and Philosophical Aspects of the* Laozi. Albany, New York: State University of New York Press, pp. 187–210.

Verellen, Franciscus 1990: "The Place of *Lao Tzu* in Early Chinese Thought". In William T. de Bary and I. Bloom (eds), *Approaches to Asian Classics*. New York: Columbia University Press, pp. 209–19.

Welch, Holmes 1957: *The Parting of the Way: Lao Tzu and the Taoist movement*. London: Methuen.

Chuang-tzu

Primary sources

Graham, Angus C. 1989 re-issue of 1981 edn: *Chuang-Tzu: The Inner Chapters*. London, Boston, Sydney, New Zealand: Mandala, Unwin Paperbacks.
—— 1982: *Chuang-tzu: Textual Notes to a Partial Translation*. London: School of Oriental and African Studies, University of London.
Hamill, Sam and J. P. Seaton (translators and eds) 1998: *The Essential Chuang Tzu*. Boston, Massachusetts: Shambhala.
Legge, James (translator) 1989, first published 1891: *The texts of Taoism, Vols 1 and 2. Part I The Tao Te Ching of Lao Tzu; The writings of Chuang Tzu*. Scotland: Tynron Press.
Merton, Thomas 1965: *The Way of Chuang Tzu*. Boston, Massachusetts: Shambhala.
Watson, Burton (translator) 1968: *The Complete Works of Chuang-tzu*. Translated from Chinese. Columbia College Program of Translations from the Oriental Classics. Records of Civilization: Sources and Studies no. LXXX. New York: Columbia University Press.
Wieger, Léon 1994: *Chuang-tzu: Nan-hua-ch'en-ching. The treatise of the transcendent master from Nan-hua*. Translated from French by Derek Bryce. Felinfach, Lampeter: Llanerch Publishers.

Secondary

Allinson, Robert E. 1989: *Chuang-Tzu for Spiritual Transformation: An analysis of the inner chapters*. Albany, New York: State University of New York Press.
Graham, Angus C. 1969: "Chuang-tzu's Essay on 'Seeing Things as Equal'". *History of Religions* 9: pp. 137–59.
Kjellberg, P. and Ivanhoe, P. 1996: *Essays on Scepticism, Relativism, and Ethics in the Zhuangzi*. Albany, New York: State University of New York Press.
Mair, Victor H. (ed.) 1983: *Experimental Essays on Chuang-tzu*. Asian Studies at Hawaii no. 29. Honolulu: University of Hawaii Press.
—— (ed.) 1983: *Chuang-tzu: Composition and Interpretation*. Symposium issue of *Journal of Chinese Religions* 11: pp. 106–17.
Rand, C. C. 1983: "*Chuang-tzu* Text and Substance". *Journal of Chinese Religions* 11: pp. 5–58.
Roth, Harold D 1993: "*Chuang tzu*". In Michael Loewe (ed.) *Early Chinese Texts: A bibliographical guide*. Berkeley, California: The Society for the Study of Early China and The Institute of East Asian Studies, University of California, pp. 56–66.
Watson, Burton 1987: "Chuang-tzu". In *ER*, 3: pp. 467–9.

Lieh-tzu

Barrett, Timothy H. 1993: "*Lieh tzu*". In Michael Loewe (ed.), *Early Chinese Texts: A bibliographical guide*. Berkeley, California: The Society for the Study of Early China and The Institute of East Asian Studies, University of California, pp. 298–308.
Graham, Angus C. (translator) 1990 first published 1960: *The Book of Lieh-tzu: A classic of the Tao*. Columbia University Press.
Wieger, Léon 1992: *Lieh-tzu Ch'ung-hu-ch'en-ching or The Treatise of the Transcendent Master of the Void*. Translated from French by Derek Bryce. Felinfach, Lampeter: Llanerch Publishers.
Wong, Eva 1995: *Lieh-tzu: A Taoist Guide to Practical Living*. Boston, Massachusetts and London: Shambhala.

Alchemy

Primary sources

Andersen, Poul 1980: *The Method of Holding the Three Ones: A Taoist manual of meditation of the fourth century A.D.* Studies on Asian Topics no. 1. London and Malmo: Curzon Press.

Bertschinger, Richard 2002 first published 1994: *The Secret of Everlasting Life: The first translation of the ancient Chinese text on immortality.* London: Vega.

Cleary, Thomas (translator) 2003, first published 1987: *Understanding Reality: A Taoist alchemical classic. The Taoist Classics: The collected translations of Thomas Cleary, Volume 2.* Boston, Massachusetts: Shambhala.

—— (translator) 2003, first published 1986: Chang Po-tuan's *The Inner Teachings of Taoism*, with commentary by Liu I-Ming. *The Taoist Classics: The collected translations of Thomas Cleary, Volume 2.* Boston, Massachusetts: Shambhala.

—— (translator) 2003, first published 1989: *The Book of Balance and Harmony. The Taoist Classics: The collected translations of Thomas Cleary, Volume 2.* Boston, Massachusetts: Shambhala.

—— (translator) 2003, first published 1996: *Practical Taoism. The Taoist Classics: The collected translations of Thomas Cleary, Volume 2.* Boston, Massachusetts: Shambhala.

—— 2003, first published 1991: *Vitality, Energy, Spirit: A Taoist Sourcebook. The Taoist Classics: The collected translations of Thomas Cleary, Volume 3.* Boston, Massachusetts: Shambhala.

—— 2003, first published 1988: *The Secret of the Golden Flower: The classic Chinese Book of Life. The Taoist Classics: The collected translations of Thomas Cleary, Volume 3.* Boston, Massachusetts: Shambhala.

—— 2003, first published 1989: *Immortal Sisters: Secrets of Taoist women. The Taoist Classics: The collected translations of Thomas Cleary, Volume 3.* Boston, Massachusetts: Shambhala.

—— 2003, first published 1988: *Awakening to the Tao: Liu I-ming. The Taoist Classics: The collected translations of Thomas Cleary, Volume 3.* Boston, Massachusetts: Shambhala.

—— (translator) 2000: *Taoist Meditation: Methods for cultivationg a healthy mind and body.* Boston, Massachusetts: Shambhala.

—— (translator) 2001: *Thunder in the Sky: Secrets on the acquisition of power.* Boston, Massachusetts: Shambhala.

Kohn, Livia 1991: *Taoist Mystical Philosophy: The Scripture of Western Ascension.* State University of New York Series in Chinese Philosophy and Culture. Albany, New York: State University of New York Press.

—— 1993: *The Taoist Experience: An anthology.* Albany, New York: State University of New York Press.

Ware, James R. (translator and ed.) 1981 first published 1966: *Alchemy, Medicine, & Religion in the China of A.D. 320: The Nei P'ien of Ko Hung (Pao-p'u-tzu).* New York: Dover Publications (1966 publication Cambridge, Massachusetts: Massachusetts Institute of Technology Press).

Wile, Douglas 1992: *Art of the Bedchamber. The Chinese sexual yoga classics including women's solo meditation texts.* Albany, New York: State University of New York Press.

Wong, Eva 1992: (translator) *Cultivating Stillness: A Taoist manual for transforming body and mind.* Boston, Massachusetts and London: Shambhala.

Secondary sources

Akahori, Akira 1989: "Drug Taking and Immortality". In Livia Kohn (ed.) in cooperation with Yoshinobu Sakade, *Taoist Meditation and Longevity Techniques.* Michigan monographs in Chinese Studies vol. 61. Ann Arbor: University of Michigan, Center for Chinese Studies pp. 73–98.

Baldrian-Hussein, Farzeen 1989–90: "Inner Alchemy: Notes on the origin and use of the term Neidan". *Cahiers d'Extrême-Asie* 5: pp. 163–90.

—— 1986: "Review of *Understanding Reality* by Thomas Cleary". *Harvard Journal of Asiatic Studies* 50: pp. 335–41.
Barrett, Timothy H. 1987: "Li Shao-chün". In *ER*, 8: p. 558.
—— 1987: "Ko Hung". In *ER*, 8: pp. 359–60.
Blofeld, John 1973: *The Secret and the Sublime: Taoist mysteries and magic*. London: Allen & Unwin.
Cooper, Jean C. 1990: *Chinese Alchemy: The Taoist Quest for Immortality*. New York: Sterling Publishing Co. and 1984: Wellingsborough, Northamptonshire: The Aquarian Press.
Coudert, Allison 1987: "Elixir". In *ER*, 5: 96–8.
Gregory, Peter N. (ed.) 1987: *Sudden and Gradual: Approaches to enlightenment in Chinese thought*. Kuroda Institute Studies in East Asian Buddhism 5. Honolulu: University of Hawaii Press.
Ishida, Hidemi 1989 "Body and Mind: The Chinese Perspective". In Livia Kohn (ed.) in cooperation with Yoshinobu Sakade, *Taoist Meditation and Longevity Techniques*. Michigan monographs in Chinese Studies, vol. 61. Ann Arbor: University of Michigan, Center for Chinese Studies, pp. 41–75.
Kohn, Livia (ed.) in cooperation with Yoshinobu Sakade (eds) 1989: *Taoist Meditation and Longevity Techniques*. Michigan monographs in Chinese Studies, vol. 61. Ann Arbor: University of Michigan, Center for Chinese Studies.
—— 1989: "Guarding the One: Concentrative Meditation in Taoism". In Livia Kohn (ed.) in cooperation with Yoshinobu Sakade, *Taoist Meditation and Longevity Techniques*. Michigan monographs in Chinese Studies, vol. 61. Ann Arbor: University of Michigan, Center for Chinese Studies, pp. 125–58.
—— 1989: "Taoist Insight Meditation: The Tang Practice of Neiguan". In Livia Kohn (ed.) in cooperation with Yoshinobu Sakade, *Taoist Meditation and Longevity Techniques*. Michigan monographs in Chinese Studies vol. 61. Ann Arbor: University of Michigan, Center for Chinese Studies, pp. 193–224.
—— 1993: *Taoist Meditation: The Mao-Shan tradition of Great Purity*. Translated from French by Julian F. Pas and Norman J. Girardot. Albany, New York: State University of New York Press.
—— 1991: "Taoist Visions of the Body". *Journal of Chinese Philosophy* 18:3 pp. 227–51.
—— 1988: "Medicine and Immortality in T'ang China". *Journal of the American Oriental Society* 108. 3: pp. 465–9.
Legeza, I. Laszlo. 1987: *Tao Magic: Secret language of diagrams and calligraphy*. London: Thames and Hudson.
Loewe, Michael 1979: *Ways to Paradise: The Chinese quest for immortality*. London: George Allen & Unwin.
Lu, K'uan-Yü (Charles Luk). 1970: *Taoist Yoga: Alchemy and Immortality*. London: Rider & Co.
Needham, Joseph *et al.* 1976: *Science and Civilisation in China Vol. 5 Part 3: Spagyrical Discovery and Invention: Historical survey, from cinnabar elixir to synthetic insulin*. Cambridge: Cambridge University Press.
—— 1980: *Science and Civilisation in China Vol. 5 Part 4: Spagyrical Discovery and Invention: Apparatus, theories and gifts*. Cambridge: Cambridge University Press.
—— with the collaboration of Lu Gwei-Djen 1983: *Science and Civilisation in China, Vol. 5, Chemistry and Chemical Technology Part 5: Spagyrical Discovery and Invention: Physiological alchemy*. Cambridge: Cambridge University Press.
—— 1971: *The Refiner's Fire: The enigma of alchemy in East and West*. The second J. D. Bernal Lecture delivered at Birckbeck College, London.
—— 1981: *Science in Traditional China: A comparative perspective*. Cambridge, Massachusetts: Harvard University Press and Hong Kong: The Chinese University Press.
Page, Michael 1988: *The Power of Ch'i: An introduction to Chinese mysticism and philosophy*. Wellingborough, Northamptonshire: The Aquarian Press.

Robinet, Isabelle 1989: "Original Contributions of *Neidan* to Taoism and Chinese Thought". In Livia Kohn (ed.) in cooperation with Yoshinobu Sakade, *Taoist Meditation and Longevity Techniques*. Michigan monographs in Chinese Studies, vol. 61. Ann Arbor: University of Michigan, Center for Chinese Studies, pp. 297–330.

—— 1989: "Visualization and Ecstatic Flight in Shanqing Taoism". In Livia Kohn (ed.) in cooperation with Yoshinobu Sakade, *Taoist Meditation and Longevity Techniques*. Michigan monographs in Chinese Studies, vol. 61. Ann Arbor: University of Michigan, Center for Chinese Studies, pp. 159–91.

—— 1998: *Harnessing the Power of the Universe*. London: Simon & Schuster.

—— 1990: "The Place and Meaning of the Notion of Taiji in Taoist Sources prior to the Ming Dynasty". In *History of Religions* pp. 373–411.

Roth, Harold D. 1999: *Original Tao: Inward Training and the foundations of Taoist mysticism*. New York and Chichester, West Sussex: Columbia University Press.

—— 1990: "The Early Taoist Concept of *Shen*: A Ghost in the Machine?" In Kidder Smith Jr. (ed.), *Sagehood and Systematizing Thought in Warring States and Han China*. Brunswick, Maine: Breckinridge Public Affairs Centre Asian Studies Program, 24, Bowdoin College.

—— 1991: "Psychology and Self Cultivation in Early Taoist Thought". *Harvard Journal of Asiatic Studies* 15 (2): pp. 599–650.

Saso, Michael 1995: *The Gold Pavilion: Taoist ways to peace, healing, and long life*. Boston: Tuttle.

Schipper, Kristofer M. 1993: *The Taoist Body*. Translated by Karen C. Duval. Berkeley, Los Angeles, London: University of California Press. First published in 1982 as *Le corps taoïste*.

Sivin, Nathan 1968: *Chinese Alchemy: Preliminary Studies*. Cambridge, Massachusetts: Harvard University Press.

—— (ed.) 1977: *Science and Technology in East Asia*. New York: Science History Publications.

—— 1987: "Chinese Alchemy". In *ER*, 1: pp. 186–90.

Strickmann, Michel (ed.) 1983: *Tantric and Taoist Studies in Honour of R. A. Stein, Vol. 2*. Brussels: Institut Belge des Hautes Études Chinoises.

Tu Wei-ming 1987: "Soul: Chinese Concepts". In *ER*, 13: pp. 447–50.

Sages, gods, ancestors and immortals

Primary sources

Chin, Yin-lien, C., Y. S. Center and M. Ross 1989: *Traditional Chinese Folktales*. Armonk, New York: M. E. Sharpe.

Eno, Robert 1996: "Deities and Ancestors in Early Oracle Inscriptions". In Donald S. Lopez Jr. (ed.), *Religions of China in Practice*. Princeton, New Jersey: Princeton University Press, pp. 41–51.

Kwok Man Ho and Joanne O'Brien (translators and eds) 1990: *The Eight Immortals of Taoism: Legends and fables of popular Taoism*. New York: Penguin Books.

Palmer, Martin and Zhao Xiaomin 1997: *Essential Chinese Mythology: Stories that change the world*. London: Thames.

Wong, Eva (translator) 1990: *Seven Taoist Masters: A folk novel of China*. Boston, Massachusetts and London: Shambhala.

—— (translator) 2001: *Tales of the Taoist Immortals*. Boston, Massachusetts and London: Shambhala.

—— (translator) 2000: *The Tao of Health, Longevity and Immortality: The teachings of Immortals Chung and Lü*. Boston, Massachusetts and London: Shambhala.

Secondary sources

Cahill, Suzanne E. 1993: *Transcendence & Divine passion: The Queen Mother of the West in Medieval China*. Stanford, California: Stanford University Press.

Fong, Mary Helena 1983: "The Iconography of the Popular Gods of Happiness, Emolument, and Longevity". *Artibus Asie* 44, 2–3: pp. 159–99.
Hansen, Valerie 1993: "Gods on Walls: A Case of Indian Influence on Chinese Lay Religion". In Patricia Buckley Ebrey and Peter Gregory (eds), *Religion and Society in T'ang and Sung China*. Honolulu: University of Hawaii Press.
Kidder Smith, Jr. (ed.) 1990: *Sagehood and Systematizing Thought in Warring States and Han China*. Brunswick, Maine: Bowdoin College Asian Studies Centre.
Kohn, Livia 1990: "Eternal Life in Taoist Mysticism". *Journal of the American Oriental Society* 110.4: pp. 623–48.
—— 1990: "Transcending Personality: From Ordinary to Immortal Life". *Taoist Resources* 2.2: pp. 1–22.
—— 1989: "The Mother of the Tao". *Taoist Religion* 1/2, pp. 37–109. Also *Taoist Resources* 1. 2. pp. 37–113.
Lagerway, John 1987: "Chen-jen". In *ER*, 3: pp. 231–3.
Robinet, Isabelle 1989: "Visualization and Ecstatic Flight in Shanqing Taoism". In Livia Kohn (ed.) in cooperation with Yoshinobu Sakade, *Taoist Meditiation and Longevity Techniques*. Michigan Monographs in Chinese Studies, vol. 6. Ann Arbor: Centre for Chinese Studies, the University of Michigan, pp. 159–91.
—— 1985–6: "The Taoist Immortals: Jesters of Light and Shadow, Heaven and Earth". *Journal of Chinese Religions* 13/14: pp. 87–107.
Roth, Harold 1987: "Huang-lao Chün". In *ER*, 6: pp. 483–4.
Sanders, Tao Tao Liu 1980: *Dragons, Gods and Spirits from Chinese Mythology*. Peter Lowe.
Seidel, Anna 1987: "Afterlife: Chinese Concepts". In *ER*, 1: pp. 124–7.
—— 1987: "Huang-ti". In *ER*, 6: pp. 484–5.
—— 1987: "Yü-huang". In *ER*, 15: p. 541.
Thompson, Laurence G. 1987: "Taoist Iconography". In *ER*, 7: pp. 50–4.
Yuan Ke 1993 reprint of 1991 edn: *Dragons and Dynasties: An introduction to Chinese mythology*. Selected and translated by Kim Echlin and Nie Zhixiong. London, New York, Victoria, Auckland, Harmondsworth: Penguin Books.
Zito, Angela 1996: "City Gods and their Magistrates". In Donald S. Lopez Jr. (ed.), *Religions of China in Practice*. Princeton, New Jersey: Princeton University Press, pp. 72–81.

Religious Taoism

Primary sources

Bokenkamp, Stephen R. 1997: *Early Daoist Scriptures*. Berkeley, Los Angeles, London: University of California Press.
Boltz, Judith M. 1987: *A Survey of Taoist Literature: Tenth to seventeenth centuries*. China Research Monograph 32. Berkeley, California: Institute of East Asian Studies, Center for Chinese Studies, University of California Press.
Johnson, David 2000 reprint of 1999 edn first published 1966, "Popular Values and Beliefs" in William Theodore de Bary and Richard Lufrano *Sources of Chinese Tradition, Vol 2: From 1600 through the twentieth century*. New York: Columbia University Press, pp. 73–141.
Lopez, Donald S. Jr. (ed.) 1996: *Religions of China in Practice*. Princeton, New Jersey: Princeton University Press.

Secondary sources

Adler, Joseph A. 2002: *Chinese Religions*. London and New York: Routledge.

Ahern, Emily M. 1973: *The Cult of the Dead in a Chinese Village*. Stanford, California: Stanford University Press.

Bell, Catherine M. 1988: "The Ritualization of texts and the Textualization of Ritual in the Codification of Taoist Liturgy". *History of Religions* 27. 4: pp. 366–92.

Bosco, J. 2003: "Popular Religion in a Southern Taiwanese Community". In Paul R. Katz and Murray Rubenstein (eds), *Religion and the Formation of Taiwanese Identities*. New York and Basingstoke: Palgrave Macmillan.

Chappell, David W. (ed.) 1987: *Buddhist and Taoist Practice in Medieval Chinese Society*. Honolulu: University of Hawaii Press.

Dean, Kenneth 1995 reprint of 1993 edn: *Taoist Ritual and Popular Cults of South-east China*. Princeton: Princeton University Press.

—— 1988: "Funerals in Fujian". *Cahiers d'Extrême-Asie* 4: pp. 217–26.

Eberhard, Wolfram 1988: *A Dictionary of Chinese Symbols: Hidden symbols in Chinese life and thought*. London and New York: Routledge.

—— 1952: *Chinese Festivals*. New York: Henry Schuman.

Groot, J. J. M. de 1964, first published 1910: *The Religious System of China: Its ancient forms, evolution, history and present aspect, manners, customs and social institutions connected therewith*, vols 1–3 *Disposal of the Dead*; vols 4–6 *On the Soul and Ancestor Worship*. New York: Paragon.

Jochim, Christian 1986: *Chinese Religion: A cultural perspective*. Upper Saddle River, New Jersey: Prentice-Hall.

Jordan, David K. 1972: *Gods, Ghosts and Ancestors: The Folk religion of a Taiwanese village*. Berkeley, Los Angeles and London: University of California Press.

—— and Daniel L. Overmyer 1986: *The Flying Phoenix: Aspects of Chinese sectarianism in Taiwan*. Princeton, New Jersey: Princeton University Press.

Katz, Paul R. and Murray A. Rubinstein 2003: *Religion and the Formation of Taiwanese Identities*. New York and Basingstoke: Palgrave Macmillan.

—— 1998, "The *Tao-te-ching* in Ritual". In Livia Kohn and Michael LaFargue (eds), *Lao-tzu and the Tao-te-ching*". Albany, New York: State University of New York Press.

Lagerway, John 1987: *Taoist Ritual in Chinese Society and History*. New York: Macmillan and London: Collier Macmillan.

—— 1987: "The Taoist Religious Community". In *ER* 14: pp. 306–17.

—— 1987: "Worship and Cultic Life: Taoist Cultic Life. In *ER* 15: pp. 482–6.

Leung, Man-Kam 1991: "The Study of Religious Taoism in the People's Republic of China (1949–1990): A bibliographic survey" *Journal of Chinese Religions* 19 (Fall): pp. 113–26.

MacInnes, Donald E. 1989: *Religion in China Today: Policy and practice*. Maryknoll, New York: Orbis Books.

Naquin, S. and Chün-fang Yü (eds) 1992: *Pilgrims and Sacred Sites in China*. Berkeley: University of California Press.

Pas, Julian F. (ed.) 1989: *The Turning of the Tide: Religion in China today*. Oxford, New York, Hong Kong: Hong Kong Branch Royal Asiatic Society in association with Oxford University Press.

Porter, Bill 1993: *Road to Heaven: Encounters with Chinese hermits*. San Francisco: Mercury House.

Sangren, P. Steven 1987: *History and Magical Power in a Chinese Town*. Stanford: Stanford University Press.

Saso, Michael 1990: *Blue Dragon, White Tiger: Taoist rites of passage*. Honolulu: University of Hawaii Press.

—— 1989 reprint of 1972: *Taoism and the Rite of Cosmic Renewal*. Pullman: Washington State University Press.

—— 2000: *Taoist Master Chuang*. Eldorado Springs: Sacred Mountain Press.
Schipper, Kristofer M. 1985: "Vernacular and Classical Ritual in Taiwan". *Journal of Asian Studies* 45: pp. 21–57.
Seidel, Anna 1978: "Buying One's way to Heaven: The Celestial Treasury in Chinese Religions". *History of Religions* 17: pp. 419–32.
Smith, Richard J. 1991: *Fortune-tellers and Philosophers: Divination in traditional Chinese society*. Boulder, Colorado, San Francisco, Oxford: Westview Press.
Stein, Rolf A. 1979: "Religious Taoism and Popular Religion from the Second to the Seventh Centuries". In Holmes Welch and Anna Seidel (eds), *Facets of Taoism: Essays in Chinese religion*. New Haven and London: Yale University Press, pp. 63–81.
Thompson, Laurence 1987: "Chinese Religious Year". In *ER*, 3: pp. 323–8.
Tsui, B. P. M. 1991: *Taoist Tradition and Change: The story of the Complete Perfection sect in Hong Kong*. Hong Kong: Christian Study Centre on Chinese Religion and Culture.
Watson, James and Evelyn S. Rawski (eds) 1988: *Death Ritual in Late Imperial China*. Nashville and New York: Abingdon Press.
Wei Yi-min, Henry and Suzanne Coutanceau 1976: *Wine for the Gods: An account of the religious traditions and beliefs of Taiwan*. Taiwan: Ch'eng Wen Publishing Company.
Wolf, Arthur P. (ed.) 1974: *Religion and Ritual in Chinese Society*. Stanford, California: Stanford University Press.
Yoshioka, Yoshtoyo 1979: "Taoist Monastic Life". In Holmes Welch and Anna Seidel (eds), *Facets of Taoism: Essays in Chinese religion*. New Haven and London: Yale University Press.

Taoism today

Bishop, Donald H. 2001 reprint of 1985 edn: "Mao Tse-tung and the Chinese Tradition". In Donald H. Bishop (ed.), *Chinese Thought: An introduction*. Delhi: Motilal Banarsidass, pp. 392–421.
Clarke, J. J. 2000: *The Tao of the West: Western transformations of Taoist thought*. London and New York: Routledge.

T'ai Chi Ch'üan/Taijiquan

Primary sources

Chang San-feng, "Zhang Sanfeng's Taiji Alchemy Secrets". In Thomas Cleary, translator, 2000: *Taoist Meditation: Methods for cultivating a healthy mind and body*. Boston, Massachusetts: Shambhala, pp. 117–22.
Chang San-feng, "Secrets of Gathering the True Essence", "Summary of the Golden Elixir" and "The Rootless Tree". In Douglas Wile (translator) 1992: *Art of the Bedchamber: The Chinese sexual yoga classics including women's solo meditation texts*. Albany, New York: State University of New York Press, pp. 169–92.
Chang San-feng, "Commentary on Ancestor Lü's Hundred-Character Tablet", "Discourses on the Teachings of Wang Che", Words on the Way", "Loving People", "On Medicine", "On Human Characters". In Thomas Cleary, translator, 2003, first published 1988: *The Taoist Classics: The collected translations of Thomas Cleary, Vol. 3*. Boston, Massachusetts: Shambhala.
Lo, Benjamin Pang Jeng, Martin Inn, Robert Amacker and Susan Foe (translators and eds) 1979: *The Essence of T'ai Chi Ch'uan: The Literary Tradition*. Berkeley, California: North Atlantic Books.
Wile, Douglas 1995: *Lost Tai-Chi Classics from the Late Ch'ing Dynasty*. Albany, New York: State University of New York Press.

BIBLIOGRAPHY

Secondary sources

Crompton, Paul 2000: *Tai Chi: An introductory guide to the Chinese art of movement*. Shaftesbury, Dorset and Boston, Massachusetts: Element.

Da Liu 1981, first published 1972: *T'ai Chi Ch'uan and I Ching: A choreography of body and mind*. London, New York, Ontario, Auckland, Harmondsworth: Arkana.

—— 1990, first published 1986: *T'ai Chi Ch'uan and Meditation*. London, New York, Ontario, Auckland, Harmondsworth: Arkana.

Delza, Sophia revised edn 1985, first published 1961: *T'ai Chi Ch'uan Body and Mind in Harmony: The integration of meaning and method*. Albany, New York: State University of New York Press.

Despeux, Catherine 1989: "Gymnastics: The Ancient Tradition". In Livia Kohn (ed.) in cooperation with Yoshinobu Sakade, *Taoist Meditiation and Longevity Techniques*. Michigan Monographs in Chinese Studies, vol. 61. Ann Arbor: University of Michigan Centre for Chinese Studies, pp. 225–61.

Galante, Lawrence 1981: *Tai Chi: The Supreme Ultimate*. York Beach, Maine: Samuel Weiser.

Miura, Kunio 1989: "The revival of Qi: Qigong in Contemporary China". In Livia Kohn (ed.) in cooperation with Yoshinobu Sakade, *Taoist Meditation and Longevity Techniques*. Michigan Monographs in Chinese Studies, vol. 61. Ann Arbor: University of Michigan Centre for Chinese Studies, pp. 331–63.

Olson, Stuart Alve 2001: *T'ai Chi according to the I Ching: Embodying the principles of the Book of Changes*. Rochester, Vermont: Inner Traditions International.

Seidel, Anna 1970: "A Taoist Immortal of the Ming Dynasty: Chang San-feng". In William Theodore de Bary and the Conference on Ming Thought, *Self and Society in Ming Thought*. Studies in Oriental Culture no. 4. New York and London: Columbia University Press.

Wong Kiew Kit 1996: *The Complete Book of Tai Chi Chuan: A comprehensive guide to the principles and practice*. Shaftesbury: Element.

Feng-shui

Brown, Simon 1996: *Principles of Feng-shui*. London: Thorsons.

Craze, Richard 1997: *The New Life Library Practical Feng Shui: The Chinese art of living in harmony with your surroundings*. London, New York, Sydney, Bath: Lorenz Books.

Dee, Jonathan 2000: *Feng Shui for the Garden*. London: Caxton Editions.

Duane, O. B. 1997: *The Origins of Wisdom*. London: Brockhampton Press.

Hale, Gill 2001, first published 2000: *The Practical Encyclopedia of Feng Shui*. London: Hermes House.

Keswick, Maggie 2003: *The Chinese Garden: History, art and architecture*. London: Frances Lincoln.

Kwok, Man-ho with Joanne O'Brien 1999, first published 1991: *Feng Shui: An introductory guide to the Chinese way to harmony*. Shaftesbury, Dorset, Boston, Massachusetts, Melbourne, Victoria: Element.

Levitt, Susan 2000: *Taoist Feng Shui: The Ancient Roots of the Chinese Art of Placement*. Rochester, Vermont: Destiny Books.

March, Andrew L. 1968: "An Appreciation of Chinese Geomancy". *Journal of Asian Studies* 27: pp. 253–67.

Sandifer, Jon 2000: *Feng Shui for Life*. Delhi: Motilal Banarsidass.

Wong, E. 1996: *Feng-shui: The ancient wisdom of harmonious living for modern times*. Boston, Massachusetts and London: Shambhala.

Wu, Baolin and Jessica Eckstein 2000: *Lighting the Eye of the Dragon: Inner Secrets of Taoist Feng Shui*. New York: St Martin's Press.

Index

Absolute, the   98, 107
Action and *Karma* Taoism   **232–3**
acupuncture   81, 93, 141, 267
afterlife   28, 160 *see also* death and the dead
alchemy   42, 83, 93, 94, 132, 135, 136, 145, 146, 150, 152, 156, 157, **161–93**, 200, 235, 267; inner/spiritual 157, 161, 162, 163, 164, 165, 166, 168, 173, 181, **181–93**, 230, 235 *see also nei-tan/neidan*, outer   161, 162, 165, 166,   **167–70** *see also wai-tan/waidan*; sexual   **179–81**
almanac   247
altars   240, 241, 242, 245, 246, 266
Analects   30, 40
ancestors   8, 11, 12, 14, 15, 16, 17, 23–4, 25, 26, 142, 149, 194, **195–7**, 242, 245, 246, 249, 255, 271; tablets of   242, 246, 260; veneration of 8, 9, 10, 11, 13, 14, 18–19, 20, 22, 28, 28–9, 150, 157–8, 172, 242, 245
animals   92, 163, 164, 166, 167, 269
animal symbols   91, **258–9**
Annals of Spring and Autumn (Lüshih Ch'un-ch'iu/Lüshi Chunqiu   23, 85–6
anthropomorphism   20, 198, 201, 203
Anyang   15, 22
Appendices see Ten Wings
art   42, 93
astronomy   93, 134

balance   8, 11, 16, 28, 35, 45, 46, 57, 62, 66, 67, 71, 72, 74, 76, 78, 81, 82, 89, 90, 92, 93, 111, 112, 135, 145, 167, 193, 225, 227, 228, 238, 240, 245, 268, 269, 270, 275; and imbalance   66, 81
"Bamboo Slip *Lao-tzu/Laozi*"   99
bellows   167, 183, 189
Big Dipper   162, 185, 186, 206, 208, 213, 256–7
Biographies of the Immortals   200
biology   42, 134
birth   78, **259–60**
Blessings, God of   204
Blue/Green Dragon   69, 78, 91, 187, 188, 189
Blue Lord in the East   25
body   8, 28, 30, 81–2, 88, 89, 92, 93, 94, 135, 142, 149, 160, 161, 163, 164–5, 167, **170–9**, 182, 183, 185, 186, 187, 189, 192–3, 234; and mind 8, 183, 185, 267, 269, 270; gates of   172, 174, 182, 190, 191; organs of   164–5
Book of Changes see I Ching/Yijing
Book of Documents (Shu Ching/Shujing)   23, 25, 38, 85
Book of Poetry or *Songs (Shih Ching/Shijing)*   23, 38, 215
Book of Rewards and Punishments   157
Book of Rituals/Rites (Li Chi/Liji)   23
breath/breathing   30, 82, 94, 136, 140, 143, 145, 161, 163, 164, 165, 166, 167, 171, 178, 182, **182–3**, 184, 189, 190, 191, 270; embryonic, womb or pre-natal   183; techniques of **182–3**
Bronze Age   12, 15, 38
Buddhism   6, 7, 9, 63, 102, 130, 131, 137–8, 143, 144, 146, 147, 150, 151, 152, 153, 153–4, 155, 157, 158, 159, 172, 198–9, 202, 208, 213, 226–8, 230, 231, 233, 235, 239, 245, 246, 248, 251, 254, 261, 263
burning of books   40, 41, 129, 132

calendar/calendrics   134, 200, 209, 238, **247–8**, **248–56** *passim*
cauldron   167, 174, 187, 189, **190–3**,
Celestial Masters   **183–9** , 141, 205, 230
Celestial Masters Taoism   130, 131, **138–9**, **142–4**, 149, 152, 164, 181, 203–4, 205, 229, **230–1**, 235, 266
Celestial Venerables   199, 202, **202–3**; of the Primordial Beginning   202–3, 205; of the Numinous Treasure   203; of *Tao* and *Te*   203 *see also* Three Pure Ones *and* Three Originals/Primordials
Central Orthodox Taoism *see* Celestial Masters Taoism *and* Way of Orthodox Unity
Chang Chan/Zhang Zhan   105
Chang Chüeh/Zhang Jue   130, 140
change   8, 11, 18, **34–64**, 78, 80, 84, 85, 107, 108, 109, 112, 113, 114, **117–19**, 146, 167, 177, 201, 238, 239, 269, 271, 274

335

INDEX

Chang Kuo-lao/Zhang Guolao   217, **219–20**
Chang Liang/Zhang Liang   130, 140
Chang Lu/Zhang Lu   139
Ch'ang'o/Chango *see* Moon, Goddess of
Chang Pao/Zhang Bao   130, 140
Chang Po-tuan/Zhang Boduan   178, 230
Chang Tao-ling/Zhang Daoling   130, **138–9**, 143, 205, 227, 230
chants/chanting   8, 150, 151, 232, 241
chaos   74, 110, 111, 178
charms   17, 230, 236, 246, 251
Ch'en/Chen dynasty   131, 148
Cheng-I Chiao-chu/Zhengyi Jiaozhu   144
Cheng-i/Zhengyi Taoism *see* Celestial Masters school
Cheng-i Meng-wei Tao/Zhengyi Mengweidao *see* Way of Orthodox Unity *and* Celestial Masters Taoism.
chen-jen/zhenren 144, 216, 223
Chen-wu Ta-ti/Zhenwu Dadi   201
chi/ji   46, 268
ch'i/qi   71, 76, 77, 81, 85, 93, 110, 111, 114, 133, 134, 146, 150, 164, 165, 171, 173, 174, 175, 177–8, 179, 180, 182, 184, 186, 187, **190–3**, 193, 203, 240, 241, 244, 271, **272–3** *see also* energy
Chiang Kai-shek   263
chiao/jiao ceremonies   233, 234, 235, **243–5**, 265
chih-jen/zhiren   223
chi-kung/qigong   245
Chin/Jin dynasty   129, 130, **144–7**, 156
Ch'in/Qin dynasty   129, **131–2**, 132, 134
Chinese New Year *see* festivals
Chinese psyche   6–7, **7–9**
ching/jing   81, 111, 164, 171, 175, **176–7**, 179, 180, 181, 184, 186, 187, **190–3**, 203, 244
Ch'ing/Qing dynasty   156, 159, 263
Chinghiz Khan   158
Ch'in Shih Huang-ti/Qinshi Huangdi   87, 129, 132
Ch'iu Ch'u-chi/Qiu Chuji   230
Chou/Zhou, Duke of   13, 22, 38, 39, 201
Chou/Zhou dynasty   12, 13, 14, 15, 17, 18, 19, 22, **22–9**, 37, 38, 39, 86, 129, 131, 134, 136, 197, 198
Chou I/Zhouyi   37–42 *see also I Ching/Yijing*
Chou I-chu/Zhouyizhu   41
Ch'üan-chen/Quanzhen Taoism *see* Complete Reality Taoism
Chuang-tzu/Zhuangzi   5, 33, 95, **102–5**, 108, 109, **113–28** *passim*, 136, 145, 146, 147, 164, 184, 186, 274
Chuang-tzu/Zhuangzi, the   5, 13, 96, 98, **102–5**, 105, 107, 108, 112, **113–28** *passim*, 146, 147, 152, 157, 183, 200, 214, 216, 223; *Inner Chapters* of 103–4; *Outer Chapters* of   103–4
Chuan-hsü/Zhuanxu   199, 201
Chu Hsi/Zhu Xi   42, 68

Ch'un Ch'iu/Chunqiu see Annals of Spring and Autumn
Chung-li Ch'üan/Zhongli Quan   217, **221**
chün-tzu/junzi   31, 62
cicada   167, 258
cinnabar   161, 164, 167, 168, 168–9, 180, 181, 189; fields   173, 174, 176, 177, 178, 180–1, 182, 185, 187, 188, 189, **190–3**, 203, 205 *see also tan-t'ien/dantian*
Classics   23, 34, 41, 132
colours   86, 91
Communist Party   263, 264, 265
Complete (or Perfect) Reality (or Realization, Perfection) Taoism   158, 181, 197, **229–30**, 233, 235, 266; Northern Branch of   230; Southern Branch of   230
conditioning   97, 117, 119, 127
Confucianism   4, 6, 7, 9, 23, 29, **30–2**, 34, 40, 63, 68, 77, 83, 87, 91, 94, 95, 96, 101, 116, 126, 130, 132, 133, 137, 138, 143, 145, 146, 147, 150, 151, 153–4, 155, 156, 157, 159, 166, 194, 226–8, 230, 231, 246, 265
Confucius   4, 6, 13, 23, 24, 29, **30–2**, 33, 38, 40, 96, 106, 116, 146, 199
consciousness   80, 127, 128, 178, 184, 185, 189, 191, 193, 225
convention(s)   103, 104, 117, 118, 122
correlates/correspondences   18, 85, 87, **91–3**
cosmology   68, 94
cosmos   35, 36, 45, 46, 52, 76, 78, 92, 108, 114–16, 133, 135, 161, 163
Count of the River   20, 28
crane   167
creation   **77–80**, 92, **110–16**, 113, 134, 177, 183, 191
Cultural Revolution   264–5

dance   8, 21, 25, 26, 27, 151, 226, 241–2, 268
Tao-tsang/Daozang see Taoist Canon
Dark Lord of the North   25
death and the dead   18, 28, 78, 93, 104, 118–19, 123, 128, 146, 160, 164, 165, 171–2, 177, 184, 191, 195, 227, 234, 242, 244, 245, 255, **261–2**
deities   8, 17, 19, 24, 26, 91, 92, 133, 139, 142–3, 156, 157, 194, **197–214**, 226, 231, 232, 233, 238, 240, 241, 242, 244, 245, 246, **248–56** *passim*, 256, 263; as dragons   210; of the body 174, 175, 182, 183, 185, 186; of the underworld 213–14; stellar   142
demonology/demons   8, 26, 134, 142, 171, 213–14, 231, 234
desires (and aversions)   72, 75, 80, 101, 109, 120, 121, 127–8, 166, 176, 178, 184, 185, 186, 192, 225
devil walls   214
diet/dietetics   134, 136, 140, 145, 146, 149, 162, 164, 182, 183, 184
differentiation   72, 78, 80, 108, 109, 112, 113, 115, 184

336

INDEX

Discussion of Trigrams (*Shuo-kua/Shuogua*) 38, 41
divination 9, 10, 14, 15, 16–17, 22, 26, 27, 35–6, 37, 38, 39, 54, 55, 59, 133, 134, 135, 142, 150, 157, 158, 227, 233, 237, **238–9**, 248, **270–5**; by divination slips 238; by divining chair 237; by spirit writing 232, 237, 238; *ch'ien/qian* method of 238
dragons/Dragon Kings 210, 258
drama 241, 244, 266
drugs 26, 136, 145, 149
dualities 66, 72, 73, 75, 76, 78, 81, 83, 84, 98, 108, 110, 112, 113, 114, 115, 127, 184, 225

Eastern Chin/Jin dynasty 130, 148
Eastern Chou/Zhou dynasty 13, 24
Eastern Wei dynasty 131
ego/egoism 75, 109, 113, 120, 127–8, 184, 186, 192, 225
egolessness 101
Eight Immortals **216–23**
eight trigrams *see* I Ching/Yijing trigrams *and Pa-kua/Bagua*
elixirs 26, 136, 139, 155, 161, 164, 165, 167, 169, 181, 183 *see also* Golden Elixir/Pill
emotions 92, 127, 178, 184, 185, 270
Emperor of the East 201, 202, 270
Emperor of the North/South/West 201
emptiness 101, 109, 112, 115, 117, 166, 184–5, 225
energy/energies 46, 71, 76, 92, 110, 116, 133, 135, 146, 156, 161, 164, 166, 172–3, 174, 175, 180–1, 182, 184, 190, 192, 193, 238, 268, 269, **270–5**; channels of 173, 179 *see also ch'i/qi* and vital energy
enlightenment/enlightened one 76, 128, 181
equilibrium 45, 72, 73, 77, 111, 113, 115, 116, 118, 127, 182, 185, 193, 269
Erh-li-t'ou/Erlitou culture 13
essence(s) 71, 111, 113, 171, 182, 191
evil 71, 76, 213–14, 234
exercise 149, 162, 164, 166, 167, 182, 183, 184, 190, 268 *see also* gymnastics
exorcism 134, 139, 142, 152, 158, 230, 231, 232, 234, **237**, 261

fang-shih/fangshi 67, 129, 132, 133, **134–6**, 146, 164, 206, 233
fa-shih/fashi see priests, Red-heads
fasting 140, 244
fate 10, 146, 147
feminine 101, 182
feng-shui 14, 83, 85, 93, 94, 133, 134, 266, **271–5**
festivals 9, 21, 28, 83, 138, 139, 230, 243, 245, **248–56**, 265; Beginning of the Three Stages 250; Chang Tao-ling/Zhang Daoling 252; Ch'ing-ming/Qingming **251–2**; Ch'ü Yüan/Quyuan 253; Dragon Boat **253**; Earth Spirits 254; First Opening of Hell 253–4; Full or Double *Yang* 255; Garments for the Dead 255; God of the Soil 250, 256; God of War 250; God of Water and Rule of Water 255–6; Hsüan-t'ien Shang-ti/Xuantian Shangdi 251; Jade Emperor **249–50**; Kitchen God 255; Kuan-sheng Ta-ti/Guansheng Dadi 253; Kuan-yin/Guanyin 251; Kuo Hsing-wang/Guo Xingwang 251; Lanterns 204, 250, 259; Lao-tzu/Laozi 251; Lü Tung-pin/Lü Dongbin 252; Mid-Autumn Moon 255; New Year 11, 21, 204, 209, 211, 212, **248–9**, 265; Pao-sheng Ta-ti/Baosheng Dadi 252; Patron of Scholars 251; Queen of Heaven (Ma-tsu/Mazu) 252; Seven Ladies 254; Shen-nung/Shennong 252; Solstice 253; Summer Solstice 253; T'ai-tzu Yeh/Taiziye 255; Three Agents 139; Yü/Yu the Great 255
feudalism 13, 17, 23–4, 131
firing process 182, **187–93**
Five Agents 29, 49–51, **84–94**, 133–4, 135, 136, 137, 140, 165, 167, 171, 173, 177, 180, 182, 184, 190, 199, 201, 206, 207, 212, 226, 239, 247, 248, 249, 257, 271 *see also wu-hsing/wuxing*
Five Bushels of Rice Taoism 130, **138–9**
Five Dynasties 155, 156
"forgetting" 112, 117, 184, 224
Former Han 129–30, 132, 134
Fu Chü/Fu Ju 223
Fu Hsi/Fu Xi 14, 38, 48, 60, 66, 92, 188, **196**
Fujian 230, 232, 235, 246, 265, 266
fu 143, 257 *see also* talismans
fu-lu 143
funerals 230, **261–2**, 266
fungi 167, 168, 169
furnace 169, 183, 187, 189, 191

geomancy 134, **271–5** *see also feng-shui*
ghosts 19, 20, 158, 171–2, 214, 236 *see also kuei/gui*
gods 8, 17, 18–19, 25, 142, 133, 135, 146, 149, 156, 157, **197–214**; of nature 19, **210**; of the door 263, 266; of the earth and soil 8, 19, 20, 21, 26, 27, 28, 29, 142, 143, 211, 246, 266; of the household 8, 19, 158, **211–12**; of the locality 19, **211–12** *see also* deities
gold 160–1, 163, 163–4, 167, 168, 169, 181
Golden Age 14, 98, 118, 125, 136, 140
Golden Elixir/Pill 14, 98, 118, 125, 136, 140
good and evil 75, 108–9, 125, 233, 245
Grand Norm 86 *see also* Hung Fan/Hongfan
Grand Unity Taoism 158
Great Treatise 38, 41, 53, 62, 67 *see also* Ta-chuan/Dazhuan
Great Wall of China 129, 131
Great Way Taoism 158
Guarding/Keeping the One 182, 184, **186**
Guodian texts 99, 101
gymnastics 136, 149, 150, 162, 164, 167, 182, 183, 190, 268 *see also* exercise

337

INDEX

Han dynasty 22, 129, **132–41**, 146
Han Hsiang-tzu/Han Xiangzi **220**
harmony 8–9, 10, 11, 14, 18, 19, 20, 21, 22, 27, 30, 35, 36, 44, 45, 46, 46–7, 62, 67, 70, 71, 72, 74, 76, 77, 80, 82, 84, 90, 92, 107, 110, 111, 112, 115, 120, 121, 122, 123, 125, 126, 128, 135, 141, 145, 146, 147, 163, 174, 175, 176, 182, 183, 185, 186, 188, 191, 193, 226, 227, 228, 233, 238, 239, 240, 246, 247, 268, 269, 270, 271, 274, 275; and disharmony 66, 71, 81
healing 138, 139, 140, 164, 230, 232, 234, 237
health 18, 146, 149, 161, 163, 177, 182, 184, 232, 245, 246, 271
Heaven 9, 20, 59, 69, 72, 75, 92, 135 149; and Earth 18, 19, 20, 25, 36, 38, 46, 47, 52–3, 60, 61, 67, 68, 72, 77, 78, 110, 113–14, 115, 135, 163, 169, 171, 172, 173, 180, 181, 186, 187, 188, 189, 192–3, 196, 201, 224, 233, 239, 258, 275; and hells 9, 172, 227, 262;
Heaven, Earth and humanity 20, 47, 56, 77, 80, 82, 83, 87, 89, 111, 135, 141, 152, 162, 240, 241, 244, 274
Hell(s) 172, 231–2, 235, 242, 243; Attack on 262; Banks of 243, 245; Gates of 232, 253–4; souls in 242, 243–4, 254, 261
herbs/herbology 141, 150, 163, 166, 167, 168, 169, 170, 183
Ho Hsien-ku/He Xiangu **221–2**
Hong Kong 229, 233, 238, 246, 266
horoscopes 247, 260
Ho-shang-kung/Heshanggong 99, 110, 111, 121–2
ho-t'u/hetu 48, 188, 257 *see also* Yellow River Map
Hou-chi/Houji 209
Hou Tse/Houze 197
Hou-tu/Houdu 213
Ho Yen/He Yan 146, 147
Hsia/Xia dynasty 13, 86
Hsiang-chuan/Xiangzhuan 40
hsien/xian 21, 171, 183 *see also* immortals
Hsin/Xin dynasty 129, 130
Hsi-tz'u/Xici see Ta Chuan/Dazhuan
Hsi Wang-mu *see* Queen Mother of the West
Hsüan-hsüeh *see* Mystery Learning
Hsüan-tsung/Xuanzong, Emperor 154–5
Hsüan-yüan chaio/Xuanyuan jiao 200
Hsü Hui/Xu Hui 148
Hsükua-chian/Xuguazhuan (Sequence of Hexagrams) 41
Hsü Mi/Xu Mi 148
Hsün Tzu/Xun Zi 68
Huai-nan-tzu/Huainanzi 77–8, 87–8, 89, 97, 130, 137–8, 184–5
Huanbei 22
Huang-ch'i/Huangqi 70
Huang-Lao Chün/Huanglaojun 136
Huang-Lao Taoism 130, **136**, 137, 140, 205–6
Huang-ti/Huangdi *see* Yellow Emperor

Huang-ti Nei-ching/Huangdi Neijing see Yellow Emperor's Classic of Internal Medicine
Hui-tsung/Huizong, Emperor 157
humanity/humanism 5, 41
hun spirits 171, 172
Hundred Character Tablet 197, 218
Hung Fan/Hongfan 85, 86 *see also* Grand Norm
hun-tun/hundun see chaos

I Ching/Yijing 17, 23, 27, **34–64**, 66–7, 77, 89, 90, 94, 118, 135, 146, 147, 167, 169, 182, 186, 187, 188, 199, 271; coin divination in 60; firm lines in 45–6, 47, **47–51**, 53–4, 56, 57, 58; hexagrams of 37, 38, 39, 40, 41, 43, 47, 53, **54–9**, 66, 73, 74, 89, 169; hexagram statements of 39, 55; Images of 37, 38, 39, 40, 41, 43, 47, 53, **54–9**, 66, 73, 74, 89, 169; Judgements of 39, 40, 42; line statements of 39, 55, **57–9**, 61; moving lines of 53, 58–9, 60; nuclear trigrams of 56–7; trigrams of 37, 38, 40, **47–54**, 54, 56, 57, 58, 66, 74, 80, 89, 168, 180–1, **186–90**, 240, 271; yarrow-stalk divination in 37, 59, 59–60, 61; yielding lines in 45–6, 47, **47–51**, 56, 57, 58 *see also* Chou I/Zhouyi
ignorance 101, 107
immanence 112, 128
immortality 14, 26, 28, 30, 76, 128, 133, 134, 135, 136, 141, 143, 146, 157, 160–93 *passim*, 205, 207, 209, 233, 250, 269,
immortals 20–1, 62, 112, 135, 136, 137, 142, 143, 163–4, 165, 169, 171, 183, 194, 207, 210, **214–23**; Land/Realm of 170, 171
incantation 25, 27
inscriptions 16; bone 16, 37, 54; bronze 37, 54
involution 184 *see also* return
Inward Training 182–3, 184
Iron Age 24

jade 161, 164–5, 167
Jade Calendar 173
Jade Emperor 157, 172, 202, 203, **204–5**, 209, 212, 232–3, 247, 248, **249–50**, 254
Jade Maiden of Obscure Brilliance 175
jen/ren 20, 32

Kao-tsung/Gaozong, Emperor 154
karma 137–8, 150, 151, 172, 198, 208–9, 232, 267
Khubilai Khan 156, 158
Kitchen God 11, 25, 157, 211, **212**, 233, 248, 255, 266
knowledge 101, 115, 127; conventional 97, 104, 224; intuitive 112, 127
Ko Ch'ao-fu/Ge Chaofu 150
Ko Hung/Ge Hong 130, **144–6**, 149, 150, 152, 165–6, 168, 169, 174, 181, 183, 223
K'ou Ch'ien-chih/Kou Qianzhi 131, 144
kua/gua 47

Kuan/Guan, General *see* War, God of
Kuan-yin/Guanyin 208, 251, 253
kuei/gui 20, 69, 172
K'unlun/Kunlun 201, 207, 223
K'unlun/Kunlun Taoism 233
Kuo Ch'ung-fu/Guo Chongfu 246
Kuo Hsiang/Guo Xiang 102, 146, 147

Lady Hao 22
Lady Tai/Dai 164, 169
Lady Wei 148, 223
laity 231, 239, 241, 245, 246, 248, 263
Lan Ts'ai-ho/Lan Caihe **221**
Lao-Chuang/Lao Zhuang Taoism 105
Lao Tan/Lao Dan 96
Lao-tzu/Laozi 5, 13, 14, 33, 95, **96–102**, **113–28** *passim*, 130, 136, 138, 139, 143, 144, 145, 146, 147, 153, 154–5, 186, **205–6**, **218–19**, 251, 274; mother of **208**
Lao-tzu pien-hua ching/Laozi bianhuajing 206
Later Chin/Qin 155
Later Chou/Zhou 155
Later Han 130, 132, 155
Later Liang 155
Later T'ang/Tang 155
lead 167, 169, 170
Legalists 132, 133, 137, 138
li 20, 32, 147, 240–1
Liang dynasty 131, 148
Li Chi/Liji see Book of Rituals/Rites
Lieh-hsien Chuan/Liexian Zhuan see Biographies of the Immortals
Lieh-tzu/Liezi 81, **105–6**, 121
Lieh-tzu/Liezi 95, **105–6**, 118, 122, 126, 157
Li Erh/Li Er *see* Lao-tzu/Laozi
life-cycle rites **259–62**, 263
Li Hsüan/Li Xuan *see* Li T'ieh-kuai/Li Tieguai
Li Hung/Li Hong 148
ling see power
Ling-pao/Lingbao Taoism 130, 148, **150–1**, 152, 202, 205, 241
Ling-pao T'ien-tsun/Lingbao Tianzun 152, 203 *see also* T'ai-shang Tao-chün/Taishang Daozun
Li Shao-chün/Li Shaojun 164–5
Literature, God of 213
Li T'ieh-kuai/Li Tieguai **218–19**
liturgy 150, 151
Liu An 137
Liu I-ming/Liu Yiming 69, 70
Liu Sung/Liu Song dynasty 130, 148
longevity 18, 30, 134, 135, 136, 139, 140, 146, 157, 161, 162–3, 164, 165, 168, 176, 177, 182, 183, 209, 214, 232, 245; God of 204
lo-shu (magic square) 257, 271
Loyang/Luoyang 24
lu 143
Lu Hsiu-ching/Lu Xiujing 130, 144, 151, 152
Lung-men/Longmen Taoism 229, 230

Lungshan/Longshan culture 12
Lü Shan San-nai Taoism 232, 234, 255
Lüshih Ch'un-ch'iu/Lüshi Chunqiu see Annals of Spring and Autumn
Lü Tung-pin/Lü Dongbin *see also* Lü Yen/Lü Yan 197, 217, **217–18**, 221, 222, 251, 252
Lü Yen/Lü Yan (Ancestor Lü) 197

macrocosmic orbit 191, **192–3**
magic 11, 17, 22, 25, 133, 134, 135, 146, 158, 227, 231, 233, 237
Ma Jung/Ma Rong 39
Mandate of Heaven 22, 23, 25, 27, 29, 135, 138
Mao Shan Taoists 148, 150, 152, 231, 237
Mao Tse-tung/Mao Zedong 264, 265
marriage **260–1**
martial arts 88, 267, 269, 270
Ma-tsu/Mazu *see* Queen of Heaven
Ma-wang-tui/Mawangdui texts 55, 99, 164, 179–80, 268–9
medicine 81, 93, 134, 145, 150, 152, 170
meditation 42, 88, 99, 136, 141, 152, 162, 163, 167, 173, 183, **184–6**, 231, 227, 267, 269, 270
mediums 158, 227, 232, 233, **236–9**, 243, 244, 248
mercury 161, 167, 169, 170, 180, 181
merit 235, 242, 245, 254
metallurgy 134, 170
metals 167, 169
microcosm and macrocosm 19, 44, 47, 71, 76, 78, 82, 92, 113, 135, 141, 163, 170–1, 184, 235, 239, 241, 274
microcosmic orbit 191, **192–3**
milfoil 37, 59–60, 66 *see also* yarrow
mind 63, 182, 183, 185, 189, 190–1, 193, 270
minerals 163, 164, 166
Ming dynasty 156, 158, 159
miracles 142, 158
Mohists 6
monasteries/monastic traditions 230, 233, 236, 263, 265, 266, 271, 272; White Cloud 230, 266
Monthly Commands 72, 85–6, 87, 89
Moon, Goddess of 213, 255
Mother of the Northern Dipper 213
mountains 144, 148, 180, 210, 257
music 21, 27, 134, 151, 226, 241
Mysterious Pass/Gate 179
Mystery Learning 147
mysticism 5, 98–9, 104, 113, 117, 124

name-giving 260
Nationalist Party 263
naturalness/naturalism 5, 62, 95, 114, 116, 117, 120, 121, **121–4**, 127, 190
nature 7–9, 10, 11, 12, 13, 14, 18, 36, 38, 41, 66, 68, 85, 88, 92, 109, 114, 121, 123, 124, 134, 145–6, 227, 268
nei-tan/neidan 161, **181–93** *see also* alchemy, inner

339

INDEX

Neolithic Age   12, 16
Neo-Taoism   130, **146–7**
non-action *see wu-wei*
Non-Being and Being   101, 108, 109, 110, 113, 146–7, 147
Northern Ch'i/Qi dynasty   131
Northern Chou/Zhou dynasty   131
Northern Sung/Song dynasty   156
Northern Wei dynasty   131
"Nourishing the Vital Principle"   164, 186
Nükua/Nügua   196
numbers   92

offerings   241, 243, **243–5**, 246, 249, 254
Official Position/Success, God of   204
oneness   113, 122, 128, 149, 185, 186, 241, 268, 274
One, The   78, 109, 110, **110–11**, 112, 114, 128, 177, 184, 185, 186
opposites   65, 70–1, **72–4**, 107, 108, 111, 115, 118, 127, 182, 193; relativity of   72, 73
order   17, 18, 21, 22, 29, 109
Orthodox Unity Taoism *see* Celestial Masters Taoism

Pa-hsien/Baxian see Eight Immortals
Pa-kua/Bagua   47–54, 188–9, **190, 222**, 273
P'an-ku/Pangu   **196**
Pao-p'u-tzu/Baopuzi   130, 144–7, **165–6**, 168, **169**; *Nei-p'ien/Neipian* of   **145**, 165–6; *Wai-p'ien/Waipian* of   **145**, 166
Pao-sheng Ta-ti/Baosheng Dadi   210, 246, 252
Pei-tou/Beidou see Big Dipper
People's Republic of China   264, 265
phoenix   258
pitch pipes   91
planets   91, 134
plants   163, 164, 166, 167
p'o/po spirits   75, 82, 171–2
polytheism   198
popular religion   4, 7, 133, 142, 154, 158, 229, 263–5
potentiality   71, 109, 110, 111, 112, 114, 116
power   197, 202, 228, 231, 235, 237, 242, 269, 272
priests/priesthood   9, 26, 142, 151, 155, 228, 231, **233–6**, 239, 241, 242, 248, 257, 261, 263, 265; Black-heads   **233–4**, 233, **233–4**; Red-heads   232, 233, **234–6**, 237, 243
processions   241, 244, 265
purification   241, 244
purity chambers   143, 146, 149

Queen Mother of the West   202, **206–7**, 223
Queen of Heaven (Ma-tsu/Mazu)   208, 246, 252, 266

reality   8, **44–7**, 65, 73, 76, 84, 110, 113, 114, 127, 134; Ultimate   5, 75, 98, 106, 107, **107–9**, 113, 137, 146, 147

rebirth   93, 137–8, 154, 171, 172, 242, 261, 267
Records of the Grand Historian see Shih Chi/Shiji
Red Guards   264
Red Lord in the South   25, 201
registers   138, 142, 143, 149, 151, 204, 231–2, 235, 236, 245
religious Taoism   **4–7, 132–59** *passim*
repentance   244
respiration *see* breathing
return   109, **183–93**, 269 *see also* reversal
ritual   9, 17, 20–1, 22, 24, 25, 26, 27, 28, 82, 226, 228, 234, 235, 236, 237, 240, **240–6**, 261, 262; for rain   234, 237
reversal   113–14, **114**, **117**, 183–93 *see also* return
Rootless Tree   **181**

sacrifice   8, 11, 13, 17, 20, 21, 24, 25, 55, 91, 138, 157; and ritual   15, 17, 18–19, 55; animal   20, 27, 157; human   13, 20, 27
sage(s)/sagehood   62, 95, 101, 103, 108, 112, 113, 115, 121, 122, **127–8**, 141, 149, 150, 177, 194, 215–16, **223–5**, 269
sage-ruler(s)   14, 22, 126–7
salvation   8, 137, 149, 150, 227, 145, 254
san-ch'ing/sanqing see Three Pure Ones
San-huang Ching/Sanhuangjing see Scripture of the Three Sovereigns
san-i/sanyi see Three Primordials *and* Three Pure Ones
san-kuan/sanguan see Three Agents
san-yüan/sanyuan see Three Pure Ones
Scripture of Great Peace   **130**, 140–1, **152**
Scripture of the Three Sovereigns   **152**
seasons   67, 73, 80, 85, 87, 91, 93
Secrets of Gathering the True Essence   **181**
self   81, 112, 173, 175, 182, 185, 187, 193; self-cultivation   99, 100, 109, 113, 116, 119
semen   173, 180, 190
senses   185, 186, 192
Seven Sages of the Bamboo Grove   147
sexual alchemy *see* alchemy
sexual practices   136, 143, 145, 162–3, 166, 168, 184, 222
shaman-diviners   20–1, 24–5, 26
shamanism   8, 9, 10–11, 26–7, 103, 131, 133, 135, 141, 142, 154, 158, 163, 198, 199, 214, 215, 223, 224, 227, 233, 234, 237, 242, 257, 266 268
Shang-ch'ing/Shangqing Taoism   88, 130, 148, **148–50**, 151, 152, 186, 203, 206, 207
Shang dynasty   12, 13, 14, **15–22**, 23, 37, 85, 86, 91, 135, 195, 198
Shang-ti/Shangdi   18–19, 20, 25, 91, 195, 198, 200
shen   111, 175, 176, **178**, 179, 182, 184, 186, 187, **190–3**, 203, 244
Shen-hsiao/Shenxiao Taoism   232, 234
sheng-jen/shengren   127, 223
shen-jen/shenren   214, 216, 223
Shen-nung/Shennong   14, 91, 196, 252

340

INDEX

shen spirits   69, 75, 81, 82, 171
shih/shi   100, 126
Shih Chi/Shiji   68, 86, 96 *see also* Ssu-ma Chien/Sima Qian
Shih Ching/Shijing see Book of Poetry/Songs
Shih-i/Shiyi *see* Ten Wings
Shu Ching/Shujing see Book of Documents
Shun   199
Shuo-kua-chuan/Shuoguazhuan see Discussions of Trigrams
silence   101, 124
silver   167
Six Dynasties   130–1, 148
Son of Heaven   18, 23
sorcery/sorcerors   8, 9, 10, 11, 25, 26–7, 142, 158, 227, 231, 237
soul(s)   20, 28, 136, 164, **171–2**, 174 5, 235, 242, 253–4, 261–2 *see also kuei/gui*
Southern Ch'i/Qi dynasty   130, 148
Southern Sung/Song dynasty   156
spirit   111, 113, 128; and matter   10
Spirit Embryo   136, 143, 174, **178–9**, 180, 182, 183, 187, 188, 191, 192, 193
spirit money   242–3, 245
spirits   8, 10–11, 16–17, 17, 18–19, 20, 22, 25, 134, 135, 139, 142, 143, 175, 228, 245; world of   8, 9, 10–11, 18, 26, 142, 231, 233, 237
spontaneity   75, 94, 101, 104, 110, 111, 114, 115, 116, 121, **121–4**, 125
Spring and Autumn period   13, 24
Ssu-ma Ch'ien/Sima Qian   15, 17, 39, 68, 100, 102–3
Ssu-ma T'an/Sima Tan   4, 6, 96
Ssu-ming/Siming   212, 251
statecraft   104, **125-6**
Steps of Yü/Yu   241–2
stillness   43, 46, 63, 78–9, 81, 109, 110, 115, 116, 120, 124, 126, 128, 184, 185, 186, 193, 224, 225, 269, 275
Stone Age   12
Sui dynasty   53
Summary of the Golden Elixir   **181**
Sung/Song dynasty   155, **156–8**
superstition   131, 264, 266
Supreme Ultimate   80, 108, 110, 268
symbols   135, 226, **256–9**
syncretism   194, 227, 230

Ta-chuan/Dazhuan   37, **38**, **41**, **46**, 53, 62 *see also* Great Treatise
T'ai-chi/Taiji   46, 80 *see also* Supreme Ultimate
T'ai Chi Ch'üan/Taijiquan   83, 120, 181, 182, 199, 232, 245, **267–70**, 275
T'ai-i/Taiyi   26, 108, 175, 202
T'ai-p'ing Ching/Taipingjing see Scripture of Great Peace
T'ai-p'ing Tao/Taipingdao *see* Way of Great Peace Taoism
T'ai-shang/Taishang   102
T'ai-shang Lao-chün/Taishang Laojun   102, 138, 203, 206 *see also* Tao-te T'ien-tsun/Daode Tianzun
T'ai-shang Tao-chün/Taishang Daozun   203 *see also* Ling-pao T'ien-tsun/Lingbao Tianzun
Taiwan   209, 229, 230, 232, 236, 237, 238, 243, 246, 254
talismans   11, 135, 139, 143, 152, 166, 168, 207, 230, 231, 233, 234, 237, 246, 248, 257
Tan/Dan *see* Chou/Zhou, Duke of
T'ang/Tang dynasty   **153–5**
tan-t'ien/dantian   173 *see also* cinnabar fields
Tao/tao   4–5, 29, 31, 38, 46–7, 62, 63, 75–6, 77, 78, 80, 81, 95–106 *passim*, **106–16**, 116–28 *passim*, 141, 143, 145, 146, 147, 148, 160, 161, 162, 163, 166, 167, 169, 174, 175, 177, 178, 179, 182, 183–4, 185, 186, 193, 198, 201, 202, 206, 214, 215, 224, 225, 232, 234, 241, 242, 245, 268, 269, 274; return to   **113–14**
Tao-chia/Daojia   4, 5, 10
Tao-chiao/Daojiao   4, 5 *see also* religious Taoism
T'ao Hung-ching/Tao Hongjing   148, 150
Taoist Canon   135, 151, **151–2**
tao-jen/daoren   215
tao-shih/daoshi   136, 230–1, 234, 235, 236, 237, 244 *see also* priests
Tao Te Ching/Daodejing   13, **95–102**, **113–28** *passim*, 136, 137, 140, 143, 146, 146–7, 147, 152, 155, 157, 164, 182, 184, 214, 216, 224, 225, 241, 267
Tao-te T'ien-tsun/Daode Tianzun   152, 203 *see also* T'ai-shang Lao-chün/Taishang Laojun
Tao-tsang/Daozang see Taoist Canon
tao-yin/daoyin   150, 183
Te/De   26, 28, 29, 30, 75, 95, 96, 98, 99, 101, 109, 113, **116–19**, 122, 126, 274
temples   83, **239–40**, 243, 246, 263, 265, 266, 271
Teng Hsiao-p'ing/Deng Xiaoping   265
Ten Heavenly Stems   91, 247
ten thousand things   110, **111**, **111–12**, 121, 177, 184
Ten Wings   **40–1**, 46, 54, 55, 59, 88 *see also* Shih-i/Shiyi
terracotta army   132
Three, the   110, **111**, 184, 185
Three Agents/Officials/Rulers   138–9, **203–4**
Three August Ones   14, **196–7**, 199
Three Gods of Happiness   **204**, 243
Three Herbs/Flowers   192
Three-in-One Taoism   231
Three Kingdoms   139, 142, 146
Three Ones *see* Three Pure Ones
Three Originals/Primordials   185, 205 *see also* Three Pure Ones *and* Celestial Venerables
Three Pure Ones   175, 185, 186, 203, 205, 235, 240, 244, 250 *see also* Three Originals/Primordials *and* Celestial Venerables
Three Treasures   111, 175, **175–8**, 184, 185, 186, **187–93**
Three Worms   172, 233

INDEX

ti/di 18–19
T'ien/Tian 25, 29, 30, 31, 108, 198
T'ien-i/Tianyi 26, 175 *see also* Three Pure Ones *and* Three Originals
T'ien-shih/Tianshi *see* Celestial Master
T'ien-shih Tao/Tianshi Dao *see* Celestial Masters Taoism
t'ien-tsun/tianzun 217
Ti-i/Diyi 26, 175 *see also* Three Pure Ones
Ti Kuai-li/Diguali 217
time 91
tortoise 167, 258
trance 10, 25
transformation(s) **34–64**, 71, 81, 92, 112, **117–19**, 177, 201 *see also* change
Transformations of Lao-tzu Scripture 206
transmutation 160–1, 169, 178, 180, 181, 182, 184, 185, 186, **187–93**, 235
trigrams *see I Ching/Yijing*
Triple/Triplex Unity 165
Tsa-kua-chuan/Zaguazhuan 41
Ts'an-t'ung Ch'i/Cantongqi see Triple/Triplex Unity
Ts'ao Kuo-chiu/Cao Guojiu 220
Tsou Yen/Zou Yan 67–8, 83, 84, 86–7, 91, 165
t'uan/tuan see I Ching/Yijing hexagram statements
T'uan-chuan/Tuanzhuan 40
Tung Chung-shu/Dong Zhongshu 68, 87, 90
turtle 167, 258
t'u-ti/tudi 211
Twelve Earthly Branches 247
Two, the 80, 110, **111**, 118, 184
tzu-jan/ziran 114, 119, **121–4** *see also* naturalness *and* spontaneity

uncarved block **123–4**
unity 7, 70, 74, 81, 82, 90, **114–16**, 150, 173, 174, 175, 180, 182, 185, 193, 268, 270; diversity in **75–7**
Unity Taoism 231–2
universe/world 36, 47, 49, 56, 68, 71, 82, 84, **114–16**, 123, 133–4, 137, 170, 173, 185; cycles of 37; interconnectedness of 8, 10, 33, **34–64**, 81, 83–4, 84, 85, 114, 133; interrelation/interaction/interdependence of parts of 18, 36, 71, 72, 76, 80, 89, 90, 92, 94, 135, 141, 177, 274, 275; patterns of 8, 18, 28, 35, 37, 44, 45, 62, 66, 92, 109, 112, 113, 147, 238, 269; rhythms of 8, 28, 44, 45, 56, 62, 63, 65, 66, 67, 71, 76, 78, 80, 92, 108, 109, 112, 113, 128, 133–4, 135, 163, 167, 173, 177, 201, 203, 224, 267, 269, 270, 274

Virtue/"Virtuality" 35, 62, 112, **116–19** *see also* Te/De
visualization 149, 164, 185
vital energy/vitality 36, 111, 113, 146, 164, 191, 268, 272 *see also ch'i/qi and* energy

Void 75, 109, 110, 178, 179, 183, 184, 190–1, **193**, 242

wai-tan/waidan 161
Wang Ch'ung-yang/Wang Chongyang 229
Wang Mang 132
Wang Pi/Wang Bi 41, 99, 109, 110, 146–7
War, God of 198, **209**, 240, 250
Warring States period 13, 134
Water, God of 210, 255–6
Way, 5, 11 *see also* Tao
Way of Great Peace Taoism 130, **140**
Way of Orthodox Unity 139 *see also* Celestial Masters Taoism
Wei Po-yang/Wei Boyang 165
Wen, King 38, 39, 48, 188
Wen-yen-chuan/Wenyanzhuan Commentary on the Words 41
Western Chin/Jin dynasty 130, 148
Western Chou/Zhou dynasty 13, 24
Western Han *see* Former Han
Western Wei dynasty 131
White Lord of the West 25
White Tiger 69, 78, 188, 189
worship 8, **245–6**
wu see shamans
Wu-chi/Wuji 80
Wu, Emperor 130, 137, 164
Wu, Empress 155
wu-hsing/wuxing **84–94** *see also* Five Agents
Wu, King 13, 27
wu-wei 95, 115, 119, **119–21**, 122, 125, 126

Yang Hsi/Yang Xi 148, 223
Yang-shao culture 12
Yao 199
yarrow 27, 37, 59–60, 66 *see also* milfoil
Yellow Emperor 13–14, 25, 86, 91, 132, 140, 163–4, 199, **200–1**, 202, 203, 205, 206, 210
Yellow Emperor's Classic of Internal Medicine 82, 93, 165, 200
Yellow Emperor Religion 200
Yellow River 15, 20
Yellow River Map 48, 188 *see also ho-t'u/hetu*
Yellow Turbans Rebellion 130, 140
yin and *yang* 8, 15, 29, 30, 32, 37, 46, 47, **49–51**, 52, 53–4, 55, 56, **57–9**, 61, **65–84**, 141, 164, 167, 168, 168–9, 169, 171, 172, 173, 174, 175, 177, 179, 180–91 *passim*, 192, 193, 196, 199, 203, 207, 215, 225, 226, 238, 239, 245, 246, 247, 248, 255, 256, 258, 260, 267, 269, 270, 271, 272, 273, 275; school of 41, 67–8, 72, 80–1, 110, 111, 112, 113, 118, 133–4, 135, 136, 137
Yin dynasty *see* Shang dynasty
Yü/Yu, Emperor 14, 86, 163–4, 197, 199, 255
Yüan/Yuan dynasty 144, 158
Yüan-shih T'ien-tsun/Yuanshi Tianzun 152, 203

342